TownsendPress
2009-2010

Sunday School COMMENTARY

King James Version

New Revised Standard Version

The Old Covenant the Law
LAW
The new Covenant the gospel

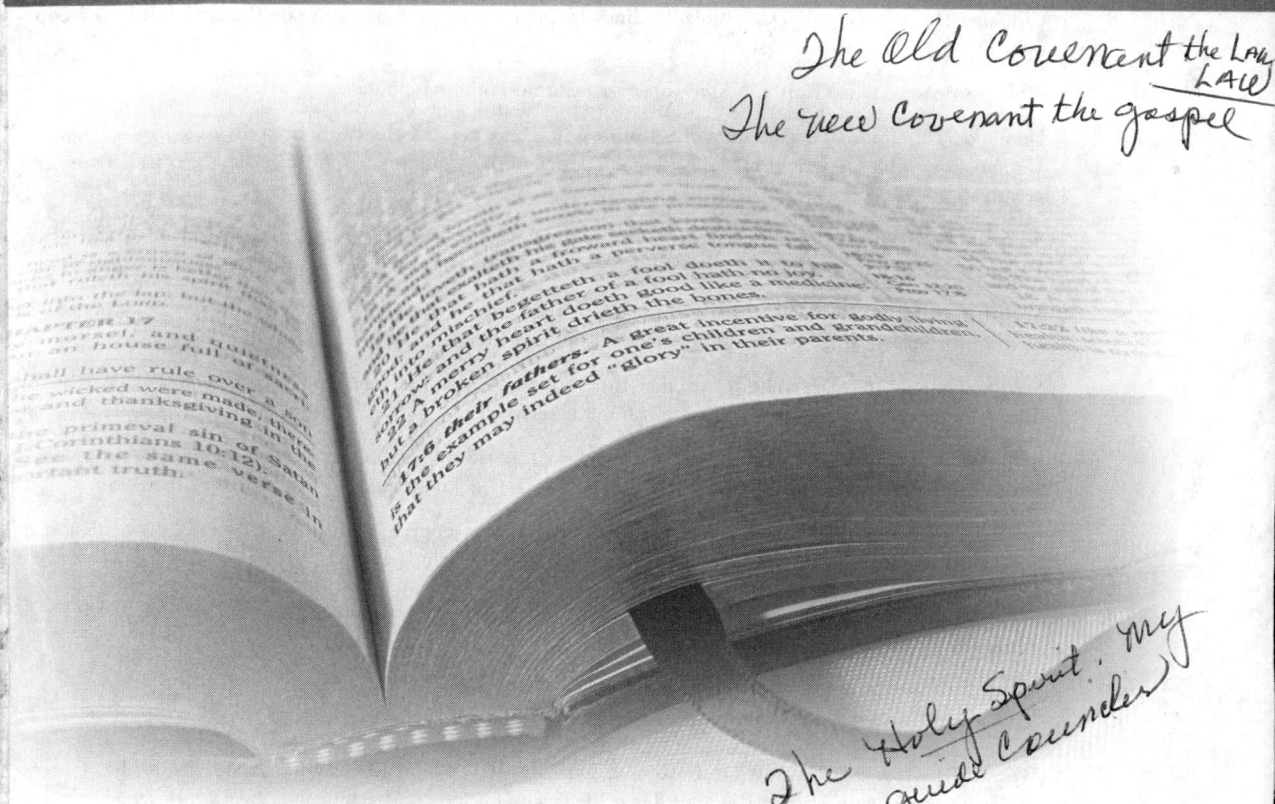

The Holy Spirit. my Helper, guide Counselor

Eighty-ninth Edition
Based on the International Lesson Series

Writers: Dr. Geoffrey V. Guns; Dr. L. Ronald Durham; Rev. Victor Michael Singletary; *Editor:* Dr. Gideon Olaleye; *Copy Editors:* Yalemzewd Worku, Tanae McKnight, Lucinda Anderson; *Layout Designer:* Royetta Davis.

ISBN: 1-932972-12-9

CONTENTS

Three-year Cycle v
List of Printed Texts vi
Preface vii
Acknowledgements viii
Know Your Writers ix

Fall Quarter, 2009—*Covenant Communities*

General Introduction 1
September: UNIT I—*Leaders in the Covenant Community*
  6 Joshua: A Leader for the People (Joshua 1:1-11, 16-17) 3
 13 Gideon: A Deliverer for the People (Judges 6:1-3, 7-14) 10
 20 Ezra: A Priest for the People (Ezra 9:5-11, 15) 17
 27 Nehemiah: A Motivator for the People (Nehemiah 2:5, 11-20) 23

October: UNIT II—*An Open Invitation to Covenant Living*
  4 Looking for Jesus (Mark 1:35-45) 30
 11 Recognizing Jesus (Mark 5:1-13, 18-20) 37
 18 Begging to Get In (Mark 7:24-30) 44
 25 Opting Out! (Mark 10:17-31) 51

November: Unit III—*The New Covenant Community*
  1 A Holy People (1 Peter 1:13-25) 58
  8 A Chosen People (1 Peter 2:1-10) 65
 15 A Suffering People (1 Peter 4:12-19) 72
 22 A Faithful People (2 Peter 1:3-15) 79
 29 A Hopeful People (2 Peter 3:1-13) 86

Winter Quarter, 2009-2010—*Christ, the Fulfillment*

General Introduction 93
December: UNIT I—*The Promised Birth Fulfilled*
  6 The Lineage of David (Ruth 4:13-17; Matthew 1:1-6) 95
 13 Prophets Foreshadow Messiah's Birth (Isaiah 7:13-17; Luke 1:30-38) 102
 20 Emmanuel Is Born (Matthew 1:18-25) 109
 27 Magi Confirm Messiah's Birth (Matthew 2:7-9, 16-23) 116

January: UNIT II—*Evidences of Jesus as Messiah*
  3 Proclaimed in Baptism (Matthew 3:1-6, 11-17) 123
 10 Strengthened in Temptation (Matthew 4:1-11) 130
 17 Demonstrated in Acts of Healing (Matthew 9:27-34; 11:2-6) 137
 24 Declared in Prayer (Matthew 11:25-30) 144
 31 Revealed in Rejection (Matthew 13:54-58) 150

February: UNIT III—*Testimonies to Jesus as Messiah*
  7 Recognized by a Canaanite Woman (Matthew 15:21-28) 157
 14 Declared by Peter (Matthew 16:13-27) 164

21 Witnessed by Disciples (Matthew 17:1-12) 171
28 Anointed by a Woman in Bethany (Matthew 26:6-13) 178

Spring Quarter, 2010—Teachings on Community

General Introduction 185

March: UNIT I—*Community with a Mission*

 7 Mission to the Community (Jonah 1:1-3; 3:1-9) 187
14 A Community to Redeem (Jonah 3:10; 4:1-5) 194
21 Family as Community (Ruth 1:1-9, 14b, 16) 200
28 Acceptance in Community (Ruth 2:5-12; 3:9-11) 207

April: UNIT II—*Teachings of Jesus*

 4 The Community Faces Pain and Joy (John 16:16-24; 20:11-16) 214
11 Love within the Community (1 John 2:9-11, 15-17) 221
18 Connecting in Community (Matthew 22:34-40) 228
25 Inclusion in Community (Luke 14:15-24) 235

May: UNIT III—*Teachings of the Church*

 2 A Faithful Community (Colossians 1:1-14) 242
 9 An Established Community (Colossians 2:1-10) 249
16 A Chosen Community (Colossians 3:12-17) 256
23 At Home in the Community (Philemon 8-18) 263
30 At Risk in the Community (Jude 3-7, 19-21, 24-25) 270

Summer Quarter, 2010—Christian Commitment in Today's World

General Introduction 277

June: UNIT I—*The Nature of Christian Commitment*

 6 Visible to God (1 Thessalonians 1:1-10) 279
13 Pleasing to God (1 Thessalonians 2:1-12) 286
20 Sustained through Encouragement (1 Thessalonians 3:1-13) 293
27 Demonstrated in Action (1 Thessalonians 4:1-12) 301

July: UNIT II—*The Foundation of Christian Commitment*

 4 God's Cosmic Plan (1 Thessalonians 5:1-11) 309
11 Glory to Christ (2 Thessalonians 1:3-12) 316
18 Chosen and Called (2 Thessalonians 2:13-17) 323
25 God's Own Faithfulness (2 Thessalonians 3:1-15) 330

August: UNIT III—*The Marks of Christian Commitment*

 1 Sharing God's Grace (Philippians 1:18b-29) 338
 8 Giving of Oneself (Philippians 2:1-13) 345
15 Living into the Future (Philippians 3:7-16) 352
22 Growing in Joy and Peace (Philippians 4:2-14) 360
29 Upheld by God (Acts 28:16-25a, 28-31) 368

CYCLE OF 2007-2010
Arrangement of Quarters According to the Church School Year,
September Through August

	Fall	Winter	Spring	Summer
2007–2008	God Created a People (Genesis) Theme: Creation	God's Call to the Christian Community (Luke) Theme: Call	God, the People, and the Covenant (1 and 2 Chronicles, Daniel, Haggai, Nehemiah) Theme: Covenant	Images of Christ (Hebrews, Gospels) Theme: Christ
2008–2009	New Testament Survey Theme: Community	Human Commitment (Luke, Old Testament) Theme: Commitment	Christ and Creation (Ezekiel, Luke, Acts, Ephesians) Theme: Creation	Call of God's Covenant Community (Exodus, Leviticus, Numbers, Deuteronomy) Theme: Call
2009–2010	Covenant Communities (Joshua, Judges, Ezra, Nehemiah, Mark, 1 and 2 Peter) Theme: Covenant	Christ the Fulfillment (Matthew) Theme: Christ	Teachings on Community (John, Ruth, New Testament) Theme: Community	Christian Commitment in Today's World (1 and 2 Thessalonians, Philippians) Theme: Commitment

LIST OF PRINTED TEXTS—2009-2010

The Printed Scriptural Texts used in the *2009-2010 Townsend Press Sunday School Commentary* are arranged here in the order in which they appear in the Bible. Opposite each reference is the page number on which Scriptures appear in this edition of the *Commentary*.

Reference	Page	Reference	Page
Joshua 1:1-11, 16-17	3	Mark 10:17-31	51
Judges 6:1-3, 7-14	10	Luke 1:30-38	102
Ruth 1:1-9, 14b, 16	200	Luke 14:15-24	235
Ruth 2:5-12	207	John 16:16-24	214
Ruth 3:9-11	207	John 20:11-16	214
Ruth 4:13-17	95	Acts 28:16-25a, 28-31	368
Ezra 9:5-11, 15	17	Philippians 1:18b-29	338
Nehemiah 2:5, 11-20	23	Philippians 2:1-13	345
Isaiah 7:13-17	102	Philippians 3:7-16	352
Jonah 1:1-3	187	Philippians 4:2-14	360
Jonah 3:1-9	187	Colossians 1:1-14	242
Jonah 3:10	194	Colossians 2:1-10	249
Jonah 4:1-5	194	Colossians 3:12-17	256
Matthew 1:1-6	95	1 Thessalonians 1:1-10	279
Matthew 1:18-25	109	1 Thessalonians 2:1-12	286
Matthew 2:7-9, 16-23	116	1 Thessalonians 3:1-13	293
Matthew 3:1-6, 11-17	123	1 Thessalonians 4:1-12	301
Matthew 4:1-11	130	1 Thessalonians 5:1-11	309
Matthew 9:27-34	137	2 Thessalonians 1:3-12	316
Matthew 11:2-6	137	2 Thessalonians 2:13-17	323
Matthew 11:25-30	144	2 Thessalonians 3:1-15	330
Matthew 13:54-58	150	Philemon 8-18	263
Matthew 15:21-28	157	1 Peter 1:13-25	58
Matthew 16:13-27	164	1 Peter 2:1-10	65
Matthew 17:1-12	171	1 Peter 4:12-19	72
Matthew 22:34-40	228	2 Peter 1:3-15	79
Matthew 26:6-13	178	2 Peter 3:1-13	86
Mark 1:35-45	30	1 John 2:9-11, 15-17	221
Mark 5:1-13, 18-20	37	Jude 3-7, 19-21, 24-25	270
Mark 7:24-30	44		

PREFACE

The *Townsend Press Sunday School Commentary*, based on the International Lesson Series, is a production of the Sunday School Publishing Board, National Baptist Convention, USA, Incorporated. These lessons were developed consistent with the curriculum guidelines of the Committee on the Uniform Series, Education Leadership Ministries Commission, National Council of the Churches of Christ in the United States of America. Selected Christian scholars and theologians—who themselves embrace the precepts, doctrines, and positions on biblical interpretation that we have come to believe—are contributors to this publication. By participating in Scripture selection and the development of the matrices for the Guidelines for Lesson Development with the Committee on the Uniform Series, this presentation reflects the historic faith that we share within a rich heritage of worship and witness.

The format of the *Townsend Press Sunday School Commentary* lessons consists of: the Unit Title, the general subject with age-level topics, Printed Text from the *King James* and the *New Revised Standard Versions* of the Bible, Objectives of the Lesson, Unifying Lesson Principle, Points to Be Emphasized, Topical Outline of the Lesson—with the Biblical Background of the Lesson, Exposition and Application of the Scripture, and Concluding Reflection (designed to focus on the salient points of the lesson), Word Power, and the Home Daily Bible Readings. Each lesson concludes with a prayer.

The *Townsend Press Sunday School Commentary* is designed as an instructional aid for persons involved in the ministry of Christian education. While the autonomy of the individual soul before God is affirmed, we believe that biblical truths find their highest expression within the community of believers whose corporate experiences serve as monitors to preserve the integrity of the Christian faith. As such, the Word of God must not only be understood, but it must also be embodied in the concrete realities of daily life. This serves to allow the Word of God to intersect in a meaningful way with those realities of life.

The presentation of the lessons anticipates the fact that some concepts and Scripture references do not lend themselves to meaningful comprehension by children. Hence, when this occurs, alternative passages of Scripture are used, along with appropriate content emphases, that are designed to assist children in their spiritual growth. There will, however, remain a consistent connection between the children, youth, and adult lessons through the Unifying Principle developed for each session.

We stand firm in our commitment to Christian growth, to the end that lives will become transformed through personal and group interaction with the Word of God. The challenge issued by the apostle Paul continues to find relevance for our faith journey: "Do your best to present yourself to God as one approved by him, a worker who has no need to be ashamed, rightly explaining the word of truth" (2 Timothy 2:15, NRSV). May we all commit ourselves to the affirmation expressed by the psalmist, "Your word is a lamp to my feet and a light to my path" (Psalm 119:105).

ACKNOWLEDGEMENTS

The *Townsend Press Sunday School Commentary* is recognized as the centerpiece of a family of church school literature designed especially to assist teachers in their presentation of the lessons as well as to broaden the knowledge base of students from the biblical perspective. Our mission has been and will always be to provide religious educational experiences and spiritual resources for our constituency throughout this nation as well as many foreign countries. To achieve this end, the collaborative efforts of many people provide the needed expertise in the various areas of the production process. Although under the employ of the Sunday School Publishing Board, personnel too numerous to list approach their respective tasks with the dedication and devotion of those who serve God by serving His people. This *Commentary* is presented with gratitude to God for all those who desire a more comprehensive treatment of the selected Scriptures than is provided in the church school quarterlies, and it is intended to be a complementary resource thereto.

We acknowledge the Executive Director of the Sunday School Publishing Board in the person of Dr. Kelly M. Smith Jr., who has given a charge to the publishing family to focus on QTC—Quality, Timeliness, and Customer care—in our interaction with our constituency. Special appreciation is appropriately accorded to Dr. Smith for his continued insightful and inspiring leadership and motivation. Through Dr. Smith's tenure at the Sunday School Publishing Board, the SSPB continues to prosper. It continues as the publisher and printer for the National Baptist Convention, USA, Inc. and its constituent components. There is a greater emphasis on addressing issues germane to the local, national, and international communities, utilizing the latest technologies to promote and distribute our materials—and doing all this based on Christian principles for the advancement of the kingdom of Jesus Christ.

The Sunday School Publishing Board consists of employees with expertise in their assigned areas whose self-understanding is that of "workers together with God," and partners with those who labor in the vineyard of teaching the Word of God in order to make disciples and nurture others toward a mature faith.

Our gratitude is expressed to Dr. L. Ronald Durham, expositor for the Fall Quarter, to Dr. Geoffrey V. Guns, Expositor for the Winter and Summer Quarters, and to Rev. Victor M. Singletary, expositor for the Spring Quarter—for their devotion to the development of the respective lessons. These three writers bring diversity and a broad spectrum of ministerial and educational experience to bear on the exposition and application of the Scripture.

Appreciation is also expressed to Dr. Kelly M. Smith Jr., Executive Director, and Mrs. Kathy Pillow, Associate Director, for their ongoing leadership. It is a credit to their leadership that the employees have embraced the mission of the Sunday School Publishing Board with a self-perspective that enhances their personal commitment to the cause of Christ as they interact with one another and intersect with the greater community of faith.

The task in which we are all involved would be meaningless and fruitless were it not for the many readers for whom this publication has been so diligently prepared. The faithfulness of our constituency has been enduring for over a century, and we consider ourselves blessed to be their servants in the ministry of the printed Word exalting the living Word, our Lord and Savior Jesus Christ. We pray that God's grace will complement our efforts so that lives will be transformed within and beyond the confines of classroom interaction as the Spirit of God manifests Himself through the intersection of teaching and learning. It is our prayer that God may grant each of us the power to live for Him and be witnesses to the saving grace of the One who died for us, even Jesus Christ, our Lord and Savior.

Wellington A. Johnson Sr.
Director of Curriculum Publishing

Dr. L. Ronald Durham ▼
Fall Quarter

Dr. L. Ronald Durham is the senior pastor of Greater Friendship Missionary Baptist Church in Daytona Beach, Florida. He has served as the moderator of the North Jersey District Missionary Baptist Association. Dr. Durham has been a teacher for our National Baptist Congress of Christian Education for over fifteen years. He is the president of the Daytona Beach Black Clergy Alliance and sits on the Halifax Hospital Board of Associates, the Daytona Beach Mayor's Kitchen Cabinet, and the Bethune Cookman University Board of Counselors.

Dr. L. Ronald Durham began his ministry at the age of sixteen, was licensed by Rev. T. H. Alexander of Union Baptist Church in Passaic, New Jersey, and was accepted on full scholarship to Shaw University in Raleigh, North Carolina. He completed his graduate and doctoral work at Evangel Christian University in Monroe, Louisiana, and holds an honorary Doctor of Divinity degree from Bethune Cookman University in Daytona Beach, Florida.

Dr. Durham pastored First Baptist Church of Anderson, New Jersey, for sixteen years and First Mt. Zion Baptist Church for eleven years, and is presently the pastor of Greater Friendship Baptist Church of Daytona Beach, Florida.

Dr. Durham is a prolific writer, a published author, and a teacher for the National Baptist Congress of Christian Education, USA, Inc. He published *The Secret Power of Prayer*, a guidebook for understanding the power of sincere prayer. He is also a writer for the Sunday School Publishing Board—having written the *Baptist Layman* for five years. He has served as one of the writers for the *Townsend Press Sunday School Commentary* and also as one of the writers of the *Baptist Teacher*. Additionally, he has contributed numerous articles for the *The Christian Education Informer*. Dr. Durham is the founder of Blacksermons.com, the premier online ministry for pastors around the world.

Dr. Geoffrey V. Guns ▼
Winter and Summer Quarters

Dr. Geoffrey V. Guns is a native of Newport, Rhode Island. He is the son of a retired Baptist pastor and co-pastor. Dr. Guns received his elementary and secondary education in the Norfolk public school system. He earned his B.S. degree in Business Administration from Norfolk State University in 1972.

In 1981, he earned his Master of Divinity degree from the School of Theology, Virginia Union University, graduating *summa cum laude*. He earned his Doctor of Ministry degree from the School of Religion, Howard University in Washington, D.C. in 1985.

Dr. Guns is the senior pastor of Second Calvary Baptist Church in Norfolk, Virginia, where he has served for the past twenty-three years. He is active in his denomination, the National Baptist Convention, USA, Inc. Dr. Guns served as the president of the

Virginia Baptist State Convention (VBSC) from 1997 to 2001 and is currently the moderator for the Tidewater Peninsula Baptist Association.

He has written articles for the *Christian Education Informer* of the Department of Christian Education of the Sunday School Publishing Board. Dr. Guns also serves as vice chairman of the Council of Christian Education for the Department of Christian Education of the Sunday School Publishing Board of the NBC. He works with the Home Mission Board of the NBC and serves as the regional representative for the Southeast region.

Dr. Guns is the author of two books: *Church Financial Management* (1997), which is published by Providence House Publishers; and *Spiritual Leadership: A Practical Guide to Developing Spiritual Leaders in the Church* (2000), published by Orman Press, Inc.

He is married to the former Rosetta Harding of Richmond, Virginia. Mrs. Guns is a licensed social worker and works as a school social worker for the City of Chesapeake public schools. They are the parents of two daughters, Kimberly Michelle Cummings and Nicole Patrice. Dr. and Mrs. Guns have one granddaughter, Kennedy Nicole Cummings.

Reverend Victor Michael Singletary▼
Spring Quarter

His paternal grand-parents, the late Sammie and the late Evelyn Joye Singletary, who instilled in him the love of the church and the importance of education, reared a native of Sumter, South Carolina, the Reverend Victor Michael Singletary. Accordingly, Rev. Singletary has a dual vocation as a Baptist clergyperson and an educator.

At Dartmouth College, where he earned an A.B. degree, Singletary obtained a dual major in History and Religion, with a certification in African & Afro-American Studies. Interestingly, his call to the ordained ministry crystallized during his undergraduate years. In response to that call, he enrolled in Union Theological Seminary in the city of New York. Singletary holds the Master of Arts Divinity degree, in which he studied church history, systematic theology, and psychiatry and religion. Afterwards, he obtained the Master of Arts degree in American History from New York University. While an administrator at Teachers College Columbia

University, he studied the History of American education, with an emphasis on political, legal, and public policy matters. He earned the Master of Education degree.

On October 1, 2000, Reverend Singletary assumed the full-time position as pastor of First Baptist Church Capitol Hill in Nashville, Tennessee. Rev. Singletary has served on several community boards: Nashville OIC, The Clinical Pastoral Education Consortium, The Boddie Chair of Excellence Board of American Baptist College, The Kelly Miller Smith Towers Board, Habitat for Humanity in Nashville, The Neighborhood Justice Center, The College Trust Fund, Tennessee CASA, and The Ennix-Jones Community Outreach Center Board. He belonged to three ministerial alliances: The Interdenominational Ministerial Fellowship, The Covenant Association, and Tying Nashville Together. Rev. Singletary is also a member of Alpha Phi Alpha Fraternity, Inc.

On May 4, 2008, Rev. Singletary concluded his tenure of seven-and-a-half years as the senior pastor of First Baptist Church Capitol Hill. He awaits the Lord's revelation of his next divine assignment.

Rev. Singletary is married to Carol Joy Lawrence, and they have a son, Curtis Joshua, and a daughter, Sariel Adya.

Covenant Communities

GENERAL INTRODUCTION

The three units in this quarter are examinations of God's covenant as manifested in communities. The lessons are considerations of the persons whom God chose as covenant leaders, the invitations God extended to enter into community, people's responses to the invitations, and the nature of God's new covenant community.

Unit I, *Leaders in the Covenant Community*, is a look at four people called to lead the Israelites in living in covenant with God: Joshua, Gideon, Ezra, and Nehemiah. Joshua was chosen by God to lead the people into the Promised Land. Gideon was called to deliver the people from the threat of the Midianites and Amalekites. The priest Ezra was called to intercede for the people who had recently returned home from exile. Nehemiah motivated people to rebuild the walls of Jerusalem.

Unit II, *An Open Invitation to Covenant Living*, is an exploration of stories from the book of Mark in which Jesus interacted with people and invited them to live in covenant with God. During a preaching tour in Galilee, many people sought Jesus, who cleansed a leper—thus giving the leper an opportunity to rejoin the community. When a demon-possessed man approached Jesus, even the demons knew who Jesus was. A Syrophoenician woman, a Gentile, convinced Jesus that He should heal her daughter. In contrast, a rich man who was seeking eternal life refused Jesus' invitation, thereby rejecting the covenant.

Unit III, *The New Covenant Community*, is an examination of 1 and 2 Peter to discern the qualities of people who are part of God's covenant community. First Peter is a portrayal of the community as a holy people who are chosen and who also suffer in order to live in covenant with God. In 2 Peter, the covenant people are described as faithful and hopeful.

*In Unit III, the children will focus on selected accounts of the early church that highlight its beginning as God's new covenant community.

LESSON 1 — September 6, 2009

JOSHUA: A LEADER FOR THE PEOPLE

DEVOTIONAL READING: 1 Timothy 2:1-6
PRINT PASSAGE: Joshua 1:1-11, 16-17

BACKGROUND SCRIPTURE: Joshua 1
KEY VERSE: Joshua 1:9

Joshua 1:1-11, 16-17—KJV

NOW AFTER the death of Moses the servant of the LORD it came to pass, that the LORD spake unto Joshua the son of Nun, Moses' minister, saying,

2 Moses my servant is dead; now therefore arise, go over this Jordan, thou, and all this people, unto the land which I do give to them, even to the children of Israel.

3 Every place that the sole of your foot shall tread upon, that have I given unto you, as I said unto Moses.

4 From the wilderness and this Lebanon even unto the great river, the river Euphrates, all the land of the Hittites, and unto the great sea toward the going down of the sun, shall be your coast.

5 There shall not any man be able to stand before thee all the days of thy life: as I was with Moses, so I will be with thee: I will not fail thee, nor forsake thee.

6 Be strong and of a good courage: for unto this people shalt thou divide for an inheritance the land, which I sware unto their fathers to give them.

7 Only be thou strong and very courageous, that thou mayest observe to do according to all the law, which Moses my servant commanded thee: turn not from it to the right hand or to the left, that thou mayest prosper whithersoever thou goest.

8 This book of the law shall not depart out of thy mouth; but thou shalt meditate therein day and night, that thou mayest observe to do according to all that is written therein: for then thou shalt make thy way prosperous, and then thou shalt have good success.

9 Have not I commanded thee? Be strong and of a good courage; be not afraid, neither be thou dismayed: for the LORD thy God is with thee whithersoever thou goest.

Joshua 1:1-11, 16-17—NRSV

AFTER THE death of Moses the servant of the LORD, the LORD spoke to Joshua son of Nun, Moses' assistant, saying,

2 "My servant Moses is dead. Now proceed to cross the Jordan, you and all this people, into the land that I am giving to them, to the Israelites.

3 Every place that the sole of your foot will tread upon I have given to you, as I promised to Moses.

4 From the wilderness and the Lebanon as far as the great river, the river Euphrates, all the land of the Hittites, to the Great Sea in the west shall be your territory.

5 No one shall be able to stand against you all the days of your life. As I was with Moses, so I will be with you; I will not fail you or forsake you.

6 Be strong and courageous; for you shall put this people in possession of the land that I swore to their ancestors to give them.

7 Only be strong and very courageous, being careful to act in accordance with all the law that my servant Moses commanded you; do not turn from it to the right hand or to the left, so that you may be successful wherever you go.

8 This book of the law shall not depart out of your mouth; you shall meditate on it day and night, so that you may be careful to act in accordance with all that is written in it. For then you shall make your way prosperous, and then you shall be successful.

9 I hereby command you: Be strong and courageous; do not be frightened or dismayed, for the LORD your God is with you wherever you go."

UNIFYING LESSON PRINCIPLE

In the midst of change and uncertainty, we need leaders who can guide us in the right direction. What are the characteristics of such leaders? Joshua, who succeeded Moses, was a strong, courageous leader whose obedience to God enabled the people to cross the Jordan into the Promised Land.

10 Then Joshua commanded the officers of the people, saying,
11 Pass through the host, and command the people, saying, Prepare you victuals; for within three days ye shall pass over this Jordan, to go in to possess the land, which the LORD your God giveth you to possess it.

.....

16 And they answered Joshua, saying, All that thou commandest us we will do, and whithersoever thou sendest us, we will go.
17 According as we hearkened unto Moses in all things, so will we hearken unto thee: only the LORD thy God be with thee, as he was with Moses.

10 Then Joshua commanded the officers of the people,
11 "Pass through the camp, and command the people: 'Prepare your provisions; for in three days you are to cross over the Jordan, to go in to take possession of the land that the LORD your God gives you to possess.'"

.....

16 They answered Joshua: "All that you have commanded us we will do, and wherever you send us we will go.
17 Just as we obeyed Moses in all things, so we will obey you. Only may the LORD your God be with you, as he was with Moses!"

TOPICAL OUTLINE OF THE LESSON

I. **Introduction**
   A. Spiritual Leaders
   B. Biblical Background

II. **Exposition and Application of the Scripture**
   A. God Calls Joshua (Joshua 1:1-9)
   B. Joshua Commands His Officers (Joshua 1:10-11)
   C. The Officers' Pledge to Joshua (Joshua 1:16-17)

III. **Concluding Reflection**

LESSON OBJECTIVES

Upon completion of this lesson, the students will know that:

1. Faith is essential in pleasing God;
2. Leaders are saddled with the responsibility of total trust in God; and,
3. Followers look up to leaders for courage.

POINTS TO BE EMPHASIZED

ADULT/YOUTH

Adult Topic: Leadership Strong and Courageous
Youth Topic: Courageous Leadership under Fire
Adult Key Verse: Joshua 1:9
Youth Key Verse: Joshua 1:7
Print Passage: Joshua 1:1-11, 16-17
—In building and developing the chosen people, God showed great concern for their social, physical, and spiritual well-being.

—God's criterion for choosing Joshua as a leader was based on Joshua's careful observance of the law given through Moses.

—Possession of land was a very significant element in the social and spiritual stability of the people because it was a crucial piece of God's covenant with Israel.

—God promised to be with Joshua as He had been with Moses; therefore, God encouraged Joshua to be strong and courageous.

—God provided for continuity of leadership of the covenant community by calling Joshua to succeed Moses.

—God commanded Joshua to unique and specific tasks and to not be frightened or dismayed.

CHILDREN

Children Topic: A Brave Leader Is Chosen

Key Verse: Joshua 1:9

Print Passage: Joshua 1:1-11

—God chose Joshua to succeed Moses as Israel's leader.

—God promised to be with Joshua in the same way that He was with Moses.

—God commanded Joshua to be strong and courageous and obey God's law.

—God promised to empower Joshua to lead the people of Israel to possess the land that God had promised to give to their ancestors.

—Joshua ordered the people to prepare the necessities needed to cross the river and possess the land God promised them.

I. INTRODUCTION

A. Spiritual Leaders

God never leaves us without guidance. Our trust in God is not predicated solely upon that which we believe but cannot see; it is also based upon that which we do see and experience firsthand. Ours is a faith based on both the tangible and the spiritual. Too often, believers discredit the work of God by failing to acknowledge His power in and through our lives. We are often guilty of self-praise for the blessings we receive at the hand of God. God desires that we put Him first in everything.

Our family values should be harmonious with God's plan for the family. A *value* is something that is important to you. Your values determine what you ought and ought not to do. As Christians, we sometimes struggle when what we want to do does not match up with God's desires for our lives. Despite sound leadership, sometimes we choose to go our own way. But God expects us to identify the negatives in our family lives and purge ourselves of them.

Spiritual leaders are God's ambassadors for affirmation of His presence among us. Through God-fearing leadership, we receive sound guidance and affirm His presence among us—thus being inspired to trust and obey His commands, both individually and collectively.

B. Biblical Background

Joshua was an Ephraimite, the son of Nun (see 1 Chronicles 7:22-27). Ironically, though he was born in Egyptian bondage, his original name, *Hoshea*, means "salvation." Joshua was one of the two spies who refused to declare that the Canaanites were too fierce for the Israelites to tackle. He opposed the majority report of his constituents, and insisted that Israel could conquer Canaan if they remained faithful to God. The nation of Israel was so angry with him that he almost suffered stoning (see Numbers 14:7-10). But Joshua remained faithful, and for his faithfulness, he not only escaped destruction, but also received assurance from God that he and Caleb would enter the Promised Land.

Moses prepared Joshua for his role as the new leader of God's chosen people. God then warned Joshua of Israel's apostasy, or falling away, but promised Joshua that he would prevail.

Upon Moses's death, Joshua, then in his nineties, became the official leader of the Hebrew nation. From this point on, Joshua's history revolved around Israel's occupation of Canaan.

II. EXPOSITION AND APPLICATION OF THE SCRIPTURE

A. God Calls Joshua
(Joshua 1:1-9)

NOW AFTER the death of Moses the servant of the LORD it came to pass, that the LORD spake unto Joshua the son of Nun, Moses' minister, saying, Moses my servant is dead; now therefore arise, go over this Jordan, thou, and all this people, unto the land which I do give to them, even to the children of Israel. Every place that the sole of your foot shall tread upon, that have I given unto you, as I said unto Moses. From the wilderness and this Lebanon even unto the great river, the river Euphrates, all the land of the Hittites, and unto the great sea toward the going down of the sun, shall be your coast. There shall not any man be able to stand before thee all the days of thy life: as I was with Moses, so I will be with thee: I will not fail thee, nor forsake thee. Be strong and of a good courage: for unto this people shalt thou divide for an inheritance the land, which I sware unto their fathers to give them. Only be thou strong and very courageous, that thou mayest observe to do according to all the law, which Moses my servant commanded thee: turn not from it to the right hand or to the left, that thou mayest prosper whithersoever thou goest. This book of the law shall not depart out of thy mouth; but thou shalt meditate therein day and night, that thou mayest observe to do according to all that is written therein: for then thou shalt make thy way prosperous, and then thou shalt have good success. Have not I commanded thee? Be strong and of a good courage; be not afraid, neither be thou dismayed: for the LORD thy God is with thee whithersoever thou goest.

Loyalty is the most necessary ingredient in the life of any organization. Without loyalty, a body of people falls apart. This is true of any organization, whether it is social, business, or religious. Allegiance is essential.

The Israelites were about to face the most important challenge of their lives as a nation. Together, they were now to cross the Jordan River to begin their conquest of the Promised Land. They were about to enter a new territory fraught with uncertainties. Many armies would oppose them and threaten to wipe them off the face of the earth. The struggle for the Promised Land would last for years. If ever there was a call for allegiance and loyalty, it was now. Joshua had to mobilize the entire nation to carry out God's orders to march in and conquer the Promised Land. If the struggle was to be successful, there had to be complete commitment, allegiance, and loyalty to the Lord.

In the first nine verses of the first chapter of Joshua, we read God's clarion call to His new leader, Joshua. God knew that the people's hearts were gripped with a deep sense of grief and anguish. They were still grieving over the passing of Moses, who had led them for so long. Moses had been the father of the nation of Israel. It was through God's guidance that Moses had founded and established the nation of Israel. And despite all their struggles and wanderings in the wilderness, the people respected and revered Moses. So God understood how profoundly their grief gripped them. Even Joshua seemed to have fallen into despair and grief. For this reason, God's call had to speak forcefully to Joshua, saying (in essence), "Moses My servant is dead! Arise! Fill the gap! Pick up the mantle of leadership! Get the people ready to cross the Jordan River and enter the Promised Land." But this call was not the only thing God had to say to Joshua. He gave Joshua and the Israelites three great promises: 1) God promised them a land flowing with milk and honey; 2) God promised them that they would conquer their enemies (verse 5); and 3) God promised that He would be with them always. These promises were enough to propel Joshua courageously forward as the leader of God's people.

The Lord swore to Joshua that He would fulfill His promise to bring the Israelites into the land promised to their forefathers. "Swearing an oath" is a custom that can be traced all the way back to ancient times. God gave approval to human custom by swearing an oath. This was to help the people to have a strong support for the mission ahead. God's first oath of promise was to Abraham (see Hebrews 6:13-18). An *oath* was "a solemn statement or claim used to validate a promise." God's oath to Joshua was an irrevocable commitment on which Joshua could depend.

B. Joshua Commands His Officers (Joshua 1:10-11)

Then Joshua commanded the officers of the people, saying, Pass through the host, and command the people, saying, Prepare you victuals; for within three days ye shall pass over this Jordan, to go in to possess the land, which the LORD your God giveth you to possess it.

The land God had promised to the Israelites was filled with powerful people who were wicked to the core. Joshua knew that the conquest of those nations would not be easy. But Joshua's excitement over God's promises and his commitment to God are evident in the command he issued to the officers of the nation of Israel. Joshua gave his officers specific instructions to mobilize the people and march them across the Jordan. As commander of the army, Joshua gave these orders to his *rank and file*—officers in charge of segments of the Israelite population.

The most important characteristic of a true Christian leader is *obedience*. Had Joshua chosen to not obey God following His command to enter the Promised Land, the Israelites' occupation of the Promised Land would have been unnecessarily delayed and would have imposed further hardship on the fledgling nation. Joshua's obedience and absence of hesitation to follow God's command revealed to the Israelites his certain anointing as their spiritual leader. There would be no question as to whether or not they would follow his commands.

There is great significance in Joshua's order to prepare the people within three days. The three-day preparation demonstrated just how organized the Israelites were, even though they were two-to-three-million strong. Consider how difficult a challenge it would be for that number of people to break camp, pack up enough food, prepare their livestock, and provide for their families' safety—all within three days. This would be the Israelites' first demonstration of their loyalty to their new leader and their belief in God's power to deliver them. The three-day challenge was meant to test the Israelites' faithfulness and fortitude.

C. The Officers' Pledge to Joshua (Joshua 1:16-17)

And they answered Joshua, saying, All that thou commandest us we will do, and whithersoever thou sendest us, we will go. According as we hearkened unto Moses in all things, so will we hearken unto thee: only the LORD thy God be with thee, as he was with Moses.

Many organizations fall apart because they fail to follow sound leadership. There are often too many chiefs and not enough Indians. But God's formula for sound leadership includes supporters who are willing to submit and to follow.

Consider the response Joshua received from his officers. The officers pledged their unflinching loyalty and obedience. They would go wherever Joshua would send them. They all agreed that they would obey Joshua in the same manner in which they obeyed Moses. Joshua had their pledge of complete loyalty and obedience, and in so doing, the tribal leaders were demonstrating their great hope and faith in God. They even prayed for Joshua—that the Lord would be with him just as He had been with Moses.

The prayer lifted by the officers confirmed their support of Joshua as God's chosen head of the Israelites. But even more, it presented a unified front to the millions of Israelites who were watching and waiting for direction. Any disagreement among the leaders would have caused the people to split and take sides. Their disagreement would lead to untold consequences. Greatness is never achieved when there is a spirit of division.

The prayer lifted by Joshua's officers should also cause us to pause and wonder how often our leaders fail because we fail to pray for them, show our loyalty to them, and obey them. Ministry leaders are often expected to plan ministry outreach and then do all the "reaching out." When the effort fails, the finger is pointed at the leadership. But we see from this lesson that every man and woman has a role to play in ministry, and without our loyalty and obedience, there is no success.

Joshua's officers demonstrated their total commitment to their commander. Further study shows that they even passed a decree that any rebel would be executed. If any officer refused to carry out the orders of Joshua, no questions would be asked; he would simply be executed. Their decree pointed out their belief in the absolute necessity of obedience to the orders of Joshua. Joshua's command to his officers was stirring, but equally stirring were the words of encouragement coming back from his followers. They promised to be strong and courageous. They only wanted one response from Joshua: that he would be just as strong a commander as they were followers.

Most people would shun the challenge of conquering a land inhabited by iniquitous people, but not Joshua. God prepared Joshua for the conquest and instilled in him the courage necessary to be an unfailing leader. Both Joshua and Caleb are a study in unflinching and unfailing faithfulness and seasoned courage. As a result of their courageous stand for God, they persevered over the doubts of the people and the size of their enemies.

III. CONCLUDING REFLECTION

Faith, trust, spiritual conviction, willingness to follow sound leadership—all these are requirements of a believer who desires to be a member of the community of faith. We must learn to recognize those leaders among us who are selfless, God-focused, and able to lead us by example.

The nation of Israel is still facing a struggle to keep their Promised Land. All the nations that surround them today are either adversaries or wary observers. No nation in the Middle East has wholeheartedly embraced Israel's right to possess the Promised Land. But God is still sending Israel capable leaders who continue to deliver them through this fearsome millennium. That is because when God chooses a leader, He fits the leader to the task.

PRAYER

Heavenly Father, we confess that we are disobedient to Your commands. We have gone astray and our disobedience has brought defeat to us. We ask that You forgive us. Enable us to remain sensitive to Your Word and always ready to obey You from henceforth. In Jesus' name we pray. Amen.

WORD POWER

Be strong (Hebrew: *kha-zak*)—this word is in the imperative mood, which means it is a command. God issued a command to Joshua and he must obey. Obedience to this command would lead to victory for Joshua. Modern society hates commands. We want to do things in our own way. Such attitudes lead to a mindset that opposes the Word of God. From home to school and to church, we have become a people bent on disobeying God. But as Joshua was commanded, we too are commanded to be strong in the work of God.

HOME DAILY BIBLE READINGS
(August 31–September 6, 2009)

Joshua: A Leader for the People

MONDAY, August 31: "Pray for Leaders" (1 Timothy 2:1-6)
TUESDAY, September 1: "Training as a Leader" (Exodus 24:12-18)
WEDNESDAY, September 2: "Misplaced Zeal" (Numbers 11:24-29)
THURSDAY, September 3: "Following without Reserve" (Numbers 32:6-13)
FRIDAY, September 4: "Commissioned to Lead" (Numbers 27:15-23)
SATURDAY, September 5: "Ready to Lead" (Deuteronomy 34:1-9)
SUNDAY, September 6: "A Leader Led by God" (Joshua 1:1-11, 16-17)

UNIT I: Leaders in the Covenant Community
CHILDREN'S UNIT: God Chooses Leaders for the People
FALL QUARTER

LESSON 2 — September 13, 2009

GIDEON: A DELIVERER FOR THE PEOPLE

DEVOTIONAL READING: **1 Corinthians 1:26-31**
PRINT PASSAGE: **Judges 6:1-3, 7-14**

BACKGROUND SCRIPTURE: **Judges 6–8**
KEY VERSE: **Judges 6:14**

Judges 6:1-3, 7-14—KJV

AND THE children of Israel did evil in the sight of the LORD: and the LORD delivered them into the hand of Midian seven years.

2 And the hand of Midian prevailed against Israel: and because of the Midianites the children of Israel made them the dens which are in the mountains, and caves, and strong holds.

3 And so it was, when Israel had sown, that the Midianites came up, and the Amalekites, and the children of the east, even they came up against them.

.....

7 And it came to pass, when the children of Israel cried unto the LORD because of the Midianites,

8 That the LORD sent a prophet unto the children of Israel, which said unto them, Thus saith the LORD God of Israel, I brought you up from Egypt, and brought you forth out of the house of bondage;

9 And I delivered you out of the hand of the Egyptians, and out of the hand of all that oppressed you, and drave them out from before you, and gave you their land;

10 And I said unto you, I am the LORD your God; fear not the gods of the Amorites, in whose land ye dwell: but ye have not obeyed my voice.

11 And there came an angel of the LORD, and sat under an oak which was in Ophrah, that pertained unto Joash the Abi-ezrite: and his son Gideon threshed wheat by the winepress, to hide it from the Midianites.

12 And the angel of the LORD appeared unto him, and said unto him, The LORD is with thee, thou mighty man of valour.

13 And Gideon said unto him, Oh my Lord, if the LORD be with us, why then is all this befallen us? and

Judges 6:1-3, 7-14—NRSV

THE ISRAELITES did what was evil in the sight of the LORD, and the LORD gave them into the hand of Midian seven years.

2 The hand of Midian prevailed over Israel; and because of Midian the Israelites provided for themselves hiding places in the mountains, caves and strongholds.

3 For whenever the Israelites put in seed, the Midianites and the Amalekites and the people of the east would come up against them.

.....

7 When the Israelites cried to the LORD on account of the Midianites,

8 the LORD sent a prophet to the Israelites; and he said to them, "Thus says the LORD, the God of Israel: I led you up from Egypt, and brought you out of the house of slavery;

9 and I delivered you from the hand of the Egyptians, and from the hand of all who oppressed you, and drove them out before you, and gave you their land;

10 and I said to you, 'I am the LORD your God; you shall not pay reverence to the gods of the Amorites, in whose land you live.' But you have not given heed to my voice."

11 Now the angel of the LORD came and sat under the oak at Ophrah, which belonged to Joash the Abiezrite, as his son Gideon was beating out wheat in the wine press, to hide it from the Midianites.

12 The angel of the LORD appeared to him and said to him, "The LORD is with you, you mighty warrior."

13 Gideon answered him, "But sir, if the LORD is with us, why then has all this happened to us? And where are all his wonderful deeds that our ancestors

UNIFYING LESSON PRINCIPLE

When situations seem hopeless, we assume there is nothing we can do. How can we face threats to our well-being—even our very existence—with confidence? In the story of Gideon—the self-described weakest member of the weakest family in Israel—it demonstrated that God calls and equips ordinary people to bring about extraordinary changes.

where be all his miracles which our fathers told us of, saying, Did not the LORD bring us up from Egypt? but now the LORD hath forsaken us, and delivered us into the hands of the Midianites.

14 And the LORD looked upon him, and said, Go in this thy might, and thou shalt save Israel from the hand of the Midianites: have not I sent thee?

recounted to us, saying, 'Did not the LORD bring us up from Egypt?' But now the LORD has cast us off, and given us into the hand of Midian."

14 Then the LORD turned to him and said, "Go in this might of yours and deliver Israel from the hand of Midian; I hereby commission you."

TOPICAL OUTLINE OF THE LESSON

I. Introduction
  A. Facing Challenges
  B. Biblical Background

II. Exposition and Application of the Scripture
  A. The Plundering of Israel (Judges 6:1-3)
  B. Their Cry and God's Rebuke (Judges 6:7-10)
  C. The Call of Gideon (Judges 6:11-14)

III. Concluding Reflection

LESSON OBJECTIVES

Upon completion of this lesson, the students will know that:

1. God will not tolerate oppressors to extinguish His chosen ones;
2. God raises up leaders for challenging times; and,
3. God listens to His chosen ones.

POINTS TO BE EMPHASIZED

ADULT/YOUTH

Adult Topic: An Unexpected Leader
Youth Topic: Confident Leadership beyond Doubt
Adult Key Verse: Judges 6:14
Youth Key Verse: Judges 6:15
Print Passage: Judges 6:1-3, 7-14

—During the period of Judges, Israel faced many trials because of their disobedience and unfaithfulness (see Judges 2).
—Gideon is an example of God's calling and equipping ordinary people to bring about extraordinary changes.
—For reassurance that God was leading him, Gideon sought proof from God a number of times.
—Corrective punishment from the Lord came at the hands of the enemies of the covenant community.
—God's raising Gideon up to deliver the covenant community followed the punishment by the Lord.
—God allowed Gideon to object to and complain about his calling.
—God gave Gideon confidence by allowing him to test God's power and promises.

CHILDREN
Children Topic: A Helpful Leader Is Chosen
Key Verse: Judges 6:14
Print Passage: Judges 6:1-3, 11-14; 7:19-21
—God allowed the enemy of the Israelites to dominate them for seven years because of their disobedience.
—After the Midianites overpowered the Israelites, they had to protect themselves by living in caves and forts in the mountains.

—An angel of God appeared to Gideon while he was threshing grain in a hidden location, and said, "God is with you."
—When Gideon doubted God's presence, the Lord commanded him to go in God's power and save the Israelites from their enemy.
—Gideon led the three hundred, carefully chosen Israelite soldiers in enacting God's plan of surprise military strategy, with which they defeated the Midianites.

I. INTRODUCTION

A. Facing Challenges

When we face challenges and trials that overpower us emotionally and spiritually, the first thing Christians do is turn to God in prayer.

Prayer should be a *daily* communication with our Creator. The intimate contact of daily prayer with God draws us into a better understanding of His purpose and His plan for our lives. It is when we lose our daily contact with God that we also lose sight of God's constant presence among us.

It is critical for the believer to accept the truth that God does not intervene on our behalf only when we pray. God is moving the world toward His preordained purpose and plan, and He can and will execute a plan for us according to our personal needs, in spite of the inconsistency of our prayers. Time and again the Bible bears proof of this truth. The Israelites would never have been blessed with repeated deliverance from paganism and apostasy had God not desired to act out of His divine love, in spite of Israel's repeated disobedience.

God's purpose and plan are far greater than our finite minds can even comprehend. When we call out to Him in prayer, we can rest assured that He is already aware of our circumstances.

B. Biblical Background

The book of Judges is a record of the period in the life of Israel when God sent judges to lead and deliver His people. Scholars agree that the period of the Judges began with the death of Joshua and ended with the coronation of Saul. This period formed a transition between God's mediating activity through Moses and Joshua and His rule through the anointed kings of the monarchy. During this period of the Judges, God raised up His chosen deliverers, whom He anointed with His Spirit, to rescue the people of Israel from their enemies. The judges (in order) were Othniel, Ehud, Shamgar, Deborah, Gideon, Tola, Jair, Jephthah, Ibzan, Elon, Abdon, and Samson. In all, they served God and Israel for more than four hundred years.

Gideon was the sixth judge of Israel, a military hero and a spiritual leader who delivered God's people from the oppression of the Midianites. As a young boy, Gideon had seen the Midianites and the Amalekites oppress his people for seven years (Judges 6:1). The Midianites and Amalekites were like invading locusts: they camped on the Israelites' land like roving bands of warriors. When harvest time came, these enemy invaders would destroy the Israelites' crops and animals, and plunder their farmhouses.

Israel's misfortune was apparently caused by the people's spiritual disobedience and their relapse into the worship of Baal. Her disobedience to God and her worship of Canaanite gods resulted in her failure to experience divine blessing and the full conquest of her enemies. Gideon witnessed all this, in preparation for the day when God would hear the cries of a repentant Israel and send His angel to anoint him as the leader of Israel, to deliver them from their enemies.

II. EXPOSITION AND APPLICATION OF THE SCRIPTURE

A. The Plundering of Israel
(Judges 6:1-3)

AND THE children of Israel did evil in the sight of the Lord: and the Lord delivered them into the hand of Midian seven years. And the hand of Midian prevailed against Israel: and because of the Midianites the children of Israel made them the dens which are in the mountains, and caves, and strong holds. And so it was, when Israel had sown, that the Midianites came up, and the Amalekites, and the children of the east, even they came up against them.

Disobedience to God always elicits a great price. For the Israelites it meant being oppressed by enemies. The Israelites' worship of the pagan god, Baal, caused God to withdraw His hedge of divine protection from them. The seven years of oppression that followed at the hands of the Midianites was God's divine chastening for Israel's idolatry and evil practices. This particular period of disobedience and subsequent oppression was a relatively brief period of persecution sandwiched in between two longer, forty-year periods of peace.

The strength of the Midianites forced the Israelites to hide themselves and their farms' produce in caves and mountain clefts during harvest time when this enemy would descend upon them in successful attempts to steal the Israelite nation's bountiful harvest. This repeated seasonal plundering of Israel's bountiful harvest crops caused impoverishment. After seven years of a losing battle, the Israelites finally cried out to the Lord for help to defeat their enemy.

Israel's cry was apparently not a cry of repentance for the sin of breaking their covenant with God. They had no idea that their oppression at the hand of the Midianites was the result of their pagan worship. All they knew was that their enemy was consistently plundering the crops.

Christians today often make the same mistake. We assume that our misery has nothing to do with our own disobedient and carnal natures. We would rather continue in sin than repent and change our ways. Yet, we petition God to save us from the pain of our carnal existence.

B. Their Cry and God's Rebuke
(Judges 6:7-10)

And it came to pass, when the children of Israel cried unto the Lord because of the Midianites, That the Lord sent a prophet unto the children of Israel, which said unto them, Thus saith the Lord God of Israel, I brought you up from Egypt, and brought you forth out of the house of bondage; And I delivered you out of the hand of the Egyptians, and out of the hand of all that oppressed you, and drave them out from before you, and gave you their land; And I said unto you, I am the Lord your God; fear not the gods of the Amorites, in whose land ye dwell: but ye have not obeyed my voice.

The apostasy of Israel was so great that they actually feared the gods of the Amorites. Baal was the chief god, but there were many others whom the Amorites worshiped. The Israelites' fear and worship of false gods had become so commonplace that even respected Israelite religious leaders were guilty of participation in the practice of offering sacrifices to these false gods.

The practice of worshiping false gods had gone on so long that Israel no longer recognized it as sin. The Israelites were apparently not aware of the moral cause behind the enemy oppression that they were now suffering. They cried unto God for help to escape their poverty and deprivation, and He heard their wailing and sent a prophet into their midst. They listened as the prophet pointed out God's terrible disappointment in their failure to remain faithful to the one true and living God. The prophet reminded the Israelites of their covenant obligations to the Lord, who had delivered them from Egypt, and he reminded them that they were not to worship false gods. Finally, he rebuked them for their disobedience.

We learn from the Israelite experience that sin loses its sting over time. Though sin is a real and potent evil that produces sorrow and distress, we see from the Israelite example that repeated sin often becomes acceptable. The sin of the Old Testament demonstrated rebellion against God. Since the penalty for sin is death (see Romans 6:23), we could only be made holy through the sacrifice of a Savior, our Lord Jesus Christ.

There is no more painful experience than to hear God recount our sins. Christians who study the Word of God know that no one will escape this painful ordeal. The Bible teaches that even those who are saved will one day stand before God and have their sins recounted.

Knowing that we too will one day face God and hear Him recount our sins, we should be highly motivated to strive to perfect our walk with Christ.

C. The Call of Gideon
(Judges 6:11-14)

And there came an angel of the Lord, and sat under an oak which was in Ophrah, that pertained unto Joash the Abi-ezrite: and his son Gideon threshed wheat by the winepress, to hide it from the Midianites. And the angel of the Lord appeared unto him, and said unto him, The Lord is with thee, thou mighty man of valour. And Gideon said unto him, Oh my Lord, if the Lord be with us, why then is all this befallen us? and where be all his miracles which our fathers told us of, saying, Did not the Lord bring us up from Egypt? but now the Lord hath forsaken us, and delivered us into the hands of the Midianites. And the Lord looked upon him, and said, Go in this thy might, and thou shalt save Israel from the hand of the Midianites: have not I sent thee?

Gideon's call or commission was executed by an angel of the Lord who appeared to him under an oak tree. It is recorded in the Scripture that Gideon was threshing his wheat at a winepress. Normally, wheat was threshed (the grain separated from the stalks) in an open area on a hard-packed threshing floor. The farmer would use his oxen to pull heavy sledges over the stalks in order to separate the wheat. The fact that Gideon was threshing wheat in a winepress tells us that he was both embarrassed by his small harvest and afraid that the Midianites would discover and seize what little he had.

The manner in which the angel addressed Gideon immediately tells us that God's presence was with Gideon. He used the singular term *thee* or *you*, and called Gideon a mighty warrior. At this point Gideon was anything but a mighty warrior, but the angel was proclaiming Gideon's potential through divine enablement, and endowing him with a new rank in the community as a military leader.

The first thing we notice is that Gideon did not question the angel's declaration that he would be a mighty warrior. Instead, Gideon questioned whether the Lord was with him. Gideon's initial response ignored the singular pronoun *you* (see Judges 6:13), and he replied, "If the Lord be with *us*, why then is all this befallen us?" It is clear that Gideon was questioning the Lord's divine promise, in view of his people's present unimaginable circumstances. But Gideon did get one thing right: he correctly concluded that the Israelites were in their present situation because the Lord put them into "the hands of the Midianites."

The second time the angel spoke, he spoke as the Lord, and He commissioned Gideon directly. God gave Gideon a direct command to go and save Israel from their enemies. God reminded Gideon that he would not be acting on his own strength, but with supernatural power from on High.

Why did God choose Gideon over other men of valor? This special task required great courage because of the fierceness of the Midianites. To test Gideon's bravery, his first assignment was to destroy his own father's altar to Baal in the family's backyard (see Judges 6:25). This act must have taken great courage because Gideon's father and his friends worshiped at that altar. Gideon and ten servants destroyed the altar in the middle of the night and erected an altar to the Lord in its place. As soon as it was built, Gideon presented an offering to the Lord (see Judges 6:27-28). When the community discovered what Gideon had done, they called his father Joash to account for his son's behavior. Joash defended his son by implying that "if he be a god, let him plead for himself." From that day on, Gideon was called *Jerubbaal*, meaning "Let Baal pleads."

Strong spiritual leaders never operate in their own strength. They rely on the strength that only their sovereign and supreme God can provide. In John 14:16-17, Jesus said, "And I will pray the Father, and He will give you another Helper, that He may abide with you forever—the Spirit of truth, whom the world cannot receive, because it neither sees Him nor knows Him; but you know Him, for He dwells with you and will be in you" (NKJV). But in Gideon's day, few people had any idea what it meant to be baptized by the Holy Spirit. They only knew God as their Sovereign Master, whom they worshiped and hoped to one day glorify in heaven. But their lack of knowledge did not mean that the Holy Spirit did not work in and through the lives of the Old Testament saints.

We often fail God when we attempt to define His power within our realm of understanding. Gideon would soon discover that the exceeding abundant power of God would use him in a mighty way.

III. CONCLUDING REFLECTION

What proof do we require of God before we will obey His commands? Three times in John 14 Jesus reminds us that love equals obedience. If we say that we love God, then we must also be willing to demonstrate that love through obedience to His will. Our love for God is to be evident in our willingness to serve Him without hesitation. Gideon and the Israelites were familiar with this verse of the Mosaic Law from Deuteronomy 6:5 (NKJV), which puts it another way: "You shall love the LORD your God with all your heart, with all your soul, and with all your strength." We know that to love God means to obey Him in every aspect of our living—to the deepest core of our personalities, with all that is within us.

PRAYER

Heavenly Father, help us to solely depend on You. Help us when we are troubled because of various situations which defy our understanding. When You looked at Gideon that day, You never left him until he subdued the enemies of Israel. In Jesus' name we pray. Amen.

WORD POWER

Turn (Hebrew: *pana*)—the word *turn* or *look* in the Key Verse is cast in the imperfect tense, which indicates a continuous action of God. It is used to describe a single action as opposed to a repeated action.

In the context of our lesson when God turned (looked) to Gideon, He never took His eye off Gideon again until Gideon defeated the Amalekites. We too are blessed with the continuous countenance of God on us. The assurance of God's eye on us should remove fear and doubt as we engage in His work.

HOME DAILY BIBLE READINGS

(September 7-13, 2009)

Gideon: A Deliverer for the People

MONDAY, September 7: "The Standards of God's Choice" (1 Corinthians 1:26-31)

TUESDAY, September 8: "Crying for Help" (Judges 6:4-10)

WEDNESDAY, September 9: "Seeking Proof of Favor" (Judges 6:14-24)

THURSDAY, September 10: "Cautious Obedience" (Judges 6:25-27)

FRIDAY, September 11: "Thinning the Ranks" (Judges 7:2-8)

SATURDAY, September 12: "Assured for the Task" (Judges 7:9-15)

SUNDAY, September 13: "Go and Deliver" (Judges 6:1-3, 7-14)

LESSON 3   **September 20, 2009**

EZRA: A PRIEST FOR THE PEOPLE

DEVOTIONAL READING: **Psalm 32:1-5**
PRINT PASSAGE: **Ezra 9:5-11, 15**

BACKGROUND SCRIPTURE: **Ezra 9**
KEY VERSE: **Ezra 9:6**

Ezra 9:5-11, 15—KJV

5 And at the evening sacrifice I arose up from my heaviness; and having rent my garment and my mantle, I fell upon my knees, and spread out my hands unto the LORD my God,

6 And said, O my God, I am ashamed and blush to lift up my face to thee, my God: for our iniquities are increased over our head, and our trespass is grown up unto the heavens.

7 Since the days of our fathers have we been in a great trespass unto this day; and for our iniquities have we, our kings, and our priests, been delivered into the hand of the kings of the lands, to the sword, to captivity, and to a spoil, and to confusion of face, as it is this day.

8 And now for a little space grace hath been shewed from the LORD our God, to leave us a remnant to escape, and to give us a nail in his holy place, that our God may lighten our eyes, and give us a little reviving in our bondage.

9 For we were bondmen; yet our God hath not forsaken us in our bondage, but hath extended mercy unto us in the sight of the kings of Persia, to give us a reviving, to set up the house of our God, and to repair the desolations thereof, and to give us a wall in Judah and in Jerusalem.

10 And now, O our God, what shall we say after this? for we have forsaken thy commandments,

11 Which thou hast commanded by thy servants the prophets, saying, The land, unto which ye go to possess it, is an unclean land with the filthiness of the people of the lands, with their abominations, which have filled it from one end to another with their uncleanness.

.....

15 O LORD God of Israel, thou art righteous: for we remain yet escaped, as it is this day: behold, we are before thee in our trespasses: for we cannot stand before thee because of this.

Ezra 9:5-11, 15—NRSV

5 At the evening sacrifice I got up from my fasting, with my garments and my mantle torn, and fell on my knees, spread out my hands to the LORD my God,

6 and said, "O my God, I am too ashamed and embarrassed to lift my face to you, my God, for our iniquities have risen higher than our heads, and our guilt has mounted up to the heavens.

7 From the days of our ancestors to this day we have been deep in guilt, and for our iniquities we, our kings, and our priests have been handed over to the kings of the lands, to the sword, to captivity, to plundering, and to utter shame, as is now the case.

8 But now for a brief moment favor has been shown by the LORD our God, who has left us a remnant, and given us a stake in his holy place, in order that he may brighten our eyes and grant us a little sustenance in our slavery.

9 For we are slaves; yet our God has not forsaken us in our slavery, but has extended to us his steadfast love before the kings of Persia, to give us new life to set up the house of our God, to repair its ruins, and to give us a wall in Judea and Jerusalem.

10 "And now, our God, what shall we say after this? For we have forsaken your commandments,

11 which you commanded by your servants the prophets, saying, 'The land that you are entering to possess is a land unclean with the pollutions of the peoples of the lands, with their abominations. They have filled it from end to end with their uncleanness.'"

.....

15 "O LORD, God of Israel, you are just, but we have escaped as a remnant, as is now the case. Here we are before you in our guilt, though no one can face you because of this."

UNIFYING LESSON PRINCIPLE

Sin, wherever it may be found, seems so prevalent that we often do not know how to deal with it. What should be our response to sin? The priest Ezra, who had opened his heart and mind to God's teachings, diligently taught the people the laws of God and responded to sin among the Israelites by fervently praying for God's forgiveness and grace.

TOPICAL OUTLINE OF THE LESSON

I. Introduction
A. Repentance
B. Biblical Background

II. Exposition and Application of the Scripture
A. The Confession Prior to Revival (Ezra 9:5-11)
B. The Desperate Plea for Forgiveness (Ezra 9:15)

III. Concluding Reflection

LESSON OBJECTIVES

Upon completion of this lesson, the students will know that:
1. The desire of sin is to enslave us;
2. Repentance is the panacea for a relationship with God; and,
3. We should uphold our leaders and church members in prayer.

POINTS TO BE EMPHASIZED

ADULT/YOUTH
Adult Topic: Getting Back on Course
Youth Topic: Faithful Leadership Calls for Obedience
Adult Key Verse: Ezra 9:6
Youth Key Verse: Ezra 9:15
Print Passage: Ezra 9:5-11, 15
—The priest Ezra felt a deep personal responsibility for and identification with the people in their disobedience to God.
—Ezra showed his awareness that the people may choose to begin a new life or to remain in sin.
—The people of Israel did not separate themselves from the paganism of the surrounding cultures.
—Ezra led the people in a prayer of confession.
—Returning to God's city requires returning to knowing and obeying God's law.
—The accomplishment of any sacred mission requires the hand of the Lord on the leader.
—Keeping God's laws requires confession and turning from sins.

CHILDREN
Children Topic: A Teaching Leader Is Chosen
Key Verse: Ezra 7:10
Print Passage: Ezra 7:1-10
—The king of Persia gave Ezra a decree allowing him to lead some Jews in returning to Jerusalem.
—The king's generous decree resulted from God blessing Ezra.
—Ezra was willing to give up his prominent position in the king's kingdom in order to return to Jerusalem to teach God's laws to the Israelites.
—Ezra devoted himself to studying, obeying, and teaching God's laws in Israel.

I. INTRODUCTION

A. Repentance

In the life of the Christian, repentance is not a one-time event. We all remember the moment when we confessed our sin and invited Christ into our hearts. *Repentance* begins with confession of our guilt and recognition that our sin is against God. But genuine repentance goes much farther. Real repentance takes full responsibility for sin—past, present, and future. It does not blame others, but quests for honest relationship with God. As long as we continue to be open and honest with God, He can continue to work with us, even after we have committed most grievous sins.

B. Biblical Background

In the book of Ezra is described the resettlement of the Hebrew people in their homeland after their long exile in Babylon. The return came about after the defeat of Babylon by the Persian Empire. The Hebrews returned from exile in two phases. The book of Ezra opens with an explanation of how the first return from exile happened. Cyrus, king of Persia, issued a proclamation allowing the exiles to return to Jerusalem to rebuild their Temple and resettle their native land. In 2 Chronicles 36:23 (NKJV), Cyrus declared that God "commanded me to build Him a house at Jerusalem." At Cyrus's direction and with his permission, about fifty thousand of the people returned to Jerusalem under the leadership of Zerubbabel.

Sixty years later, Ezra arrived on the scene. As priest, Ezra was chosen by God to bring the remaining exiles home to Jerusalem. The theme of the book of Ezra is a restoration of the remnant of God's chosen people. God acted to preserve a remnant of the Jews, even when they were being held captive in a pagan land.

II. EXPOSITION AND APPLICATION OF THE SCRIPTURE

A. The Confession Prior to Revival
(Ezra 9:5-11)

And at the evening sacrifice I arose up from my heaviness; and having rent my garment and my mantle, I fell upon my knees, and spread out my hands unto the LORD my God, And said, O my God, I am ashamed and blush to lift up my face to thee, my God: for our iniquities are increased over our head, and our trespass is grown up unto the heavens. Since the days of our fathers have we been in a great trespass unto this day; and for our iniquities have we, our kings, and our priests, been delivered into the hand of the kings of the lands, to the sword, to captivity, and to a spoil, and to confusion of face, as it is this day. And now for a little space grace hath been shewed from the LORD our God, to leave us a remnant to escape, and to give us a nail in his holy place, that our God may lighten our eyes, and give us a little reviving in our bondage. For we were bondmen; yet our God hath not forsaken us in our bondage, but hath extended mercy unto us in the sight of the kings of Persia, to give us a reviving, to set up the house of our God, and to repair the desolations thereof, and to give us a wall in Judah and in Jerusalem. And now, O our God, what shall we say after this? for we have forsaken thy commandments, Which thou hast commanded by thy servants the prophets, saying, The land, unto which ye go to possess it, is an unclean land with the filthiness of the people of the lands, with their abominations, which have filled it from one end to another with their uncleanness.

Consider how long the Jews had been in exile, and the impact that experience had on their worship of God. The Babylonians did not permit captives to worship as they saw fit. Instead, they were forced to conform to the pagan worship of their captors. For fifty years or more, they were forced either to abandon all of their worship rituals and practices or be condemned to death.

What does it take to revive a dead faith? It takes a loving God's intervention. In spite of their exposure to the heathen practices of the Babylonians, God preserved a remnant of the covenant faith. That remnant would be the catalyst to restore the Hebrew nation to a right relationship with its creator.

We learn a valuable lesson about the providence or divine intervention of God when we notice that God used several different Persian kings in the book of Ezra to play a significant role in returning God's covenant people to their homeland. The first step was to conquer the Hebrews' oppressors. God used Persia, a nation known for its religious tolerance, to conquer Babylon. Step two was the restoration of the Temple in Jerusalem. God used the kindness of King Cyrus to send fifty thousand home to complete the reconstruction project. God's use of Persia's conquest of Babylon and the compassion of King Cyrus demonstrates that He can use the unrighteous as well as the righteous to work His ultimate will in the lives of His people.

The final step in the return to Jerusalem came over fifty years later. When Ezra finally returned to Jerusalem, it was during the reign of Artaxerxes. Fifty-seven years had passed since the rebuilding of the Temple in 515 BC under the reign of Darius I. Though Ezra held no official position within the government when he returned home, he had the blessing of the pagan king, and because of that favor, Ezra was given a free hand in what he desired to do. His favor was yet another affirmation that God was with him. Thus God used an obedient priest, Ezra, a man well-versed in the Law of God, to re-teach the ways of Yahweh. From our text we learn of Ezra's great faith in God as he confessed the sins of his people.

Ezra was a man of faith. He knew the magnitude of the sin of his people, and for that reason he prayed for their forgiveness. At the evening sacrifice, he was on his knees pleading for God's pardon. Physical postures of prayer are often described in the Bible: 1) kneeling is a sign of humble respect; and 2) raising one's hand is a sign of openness, total surrender to the Lord, and recognizing that all gifts are from the Lord's hand. The prayer of Ezra was not frivolous. He really meant business with the Lord. Ezra felt an overwhelming sense of shame. His prayer was one of confession; though Ezra had not participated in this sin himself, he identified with the sin of his people.

As we come to verse 7, Ezra acknowledged that the people's sinful actions were part of their history, including kings, priests, and the people. A thorough confession of sin must not sweep anything under the rug. Ezra noted that their sin brought upon them loss of life, property, freedom, and honor. The reference to "a wall in Judah" as found in verse 9 could also mean "a peg." It is a metaphor which describes the mercy of the Lord. It means that the Israelites were not totally forgotten by God. God is truly a God of mercy and He left them a place to occupy.

Ezra confessed the sins of the nations by referring to what the prophets had preached. Moses is called a prophet in Deuteronomy 18:15 and 34:10, and Hosea 12:13.

B. The Desperate Plea for Forgiveness (Ezra 9:15)

O Lord God of Israel, thou art righteous: for we remain yet escaped, as it is this day: behold, we are before thee in our trespasses: for we cannot stand before thee because of this.

As we read verse 15, we can feel Ezra's expression of the pain of confession and the complete and utter shame of sin. *Atonement* is the only way to release the sinner from that kind of pain. The fact that we cannot atone from sin until we first offer God a sincere confession of guilt has been the stumbling block for many so-called Christians.

Two counterfeit forms of repentance are often passed off as the real thing. The first is the regret expressed when a person is caught in sin. This type of counterfeit confession is prompted by a sense of embarrassment. The second is an admonition that you will "try to do better next time," a confession that is seldom accompanied by sincerity.

Genuine repentance involves several things. The first step is, of course, *confession*—not just a statement of one's wrongdoing, but also a genuine acknowledgement that one has sinned against God. Ezra realized that there was no rational explanation for sin. We cannot explain away our transgression with a confession that we will be more careful next time. And we cannot place the blame on someone else, even if that person was an accomplice to our sin. When the blame is placed on someone else, our repentance is rendered incomplete. A truly repentant person takes full responsibility for his or her actions no matter what happened, who was involved, or who exposed him or her to the temptation. As we read verse 15, we are certain Ezra realized that true repentance requires total honesty with God.

Ezra's prayer was not only a confession of his own sin, but the sins of his nation. He recognized the interconnectivity of all their sins and the great need for nationwide repentance. Thus he assumed the role of intercessor and prayed for his country and its leadership. *Intercessory prayer* for others is an essential part of the prayer life of any Christian. Yet, those who develop a healthy and consistent prayer life often fall short in their responsibility to pray for our leaders. It is stated in the Scripture, "The powers that be are ordained of God" (Romans 13:1). In other words, they exist either by God's sovereign will or permissive will. And it is our duty to pray for the overall effectiveness of leadership within the perfect will of God.

Belief and *repentance* are so interconnected that you cannot have one without the other. They are like two sides of the same coin. Charles Ryrie explains it this way: "Repentance focuses on changing one's mind about one's former conception of God and disbelief in Jesus Christ. Faith in Christ focuses on receiving Christ as your personal Savior."

Ezra ended his plea by saying that God is righteous. In other words, the righteousness of God prevailed. Israel had sinned, yet God in His righteousness kept a remnant for His own sake.

III. CONCLUDING REFLECTION

The Adamic nature is still in each and every one of us. The sinful nature of human beings is to rebel against God. Since Adam, the drifting away from God has continued to the present. However, we see Ezra as an uncompromising leader. He did not participate in the sins of his generation, yet he pleaded for their forgiveness. He did not take himself out and play the "holier than thou" attitude card. Ezra's life became a mirror for Christians in our time. He belonged to a sinful generation, yet he did not partake of their wantonness. As a teaching scribe, he led his people on a road to repentance by taking the lead. He personally fasted for days without involving anybody. We too can do the same for our generation.

It is important for us to understand that once we receive Christ, we will continue to grow in Christian faith and character. Our repentance is a change of mind that leads to a change in behavior. God is looking for us to be totally honest about our sin. He wants us to be honest about our weaknesses, our failures, and our frustrations. Honesty with God promotes fellowship with God. God wants us to understand that sin enslaves us and separates us from Him. The only way to release the chains of sin and reunite oneself with God is to have a heart of repentance and a spirit of continual confession. Only the repentant heart receives God's forgiveness.

PRAYER

Father in heaven, we thank You for Your loving kindness. We have sinned. We have chosen our part and there has been no peace. Forgive us, Father, and help us to remain faithful even to the end. In Jesus' name we pray. Amen.

WORD POWER

Ashamed (Hebrew: *buwsh* [bush])—means "to be disconcerted, be disappointed, to fail in hope and expectation." Ezra personally felt ashamed to look God in the face when he reflected over the sin of his people. Sin causes a sense of shame and renders relationship with God impossible. This is the reason Ezra singularly pleaded for God's forgiveness. The sense of shame led to genuine repentance. *Repentance* is agreeing with God: "You are right, and I am wrong; You are holy, and I am vile."

HOME DAILY BIBLE READINGS
(September 14-20, 2009)

Ezra: A Priest for the People

MONDAY, September 14: "Confession and Forgiveness" (Psalm 32:1-5)
TUESDAY, September 15: "Skilled in the Law of Moses" (Ezra 7:1-6)
WEDNESDAY, September 16: "A Heart Set on Study" (Ezra 7:7-10)
THURSDAY, September 17: "Guided by God's Hand" (Ezra 7:25-28)
FRIDAY, September 18: "Seeking God's Protection" (Ezra 8:21-23)
SATURDAY, September 19: "Hearing the Law of God" (Nehemiah 8:1-12)
SUNDAY, September 20: "A Fervent Prayer for the People" (Ezra 9:5-11, 15)

Blessed — Happy

LESSON 4　　　　　　　　　　　　**September 27, 2009**

NEHEMIAH: A MOTIVATOR FOR THE PEOPLE

DEVOTIONAL READING: **Isaiah 62:1-7**
PRINT PASSAGE: **Nehemiah 2:5, 11-20**

BACKGROUND SCRIPTURE: **Nehemiah 2**
KEY VERSE: **Nehemiah 2:18**

Nehemiah 2:5, 11-20—KJV

5 And I said unto the king, If it please the king, and if thy servant have found favour in thy sight, that thou wouldest send me unto Judah, unto the city of my fathers' sepulchres, that I may build it.

.....

11 So I came to Jerusalem, and was there three days.

12 And I arose in the night, I and some few men with me; neither told I any man what my God had put in my heart to do at Jerusalem: neither was there any beast with me, save the beast that I rode upon.

13 And I went out by night by the gate of the valley, even before the dragon well, and to the dung port, and viewed the walls of Jerusalem, which were broken down, and the gates thereof were consumed with fire.

14 Then I went on to the gate of the fountain, and to the king's pool: but there was no place for the beast that was under me to pass.

15 Then went I up in the night by the brook, and viewed the wall, and turned back, and entered by the gate of the valley, and so returned.

16 And the rulers knew not whither I went, or what I did; neither had I as yet told it to the Jews, nor to the priests, nor to the nobles, nor to the rulers, nor to the rest that did the work.

17 Then said I unto them, Ye see the distress that we are in, how Jerusalem lieth waste, and the gates thereof are burned with fire: come, and let us build up the wall of Jerusalem, that we be no more a reproach.

18 Then I told them of the hand of my God which was good upon me; as also the king's words that he had spoken unto me. And they said, Let us rise up and build. So they strengthened their hands for this good work.

Nehemiah 2:5, 11-20—NRSV

5 Then I said to the king, "If it pleases the king, and if your servant has found favor with you, I ask that you send me to Judah, to the city of my ancestors' graves, so that I may rebuild it."

.....

11 So I came to Jerusalem and was there for three days.

12 Then I got up during the night, I and a few men with me; I told no one what my God had put into my heart to do for Jerusalem. The only animal I took was the animal I rode.

13 I went out by night by the Valley Gate past the Dragon's Spring and to the Dung Gate, and I inspected the walls of Jerusalem that had been broken down and its gates that had been destroyed by fire.

14 Then I went on to the Fountain Gate and to the King's Pool; but there was no place for the animal I was riding to continue.

15 So I went up by way of the valley by night and inspected the wall. Then I turned back and entered by the Valley Gate, and so returned.

16 The officials did not know where I had gone or what I was doing; I had not yet told the Jews, the priests, the nobles, the officials, and the rest that were to do the work.

17 Then I said to them, "You see the trouble we are in, how Jerusalem lies in ruins with its gates burned. Come, let us rebuild the wall of Jerusalem, so that we may no longer suffer disgrace."

18 I told them that the hand of my God had been gracious upon me, and also the words that the king had spoken to me. Then they said, "Let us start building!" So they committed themselves to the common good.

19 But when Sanballat the Horonite, and Tobiah the servant, the Ammonite, and Geshem the Arabian, heard it, they laughed us to scorn, and despised us, and said, What is this thing that ye do? will ye rebel against the king?

20 Then answered I them, and said unto them, The God of heaven, he will prosper us; therefore we his servants will arise and build: but ye have no portion, nor right, nor memorial, in Jerusalem.

19 But when Sanballat the Horonite and Tobiah the Ammonite official, and Geshem the Arab heard of it, they mocked and ridiculed us, saying, "What is this that you are doing? Are you rebelling against the king?"

20 Then I replied to them, "The God of heaven is the one who will give us success, and we his servants are going to start building; but you have no share or claim or historic right in Jerusalem."

TOPICAL OUTLINE OF THE LESSON

I. **Introduction**
   A. A Leader with Integrity
   B. Biblical Background

II. **Exposition and Application of the Scripture**
   A. Request for a Purpose-fulfilling Journey (Nehemiah 2:5)
   B. Assessing the Challenges (Nehemiah 2:11-16)
   C. Issuing a Challenge (Nehemiah 2:17-20)

III. **Concluding Reflection**

LESSON OBJECTIVES
Upon completion of this lesson, the students will know that:
1. Leaders should win the trust of their followers in order to move forward;
2. We must depend on God at all times; and,

3. Leaders can embolden the faith of their followers through their actions.

POINTS TO BE EMPHASIZED
ADULT/YOUTH
Adult Topic: Overcoming Problems
Youth Topic: Strategic Leadership for Accomplishment
Adult Key Verse: Nehemiah 2:18
Youth Key Verse: Nehemiah 2:17
Print Passage: Nehemiah 2:5, 11-20
—Nehemiah was deeply saddened by the ruin and neglect of the sacred home of his people.
—Nehemiah interceded for the people both with God and the king and was heard.
—The people were highly motivated by Nehemiah's efforts and encouraging words.
—Nehemiah prayed in order to clarify his resolve and his request.
—Nehemiah inspected the walls of Jerusalem and they had been destroyed.
—Nehemiah foresaw possible problems and began preparing for solutions before the problems arose.
—Most of the people committed themselves to rebuilding the wall.

CHILDREN

Children Topic: A Praying Leader Is Chosen
Key Verse: Nehemiah 1:4
Print Passage: Nehemiah 2:1-8
—When Nehemiah the cupbearer was performing his duties, the king noticed his unhappiness.
—When the king inquired about Nehemiah's sadness, Nehemiah asked for permission to go to Jerusalem and rebuild the city of his deceased ancestors.
—The king gave Nehemiah permission to go to Jerusalem and rebuild the city.
—The king gave Nehemiah the materials he needed to rebuild the city and letters of authority to present to the governors of Judah.
—Nehemiah prayed for God's guidance in responding to the king.

I. INTRODUCTION
A. A Leader with Integrity

Life can be overwhelming at times, for the individual and even for a nation. When we are faced with vast and crushing challenges, we need bold leaders to lead us through our difficult times. But bold leadership is not enough. Leaders with uncontrolled boldness can violate the rights of people. We need leaders who are righteous as well. Yet righteousness alone is not enough, because without initiative and courage, nothing is accomplished. We therefore need leaders who are both bold *and* righteous. Boldness is controlled by righteousness. A God-chosen leader must possess a type of wisdom to be able to distinguish between right and wrong. He or she must be able to act decisively and boldly to carry out righteous acts.

B. Biblical Background

The rebuilding of the city walls around Jerusalem is described in the historical book of Nehemiah. The book is named for its major personality, a Jewish servant of a Persian king who became a visionary and effective leader to the Jews. Nehemiah organized and led the people to rebuild the walls of Jerusalem.

This period in the life of the Jews is known as the post-exilic period—the years after the return of the covenant people to their homeland following seventy years of captivity in Babylon. At first, the people were excited about rebuilding and restoring their city. But the work was slow and tiresome, and the living conditions were primitive. Without the outer wall around Jerusalem, enemies entered at will and often exploited the Jews in their plight. The political and religious climate in Jerusalem was now one of despair. Years of attempts at reconstruction only led to failure and frustration.

Aroused by deep concern, Nehemiah began to fast and pray, and asked the Lord for a solution. He knew that he would eventually have to bring up the subject to the king and ask his help for the distressed Jews back in Jerusalem. But Nehemiah would not seek *foreign aid* from the king. He wanted to personally help his fellow countrymen with the king's permission. Would the king permit such a request from a cupbearer, or would he be so displeased that he would imprison Nehemiah or, worse, have him executed? The seriousness of Nehemiah's request caused him to fast and pray for four months, and to carefully plan his strategy for approaching King Artaxerxes.

II. EXPOSITION AND APPLICATION OF THE SCRIPTURE

A. Request for a Purpose-fulfilling Journey
   (Nehemiah 2:5)

And I said unto the king, If it please the king, and if thy servant have found favour in thy sight, that thou wouldest send me unto Judah, unto the city of my fathers' sepulchres, that I may build it.

A study of Nehemiah's prayer in 1:5-11 helps us to better understand this courageous biblical character. Nehemiah's prayer is one of the most moving in all of the Old Testament. It reveals the close relationship that existed between God and this chosen visionary leader.

We must not take Nehemiah's request of King Artaxerxes lightly. While it is true that the Persians were known for their religious tolerance, it was also true that they had no desire to see the conquered Jews return to their original position of power and influence. The fact that Nehemiah had favor with the king demonstrates only that Nehemiah was rewarded for his faithfulness to his duty in the palace. In no way did that favor guarantee that Nehemiah would receive a favorable response to his request for permission to leave the palace and return home to rebuild the wall of his beloved Jerusalem.

Nevertheless, Nehemiah waited four months for the right moment, and then carefully chose his words before the king. And out of respect for Nehemiah, the king not only allowed him to leave the palace and return to his homeland of Judah, but he sent Nehemiah as the new governor of the province, with full authority from the king.

Nehemiah did not approach the king based on his personal relationship with him; rather, he appealed to the God of heaven to reach out to the heart of the king. The sentence in verse 4 indicates that even before Nehemiah approached the king, he breathed a little word in prayer. This is an encouragement to us not to take situations in life without first consulting with the God of heaven. Respectively and with godly courage he asked the king, "If it please the king…" In other words, he said, "Let the king be pleased to send me to Judah." Nehemiah asked the king to share in his concern for Jerusalem and to become a partner in getting the city and its inhabitants back where they should be.

As a God-minded leader, Nehemiah revealed his purpose, which was, "That I may build it (Jerusalem)." The sepulchers of his ancestors were very important to him. He believed the dead and the living deserve rest. That was a big job and a big goal. Nehemiah was not just going on a fact-finding trip, or to give order to the leaders of Jerusalem. He went there to get the job done. Visionary leaders must learn how to roll back their sleeves and take positions to lead others by example.

B. Assessing the Challenges
   (Nehemiah 2:11-16)

So I came to Jerusalem, and was there three days. And I

arose in the night, I and some few men with me; neither told I any man what my God had put in my heart to do at Jerusalem: neither was there any beast with me, save the beast that I rode upon. And I went out by night by the gate of the valley, even before the dragon well, and to the dung port, and viewed the walls of Jerusalem, which were broken down, and the gates thereof were consumed with fire. Then I went on to the gate of the fountain, and to the king's pool: but there was no place for the beast that was under me to pass. Then went I up in the night by the brook, and viewed the wall, and turned back, and entered by the gate of the valley, and so returned. And the rulers knew not whither I went, or what I did; neither had I as yet told it to the Jews, nor to the priests, nor to the nobles, nor to the rulers, nor to the rest that did the work.

Nehemiah exhibited many characteristics necessary for effective leadership. He knew how to set reasonable and attainable goals. He had a sense of mission and was willing to get involved. He was willing to rearrange his priorities to attain his goal. He trusted God's timing. He was a praying man. He identified himself as one with his people, and assured them that God was in the project. He was not afraid to use the authority of his position. He displayed self-confidence in the face of obstacles, and he never succumbed to arguing with his opponents. But above all, he took time to plan.

Nehemiah's journey to Jerusalem probably took about two months, even in taking the shortest route possible. Ezra's earlier trip had taken four to five months. Nehemiah took with him his letters of authority from the king. But as soon as he arrived, he was met with opposition. When Sanballat heard that Nehemiah had arrived to help Israel, he was very displeased. He and his counterpart, Tobiah, began to scheme about how they might stop Nehemiah from achieving his goal. The thought among biblical scholars is

that these two were hoping to gain control of Judah. In fact, an ancient papyrus that still exists today refers to Sanballat as "governor of Samaria." Nonetheless, Nehemiah was undaunted. He knew that God had brought him to this moment in Israel's history.

This enormous task of rebuilding the wall called for unusual organizational skills. When Nehemiah arrived in Jerusalem, he had to have a plan. He knew that before he could share God's plan with the people, he would have to do some research on the situation. To avoid letting others know of his idea in advance, he decided to make his assessment of the city at night. He rode his horse from the Valley Gate in the southwest wall, east to the Jackal Well, an unknown site, and then to the Dung Gate in the southeast part of the city. (This could have been the Potsherd Gate referred to in Jeremiah 19:2.) Then he went north to the Fountain Gate on the eastern wall. The gates of the city of Jerusalem defined its many areas. We do not know exactly how many gates there were in the city because it varied from century to century. The King's Pool referred to in 3:15 may be the same as the Pool of Siloam, which was near the king's garden. The rubble in that area was so bad that it kept him from continuing on horseback. It is stated in the record that he "went up by way of the valley" (probably the Kidron Valley) and either went around the entire wall or, more likely, retraced his steps along the eastern wall. This careful assessment allowed Nehemiah to properly prepare a workable plan for this enormous task. Following this secret survey, Nehemiah was now ready to make known his plan to the people.

The word *sepulchres* (also spelled *sepulchers*) in verse 5 refers to the tombs of Judah's forefathers in Jerusalem. Sepulchers were built to house the bodies of deceased religious leaders and prominent families in the religious community. These tombs were often on the outskirts of the city, although in history it is recorded that David was buried within the city walls. So important were the graves of ancestors that Joseph's bones were carried for forty years until they found their final resting place in Shechem, north of Jerusalem. In returning home to rebuild the Temple, Nehemiah also reclaimed the tombs of his ancestral leaders.

According to verse 16, Nehemiah did not inform the leaders of the people about his mission. Only very few knew about his mission. The lesson here is that no matter how important a project is, leaders must learn to trust few people in the initial stage of the project. People with limited vision have unlimited power to shoot down good ideas.

C. Issuing a Challenge
(Nehemiah 2:17-20)

Then said I unto them, Ye see the distress that we are in, how Jerusalem lieth waste, and the gates thereof are burned with fire: come, and let us build up the wall of Jerusalem, that we be no more a reproach. Then I told them of the hand of my God which was good upon me; as also the king's words that he had spoken unto me. And they said, Let us rise up and build. So they strengthened their hands for this good work. But when Sanballat the Horonite, and Tobiah the servant, the Ammonite, and Geshem the Arabian, heard it, they laughed us to scorn, and despised us, and said, What is this thing that ye do? will ye rebel against the king? Then answered I them, and said unto them, The God of heaven, he will prosper us; therefore we his servants will arise and build: but ye have no portion, nor right, nor memorial, in Jerusalem.

We must bear in mind that the people had been struggling for almost a hundred years to rebuild Jerusalem. If Nehemiah was going to get the job done, he first had to inspire his discouraged countrymen. First he challenged them to note their deplorable circumstances. They were troubled and disgraced (see 1:3). They were open to invasion and attack by anyone who chose to plunder their possessions. Then Nehemiah shared his story of how God had prepared the heart of King Artaxerxes to receive his request and grant him the favor of becoming their new governor to spearhead the project.

When Nehemiah gave his challenge to the people, the people's negative feelings instantly became positive. All of their despair turned into hope.

Today's spiritual leaders are often dissuaded by followers who fail to catch God's vision. Some leaders attempt to honor God's plan without faith community support, and some may even experience some semblance of success. But God's plan is always for unity—a unity that promotes oneness, harmony, and agreement (see Acts 2:1). Those who do not permit a leader to lead run the risk of missing the greatest blessings God has for His people.

Somehow Sanballat and Tobiah got the word that Nehemiah had come back to rebuild the wall of Jerusalem. These two men were unhappy about his coming. Then the opposition grew to three. Geshem, a leader among the Arabs, teamed up with Nehemiah's enemy. But Nehemiah (in verse 20) ignored his opponents. They accused Nehemiah of rebelling against the king, but Nehemiah's motive was not rebellion—he was ready to carry out the mandate of God.

III. CONCLUDING REFLECTION

Overcoming overwhelming odds requires great faith. Consider the man at the Pool of Bethesda who waited thirty-eight years for his healing. Failure was never an option.

As Christians, we must learn to trust God with the same level of faith Nehemiah had, even when the way seems impossible. But if there is one lesson in this study worthy of our attention, it is the lesson on obedience. Nehemiah obeyed God. The people obeyed Nehemiah. The leader cannot achieve any success without the cooperation of the followers. John Maxwell once said, "If you are leading and no one is following, you are only taking a walk." It is important for the leader to secure the cooperation of the followers, just as Nehemiah did in our text. There will be no maximum cooperation; there will still be few who will not go along. However, a leader must not waver. In Nehemiah's time, Sanballat, Tobiah, and Geshum ganged up against Nehemiah, but he pressed on. We must realize that the presence of detractors is a blessing in disguise. It kept Nehemiah vigilant and prayerful. As we engage in the Lord's work, the constant barrage of the enemy should keep us focused and on our knees.

PRAYER

Our Father, thank You for leaders like Nehemiah who by Your enablement weather through impossible tasks. He focused on You, even though he was in the midst of enemies who did not hide their agenda. Help us, O God, to remain focused on You. In Jesus' name we pray. Amen.

WORD POWER

Strengthened (Hebrew: *chazak* [kha-zak])—means "to be strong, grow strong, prevail upon, press on." In the Key Verse, the word *strengthened* carries the idea of continuous effort, or relentless effort to see the job carried to its completion. The people did not stop for a second while building the walls. It was a united effort. Nehemiah was not idle. He was there, encouraging his men and warning them about the ploy of the enemy.

HOME DAILY BIBLE READINGS
(September 21-27, 2009)

Nehemiah: A Motivator for the People

MONDAY, September 21: "Hope for God's Vindication" (Isaiah 62:1-7)

TUESDAY, September 22: "Mourning over Jerusalem" (Nehemiah 1:1-4)

WEDNESDAY, September 23: "Confession and Petition to God" (Nehemiah 1:5-11)

THURSDAY, September 24: "Identifying the Problem" (Nehemiah 2:1-4)

FRIDAY, September 25: "Preparing for the Task" (Nehemiah 2:6-10)

SATURDAY, September 26: "Dealing with Opposition" (Nehemiah 4:15-23)

SUNDAY, September 27: "Rallying Support" (Nehemiah 2:5, 11-20)

LESSON 5 — October 4, 2009

LOOKING FOR JESUS

DEVOTIONAL READING: Ezekiel 34:11-16
PRINT PASSAGE: Mark 1:35-45

BACKGROUND SCRIPTURE: Mark 1:35-45
KEY VERSE: Mark 1:37

Mark 1:35-45—KJV

35 And in the morning, rising up a great while before day, he went out, and departed into a solitary place, and there prayed.

36 And Simon and they that were with him followed after him.

37 And when they had found him, they said unto him, All men seek for thee.

38 And he said unto them, Let us go into the next towns, that I may preach there also: for therefore came I forth.

39 And he preached in their synagogues throughout all Galilee, and cast out devils.

40 And there came a leper to him, beseeching him, and kneeling down to him, and saying unto him, If thou wilt, thou canst make me clean.

41 And Jesus, moved with compassion, put forth his hand, and touched him, and saith unto him, I will; be thou clean.

42 And as soon as he had spoken, immediately the leprosy departed from him, and he was cleansed.

43 And he straitly charged him, and forthwith sent him away;

44 And saith unto him, See thou say nothing to any man: but go thy way, shew thyself to the priest, and offer for thy cleansing those things which Moses commanded, for a testimony unto them.

45 But he went out, and began to publish it much, and to blaze abroad the matter, insomuch that Jesus could no more openly enter into the city, but was without in desert places: and they came to him from every quarter.

Mark 1:35-45—NRSV

35 In the morning, while it was still very dark, he got up and went out to a deserted place, and there he prayed.

36 And Simon and his companions hunted for him.

37 When they found him, they said to him, "Everyone is searching for you."

38 He answered, "Let us go on to the neighboring towns, so that I may proclaim the message there also; for that is what I came out to do."

39 And he went throughout Galilee, proclaiming the message in their synagogues and casting out demons.

40 A leper came to him begging him, and kneeling he said to him, "If you choose, you can make me clean."

41 Moved with pity, Jesus stretched out his hand and touched him, and said to him, "I do choose. Be made clean!"

42 Immediately the leprosy left him, and he was made clean.

43 After sternly warning him he sent him away at once,

44 saying to him, "See that you say nothing to anyone; but go, show yourself to the priest, and offer for your cleansing what Moses commanded, as a testimony to them."

45 But he went out and began to proclaim it freely, and to spread the word, so that Jesus could no longer go into a town openly, but stayed out in the country; and people came to him from every quarter.

We often seek out people we believe can help us solve our problems. Where can we find such people? The people of Galilee realized that Jesus had the words of life and a healing touch that they sought, so they went looking for Him.

TOPICAL OUTLINE OF THE LESSON

I. Introduction
  A. Stress and Peace
  B. Biblical Background

II. Exposition and Application of the Scripture
  A. Jesus' Prayer Model (Mark 1:35-37)
  B. A Purposeful Leader (Mark 1:38-39)
  C. A Focused and Compassionate Leader (Mark 1:40-45)

III. Concluding Reflection

LESSON OBJECTIVES

Upon completion of this lesson, the students will know that:

1. The love of God is constant in spite of our conditions;
2. The only way to hope is dependence on Christ; and,
3. God can heal us in His own terms and times.

andrew
James
John

POINTS TO BE EMPHASIZED

ADULT/YOUTH

Adult Topic: In Search of a Leader
Youth Topic: Searching for True Treasure
Adult Key Verse: Mark 1:37
Youth Key Verse: Mark 1:45
Print Passage: Mark 1:35-45

—Mark's gospel is often focused on narratives that disclose Jesus' divine authority and identity.

—The healing of the person with leprosy not only restored his physical health but also made possible the restoration of his social situation.

—Described in the passage is the extension of Jesus' ministry into all of Galilee because of people's growing recognition of His teaching and healing; He was not merely a local healer and teacher in Capernaum.

—Jesus went about Galilee preaching the Gospel and demonstrating His power.

—Jesus healed the man plagued by leprosy.

—Jesus admonished the man not to tell anybody, but he told everybody.

CHILDREN

Children Topic: A Leper Is Touched
Key Verse: Mark 1:41
Print Passage: Mark 1:35-45

—Because of Jesus' ministry and message, people sought Jesus.

—Jesus responds to the needs of persons, including a leper.

—The man with leprosy who was healed joyously shared his good news with others.

—People may become disciples of Jesus after Jesus intervenes in their lives.

I. INTRODUCTION

A. Stress and Peace

Stress is the intangible partner of life's progress. It is defined as "the normal internal physiological mechanism that makes us change." But when we are stressed, it feels like anything but normal. The more demanding life becomes, the more stressed we become in our attempts to keep up with life's pace.

Stress is actually a by-product of the challenges we face in life—whether they are physical, emotional, or spiritual. People readily say that if they could find a way to deal with all of life's challenges, they would have no stress.

But there is already a way to deal with life's challenges! God calls us to humble ourselves and trust Him with life's unavoidable pressures. Jesus' solution for stress management is to cast "all your care upon Him, for He cares for you" (1 Peter 5:7, NKJV). Christ wants us to give Him the responsibility for things we have no control over.

God desires us to be at peace with our surroundings. But the only possible way to experience peace when life is so tumultuous is to let Christ carry us through each phase of the battle.

B. Biblical Background

The gospel of Mark is often focused on narratives that disclose Jesus' divine authority and identity. It is a focus more on what Jesus does than on what He says. And although the book of Mark is the shortest of the Gospels, its direct style pays close attention to matters of human interest. The book is divided into two parts: Jesus' ministry in Galilee and Jesus' ministry in Judea.

Jesus began to gather the disciples who would come under His tutelage—shortly after His baptism in the Jordan River and His forty days alone in the wilderness. When Jesus healed the man with the unclean spirit in the synagogue, His fame spread rapidly. From that day forward, there was never a time when Jesus did not attract a crowd. Jesus sought refuge in the home of Simon and Andrew, and while He was there, He healed Simon's mother-in-law of a fever.

II. EXPOSITION AND APPLICATION OF THE SCRIPTURE

A. Jesus' Prayer Model
(Mark 1:35-37)

And in the morning, rising up a great while before day, he went out, and departed into a solitary place, and there prayed. And Simon and they that were with him followed after him. And when they had found him, they said unto him, All men seek for thee.

Trusting Christ with our lives is easy when we closely examine Mark's record of His actions. Following the healing of the multitude at the synagogue and the home of Simon and Andrew, Jesus sought some solitude early the next morning for time alone to pray. What does this tell us about our Savior? It tells us that He is ever replenishing His power to deal with our disappointments. Also, He prayed because of the enormous task of saving people. From this text we also learn that the servant of God gets his or her power directly from the Father.

Jesus was actually in the habit of setting aside early-morning prayer time. His prayer life must have made a great impact upon the disciples, because Mark gave a detailed description of the observation, which was probably passed on to him by Peter. Mark felt it was important to record not only what Jesus' ministry was like, but also what His prayer life was like.

Notice that Jesus departed to a solitary place to pray. When we want clear communication with God, we must be willing to remove the worldly and earthly distractions that act as a buffer between God and us. And if Jesus needed time to pray, consider how much more imperative it is that we need to make time to pray. "Early morning" is an important phrase; it shows the importance of prayer in Jesus' life. Jesus' prayer life was successful for four important reasons: it was planned, private, early, and prolonged. This is unlike our prayers which are short, distracted, and often interrupted by phones, television, and all other electronic gadgets. Jesus got up early enough, got far enough away, and stayed at it a long time. Jesus took time to pray. Admittedly, finding time to pray is not easy—but prayer is the vital link between us and God. Like Jesus, we must break away from other mundane engagements to talk with God, even if it involves waking up early before others in our household.

B. A Purposeful Leader
(Mark 1:38-39)

And he said unto them, Let us go into the next towns, that I may preach there also: for therefore came I forth. And he preached in their synagogues throughout all Galilee, and cast out devils.

The disciples were astonished when they could not find Jesus nearby. At that point Peter and others began looking around for Him. Even though it is not indicated in the text the location where He was found, the disciples knew where to look for Him. Their search underscores one important fact, which is that a leader must find a place of solitude to commune with God. Also, the followers should not second guess where their leader is. In our time, followers in both secular and religious places have faced disappointment when they realized the hideouts of their leaders. The disappointments have caused distress among many followers and many have dropped out of the church.

Followers as well as leaders have stressful moments. The most effective way a believer prepares for the stress of life is to seek Christ. We surround ourselves with His protection when we seek Him early in life. But that seems to be the hardest step for most people to take in seeking Christ. Some people have a terrible time admitting that life is too complicated and too challenging for them to face it alone, without the Savior.

Once Jesus began performing miracle after miracle, the groundswell of seekers was difficult to contain. Everyone with a problem sought Him for help. It was the visual experience of Christ's power that motivated them to seek Him. Though the Bible does not dwell on those who were not healed, there had to be many who left their encounter with Jesus the same way they came—destitute and disappointed. Mark recorded such an experience in the sixth chapter during Jesus' visit to Nazareth, which was His home country. During that visit, Jesus could not heal the multitude because of their unbelief (verse 5). Only a few were able to overcome the stumbling block that Jesus was a mere carpenter's son, and take the giant spiritual leap of faith that brought them to believe in Him as the Son of God. This occurrence is recorded only once in Scripture. Mark documented the event that we might know the importance of complete submission to Christ as the prerequisite to salvation.

C. A Focused and Compassionate Leader (Mark 1:40-45)

And there came a leper to him, beseeching him, and kneeling down to him, and saying unto him, If thou wilt, thou canst make me clean. And Jesus, moved with compassion, put forth his hand, and touched him, and saith unto him, I will; be thou clean. And as soon as he had spoken, immediately the leprosy departed from him, and he was cleansed. And he straitly charged him, and forthwith sent him away; And saith unto him, See thou say nothing to any man: but go thy way, shew thyself to the priest, and offer for thy cleansing those things which Moses commanded, for a testimony unto them. But he went out, and began to publish it much, and to blaze abroad the matter, insomuch that Jesus could no more openly enter into the city, but was without in desert places: and they came to him from every quarter.

A leader is ineffective unless he or she is also willing to take on the role of servant. Notice that Jesus was the one who suggested that they continue on their journey into new towns where His message could be spread and His power demonstrated. God sends leaders with a specific purpose. Jesus' purpose was "to seek and to save that which was lost" (Luke 19:10)—to redeem humankind and open the door to reconciliation with the Creator. Jesus knew this to be His purpose, and He would not shy away from the task. Other than quiet prayer time and sleep, Jesus took little time for rest, because He was compelled by the brevity of His earthly existence. He was fully aware of humans' apostasy, and therefore He must go on preaching in other towns and villages to fulfill His role as Savior of the world.

Jesus' fame spread like a wild fire, and the disciples' concern was glaring in the statement, "Everyone is looking for you." The mission ahead of Jesus was very important to Him; He refused to wait, but urged them to go to the next towns and villages. Jesus took seriously His mission to reach "the next town." He stressed His mission by saying, "for this purpose I came" (John 12:27, NKJV). Jesus modeled singleness of purpose. He would not allow anything to distract Him.

While going to the next town in Galilee Jesus came across a leper. In keeping with Levitical laws as recorded in Leviticus 13 and 14, Jewish leaders declared people with leprosy unclean. This meant that lepers were unfit to participate in any religious and social engagements. Some people even threw rocks at lepers to keep them away from society. The Law declared that anyone who touched a leper was ceremonially unclean. But Jesus was moved with compassion. Jesus not only healed but touched him. The interpretation of Jesus touching the leper is that the real value of a person is inside, and not outside. It is possible to be—and we have seen around us—a person who is physically challenged yet inwardly is a great person. How often it is that we see the need but remained unmoved, untouched, and uninvolved. The Bible has over four hundred passages encouraging us to care for the poor and the helpless (see Deuteronomy 8:2; 15:7-11).

Every leader called by God has a specific purpose. All ministries are not the same. Some leaders are called to revive; some are called to heal; some are called to organize; some are called to teach. God equips the leader with the tools necessary to fulfill his or her calling according to God's plan. Many leaders fail in ministry because rather than prayerfully seek God's specific purpose for their lives, they attempt to model their ministries after another. A good example is the proliferation of pastors in some denominations and the absence of mission workers. Jesus' ministry was a ministry of missions. He was sent *to the people.* Had His been a pastoral ministry, the people would have come to Him. The apostle Paul had a mission ministry. By comparison, the disciple Peter had a pastoral ministry.

We recognize effective leaders by their ministry results, just as we derive our hope from recognizing that God responds to our needs and our wounds. On some occasions God's plan for our "healing" may not always take on the form we anticipated. Healing comes in many forms. Consider Paul, who prayed three times for God to remove his "thorn in the flesh" (see 2 Corinthians 12:7-8). But God's response to his request was, "My grace is sufficient for thee: for my strength is made perfect in weakness" (2 Corinthians 12:9). Paul's healing took on spiritual form, as attested by his response (in that same verse): "Most gladly therefore will I rather glory in my infirmities, that the power

of Christ may rest upon me."

As human beings, we do not use the same litmus test for great leaders that God uses. When God told Samuel to visit the prominent and respected citizen of Bethlehem, Jesse (see 1 Samuel 16:1-13)—to find a replacement for the demented king Saul—Samuel was willing to anoint the first son of Jesse, Eliab, because he was impressed with Eliab's sheer size. But God rejected Eliab. Subsequently, each of Jesse's sons was rejected by God, and all for the same reason. Samuel was looking at the outward man, his countenance, but God was searching inwardly for a leader. It was not until Jesse brought His youngest son, David, into Samuel's presence that Samuel understood God's choice.

Nothing has changed since biblical times. Humankind is still impressed with leaders who are eloquent, fair in appearance, and full of promises. That is why Franklin D. Roosevelt never let the public know, during his last campaign for the White House, that he was in a wheelchair. If we are to follow God's plan for our redemption and regeneration as a people, we must learn to view leadership through the same perspective as God. And what is that perspective? We should seek leaders who emulate Christ, the Savior.

III. CONCLUDING REFLECTION

God never intended for us to live stress-filled lives. Jesus experienced incredible pressures while living on earth in human form, but it is recorded in the Bible that His release mechanism was to withdraw from the crowds to pray. We too can manage our stress by withdrawing to a quiet place for prayer and communion with God. God cares about the intimate details of our lives, and He assumes complete responsibility for every person who is committed to Him. We must learn to trust God's promise of help and provision. The lyric writer William J. Kirkpatrick wrote, "'Tis so sweet to trust in Jesus, just to take Him at His Word; Just to rest upon His promise; Just to know 'Thus saith the Lord.'" The writer knew that things can be difficult for *us,* but nothing is too hard for God. Believing and resting in that truth will protect us—mind, heart, and spirit.

Our knowledge of who God is determines the amount of time we spend in our prayer closets. At the time of this writing, the political debates are going strong. We take time to listen to candidates. Ninety minutes of debate means nothing to us. But when it comes to talking to God, we rush at it and rush out of His presence.

PRAYER

Father in heaven, we are grateful for Your lovingkindness. The urge to seek You comes from You. May we not brush aside Your promptings. May we seek You as the saints of old did. In Jesus' name we pray. Amen.

WORD POWER

Seek (Greek: *Zeteo*)—carries the idea of intense search in order to find out, seeking traces of divine majesty and power. This type of seeking is to strive after something until it is found. The people mentioned in our Key Verse were seeking Jesus with all their hearts because they realized what He had done for them. These people were true seekers and we too should emulate their desire to see Jesus.

HOME DAILY BIBLE READINGS
(September 28–October 4, 2009)

Looking for Jesus

MONDAY, September 28: "The Shepherd's Search" (Ezekiel 34:11-16)

TUESDAY, September 29: "Seek the Lord" (1 Chronicles 16:8-13)

WEDNESDAY, September 30: "Set Your Mind and Heart" (1 Chronicles 29:17-19)

THURSDAY, October 1: "Seeking God and God's Law" (1 Chronicles 28:6-10)

FRIDAY, October 2: "Seeking God's Face" (2 Chronicles 7:12-18)

SATURDAY, October 3: "The Search that Brings Peace" (2 Chronicles 14:1-7)

SUNDAY, October 4: "Search for Healing" (Mark 1:35-45)

LESSON 6

October 11, 2009

RECOGNIZING JESUS

DEVOTIONAL READING: **Luke 7:18-23**
PRINT PASSAGE: **Mark 5:1-13, 18-20**

BACKGROUND SCRIPTURE: **Mark 5:1-20**
KEY VERSE: **Mark 5:19**

Mark 5:1-13, 18-20—KJV

AND THEY came over unto the other side of the sea, into the country of the Gadarenes.

2 And when he was come out of the ship, immediately there met him out of the tombs a man with an unclean spirit,

3 Who had his dwelling among the tombs; and no man could bind him, no, not with chains:

4 Because that he had been often bound with fetters and chains, and the chains had been plucked asunder by him, and the fetters broken in pieces: neither could any man tame him.

5 And always, night and day, he was in the mountains, and in the tombs, crying, and cutting himself with stones.

6 But when he saw Jesus afar off, he ran and worshipped him,

7 And cried with a loud voice, and said, What have I to do with thee, Jesus, thou Son of the most high God? I adjure thee by God, that thou torment me not.

8 For he said unto him, Come out of the man, thou unclean spirit.

9 And he asked him, What is thy name? And he answered, saying, My name is Legion: for we are many.

10 And he besought him much that he would not send them away out of the country.

11 Now there was there nigh unto the mountains a great herd of swine feeding.

12 And all the devils besought him, saying, Send us into the swine, that we may enter into them.

13 And forthwith Jesus gave them leave. And the unclean spirits went out, and entered into the swine: and the herd ran violently down a steep place into the sea, (they were about two thousand;) and were choked in the sea.

Mark 5:1-13, 18-20—NRSV

THEY CAME to the other side of the sea, to the country of the Gerasenes.

2 And when he had stepped out of the boat, immediately a man out of the tombs with an unclean spirit met him.

3 He lived among the tombs; and no one could restrain him any more, even with a chain;

4 for he had often been restrained with shackles and chains, but the chains he wrenched apart, and the shackles he broke in pieces; and no one had the strength to subdue him.

5 Night and day among the tombs and on the mountains he was always howling and bruising himself with stones.

6 When he saw Jesus from a distance, he ran and bowed down before him;

7 and he shouted at the top of his voice, "What have you to do with me, Jesus, Son of the Most High God? I adjure you by God, do not torment me."

8 For he had said to him, "Come out of the man, you unclean spirit!"

9 Then Jesus asked him, "What is your name?" He replied, "My name is Legion; for we are many."

10 He begged him earnestly not to send them out of the country.

11 Now there on the hillside a great herd of swine was feeding;

12 and the unclean spirits begged him, "Send us into the swine; let us enter them."

13 So he gave them permission. And the unclean spirits came out and entered the swine; and the herd, numbering about two thousand, rushed down the steep bank into the sea, and were drowned in the sea.

UNIFYING LESSON PRINCIPLE

At times, our problems are so overwhelming and sometimes cause such alienation that we do not know where to turn. What help is available? Mark's account of the Gerasene demoniac is an illustration that Jesus is able to break the chains that bind and isolate us and bring us back into community.

.....

18 And when he was come into the ship, he that had been possessed with the devil prayed him that he might be with him.
19 Howbeit Jesus suffered him not, but saith unto him, Go home to thy friends, and tell them how great things the Lord hath done for thee, and hath had compassion on thee.
20 And he departed, and began to publish in Decapolis how great things Jesus had done for him: and all men did marvel.

.....

18 As he was getting into the boat, the man who had been possessed by demons begged him that he might be with him.
19 But Jesus refused, and said to him, "Go home to your friends, and tell them how much the Lord has done for you, and what mercy he has shown you."
20 And he went away and began to proclaim in the Decapolis how much Jesus had done for him; and everyone was amazed.

TOPICAL OUTLINE OF THE LESSON

I. Introduction
  A. Coping in Times of Stress
  B. Biblical Background

II. Exposition and Application of the Scripture
  A. Jesus Encounters Unclean Spirits
     (Mark 5:1-5)
  B. Jesus' Authority over Evil Spirits
     (Mark 5:6-13)
  C. Jesus Commissions the Healed Man
     (Mark 5:18-20)

III. Concluding Reflection

LESSON OBJECTIVES

Upon completion of this lesson, the students will know that:

1. Jesus is still healing today through His faithful servants;
2. The demons recognize the presence of Christ and the Holy Spirit; and,
3. Jesus is a bondage broker for both mental and physical problems.

POINTS TO BE EMPHASIZED
ADULT/YOUTH

Adult Topic: Restored to Wholeness
Youth Topic: The Treasure of True Freedom
Adult/Youth Key Verse: Mark 5:19
Print Passage: Mark 5:1-13, 18-20

—This story sets an example for the wideness of God's mercy for individuals on the edge of society.
—The intense desire of Legion to drive Jesus away is characteristic of other stories in which demons encounter the Holy One of God.
—Jesus found the Gerasene demoniac living in the tombs among the dead.
—True freedom means breaking not only human shackles but also demonic bonds.
—The demon in the man asked Jesus, "What do you want with me?" Jesus told the demon to come out and asked him his name.

—The demon gave his name as "Legion" and asked Jesus not to torment him.

—Often, people are more concerned with economic prosperity than with human freedom.

CHILDREN
Children Topic: Caring for Outsiders
Key Verse: Mark 5:6
Print Passage: Mark 5:1-13, 18-20

—Jesus did not shun anyone who came in search of Him.

—Jesus took time to reach out to people in need.

—Persons who receive life transformations from Jesus are prone to follow Jesus.

—Jesus delivered the man and cast the demons into the herd of pigs, which died in the sea.

I. INTRODUCTION

A. Coping in Times of Stress

There are many times in our lives when we feel bound or buffeted by emotional or psychological dynamics that seem to be out of our control. But seldom do we admit it because of the stigma that is attached to mental illness. Society expects us to cope, no matter how critical our circumstances.

It is important for believers to understand that God knows our dilemmas when we are mentally challenged. That's why God emphasized in His Word that He desires control over all of our being—physically (body), emotionally (mind), and spiritually (soul).

B. Biblical Background

The story of the healing of the demon-possessed man takes place in Gadara, the home of the Gadarenes. Gadara was the capital of the Roman province of Perea, a city on the east side of the Jordan River, about six miles from the Sea of Galilee. In Greco-Roman times, it was part of the ancient ten-city commercial and geographical confederacy known as the Decapolis (verse 20). The Decapolis suffered many attacks and conquests prior to Pompey's liberation of the area. It was Pompey, himself, who ordered the rebuilding of Gadara, probably because of the natural hot and cold springs that ran through the area—which the heathens believed were therapeutic, and the Jews believed were a gift from God.

The "healing" waters of Gadara drew people from hundreds of miles away. This made Gadara a city of bustling commerce that thrived on tourism. This also made Gadara a great place from which to spread Christ's message of redemption and hope. This may also explain why the healing of the demonic man in Gadara became one of the most celebrated events in ancient times.

II. EXPOSITION AND APPLICATION OF THE SCRIPTURE

A. Jesus Encounters Unclean Spirits
(Mark 5:1-5)

AND THEY came over unto the other side of the sea, into the country of the Gadarenes. And when he was come out of the ship, immediately there met him out of the tombs a man with an unclean spirit, Who had his dwelling among the tombs; and no man could bind him, no, not with chains: Because that he had been often bound with fetters and chains, and the chains had been plucked asunder by him, and the fetters broken in pieces: neither could any man tame him. And always, night and day, he was in the mountains, and in the tombs, crying, and cutting himself with stones.

The Spirit of God controls people to varying degrees; conversely, evil spirits also control people to varying degrees. Some people are extremely controlled, while others are only slightly controlled. It is recorded in Mark 16:9 that Mary Magdalene was possessed by seven devils. In Matthew 12:45, Jesus refers to one devil being replaced by seven devils, and the latter state being far worse.

Demons are fallen angels who joined the kingdom of Satan in rebellion against God. They can possess a person's mind, body, and soul. While the origin of demons is not explicitly discussed in the Bible, the New Testament does speak of the fall and later imprisonment of a group of angels who followed Satan. This fall occurred before the creation of the world, leaving Satan and his angels free to contaminate the human race with their wickedness (Genesis 3).

Because the Jews believed that God's power was limitless, there is little mention of demons in the Old Testament. In fact, they sometimes attributed the world of fallen angels to God Himself. Micaiah, the prophet, spoke of a "lying spirit" from the Lord in 1 Kings 22:21-23. In 1 Samuel 16:15-16, Saul's torment is attributed to a "distressing (or evil) spirit from God."

One of the primary purposes of Jesus' ministry on earth was to overcome the power of Satan and the demonic realm (see Matthew 12:25-29; 1 John 3:8). There was a fierce conflict between Jesus and Satan while He was on earth. Jesus' enemies even accused Him of being in alliance with Satan and his demons (see Mark 3:22, John 8:48). But Christ's works of goodness and righteousness demonstrated that this was not true.

The demonic man in Mark's record was possessed by a *legion* of demons. The word *legion* means "hordes" or "a multitude." This tormented man had been rejected by his family and cast out of the community by his fellow brothers and sisters. He was so full of demons that when he saw Jesus, he ran to Him. Fearing that Jesus would cast him into hell, Legion immediately acknowledged Jesus as the Son of God and begged for mercy. Since the demon-possessed man had never met Jesus and knew nothing of His teachings, the fact that he acknowledged Christ as the Son of God reveals that God can get through to the heart of anyone, even when the mind is tormented.

The extreme malady of this man is described in verse 5. He was bereft of reason, strong and dangerous. Mark said that this madness was caused by unclean spirits. The man would lacerate himself with stones and any other objects at his disposal. However when he saw Jesus afar off he ran to meet him and worshiped. The power and authority of

Jesus has no limitations. The man under the control of the evil spirit and the evil spirit in him recognized the Son of God. They both bowed down before Him. It is true that "at the name of Jesus every knee should bow" (Philippians 2:10).

From this valuable lesson (from Mark) Christians learn that no matter how mentally unstable a person may feel, God is able to get His message of hope to the heart. Jesus did not have to speak because His presence in any situation and anywhere is recognized.

B. Jesus' Authority over Evil Spirits
(Mark 5:6-13)

But when he saw Jesus afar off, he ran and worshipped him, And cried with a loud voice, and said, What have I to do with thee, Jesus, thou Son of the most high God? I adjure thee by God, that thou torment me not. For he said unto him, Come out of the man, thou unclean spirit. And he asked him, What is thy name? And he answered, saying, My name is Legion: for we are many. And he besought him much that he would not send them away out of the country. Now there was there nigh unto the mountains a great herd of swine feeding. And all the devils besought him, saying, Send us into the swine, that we may enter into them. And forthwith Jesus gave them leave. And the unclean spirits went out, and entered into the swine: and the herd ran violently down a steep place into the sea, (they were about two thousand;) and were choked in the sea.

The man in our text was possessed with evil spirits. The presence of demons or evil spirits is a common phenomena in the Bible (see Mark 1:23, 32-34; Revelation 16:13-16). They are fallen angels, and servants of Satan (see Matthew 12:26-27; 25:41). There is only one devil but a countless number of demons who serve the devil and make his power practically universal. As Jesus was approaching, the man possessed by the evil spirits saw Jesus in the distance. He ran and fell on his knees. The irony of it is that the demons recognized Jesus and they begged Him and requested that they not be tortured. The demons had been torturing this man for a long time, but they would not want to be tortured.

Jesus knew the evil spirit and asked him to identify himself by his name. He was a *legion*, meaning that there were many spirits. He begged Jesus not to destroy them or send them out. This incident took place southeast of the Sea of Galilee in the region of the Gerasenes. Jesus expelled them and they ran into the herd of pigs.

Satan is alive and he has uncountable evil spirits at his disposal. The fact that we cannot see them with our naked eyes does not mean they are not in operation. They prefer not to be identified. In our modern world, we have relegated demon possession to primitive religions. But the fact that our Lord recognized them and disallowed them from operating should tell us not to dismiss their presence.

Paul, in his epistle to the church in Ephesus, warned that we are not fighting against flesh and blood but against principalities and powers—against wicked spirits in high places.

C. Jesus Commissions the Healed Man
(Mark 5:18-20)

And when he was come into the ship, he that had been possessed with the devil prayed him that he might be with him. Howbeit Jesus suffered him not, but saith unto him, Go home to thy friends, and tell them how great things the Lord hath done for thee, and hath had compassion on thee. And he departed, and began to publish in Decapolis how great things Jesus had done for him: and all men did marvel.

It would be natural for a man healed of such an infirmity to desire to remain in the

Matt 12:31 Blasphemy —

LEGION — 3000 – 6000

presence of his healer. This man, motivated by his tremendous gratitude, wanted to follow Christ and become a disciple. But because they were in the Decapolis, Jesus knew that this man's testimony would be far more valuable to the spread of the Gospel, as it would easily spread through the cities of commerce of the area. So Jesus commissioned the healed man to "Go home to thy friends and tell them…" (verse 19). Four important words in verse 20 captured the reaction of the people: "all men did marvel"; this man's testimony had a profound impact on this area of antiquity.

All believers enjoy being in the presence of Jesus Christ. This explains why more Christians worship God than serve Him. We enjoy the experience of one-on-one contact with God's Spirit and becoming enjoined to the joyful celebration of His goodness. But Jesus teaches us, through His response to this once demon-possessed man, that worship is only half of our Christian experience. The other half is service. Many churches have a sign over their doors that read, "Enter to worship; depart to serve." This is the oversimplified commission of Jesus Christ to all believers who aspire toward a more full and complete relationship with God.

When Peter and John were on the Mount of Transfiguration with Jesus, Peter said, "Master, it is good for us to be here" (Mark 9:5). Their worship experience on that mountaintop with Elias, Moses, and Jesus left them in awe of God. Peter and John's desire was to build a monument or place of worship on that mountain. But Jesus quickly made them come down from the mountaintop, and He began to teach them of the urgency of their service to God.

Our "healing" experience, whether we are healed mentally, physically, spiritually, or in all three arenas, is the fuel that forms our effective witness. Our mountaintop experience should compel us to go down into the valley to share our strong testimony of victory. Our minds formulate our testimony as we overcome adversity through Jesus Christ, but a bottled-up testimony does nothing to serve the kingdom of God.

The medical community has focused much attention in recent years on what is known as bipolar disorder. Doctors are finally able to name this crippling mental disorder that has plagued so many for centuries. Is it possible that the demonic man in our text could have suffered from bipolar disorder? We know that Job had boils (see Job 2:7); King Asa had gout (see 2 Chronicles 16:12); Simon Peter's mother had a persistent fever (see Luke 4:38-39); King Hezekiah had dysentery (see 2 Kings 20:1); and King Saul probably suffered from manic depression (see 1 Samuel 16:14-23). Diseases of the Bible are sometimes difficult to recognize today because of translation inadequacies, but most of the diseases mentioned still exist today.

Sickness among Christians raises many questions. Some wonder why their faith does not cure them. While faith can cure a believer, there are many times when the power of illness over the body causes us to lose the battle for complete physical or mental wellness. The failure to get well is not a confirmation that we have too small a faith. Christ said, "In the world ye shall have tribulation: but be of good cheer; I have overcome the world" (John 16:33). This declaration of Christ makes it clear that our victory over illness does not mean that we will always recover physically. Instead, Christ's declaration promises that if we endure to the end, we will spend eternity with Him.

III. CONCLUDING REFLECTION

God desires for us to be physically, emotionally, and spiritually well. Sickness comes as a result of Satan's attempt to separate us from God. But we can win the final battle if, throughout life's challenges, we keep our minds focused on Christ. Even through extreme illnesses such as cancer, heart failure, lupus, diabetes, bipolar disorder, and all the other "attacks" on our bodies, we can weather our storms as long as we have Christ. It may be an uphill battle that seems to elude our efforts at recovery, but in the end—we will win!

Christ is the only way to win the final battle against Satan. Whether one suffers from mental, physical, or spiritual infirmities, giving ourselves over to Christ wholly guarantees that we *will* have the final victory.

Jesus told this man that was healed, "Go home and tell." This is the mandate for every one of us. We must be willing to share the testimony of what Christ has done for us.

When was the last time you told your neighbor what Christ did in your life? What exactly did you remember He did for you? Is it worth sharing? No matter how small you think the miracle is, you should try to share it with your friends and your church.

PRAYER

Father in heaven, we thank You for various healings and helps we have received from You. Forgive us for failing to share the Good News. Help us to heed Your command to go and tell others of Your love. In Jesus' name we pray. Amen.

WORD POWER

Go (Greek: *hupago*)—is cast in the imperative mood, meaning it is a command. At this point the Lord Jesus did not advise the man to go. He could take the advice or ignore it, but in this instance the Lord issued a command. It carries the idea of "go away from me," or "depart from this place of your healing and spread the news of your healing."

HOME DAILY BIBLE READINGS
(October 5-11, 2009)
Recognizing Jesus

MONDAY, October 5: "The Lord's Work for Freedom" (Luke 7:18-23)

TUESDAY, October 6: "A Bondage Imposed" (Exodus 1:8-14)

WEDNESDAY, October 7: "I Will Free You!" (Exodus 6:2-7)

THURSDAY, October 8: "The Hope for Redemption" (Romans 8:18-25)

FRIDAY, October 9: "Freed from the Fear of Death" (Hebrews 2:14-18)

SATURDAY, October 10: "Christ Has Set Us Free" (Romans 8:9-17)

SUNDAY, October 11: "A Shackled Man Set Free" (Mark 5:1-13, 18-20)

LESSON 7

October 18, 2009

BEGGING TO GET IN

DEVOTIONAL READING: **2 Corinthians 8:1-7**
PRINT PASSAGE: **Mark 7:24-30**

BACKGROUND SCRIPTURE: **Mark 7:24-30**
KEY VERSE: **Mark 7:26**

Mark 7:24-30—KJV

24 And from thence he arose, and went into the borders of Tyre and Sidon, and entered into an house, and would have no man know it: but he could not be hid.

25 For a certain woman, whose young daughter had an unclean spirit, heard of him, and came and fell at his feet:

26 The woman was a Greek, a Syrophenician by nation; and she besought him that he would cast forth the devil out of her daughter.

27 But Jesus said unto her, Let the children first be filled: for it is not meet to take the children's bread, and to cast it unto the dogs.

28 And she answered and said unto him, Yes, Lord: yet the dogs under the table eat of the children's crumbs.

29 And he said unto her, For this saying go thy way; the devil is gone out of thy daughter.

30 And when she was come to her house, she found the devil gone out, and her daughter laid upon the bed.

Mark 7:24-30—NRSV

24 From there he set out and went away to the region of Tyre. He entered a house and did not want anyone to know he was there. Yet he could not escape notice,

25 but a woman whose little daughter had an unclean spirit immediately heard about him, and she came and bowed down at his feet.

26 Now the woman was a Gentile, of Syrophoenician origin. She begged him to cast the demon out of her daughter.

27 He said to her, "Let the children be fed first, for it is not fair to take the children's food and throw it to the dogs."

28 But she answered him, "Sir, even the dogs under the table eat the children's crumbs."

29 Then he said to her, "For saying that, you may go—the demon has left your daughter."

30 So she went home, found the child lying on the bed, and the demon gone.

BIBLE FACT

SYROPHENICIAN: A *Syrophenician* was a Gentile born in the Phoenician part of Syria. In our Printed Text, when our Lord retired into the borderland of Tyre and Sidon (see Mark 7:26), a Greek ("a Syrophenician by nation"—Mark 7:26) woman pressed through the crowd and came to Jesus and earnestly besought Him, on behalf of her daughter—who was grievously afflicted with a demon. Her faith in Jesus was severely tested by His answer and seeming reproach that it was not meet to cast the children's bread to dogs (see Mark 7:27). But the woman stood the test, and her petition was graciously granted. Do not give up even when you think all hope is gone.

UNIFYING LESSON PRINCIPLE

We are sometimes astonished by the faith and tenacity that people exhibit. What motivates people to maintain such an attitude? The woman of Syrophenicia believed that Jesus could heal her daughter, so she persisted despite Jesus' challenging questions.

TOPICAL OUTLINE OF THE LESSON

I. Introduction
A. A Solution to Problems
B. Biblical Background

II. Exposition and Application of the Scripture
A. The Petition of a Gentile Woman (Mark 7:24-26)
B. The Petition Rejected (Mark 7:27)
C. The Petitioner's Persistence Rewarded (Mark 7:28-30)

III. Concluding Reflection

LESSON OBJECTIVES

Upon completion of this lesson, the students will know that:

1. Adversity can teach us to develop faith in God;
2. The silence of God is an answer in disguise; and,
3. The love of God is universal to those who come through Jesus Christ.

By Birth this Gentile woman, Was a Syrian from the region of Phoenicia

POINTS TO BE EMPHASIZED

ADULT/YOUTH

Adult Topic: Pleading for Mercy

Youth Topic: Determined to Find True Treasure

Adult Key Verse: Mark 7:26

Youth Key Verse: Mark 7:28

Print Passage: Mark 7:24-30

—The thrust of this passage suggests that Jesus was open to considering an opinion different from the one He initially expressed.

—Jesus may have been testing the woman or ironically expressing the ethnocentrism of the Jews when He seemed to connect the derogatory term "dogs" to the Gentiles.

—Whatever the complexities and ambiguities of this passage, the primary message—consistent with Jesus' eventual response to the woman and His healing of her daughter—seems to be this: Jesus recognized the claims of the Gentiles to share in the salvation of the Gospel.

—The Syrophenician woman begged Jesus to cast out the unclean spirit from her daughter.

—The woman persisted in her faith.

CHILDREN

Children Topic: A Woman's Faith

Key Verse: Mark 7:25

Print Passage: Mark 7:24-30

—Having faith can make a difference in one's approach to a situation.

—Jesus recognizes the faith of all persons and rewards it.

—Serious situations sometimes call for unusual courage and action.

—The woman with the sick daughter interceded with Jesus on her child's behalf.

—The Syrophenician woman was an outsider.

Fall 2009–TOWNSEND PRESS COMMENTARY | 45

I. INTRODUCTION

A. A Solution to Problems

Christians recognize their dependence upon their Creator. We have every reason to express our gratitude for God's blessings. But there are times in the life of every Christian when one feels separated from God. These are often the times when we are going through trials and tribulations, and we are patiently or impatiently awaiting God's answer to our prayers of deliverance. However, even in those difficult periods of our lives, we take comfort in our ability to communicate with God.

Consider the sinner who does not know God. Unbelievers go through the same testing periods as Christians. But they have no basis for a rewarding fellowship with God because they have not met the conditions set forth in the Bible for effectiveness in prayer. Consequently, they remain separated from their source of deliverance.

The Syrophenician woman faced such a crisis. Her daughter lay ill, possessed by a demon. As a mother, she no doubt had done everything in her power to heal the desperate situation. When she heard news of Jesus' widespread fame as a healer, she recognized that Jesus was the solution to her dilemma.

B. Biblical Background

Mark recorded a somewhat unusual story of a Syrophenician woman and her encounter with Jesus. The woman was from Phenicia, a nation northeast of Palestine which had been incorporated into the Roman province of Syria. Thus she was called a Syrophenician. As a Gentile during the earthly ministry of Jesus, she was labeled an outsider and a foreigner.

The Jews' hatred of the Gentiles developed over their long covenant history with God as His chosen people. The Gentiles had not always been looked upon with hostility. Early in Hebrew history, the Gentiles were treated cordially by the Israelites (see Deuteronomy 10:19). Jewish men often married Gentile women (Boaz married Ruth; David married Bathsheba). However, after the Jews returned from captivity in Babylon to their homeland, the prophets discouraged the practice of intermarriage in order to preserve their covenant worship of the one true and living God (see Ezra 9:12; 10:2-44; Nehemiah 10:30). By the time of the New Testament, the separation between Jew and Gentile had become so strict that the Jews despised all Gentiles. The persecution by the Greeks and Romans from about 400 BC until the time of Jesus Christ's ministry caused the Jews to retaliate with the greatest hatred ever, and forbid any contact with foreigners.

The Scriptures record that it was Jesus' idea to go into the area of Tyre and Sidon. These two cities, one established in 2750 BC and the other in 4000 BC, still exist today and are part of the country of Lebanon. Ancient Tyre and Sidon were commercial cities famous for their export of purple-dyed cloth, a symbol of royalty. These cities were also known for athletic games and competitions, and drew athletes, as well as *Gentiles* from the entire known ancient world. Jesus often took His message of salvation to commerce cities to facilitate the spread of the Gospel. Though it is stated in this Scripture that Jesus went there to escape the throngs of Jewish followers and find some rest, as the all-knowing Messiah, He had to expect that His message would gain notoriety in these commerce cities.

II. EXPOSITION AND APPLICATION OF THE SCRIPTURE

A. The Petition of a Gentile Woman
(Mark 7:24-26)

And from thence he arose, and went into the borders of Tyre and Sidon, and entered into an house, and would have no man know it: but he could not be hid. For a certain woman, whose young daughter had an unclean spirit, heard of him, and came and fell at his feet: The woman was a Greek, a Syrophenician by nation; and she besought him that he would cast forth the devil out of her daughter.

Prayer is our method of communication with God. The most meaningful prayer comes from a heart that places its complete trust in Jesus Christ as Lord and Savior. God speaks to us through the Bible and we, in turn, speak to Him through trusting and believing prayer. The Bible assures us that God is all-knowing, all-wise, and all-powerful, and accordingly He can hear and help us. Our confident prayer lives are built on the foundation of Christ's work as recorded in the Scriptures. The more aware we are of God's holiness, the more conscious we are of our own sinfulness.

The sinner knows nothing of this relational experience with Deity until he or she connects spiritually with Jesus Christ. Sinners must confess their sins to God and "get right" with Him before God can hear and answer their prayers.

This was the plight of the Greek woman from Syrophenicia. She could do nothing to help her demon-possessed daughter. She was disconnected from the God of the Jews, and forbidden to enter into Jewish territory or worship the God of the Jews. But she knew that she needed to connect with Christ if she was to have any hope of her petition being granted.

Mark said that Jesus desired to be alone to rest. It seemed logical to withdraw to the northern Gentile area for respite, because no Jew was likely to enter into a Gentile area. But it wasn't long before word spread of His location and a crowd gathered outside the residence where He was staying. Among them was the woman from Syrophenicia. When she heard that Jesus was in the area, she pressed her way through the crowd, determined to connect with the Son of God.

B. The Petition Rejected
(Mark 7:27)

But Jesus said unto her, Let the children first be filled: for it is not meet to take the children's bread, and to cast it unto the dogs.

Jesus rejected her request on the spot. Rejection is painful; it alienates the rejected and leaves the one rejected in emotional pain. The woman's life was a constant torment because of her sick daughter. All of her hope lay in Jesus' response to her request for her daughter's healing. And all of her hope seemed dashed by Jesus' response.

This woman had two strikes against her. First, she had a demonic daughter whose illness caused her family to be ostracized from the community where she lived. Both the daughter and the mother suffered the pains of complete rejection. Second, she was a Gentile by race. She was from one of the seven nations driven out of the land of Canaan in the Old Testament. They and the Jews were bitter ancestral enemies. They despised and hated each other. In approaching Jesus, she knew that she was coming to a Jew who was assumed to be her enemy.

But notice that Jesus let her come; He did not stop her. Others rejected her and her daughter and had nothing to do with them, but Jesus let her come, despite His need for rest. Even the disciples objected to her (see Matthew 15:23). But Jesus allowed her to interrupt Him. She stood alone in the world as rejected as a person could be, but Jesus received her.

And yet, Jesus seemed to reject her request. As Christians, it is important for us to understand what was happening in this situation, or we risk wrongly interpreting Jesus' response to her petition. To petition Jesus, a believer must first know Jesus is the Savior. This woman's concept of Jesus was limited. She had heard that the Jews expected a Messiah, a descendant of King David, who was to work miracles for them. And she had heard about Jesus—that He was performing miracles and delivering people from their sickness. But seeing Jesus only as a miracle worker and healer was an inadequate concept of Him. It prohibited Him from helping her. What the woman needed was to grow in her understanding of just who Jesus really was.

Jesus listened to the cry of this rejected woman and knew every thought of her heart. He knew that she needed an understanding of His true Messianic purpose. So He began to lead her step-by-step to understand His lordship and to confess her faith in a humble and worshipful spirit. He wanted to help turn her rejection into acceptance and deliverance. His seeming rejection of her request was carefully executed to invoke her confession of faith.

Jesus said, "Let the children first be filled" (verse 27). The Jews are the first children of God, the covenant people of God, to whom Jesus had been sent first. Jesus had come primarily to the house of Israel during His earthly ministry, and had to concentrate His ministry on Israel if He was to achieve His purpose. Jesus made this statement to the Greek woman for two reasons: first, the woman needed to learn the importance of persistence, humility, and trust; and second, the woman needed to learn that there was only one true religion and one true Messiah. She was a Greek from a proud pagan society who worshiped false gods. Though she had recognized Jesus as the Son of David, as the miracle worker of the Jews who was delivering them from their diseases, she also needed to recognize that Jesus was the *only* Messiah and the *only* hope for all mankind. She had to learn the same lesson that the Samaritan woman at the well had to learn (see John 4:22).

Jesus' words that followed seem harsh, on the surface. He said, "It is not meet to take the children's bread, and to cast it unto the dogs" (verse 27). But we know that Jesus never spoke harshly. So what did Jesus mean? Jesus was saying that it was not right to take the bread of the Gospel that belonged to the true worshipers of God and give it to the *dogs*, or the *heathens*. The woman had to reconcile the fact that her people, the Greeks, hated the Jews, the true worshipers of God, and thus were heathens. She had to humbly surrender herself to Jesus as the Master of her life.

C. The Petitioner's Persistence Rewarded
(Mark 7:28-30)

And she answered and said unto him, Yes, Lord: yet the dogs under the table eat of the children's crumbs. And he said unto her, For this saying go thy way; the devil is gone out of thy daughter. And when she was come to her house, she found the devil gone out, and her daughter laid upon the bed.

Rejection often casts a forlorn shadow and sends the rejected away, but not this persistent woman. Notice that she responded by calling Jesus *Lord*, and worshiping Jesus as Lord! She had called Jesus *Lord* before, but only out of respect. The woman understood Jesus' test and persistently replied that even during the meal "the dogs" consumed the children's crumbs that fell from the table.

Many sinners come to church seeking all manner of help, from financial to physical, and even spiritual. They are troubled, and they come because they have heard that the church dispenses help to those in need. But most of them leave unchanged, because they have come for all the wrong reasons. They come desiring only a handout. And they miss Jesus' greater gift of salvation.

In Ephesians 6:18, we are admonished to pray with "all prayer and supplication." *Supplication* is an intense petition to God. It means "to beg, humbly and earnestly." Solomon offered a prayer of supplication (see 1 Kings 8:28-59). David said "The LORD hath heard my supplication; the LORD will receive my prayer"

(Psalm 6:9). Supplication, then, is persistence in our petitions to God. Persistence paid off for Solomon, who built the Temple of God. Persistence paid off for David, who overcame his adversaries and became the king of Israel.

Spiritual growth is often likened to a journey. A person comes to faith and then begins walking with God, step-by-step, year-by-year, moving into ever-higher areas of spiritual maturity. But for many people, the journey seems to fade along the way. Perhaps they feel that it has become too difficult, or they get sidetracked by distractions, or detoured by sin. Perhaps they feel that they have reached a dead end and can go no further. Whatever the case, their spiritual lives remain at a standstill and their journey is incomplete. Prayer is the tool God offers us to get us through those times when our faith is challenged and we find ourselves discouraged. Whatever steps are needed to restore our faith, the Scriptures encourage us to finish the journey (see Hebrews 6:11). God is ready to help us (see Philippians 1:8), but He cannot do our praying for us. The believer is the only one who can take the steps of faith and obedience that lead to maturity in Christ.

This Gentile woman's persistence is the greatest of all points in this lesson, for it reveals that persistence in our petitions to Jesus pays off. She believed Jesus could meet her need, and she would not let Him go until He had met her need. Her belief was so strong that she overcame silence, irritation, opposition, apparent rebuff, and the claim of others that she was undeserving.

When Jesus saw the persistence of this woman, He told her to go home—that her child was already healed. This miracle shows that Jesus' power over demons is so great that He does not need to be present physically in order to heal someone. Jesus' power has no limitation and nothing can hinder His work.

III. CONCLUDING REFLECTION

Adversity is never meant to discourage Christians, but instead to challenge our faith to operate on a new level. When we encounter situations that test our faith, that is the time to remain persistent. We must plant our spiritual feet firmly in the knowledge that Christ can and will deliver us, and press for that deliverance. Persistent prayer builds spiritual character and can bring about a change in God's response to our situation. Seeming rejection to our petitions may be God's response to a weak and anemic faith that needs repair.

PRAYER

Heavenly Father, when our requests are not immediately met, help us (Your children) to remain faithful and persistent. The Syrophenician woman helps us to see that our condition is not beyond Your control. And You don't have to be present before You answer us. In Jesus' name we pray. Amen.

WORD POWER

Besought (Greek: *Erotao*)—this word means: "ask, request, entreat, beg, etc." However, the word *besought* in the context of the lesson means that the woman kept on asking unashamed. The presence of the Jews and other people did not stop this woman in her earnestness. Even when Jesus made a statement that could make her uncomfortable and become resentful, she kept on asking. How often do we become discouraged when our requests are not immediately met? We become impatient. Having persistence means we can trust that God is alive.

HOME DAILY BIBLE READINGS
(October 12-18, 2009)

Begging to Get In

MONDAY, October 12: "Excelling in Generosity" (2 Corinthians 8:1-7)

TUESDAY, October 13: "Inquiring Nations" (Isaiah 11:1-10)

WEDNESDAY, October 14: "A Light to the Nations" (Isaiah 42:5-9)

THURSDAY, October 15: "Salvation to All the Earth" (Isaiah 49:1-6)

FRIDAY, October 16: "God's Glory among Nations" (Isaiah 66:18-20)

SATURDAY, October 17: "Great among the Nations" (Malachi 1:9-11)

SUNDAY, October 18: "A Gentile's Faith Rewarded" (Mark 7:24-30)

LESSON 8

October 25, 2009

OPTING OUT!

DEVOTIONAL READING: **Proverbs 11:1-7**
PRINT PASSAGE: **Mark 10:17-31**

BACKGROUND SCRIPTURE: **Mark 10:17-31**
KEY VERSE: **Mark 10:21**

Mark 10:17-31—KJV

17 And when he was gone forth into the way, there came one running, and kneeled to him, and asked him, Good Master, what shall I do that I may inherit eternal life?

18 And Jesus said unto him, Why callest thou me good? there is none good but one, that is, God.

19 Thou knowest the commandments, Do not commit adultery, Do not kill, Do not steal, Do not bear false witness, Defraud not, Honour thy father and mother.

20 And he answered and said unto him, Master, all these have I observed from my youth.

21 Then Jesus beholding him loved him, and said unto him, One thing thou lackest: go thy way, sell whatsoever thou hast, and give to the poor, and thou shalt have treasure in heaven: and come, take up the cross, and follow me.

22 And he was sad at that saying, and went away grieved: for he had great possessions.

23 And Jesus looked round about, and saith unto his disciples, How hardly shall they that have riches enter into the kingdom of God!

24 And the disciples were astonished at his words. But Jesus answereth again, and saith unto them, Children, how hard is it for them that trust in riches to enter into the kingdom of God!

25 It is easier for a camel to go through the eye of a needle, than for a rich man to enter into the kingdom of God.

26 And they were astonished out of measure, saying among themselves, Who then can be saved?

27 And Jesus looking upon them saith, With men it is impossible, but not with God: for with God all things are possible.

28 Then Peter began to say unto him, Lo, we have left all, and have followed thee.

Mark 10:17-31—NRSV

17 As he was setting out on a journey, a man ran up and knelt before him, and asked him, "Good Teacher, what must I do to inherit eternal life?"

18 Jesus said to him, "Why do you call me good? No one is good but God alone.

19 You know the commandments: 'You shall not murder; You shall not commit adultery; You shall not steal; You shall not bear false witness; You shall not defraud; Honor your father and mother.'"

20 He said to him, "Teacher, I have kept all these since my youth."

21 Jesus, looking at him, loved him and said, "You lack one thing; go, sell what you own, and give the money to the poor, and you will have treasure in heaven; then come, follow me."

22 When he heard this, he was shocked and went away grieving, for he had many possessions.

23 Then Jesus looked around and said to his disciples, "How hard it will be for those who have wealth to enter the kingdom of God!"

24 And the disciples were perplexed at these words. But Jesus said to them again, "Children, how hard it is to enter the kingdom of God!

25 It is easier for a camel to go through the eye of a needle than for someone who is rich to enter the kingdom of God."

26 They were greatly astounded and said to one another, "Then who can be saved?"

27 Jesus looked at them and said, "For mortals it is impossible, but not for God; for God all things are possible."

28 Peter began to say to him, "Look, we have left everything and followed you."

People wonder whether eternal life exists, and how they may obtain it. What leads to eternal life? Jesus teaches that to become true followers and so inherit eternal life we must submit our possessions and ourselves to God.

29 And Jesus answered and said, Verily I say unto you, There is no man that hath left house, or brethren, or sisters, or father, or mother, or wife, or children, or lands, for my sake, and the gospel's,

30 But he shall receive an hundredfold now in this time, houses, and brethren, and sisters, and mothers, and children, and lands, with persecutions; and in the world to come eternal life.

31 But many that are first shall be last; and the last first.

29 Jesus said, "Truly I tell you, there is no one who has left house or brothers or sisters or mother or father or children or fields, for my sake and for the sake of the good news,

30 who will not receive a hundredfold now in this age—houses, brothers and sisters, mothers and children, and fields with persecutions—and in the age to come eternal life.

31 But many who are first will be last, and the last will be first."

TOPICAL OUTLINE OF THE LESSON

I. Introduction
  A. Materialism
  B. Biblical Background

II. Exposition and Application of the Scripture
  A. The Three Flaws (Mark 10:17-22)
  B. The Needle Nemesis Overcome (Mark 10:23-26)
  C. The Reward for Obedience (Mark 10:27-31)

III. Concluding Reflection

LESSON OBJECTIVES

Upon completion of this lesson, the students will know that:

1. Faith in earthly treasure can impede entrance into heaven;
2. We have a misguided view of earthly treasures; and,
3. Where our treasure is determines our values.

POINTS TO BE EMPHASIZED

ADULT/ YOUTH

Adult Topic: The Gain in Giving

Youth Topic: True Treasure Costs

Adult Key Verse: Mark 10:21

Youth Key Verses: Mark 10:29-30

Print Passage: Mark 10:17-31

—The story of the rich man is an illustration of the grip of wealth on a person's loyalties and allegiances.

—The Ten Commandments serve as a summary of the whole Mosaic law.

—From the following question is implied this passage: In what sense do wealth and possessions hinder love of God and neighbor?

—The man asked Jesus what he must do to inherit eternal life.

—Jesus questioned why he called Him "good" and asked him about the commandments.

—The man said that he kept the commandments.

—Jesus told him to sell all he had, give to the poor, and follow Him. The man went away grieving.

CHILDREN

Children Topic: A Rich Man Refuses to Follow

Key Verse: Mark 10:22

Print Passage: Mark 10:17-31

—The rich man did not realize when he came to Jesus that inheriting eternal life would involve sacrifice.

—The rich man had performed the letter of the law.

—Treasures on earth are less significant than treasures in heaven.

—The rich man's grief did not keep him from walking away from Jesus.

—Some decisions are difficult to make and require great sacrifice.

I. INTRODUCTION

A. Materialism

There is much talk about materialism in America. Most define *materialism* as "the desire for possessions." But the desire to acquire wealth through possessions is not the definition of materialism; it is the definition of consumerism. *Consumerism* is a by-product of materialism. *Materialism* is the belief that nothing exists and has value unless it is made of matter. Therefore, the consumer believes his or her wealth is predicated upon the volume of his or her material possessions.

Materialism holds to the position that matter simply exists and does not need God to explain its existence or give it meaning. But Judeo-Christian *theism* stands in stark contrast to that theory. *Theism* is "the belief in God as the Creator of the universe"; and while it is true that we cannot explain it or reason it out, we believe that God is absolute in His existence and His authority.

The rich man in our text was struggling with materialism. He had become a consumer with great material wealth, and he would not permit his professed faith in Christ to devalue his enormous possessions. He struggled with the common malady of putting *self* before Christ.

B. Biblical Background

The ancient term "eye of the needle" was a figure of speech used by Jesus to illustrate the extreme difficulty of a wealthy person's attaining salvation. Jesus said, "It is easier for a camel to go through the eye of a needle, than for a rich man to enter into the kingdom of God" (Matthew 19:24). Much has been written in an attempt to explain that statement. Some theologians suggest that the "needle's eye" was a narrow gate adjacent to one of the main gates of Jerusalem. A camel could pass through this gate, but not without extreme difficulty. The camel would first have to be stripped of the goods it was carrying, and then it had to bow low to its knees and crawl through the gate. There is no historical evidence, however, to support this theory.

Too much wealth can be detrimental to the moral and spiritual health of a believer. We must beware of the impact of wealth on our relationship with Christ.

II. EXPOSITION AND APPLICATION OF THE SCRIPTURE

A. The Three Flaws
(Mark 10:17-22)

And when he was gone forth into the way, there came one running, and kneeled to him, and asked him, Good Master, what shall I do that I may inherit eternal life? And Jesus said unto him, Why callest thou me good? there is none good but one, that is, God. Thou knowest the commandments, Do not commit adultery, Do not kill, Do not steal, Do not bear false witness, Defraud not, Honour thy father and mother. And he answered and said unto him, Master, all these have I observed from my youth. Then Jesus beholding him loved him, and said unto him, One thing thou lackest: go thy way, sell whatsoever thou hast, and give to the poor, and thou shalt have treasure in heaven: and come, take up the cross, and follow me. And he was sad at that saying, and went away grieved: for he had great possessions.

The young man in our text was quite a rarity. He was conscientious, responsible, and dependable—traits that are rare in our youths and adults. As a result of his exceptional character and reputation, he had already attained a position of leadership. When he approached Jesus, it was instantly evident to the Master that this young man was sincere in his desire to obtain eternal life. Jesus shocked the young man; when His disciples and the crowd had gathered around Him, Jesus let the young man know that sincerity, eagerness, and a desire for eternal life were not enough. He made it clear that to inherit eternal life takes much more than just being desperate to possess it.

Jesus carefully and methodically pointed out the flaws in this man's faith. The *first flaw* was that the young man did not praise Jesus Christ as the only begotten son of God. The young man had praised and honored Jesus as a good teacher and an honored rabbi. He did not consider Jesus to be the divine Son of God. He addressed Jesus as a mere man, worthy of respect, but not his Redeemer. Jesus corrected his error by saying, "Why callest thou me good? there is none good but one, that is, God" (verse 18). He was saying to the young man, "God alone is good. No man is good, not in comparison to God, not good enough to stand before God in righteousness. If I am but a mere man, a good teacher, then I am not 'good' and do not have the words to eternal life. *But if I am God*, then you can address me as 'good' and I do have the words to eternal life."

The *second flaw* was found in the young man's essential question, "What *good thing* shall I do?" (see verse 17). This man had a religion of works and not of faith. Though he quoted five of the Ten Commandments, he misunderstood God's law and had a tragic sense of self-righteousness. People cannot secure eternal life by being good and living moral and clean lives. God keeps no tally sheet of our good deeds.

It is stated in the Scriptures that Jesus beheld him and loved him for his sincerity. But Jesus' love for him was not enough to save him. The *third flaw* was this: he had not wholly and completely surrendered to Jesus Christ as Lord and Savior. *Giving everything* was the one thing that the young man could not do. Some say his rejection of Jesus showed that he was hoarding wealth instead of distributing it.

What the young man needed to hear was just what Jesus said (essentially): "If thou wilt be perfect" then demonstrate to all publicly and without question, that you love your neighbor. "Go and sell all you have and give the money to the poor . . . and come, follow me" (verse 21, TLB).

We struggle so much to protect the glorious truth that humankind is saved by grace and grace alone, that we often forget and neglect another great truth: *to follow Christ is to put Him first, above all else.* We must deny self completely. Once we learn to deny self, Christ is able to grant us the keys to eternal life.

B. The Needle Nemesis Overcome
(Mark 10:23-26)

And Jesus looked round about, and saith unto his disciples, How hardly shall they that have riches enter into the kingdom of God! And the disciples were astonished at his words. But Jesus answereth again, and saith unto them, Children, how hard is it for them that trust in riches to enter into the kingdom of God! It is easier for a camel to go through the eye of a needle, than for a rich man to enter into the kingdom of God. And they were astonished out of measure, saying among themselves, Who then can be saved?

When the young man walked away grieved, Jesus warned those around Him of the dangers of wealth. Wealth has many pitfalls, both for those seeking it and for those who have already obtained it. The quest for wealth can enslave us and blind us to our Christian duty. Jesus used the analogy of pushing a camel through the eye of a needle to demonstrate that the terrible peril of wealth can easily bar a person from the kingdom of God.

Consumerism is a tool of Satan's. He tantalizes us with objects that play to our selfish desires. Riches—cars, money, the latest technological gadgetry, fashion—can pose a serious problem to any person's relationship with God. These *things* can cause a person to place far too much value on wealth. We can surround ourselves with possessions, but they only serve to hide our true condition—that we are helplessly and hopelessly lost without Christ.

Possessions are earthly things, and we cannot take them with us when we leave this life. When we stand before God on the Day of Judgment, what will be present as proof of our faithfulness? The real valuable possessions we have are our integrity and our righteousness through Jesus Christ. And on that day, God will evaluate our character and how we lived our lives—either to His glory or to our shame.

The tension between wealth and faith is noted in James 2:5-6. None of us is exempt from the distracting and distorting effect of growing affluence. While God does not condemn wealth, He clearly warns us that we cannot pursue wealth or trust in it while also pursuing God and trusting in Him.

Most Christians are well-aware of their responsibility to financially support the work of the church. But once they have fulfilled their obligation, many Christians assume that the rest of their income is of no concern to God. God is as concerned with the money we keep as He is with the money we give to His church.

C. The Reward for Obedience
(Mark 10:27-31)

And Jesus looking upon them saith, With men it is impossible, but not with God: for with God all things are possible. Then Peter began to say unto him, Lo, we have left all, and have followed thee. And Jesus answered and

said, Verily I say unto you, There is no man that hath left house, or brethren, or sisters, or father, or mother, or wife, or children, or lands, for my sake, and the gospel's, But he shall receive an hundredfold now in this time, houses, and brethren, and sisters, and mothers, and children, and lands, with persecutions; and in the world to come eternal life. But many that are first shall be last; and the last first.

No man can save himself. Theism teaches us that God alone can save, through Jesus Christ, who paid the price for the penalty of our sin. Human beings cannot withstand the natural urge to seek the comforts of this life. Satan makes it too entangling and too pleasing. But Christ teaches that if we allow our spirits to set our affections on things above, and not on things on the earth (see Colossians 3:1-2), we will inherit eternal life.

The materialists do not believe in the existence of eternal life. Their finite minds cannot comprehend a time that has no beginning and no ending, any more than they can comprehend the concept of endless outer space.

But eternal life and eternal death are foundational truths of Scripture. Though eternal life is not a tangible gift that can be proven through visual reference, it is the theistic belief in a glorious and endless future promised to God's people. Jesus made it clear that eternal life comes only to those who make a total commitment to Him (see Matthew 19:16-21; Luke 18:18-22). The closest proof we have of eternal life is summarized by John (17:3, NKJV), where he said, "And this is eternal life, that they may know You, the only true God, and Jesus Christ whom You have sent." Those who know Christ have tasted of the gift of eternal life.

Materialism prevents the church from flourishing as it should. The law of materialism teaches a visible return for investment. This philosophy has infiltrated the level of giving in most churches. But God expects us to invest in His process of kingdom building. The practice of the tithe (ten percent of one's assets) was an ancient practice among many nations in ancient biblical times, even before the formation of the Hebrew nation under Mosaic Law. The first tithe recorded in biblical history is in Genesis 14:17-20, when Abraham gave Melchizedek a tithe of all the goods he had obtained in battle. Jacob, also long before the Law of Moses, promised that he would give to the Lord a tenth of all he received (see Genesis 28:22). The custom of the tithe was practiced by Jesus and His followers. Jesus taught that believers are to be generous in sharing their material possessions with the poor.

In the prophet Malachi's day, the postexilic Israelites were withholding their tithes and offerings (see Malachi 3:8-10). They apparently preferred to keep more for themselves and give God less. But in doing so, they were not only robbing God—they were robbing from the priests and the poor.

Could the same be true of today's believers? Christians are called to have a sense of responsibility for the poor and for public worship. Obedience to God is more than just a private religious experience. There are social implications as well. We are called by God to pool our resources and address the greater needs of the church and the community that surrounds it. Our giving is to be voluntary, cheerful, willing, and given in the light of our accountability to God. Our gifts should be systematic and never limited to just ten percent of our income, for we recognize that all we have belongs to God.

Our giving, then, springs from a love of Christ rather than a slavish obedience to the tithe's percentage standard of ten percent. Those who learn this truth will freely give beyond the tithe, even to all that they have!

III. CONCLUDING REFLECTION

Would your friends describe you as generous? Do you cling to your possessions as though you deserve them? You may think you are living a clean life, but will your lifestyle dash your hope of an eternal home in heaven? Jesus made it clear that a person's service to others is an indication of his or her fitness for eternal life. Those who selfishly hoard their possessions are missing the chance to give their all for Christ.

There is no medicine, no philosophy, no politics, and no social movement that can motivate a soul to be unselfish. Only Christ can change a soul and turn it into a generous person.

Peter made a statement that should arrest our attention (verse 28, NIV): "We have left everything to follow you!" Jesus answered him, "No one who has left home or brothers or sisters . . . for me and the gospel will fail to receive a hundred times as much" (verses 29-30, NIV). We cannot "over-give" to God; whatever we give to Him is an investment which will yield an eternal dividend.

PRAYER

Heavenly Father, we know Your love for us is beyond our comprehension. Help us to love You in return because of all You have done and will do for us. Forgive us for our selfishness. In Jesus' name we pray. Amen.

WORD POWER

Lackest (Greek: *hustero*)—means "to be left behind in the race and so fail to reach the goal; to fall short of the end; fail to become a partaker." The wealth of the man was an impediment to his way to eternal life. Jesus loved him *(agapao)* but he could not see the love because of his wealth. The love of God is always available but we fail to reciprocate it.

HOME DAILY BIBLE READINGS
(October 19-25, 2009)

Opting Out!
MONDAY, October 19: "Generosity and Its Rewards" (Proverbs 11:24-28)
TUESDAY, October 20: "A Discerning Mind" (1 Kings 3:5-14)
WEDNESDAY, October 21: "The Little of the Righteous" (Psalm 37:12-19)
THURSDAY, October 22: "Trusting in Wealth" (Psalm 49:1-7)
FRIDAY, October 23: "Take Refuge in God" (Psalm 64:5-10)
SATURDAY, October 24: "Rich toward God" (Luke 12:13-21)
SUNDAY, October 25: "Wealth and the Kingdom" (Mark 10:17-31)

LESSON 9

November 1, 2009

A HOLY PEOPLE

DEVOTIONAL READING: **Deuteronomy 7:6-11**

PRINT PASSAGE: **1 Peter 1:13-25**

BACKGROUND SCRIPTURE: **1 Peter 1**

KEY VERSES: **1 Peter 1:15-16**

1 Peter 1:13-25—KJV

13 Wherefore gird up the loins of your mind, be sober, and hope to the end for the grace that is to be brought unto you at the revelation of Jesus Christ;

14 As obedient children, not fashioning yourselves according to the former lusts in your ignorance:

15 But as he which hath called you is holy, so be ye holy in all manner of conversation;

16 Because it is written, Be ye holy; for I am holy.

17 And if ye call on the Father, who without respect of persons judgeth according to every man's work, pass the time of your sojourning here in fear:

18 Forasmuch as ye know that ye were not redeemed with corruptible things, as silver and gold, from your vain conversation received by tradition from your fathers;

19 But with the precious blood of Christ, as of a lamb without blemish and without spot:

20 Who verily was foreordained before the foundation of the world, but was manifest in these last times for you,

21 Who by him do believe in God, that raised him up from the dead, and gave him glory; that your faith and hope might be in God.

22 Seeing ye have purified your souls in obeying the truth through the Spirit unto unfeigned love of the brethren, see that ye love one another with a pure heart fervently:

23 Being born again, not of corruptible seed, but of incorruptible, by the word of God, which liveth and abideth for ever.

24 For all flesh is as grass, and all the glory of man as the flower of grass. The grass withereth, and the flower thereof falleth away:

25 But the word of the Lord endureth for ever. And this is the word which by the gospel is preached unto you.

1 Peter 1:13-25—NRSV

13 Therefore prepare your minds for action; discipline yourselves; set all your hope on the grace that Jesus Christ will bring you when he is revealed.

14 Like obedient children, do not be conformed to the desires that you formerly had in ignorance.

15 Instead, as he who called you is holy, be holy yourselves in all your conduct;

16 for it is written, "You shall be holy, for I am holy."

17 If you invoke as Father the one who judges all people impartially according to their deeds, live in reverent fear during the time of your exile.

18 You know that you were ransomed from the futile ways inherited from your ancestors, not with perishable things like silver or gold,

19 but with the precious blood of Christ, like that of a lamb without defect or blemish.

20 He was destined before the foundation of the world, but was revealed at the end of the ages for your sake.

21 Through him you have come to trust in God, who raised him from the dead and gave him glory, so that your faith and hope are set on God.

22 Now that you have purified your souls by your obedience to the truth so that you have genuine mutual love, love one another deeply from the heart.

23 You have been born anew, not of perishable but of imperishable seed, through the living and enduring word of God.

24 For "All flesh is like grass and all its glory like the flower of grass. The grass withers, and the flower falls,

25 but the word of the Lord endures forever." That word is the good news that was announced to you.

TOPICAL OUTLINE OF THE LESSON

I. **Introduction**
   A. Identifying with Jesus
   B. Biblical Background

II. **Exposition and Application of the Scripture**
   A. Called to Reflect Christ (1 Peter 1:13-16)
   B. Called to Reverence God (1 Peter 1:17-21)
   C. Called to Love One Another (1 Peter 1:22-25)

III. **Concluding Reflection**

LESSON OBJECTIVES

Upon completion of this lesson, the students will know that:

1. We should desire holiness as stipulated in the Scriptures;
2. Through faith in Jesus we possess righteousness; and,
3. We are called to reflect the presence of Christ at all times.

POINTS TO BE EMPHASIZED

ADULT/YOUTH

Adult Topic: The Beauty of Nonconformity

Youth Topic: Called to Be Holy

Adult/Youth Key Verses: 1 Peter 1:15-16

Print Passage: 1 Peter 1:13-25

—The writer of the biblical text admonished readers to experience God's sacrificial love, obey the Gospel, and cultivate mutual love.

—In 1 Peter, readers are admonished to anchor their hope on the resurrection of Jesus and the anticipation of His return.

—The concept of holiness demands accountability toward God and ethical obligations to one another.

—Extreme obedience requires preparing one's mind for action, being self-disciplined, being like children, living in reverent fear, obeying truth, and loving one another.

—Holiness includes both aiming toward moral perfection and receiving the divine commission.

—Being in God's covenant community means being in exile in the world.

—Sin establishes an ownership over people, necessitating God's ransoming them.

CHILDREN

Children Topic: Waiting and Watching

Key Verse: 1 Peter 1:15

Print Passage: Acts 1:6-14; 2:1-4; 1 Peter 1:15

—Jesus told the disciples to wait for the power of the Holy Spirit.

—The disciples gathered for prayer while they waited.

—Among the disciples were the eleven apostles and several women.

—When the Spirit finally came, the disciples received power to become holy people.

Holy — Set apart to the
in the service of God
Spiritually pure

—The disciples did not delay acting in the Spirit's power.

—In 1 Peter, believers are called on to develop holiness in their lives.

I. INTRODUCTION

A. Identifying with Jesus

Have you ever been embarrassed or afraid to identify publicly with Jesus Christ because of possible rejection? That is the price of salvation. Christians suffer persecution. The Scriptures are clear that one of the prices for authentic discipleship is the certainty that we will experience rejection and persecution.

Christians have been under attack, not just in foreign countries like China and Afghanistan, but also right here in the United States. We are attacked for our representation of scriptural values as outlined in our instruction manual, the Holy Bible, despite the fact that those values have their root in the substitutionary death of Christ on the cross for the sins of humankind, and Christ's resurrection from the grave.

The purpose of Peter's epistle was to encourage the downhearted Christians who were severely persecuted. Most early Christians considered persecution a privilege. God allowed persecution to fall on both the Old and New Testament saints as a part of His discipline designed for their spiritual growth in righteousness and holiness (see Hebrews 10:32-34). God has told us clearly that we must suffer persecutions as followers of Christ (see John 15:20), and the Christian should see in such sufferings God's appointed means of testing faith, purifying character, and developing humility and compassion. What happens *in* us is much more important than what happens *to* us.

B. Biblical Background

Peter was the most prominent of Jesus' twelve disciples. The New Testament paints him, not as a big, blundering fisherman, but as a complex and many-sided personality—a pioneer in the early church.

Peter's given name was Simon or Symeon. His brother, Andrew, was also a disciple of Jesus. We know that Peter married, because Jesus healed his mother-in-law (see Matthew 8:14-15). According to the gospel of John, both Peter and Andrew were followers of John the Baptist until they met Jesus. Peter was the first apostle, however, to recognize Jesus as the Messiah (see Matthew 16:13-17).

Peter began this first epistle (written in Rome) on a positive note, praising God for the blessings of a "living hope"—the resurrected Christ. The remainder of his letter can be divided into three parts: blessings, duties, and trials. In the first part, which is the focus of this lesson, Peter called upon all Christians to live holy and blameless lives as God's chosen people.

As Christians read this epistle, we clearly sense that the life, death, and resurrection of Jesus Christ have been deeply etched into the writer's memory. Thus, there is no question that Simon Peter was the author, though he was a Galilean fisherman by trade. Since Greek was not Peter's native tongue, it is believed that he had help with putting his words on paper. That help came from Silvanus, a former associate of Paul, who played an important role in bringing Peter's first epistle to completion while he was in Rome.

Though the Pharisees held a powerful grip on Jewish society in biblical times, one thing is certain: the writer sensed the triumphant outcome of God's purpose for the world and the triumphant future we have through the resurrection of Jesus Christ. Jesus endured temptations, the gainsaying of sinners, and finally the Cross. Peter passed on his assurance that Jesus was compassionate and sympathetic with people (see Hebrews 2:18). Peter emphasized that any persecution we suffer helps us to grow in ability and to sympathize with others.

II. EXPOSITION AND APPLICATION OF THE SCRIPTURE

A. Called to Reflect Christ
(1 Peter 1:13-16)

Wherefore gird up the loins of your mind, be sober, and hope to the end for the grace that is to be brought unto you at the revelation of Jesus Christ; As obedient children, not fashioning yourselves according to the former lusts in your ignorance: But as he which hath called you is holy, so be ye holy in all manner of conversation; Because it is written, Be ye holy; for I am holy.

Persecution can cause either growth or bitterness in the Christian life. Our response determines the result. In writing to the Jewish believers struggling in the midst of persecution, Peter encouraged them to conduct themselves courageously for Christ. He pointed out that both their character and conduct must be above reproach at all times.

Christians who are born-again must imitate Christ who has called them. The fruit of their character will be conduct that is rooted in submission as citizens to government, servants to masters, wives to husbands, husbands to wives, and Christians—one to another. To understand the complexities of being a

suffering servant, Peter made it clear that we must first learn the art of submission.

At the time of Peter's writing, Christians were suffering terrible persecution. They had lost their homes, property, money, possessions, and friends. Many were forced to flee for their lives. Their persecution stemmed from their open proclamation of salvation through Jesus Christ and the hope of eternal life in Him.

It was not the message of salvation, hope, and eternal life that caused the uprising against the early Christians. It was their insistence on repentance as the prerequisite for salvation. The world was not willing to accept that righteousness and godliness were an essential part of their salvation, and that they must be prepared to give Christ all of themselves. Thus, the early Christians fled, sometimes to other countries, and often with disappointment and fear. They needed desperately to be encouraged and strengthened if they were to survive their scattering.

Peter challenged the early Christians to keep their eyes on Jesus and the glorious message of His Gospel. But he knew that would not be enough for their survival. Thus, he also encouraged them to act: to dedicate their lives to God and keep themselves—mind, body, and soul—concentrated upon obedience to the teachings of Jesus.

The command to *gird up one's loins* was a familiar term used to describe the method by which farmers would turn their loose tunics into working garments in preparation for harvest. The back hem of the tunic would be pulled up through the legs and tucked into the belt at the waist to create pants. This "girding" was necessary in order for the farmer to work in the fields. Peter used this familiar term to command Christ's followers to gather up their loose thoughts, be sober-minded, concentrate on the example set by Jesus, and be prepared for obedient service in the kingdom of God.

Peter called all believers to be holy, and to live holy. In other words, we are called to reflect Christ. Believers reflect Christ in a variety of ways. Our regenerated spirit allows us to respond to Christ with complete faith in every aspect of our daily living—in our conversation (see Philippians 1:27), by our forgiving spirits (see Matthew 6:14), in intercessory prayer (see James 5:16), by our giving (see Luke 6:38), by our truthfulness (see Proverbs 14:5), by our faithfulness (see Exodus 15:26; Psalm 119:4), by our continual repentance (see 1 John 1:9), by our humility (see Philippians 2:3), and by our worship (see Psalm 29:2; Hebrews 10:25).

It is a challenge for Christians to reflect Christ in an evil and corrupt world, but Peter reminded us that we must cling to the promise that we will one day be delivered from its grasp. Until then, we must focus our minds on the perfect hope we have in Christ. Those who sincerely believe in the resurrection of Jesus Christ as Lord and Savior, and have been made partakers of God's Spirit, will reflect the character of God through their emulation of Jesus Christ. Believers are able to live in a Christlike manner because of God's provision of the Holy Spirit planted within us at redemption. We are empowered, by the aid of the Holy Spirit within us, to love Him and others, as Christ loves us. Our Christlike actions may often be countercultural. We may sometimes be forced to separate ourselves from cultural celebrations, and non-Christian practices that society deems acceptable. We must choose carefully the government freedoms we exercise, knowing that everything of which the world approves does not necessarily have God's approval. And as a result of setting ourselves apart, we must be prepared to endure persecution as good soldiers of the Cross.

B. Called to Reverence God
(1 Peter 1:17-21)

And if ye call on the Father, who without respect of persons judgeth according to every man's work, pass the time of your sojourning here in fear: Forasmuch as ye know that ye were not redeemed with corruptible things, as silver and gold, from your vain conversation received by tradition from your fathers; But with the precious blood of Christ, as of a lamb without blemish and without spot: Who verily was foreordained before the foundation of the world, but was manifest in these last times for you, Who by him do believe in God, that raised him up from the dead, and gave him glory; that your faith and hope might be in God.

Where do Christians find the strength to face persecution? Peter wrote that our strength is found in our fear of God. Fear can be helpful or harmful. When fear is caused by a sense of danger, it can be an unpleasant and often harmful emotion. Believers are instructed not to fear wicked men (see Matthew 10:28, Philippians 1:28) because they cannot harm us.

On the other hand, the fear of God is a feeling of reverence, awe, and respect. The believer has every reason to fear God, because we stand before Him condemned in our sins. He is our heavenly Father *and* our earthly Judge. The fear we experience when we consider the power of God is the one emotion that causes us to cry out for God's mercy. It is similar to the relational fear a child has toward his earthly father. As with a child's earthly father, we need to fear God only if we disobey Him. If we reverence God, and follow His commands out of respect, we will endure any temptation and persecution for His sake. Our reverence for God should always arouse in us a desire for obedient service and sincere worship.

Peter emphasized that we find the courage to trust in God's power because He demonstrated His power with the resurrection of His Son, Jesus Christ. The same God who brought up Jesus Christ from the dead is able to raise us up also. God has proven His power over death and His omniscience and omnipotence in the face of all enemies. Those who believe in the resurrection of Jesus Christ live with the surety that eternal life will be ours also.

C. Called to Love One Another (1 Peter 1:22-25)

Seeing ye have purified your souls in obeying the truth through the Spirit unto unfeigned love of the brethren, see that ye love one another with a pure heart fervently: Being born again, not of corruptible seed, but of incorruptible, by the word of God, which liveth and abideth for ever. For all flesh is as grass, and all the glory of man as the flower of grass. The grass withereth, and the flower thereof falleth away: But the word of the Lord endureth for ever. And this is the word which by the gospel is preached unto you.

Consider the power of love; there is no greater force between two people. When we love another, we will do anything for that person. There is no greater bond on earth than love.

There are many words for "love"—*eros*, *phileo*, and *agape*. *Eros* love is sensual, as in the love between a man and a woman. *Phileo* love is brotherly love. *Agape* love is the sacrificial love God has for us. *Philarguria* is love of money.

All believers have a relational bond of *phileo* love. It is stated in Romans 12:10, "Be kindly affectioned one to another with brotherly love; in honour preferring one another." From Philippians 2:3, we learn that brotherly love is expressed in the way we treat each other—without strife between us, always putting the other ahead of ourselves. And it is implied in Hebrews 13:1 that if we do not continually cultivate our love for each other, it can diminish.

Love is totally sacrificial and committed to another. It is the fruit of the Spirit that dwells in us (see Galatians 5:22). An examination of the fruits of the Spirit reveals that joy is love *enjoying*, longsuffering is love *resting*, patience is love *waiting*, kindness is love *reacting*, goodness is love *choosing*, faithfulness is love *keeping its word*, gentleness is love *being able to empathize*, and temperance is love *being in charge or self-controlled*. This kind of love does not come from humanity, but from God. We cannot muster this up on our own; it comes from an outflow of the Holy Spirit within us.

God expressed His love through Creation, through the gift of free will, through our adoption by the blood of Jesus Christ. We express our love for Him by our faithful and consistent worship, by our selfless service, and in our unfeigned love for our Christian brothers and sisters. The word *unfeigned* means "genuine, sincere, without pretense or hypocrisy." If a Christian has to pretend to love another, that love is not real; it is play-acting.

Peter also said that we are to love each other fervently. We must be careful here to choose the right modern definition of the word *fervent*. Our relational bond is not "showing warmth of feeling," but rather "hot, glowing, and intense." In other words, we burn with the desire to be of one accord. It means that we are willing to stretch love to the fullest, and in an all-out manner.

III. CONCLUDING REFLECTION

Christ's resurrection from the dead was God's proclamation to all humankind that He accepted Jesus' atoning death on the cross for all the sins of humanity. The Father's mandate had been completely satisfied. The barrier of sin had been removed. The Resurrection was all the proof needed that God acknowledged His Son's death as the final payment for the sins of man.

Our joy in the Lord should be full and expressive, despite persecution and suffering, knowing that the Resurrection definitively proves God's promise that if we live according to Christ's righteousness, we will have access to the Tree of Life.

PRAYER

Heavenly Father, we want to be holy as You are holy. You have provided the way for us to become holy through the Lord Jesus Christ. Help us to draw near through Your Son. And help us to remain with Him. In Jesus' name we pray. Amen.

WORD POWER

As (Greek: *kata*)—means "according to," or "after the pattern of the one who called you." In this context it denotes diffusion of one personality into another (God). It is becoming like God. We are called to be holy as God is holy.

HOME DAILY BIBLE READINGS
(October 26–November 1, 2009)

A Holy People
MONDAY, October 26: "Chosen by a Loving God" (Deuteronomy 7:6-11)
TUESDAY, October 27: "Keeping the Covenant" (Exodus 19:1-6)
WEDNESDAY, October 28: "A Reminder to Obey" (Numbers 15:37-41)
THURSDAY, October 29: "Waiting for the Holy Spirit" (Acts 1:1-11)
FRIDAY, October 30: "Filled with the Holy Spirit" (Acts 2:1-4)
SATURDAY, October 31: "Born into a Living Hope" (1 Peter 1:1-12)
SUNDAY, November 1: "Called to Holy Living" (1 Peter 1:13-25)

LESSON 10   November 8, 2009

A CHOSEN PEOPLE

DEVOTIONAL READING: **Deuteronomy 10:10-15**

PRINT PASSAGE: **1 Peter 2:1-10**

BACKGROUND SCRIPTURE: **1 Peter 2:1-17**

KEY VERSE: **1 Peter 2:9**

1 Peter 2:1-10—KJV

WHEREFORE LAYING aside all malice, and all guile, and hypocrisies, and envies, and all evil speakings,
2 As newborn babes, desire the sincere milk of the word, that ye may grow thereby:
3 If so be ye have tasted that the Lord is gracious.
4 To whom coming, as unto a living stone, disallowed indeed of men, but chosen of God, and precious,
5 Ye also, as lively stones, are built up a spiritual house, an holy priesthood, to offer up spiritual sacrifices, acceptable to God by Jesus Christ.
6 Wherefore also it is contained in the scripture, Behold, I lay in Sion a chief corner stone, elect, precious: and he that believeth on him shall not be confounded.
7 Unto you therefore which believe he is precious: but unto them which be disobedient, the stone which the builders disallowed, the same is made the head of the corner,
8 And a stone of stumbling, and a rock of offence, even to them which stumble at the word, being disobedient: whereunto also they were appointed.
9 But ye are a chosen generation, a royal priesthood, an holy nation, a peculiar people; that ye should shew forth the praises of him who hath called you out of darkness into his marvellous light:
10 Which in time past were not a people, but are now the people of God: which had not obtained mercy, but now have obtained mercy.

1 Peter 2:1-10—NRSV

RID YOURSELVES, therefore, of all malice, and all guile, insincerity, envy, and all slander.
2 Like newborn infants, long for the pure, spiritual milk, so that by it you may grow into salvation—
3 if indeed you have tasted that the Lord is good.
4 Come to him, a living stone, though rejected by mortals yet chosen and precious in God's sight, and
5 like living stones, let yourselves be built into a spiritual house, to be a holy priesthood, to offer spiritual sacrifices acceptable to God through Jesus Christ.
6 For it stands in scripture: "See, I am laying in Zion a stone, a cornerstone chosen and precious; and whoever believes in him will not be put to shame."
7 To you then who believe, he is precious; but for those who do not believe, "The stone that the builders rejected has become the very head of the corner,"
8 and "A stone that makes them stumble, and a rock that makes them fall." They stumble because they disobey the word, as they were destined to do.
9 But you are a chosen race, a royal priesthood, a holy nation, God's own people, in order that you may proclaim the mighty acts of him who called you out of darkness into his marvelous light.
10 Once you were not a people, but now you are God's people; once you had not received mercy, but now you have received mercy.

BIBLE FACT

CHOSEN: Of all Christian doctrines, this is one of the greatest. Many have yet to understand the blessing of being "chosen" by God. Many who understood are living beneath its comprehensive meaning. Many enjoy the *judicial* part of it but not the *actual* part. To enjoy the "actual" is an intimate relationship with God. It is living and manifesting the glory of God.

TOPICAL OUTLINE OF THE LESSON

I. Introduction
  A. Spiritual Community
  B. Biblical Background

II. Exposition and Application of the Scripture
  A. Stripping Off the Old Nature
    (1 Peter 2:1-3)
  B. Building Your Spiritual House
    (1 Peter 2:4-8)
  C. Declaring Your Loyalty
    (1 Peter 2:9-10)

III. Concluding Reflection

LESSON OBJECTIVES

Upon completion of this lesson, the students will know that:

1. As children of God, we must lay aside offensive attitudes;
2. Our lives are books before the unbelieving world; and,
3. Our identification with Christ leaves us with no alternative but to please God.

POINTS TO BE EMPHASIZED

ADULT/YOUTH

Adult Topic: Chosen to Proclaim
Youth Topic: From No People to Chosen People
Adult/Youth Key Verse: 1 Peter 2:9
Print Passage: 1 Peter 2:1-10

—Peter called the people to come together in faith and form a new community.
—Peter claimed that salvation is an ongoing process of being built into "a spiritual house."
—Images in verses 9 and 10 are found in Exodus 19:6 and Hosea 1:9; 2:23.
—To "proclaim the mighty acts" of God is the basis of witness and service to Christ in the world.
—In the new community, Christians can accept the living stone of Jesus, who is the cornerstone that has been rejected by worldly people because it makes them stumble and fall (see Psalm 118:22).
—God calls Christians out of darkness into Jesus' marvelous light.
—Once people lived in the worldly community without mercy, but now they live as Christians who have received mercy from God in their community.

CHILDREN

Children Topic: Sharing Possessions
Key Verse: Acts 4:32
Print Passage: Acts 4:31-37; 1 Peter 2:9

—Filled with the Holy Spirit, the disciples proclaimed God's Word.
—The believers found joy and power in one another.
—The disciples shared everything they possessed so that no believer was in need.

—The disciples began to identify themselves as God's people empowered to bear witness to Jesus.

—First Peter is a reminder to believers that God has chosen them to share the Gospel.
—Believers' acts help others know their identity.

I. INTRODUCTION

A. Spiritual Community

God's spiritual community, the church, is a body of baptized believers who share the common experience of redemption from sin by the blood of Jesus Christ. Often referred to by the apostle Paul as the body of Christ, the faith community's purpose is to act as a unified body despite our varied gifts, ministries, and personalities.

The word *church* (*Ekklesia*) refers to all who follow Christ, without respect to locality, race, or gender. The local church is the visible church to come. And in a world where change happens faster than textbooks can record it, the church must be accountable to its timeless mission. Unless we are willing to make the changes that will equip the church to evangelize, the relevancy of the Gospel will likely never reach those who are lost. Those changes include our willingness to purge ourselves of the sins that have continued throughout time to infiltrate our ranks.

Even though the Christian church is the largest institution ever to exist in world history, we are slowly losing our effectiveness even among believers. Christians no longer cling to denominational lines as tenaciously as they once did. Instead, they seek a Bible-believing church that teaches the relevance of the Scriptures in today's world—a church whose teachings are practical and applicable. And in their searching, if they discern that the body of Christ has become caught up in malice, guile, hypocrisy, envies, and evil speaking (see verse 1), they may soon become discouraged. This is the dilemma of the church today. Because of the corporate church's failings, believers are choosing to worship God at home. Corporate fellowship is infested with carnal disease, and consequently is driving away those who seek Christ.

B. Biblical Background

Our Scripture text refers to both a holy priesthood and a royal priesthood in describing the relationship between God and redeemed human beings. The priesthood was a familiar point of reference for the Jew. From the days of Moses, when God appointed the house of Aaron as the priests of the young Hebrew nation, all priests held a position of distinction and respect as representatives of the Most High God.

There is a strong parallel between the old Levite priesthood of the Old Testament and the new priesthood of which Peter spoke in the New Testament. The Old Testament priesthood was led by the high priest. It was a hereditary position held by a man. The high priest was consecrated by God to lead the people of God in sincere worship. The High Priest was distinguished from his fellow priests by the garments he wore and the duties he performed as the spiritual head of God's people, all of which sanctified him to minister in God's name. As long as the priests and the people remained loyal to God and His Law, the priests were highly respected and exercised a healthy influence in the land. Priesthood and holiness were meant to be inseparable. But the sinful nature of the priests allowed corruption to enter the God-ordained office. Eventually they, too, fell into idol worship and departed from worship of the one true and living God.

While the priests of the Old Testament went through a series of rituals to purify themselves, Jesus is our Lamb without blemish. He is distinguished and set apart from all others by His own divine purity and perfection. This office of the High Priest was permanently filled in Jesus Christ, the Son of God, who became a man that He might offer Himself as the final and permanent sacrifice for our sins. Hence, there is no longer a need for us to offer sacrifices to atone for our sins.

II. EXPOSITION AND APPLICATION OF THE SCRIPTURE

A. Stripping Off the Old Nature
(1 Peter 2:1-3)

WHEREFORE LAYING aside all malice, and all guile, and hypocrisies, and envies, and all evil speakings, As newborn babes, desire the sincere milk of the word, that ye may grow thereby: If so be ye have tasted that the Lord is gracious.

Two strong words are used here to emphasize the actions of a true believer. First the believer must "lay aside" or *strip off* some things. And then the believer must "desire" or *crave* the Word of God.

The Greek word for "laying aside" (*apothemenoi*) means "to put off one's clothing." It parallels the ritual cleansing done by the high priest before he put on his "spiritual" garments. The priest would go through a ritual cleansing to remove what defiled his priestly functions.

Peter made it clear that there are some things that defile the believer. Five are mentioned in this passage of Scripture: malice, guile, hypocrisy, envy, and evil speaking. All of these sins prevent us from becoming spiritual partners with our High Priest, Jesus Christ, in the work of building the church community. Believers cannot lead with a strong faith until we first learn to eliminate what defiles our relationship—not only with Christ, but with our brothers and sisters in the household of faith.

The word *malice,* meaning "wickedness," addresses a sin that strikes at the very heart of our vices. We must eradicate all feelings of deep-seated resentment and bitterness toward another.

The word *guile* means "to deceive or mislead." True believers will not set a trap for a fellow Christian, bait him or her with deceiving remarks, or be two-faced in his or her relationships. He will not use flattery, false information, suggestive conversation, enticing words, or outright lies to achieve any goal.

The word *hypocrisy* means "to pretend" or "put on a show." Church is not a stage for performances, and the true believer will never wear a mask to hide his or her real self. We are called to be honest and forthright, open and sincere. Jesus warned that believers must strip off any semblance of hypocrisy (see Matthew 23:14, 33).

The word *envies* in verse 1 means "one who covets what another has." Covetousness is one of the condemned sins in the Ten Commandments. The person who envies another is openly declaring his or her dissatisfaction with God, and his or her resentment toward God for blessing others. Covetousness can ultimately lead to lawlessness, but the greatest damage is done when we allow envy to dictate our relationship with others in the church.

The term *evil speakings* (*katalalias*) means "criticism, backbiting, judging, gossip, and condemnation." Believers are called to build up rather than to tear down. Grumblings in the church serve to divide the worshipers and cause *camps* of discontent.

Believers are called to crave the Word of God in its purest form, devoid of human misinterpretation or convenient exclusion.

B. Building Your Spiritual House
(1 Peter 2:4-8)

To whom coming, as unto a living stone, disallowed indeed of men, but chosen of God, and precious, Ye also, as lively stones, are built up a spiritual house, an holy priesthood, to offer up spiritual sacrifices, acceptable to God by Jesus Christ. Wherefore also it is contained in the scripture, Behold, I lay in Sion a chief corner stone, elect, precious: and he that believeth on him shall not be confounded. Unto you therefore which believe he is precious: but unto them which be disobedient, the stone which the builders disallowed, the same is made the head of the corner, And a stone of stumbling, and a rock of offence, even to them which stumble at the word, being disobedient: whereunto also they were appointed.

Peter painted a marvelous picture of the living church of Jesus Christ. The reference to the living stone refers to Jesus Christ Himself, who is the foundation upon which the church is built. God looks on His church (all believers) as that of a building whose cornerstone is Christ. If a person desires to be part of God's building, he or she must first place his or her life on the foundation stone—Jesus Christ.

In biblical times, buildings were often made of cut, squared stone. By uniting the two intersecting walls, a cornerstone helped to align the whole building and tie it together. In his address before the Jewish Sanhedrin council, the apostle Peter quoted Psalm 118:22 and boldly proclaimed that Jesus Christ of Nazareth, crucified and raised from the dead, was the stone rejected by the builders who had now become the chief cornerstone (see Acts 4:11). This chief cornerstone, Jesus Christ, is the foundation of the church, because "there is none other name under heaven given among men, whereby we must be saved" (Acts 4:12), and in Him "the whole building is joined together and rises to become a holy temple in the Lord" (Ephesians 2:21, NIV). The ones who believe in Jesus Christ as Lord see in Him a solid Rock on which to build their lives.

The living stone is still being rejected today. Human beings still struggle with the requirement of repentance through Jesus Christ as the prerequisite to salvation. The sinner feels that Christ is an "unsuitable stone" for His life's building, and not worth the price. Human beings reject Christ because they prefer to build their own lives according to their own personal desires, rather than to accept the living stone as God's choice for the foundation of their lives. Notice too that the living stone is the preeminent stone—the first stone that was laid. Christ is the captain of salvation, the author of eternal life, the Alpha and Omega (beginning and ending) of all who come after Him (see Revelation 1:8).

C. Declaring Your Loyalty
(1 Peter 2:9-10)

But ye are a chosen generation, a royal priesthood, an holy nation, a peculiar people; that ye should shew forth the praises of him who hath called you out of darkness into his marvellous light: Which in time past were not a people, but are now the people of God: which had not obtained mercy, but now have obtained mercy.

Believers are called to place their complete trust and loyalty in Christ. Our confidence comes from knowing who we are as children of God. We believe in God's Son Jesus Christ as the Messiah, our Lord and Savior. We are set apart as the "chosen generation" of God because we trust Christ as our Redeemer and our Intercessor.

The Greek word for a "chosen generation" (*genos eklekton*) means "chosen or elected race." Peter took the term from the Old Testament where God called Israel by the same name (see Isaiah 43:20-21). The idea of a separate race sounds shocking and divisive to some people. How can God create a new race of people? Yet that is exactly what the Scriptures confirm. This new race comes from all areas of the world, because its prequalification has nothing to do with culture, or language, or ethnicity, or human values. This new race is built solely on the Word of God and God's plan for the salvation of this new race of people. This newly birthed race is identified, not by outward appearance, but by the Spirit of God that dwells in each new member of the race. God is implanting His divine nature within each member of this new race called "Christians." We are completely born-again and renewed to new life in Christ Jesus (see John 3:3-6).

The idea of a daily relationship and constant communication with God is a foreign concept for the unbeliever. God seems untouchable and unreachable. That is because without Christ, a person has no access to God. Men may think they are praying to a God who hears, but unless they believe first on Jesus Christ as Savior and Intercessor, God's hands are tied. God cannot and will not respond to those who reject His Son.

The royal priesthood is made up of *believers* who are given open access to God's presence. We are admonished to live in God's presence continually, to petition Him unendingly, and to obey Him entirely. The use of the word *royal* means that we are priests of the royalty, who belong to the sovereign majesty of the universe, the King of Kings, and we reign with Christ who serves and worships the Father unceasingly. Ours is a cherished open communication in which we walk in the presence of God. Each of us is part of the priesthood that contributes to the development of opportunities and ministries that meet the needs of believers and their families, and reaches out to the unsaved community.

The church—Christ's royal priesthood—must change if we are to continue to lead all people to Christ. With changing demographics, monetary needs, family structures, and other important considerations, the church must be purged and ready to accept the challenge to minister to those within its reach. The mission of each individual church may vary according to the needs of the community, but the message must never vary. We must change, but we must also stay the same. On the surface that may sound ambiguous, but it is not. The church has only one mission, but we have many avenues in which to accomplish it. We must exercise our spiritual gifts, step forward in faith, incorporate newcomers, and move out of our comfort zones. A new identity will have to be forged for this new race of God's people. The key is the recognition of our mission, and our willingness to change our methods to accomplish our goals for Christ. George Barna once said, "The ministry is not called to fit the church's structure; the structure of the church exists to further effective ministry."

III. CONCLUDING REFLECTION

The foundation stones of human beings pass away—they fade with time. But God is eternal, and His living stone will never deteriorate or waste away. Christ, the cornerstone of our salvation, will exist forever.

PRAYER

Father in heaven, thank You for making us Your children. We are a new generation, a royal priesthood, and a peculiar people. Help us to live up to the knowledge of the truth that has been released to us. In Jesus' name we pray. Amen.

WORD POWER

Chosen (Greek: *Ekletos* [ek-lek-tos])— in Greek it is a compound word, meaning it is a combination of a preposition (*ek*) and a noun. The word *ek* means "out." *Eklektos* means "select out," "favorite among others," "a private property belonging to God." When we understand that truly we are a private property of God then nothing should trespass on this property.

HOME DAILY BIBLE READINGS
(November 2-8, 2009)

A Chosen People
MONDAY, November 2: "Chosen Out of All People" (Deuteronomy 10:10-15)
TUESDAY, November 3: "A Happy People" (Psalm 33:4-12)
WEDNESDAY, November 4: "Hope in God and God's Love" (Psalm 33:13-22)
THURSDAY, November 5: "Chosen as God's Witnesses" (Acts 10:34-43)
FRIDAY, November 6: "A People One in Heart and Soul" (Acts 4:31-37)
SATURDAY, November 7: "Free Servants of God" (1 Peter 2:11-17)
SUNDAY, November 8: "God's Own People" (1 Peter 2:1-10)

Christ will lead you into many situations, that will seem impossible, but don't try to avoid them, stay in the middle of them, for there is where you will experience God

LESSON 11   November 15, 2009

A SUFFERING PEOPLE

DEVOTIONAL READING: 1 Corinthians 12:20-26

PRINT PASSAGE: 1 Peter 4:12-19

BACKGROUND SCRIPTURE: 1 Peter 4

KEY VERSE: 1 Peter 4:19

1 Peter 4:12-19—KJV

12 Beloved, think it not strange concerning the fiery trial which is to try you, as though some strange thing happened unto you:

13 But rejoice, inasmuch as ye are partakers of Christ's sufferings; that, when his glory shall be revealed, ye may be glad also with exceeding joy.

14 If ye be reproached for the name of Christ, happy are ye; for the spirit of glory and of God resteth upon you: on their part he is evil spoken of, but on your part he is glorified.

15 But let none of you suffer as a murderer, or as a thief, or as an evildoer, or as a busybody in other men's matters.

16 Yet if any man suffer as a Christian, let him not be ashamed; but let him glorify God on this behalf.

17 For the time is come that judgment must begin at the house of God: and if it first begin at us, what shall the end be of them that obey not the gospel of God?

18 And if the righteous scarcely be saved, where shall the ungodly and the sinner appear?

19 Wherefore let them that suffer according to the will of God commit the keeping of their souls to him in well doing, as unto a faithful Creator.

1 Peter 4:12-19—NRSV

12 Beloved, do not be surprised at the fiery ordeal that is taking place among you to test you, as though something strange were happening to you.

13 But rejoice insofar as you are sharing Christ's sufferings, so that you may also be glad and shout for joy when his glory is revealed.

14 If you are reviled for the name of Christ, you are blessed, because the spirit of glory, which is the Spirit of God, is resting on you.

15 But let none of you suffer as a murderer, a thief, a criminal, or even as a mischief maker.

16 Yet if any of you suffers as a Christian, do not consider it a disgrace, but glorify God because you bear this name.

17 For the time has come for judgment to begin with the household of God; if it begins with us, what will be the end for those who do not obey the gospel of God?

18 And "If it is hard for the righteous to be saved, what will become of the ungodly and the sinners?"

19 Therefore, let those suffering in accordance with God's will entrust themselves to a faithful Creator, while continuing to do good.

BIBLE FACT

SUFFERING: Suffering is one area of human existence that is disliked with a passion. We cannot understand why we suffer since we claim to serve a loving God. However, when we look at the suffering of Jesus in the hands of sinners, our own suffering fades to the background. We cannot understand the total reason for suffering, but we can depend on the mercy of God to weather through the storm of suffering (see 1 Peter 4:19).

UNIFYING LESSON PRINCIPLE

Life tests us in many ways. How are we to respond to the trials and sufferings that come our way? Peter believed that those who suffer as Christians are to rejoice as they follow Christ even as the apostles did when they were arrested for teaching people about Jesus.

TOPICAL OUTLINE OF THE LESSON

I. Introduction
   A. Suffering
   B. Biblical Background

II. Exposition and Application of the Scripture
   A. Suffering that Is Worth Celebrating
      (1 Peter 4:12-14)
   B. The Right Kind of Suffering
      (1 Peter 4:15-16)
   C. Purifying Suffering
      (1 Peter 4:17-18)
   D. Stay Committed to Christ
      (1 Peter 4:19)

III. Concluding Reflection

LESSON OBJECTIVES

Upon completion of this lesson, the students will know that:

1. We should not attribute punishment to sin;
2. Opposition should not deter us from sharing our faith in Christ; and,
3. Suffering should lead to soul searching and a return to the Lord.

POINTS TO BE EMPHASIZED

ADULT/YOUTH
Adult Topic: **Facing Opposition**
Youth Topic: **Feel the Pain!**
Adult/Youth Key Verse: **1 Peter 4:19**
Print Passage: **1 Peter 4:12-19**

—Biblical leaders such as Paul, Peter, Stephen, and others suffered for their faith.
—Believers may suffer because of living in accordance to the will of God.
—It is implied in this text that all people suffer, but Christians can find joy in suffering.
—Peter believed that suffering was of a limited duration compared to the joy of eternity.
—Doing good is the godly positive response to suffering.
—Suffering for godly principles is reason to praise and thank God.
—Peter instructed Christians to avoid a lifestyle that reaps deserved personal suffering.

CHILDREN
Children Topic: **Speak Out!**
Key Verse: **Acts 5:29**
Print Passage: **Acts 5:12-13, 17-21, 26-29, 40;**
1 Peter 4:16

—Peter and John were arrested for acting on their faith.
—Peter and John refused to keep quiet about Jesus, even when beaten.
—The Holy Spirit did many "signs and wonders" through the apostles.
—In 1 Peter, believers are encouraged to rejoice when they suffer on behalf of Christ.

I. INTRODUCTION

A. Suffering

The church is guilty of distorting the Gospel of Jesus Christ on the subject of suffering. Christian leaders around the world preach deliverance from suffering as a "gift" to those who repent and live right. While it is true that much pain in the lives of human beings comes from the sin of disobedience to God's will (alcoholism, drug addiction, sexually transmitted diseases, murder, theft, etc.)—and our lives are greatly improved through the application of repentance and obedience—the tough pill for most Christians to swallow is the idea that suffering continues as consequence even after deliverance from sin.

Many familiar hymns are sung in the reflection of the paradox between salvation and suffering. One such hymn is a confession that as Christians, "We wonder why others prosper, living so wicked year after year" ("Farther Along," W. B. Stevens). The idea that salvation solves all problems is a falsehood. The correct biblical interpretation is the idea that salvation makes us partners with God in our tribulation, and therefore we are able to endure. Spoken of in 2 Corinthians 1:4 is our God "who comforts us in all our tribulation, that we may be able to comfort those who are in any trouble, with the comfort with which we ourselves are comforted by God" (NKJV). There is a difference between feeling comfortable and being comforted. The Bible clearly does not promise escape from storms, but rather "shelter in the time of storm." Never have we been promised in the Word that suffering would be eradicated for the believer, but we were promised that we would have a Comforter (the Holy Spirit) who soothes us in the midst of our trials. The Comforter soothes us in various ways—through Scripture, hymns, and the testimonies of other believers who have weathered similar storms. Through the Holy Spirit, God provides the believer with permanent consolation even in the midst of excruciating pain. A mother can find peace while dealing with a wayward child; a husband can find peace after the death of his wife; a wife can find peace even if her husband divorces her; a cancer patient can find peace in the midst of terminal illness; a businessman can experience peace, even in the midst of bankruptcy. All this is possible by the power of the Holy Spirit.

Peace is never the absence of pain, but rather the ability to endure it by God's grace. This peace is often difficult to explain to someone who has never experienced it. But for the believer who has learned to hold to God's unchanging hand, the deeper the sorrow, the more potent and powerful is God's peace. Our physical and mental well-being may remain challenged by our circumstances, but our souls are delivered to a place of respite and reprieve. There is a place where the sorrowing heart and the peaceful soul can reside together, and it is found in the bosom of Jesus Christ.

wear this world as a loose garment, knowing that at any day, the end will be staring us in the face

B. Biblical Background

Suffering has been part of human experience since the fall of Adam in the Garden of Eden (see Genesis 3). One third of the book of Psalms is laments or expressions of grief and includes graphic descriptions of suffering. Psalm 22, a cry for deliverance made by David, is a revelation of the presence of God's power in the midst of trials. Verse 1 is a seeming declaration of abandonment. Yet, it is revealed in verses 4 and 5 that David's soul had already found comfort in the testimonial faith of his forefathers who "trusted in thee and were not confounded."

We know that all suffering is not the result of disobedience, because it is recorded in Hebrews 5:8 that Jesus learned obedience by the things He suffered. It is stated in Hebrews 2:10 that Jesus was perfected through suffering. Of one thing we can be certain—suffering has the potential to demonstrate God's power. Second Corinthians 12:9 reads, "My grace is sufficient for thee: for my strength is made perfect in weakness."

Suffering helps the believer to identify with Christ. This is how we, as believers, share in the suffering of Christ and become one with Him. We become bonded together through the experience of suffering. Christ is our greatest example of a suffering servant, who endured suffering for the sake of others and proclaimed that suffering was His mission (see Matthew 17:12; Luke 24:46). Isaiah portrayed Christ as a sin bearer in Isaiah 53:5 when he wrote, "With his stripes we are healed." As His followers, Christ challenges us to suffer for others. We suffer for Christ when we forgive our enemies and refuse to retaliate against them. We suffer for Christ when we sacrifice more than the tithe to further the spread of the Gospel. We suffer for Christ when we commit our time and talents to mission work, here and abroad.

The disciples suffered persecution and torture for the sake of Christ. Though there is no definitive proof of the fates of eleven of Christ's disciples (Judas's death was self-inflicted), tradition has it that many of them met with violent death. Andrew was believed to be crucified in a spread-eagle fashion; Peter was believed to have been crucified upside-down at his own request; James is believed to have died at the hand of the sword (see Acts 12:2).

II. EXPOSITION AND APPLICATION OF THE SCRIPTURE

A. Suffering that Is Worth Celebrating (1 Peter 4:12-14)

Beloved, think it not strange concerning the fiery trial which is to try you, as though some strange thing happened unto you: But rejoice, inasmuch as ye are partakers of Christ's sufferings; that, when his glory shall be revealed, ye may be glad also with exceeding joy. If ye be reproached for the name of Christ, happy are ye; for the spirit of glory and of God resteth upon you: on their part he is evil spoken of, but on your part he is glorified.

Peter was addressing the pressing question of the early church that Christian men and women today still ponder: "Why do Christians suffer?" Referred to as "fiery trials" in the text, Peter first corrected the erroneous belief that all suffering was the result of unforgiveness. As believers, we are sometimes surprised by the level of suffering we endure in the course of our lifetime on earth. Many wonder why God allows persecution and suffering at all. But as genuine believers, we must understand that we are forced to live in a corrupt world that does not understand the concept of righteousness and living holy. As a result, we must come to expect animosity, resentment, and even hatred toward those who profess Christ as Lord.

Some Christians can deal with persecution, but they question why believers must suffer the same illnesses and tragedies that befall the unbeliever. Again, we must realize that we live in a corrupt and vile world full of sickness and disease—and while the "effectual fervent prayer of a righteous man availeth much" (James 5:16), our souls are housed in a transitory shell that was never intended as our permanent dwelling place.

When we suffer, we are sharing in Christ's suffering. Jesus was rejected by men because He lived and proclaimed the righteousness and salvation of God. When we suffer for following Christ, we are suffering for the very same reason. We are denying self and taking up the cross of Christ. Sacrificial suffering is cause for celebration. We "count it all joy" when the world attacks us for our faithfulness to Christ. Jesus Himself said, "Blessed are ye, when men shall revile you, and persecute you, and shall say all manner of evil against you falsely, for my sake. Rejoice, and be exceeding glad: for great is your reward in heaven: for so persecuted they the prophets which were before you" (Matthew 5:11-12). Our persecution is a blessing because it affirms our faith in Christ, and His presence within our hearts.

B. The Right Kind of Suffering
(1 Peter 4:15-16)

But let none of you suffer as a murderer, or as a thief, or as an evildoer, or as a busybody in other men's matters. Yet if any man suffer as a Christian, let him not be ashamed; but let him glorify God on this behalf.

Peter reminded us that we can bring persecution and shame upon ourselves if we defiantly break the laws of our society. Disobedience to local, state, and federal rules and regulations is not what the Bible means by suffering. This type of suffering is not of God. A good example is the illegal bombings of abortion clinics. While the laws permitting abortion run counter to our belief in the sanctity of life, the believers must not break the law and endanger others to prove their protest of this type of murder. Objections to man-made laws must be voiced by peaceful protest.

If we live right, as obedient members of society, and according to God's Law, we will have no need of shame when others deride us for our lifestyle. Believers should never be ashamed of their Christian faith. The believer honors the name of Jesus Christ by glorifying God and standing up for Him in all situations. Paul said in Romans 1:16, "For I am not ashamed of the gospel of Christ: for it is the power of God unto salvation to every one that believeth."

C. Purifying Suffering
(1 Peter 4:17-18)

For the time is come that judgment must begin at the house of God: and if it first begin at us, what shall the end be of them that obey not the gospel of God? And if the righteous scarcely be saved, where shall the ungodly and the sinner appear?

These two verses refer not to final judgment but to God's refining discipline (see Hebrews 12:7-8). The sovereign God, in His own way, allows believers to sin and then experience the consequences. It is difficult for Christians to grasp the idea that suffering purifies the soul. Consider that when a believer's life is going well for him or her, he or she tends to feel more secure, and consequently partakes of the world more and more. When this happens, the believer focuses less and less on God. An easy life can weaken a believer's prayer life, church attendance, and commitment for service to God, and can also create an air of complacency and self-satisfaction in the believer. But when trouble comes our way, it awakens in us the need to stay connected to God. God can use persecution to draw us closer to Him and revive us or stir us up.

There are several reasons why God allows suffering: (1) it shows our potential for sinning; (2) it serves as an encouragement to turn from sin; (3) it helps us become fighters against the enemy of our souls (Satan); (4) it helps us stay focused and faithful to the end; and (5) it helps us encourage others who are suffering.

During Old Testament times, *purification* was "the act of making oneself clean and pure before God." The Mosaic Law provided instructions for both physical and spiritual cleansing. These laws and regulations were much more than sanitary instructions, because they included religious and spiritual cleansing as well. By the time Jesus began His earthly ministry, so much had been added to the purification laws that they became a burden for the people to obey them. Jesus denounced the purification rituals and taught that defilement and uncleanness came from within. In other words, defilement came from the inner motives of the mind and the heart (see Mark 7:14-23). Jesus taught that genuine purification is possible only by following Him and giving heed to His message of love and redemption (see John 15:3). If this is the process of purification in the new dispensation, then God can and will use any means necessary, including suffering, to "purify" the soul of a believer and restore his or her right relationship with God.

D. Stay Committed to Christ (1 Peter 4:19)

Wherefore let them that suffer according to the will of God commit the keeping of their souls to him in well doing, as unto a faithful Creator.

If a believer's suffering is in the will of God, then the believer ought to trust God for his or her ultimate care. We know that through suffering, God is either glorifying the name of Jesus Christ or purifying the life of the believer—in order that the believer would remain "stedfast, unmoveable, always abounding in the work of the Lord" (1 Corinthians 15:58).

Notice that it is the believer who must *commit* his or her soul to God's keeping. The word *commit* (*paratithesthosan*) means "to deposit or entrust into the hands of," as an investor does with a banker. We must learn to deposit our whole being into God's hands, knowing that He will not fail us—that He will deliver us through our storms, whether the end results in recovery this side of heaven, or victory in glory. It is imperative that the believer staunchly believe that no matter how bleak the circumstances, in the end God will have the victory in the life of every Christian.

God's plan for His saints will never be defeated. When we commit our souls to Him, we take a giant leap of faith and learn to place all of our trust where it belongs—with our Creator. The Bible is replete with examples of saints who learned to trust God completely. The apostle Paul took such a leap of faith in spite of his infirmity. David took such a leap of faith in spite of his depression and persecution. The three Hebrew boys took such a leap of faith in spite of the king's threat to throw them into the fiery furnace. These are just a few examples that should strengthen our resolve to lean on God's everlasting arms.

III. CONCLUDING REFLECTION

In 1874, a passenger steamship was on its way to Europe. There was a family from Chicago on board—Mrs. H. G. Spafford and her four young daughters. The father, a Chicago lawyer, was too busy to go with them but intended to come later, on another ship. In the middle of the Atlantic Ocean, the steamship collided with another vessel, and nearly every passenger was lost at sea, including Mrs. Spafford's four girls. The mother was rescued, and when she got to England she cabled her husband of the tragic loss. Her message read, "Saved alone." Mr. Spafford left immediately for England to retrieve his sorrowing wife. On the way across the Atlantic Ocean, at about the point at which his daughters were lost at sea, he penned these words in their memory: "When peace like a river, attendeth my way, When sorrows like sea billows roll, Whatever my lot, Thou has taught me to say; 'It is well, it is well with my soul" (Hymn: "It is Well with My Soul," by H. G. Spafford, *Gospel Pearls*, #26).

As Christians, we must strengthen our resolve to "endure hardness, as a good soldier of Jesus Christ" (2 Timothy 2:3). Our promised reward comes, not in this life, but in the life hereafter.

PRAYER

Father in heaven, we are grateful to You for helping us in ways we do not understand. It is hard for us to understand why You allow us to suffer. Father, help us to stay close and commit our souls to You. In Jesus' name we pray. Amen.

WORD POWER

Commit (Greek: *paratithemi* [pa-ra-ti-the-mi])—it is a compound word, meaning it has a preposition: *para* ("alongside"); *tithemi* ("I put"). It is an old accounting word. It is used for a depositor who takes money or gold to the bank. He or she commits his or her treasure to the banker. Jesus used this word when He was on the cross—where He committed His soul to God (see Luke 23:46). Have you committed your soul to God?

HOME DAILY BIBLE READINGS
(November 9-15, 2009)

A Suffering People

MONDAY, November 9: "Suffering Together" (1 Corinthians 12:20-26)

TUESDAY, November 10: "Choosing to Share in Suffering" (Hebrews 11:23-28)

WEDNESDAY, November 11: "Strengthened in Distress" (Philippians 4:10-14)

THURSDAY, November 12: "Faithfully Obeying God" (Acts 5:27-32)

FRIDAY, November 13: "Living by the Will of God" (1 Peter 4:1-6)

SATURDAY, November 14: "Glorifying God in All Things" (1 Peter 4:7-11)

SUNDAY, November 15: "Sharing Christ's Sufferings" (1 Peter 4:12-19)

LESSON 12   November 22, 2009

A FAITHFUL PEOPLE

DEVOTIONAL READING: **Luke 19:12-26**
PRINT PASSAGE: **2 Peter 1:3-15**

BACKGROUND SCRIPTURE: **2 Peter 1:3-15**
KEY VERSE: **2 Peter 1:3**

2 Peter 1:3-15—KJV

3 According as his divine power hath given unto us all things that pertain unto life and godliness, through the knowledge of him that hath called us to glory and virtue:

4 Whereby are given unto us exceeding great and precious promises: that by these ye might be partakers of the divine nature, having escaped the corruption that is in the world through lust.

5 And beside this, giving all diligence, add to your faith virtue; and to virtue knowledge;

6 And to knowledge temperance; and to temperance patience; and to patience godliness;

7 And to godliness brotherly kindness; and to brotherly kindness charity.

8 For if these things be in you, and abound, they make you that ye shall neither be barren nor unfruitful in the knowledge of our Lord Jesus Christ.

9 But he that lacketh these things is blind, and cannot see afar off, and hath forgotten that he was purged from his old sins.

10 Wherefore the rather, brethren, give diligence to make your calling and election sure: for if ye do these things, ye shall never fall:

11 For so an entrance shall be ministered unto you abundantly into the everlasting kingdom of our Lord and Saviour Jesus Christ.

12 Wherefore I will not be negligent to put you always in remembrance of these things, though ye know them, and be established in the present truth.

13 Yea, I think it meet, as long as I am in this tabernacle, to stir you up by putting you in remembrance;

14 Knowing that shortly I must put off this my tabernacle, even as our Lord Jesus Christ hath shewed me.

2 Peter 1:3-15—NRSV

3 His divine power has given us everything needed for life and godliness, through the knowledge of him who called us by his own glory and goodness.

4 Thus he has given us, through these things, his precious and very great promises, so that through them you may escape from the corruption that is in the world because of lust, and may become participants of the divine nature.

5 For this very reason, you must make every effort to support your faith with goodness, and goodness with knowledge,

6 and knowledge with self-control, and self-control with endurance, and endurance with godliness,

7 and godliness with mutual affection, and mutual affection with love.

8 For if these things are yours and are increasing among you, they keep you from being ineffective and unfruitful in the knowledge of our Lord Jesus Christ.

9 For anyone who lacks these things is nearsighted and blind, and is forgetful of the cleansing of past sins.

10 Therefore, brothers and sisters, be all the more eager to confirm your call and election, for if you do this, you will never stumble.

11 For in this way, entry into the eternal kingdom of our Lord and Savior Jesus Christ will be richly provided for you.

12 Therefore I intend to keep on reminding you of these things, though you know them already and are established in the truth that has come to you.

13 I think it right, as long as I am in this body, to refresh your memory,

14 since I know that my death will come soon, as indeed our Lord Jesus Christ has made clear to me.

UNIFYING LESSON PRINCIPLE

We all have faith in something or someone, but we often find it hard to develop this faith. How can we support and strengthen a growing and effective faith? From Peter's second letter we learn that goodness, knowledge, self-control, endurance, godliness, mutual affection, and love all undergird a growing faith. In the book of Acts, we see the example of Philip, a faithful follower who led others to Jesus.

15 Moreover I will endeavour that ye may be able after my decease to have these things always in remembrance.

15 And I will make every effort so that after my departure you may be able at any time to recall these things.

TOPICAL OUTLINE OF THE LESSON

I. Introduction
  A. Our Imperfections
  B. Biblical Background

II. Exposition and Application of the Scripture
  A. Divine Power Bestows Divine Nature (2 Peter 1:3-4)
  B. Moral Excellences Worth Adding (2 Peter 1:5-11)
  C. The Importance of These Moral Excellences (2 Peter 1:12-15)

III. Concluding Reflection

LESSON OBJECTIVES

Upon completion of this lesson, the students will know that:

1. It is required for believers in Christ to demonstrate their faith in public;
2. We must resist the evil one (Satan) at all costs; and,
3. Christianity is a way of life and not a religion.

POINTS TO BE EMPHASIZED

ADULT/YOUTH

Adult Topic: Pursuing Virtue
Youth Topic: Got What It Takes?
Adult Key Verse: 2 Peter 1:3
Youth Key Verse: 2 Peter 1:8
Print Passage: 2 Peter 1:3-15

—Believers are "participants of the divine nature" (verse 4). Created in the image of God, they seek to reflect the godly perspective in all they do.
—That God takes the initiative in granting and supplying the people's needs is a common theme in the biblical story.
—Peter said that God, with the same powers used to create the world, has given Christians all the resources necessary for them to live a godly life.
—The goal of the Christian life is to escape the corruption that is in the world of lust and participate in God's holy nature.
—Faith, as dependence on God for spiritual regeneration, is the very root and basis of the Christian life.
—To develop these virtues keeps Christians from ineffective and unfruitful lives.
—Developing these virtues confirms to Christians that God has chosen them as God's obedient and holy people.

CHILDREN

Children Topic: Following Directions
Key Verses: Acts 8:26, 27
Print Passage: Acts 8:26-32; 2 Peter 1:3

—At the direction of God, Philip went out on a mission.

—When Philip met an Ethiopian reading the book of Isaiah, he asked if the man understood the words he was reading.

—The Ethiopian invited Philip to explain Isaiah's message.

—In 2 Peter, believers are reminded that God has provided everything essential for life.

—God intervened so the Ethiopian eunuch would encounter Philip.

I. INTRODUCTION

A. Our Imperfections

It is common today to excuse people for their faults. The familiar attitude most people take is that "nobody is perfect." What else can people be expected to be but human, weak, and fallible? The attitude is that when we stand before God, we may not be perfect, but we are good enough. There seems to be a moral and ethical lethargy that permeates our society. The pursuit of virtue has been blinded by sin, and we are in need of a "perception checkup." It is not that people are thoroughly evil, or that they never do any moral good. Humankind is capable of impressive acts of kindness, courage, and justice. But in the light of God's morally perfect will, our moments of moral lucidness are fleeting at best. The only true and constant standards are those that are ultimately determined by God Himself. Like a carpenter using a plumb line, only God can evaluate the whole earth and perfectly measure the integrity of His creation. When we juxtapose our morality on God's, our imperfections become glaringly obvious. We quickly see that our goodness and kindness are exceptions rather than the rule.

B. Biblical Background

While 1 Peter deals with problems from the outside, 2 Peter deals with problems from within. Peter wrote to warn believers about the false teachers who were peddling damaging doctrine among the body of Christ. He began his narrative by urging them to keep a close watch on their own personal lives.

The Christian life demands diligence from the believer in the pursuit of moral excellence, knowledge, self-control, perseverance, godliness, brotherly kindness, and a selfless love for all. By contrast, false teachers train their followers in arrogance, greed, and covetousness. These false teachers scoff at the thought of a future judgment and live their lives as though the present is the only pattern they need to follow.

Peter reminded believers that although God may be longsuffering in sending His final judgment, His judgment will ultimately come. Believers should live godly, blameless, and steadfast lives, awaiting the sure coming of our Lord.

II. EXPOSITION AND APPLICATION OF THE SCRIPTURE

A. Divine Power Bestows Divine Nature
(2 Peter 1:3-4)

According as his divine power hath given unto us all things that pertain unto life and godliness, through the knowledge of him that hath called us to glory and virtue: Whereby are given unto us exceeding great and precious promises: that by these ye might be partakers of the divine nature, having escaped the corruption that is in the world through lust.

Peter explained that divine power can only emanate from divine nature. To understand the essence of our power as believers, we must first fully comprehend the divine nature of Christ. Our understanding is accomplished by metaphorically "climbing" a ladder of truths till we reach the top. Once we accept each truth about Christ, we are ready to receive His divine power.

The first truth is that Christ is the Son of God. It is declared in Matthew 1:23 that Christ is "God with us." And as the Son of God, Jesus existed before His incarnation (see John 8:58). Peter revealed Jesus' divine birthright when he proclaimed in Matthew 16:16 that "Thou art the Christ, the Son of the living God." John declared in 3:16 that Jesus was the only begotten Son of God.

Second, as the Son of God, Jesus has certain powers that are unique to Him alone. Christ has the power to forgive sins (see John 3:35; 5:22), the power to baptize believers in the Holy Spirit (see Mark 1:8; John 20:22), and the power to mediate between the Father and our estranged sinful world (see 1 Timothy 2:8) and reconcile humanity back to God.

Third, as believers we must worship Him (see Philippians 2:10-11); we cannot keep the first commandment of God without worshiping Christ (see Exodus 20:3-6).

Fourth, believers must accept that Jesus Christ rules over them in all things (see Colossians 1:15-17), and must be obeyed in all things (see Philippians 2:10).

Once the believer understands and accepts the divine nature of Christ and repents, he or she opens the door to forgiveness and the ability to receive Christ's divine power through the Holy Spirit. By the divine power of Christ, we are able to sustain a repentant spirit that moves us daily toward a closer relationship with the Father. This lifetime process of purging and cleansing is the "maintenance agreement" we sign at conversion.

However, consider what kinds of acts we have engaged in: the lies we have told, the ways we have cheated, abuse to our families, manipulating situations to our advantage, selfish acts, wasteful spending on trivial luxuries, ignoring the poor, damaging our environment, power plays, arrogance, and lack of faith. The question is this: When the smoke clears, how much of your life as a believer will be left? Will your life's story be a pile of burned rubble, or will your life be a story of God's divine nature exercised through you?

B. Moral Excellences Worth Adding
(2 Peter 1:5-11)

And beside this, giving all diligence, add to your faith virtue; and to virtue knowledge; And to knowledge temperance; and to temperance patience; and to patience godliness; And to godliness brotherly kindness; and to brotherly kindness charity. For if these things be in you, and abound, they make you that ye shall neither be barren nor unfruitful in the knowledge of our Lord Jesus Christ. But he that lacketh these things is blind, and cannot see afar off, and hath forgotten that he was purged from his old sins. Wherefore the rather, brethren,

give diligence to make your calling and election sure: for if ye do these things, ye shall never fall: For so an entrance shall be ministered unto you abundantly into the everlasting kingdom of our Lord and Saviour Jesus Christ.

Our part in salvation involves *seven things*. The *things* of the believer's life are of critical importance and are to be added to our salvation. The Greek word for *add* (*epichoregesate*) means "in addition to." Peter was saying that salvation is not the end of our spiritual growth; it is the beginning. Notice too that we are to add these moral excellences "with all diligence."

The first to be added are *virtue* and *good character*. We are called to abound in virtue (see 1 Thessalonians 4:1-7) as a more excellent way (see 1 Corinthians 12:31).

The second to be added is *knowledge*, or practical intelligence and insight. Our faith's power is limited if we do not seek to add to our faith the knowledge necessary to execute our responsibilities as believers in Jesus Christ. Faith without knowledge will lead to little "works," and we know that faith without works is dead (see James 2:18, 26).

Third, the believers must add *temperance* to their Christian repertoire of morality. *Temperance* is "the control of one's body and the lusts of the flesh." God requires believers to have self-control over their appetites and passions. Temperance grooms believers to restrain themselves, especially against sexual urges (see 1 Corinthians 7:9), but also against any other temptations the believers have to face (see 1 Corinthians 9:25).

Fourth, we are to add *patience*, or endurance and constancy. Without patience, the more our faith is challenged, the weaker we become. This could explain why there seems to be a revolving door in most sanctuaries; believers come confessing their faith, but with little patience to endure the trials that ensue, they soon exit in search of some other means of deliverance.

The fifth requirement of a seasoned believer is *godliness*, which means "living like Christ and being a godly person." Sixth on the list of necessary *things* is *brotherly kindness*. We are called to have a "Philadelphian" relationship with all believers—to cherish the common bond that we have in Jesus Christ. This is a deep affection that nourishes and nurtures one another for the sake of building up the body of Christ.

The seventh and final thing we must acquire in our walk with Christ is this thing called *charity*, or love. Peter called us to have the Spirit of God dwelling in us, to the extent that we are able to respond to everyone with the same love the Father has for us.

We are not capable of assessing our own needs without the help of God. By God's indwelling of the Holy Spirit, we are able to see beyond our human limitations, to the glory that God wants us to experience. Peter explained that we are barren and unfruitful in life, blind to God's purpose. And again, he challenged believers to be *diligent* in their quest to solidify salvation.

We do not know how to keep from failing in life, unless we become one with Christ. We do not know how to guarantee ourselves access to eternal life. But all of our spiritual needs are met in Christ Jesus, if we add *these things* to our lives in abundance. The word *abound* means "to increase to overflow." Peter said that if we abound in these things that represent the morality and character of God, God will pour out His power upon us. The believer must never be satisfied with life as it is. Our spiritual quest should never become stagnant, nor should we just be satisfied with knowing Jesus. If the Spirit of Christ is truly in us, then it will constrain us from evil and propel us toward perfection.

C. The Importance of These Moral Excellences (2 Peter 1:12-15)

Wherefore I will not be negligent to put you always in remembrance of these things, though ye know them, and be established in the present truth. Yea, I think it meet, as long as I am in this tabernacle, to stir you up by putting you in remembrance; Knowing that shortly I must put off this my tabernacle, even as our Lord Jesus Christ hath shewed me. Moreover I will endeavour that ye may be able after my decease to have these things always in remembrance.

Great coaches often review the rudiments of the sport with their teams in order for the team to win. Peter was doing the same thing for us here as followers of Christ. When questioned, most believers will tell you that living a Christlike life is of the utmost importance to them, but their actions often tell a different story. They wear one suit of external clothing in the presence of other Christians, but change their garments as soon as they are out of earshot and eyeshot. To be fair, we all fall prey to the carnal flesh. But the true believer who presses daily to put on the garment of salvation and add to it the virtues of a Christlike life will experience less and less incidences of sin.

We are on a journey, striving daily to move our faith one notch higher and a little closer to heaven. It takes constant work to achieve the goal. This reveals how important it is to work at our faith. Peter committed to preaching and teaching about spiritual growth after salvation, so that all believers would be reminded to work on their "spiritual building." Notice that Peter's commitment was so steadfast and sure that he declared a lifelong pledge to the task. He would not be deterred!

Peter referred to the body of the believer as a tabernacle. In the Old Testament, the *tabernacle* was a portable holy place of worship, and God's residence among the Israelites in the wilderness. God instructed Moses with specifics on how the temporary wilderness tabernacle would be erected, the details of which are recorded in the book of Exodus. The care of the tabernacle was equally detailed, with various families of the tribe of Levi commissioned for different tasks. Levitical families were commissioned to care for the boards, the pillars, the pins, and even the cords of the draperies. God left no detail of the tabernacle unaddressed. The tabernacle was to be kept in perfect condition.

Our tabernacles, or our bodies, are to be kept in the same impeccable condition. We have Jesus Christ as the example of just how perfect those tabernacles are to be kept. Jesus Christ was the first tabernacle to take on human form. The Bible declares that "the Word (Jesus) was made flesh, and dwelt among us" (John 1:14). The Greek word for "dwelt" is *tabernacled*. In our text, Paul referred to the believer's body as the tabernacle of God. Second Corinthians 5:1 reads, "For we know that if our earthly house of this tabernacle were dissolved, we have a building of God, an house not made with hands, eternal in the heavens." The clear inference is that our bodies are God's temporary tabernacles on earth in this new dispensation, and Peter was calling all believers to be as diligent in the care of their tabernacles as the Levites were of the temporary tabernacle in the wilderness.

III. CONCLUDING REFLECTION

The good news is that God has reached out to us despite our imperfect ways. God's attitude is not one of rejection, but one of love. He does not say, "They're not good enough for Me." Instead, He demonstrates His grace and compassion by saying, "I will make them into good people—people as good as I AM—and I will do it by means of My Son, Jesus Christ."

We are called to a great work of sharing Christ with the world. And if we are to represent Christ effectively, we must live by the high standards of a Christlike servant of the Most High God. Our diligence in adding *these moral excellences* will hasten the day when we can truly say, "I can do all things through Christ which strengtheneth me" (Philippians 4:13).

PRAYER

Our Father in heaven, thank You for saving us from our wicked ways and giving us eternal life. Help us to understand our mission in the world. Let our lives speak to our confessions. As people watch us, let them see that we are Your representatives. In Jesus' name we pray. Amen.

WORD POWER

Hath Given (Greek: *dedoreomai* [de-do-reo-mai])—the grammatical analysis reveals that the Gift (Jesus) was given and there was no human effort applied. It was a gift bestowed freely or gratuitously, or a gift granted without a pre-existing condition. Peter helped us again to understand that the love of God is beyond human comprehension.

HOME DAILY BIBLE READINGS
(November 16-22, 2009)

A Faithful People

MONDAY, November 16: "Trustworthiness" (Luke 19:12-26)

TUESDAY, November 17: "Integrity" (Psalm 101:1-4)

WEDNESDAY, November 18: "Truthfulness" (Proverbs 14:2-5)

THURSDAY, November 19: "Courage" (Daniel 6:6-10)

FRIDAY, November 20: "Readiness" (Matthew 24:42-47)

SATURDAY, November 21: "Willingness" (Acts 8:26-40)

SUNDAY, November 22: "Godliness" (2 Peter 1:3-15)

LESSON 13 — November 29, 2009

A HOPEFUL PEOPLE

DEVOTIONAL READING: **Psalm 42**
PRINT PASSAGE: **2 Peter 3:1-13**

BACKGROUND SCRIPTURE: **2 Peter 3**
KEY VERSE: **2 Peter 3:9**

2 Peter 3:1-13—KJV

THIS SECOND epistle, beloved, I now write unto you; in both which I stir up your pure minds by way of remembrance:

2 That ye may be mindful of the words which were spoken before by the holy prophets, and of the commandment of us the apostles of the Lord and Saviour:

3 Knowing this first, that there shall come in the last days scoffers, walking after their own lusts,

4 And saying, Where is the promise of his coming? for since the fathers fell asleep, all things continue as they were from the beginning of the creation.

5 For this they willingly are ignorant of, that by the word of God the heavens were of old, and the earth standing out of the water and in the water:

6 Whereby the world that then was, being overflowed with water, perished:

7 But the heavens and the earth, which are now, by the same word are kept in store, reserved unto fire against the day of judgment and perdition of ungodly men.

8 But, beloved, be not ignorant of this one thing, that one day is with the Lord as a thousand years, and a thousand years as one day.

9 The Lord is not slack concerning his promise, as some men count slackness; but is longsuffering to us-ward, not willing that any should perish, but that all should come to repentance.

10 But the day of the Lord will come as a thief in the night; in the which the heavens shall pass away with a great noise, and the elements shall melt with fervent heat, the earth also and the works that are therein shall be burned up.

11 Seeing then that all these things shall be dissolved, what manner of persons ought ye to be in all holy conversation and godliness,

2 Peter 3:1-13—NRSV

THIS IS now, beloved, the second letter I am writing to you; in them I am trying to arouse your sincere intention by reminding you

2 that you should remember the words spoken in the past by the holy prophets, and the commandment of the Lord and Savior spoken through your apostles.

3 First of all you must understand this, that in the last days scoffers will come, scoffing and indulging their own lusts

4 and saying, "Where is the promise of his coming? For ever since our ancestors died, all things continue as they were from the beginning of creation!"

5 They deliberately ignore this fact, that by the word of God heavens existed long ago and an earth was formed out of water and by means of water,

6 through which the world of that time was deluged with water and perished.

7 But by the same word the present heavens and earth have been reserved for fire, being kept until the day of judgment and destruction of the godless.

8 But do not ignore this one fact, beloved, that with the Lord one day is like a thousand years, and a thousand years are like one day.

9 The Lord is not slow about his promise, as some think of slowness, but is patient with you, not wanting any to perish, but all to come to repentance.

10 But the day of the Lord will come like a thief, and then the heavens will pass away with a loud noise, and the elements will be dissolved with fire, and the earth and everything that is done on it will be disclosed.

11 Since all these things are to be dissolved in this

UNIFYING LESSON PRINCIPLE

Even in the toughest situations, an encouraging word from a friend can make all the difference in how we respond to challenges that confront us. How, then, can we encourage others to keep persevering when barriers seem insurmountable? Peter taught people to live as they awaited Christ's return, and Paul and Barnabas taught people to hold fast to their faith.

12 Looking for and hasting unto the coming of the day of God, wherein the heavens being on fire shall be dissolved, and the elements shall melt with fervent heat?

13 Nevertheless we, according to his promise, look for new heavens and a new earth, wherein dwelleth righteousness.

way, what sort of persons ought you to be in leading lives of holiness and godliness,

12 waiting for and hastening the coming of the day of God, because of which the heavens will be set ablaze and dissolved, and the elements will melt with fire?

13 But, in accordance with his promise, we wait for new heavens and a new earth, where righteousness is at home.

TOPICAL OUTLINE OF THE LESSON

I. Introduction
A. Jesus Will Return
B. Biblical Background

II. Exposition and Application of the Scripture
A. Dealing with Scoffers (2 Peter 3:1-7)
B. Reaffirmation of Christ's Return (2 Peter 3:8-10)
C. The Readiness of Those Who Await Christ (2 Peter 3:11-13)

III. Concluding Reflection

LESSON OBJECTIVES

Upon completion of this lesson, the students will know that:

1. The return of Christ is guaranteed and it can occur at any time;
2. Christ's return should spur us on to witnessing with zeal; and,
3. Scoffers will continue to be on the rise.

POINTS TO BE EMPHASIZED
ADULT/YOUTH

Adult Topic: The Best Is Yet to Come

Youth Topic: Got Hope?

Adult Key Verse: 2 Peter 3:9

Youth Key Verse: 2 Peter 3:13

Print Passage: 2 Peter 3:1-13

—The Old and New Testaments have a consistent message of God's reign.

—Brief descriptions of the last days and the end of times tell us *that* Christ will come again but do not give us a precise description of *when* and *how* Christ will come.

—The element of surprise continues to be associated with the day of the Lord.

—God's desire is that *all* will come to receive the mercy and redemption before the Day of Judgment arrives.

—Peter was writing to encourage persecuted Christians to help them endure criticisms of their faith.

—People should not doubt God's works just because their schedules do not match God's schedule.

—What may appear as God's slowness to bring culmination is really God's patient and loving desire for all to be saved.

—People cannot predict when God will end the world because the end will come unexpectedly.

—Since the end of the world is coming, bringing all humans into account with God, Christians are to be diligent to live holy and godly lives.

CHILDREN
Children Topic: Encouraging Others
Key Verse: Acts 14:22
Print Passage: Acts 14:21-28; 2 Peter 3:18
—On a joint missionary journey from Antioch, Paul and Barnabas visited several cities in Asia Minor.

—Although rejected by many people, the missionaries did not lose courage.
—Paul and Barnabas were frequently persecuted, as were those who accepted the Gospel.
—When Paul and Barnabas returned to the cities visited earlier, they encouraged the young churches.
—Going back to Antioch, the apostles reported the positive results of their efforts among Gentiles.
—In 2 Peter, believers are encouraged to be faithful and grow in Christ.

I. INTRODUCTION

A. Jesus Will Return

Just a short time after Christ's miraculous resurrection, the disciples and their followers found themselves anxiously awaiting Christ's return. Their hearts were heavy; they were both bewildered and confused. Their thoughts must have raced back to the teachings of Jesus in an attempt to find some sense of hope in the midst of a seemingly hopeless situation. Upon reflection, all of them undoubtedly assumed that Christ's promise of His return would be fulfilled in their lifetimes. The New Testament Christians who followed them were filled with the same anticipation and expectancy of Jesus' return.

In 2 Peter 3, Peter refuted the mockers' denial of Christ's return (verses 1-7), presented the correct view concerning Christ's return (verses 8-13), and concluded with timely exhortations to his readers in view of the dark and dangerous days facing them (verses 14-18). Peter underscored how important it is for Christians to stay focused on the promise of Christ's return. A close connection with the body of Christ is the best way to prevent becoming detached or desensitized to God's promises that are yet to be fulfilled.

B. Biblical Background

Many denominations of Christianity have differing views on the exact details of Christ's second coming. Only a handful of Christian organizations dare to claim complete and authoritative interpretation of the symbolic and prophetic biblical resources. The cause of this hesitancy rests with Christ's own words: "Watch therefore, for ye know neither the day nor the hour wherein the Son of man cometh" (Matthew 25:13).

The second coming of Christ is mentioned over three hundred times in the New Testament. The night before His crucifixion, Jesus told His disciples that He would return (see John 14:3). When Jesus ascended into heaven, two angels appeared to His followers, saying that He would return in the same manner as they had seen Him depart (see Acts 1:11).

The words *Second Coming* do not appear in the Bible, though the Bible does refer to Christ's return as the "second time" (see Hebrews 9:28). However, the words *Second Coming* have come to identify Christ's impending return.

II. EXPOSITION AND APPLICATION OF THE SCRIPTURE

A. Dealing with Scoffers
(2 Peter 3:1-7)

THIS SECOND epistle, beloved, I now write unto you; in both which I stir up your pure minds by way of remembrance: That ye may be mindful of the words which were spoken before by the holy prophets, and of the commandment of us the apostles of the Lord and Saviour: Knowing this first, that there shall come in the last days scoffers, walking after their own lusts, And saying, Where is the promise of his coming? for since the fathers fell asleep, all things continue as they were from the beginning of the creation. For this they willingly are ignorant of, that by the word of God the heavens were of old, and the earth standing out of the water and in the water: Whereby the world that then was, being overflowed with water, perished: But the heavens and the earth, which are now, by the same word are kept in store, reserved unto fire against the day of judgment and perdition of ungodly men.

The coming of Jesus Christ to earth was the pivotal point in human history. Peter recorded the view of biblical scoffers of Christ's deity who believed that "since the fathers fell asleep, all things continue as *they were* from the beginning of the creation" (verse 4). The *fathers* to whom Peter referred are the Old Testament patriarchs and prophets.

The scoffers of the New Testament adhered to a philosophy of *uniformitarianism*. This philosophy has gripped both the scientific world and the scholastic world for a long time. Their denial of the possibility of a supernatural reappearance of Jesus is based on the fact that nothing of that nature has occurred in the past. Several Christian and even secular documents of the first two centuries report the dismay that spread among Christians when the promise of Jesus' second coming was unfulfilled. Peter rebutted the uniformitarian argument by recalling the very Old Testament event of the Flood to disprove their claims. The Flood was a supernatural event that came suddenly and unexpectedly upon the world, just as the *parousia* (return of Christ) will come.

As Christians, we are presently living in the age of grace, when God's mercy is flowing out to the world through His Son Jesus Christ (see Hebrews 1:2). But this age of grace will not last forever. While it is true that God's longsuffering toward sinners is proof of His agape love for humankind, the Bible does warn us that Judgment Day will come. The mere knowledge of God's plan to judge the earth should motivate Christians to work toward the redemption of all people. Once we the believers understand God's future plan, we have two choices: 1) we can attach ourselves to the world and be destroyed with it; or 2) we can attach ourselves to Jesus Christ and enter into the glory of the new world that is soon to come.

In 2 Timothy 3:1, we are reminded that in the last days it will become increasingly difficult to be a Christian. Peter's discussion of scoffers in the last days who will laugh at the idea of Christ returning to earth is supported by Jude's revelation (see 1:18-19). These scoffers are already evident in our present day. Guided by their own lusts and finite mental capacity, they live as though they have power over their own future. These are the people to whom we are called to witness, and for the unseasoned Christian, it can be a disenchanting and even frightening experience to share Christ with these hardened sinners. Trigger words such as *eternal judgment* and *hell* often provoke their laughter and amusement. They ridicule the return of Jesus Christ, not just because of the length of time that has passed since Christ's resurrection, but also because they see no vivid change in the world today, despite the proliferation of believers. They mock our belief and argue that if God really cared about the world, He would have done something about our taxing conditions by now—poverty, lawlessness, sickness, natural catastrophes, etc. They would rather be self-reliant and depend upon the laws of nature to run the world and keep it stable. They argue, "Why should we get excited about Christ's return when the world has been functioning for millions of years?" These unbelievers are much like the rich farmer, with his barns full to bursting from a bountiful harvest, who arrogantly proclaimed to his own soul, "take thine ease, eat, drink, and be merry" (Luke 12:19). These same scoffers will turn to the church when life's twists and turns make them squirm and cry out for help. They use Christ's mercy as a tool against the believer, in an attempt to get the church to meet their needs. And too often, once the need is met, our testimony of the need for repentance and salvation goes unheeded.

Scoffers can wear Christians down if we are not careful. Jesus said, "Behold, I come quickly: hold that fast, which thou hast, that no man take thy crown" (Revelation 3:11). It is clear that it takes diligence and determination on the part of the believer to prevent being drawn into the world of the jeering crowd.

B. Reaffirmation of Christ's Return (2 Peter 3:8-10)

But, beloved, be not ignorant of this one thing, that one day is with the Lord as a thousand years, and a thousand years as one day. The Lord is not slack concerning his promise, as some men count slackness; but is longsuffering to us-ward, not willing that any should perish, but that all should come to repentance. But the day of the Lord will come as a thief in the night; in the which the heavens shall pass away with a great noise, and the elements shall melt with fervent heat, the earth also and the works that are therein shall be burned up.

Among Christian groups, various opinions exist about the second coming of Jesus Christ. Some actually believe that Jesus was referring to the Day of Pentecost and the descent of the Holy Spirit (the Comforter). Others believe Jesus was referring to the coming of Christ into the heart of the believer at conversion. Still others believe Jesus was referring to the believer's transition from death to eternal life. But a careful examination of the New Testament confirms that the Second Coming will be a climactic and historical event.

First Thessalonians 4:16 is perhaps the most familiar of texts affirming Christ's return. As we decipher it we realize that, though Christ will come "as a thief in the night" to those who are not *watching,* He will be as visible as a mighty storm to those who have been faithful in waiting with expectancy. The faithful will see Christ come with "a shout," "the voice of the archangel," and the "trump of God." The shout may be the sound of lightning and thunder (see Matthew 24:27), or it may be the shout of believers heard around the world as our eyes behold His glory.

The archangel Michael (see Jude 1:9) will announce Christ's second coming. Angels are observers. The Bible teaches us that angels are spectators of God's activities in the world and that they are especially keen on observing the unfolding of His plan of redemption. They were present at the birth and resurrection of Christ. And we see that the archangel Michael will be present at His second coming. The archangel's role is that of a warrior (see Daniel 10:13; Revelation 12:7-8). Often referred to as the good *angel of death*, Michael's duty is to clear the way of oppressors who would attempt to war against God's plan for humankind. No more fitting angel could be chosen to announce the coming of Christ in glory.

Finally, Christ's return will be announced with the trump of God. The first trump of God was at Mt. Sinai, with its tremendous impact for Israel. In 1 Corinthians 15:52, the apostle Paul used the sounding of the trump of God to signal the time when the believers will be raptured. This second sounding of the trump of God will mark the completion of the work of the church, and renewal of His relations with Israel.

C. The Readiness of Those Who Await Christ (2 Peter 3:11-13)

Seeing then that all these things shall be dissolved, what manner of persons ought ye to be in all holy conversation and godliness, Looking for and hasting unto the coming of the day of God, wherein the heavens being on fire shall be dissolved, and the elements shall melt with fervent heat? Nevertheless we, according to his promise, look for new heavens and a new earth, wherein dwelleth righteousness.

In the second century, there was a Christian sect called the *Montanists*, who believed that Christ would return during their lifetime, and that the New Jerusalem would come down out of heaven. One Roman leader was so certain that the end of the world was only two days away that he and his followers disposed of their houses and all other belongings in preparation. Some time between AD 375–AD 400, a student of Hilary of Poitiers, Saint Martin of Tours, braced his followers for a definite end of the world no later than AD 400. He also stated, "There is no doubt that the Antichrist has already been born." The middle of the first millennium saw a number of doomsday predictions, including that of Hippolytus of Rome, the "antipope" who temporarily defected from the Catholic Church to protest its reformation, whose math convinced him that the Second Coming would occur six thousand years after Creation, or AD 500. There have been many more such predictions that have come and gone (*End of Days: Predictions and Prophecies about the End of the World*, by Sylvia Browne).

Jesus stated emphatically that only the Father knew the time of Christ's return. It is recorded in Matthew 24:36, "But of that day and hour knoweth no man." The purpose for this secrecy is to leave the believer in constant expectancy. We have no way of knowing the timing for this event that will rock our world. We could shrug our shoulders and casually wait for that important day. But Jesus admonished us to *keep watch* (Matthew 24:42—"Watch therefore…"). The best way to keep watch is to have some idea of what you are looking for, and to know what your role is during the waiting period.

In the parable of the Master and the porter (see Mark 13:33-37), Jesus reinforced the need for Christians to be porters or watchers. He used the same reference to porters or gatekeepers in the parable of the Shepherd and His fold (see John 10:3). In the parable in the book of

Mark, the master leaves on a far journey and commands the porter to watch over his assets while he is gone, and he warns the porter to remain alert. There is an allusion to the four Roman watches of the night—beginning at 9 p.m. (evening), and 12 midnight (midnight), 3 a.m. (cockcrowing), and 6 a.m. (morning)—to reinforce the importance of staying faithful and awake. Of course, the Master taking the far journey is Jesus Christ, the Son of Man, who at His ascension gave His followers all authority to witness for Him. We know not whether the world is in the season of evening or midnight or cockcrowing, but we do know that the morning will come when the Master will return. And as we look out on the condition of the world, we know that it cannot be too far into the future.

III. CONCLUDING REFLECTION

As believers, we must not let the stretch of two millenniums water down our excitement of one day seeing Jesus face-to-face. No matter how long we must "tarry," our charge is to keep alive the message of salvation through Jesus Christ, to remain energized and eager for Christ's return, and to spend our time living in godly and holy preparation for that climactic event. We are to exercise the gift of longsuffering, and patiently perform our duties as Christians.

We must remember that in eternity there is no time, i.e. past or future, but only the present. Thus, "time" and "delay" are virtually meaningless to God. Believers must learn to adjust to God's timetable, which will greatly help us in facing the centuries that have passed since New Testament times.

PRAYER

Our Father in heaven, we thank You for this lesson today. Help us O God to always be mindful of the second coming of our Savior. Help us to share the Good News with those we come in contact with. In Jesus' name we pray. Amen.

WORD POWER

Scoffers (Greek: *empaiktes* [em-paik-tes]) —it means "mockers, those who reproach others (Christians)." The aim of a scoffer is to depreciate the truth about God in the sight of a multitude. They are superficial thinkers. They try to make believers in Christ look like fools. A scoffer's desire is to water down the truth. This is the reason why Peter alerted us to their presence in our midst. Beyond their aim they reproach the name of Christ.

HOME DAILY BIBLE READINGS
(November 23-29, 2009)

A Hopeful People
MONDAY, November 23: "I Shall Again Praise God" (Psalm 42)
TUESDAY, November 24: "Be Strong, Take Courage" (Psalm 31:21-24)
WEDNESDAY, November 25: "God Is My Hope" (Psalm 71:1-6)
THURSDAY, November 26: "Hope in God's Word" (Psalm 119:81-88)
FRIDAY, November 27: "Hoping against Hope" (Romans 4:16-24)
SATURDAY, November 28: "Strengthen and Encourage" (Acts 14:21-28)
SUNDAY, November 29: "Waiting for the Day of God" (2 Peter 3:1-13)

Christ, the Fulfillment

GENERAL INTRODUCTION

Matthew's gospel serves as confirmation of the fulfillment of God's promise to send the Messiah. Throughout its pages, references are made to Old Testament prophecies that were fulfilled in Jesus. The writer gave other evidence through events and persons' reactions that point to Jesus as the Christ.

Unit I, *The Promised Birth Fulfilled,* is a consideration of the Messiah's lineage and Isaiah's prophecy of Immanuel's birth. Gabriel's message to Mary and the visit of the magi are further confirmations of the coming of the Messiah. The magi's audience with Herod also sets into motion the king's ruthless act of killing innocent male infants and the holy family's escape to Egypt, both foretold in prophecy.

Unit II, *Evidences of Jesus as Messiah,* is a focus on some of the events in Jesus' life that helped identify Him as Messiah. The study includes Jesus' baptism, temptation, the healing of persons who were blind and mute, a prayer of thanks to the Father, and rejection by persons in His hometown. (Note: On the second Sunday of December, the children will focus on the angel's visit to Mary rather than Isaiah's prophecy.)

Unit III, *Testimonies to Jesus as Messiah,* is an examination of the witness of specific persons who helped confirm Jesus as the Messiah. A Canaanite woman recognized Jesus' power. Impetuous Peter spoke out in faith, though he did not understand what he was saying. Peter, James, and John witnessed Christ's transfiguration. Mary of Bethany showed her faith by her act of anointing Jesus.

LESSON 1   December 6, 2009

THE LINEAGE OF DAVID

DEVOTIONAL READING: 2 Samuel 7:8-17
PRINT PASSAGE: Ruth 4:13-17; Matthew 1:1-6
KEY VERSE: Ruth 4:17

BACKGROUND SCRIPTURE: Ruth 4:13-17;
Matthew 1:1-17

Ruth 4:13-17; Matthew 1:1-6—KJV

13 So Boaz took Ruth, and she was his wife: and when he went in unto her, the LORD gave her conception, and she bare a son.

14 And the women said unto Naomi, Blessed be the LORD, which hath not left thee this day without a kinsman, that his name may be famous in Israel.

15 And he shall be unto thee a restorer of thy life, and a nourisher of thine old age: for thy daughter in law, which loveth thee, which is better to thee than seven sons, hath born him.

16 And Naomi took the child, and laid it in her bosom, and became nurse unto it.

17 And the women her neighbours gave it a name, saying, There is a son born to Naomi; and they called his name Obed: he is the father of Jesse, the father of David.

.....

THE BOOK of the generation of Jesus Christ, the son of David, the son of Abraham.

2 Abraham begat Isaac; and Isaac begat Jacob; and Jacob begat Judas and his brethren;

3 And Judas begat Phares and Zara of Thamar; and Phares begat Esrom; and Esrom begat Aram;

4 And Aram begat Aminadab; and Aminadab begat Naasson; and Naasson begat Salmon;

5 And Salmon begat Booz of Rachab; and Booz begat Obed of Ruth; and Obed begat Jesse;

6 And Jesse begat David the king; and David the king begat Solomon of her that had been the wife of Urias.

Ruth 4:13-17; Matthew 1:1-6—NRSV

13 So Boaz took Ruth and she became his wife. When they came together, the LORD made her conceive, and she bore a son.

14 Then the women said to Naomi, "Blessed be the LORD, who has not left you this day without next-of-kin; and may his name be renowned in Israel!

15 He shall be to you a restorer of life and a nourisher of your old age; for your daughter-in-law who loves you, who is more to you than seven sons, has borne him."

16 Then Naomi took the child and laid him in her bosom, and became his nurse.

17 The women of the neighborhood gave him a name, saying, "A son has been born to Naomi." They named him Obed; he became the father of Jesse, the father of David.

.....

AN ACCOUNT of the genealogy of Jesus the Messiah, the son of David, the son of Abraham.

2 Abraham was the father of Isaac, and Isaac the father of Jacob, and Jacob the father of Judah and his brothers,

3 and Judah the father of Perez and Zerah by Tamar, and Perez the father of Hezron, and Hezron the father of Aram,

4 and Aram the father of Aminadab, and Aminadab the father of Nahshon, and Nahshon the father of Salmon,

5 and Salmon the father of Boaz by Rahab, and Boaz the father of Obed by Ruth, and Obed the father of Jesse,

6 and Jesse the father of King David. And David was the father of Solomon by the wife of Uriah.

UNIFYING LESSON PRINCIPLE

Genealogy is a popular hobby because people want to know who they are and where they came from. Why are we so fascinated with our family heritage? We want to be able to make connections, just as the Bible traces Jesus' human family through King David.

TOPICAL OUTLINE OF THE LESSON

I. **Introduction**
   A. The Importance of Origin
   B. Biblical Background

II. **Exposition and Application of the Scripture**
   A. Ruth Marries Boaz (Ruth 4:13)
   B. Ruth's Mother-in-law Is Blessed (Ruth 4:14-16)
   C. Ruth's Descendants (Ruth 4:17)
   D. Ruth's Ancestors (Matthew 1:1-6)

III. **Concluding Reflection**

LESSON OBJECTIVES

Upon completion of this lesson, the students will know that:

1. The origin birth of Christ is discussed in the book of Ruth;
2. God can bring blessing out of tragedy; and,
3. Matthew linked the birth of Jesus to the life of Ruth.

POINTS TO BE EMPHASIZED

ADULT/YOUTH

Adult Topic: A Son Is Born
Youth Topic: Skeletons in Jesus' Closet?
Adult Key Verse: Ruth 4:17
Youth Key Verse: Matthew 1:1
Print Passage: Ruth 4:13-17; Matthew 1:1-6

—Tamar (Matthew 1:3), Rahab (verse 5), and Ruth (verse 5) are surprise entries in Jesus' ancestral genealogy.
—Matthew 1:2-6 is based on the genealogical list in 1 Chronicles 1–2.
—In the book of Matthew, Jesus' genealogy is traced back to God's call of Abraham.
—Jesus' genealogy shows His inclusive and diverse family heritage.
—Jesus' birth fulfilled God's promise that He would establish the kingdom of David forever.

CHILDREN

Children Topic: The Family Tree
Key Verse: Ruth 4:14
Print Passage: Ruth 4:13-17; Matthew 1:1-6

—Jesus Christ is a descendant of Abraham.
—God blessed the family of Boaz and Ruth with a son who became one of Jesus' ancestors.
—Ruth, Naomi's daughter-in-law, was an integral part of Naomi's family.
—Ruth is an example of someone who became a follower of God.
—The birth of a child extends the life of a family.
—A summary of the ancestry of Jesus is provided in Matthew 1:1-17.

I. INTRODUCTION

A. The Importance of Origin

In 1976, Alex Haley published his highly acclaimed book *Roots: The Saga of an American Family*. Haley was born in Ithaca, New York, in 1921. After his birth his family moved to Henning, Tennessee, where he spent the first five years of his life and where he is buried today. Alex Haley's remarkable book was a groundbreaking literary masterpiece in which he retells and retraces the story of his family, beginning with the capture and enslavement of Kunta Kinte, Alex's great-great-grandfather. Kunta Kinte was kidnapped in 1767 from the tiny nation of Gambia, West Africa, and transported to Maryland, where he was eventually sold into slavery. Haley spent ten years conducting research about his family. His work eventually carried him to the tiny village in Gambia where Kunta Kinte was born and lived until the day of his capture. Haley's work and publication of *Roots* spawned new interest in genealogical research.

Now think for a moment that God's Word provides us the historical background of our spiritual heritage. It is pointed out in our lesson that God has provided us with exact information for understanding our spiritual and historical origins in Jesus Christ.

B. Biblical Background

In today's lesson, we are introduced to a small, but important portion of the genealogical tree of Jesus Christ. The lesson comes from the book of Ruth, a short book of eighty-five verses in which events are described that occurred sometime between the period of the Judges and rise of Samuel—the last judge of Israel (see Ruth 1:1). There are three main characters in the lesson: Naomi and Ruth, two women whose lives became forever entwined through a series of marriages and family deaths, and a man named Boaz, who took on the role of kinsman-redeemer.

The story of Ruth and Naomi is one of the most remarkable and loved stories in the Old Testament. It is a detailed account of a Hebrew woman whose husband and sons left Judah and migrated to the land of Moab because of a famine (see Ruth 1:1). While living in Moab their sons married Moabite women, one of whom was named Orpah and the other was named Ruth (see Ruth 1:4). Eventually, Naomi's husband and sons died, leaving her in a strange land with no financial support and very few real assets (see Ruth 1:3, 5). She was befriended by the widow of one of her sons who pledged Naomi her unqualified support and love (see Ruth 1:16-17). The lesson holds several valuable principles for all believers. First, we will learn that God is faithful. Naomi felt that her life was over, but God, who is faithful to His promises, had other plans. Second, we will see that the plan of God for His people is greater than the trials and troubles that we sometimes find ourselves in. It was through the birth of the son of Ruth and Boaz that David would be born. Third, we will learn the lesson of the Hebrew redeemer, which is a type of the redeemer to come who was Jesus Christ.

II. EXPOSITION AND APPLICATION OF THE SCRIPTURE

A. Ruth Marries Boaz
(Ruth 4:13)

So Boaz took Ruth, and she was his wife: and when he went in unto her, the LORD gave her conception, and she bare a son.

In Ruth 4:1-9, there is the description of the events that led up to the final hurdle Boaz had to jump before he could marry Ruth. He would marry Ruth and raise up the name of his dead kinsman, Mahlon. There is at least a nine-month span that is covered in verse 13. Boaz "took" Ruth to be his wife and "went in unto her," signifying the consummation of the marriage. Their marriage was immediately blessed by the Lord. The Lord gave her conception. This act of conception stands in stark contrast to the ten-year marriage of Ruth to Mahlon (see Ruth 1:4) in which there were no children born. Naomi's sons were married for ten years before they died, and neither one of them had a child.

Ruth's conception moved her from a state of barrenness to blessedness. For ten years she had been unable to bear a son, but now in the course of a few months, God opened her womb and she conceived. The birth of the son can only be interpreted as the grace of God. The birth of a son looks back in Israel's history to the time God visited Sarah and she conceived and gave birth to a son.

B. Ruth's Mother-in-law Is Blessed
(Ruth 4:14-16)

And the women said unto Naomi, Blessed be the LORD, which hath not left thee this day without a kinsman, that his name may be famous in Israel. And he shall be unto thee a restorer of thy life, and a nourisher of thine old age: for thy daughter in law, which loveth thee, which is better to thee than seven sons, hath born him. And Naomi took the child, and laid it in her bosom, and became nurse unto it.

The scene moves from Ruth and Boaz to Naomi, whom the women of the village proclaimed as highly blessed and favored. Why did the women bless Naomi? First, because when Naomi returned to Bethlehem she returned as a broken, dejected, and despondent woman. In ancient Hebrew tradition, her life was all but over. She had no husband and had no sons to produce grandchildren—and on top of all that she was an old woman, with no prospects for future marriage. However, when Boaz became the kinsman-redeemer it gave Naomi hope for the future.

Second, the Lord had given Naomi a kinsman-redeemer who would bring up sons in the name of her deceased son Mahlon. In ancient Hebrew tradition, the primary role of the next of kin was to rescue a relative from danger, avenge the blood of a slain relative, or marry the wife of a deceased relative. According to the Old Testament tradition, there were at least four cases that were covered by the Law about the next of kin (see Leviticus 25:25, 48-50; 27:13; Numbers 35:12ff.). In the case of Ruth and Naomi, the next of kin wanted to buy back the land of her deceased husband, but he did not want to marry Ruth. This opened the door for Boaz to step in and perform both acts of buying the land and marrying Ruth (see Deuteronomy 25:5-10).

Third, the women declared that the name of the son would be famous in Israel. This was a forward look to the time of David, who would become the most famous king in Israel's history.

Fourth, the women blessed Naomi because of her relationship with Ruth. The baby born to Ruth and Boaz was seen as "a restorer of life" for Naomi (Hebrew *shuwb*, pronounced *shoob*—literally means "to bring back to life or renew"). Naomi died emotionally and spiritually when her husband and sons died. The son of Naomi's old age would bring her back to life and sustain her, which is the meaning of the word *nourisher*.

The greatest blessing that Naomi had was her relationship with Ruth, who had made a vow never to leave nor to stop following her (see Ruth 1:16-17). Ruth did not just make a pledge of support, but entered into covenant with her mother-in-law. The women recognized the unconditional love of Ruth. This was love that was not expressed in words but through concrete actions. Her love was a type of the love that God demonstrated through the cross of Jesus Christ (see John 3:16; Romans 5:8-10; 1 John 4:10). Ruth followed Naomi back to Bethlehem without any guarantees that her life would be any better. Ruth could have remained with her own people in her own land, but she chose the uncertainty of Judah. The women celebrated Ruth's love for Naomi by reminding her that the love she received from Ruth was greater than that of seven sons. *Seven* is the number of completion, and in their eyes, there was nothing greater than what Ruth had already demonstrated. The child who would sustain Naomi was sustained by Naomi, who became his nurse (see Ruth 4:16).

Every grandparent can relate to the joy that Naomi must have felt. There is no greater joy than to see the Lord bless a family with new generations: it means the continuation of the family name and tradition. Naomi's bitterness and barrenness were turned into absolute joy through the birth of the son born to Ruth and Boaz.

Ruth's love for her mother-in-law was known and became the talk of the town. God brought blessings out of Naomi's tragedy even greater than that of seven sons, or an abundance of heirs. Even in tough times, Naomi maintained her trust in God, and God in His time gave her unbelievable blessings. Even in our sorrow and calamity, God can bring blessing.

C. Ruth's Descendants
(Ruth 4:17)

And the women her neighbours gave it a name, saying, There is a son born to Naomi; and they called his name Obed: he is the father of Jesse, the father of David.

The women who were Naomi's neighbors gave the baby a name. They declared that a son had been born to Naomi. They called the son who was born to Ruth and Boaz "Obed." He became the father of Jesse and the grandfather of David. God used a woman of non-Hebrew heritage to be the birth mother of the grandfather of King David. Through this line would come the fulfillment of God's promise to David that his throne and kingdom would last forever (see 2 Samuel 7:12-14). The Messiah/Redeemer of the world would be born through David.

D. Ruth's Ancestors
(Matthew 1:1-6)

THE BOOK of the generation of Jesus Christ, the son of David, the son of Abraham. Abraham begat Isaac; and Isaac begat Jacob; and Jacob begat Judas and his

brethren; And Judas begat Phares and Zara of Thamar; and Phares begat Esrom; and Esrom begat Aram; And Aram begat Aminadab; and Aminadab begat Naasson; and Naasson begat Salmon; And Salmon begat Booz of Rachab; and Booz begat Obed of Ruth; and Obed begat Jesse; And Jesse begat David the king; and David the king begat Solomon of her that had been the wife of Urias.

This portion of our lesson comes from the opening chapter of the gospel according to Matthew. Who was Matthew and why did he write? Tradition has it that the writer of this gospel is the same Matthew who was the disciple of Jesus who was the tax collector (see Matthew 10:3). He wrote to provide believers with the message of Jesus' teachings. Matthew's is first in the canon of the New Testament and is often referred to as the church's gospel because of its emphasis on the teachings of Jesus. One of the unique features of the gospel of Matthew is its portrayal of Jesus as the royal heir to the throne of David (see 2 Samuel 7:12-14). Matthew took great care to point out that Jesus was not a pretender to the throne of David; rather, He was the living fulfillment of God's promise that began with Abraham (see Genesis 12:1-3; 17:1-13). Through the covenant made with Abraham, all of the families of the earth would be blessed. Matthew began with a simple statement that what one was about to read was the book (Greek: *biblos*—literally "book" or "record") about the origin of Jesus Christ. He used the Greek word *Christos,* which denotes "an office" or "title" more than being a proper name. The title is a translation from the Hebrew word for "Messiah."

The KJV uses the word *generations.* However, the more literal translation is the word *genesis,* which means "beginnings" or "origins." Matthew stated that the record he was about to present was the record or book of the beginnings of Jesus Christ, whose heritage can be traced back in time through two of Israel's most revered people—Abraham (the chief father of the nation) and David, her most revered king. The generations of Jesus cover forty-two generations (see Matthew 1:17).

Many Christians skip this portion of the Gospel because they feel it does not offer much in terms of sound spiritual food. However, nothing could be further from the truth. There are several valuable lessons to be gleaned from studying this list of names. New Testament scholar Darrell L. Bock stated that Matthew's genealogy is important culturally. He pointed out that genealogies communicate a person's social standing and status within the community.

There are several key points about the opening verses of this genealogy in the book of Matthew. First, note the name of *Judah,* who was the third son born to Jacob and Leah (see Genesis 29:35). He was also the son that Jacob blessed, saying that the scepter would never depart from Judah (see Genesis 49:9-10). The tribes of Judah and Benjamin were the only two surviving tribes. In 722 BC, the ten tribes of the Northern Kingdom were removed and carried into exile and absorbed into Assyrian culture (according to 2 Kings 17). The tribes from the north never re-emerged in the history of Israel. Second, in the list of descendants, four of the people were women who had questionable characters and motives: Tamar (compare verse 3 to Genesis 38); Rahab (compare verse 5 to Joshua 2); Ruth (compare verse 5 to Ruth 1–4), a Moabite woman; and last Bathsheba, who was not mentioned by name (compare verse 6 to 2 Samuel 11-12). The inclusion of these women by Matthew points out that God's work includes people of all backgrounds and races. This is good news because it points to the inclusive nature of God, who is not a respecter of persons and who is willing to use anyone who will submit to His will and purpose (see Acts 10:34).

III. CONCLUDING REFLECTION

What are we to make of Matthew's inclusion of the forty-two names that form the genealogical heritage of Jesus Christ? One thought is quite clear: it teaches us lessons about the sovereignty of God. This means that God is free to choose whomever He wants to choose to accomplish His will and purpose. Second, we learn that God often works in ways that contradict and stand diametrically opposed to how we would choose people. God does not look at the outward person but at the heart and spirit (see 2 Samuel 16:1-13). Finally, from the story of Ruth and Boaz we learn that even when life takes a horrible turn, it is never an indication that all is lost. God is able to reverse our worst days of pain and brokenness and turn our latter days into our most glorious moments.

PRAYER

Lord God, we honor You with our hearts as well as our lips. Grant that we will be more willing to submit to Your will for our lives. In the name of Jesus Christ we pray. Amen.

WORD POWER

Naomi [*Na-o-mi*]—means "sweetness, pleasantness, or someone to rejoice with." However, calamity struck her life in a foreign land. When she returned her neighbors called her Naomi, but she said "My name is mara"—which means "bitterness." Do not lose hope in God by calling yourself a name which is contrary to God's expectation in your life.

HOME DAILY BIBLE READINGS
(November 30–December 6, 2009)

The Lineage of David
MONDAY, November 30: "I Have Been with You" (2 Samuel 7:8-11b)
TUESDAY, December 1: "I Will Establish Forever" (2 Samuel 7:11c-17)
WEDNESDAY, December 2: "Instruction for the People" (2 Samuel 7:18-22)
THURSDAY, December 3: "God's Name Magnified Forever" (2 Samuel 7:23-26)
FRIDAY, December 4: "The Lord Sits Enthroned" (Psalm 9:7-11)
SATURDAY, December 5: "Steadfast Love to His Anointed" (Psalm 18:43-50)
SUNDAY, December 6: "Jesus, Son of David" (Ruth 4:13-17; Matthew 1:1-6)

LESSON 2   December 13, 2009

PROPHETS FORESHADOW MESSIAH'S BIRTH

DEVOTIONAL READING: **Micah 5:1-5a**
PRINT PASSAGE: **Isaiah 7:13-17; Luke 1:30-38**
KEY VERSE: **Isaiah 7:14**

BACKGROUND SCRIPTURE: **Isaiah 7:13-17;**
Luke 1:26-38

Isaiah 7:13-17; Luke 1:30-38—KJV

13 And he said, Hear ye now, O house of David; Is it a small thing for you to weary men, but will ye weary my God also?

14 Therefore the Lord himself shall give you a sign; Behold, a virgin shall conceive, and bear a son, and shall call his name Immanuel.

15 Butter and honey shall he eat, that he may know to refuse the evil, and choose the good.

16 For before the child shall know to refuse the evil, and choose the good, the land that thou abhorrest shall be forsaken of both her kings.

17 The LORD shall bring upon thee, and upon thy people, and upon thy father's house, days that have not come, from the day that Ephraim departed from Judah; even the king of Assyria.

.....

30 And the angel said unto her, Fear not, Mary: for thou hast found favour with God.

31 And, behold, thou shalt conceive in thy womb, and bring forth a son, and shalt call his name JESUS.

32 He shall be great, and shall be called the Son of the Highest: and the Lord God shall give unto him the throne of his father David:

33 And he shall reign over the house of Jacob for ever; and of his kingdom there shall be no end.

34 Then said Mary unto the angel, How shall this be, seeing I know not a man?

35 And the angel answered and said unto her, The Holy Ghost shall come upon thee, and the power of the Highest shall overshadow thee: therefore also that holy thing which shall be born of thee shall be called the Son of God.

36 And, behold, thy cousin Elisabeth, she hath also

Isaiah 7:13-17; Luke 1:30-38—NRSV

13 Then Isaiah said: "Hear then, O house of David! Is it too little for you to weary mortals, that you weary my God also?

14 Therefore the Lord himself will give you a sign. Look, the young woman is with child and shall bear a son, and shall name him Immanuel.

15 He shall eat curds and honey by the time he knows how to refuse the evil and choose the good.

16 For before the child knows how to refuse the evil and choose the good, the land before whose two kings you are in dread will be deserted.

17 The LORD will bring on you and on your people and on your ancestral house such days as have not come since the day that Ephraim departed from Judah—the king of Assyria."

.....

30 The angel said to her, "Do not be afraid, Mary, for you have found favor with God.

31 And now, you will conceive in your womb and bear a son, and you will name him Jesus.

32 He will be great, and will be called the Son of the Most High, and the Lord God will give to him the throne of his ancestor David.

33 He will reign over the house of Jacob forever, and of his kingdom there will be no end."

34 Mary said to the angel, "How can this be, since I am a virgin?"

35 The angel said to her, "The Holy Spirit will come upon you, and the power of the Most High will overshadow you; therefore the child to be born will be holy; he will be called Son of God.

36 And now, your relative Elizabeth in her old age

People often look for proof or signs that God is involved in our world. What proof do we have of such involvement? Isaiah prophesied of the coming Messiah who would be Immanuel ("God with us"), and Luke centuries later told how God sent the angel to reveal good news to Mary.

conceived a son in her old age: and this is the sixth month with her, who was called barren.

37 For with God nothing shall be impossible.

38 And Mary said, Behold the handmaid of the Lord; be it unto me according to thy word. And the angel departed from her.

has also conceived a son; and this is the sixth month for her who was said to be barren.

37 For nothing will be impossible with God."

38 Then Mary said, "Here am I, the servant of the Lord; let it be with me according to your word." Then the angel departed from her.

TOPICAL OUTLINE OF THE LESSON

I. Introduction
   A. Signs
   B. Biblical Background

II. Exposition and Application of the Scripture
   A. An Unsolicited Sign (Isaiah 7:13-14)
   B. An Unforeseen Development (Isaiah 7:15-17)
   C. The Message Delivered (Luke 1:30-33)
   D. The Method Explained (Luke 1:34-38)

III. Concluding Reflection

LESSON OBJECTIVES

Upon completion of this lesson, the students will know that:

1. Jesus fulfilled the prophetic message found in the Old Testament books;
2. God came in the form of the Son to deliver us from sin and eternal death; and,
3. God can still give any sign to us in order to assure us of His omnipresence.

POINTS TO BE EMPHASIZED

ADULT/YOUTH

Adult Topic: An Unexpected Sign

Youth Topic: Guess Who Is Coming to Dinner

Adult Key Verse: Isaiah 7:14

Youth Key Verse: Luke 1:35

Print Passage: Isaiah 7:13-17; Luke 1:30-38

—"Young woman" in Isaiah 7:14 is *almah* (Hebrew: "young woman"), not *bethulah* (Hebrew: "virgin"), although the *Septuagint* (LXX) uses *parthenos* (Greek: "virgin").

—"Jesus" is a Greek transcription of the Hebrew name "Joshua," which means "God saves."

—"House of Jacob" (Luke 1:33) refers to the people of Israel, while "house of David" (Luke 1:27; Isaiah 7:13) refers to the royal line.

—Luke understood the annunciation in terms of fulfillment of Isaiah's prophecy.

—God sent the angel to deliver God's message to Mary and to fulfill God's purpose.

—Mary was humble before the Lord and accepted the angel's words as truth.

—Mary was assured that God would perform the birth by way of the Spirit.

CHILDREN
Children Topic: Receiving Good News
Key Verse: Luke 1:35
Print Passage: Luke 1:26-38
—Isaiah foretold the birth of Immanuel.

—The angel Gabriel brought good news to Mary.

—Gabriel told Mary that she would give birth to a holy child who would be called Son of God.

—The angel told Mary that Elizabeth was with child in her old age.

—This story is an example of how God performs miracles in people's lives.

I. INTRODUCTION
A. Signs

What are signs? *Signs* are "events, words, or miraculous occurrences that point beyond themselves to something far greater." Signs can be miraculous events such as God's great act of deliverance and salvation of the children of Israel at the Red Sea (see Exodus 14), or the feeding of the children of Israel with manna for forty years in the wilderness (see Exodus 16:35). In Genesis 1:14, God created the sun and moon to divide the day from night. They were to serve as signs for the seasons and years. Just prior to crossing the Jordan River, God commanded Joshua to take twelve stones from the riverbed and carry them as constant reminders of how God opened the waters of the river for the children of Israel to cross on dry ground (see Joshua 4:5-7). Can you think of other occasions when God used signs to encourage, inform, and direct His people?

B. Biblical Background

Today's lesson comes from two passages: Isaiah 7:13-17 and Luke 1:26-38. Isaiah was one of several Old Testament prophets whom God used to announce the coming of the Messiah/King who would fulfill the promise made to King David (see 2 Samuel 7:12-15). Isaiah preached during a very difficult time in Judah's history. The events described in chapter seven occurred somewhere around 735 BC and prior to the fall of Samaria in 722 BC.

The second half of the lesson comes from the gospel of Luke. In this passage, we meet the young woman God chose to be the birth mother of the Messiah. This passage serves as one of the traditional Advent readings that remind us of the graciousness of God. In the story, we see a God who chooses without any regard for social status or personal achievement.

One of the central points of the passage in the book of Luke is the greatness of God's power. A main tenet of the lesson is the proclamation of the Virgin Birth. The Virgin Birth is a proclamation that there is nothing too hard for God (see Jeremiah 32:17, 27). Mary and Joseph came to realize through the birth of Jesus that God can do anything but fail.

II. EXPOSITION AND APPLICATION OF THE SCRIPTURE

A. An Unsolicited Sign
(Isaiah 7:13-14)

And he said, Hear ye now, O house of David; Is it a small thing for you to weary men, but will ye weary my God also? Therefore the Lord himself shall give you a sign; Behold, a virgin shall conceive, and bear a son, and shall call his name Immanuel.

The crisis that Ahaz faced grew more ominous by the day. God spoke to Ahaz and told him to ask for a sign that He would deliver him and the nation of Judah from the hands of their enemies (see Isaiah 7:11). This sign could be as great or as insignificant as he wanted it to be. Through an act of false piety, Ahaz told the prophet that he would not dare tempt God. He was referring to the Law when Israel tested God in the wilderness (see Numbers 14:22; Deuteronomy 6:16). In this instance, God was not being tempted; rather, God wanted Ahaz to trust Him and believe that He could deliver the nation. Ahaz, as well as the whole house of David, had wearied God with their failure to live up to the example of King David. There was no trust in the land. God had grown weary of trying to get the king to do something that was simply not in him—trusting the only true God.

God told Ahaz that He would give a sign anyway. A virgin would conceive and bear a son and call his name *Immanuel*, meaning that "God is with us." Throughout the centuries, this verse has been hotly debated among biblical scholars as to what exactly Isaiah meant. The most important question revolves around how to interpret the meaning of the word *virgin*. The second relates to the time of the fulfillment of the prophecy. Was Isaiah referring to an event that was contemporary to his time or was there a larger, far more significant meaning to his proclamation? The first question regarding the word *virgin* has never been settled to the satisfaction of some more liberal scholars. At the heart of the debate is the issue about the possible correct translation of the Hebrew word *almah*. This word has three possible translations: first, it can refer to a young woman. Second, it can refer to a young woman who is at an age where she can marry. Third, it can refer to a virgin. The traditional translation of the word *almah* has been "virgin," based upon the context and the nature of the prophecy of Isaiah. We do not know whether Ahaz would have requested this sign, but what is critical is that the sign God gave had to be unquestionable.

The *Septuagint*, which is the Greek translation of the "Hebrew Scriptures," translated these words as *virgin*. This is the word which is used in Matthew 1:23. We must consider that the great meaning of Isaiah's message was the sign of the Virgin Birth, pointing to the future coming of the Lord Jesus Christ.

The second question concerns the nature of the prophecy. We must understand that all prophetic preaching was first contextual. That is, the prophet preached to his generation and to the conditions of his day. The message of Isaiah was addressed to Ahaz and the people of Judah. The sign that God offered was specifically for him. We do not know who this young woman was and much time and effort has been wasted trying to figure out her identity.

However, there is a larger, weightier aspect to the prophecy which pointed beyond the time of Isaiah to another point in time. The words looked forward in time to an event that had eternal consequences.

B. An Unforeseen Development
   ### (Isaiah 7:15-17)

Butter and honey shall he eat, that he may know to refuse the evil, and choose the good. For before the child shall know to refuse the evil, and choose the good, the land that thou abhorrest shall be forsaken of both her kings. The Lord shall bring upon thee, and upon thy people, and upon thy father's house, days that have not come, from the day that Ephraim departed from Judah; even the king of Assyria.

The coming of Immanuel in the days of Isaiah came as a mixed bag of blessings and curses. On the one hand, the birth of the child would mean deliverance for Judah and at the same time his presence meant doom. The land which was under extreme military pressure was experiencing food shortages. The interpretation of the words "butter and honey" in verse 15 is very ambiguous and scholars have never agreed as to exactly what they meant. Some say they pointed to a time when there would be a lack of food in the land and they cite 7:21-22 as the foundation for this position. Others hold that the verses are a play on the words "land flowing with milk and honey." Therefore, the latter interpretation sees this as pointing to a time of plenty in the midst of military size because the population would have been greatly reduced by the conflict (see 7:1-6). Both interpretations are possible.

What is clear is that Isaiah saw a time when the two chief antagonists of Judah would be reduced to nothing (verse 16). The two kings would be dethroned and their kingdoms destroyed or conquered. Ahaz spent time worrying about the wrong enemy. Israel and Syria would both be swept up by the might of the Assyrians and it would not be long before their attention would turn to Judah as well. Isaiah prophesied that instead of peace coming, there would come a time unseen in the nation since the time that the ten tribes in the north split and formed their own kingdom under Jeroboam I (verse 17; see also 2 Kings 12:1ff.).

C. The Message Delivered
   ### (Luke 1:30-33)

And the angel said unto her, Fear not, Mary: for thou hast found favour with God. And, behold, thou shalt conceive in thy womb, and bring forth a son, and shalt call his name JESUS. He shall be great, and shall be called the Son of the Highest: and the Lord God shall give unto him the throne of his father David: And he shall reign over the house of Jacob for ever; and of his kingdom there shall be no end.

In the sixth month of Elizabeth's pregnancy the angel Gabriel was sent by God to deliver a very important message to a young woman named Mary (see Luke 1:26). He told Mary not to be afraid (Greek: *phobeo*—literally "to be struck with fear or amazement"). This was an obvious indication that Mary was completely startled and afraid by the sudden appearance of Gabriel. He repeated his earlier statement that Mary had found favor (Greek: *Charis*—literally "goodwill" or "loving-kindness," most commonly translated as "grace"). This favor was not from anything that Mary had done nor merited, nor did it have anything to do with her faith or piety (see Ephesians 2:8-10). God chose Mary based upon His own prerogatives and sovereign will and purpose (see 1 Corinthians 1:26-29).

In verse 31, we hear the message from God. In these words stands one of the central tenets of the Christian faith—the virgin birth of the Lord Jesus Christ. Mary would conceive and bear a Son, and His name would be Jesus (see Isaiah 7:14). Not only had Mary found favor, but God's favor had put her in an enviable and difficult position.

Given in verses 32-33 is a fivefold description of the Child that Mary would bear. First, He would be great (Greek: *megas*—literally "unsurpassing"). The greatness of Jesus exceeded the greatness of John the Baptist who would be great in the eyes of humankind (see Luke 1:15). Second, Jesus would be called the "Son of the Highest," which was a clear reference to God. Jesus was the Son of God before His coming into the world. He was in the very beginning with God (see John 1:1-3). Third, Jesus would receive the throne of His father, David. This is a statement that fulfilled the promise made to David in 2 Samuel 7:12-14. We refer to these words as the Davidic covenant. Fourth, He would reign over the house of Jacob. Fifth, there would be no end to His kingdom. Jesus would rule and reign forever (see Isaiah 9:7; Hebrews 1:3).

D. The Method Explained
(Luke 1:34-38)

Then said Mary unto the angel, How shall this be, seeing I know not a man? And the angel answered and said unto her, The Holy Ghost shall come upon thee, and the power of the Highest shall overshadow thee: therefore also that holy thing which shall be born of thee shall be called the Son of God. And, behold, thy cousin Elisabeth, she hath also conceived a son in her old age: and this is the sixth month with her, who was called barren. For with God nothing shall be impossible. And Mary said, Behold the handmaid of the Lord; be it unto me according to thy word. And the angel departed from her.

Baffled and startled by the news, Mary wanted to know how she could possibly be pregnant. She had never *known* a man. Gabriel responded that the power of the Holy Spirit would completely overshadow her and impregnate her womb; and to prove that this message was true, Gabriel announced to Mary that her elderly cousin Elizabeth was in the sixth month of her pregnancy. The woman who had been called *barren* (that is, unable to bear children) was expecting a child (see Luke 1:7).

In verse 37, further explanation of proof to Mary is offered regarding the truthfulness of Gabriel's announcement. Elizabeth was pregnant in her old age and Mary would conceive through miraculous means. Who else but God could perform such feats? Nothing is beyond the realm of possibility with God (see Matthew 19:26; Mark 10:27; Luke 18:27). Mary was convinced of the message and her mission and she submitted her life totally to God's will: "Be it unto me according to thy word." The lesson is clear—believers must learn to take God at His Word and trust Him even when the circumstances say something that is completely contrary to what we see (see Acts 27:21-25).

III. CONCLUDING REFLECTION

The Virgin Birth is the centerpiece of our belief regarding the sinlessness of Jesus Christ. In theological terms, we think of the Virgin Birth as foundational to our belief about the Incarnation. What does this mean? It means that when Jesus Christ came into the world in human flesh, He was at the same time both God and Man—fully divine and fully human at the same time (see John 1:14; 2 Corinthians 8:9; Philippians 2:5-11). The attestation of His humanness and divinity is present throughout the Gospels. The Virgin Birth then underscores the foundational belief that Jesus was fully human, tempted in all points as we are, yet without sin (see Hebrews 4:14-15). There are people in the world who would deny this miraculous event. If we deny the reality of this truth, we then deny everything in the Gospels and we are still in our sins.

We must not confuse the Virgin Birth with the Roman Catholic belief of the "Immaculate Conception." This is a belief that holds that Mary was born sinless and therefore that is the primary reason that she was selected to be the birth mother of the Lord Jesus Christ. This of course goes against every fundamental teaching of Scripture regarding the sinfulness of human beings (see Psalm 51:5; Isaiah 53; Romans 3:23). The birth of Jesus Christ reminds us that God was willing to enter the world of human brokenness and heal us of our sins.

The fact that God entered this world in physical form through His Son should calm every fear and doubt. Ahaz was afraid when Israel and Syria were plotting to bring his kingdom down. The prophet encouraged him to know that God had come to help him. The same God of Ahaz is still on the throne. No doubt there are situations in our lives which bewilder us, but the moment we remember that God is with us we must be courageous. Are you currently in any situation which defies your understanding? The presence of God permeates the earth. You are just one prayer away from victory.

PRAYER

Heavenly Father, we thank You for Your amazing grace and love that was manifested through Jesus Christ. We honor You and praise You for the greatness and the goodness of Your love. In Jesus' name we pray. Amen.

WORD POWER

Immanuel (Hebrew:`*Immanuw`el*)—this is a compound word. The first part (*Immanuw*) means "with us." The second part*(el)* means "God." When combined it means "God with us," or "united to us." This name describes God's manifested attributes. In the context where this name first appears, Ahaz was afraid of Syria and Israel, and the prophet told him, "God is with us." Therefore, if God is with us, why are we afraid? The fact that God is with us is the reason why we should not be afraid.

HOME DAILY BIBLE READINGS
(December 7–13, 2009)

Prophets Foreshadow Messiah's Birth

MONDAY, December 7: "A Ruler from Bethlehem" (Micah 5:1-5a)

TUESDAY, December 8: "I Sent You Prophets" (Matthew 23:29-39)

WEDNESDAY, December 9: "Preparing the Way" (Mark 1:1-8)

THURSDAY, December 10: "The Lord Is with You" (Luke 1:26-29)

FRIDAY, December 11: "What Prophets Desired to See" (Luke 10:21-24)

SATURDAY, December 12: "Prophets from of Old" (Luke 1:68-75)

SUNDAY, December 13: "The Promise Fulfilled" (Isaiah 7:13-17; Luke 1:30-38)

LESSON 3   December 20, 2009

EMMANUEL IS BORN

DEVOTIONAL READING: Galatians 4:1-7
PRINT PASSAGE: Matthew 1:18-25

BACKGROUND SCRIPTURE: Matthew 1:18-25
KEY VERSE: Matthew 1:21

Matthew 1:18-25—KJV

18 Now the birth of Jesus Christ was on this wise: When as his mother Mary was espoused to Joseph, before they came together, she was found with child of the Holy Ghost.

19 Then Joseph her husband, being a just man, and not willing to make her a publick example, was minded to put her away privily.

20 But while he thought on these things, behold, the angel of the Lord appeared unto him in a dream, saying, Joseph, thou son of David, fear not to take unto thee Mary thy wife: for that which is conceived in her is of the Holy Ghost.

21 And she shall bring forth a son, and thou shalt call his name JESUS: for he shall save his people from their sins.

22 Now all this was done, that it might be fulfilled which was spoken of the Lord by the prophet, saying,

23 Behold, a virgin shall be with child, and shall bring forth a son, and they shall call his name Emmanuel, which being interpreted is, God with us.

24 Then Joseph being raised from sleep did as the angel of the Lord had bidden him, and took unto him his wife:

25 And knew her not till she had brought forth her firstborn son: and he called his name JESUS.

Matthew 1:18-25—NRSV

18 Now the birth of Jesus the Messiah took place in this way. When his mother Mary had been engaged to Joseph, but before they lived together, she was found to be with child from the Holy Spirit.

19 Her husband Joseph, being a righteous man and unwilling to expose her to public disgrace, planned to dismiss her quietly.

20 But just when he had resolved to do this, an angel of the Lord appeared to him in a dream and said, "Joseph, son of David, do not be afraid to take Mary as your wife, for the child conceived in her is from the Holy Spirit.

21 She will bear a son, and you are to name him Jesus, for he will save his people from their sins."

22 All this took place to fulfill what had been spoken by the Lord through the prophet:

23 "Look, the virgin shall conceive and bear a son, and they shall name him Emmanuel," which means, "God is with us."

24 When Joseph awoke from sleep, he did as the angel of the Lord commanded him; he took her as his wife,

25 but had no marital relations with her until she had borne a son; and he named him Jesus.

BIBLE FACT

The birth of Jesus Christ displays the victory of God over Satan. In the Garden of Eden, Satan plotted against God by deceiving Adam and Eve—but God had a greater plan: to bring the right relationship of humankind back to Himself. No Christian should feel isolated because the Christmas season is a reminder of God's love. It is a season of breaking down isolation and drawing closer to God. Christians should go beyond themselves by displaying love in concrete ways to believers and unbelievers.

3 titles,
Savior — Messiah — Lord
Christ — anointed one — Yahweh

UNIFYING LESSON PRINCIPLE

People can feel all alone in their lives. Who can break down the walls that isolate us? Scripture proclaims that Jesus came to be God with us.

TOPICAL OUTLINE OF THE LESSON

I. Introduction
   A. Christmas
   B. Biblical Background

II. Exposition and Application of the Scripture
   A. The Miraculous Conception (Matthew 1:18-19)
   B. The Angelic Announcement (Matthew 1:20-21)
   C. The Prophetic Fulfillment (Matthew 1:22-23)
   D. The Willing Obedience of Joseph (Matthew 1:24-25)

III. Concluding Reflection

LESSON OBJECTIVES

Upon completion of this lesson, the students will know that:

1. Jesus came to redeem us from our estrangement from God;
2. The birth of Jesus is miraculous, and no other religion can claim that about their leader; and,
3. Joseph displayed uncommon courage and obedience.

POINTS TO BE EMPHASIZED

ADULT/YOUTH

Adult Topic: A Unique Birth
Youth Topic: Look Who Just Dropped In
Adult Key Verse: Matthew 1:21
Youth Key Verse: Matthew 1:24
Print Passage: Matthew 1:18-25

—The word *righteous* (verse 19) is theologically important in Matthew's gospel.
—Unlike Luke's gospel, the angel who spoke to Joseph remains unnamed.
—New Testament writers lift up Jesus Christ as He who fulfills many Old Testaments texts (such as Isaiah 7:14).
—Matthew placed Jesus within the fabric of God's whole salvation story.
—Matthew showed God as one who keeps His promise to redeem humanity from sin.
—The angel announced Jesus' birth as fulfillment of the Old Testament promise of Emmanuel.
—Jesus was born into humble surroundings but was as Matthew asserted, of royal lineage, the house of David.

CHILDREN

Children Topic: What a Special Day!
Key Verse: Matthew 1:21
Print Passage: Matthew 1:18-25

—The angel told Joseph about Mary's baby.
—Old Testament prophets foretold the virgin birth of *Emmanuel*, which means "God is with us."
—Joseph was obedient to God.
—Mary conceived God's Son by the power of the Holy Spirit.
—Jesus' birth fulfilled God's promise to be with us and save people from their sins.

I. INTRODUCTION

A. Christmas

This is the final Sunday in the Advent Season. In five days, the world will pause to celebrate Christmas. The celebration of Christmas is the most joyous time of the year. The music is special: "Hark the Herald Angels Sing," "Joy to the World," or the soft melody of "Silent Night." When these great Christmas hymns are sung, it gives us a sense of being among the shepherds and wise men that came from the east to bring gifts to the Christ child.

Christmas is excitement personified. It is "Jingle Bells," "Sleigh Ride," "tiny tots with their faces all aglow," and "folks dressed up like Eskimos." Christmas means mistletoe, plenty of good things to eat, crowded malls, and panicky husbands and boyfriends looking for that perfect gift. It is traffic jams, long lines to charge our gifts, and stockings all hung by the chimney with care. Yes—there is no season like the Christmas season.

Christmas is also the extension of love and compassion as those who are blessed give to those who are less fortunate. It is a time of goodwill and peace on earth. Yet in the midst of all of this celebration, there are many people who are draped in sadness—for this time of the year reminds them of some family tragedy, or some loneliness as they seek to find companionship for the holidays.

B. Biblical Background

The events surrounding the birth of Jesus Christ form the foundational cornerstone of the Christian faith. Matthew told the story of the birth of Jesus from Joseph's perspective. Luke told the story of the birth of Jesus from Mary's perspective. Both accounts are important because they give us the full picture of God's great act of salvation.

The miraculous birth of Jesus is referred to as the "Immaculate Conception." In theological terms, we think of the coming of Jesus as the Incarnation. Jesus Christ, the eternal God of creation, disrobed Himself of heavenly power, stepped out of eternity into time, and became like each of us. The Incarnation is an affirmation that the omnipotent God emptied Himself of His divinity and became a human being (see Philippians 2:5-11). It is an affirmation that God saw our pain and came into the world to lift us from our dungeons of despair. The Incarnation affirms both the humanity and divinity of Jesus. The word *incarnation* affirms that "God was in Christ, reconciling the world unto himself" (2 Corinthians 5:19). The Incarnation affirms (in Galatians 4:4) that "When the fulness of the time, was come, God sent forth his Son." The Incarnation affirms the truth of 2 Corinthians 8:9: "For ye know the grace of our Lord Jesus Christ, that, though he was rich, yet for your sakes he became poor, that ye through his poverty might be rich." The Incarnation is an affirmation that Jesus took upon Himself the form of man, humbled Himself, and became obedient unto death—even the death of the Cross. Christmas opened the door and set the stage for the fulfillment of the promise of God that went back to Genesis 3:15—that there would come one who would bruise the head of Satan.

II. EXPOSITION AND APPLICATION OF THE SCRIPTURE

A. The Miraculous Conception
(Matthew 1:18-19)

Now the birth of Jesus Christ was on this wise: When as his mother Mary was espoused to Joseph, before they came together, she was found with child of the Holy Ghost. Then Joseph her husband, being a just man, and not willing to make her a publick example, was minded to put her away privily.

Matthew followed the listing of the generations of Jesus with an account of the circumstances surrounding the birth (Greek: literally *genesis,* meaning "beginning") of Jesus Christ. Mary and Joseph were engaged to be married. In ancient Jewish culture, engagement amounted to a firm and complete commitment to marry. Usually, this arrangement would last for one year and at the end of the engagement the bride would go to her husband's home and the marriage would be consummated. According to Deuteronomy 22:23-24, Mary violated the Law and should have been put to death as an adulteress for violating the marriage vows. Matthew took great care to point out that this conception did not involve sexual intercourse, but was the result of the Holy Spirit. The full impact of the shame and humiliation that Joseph faced could not be captured by the brief words that Matthew used to tell the story.

In verse 19, we are informed that Joseph was a just and honorable man. This statement points to his standing before the Law. At this point, Mary was obviously showing signs of being pregnant or had told Joseph of the pregnancy. We are not told how he found out—only that he discovered that the woman he planned to spend his life with was pregnant and he was not the father. Joseph had two options before him. First, he could demand that Mary be brought to the gate of the city and be charged before the elders with violating her marriage vows. At that point she could be stoned for her transgression (see Deuteronomy 22:20-22). Second, he could do as he proposed in his heart; he could put her away privately without bringing public shame to Mary or her family, especially her father. The private act could be done in the presence of two or three witnesses, thereby being firmly established (see Deuteronomy 17:6).

B. The Angelic Announcement
(Matthew 1:20-21)

But while he thought on these things, behold, the angel of the Lord appeared unto him in a dream, saying, Joseph, thou son of David, fear not to take unto thee Mary thy wife: for that which is conceived in her is of the Holy Ghost. And she shall bring forth a son, and thou shalt call his name JESUS: for he shall save his people from their sins.

Once Joseph found out about Mary's pregnancy, he spent several days pondering the course of action to take. While he was thinking about what to do, the angel of the Lord appeared to him in a dream. It was not Gabriel or Michael, both of whom were and are archangels (see Daniel 8:15-26; 10:13;

Luke 1:26; Revelation 12:7-8). This is one of the myriad of angels that God has available at His disposal. The angel told Joseph that the child that Mary was carrying in her womb was not of human origin. He was conceived by the Holy Spirit.

Dreams are sometimes used as the medium through which God communicates to people (see Genesis 20:3, 6). Dr. Michael L. Wilkins remarked that "In the Old Testament, dreams were believed to come from natural (Ecclesiastes 5:3), divine (Genesis 28:12; Daniel 2:19), and evil (Deuteronomy 13:1-2; Jeremiah 23:32) sources. God used dreams to point to events that are currently happening, or they pointed to future events. In the birth narratives of Matthew's gospel, dreams played a very important role. First, to inform Joseph that God had chosen Mary. Second, the dream spoke peace to his heart and reassured him that he could take Mary to be his wife."

There are two statements that connected Joseph to the fulfillment of prophecy regarding the Messiah: first, the angel called him a son of David; this clearly was an allusion to the promise that God had made to David in Abraham (see Genesis 12:1-3; 2 Samuel 7:12-14; also compare to Matthew 1:1, 17). David was Israel's most revered king. He was the standard by which all of the other kings of Judah and Israel were measured.

When Mary's child was born, Joseph was to name Him Jesus because He would save His people from their sins. The name *Jesus* means "Jehovah is salvation" (see Psalm 130:7-8; Isaiah 12:1-2; 45:21-22; Jeremiah 23:6; 33:16; Zechariah 9:9; John 1:29). The name *Jesus* is the same name for "Joshua" in the Old Testament. Frederick Brunner noted that in Jesus' name, "the church has believed

we possess the two deepest definitions of the two major Christological truths: (1) *who* Jesus essentially is, and (2) *what* Jesus existentially *does*." Here in one full sweep, Matthew stated what had become an essential truth of the Christian faith: Jesus was both fully God and fully man. He had come to fulfill a divine mission and purpose, which was to save not just a people, but specifically *His* people, the chosen people—those who were the seed of Abraham and the offspring of David. Jesus saves from sins (see Ephesians 1:7; 1 Timothy 1:15; Revelation 1:5).

C. The Prophetic Fulfillment (Matthew 1:22-23)

Now all this was done, that it might be fulfilled which was spoken of the Lord by the prophet, saying, Behold, a virgin shall be with child, and shall bring forth a son, and they shall call his name Emmanuel, which being interpreted is, God with us.

Everything told to Mary and Joseph was in fulfillment of the words of prophecy (see Isaiah 7:12-14; 9:6-7). There are a number of prophecies in the Old Testament regarding the Messiah. There are more in the book of Isaiah than any other Old Testament book. The words that Matthew recorded were spoken by the Lord and the prophet. The specific words referred to are found in Isaiah 7:14 (see the previous lesson for more discussion about these words).

Jesus' birth was unlike any other birth. Ancient history is full of the sagas of heroes who were born through some form of miraculous conception. Caesar claimed such a birth. Unlike Jesus, Caesar never claimed divine sonship nor did he claim to be a global Savior. The central affirmation of the New Testament witness is that Jesus was born of a virgin. For nearly two thousand years men and women have debated the historicity of the Virgin Birth. The natural mind cannot comprehend such a stupendous feat (see 1 Corinthians 2:14-16). Yet, the God who created the universe out of nothing can certainly cause birth without a man's input. The Virgin Birth points to the absolute uniqueness of Jesus Christ. "His conception, ministry, and resurrection are nothing short of declarations of His divine nature, which impels us to regard His claims upon our lives as second to none." Without the Virgin Birth there could never be the possibility of a sinless Savior who took upon Himself our sins and became what sin was for us (see 2 Corinthians 5:21; Hebrews 4:15). He knew no sin, yet He understood the heaviness of the weight of the world's sin.

D. The Willing Obedience of Joseph (Matthew 1:24-25)

Then Joseph being raised from sleep did as the angel of the Lord had bidden him, and took unto him his wife: And knew her not till she had brought forth her firstborn son: and he called his name JESUS.

Joseph awoke from his sleep and followed the commands of the angel exactly as they were given. Throughout this birth narrative Matthew attributed a very special place to Joseph. He was not just the betrothed husband of Mary; he was an honorable man, righteous and committed to obeying God. Joseph was the perfect earthly father for Jesus. Joseph took Mary to be his wife and she remained a virgin throughout the pregnancy. We have no way of knowing how Joseph reacted, what he thought about the events that had occurred in his life, or

his feelings about having to be patient during the period of Mary's pregnancy. Anything that is said is speculative guessing. We do know that Joseph obeyed God's command to keep Mary pure, and when the child was born, Joseph named Him Jesus.

Joseph has remained a mystery to us. We know nothing else about him. He and Mary eventually had other children (see Matthew 12:46; 13:55-56; Mark 6:3). We know that Joseph was a man whose heart was filled with compassion and concern, particularly when it came to his treatment of Mary. Therefore, we can draw several conclusions from the actions of Joseph that will be helpful to any inquiring mind today.

First, he loved his wife dearly. He would not do anything to hurt, harm, or humiliate her or her family. Second, he was a godly man. He was spiritually sensitive to the voice of the Holy Spirit. God spoke and he listened. Third, he was committed to serving God. Joseph never questioned what God was doing; he simply followed the commands as they were given to him. Is it any wonder that God chose Joseph to be the earthly father for His Son?

III. CONCLUDING REFLECTION

In Mary and Joseph, we see the earliest signs of discipleship. God asked both of them to do something that went against their own culture, values, and traditions. He called upon them to accept a new life together that would put them both at risk of being talked about and publicly humiliated. Yet, rather than turn away, they both readily accepted the assignment to serve God by becoming the birth mother and earthly father of the Son of God. Mary and Joseph can teach us lessons about radical obedience to God under any and all circumstances.

Can you remember the times in your life when God called upon you to do something or go somewhere that was outside of the norm? In this instance, to hear and obey puts us in the same category as the great saints of old: even Mary and Joseph. And lest we forget, Christmas is about Christ and it is from that perspective that we must understand the season. In the account of Matthew's birth narrative, the birth of Jesus was the long-awaited and anticipated fulfillment of the messianic ... in ... of ... nd ... m ... he ... he ... nt ... ph ... on:

"She shall bring forth a son, and thou shalt call his name JESUS: for he shall save His people from their sins" (verse 21). Here we see the purpose of the life and ministry of Jesus Christ, which was salvation and redemption. Jesus did not come nearly two thousand years ago so that there would be carols to sing and gifts to give, but that the world through Him might be saved.

Jesus means "the Lord saves." If it were not for the coming of Jesus to the world we would still be wretched and heading to hell. No matter how good we may be, we are incapable of eliminating the sinful nature which resides in each of us. As you celebrate this Christmas, make Jesus the utmost center of your activities.

PRAYER

Lord, we are grateful for yet another year. As we celebrate this Christmas, help us to make You the desire of our hearts. In Jesus' name we pray. Amen.

which precedes *save* makes it more emphatic. He ...lames were significant in biblical times. In Africa ...mes signify the hope of the parent. Jesus is priest, ...ums up His mission in life in one word.

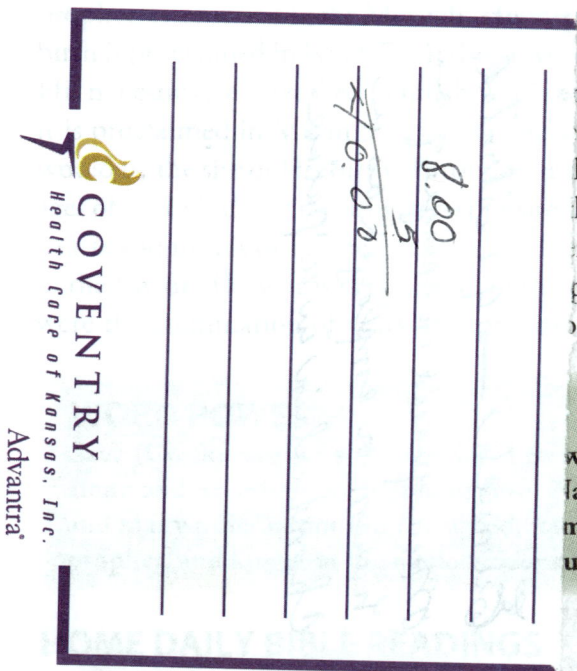

Emmanuel Is Born
MONDAY, December 14: "The Fullness of Time" (Galatians 4:1-7)
TUESDAY, December 15: "God with Me Wherever I Go" (Genesis 35:1-4)
WEDNESDAY, December 16: "May God Not Leave Us" (1 Kings 8:54-61)
THURSDAY, December 17: "God Ahead of Us" (2 Chronicles 13:10-15)
FRIDAY, December 18: "A Greater One with Us" (2 Chronicles 32:1-8)
SATURDAY, December 19: "God Is with Us" (Isaiah 8:5-10)
SUNDAY, December 20: "Jesus, Emmanuel" (Matthew 1:18-25)

LESSON 4   December 27, 2009

MAGI CONFIRM MESSIAH'S BIRTH

DEVOTIONAL READING: **Proverbs 9:7-12**
PRINT PASSAGE: **Matthew 2:7-9, 16-23**

BACKGROUND SCRIPTURE: **Matthew 2**
KEY VERSE: **Matthew 2:10**

Matthew 2:7-9, 16-23—KJV

7 Then Herod, when he had privily called the wise men, enquired of them diligently what time the star appeared.

8 And he sent them to Bethlehem, and said, Go and search diligently for the young child; and when ye have found him, bring me word again, that I may come and worship him also.

9 When they had heard the king, they departed; and, lo, the star, which they saw in the east, went before them, till it came and stood over where the young child was.

…..

16 Then Herod, when he saw that he was mocked of the wise men, was exceeding wroth, and sent forth, and slew all the children that were in Bethlehem, and in all the coasts thereof, from two years old and under, according to the time which he had diligently enquired of the wise men.

17 Then was fulfilled that which was spoken by Jeremy the prophet, saying,

18 In Rama was there a voice heard, lamentation, and weeping, and great mourning, Rachel weeping for her children, and would not be comforted, because they are not.

19 But when Herod was dead, behold, an angel of the Lord appeareth in a dream to Joseph in Egypt,

20 Saying, Arise, and take the young child and his mother, and go into the land of Israel: for they are dead which sought the young child's life.

21 And he arose, and took the young child and his mother, and came into the land of Israel.

22 But when he heard that Archelaus did reign in Judaea in the room of his father Herod, he was afraid to go thither: notwithstanding, being warned of God in a dream, he turned aside into the parts of Galilee:

23 And he came and dwelt in a city called Nazareth: that it might be fulfilled which was spoken by the prophets, He shall be called a Nazarene.

Matthew 2:7-9, 16-23—NRSV

7 Then Herod secretly called for the wise men and learned from them the exact time when the star had appeared.

8 Then he sent them to Bethlehem, saying, "Go and search diligently for the child; and when you have found him, bring me word so that I may also go and pay him homage."

9 When they had heard the king, they set out; and there, ahead of them, went the star that they had seen at its rising, until it stopped over the place where the child was.

…..

16 When Herod saw that he had been tricked by the wise men, he was infuriated, and he sent and killed all the children in and around Bethlehem who were two years old or under, according to the time that he had learned from the wise men.

17 Then was fulfilled what had been spoken through the prophet Jeremiah:

18 "A voice was heard in Ramah, wailing and loud lamentation, Rachel weeping for her children; she refused to be consoled, because they are no more."

19 When Herod died, an angel of the Lord suddenly appeared in a dream to Joseph in Egypt and said,

20 "Get up, take the child and his mother, and go to the land of Israel, for those who were seeking the child's life are dead."

21 Then Joseph got up, took the child and his mother, and went to the land of Israel.

22 But when he heard that Archelaus was ruling over Judea in place of his father Herod, he was afraid to go there. And after being warned in a dream, he went away to the district of Galilee.

23 There he made his home in a town called Nazareth, so that what had been spoken through the prophets might be fulfilled, "He will be called a Nazorean."

TOPICAL OUTLINE OF THE LESSON

I. Introduction
   A. Historical Data of Jesus' Birth
   B. Biblical Background

II. Exposition and Application of the Scripture
   A. Herod, the Wise Men, and Divine Guidance (Matthew 2:7-9)
   B. The Slaughter of the Children (Matthew 2:16-18)
   C. The Warning from the Lord (Matthew 2:19-21)
   D. The Returning to Nazareth (Matthew 2:22-23)

III. Concluding Reflection

LESSON OBJECTIVES

Upon completion of this lesson, the students will know about:

1. The hidden ambition of Herod the king;
2. How God, through a peculiar star, guided the wise men;
3. The foolishness of Herod for committing a horrendous crime; and,
4. The homecoming of Jesus through divine guidance.

POINTS TO BE EMPHASIZED

ADULT/YOUTH

Adult Topic: Searching for a Child

Youth Topic: Kings at the Front Door

Adult/Youth Key Verse: Matthew 2:10

Print Passage: Matthew 2:7-9, 16-23

—Rama (verse 18) was a few miles north of Jerusalem, the hometown of Elkanah—father of Samuel.

—Verse 20 contains the only New Testament use of the phrase "land of Israel."

—Matthew is the only gospel to include the story of the magi who are Gentiles—that is, not Jews.

—The magi, or wise men, were aware of the divine activity of God in the birth of Jesus.

—God directed the wise men to Jesus, where they worshiped and brought gifts to Him.

—God spoke to the wise men in a dream to go home another way.

CHILDREN

Children Topic: Worship the King!

Key Verse: Matthew 2:11

Print Passage: Matthew 2:1-12

—The magi searched for and found Jesus by following the star.

—The magi found that Jesus was worth seeking.

—When the magi found Jesus, they worshiped Him and gave Him gifts.

—The wise men inquired of King Herod where the King of the Jews had been born.

I. INTRODUCTION

A. Historical Data of Jesus' Birth

Only Matthew and Luke included the birth narratives of Jesus Christ. Mark and John chose not to include birth narratives as part of their gospels. According to the biblical accounts of the birth of Jesus, He was born prior to the death of Herod the Great, which occurred sometime during 4 BC. Therefore, Jesus could not have been born after 4 BC. It is stated in Matthew 2:1-2 (NASB): "After Jesus was born in Bethlehem of Judea in the days of Herod the king, magi from the east arrived in Jerusalem, saying, 'Where is He who has been born King of the Jews? For we saw His star in the east and have come to worship Him.'"

Luke's historical time marker for the birth of Jesus was a census that was connected to Quirinius (sometimes spelled as Cyrenius), who was governor of Syria at the time. The census was decreed by Caesar Augustus and was imposed upon all of those subject to Roman rule. The exact date of the census has been debated and cannot be determined with certainty.

What can be stated with certainty is that both Jesus and John the Baptist were born during the latter days of Herod's reign. The slaughter by Herod of innocent baby boys, two years of age and younger, was in keeping with his murderous, paranoid personality and his insecurity surrounding his throne.

There were originally two dates used to celebrate the birth of Jesus. In the Eastern Church the date was January 6, which has come to be associated with the celebration of the Epiphany. In the Western church, the date was December 25. The Christian church has, since the fourth century, celebrated December 25 as the birthday of Jesus Christ. The celebration originally began as a Nativity festival in the Western church. Williston Walker writes of the church's celebration of Christmas: "The date was partly determined by the idea that the birth of the world occurred on the vernal equinox (March 25) and correspondingly its new birth in the Saviour would have been at the same moment. This was understood as the conception by the Virgin, and hence the actual birth would be nine months later, December 25."

This is a traditional date and has nothing to do with the actual date of Jesus' birth. We simply do not know for sure, but that in no way lessens the significance of the celebration of the birth of Jesus Christ on December 25 each year.

B. Biblical Background

Herod the Great was the founder and first king of the Herodian Dynasty and was king of all Israel from 37–4 BC. Herod was without a doubt the greatest of the Herodian kings. His kingdom rivaled David's and Solomon's in size, grandeur, and wealth. His success can be attributed to his diplomatic and uncanny ability to get along with Roman rulers, regardless of who they were at the time. He was an Edomite from Edom; they were the descendants of Esau. His Jewish heritage was always the subject of debate among Jews, who regarded him with suspicion. Moshe Pearlman states, "There had been constant enmity between the Jews and Edomites and at the end of the second century BCE, Idumea had been conquered by the Jewish state and became part of Judea." Years later Herod's grandfather, Antipater I, who converted to Judaism, was appointed governor of the Idumean province.

He was followed by his son Antipater II and finally, Herod succeeded him, becoming the first Herodian king of Judea.

Herod was a man of many personalities. He was gracious, yet harsh, ruthless, insecure, scheming, cunning, and, above all, a master politician. All of these traits can be seen in this week's lesson. One of the eternal truths from today's lesson is the indestructibility of the purpose of God. Herod believed that by killing all of the males who were two years of age and younger, he would stop the ascendancy of Jesus Christ to be King of Kings and Lord of Lords. His efforts failed. This is a powerful lesson for all who labor in the vineyard that one's labor is never in vain.

II. EXPOSITION AND APPLICATION OF THE SCRIPTURE

A. Herod, the Wise Men, and Divine Guidance (Matthew 2:7-9)

Then Herod, when he had privily called the wise men, enquired of them diligently what time the star appeared. And he sent them to Bethlehem, and said, Go and search diligently for the young child; and when ye have found him, bring me word again, that I may come and worship him also. When they had heard the king, they departed; and, lo, the star, which they saw in the east, went before them, till it came and stood over where the young child was.

The arrival of the wise men from the east created a lot of talk in Jerusalem. They had come in search of the one who had been born King of the Jews (see Matthew 2:2). Their question aroused a great deal of anxiety and tension in the king's court and throughout the city (verse 3). The citizens of Jerusalem were all too familiar with Herod's ruthless and callous reputation and his lack of tolerance for anyone who had any claim to his throne. The Jewish religious leaders gave him the prophecies concerning where the Christ Child would be born. Upon finding out the news, Herod held a private meeting with the wise men to build a relationship and hopefully get them to confide in him. His intentions were completely false. He wanted to know the exact day and time that the star had appeared (verse 2). Information regarding the star would enable Herod to determine the age of the child. He already knew where the child would be born (verses 5-6). We are not privileged to have information regarding the conversation between Herod and the wise men.

Herod commissioned the wise men to go and search diligently for the child. The language suggests that he wanted to find the exact place so that there would be no mistake about the identity of the child. His request to the wise men was spoken with imperative authority: "Bring me word again, that I may come and worship him also" (see verse 8). Herod had no intention of worshiping Jesus. But the wise men had no way of knowing that Herod was a fraud.

After their meeting with Herod, the wise men proceeded to Bethlehem, which is six miles south of Jerusalem. As they traveled, the star that they had seen in the east reappeared. There has been a lot of discussion and debate among scholars about the star in this verse. Michael J. Wilkins offers the suggestion that the supernatural phenomenon of the "star" may have actually been an angel sent to announce the birth of the Messiah, and also to guide them to the place where Jesus was born and living. This is a possibility, given the role that angels played in the lives of God's people (see Exodus 23:20; Job 38:7; Daniel 8:10; Revelation 1:16, 20; 2:1; 3:1). Whatever the case may have been, the fact is that the wise men were guided by divine power.

B. The Slaughter of the Children
(Matthew 2:16-18)

Then Herod, when he saw that he was mocked of the wise men, was exceeding wroth, and sent forth, and slew all the children that were in Bethlehem, and in all the coasts thereof, from two years old and under, according to the time which he had diligently enquired of the wise men. Then was fulfilled that which was spoken by Jeremy the prophet, saying, In Rama was there a voice heard, lamentation, and weeping, and great mourning, Rachel weeping for her children, and would not be comforted, because they are not.

God warned the wise men in a dream that Herod's intentions were corrupt and false. Rather than report back to Herod, they went back to Persia via another route. We are not told the length of time Herod had waited for the report from the wise men. At some point he realized that they were not coming back. How he came to this conclusion is not known. He may have sent out an envoy to find the entourage of the wise men who could not hide in a small town such as Bethlehem. The one who had built his legacy upon deception got a taste of his own medicine. His plan backfired.

He was exceedingly mad to the extent that he lost complete control. There was but one course of action open to him: to kill every male child born during the time frame mentioned by the wise men. Remember, the events covered in this part of the birth narrative did not take place on the night that Jesus was born. He was probably a few months to maybe even a year or more old at the time. Herod sent out his soldiers with specific instructions to kill every male child in Bethlehem that was two years old and younger. Not only were they to kill all of the male children in Bethlehem, but also those who lived within local proximity of the town. Matthew stated that these events were the fulfillment of Jeremiah 31:15 that foretold of the slaughter of the innocents. These events are another example of Herod's insecurity and hardheartedness.

C. The Warning from the Lord
(Matthew 2:19-21)

But when Herod was dead, behold, an angel of the Lord appeareth in a dream to Joseph in Egypt, Saying, Arise, and take the young child and his mother, and go into the land of Israel: for they are dead which sought the young child's life. And he arose, and took the young child and his mother, and came into the land of Israel.

Joseph and Mary departed from Bethlehem shortly after the wise men left to return to their own country. We are told that God warned Joseph in a dream of the plot of Herod, and he was to arise and go to Egypt and remain there until he was told it was safe to return (see Matthew 2:7, 13-15). We are not told the length of time that the family spent in Egypt. It may have been a year or as little as a few months. This is the fourth time that an angel of the Lord appeared to Joseph in a dream (see Matthew 1:20; 2:13, 19, 22). The ones who had sought to kill Jesus were dead. However long it was, they stayed until Herod was dead. He died sometime during 4 BCE. The use of the plural designated not only Herod in the plot to kill Jesus, but also the Jewish religious leaders. Joseph was obedient to the voice of God. He took Mary and Jesus and they returned to the "land of Israel."

D. The Returning to Nazareth
(Matthew 2:22-23)

But when he heard that Archelaus did reign in Judaea in the room of his father Herod, he was afraid to go thither: notwithstanding, being warned of God in a dream, he turned aside into the parts of Galilee: And he came and dwelt in a city called Nazareth: that it might be fulfilled which was spoken by the prophets, He shall be called a Nazarene.

Nazareth was the hometown of Jesus. His living in Nazareth was in fulfillment of a prophecy (see Isaiah 11:1). Nazareth is significant in Christian tradition for several reasons. Christian tradition holds that the announcement of the birth of Christ was made to Mary in Nazareth. During the sixth month of Elizabeth's pregnancy with John, the angel Gabriel was sent by God to a city in Galilee named Nazareth (see Luke 1:26). The angel of the Lord announced to Mary that God had highly favored her and that in her womb would be a child who would be called the Son of the Most High.

Jesus was reared and spent the early years of His life in Nazareth. When Joseph and Mary returned from Egypt, they settled in Nazareth (see Matthew 2:19-23).

The town of Nazareth is located in lower Galilee about seventy miles north of Jerusalem. The small town sat on a plateau that sits about thirteen hundred feet above sea level. Nazareth is located in the hills that form the northern boundary of the Valley of Jezreel. It is about four miles southeast of Sepphoris, the city Herod Antipas used as his capital before moving it to Tiberius. Nazareth was such an insignificant place that one of Jesus' own disciples, Nathanael, remarked, "Can anything good come out of Nazareth?" (John 1:46, NKJV).

III. CONCLUDING REFLECTION

The birth narratives of Jesus make for excellent drama. They tell us a story that is full of intrigue with a plot that has several twists and turns. For Christians, the story of the miraculous conception and the events surrounding the birth of Jesus Christ are at the heart of our faith. In this lesson, we learn something of the universal appeal of Jesus. The wise men were the most unlikely people to come searching for Jesus and to be among His first worshipers. Did their worship and commitment to find Jesus look forward to the time when the Gospel message would go into the entire world (see Matthew 28:19-20)? We are called to be disciples of the Lord Jesus Christ. Our commitment to serving Him can be no less than the commitment of the wise men to find Him.

A second lesson we learn from this story is about radical obedience. Joseph had every right and reason to divorce Mary. But, each time and at each major turn the angel of the Lord was there to give guidance and direction regarding the course of action he was to pursue. Joseph did exactly as the angel of the Lord instructed, without question and without wavering. When we are obedient to the heavenly commands, God will guide and direct our footsteps as we achieve His purposes in the world.

Finally, this lesson points to the sovereignty of God. It also depicts His mighty power to achieve His purposes in the world. Herod was an unwilling participant in this divine drama. God's plan cannot be overcome by human devices and strategies. He will always accomplish that which He sets out to do. These should be very powerful words of encouragement for those who work in ministry.

PRAYER

Our Father, we are grateful to You for sending us our Savior. Our lives have been changed. We are eternally saved in You. As we rejoice, help us to share this joy with the unconverted souls, so that they too can join us. In Jesus' name we pray. Amen.

WORD POWER

Rejoice (Greek: *chairo* [ka-i-ro]) —means "to be cheerful, i.e. calmly happy, or well off, or pleasantly happy or surprisingly happy." The wise men were following divine guidance (the star). They did not disobey the instruction given by the angel. They went with joy and were pleasantly surprised. We are the objects of the Good News. The rejoicing should let others know about the saving knowledge of Christ.

HOME DAILY BIBLE READINGS
(December 21–27, 2009)

Magi Confirm Messiah's Birth

MONDAY, December 21: "The Beginning of Wisdom" (Proverbs 9:7-12)

TUESDAY, December 22: "Give Me Wisdom" (2 Chronicles 1:7-12)

WEDNESDAY, December 23: "Gaining a Wise Heart" (Psalm 90:11-17)

THURSDAY, December 24: "Those Who Find Wisdom" (Proverbs 3:13-23)

FRIDAY, December 25: "Where Is the Child?" (Matthew 2:1-6)

SATURDAY, December 26: "Overwhelmed with Joy" (Matthew 2:10-15)

SUNDAY, December 27: "Finding and Protecting Jesus" (Matthew 2:7-9, 16-23)

LESSON 5   January 3, 2010

PROCLAIMED IN BAPTISM

DEVOTIONAL READING: Acts 8:26-38
PRINT PASSAGE: Matthew 3:1-6, 11-17

BACKGROUND SCRIPTURE: Matthew 3
KEY VERSE: Matthew 3:17

Matthew 3:1-6, 11-17—KJV

IN THOSE days came John the Baptist, preaching in the wilderness of Judaea,

2 And saying, Repent ye: for the kingdom of heaven is at hand.

3 For this is he that was spoken of by the prophet Esaias, saying, The voice of one crying in the wilderness, Prepare ye the way of the Lord, make his paths straight.

4 And the same John had his raiment of camel's hair, and a leathern girdle about his loins; and his meat was locusts and wild honey.

5 Then went out to him Jerusalem, and all Judaea, and all the region round about Jordan,

6 And were baptized of him in Jordan, confessing their sins.

…..

11 I indeed baptize you with water unto repentance: but he that cometh after me is mightier than I, whose shoes I am not worthy to bear: he shall baptize you with the Holy Ghost, and with fire:

12 Whose fan is in his hand, and he will throughly purge his floor, and gather his wheat into the garner; but he will burn up the chaff with unquenchable fire.

13 Then cometh Jesus from Galilee to Jordan unto John, to be baptized of him.

14 But John forbad him, saying, I have need to be baptized of thee, and comest thou to me?

15 And Jesus answering said unto him, Suffer it to be so now: for thus it becometh us to fulfil all righteousness. Then he suffered him.

16 And Jesus, when he was baptized, went up straightway out of the water: and, lo, the heavens were opened unto him, and he saw the Spirit of God descending like a dove, and lighting upon him:

17 And lo a voice from heaven, saying, This is my beloved Son, in whom I am well pleased.

Matthew 3:1-6, 11-17—NRSV

IN THOSE days John the Baptist appeared in the wilderness of Judea, proclaiming,

2 "Repent, for the kingdom of heaven has come near."

3 This is the one of whom the prophet Isaiah spoke when he said, "The voice of one crying out in the wilderness: 'Prepare the way of the Lord, make his paths straight.'"

4 Now John wore clothing of camel's hair with a leather belt around his waist, and his food was locusts and wild honey.

5 Then the people of Jerusalem and all Judea were going out to him, and all the region along the Jordan,

6 and they were baptized by him in the river Jordan, confessing their sins.

…..

11 "I baptize you with water for repentance, but one who is more powerful than I is coming after me; I am not worthy to carry his sandals. He will baptize you with the Holy Spirit and fire.

12 His winnowing fork is in his hand, and he will clear his threshing floor and will gather his wheat into the granary; but the chaff he will burn with unquenchable fire."

13 Then Jesus came from Galilee to John at the Jordan, to be baptized by him.

14 John would have prevented him, saying, "I need to be baptized by you, and do you come to me?"

15 But Jesus answered him, "Let it be so now; for it is proper for us in this way to fulfill all righteousness." Then he consented.

16 And when Jesus had been baptized, just as he came up from the water, suddenly the heavens were opened to him and he saw the Spirit of God descending like a dove and alighting on him.

17 And a voice from heaven said, "This is my Son, the Beloved, with whom I am well pleased."

TOPICAL OUTLINE OF THE LESSON

I. Introduction
A. John the Baptist: A Humble Prophet
B. Biblical Background

II. Exposition and Application of the Scripture
A. John Prepares the Way (Matthew 3:1-6)
B. John Testifies to the Power of Jesus (Matthew 3:11-12)
C. Jesus' Baptism and Heavenly Attestation (Matthew 3:13-17)

III. Concluding Reflection

LESSON OBJECTIVES

Upon completion of this lesson, the students will:

1. Learn to be dedicated to God's service;
2. Learn how to testify for Jesus with integrity; and,
3. Know that the power of ministry comes when they recognize their limitations.

POINTS TO BE EMPHASIZED

ADULT/YOUTH

Adult Topic: Declaring Identity
Youth Topic: Splitting the Heavens
Adult/Youth Key Verse: Matthew 3:17
Print Passage: Matthew 3:1-6, 11-17

—Matthew quoted Isaiah 40:3 to show Jesus as the fulfillment of the messianic hope.
—John's message, "Repent," and the people's response, "confessing their sins," demonstrated the life change expected of those who were baptized.
—While John baptized with water, he recognized that Jesus would perform a baptism of the Holy Spirit and judgment.
—The voice from heaven gave evidence that Jesus' actions were pleasing to His heavenly Father (see also Psalm 2:7).
—Jesus came to John to be baptized, yet John felt the need to be baptized by Jesus.
—Jesus' baptism, a public way of identifying with a certain way of living, was the first public declaration of His sonship.
—Jesus accepted that He was the fulfillment of the Jewish faith and identified with it as the way God had chosen for Him to live.

CHILDREN

Children Topic: Taking on the Task
Key Verse: Matthew 3:17
Print Passage: Matthew 3:1-6, 13-17

—Baptism was important to Jesus.
—Jesus showed humility and obedience to God when He came to John for baptism.
—John recognized his unworthiness before Jesus.
—The voice from heaven confirmed Jesus as God's Son.

I. INTRODUCTION

A. John the Baptist: A Humble Prophet

John the Baptist appeared in first-century Judea as a towering figure. He is one of the few New Testament personalities who were so prominent that he appears in non-biblical writings or "extra-biblical writings." Indeed, prior to the start of the ministry of Jesus, John the Baptist was probably the most influential religious personality in Israel. He was the son of a priestly family. His mother Elizabeth was the relative of Mary, the mother of Jesus. His father Zechariah was from the lineage of Aaron (see Luke 1:5-25, 57-80). It was foretold that he would live a hermitic life as a Nazarite (see Luke 1:15; compare it with Numbers 6:13). Jewish historian Josephus recorded that John was so popular that even Herod Antipas feared him and thought that John might one day lead a rebellion against him. John was such a popular preacher that men and women would go out into the wilderness of Judea to hear him preach and to be baptized by him. John's ministry was carried on in an area near the Jordan River. Some scholars believed that the location of John's activities was north of the Dead Sea and east of Qumran—the site where the Dead Sea scrolls were found and where there was a community of Essenes.

John's ministry marked the end of an era of preparation and the beginning of God's decisive entrance into human history in the person of His Son Jesus Christ. John's baptism was in preparation for the greater baptism that would come in Jesus Christ. John's baptism symbolized cleansing from all sin; it was preparation for a deeper cleansing of the spirit from all unrighteousness and rebellion against God. John's baptism was preparation for the Messiah.

B. Biblical Background

Each of the Gospels is an attestation to the magnetic persona and preaching power of John the Baptist. In the days immediately preceding the ministry of Jesus Christ, John the Baptist was the most prominent religious person in Israel for three reasons.

First, he was highly regarded and respected among the people of his day. Josephus wrote glowingly of him and kings feared his presence. He was not just another preacher in Judea; rather, he had been specifically chosen, anointed, and set apart by God from his mother's womb to be the forerunner for the coming Messiah.

Second, God used John's preaching to specifically set the stage for the coming of Jesus. His preaching and summons to repentance aroused a deep yearning in the hearts of men and women for God. Revival swept the land, and people flocked to the place where John was preaching and baptizing. Remember, Jews did not practice baptism prior to John's ministry. Jews practiced ritual bathing—which was a custom that went back to the time of the Exodus.

Third, John's ministry marked the end of an era of preparation and the beginning of God's decisive entrance into human history in the person of His Son Jesus Christ. John's ministry was the old thing passing away and Jesus represented "all things becoming new."

II. EXPOSITION AND APPLICATION OF THE SCRIPTURE

A. John Prepares the Way
(Matthew 3:1-6)

IN THOSE days came John the Baptist, preaching in the wilderness of Judaea, And saying, Repent ye: for the kingdom of heaven is at hand. For this is he that was spoken of by the prophet Esaias, saying, The voice of one crying in the wilderness, Prepare ye the way of the Lord, make his paths straight. And the same John had his raiment of camel's hair, and a leathern girdle about his loins; and his meat was locusts and wild honey. Then went out to him Jerusalem, and all Judaea, and all the region round about Jordan, And were baptized of him in Jordan, confessing their sins.

John the Baptist was the son of a Jewish priest named Zechariah and his wife Elizabeth. In Luke 1:36, we are told that Elizabeth was the relative of Mary, the birth mother of Jesus. The passage contains several important details about the ministry of John. First, his ministry consisted of preaching repentance in preparation for the coming Messiah. Second, John preached that it was time for the Jewish people to change directions. Third, John preached that the kingdom of heaven was near. This did not refer to an earthly location but to the coming of God's rule upon the earth. There is no difference between the phrases "Kingdom of God" and "Kingdom of Heaven"; they both refer to the same thing—God's rule on the earth and in the hearts and lives of His people.

In Isaiah 40:3, the prophet foretold of John's coming over five hundred years before his birth. John's task was to prepare the nation of Israel for the coming of God's anointed Messiah. He was a powerful voice crying in the wilderness to "prepare the way of the Lord." God designed John's preaching—which conjured a desire in people's hearts for God—to set the stage for the coming of Jesus. Jews did not practice baptism prior to John's ministry, but practiced ritual bathing—which involved physically washing with water as a sign of consecration and spiritual cleansing. Baptizing was something altogether different and new in the land.

John lived a simple life which was evidenced by his clothing and diet. He wore garments made of camel's hair with a leather belt around his waist. His diet consisted largely of locusts and wild honey. In verses 5 and 6, we are given some indication of the impact of John's ministry. People came from all over the Jordan Valley, which geographically extends north nearly sixty miles to the Sea of Galilee. Further, John's influence reached into the major metropolis of Jerusalem which was in Judea and was located about twenty miles to the west of the Jordan River Valley. People went to see this strange man whose preaching attracted men and women from across the social and economic spectrum. Many people confessed their sins and were baptized by John in the Jordan River. God used John to prepare the hearts and minds of the people to receive the message of Jesus.

B. John Testifies to the Power of Jesus (Matthew 3:11-12)

I indeed baptize you with water unto repentance: but he that cometh after me is mightier than I, whose shoes I am not worthy to bear: he shall baptize you with the Holy Ghost, and with fire: Whose fan is in his hand, and he will throughly purge his floor, and gather his wheat into the garner; but he will burn up the chaff with unquenchable fire.

Christian discipleship begins with the act of baptism. Once we take the initial step to start out as a disciple of the Lord Jesus Christ, we then move toward total consecration to His service. Service is what we are called to do. Jesus models for us this act of consecration (or being set apart) for service. Jesus did not need to be sanctified, for He was already spotless and sinless. He needed no inner cleansing; He modeled what we must do. John baptized with water for repentance, but Jesus' baptism was and is with the Holy Spirit and fire.

What does it mean to experience the baptism of the Holy Spirit? Talk to one hundred believers and you will get one hundred different answers. Let's understand the meaning by looking at the text. The Holy Spirit is the third person of the Godhead: Father, Son, and Holy Spirit.

To baptize means "to dip, to immerse, to wash, to submerge, to place into." When we are baptized, we are immersed into the body of Christ. We become one with the Father, Son, and Holy Spirit, and all believers. *Fire* is used as a symbol and sign of cleansing and purification, but it can also refer to divine judgment and wrath.

Therefore, what John declared is that Jesus will immerse our lives under the very power of the Holy Spirit, so as to cleanse and consecrate us for the work of ministry. Since we cannot do this work of ministry under our own strength, we will receive the power of the Holy Spirit (see Acts 1:8).

Preparation must precede consecration. God will prepare us, but He must also consecrate us. Baptism of the Holy Spirit is God's special anointing upon our lives and work. Spiritual preparation and consecration lead to confidence in the work of ministry.

C. Jesus' Baptism and Heavenly Attestation (Matthew 3:13-17)

Then cometh Jesus from Galilee to Jordan unto John, to be baptized of him. But John forbad him, saying, I have need to be baptized of thee, and comest thou to me? And Jesus answering said unto him, Suffer it to be so now: for thus it becometh us to fulfil all righteousness. Then he suffered him. And Jesus, when he was baptized, went up straightway out of the water: and, lo, the heavens were opened unto him, and he saw the Spirit of God descending like a dove, and lighting upon him: And lo a voice from heaven, saying, This is my beloved Son, in whom I am well pleased.

The ministry of Jesus began at this point. John's ministry was the signal that Jesus was to begin His mission of seeking and saving the lost. He left Galilee and went down to the Jordan River Valley. He submitted to the baptism of John because it would fulfill all righteousness. John did not want to baptize Jesus. Yet, our Lord said, "John, let it be so, for I must fulfill all righteousness." In order to fulfill all righteousness, Jesus had to start at the very beginning. *To fulfill* means "to finish, to bring to completion, and to arrive at the fullest possible measure"—it means going through the process from start to finish.

Jesus was not baptized because He needed to repent. He was not baptized because He was looking to be forgiven of some sin in His life. He was and is the One without sin, who knew no sin—yet He became sin for us. St. Augustine declared, "No baptism was necessary for Christ, but he freely received the baptism of a servant (John) to draw us toward His baptism."

This was the beginning, the kickoff of the divine plan of salvation for the world. Listen: there is always a starting point in your Christian service. You may be nearing retirement age, but for God this can be the starting point. You may be a college freshman, a high school senior, a middle school freshman—but in God's plans, this is the beginning of your life of service.

For Jesus, the beginning was His baptism by John the Baptist. One of the greatest disservices we do to the kingdom's work is rushing men and women to levels of service they are not ready for, either spiritually or emotionally. There has to be a period of training and skill development, a time of growth in the Lord. But in the church, we rush people along, and wonder why ministries get twisted, sidetracked, and distorted.

The Gospels all report that the heavens opened and there came a voice from heaven that declared, "This is my beloved Son, in whom I am well pleased" (Matthew 3:17). In the Father's voice, we hear a heavenly proclamation and a loving attestation. The text literally means that "God declares, 'This is my priceless Son in whom I am well pleased.'" God took great pleasure in His Son, Jesus Christ. On that day there was a theophany of God's voice speaking through the open heavens.

The Apostolic and African church fathers understood the opening of the heavens in two ways. First, they said it was a sign that God had opened the channel between heaven and earth. The four-hundred-year silence between earth and heaven had ended. Second, they said it meant that God had poured out upon Jesus divine favor and power.

He was the One who would take away the sins of the world. He was the One who would give His life as a ransom for the sins of many. He was the One who would shed His blood at Calvary for the sin of every person.

When Jesus walked on the face of the earth, He left us with an example of how to live well-pleasing to the Father. He said, in John 8:29, "He that sent me is with me: the Father hath not left me alone; for I do always those things that please him."

Jesus was approved by God. The sign of God's approval was manifested and demonstrated in the work that He did. Jesus did things that people had never seen before. In fact, they said they were strange things. In his first sermon preached on Pentecost, Peter stated in Acts 2:22: "Ye men of Israel, hear these words; Jesus of Nazareth, a man approved of God among you by miracles and wonders and signs, which God did by him in the midst of you, as ye yourselves also know." He was God's anointed and gifted Messiah, who had power with God.

Men and women looked at the life of Jesus and knew that there was something different about this man. His teachings were with power and authority and not as the scribes and Pharisees. He came across as someone who cared deeply about the common men and women—who heard Him gladly. It is noted in Mark 7:37 (NASB), "They were utterly astonished, saying, 'He has done all things well; He makes even the deaf to hear, and the dumb to speak.'"

III. CONCLUDING REFLECTION

Observe that in this life of discipleship we cannot become nor achieve everything God wills for our lives by taking shortcuts. Discipleship is not like a game of "Sorry, you draw the number eleven and you can exchange places with another player on the board." It's not Monopoly, where we take the card that says, "Proceed past 'Go' and collect two hundred dollars on the way." You cannot become a corporate CEO having never held a job. I cannot declare myself to be the next Tiger Woods when I have only played one game of golf in the past five years. Many of us want to bypass the starting point of discipleship and commitment and get the seats next to the Master on the right hand and the left.

God has a master plan for our lives. It starts with baptism, growth, and committing ourselves to deep spiritual cleansing in Him. God has a direction that He wants our lives to follow as we reach the next level. Jesus began at the starting point, which was His baptism by John.

PRAYER

Heavenly Father, help us, O God, to carry out our assignments with a sense of purpose and urgency. Remind us to always remember that we are not here to please ourselves. We are here on a mission for You. In Jesus' name we pray. Amen.

WORD POWER

Condemn (Greek: *krino* [kri-no]): —means "to separate, to put asunder, to pronounce opinion concerning right and wrong." The word *condemn* is in the subjunctive mood (possibility and potentiality), which means the action described may or may not happen, depending upon circumstances. Jesus did not come to condemn, but He may condemn or judge, depending on the circumstances.

HOME DAILY BIBLE READINGS
(December 28, 2009–January 3, 2010)

Proclaimed in Baptism
MONDAY, December 28: "The Origin of John's Baptism" (Matthew 21:23-27)
TUESDAY, December 29: "John, More than a Prophet" (Luke 7:24-30)
WEDNESDAY, December 30: "John's Testimony of Jesus" (John 1:24-34)
THURSDAY, December 31: "Calling on the Name of Jesus" (Romans 10:8-17)
FRIDAY, January 1: "The Necessity of Repentance" (Matthew 3:7-10)
SATURDAY, January 2: "Buried and Raised with Christ" (Romans 6:1-11)
SUNDAY, January 3: "Jesus Baptized by John" (Matthew 3:1-6, 11-17)

LESSON 6   January 10, 2010

STRENGTHENED IN TEMPTATION

DEVOTIONAL READING: Hebrews 2:10-18
PRINT PASSAGE: Matthew 4:1-11

BACKGROUND SCRIPTURE: Matthew 4:1-11
KEY VERSE: Matthew 4:10

Matthew 4:1-11—KJV

THEN WAS Jesus led up of the Spirit into the wilderness to be tempted of the devil.

2 And when he had fasted forty days and forty nights, he was afterward an hungred.

3 And when the tempter came to him, he said, If thou be the Son of God, command that these stones be made bread.

4 But he answered and said, It is written, Man shall not live by bread alone, but by every word that proceedeth out of the mouth of God.

5 Then the devil taketh him up into the holy city, and setteth him on a pinnacle of the temple,

6 And saith unto him, If thou be the Son of God, cast thyself down: for it is written, He shall give his angels charge concerning thee: and in their hands they shall bear thee up, lest at any time thou dash thy foot against a stone.

7 Jesus said unto him, It is written again, Thou shalt not tempt the Lord thy God.

8 Again, the devil taketh him up into an exceeding high mountain, and sheweth him all the kingdoms of the world, and the glory of them;

9 And saith unto him, All these things will I give thee, if thou wilt fall down and worship me.

10 Then saith Jesus unto him, Get thee hence, Satan: for it is written, Thou shalt worship the Lord thy God, and him only shalt thou serve.

11 Then the devil leaveth him, and, behold, angels came and ministered unto him.

Matthew 4:1-11—NRSV

THEN JESUS was led up by the Spirit into the wilderness to be tempted by the devil.

2 He fasted forty days and forty nights, and afterwards he was famished.

3 The tempter came and said to him, "If you are the Son of God, command these stones to become loaves of bread."

4 But he answered, "It is written, 'One does not live by bread alone, but by every word that comes from the mouth of God.'"

5 Then the devil took him to the holy city and placed him on the pinnacle of the temple,

6 saying to him, "If you are the Son of God, throw yourself down; for it is written, 'He will command his angels concerning you,' and 'On their hands they will bear you up, so that you will not dash your foot against a stone.'"

7 Jesus said to him, "Again it is written, 'Do not put the Lord your God to the test.'"

8 Again, the devil took him to a very high mountain and showed him all the kingdoms of the world and their splendor;

9 and he said to him, "All these I will give you, if you will fall down and worship me."

10 Jesus said to him, "Away with you, Satan! for it is written, 'Worship the Lord your God, and serve only him.'"

11 Then the devil left him, and suddenly angels came and waited on him.

BIBLE FACT

The word *temptation* in its original meaning means "putting to the proof, and the testing of character or quality." In our day, we see temptation in a different light. Conquering temptation leads to achieving a higher, nobler personhood. Jesus was tempted, but He overcame it. Holiness is the catalyst which neutralizes the power of temptation.

TOPICAL OUTLINE OF THE LESSON

I. Introduction
  A. Temptation
  B. Biblical Background

II. Exposition and Application of the Scripture
  A. The First Temptation—Satan (Matthew 4:1-4)
  B. The Second Temptation (Matthew 4:5-7)
  C. The Third Temptation (Matthew 4:8-11)

III. Concluding Reflection

LESSON OBJECTIVES

Upon completion of this lesson, the students will know that:

1. The temptation of Jesus by Satan was real;
2. Jesus overcame the temptations by the Word of God; and,
3. We too can overcome any temptation by resisting Satan.

POINTS TO BE EMPHASIZED

ADULT/YOUTH

Adult Topic: Facing Temptation
Youth Topic: Who Am I Anyway?
Adult Key Verse: Matthew 4:10
Youth Key Verse: Matthew 4:11
Print Passage: Matthew 4:1-11

—That Jesus was tempted even though He was being "led by the Spirit" indicates that temptation itself is not sin.
—Jesus repelled temptation by quoting the Word of God.
—Jesus was tempted at all points as we are, yet was without sin (Hebrews 4:15).
— After baptism, Jesus was led into the wilderness where He fasted for forty days.
—Jesus was tempted to meet His physical needs.
—In overcoming temptation, Jesus put God first to fulfill His mission.

CHILDREN

Children Topic: Resisting Wrong
Key Verse: Matthew 4:10
Print Passage: Matthew 4:1-11

—Jesus' time of temptation followed the high moment of His baptism.
—Jesus called on Scripture to respond to the devil's temptation.
—The devil tried to test Jesus' power and authority as God's Son.
—Jesus was not fooled by the devil's use of Scripture.

I. INTRODUCTION

A. Temptation

The inability to resist and ward off temptation is one of the most powerful deterrents to our spiritual growth (see James 1:14). *Lust* is one of the primary roots of temptation (see 1 John 2:16). Satan uses temptation to hinder our growth, keeping us and our churches stunted and unable to fulfill the Great Commission. He does this with such cunning skill that by the time we realize what has happened, the tragic consequences have already started to take hold. All of us will at some point face the temptation to compromise our beliefs or engage in behavior that is the opposite of what God's Word teaches.

Temptation is a force and evil so powerful that it was the first spiritual battle that Jesus fought and won. The temptations of Jesus were the first real tests of His resolve and commitment to the heavenly anointing. We can learn several valuable lessons from the temptations of our Lord and Master. The battle against temptation is the first major spiritual conflict that we face after conversion, and it is one that we will all face again and again. The enemy never tires or grows weary in his attacks against us. The presence of temptation must never be viewed as a sign that there is something morally or spiritually wrong in our lives. Jesus was tempted in all points just as we are, yet He would not give in (see Hebrews 4:15). He is our model for what should be our response when we face temptations.

In today's lesson, we will learn several important things that will equip us with practical skills that will empower us to respond when temptation comes. Second, we will learn from the life of Jesus that all of God's people will face temptation. Third, we will learn that Satan is a relentless foe, who never grows weary of attacking the people of God. Finally, we will discover how God's Word was used by Jesus to overcome the attacks of the devil.

B. Biblical Background

Each of the Synoptic Gospels ("seeing with the same eye") is a record of some aspects of the temptation of Jesus. The book of Mark, which is the earliest of the four gospels, has the shortest account of the event (see Mark 1:12-13). In the book of Mark, Jesus was immediately driven into the wilderness for forty days where He was tempted by Satan, lived among the wild beasts, and was ministered to by the angels. Luke, as did Matthew, added more details of the temptation. In the book of Luke, the temptation to bow before him is placed second (see Matthew 4:1-11 and compare with Luke 4:1-13).

At His baptism, Jesus was anointed with the Holy Spirit. He received the divine affirmation by the Father of His Sonship—"This is My beloved Son in whom I am well pleased." After His baptism by John, Jesus was led by the Holy Spirit into the wilderness. "Then was Jesus led up of the Spirit into the wilderness to be tempted of the devil" (Matthew 4:1).

II. EXPOSITION AND APPLICATION OF THE SCRIPTURE

A. The First Temptation—Satan
(Matthew 4:1-4)

THEN WAS Jesus led up of the Spirit into the wilderness to be tempted of the devil. And when he had fasted forty days and forty nights, he was afterward an hungred. And when the tempter came to him, he said, If thou be the Son of God, command that these stones be made bread. But he answered and said, It is written, Man shall not live by bread alone, but by every word that proceedeth out of the mouth of God.

In the first temptation, Satan attacked Jesus at the point of physical need. Jesus came from Galilee, most likely Nazareth, and was baptized by John in the Jordan (see Matthew 3:13). Immediately after His baptism, Jesus was led by the Holy Spirit up into the wilderness of Judea for a time of reflection and preparation for the work of redemption (verse 1). *He was tempted* literally means "to try, to test, to determine the quality of a thing." He was not tempted to sin, because God would never tempt anyone to commit evil (see James 1:13). The act of testing was a time of submission to the will of the Father. Jesus was well-aware of what lay ahead—that in His flesh He must be prepared to endure the scorn and shame of the Cross. The *devil* (Greek: *diabolos* [pronounced di-ab-ol-os]), literally means "one that slanders or stands opposed to the purposes of God."

Jesus spent forty days fasting. *Fasting* is "the act of depriving the body of food and nourishment for spiritual purposes or during periods of deep sorrow" (see 2 Samuel 12:21-23; Esther 4:16). At the end of Jesus' fasting, the devil attacked Jesus where He appeared to be the most vulnerable. The usual fast lasted from sunrise to sunset (see 2 Samuel 1:12). Jesus fasted forty days and nights, which was a total fast (see Exodus 34:28, which describes the length of time that Moses fasted).

The tempter approached Jesus and said, "If thou be the Son of God ...." The phrase is stated in such a manner as not to raise doubt in the mind of Jesus regarding who He was, but to question whether being the Son of God would guarantee that the Father would come to the Son's assistance. The devil knew full well who Jesus was and what His purpose was on the earth. There was a belief in ancient Israel that when the Messiah came, He would do things not seen since the time of Moses (i.e., producing manna from heaven).

This is how the enemy comes to us—he comes when he thinks we are at our weakest points, when life becomes a struggle and we could easily give in. The devil will sometimes approach during times of high spiritual moments. The end of a fast is not a time of weakness, but one of great spiritual depth and power. Satan comes as an angel of light with conflicting and confusing messages (see 2 Corinthians 11:14). He approached Jesus and wanted Him to do something that would meet an immediate need, and which would lead to absolute disobedience to the will of the Father.

Jesus responded by quoting Deuteronomy 8:3—which reflects back to the life of Israel's sojourn in the wilderness when God fed them with manna from heaven: "And he humbled thee, and suffered thee to hunger, and fed thee with manna, which thou knewest not, neither did thy fathers know; that he might make thee know that man doth not live by bread only, but by every word that proceedeth out of the mouth of the LORD." Jesus wanted it to be clear that we need bread, but bread is not all we need. God will provide the bread (see Philippians 4:19).

What are the key lessons that we can take from the first temptation? First, there is no substitute for spiritual preparation for ministry and service to the Lord Jesus Christ. Second, pulling away from the noise and din of the crowd is one way that we can hear more clearly the voice of God. Third, we must be prepared during these times of intense spiritual preparation for attacks by the devil. Fourth, our greatest weapon is the Word of God, which is the sword of the Spirit (see Ephesians 6:17; compare with Revelation 12:10-11).

B. The Second Temptation
(Matthew 4:5-7)

Then the devil taketh him up into the holy city, and setteth him on a pinnacle of the temple, And saith unto him, If thou be the Son of God, cast thyself down: for it is written, He shall give his angels charge concerning thee: and in their hands they shall bear thee up, lest at any time thou dash thy foot against a stone. Jesus said unto him, It is written again, Thou shalt not tempt the Lord thy God.

In the second temptation, Satan attacked Jesus' personal confidence in the Father. This temptation appears third in Luke's account of the temptation. The Holy City was Jerusalem. David captured the city when it was ruled by the Jebusites and made it his capital (see 2 Samuel 5:1-9). During the reign of King Solomon, the first Temple was built and dedicated (see 1 Kings 7:1-38). The Temple, along with Jerusalem, was destroyed by the Babylonians in 588/87 BCE (see 2 Kings 25:8-18). Eventually, the Temple was rebuilt during the period of the restoration under the leadership of Zerubbabel sometime around 520 BCE (see the book of Zechariah). During the reign of Herod the Great, the platform upon which the Temple sat was enlarged and expanded. The pinnacle of the Temple was located at the southeastern part of the Temple platform overlooking the Kidron Valley.

We are not told how Satan transported himself and Jesus. Evidently, Satan did not appear in the form that we have become so accustomed to—red suit and pitchfork. We are told that they simply appeared at the Temple. Satan took Jesus to the place where there would be the greatest concentration of people and where He could claim an instant following. Again, it was all about yielding to the temptation of the devil. Jerusalem and its magnificent Temple were the centers of Jewish religious and political life—they were the perfect backdrop. Here, Satan revealed his knowledge and his ability to use the Scriptures to confuse and confound many believers. He quoted from Psalm 91:11-12 urging Jesus to hurl Himself down, and telling Him that before He could hit the ground the angels of God would catch Him and bear Him up.

Again, Jesus responded to the devil's overture with the Word of God by saying, "It is written again, Thou shalt not tempt the Lord thy God" (Matthew 4:7). A similar quote is found in Deuteronomy 6:16. This passage is a look back into Israel's history during the wilderness wanderings when they tried God's patience unnecessarily. They complained about not having water and God had Moses to strike a rock to give them water (see Exodus 17:1-7).

What are the lessons we can learn from this second temptation? First, the devil is shrewd enough to know that men and women can be tempted with plaudits and praises of humankind. Second, there are no easy roads and flowery beds of ease when it comes to achieving the purposes of God. Third, once we begin to attract people with the spectacular, we must continue to do so. Fourth, there is no substitute for knowing the Word of God and being skilled in its use because our adversary is just as skilled. Fifth, there are some things that God will not do in our lives, no matter how much we name it, claim it, speak it, and stand on it. It is not going to happen. We have to know when we are in God's will and when we have just stepped outside of it. Sometimes, we can put ourselves in jeopardy thinking that God will deliver us, when we have simply set ourselves up for a major, catastrophic spiritual meltdown.

C. The Third Temptation
(Matthew 4:8-11)

Again, the devil taketh him up into an exceeding high mountain, and sheweth him all the kingdoms of the world, and the glory of them; And saith unto him, All these things will I give thee, if thou wilt fall down and worship me. Then saith Jesus unto him, Get thee hence, Satan: for it is written, Thou shalt worship the Lord thy God, and him only shalt thou serve. Then the devil leaveth him, and, behold, angels came and ministered unto him.

In the third and final temptation, the devil attacked Jesus over whom He should give His highest loyalty and devotion to (verses 8-10). Again, the devil took Him up into an exceedingly high mountain, and showed Him all the kingdoms of the world, and the glory of them, and told Jesus: "All these things will I give thee, if thou wilt fall down and worship me" (verse 9).

If the first two temptations would not work, the devil was willing and ready to try something else. We are not told the location of this "exceeding high mountain" nor what kingdoms were included. Wherever it was, Jesus could clearly see all the kingdoms of the world. This included kingdoms that were great and small. Not only did the devil show Jesus the kingdoms—he showed Jesus the glory and splendor that made each one of them great. Is it possible that the devil wanted Jesus to sense and see that He could rule and control the entire world if He would just bow and worship him? Is it possible that what the devil offered was a more palatable method to achieve worldwide redemption by simply giving to him what was the exclusive right of God—human worship? For Jesus to bow and worship the devil would be to ascribe to him a worth that he was not due. All worship is to be given to God and Him only (see Psalm 95:1-7).

In this third temptation, we see the skill of Jesus in using the Word of God to defeat the power of darkness. Jesus quoted from Deuteronomy 6:13; then Jesus said to Satan, "Get thee hence, Satan: for it is written, Thou shalt worship the Lord thy God, and him only shalt thou serve" (Matthew 4:10).

What are some lessons we learn from Jesus in this third temptation? First, we learn that God and God alone is the object of our worship. Second, we are not to sell ourselves out to the power of darkness to achieve ends that promote good and righteousness. Third, the devil is relentless and will continue to offer us plums that he believes will entice us to turn aside from the true and living God. Fourth, there is no substitute for knowledge of and application of the Scriptures in our daily lives. Fifth, God will always send ministering angels to bolster our confidence and trust in Him when we face the onslaughts of the devil.

III. CONCLUDING REFLECTION

We may never face the kind of temptations that Jesus faced. Yet, every believer is continually faced with the reality of temptation. Jesus was tempted neither to commit some grievous sin nor deny His messianic mission; He was not asked to deny that He was the Son of God. Rather, He was challenged to turn aside from His true and only purpose for coming into the world. Many times believers are distracted from the larger and greater mission of the church, which is the Great Commission (see Matthew 28:19-20). When the prospects of personal gain and glory are presented as more plausible alternatives to sacrifice and service and we yield, have we not submitted to the devil?

PRAYER

Father in heaven, we thank You for helping us to understand the purpose of Jesus. He was tempted, yet He did not fail. Help us to stand against the wiles of the enemy—Satan. In Jesus' name we pray. Amen.

WORD POWER

Tempt (Greek: *peirazo* [pi-rad-zo])—means "to scrutinize or entice for the purpose of ascertaining one's quality." It also means "to endeavor." In the context of this lesson, Satan enticed Jesus for the purpose of lording it over Him, and also to ascertain the qualities of Jesus. Temptation will come and entice us to yield; however, we must yield to the hand of God. Jesus quoted Scriptures to ward off the evil one, so we too must stand against the evil one by quoting accurately the Word of God back to Satan.

HOME DAILY BIBLE READINGS
(January 4–10, 2010)
Strengthened in Temptation

MONDAY, January 4: "Enduring Trials and Temptations" (James 1:12-16)

TUESDAY, January 5: "Times of Testing" (Luke 8:5-8, 11-15)

WEDNESDAY, January 6: "Restore Others but Take Care" (Galatians 6:1-5)

THURSDAY, January 7: "Stay Awake and Pray" (Matthew 26:36-46)

FRIDAY, January 8: "The Way to Pray" (Matthew 6:9-15)

SATURDAY, January 9: "Our Temptation and God's Faithfulness" (1 Corinthians 10:6-13)

SUNDAY, January 10: "Jesus' Victory over Temptation" (Matthew 4:1-11)

LESSON 7   January 17, 2010

DEMONSTRATED IN ACTS OF HEALING

DEVOTIONAL READING: Luke 5:27-32
PRINT PASSAGE: Matthew 9:27-34; 11:2-6

BACKGROUND SCRIPTURE: Matthew 9:27-34; 11:2-6
KEY VERSE: Matthew 11:5

Matthew 9:27-34; 11:2-6—KJV

27 And when Jesus departed thence, two blind men followed him, crying, and saying, Thou Son of David, have mercy on us.

28 And when he was come into the house, the blind men came to him: and Jesus saith unto them, Believe ye that I am able to do this? They said unto him, Yea, Lord.

29 Then touched he their eyes, saying, According to your faith be it unto you.

30 And their eyes were opened; and Jesus straitly charged them, saying, See that no man know it.

31 But they, when they were departed, spread abroad his fame in all that country.

32 As they went out, behold, they brought to him a dumb man possessed with a devil.

33 And when the devil was cast out, the dumb spake: and the multitudes marvelled, saying, It was never so seen in Israel.

34 But the Pharisees said, He casteth out devils through the prince of the devils.

.....

2 Now when John had heard in the prison the works of Christ, he sent two of his disciples,

3 And said unto him, Art thou he that should come, or do we look for another?

4 Jesus answered and said unto them, Go and shew John again those things which ye do hear and see:

5 The blind receive their sight, and the lame walk, the lepers are cleansed, and the deaf hear, the dead are raised up, and the poor have the gospel preached to them.

6 And blessed is he, whosoever shall not be offended in me.

Matthew 9:27-34; 11:2-6—NRSV

27 As Jesus went on from there, two blind men followed him, crying loudly, "Have mercy on us, Son of David!"

28 When he entered the house, the blind men came to him; and Jesus said to them, "Do you believe that I am able to do this?" They said to him, "Yes, Lord."

29 Then he touched their eyes and said, "According to your faith let it be done to you."

30 And their eyes were opened. Then Jesus sternly ordered them, "See that no one knows of this."

31 But they went away and spread the news about him throughout that district.

32 After they had gone away, a demoniac who was mute was brought to him.

33 And when the demon had been cast out, the one who had been mute spoke; and the crowds were amazed and said, "Never has anything like this been seen in Israel."

34 But the Pharisees said, "By the ruler of the demons he casts out the demons."

.....

2 When John heard in prison what the Messiah was doing, he sent word by his disciples

3 and said to him, "Are you the one who is to come, or are we to wait for another?"

4 Jesus answered them, "Go and tell John what you hear and see:

5 the blind receive their sight, the lame walk, the lepers are cleansed, the deaf hear, the dead are raised, and the poor have good news brought to them.

6 And blessed is anyone who takes no offense at me."

UNIFYING LESSON PRINCIPLE

Although we live in a world where many people want to be able to explain all events scientifically, many mysteries remain. To whom can we turn when we are confronted by the inexplicable? Jesus performed healing miracles that led people to place their faith in Him.

TOPICAL OUTLINE OF THE LESSON

I. Introduction
A. The Uniqueness of Jesus
B. Biblical Background

II. Exposition and Application of the Scripture
A. Jesus Heals Two Blind Men (Matthew 9:27-31)
B. Jesus Heals a Dumb Demoniac (Matthew 9:32-34)
C. John Sends a Message and Jesus Responds (Matthew 11:2-6)

III. Concluding Reflection

LESSON OBJECTIVES

Upon completion of this lesson, the students will know that:

1. Jesus fulfilled His mission through healing;
2. Jesus fulfilled His mission through teaching;
3. John confirmed the identity of Jesus; and,
4. We are to endeavor to complete our own missions.

POINTS TO BE EMPHASIZED

ADULT/YOUTH

Adult Topic: **Works of Healing**
Youth Topic: **Yes, Lord**
Adult Key Verse: **Matthew 11:5**
Youth Key Verse: **Matthew 9:30**
Print Passage: **Matthew 9:27-34; 11:2-6**

—Jesus connects faith with healing.
—Jesus made no empty claims about His identity. He invited the disciples and John to examine the evidence.
—"Son of David" was a designation frequently used for the Messiah (Matthew 9:27), though Jesus did not refer to Himself by that title.
—In spite of a charge from Jesus to tell no one about their healing, they spread His fame in all that land.
—Matthew showed that Jesus was a healer, but never for show; He healed out of compassion.
—Matthew demonstrated that Jesus can heal sickness and disease that cripple human life and stifle human potential, thereby affirming that Jesus has power over all of life's adversities.

CHILDREN

Children Topic: **Healing People**
Key Verse: **Matthew 9:33**
Print Passage: **Matthew 9:27-34**

—The two blind men showed persistence in getting Jesus' attention.
—Jesus asked the two for a statement of belief in His ability to heal them.
—The opening of their eyes to sight supported their statement of belief.
—The crowds were amazed and could not explain the healing of the man who was mute.
—The Pharisees believed that Jesus' good act of healing was evil.

I. INTRODUCTION

A. The Uniqueness of Jesus

Today's lesson is an introduction to the Jewish concept of the Messiah. We know from the Gospels that the ministry of Jesus consisted not only of preaching and teaching, but also of healing and performing mighty works of power (see Matthew 4:21-23; John 3:1-5; Acts 2:22). He healed all kinds of diseases and maladies. This was one of the contributing factors for His local popularity and large following in Galilee.

Further, there was clearly an atmosphere of joy in Galilee that in Jesus of Nazareth, the long-awaited Messiah, had appeared. On the road to Jerusalem, as they were entering the city on what has come to be known as Palm Sunday, the crowd greeted Jesus as the coming King-Messiah (see Luke 19:37-38).

It is clear that Jesus did not encourage His disciples or anyone else to call Him *Messiah*. Yet, He never discouraged people from referring to Him as the Messiah. Peter's confession at Caesarea Philippi was a decisive turning point in the messianic awareness of the disciples. We learn more about this in a future lesson. Prior to that time the disciples knew that they were walking with someone unique and different in every way (see Matthew 7:29; 8:27). In the first pronouncement of His passion, Jesus began the process of changing the messianic beliefs of His disciples to reflect the reality of a Messiah who would face suffering and death (see Mark 8:27-33).

B. Biblical Background

During the time of Jesus' ministry, there were several messianic movements circulating within the nation of Israel. All of these movements had a major impact upon the life of the Jewish nation. The belief in the Messiah as the son of David was very much alive during the time of the ministry of Jesus. In fact, Jesus was referred to as the Son of David (see Matthew 9:27; Luke 18:38). Jesus never used the title of Messiah/Christ to refer to Himself. When He was tried by the Jewish Sanhedrin Court one of the charges against Him was His claiming to be the Christ (see Luke 22:66-67). The word *Messiah* is the English translation of a Hebrew word (*mashia*), which means "the Lord's anointed" or "anointed one." The concept of the Messiah was a very important development in Israel—for it was the belief in the Messiah that provided the hope Israel needed to sustain itself during its days of trial and difficulty. The word *Messiah* is found in only two Old Testament verses: Daniel 9:25-26.

The selection of David to be Israel's second king figured prominently in the development of David as the prototype of the Messiah for several reasons. First, David was the one chosen by God (see 1 Samuel 16:1-12). Second, Samuel was told to anoint the man whom God had chosen (see 1 Samuel 16:3). Third, God's choice of David was different than that of Samuel (see 1 Samuel 16:6-13).

David's greatest desire was to build a house for the Lord so that the ark of the covenant would have a dwelling place (see 1 Chronicles 28-29). Instead of a physical house, God built a spiritual house for David to last forever.

II. EXPOSITION AND APPLICATION OF THE SCRIPTURE

A. Jesus Heals Two Blind Men (Matthew 9:27-31)

And when Jesus departed thence, two blind men followed him, crying, and saying, Thou Son of David, have mercy on us. And when he was come into the house, the blind men came to him: and Jesus saith unto them, Believe ye that I am able to do this? They said unto him, Yea, Lord. Then touched he their eyes, saying, According to your faith be it unto you. And their eyes were opened; and Jesus straitly charged them, saying, See that no man know it. But they, when they were departed, spread abroad his fame in all that country.

This is the first miracle of Jesus giving sight to the blind in the book of Matthew. There are more of these miracles than there are of any other single category of miracles in the ministry of Jesus. The giving of sight was a divine activity (see Exodus 4:11; Psalm 146:8) and it has messianic significance (see Isaiah 29:18; 35:5; 42:7). Jesus continued His ministry, and as He moved about Capernaum two blind men began to follow Him. How did they follow Jesus? They may have followed the noise of the crowd, or they could have been led along by someone. No other details about the two men are provided. Nothing is reported about their families, homes, or how long they had been in that condition. What is central is that Jesus passed by them and this may have been their only chance to be healed and regain their sight.

Graham Twelftree points out that the word *followed* was one of Matthew's favorite words, and he used it to indicate that discipleship was an important theme for including this story in the Gospel. It is used twenty times and in this instance, it means that the two blind men followed with the intention of becoming disciples of Jesus. They cried out loudly trying to get the attention of Jesus—"Thou Son of David, have mercy on us." The use of this title indicates their belief that Jesus was the Messiah. How they came to that knowledge we do not know. However, they continued to follow Him into the house. Jesus said to them: "Do you believe that I am able to do this?" (verse 28, NASB). It was a question of faith in the power of God to open their blind eyes through faith in Jesus. Their affirmation of confidence in Jesus became the ground upon which they were healed. Jesus said, "Be it done to you according to your faith" (Matthew 9:29, NASB). And their eyes were opened. They were healed because they believed without reservation that Jesus could heal them of their blindness.

Jesus told the two men not to say anything about what had happened to them. It is clear that they would have had no idea of the events that transpired during the miracle—after all, they were blind. Why Jesus told them not to say anything about the miracle is a mystery and any answer would be more conjecture than fact. What is clear is that they disobeyed the Lord's stern command. They told people wherever they went. And clearly there would have been an interest on the part of their families and friends as to how they received their sight. This is a clear message about discipleship and the role of the one whose life has been touched by Jesus. They could not contain themselves. They had to tell someone what had happened. They went out and spread the word abroad; everywhere they went, they told people that Jesus had given them their sight.

B. Jesus Heals a Dumb Demoniac
(Matthew 9:32-34)

As they went out, behold, they brought to him a dumb man possessed with a devil. And when the devil was cast out, the dumb spake: and the multitudes marvelled, saying, It was never so seen in Israel. But the Pharisees said, He casteth out devils through the prince of the devils.

Jesus continued to move about. We are not told whether this was the same day or on a new day. What took place now occurred after He left the house. Jesus was confronted with large numbers of people living in pain and misery, people broken by despair and the disappointments of life. He often encountered large numbers of diseased and hurting people (see John 5:1ff.). A dumb man, who was demon-possessed, was brought to Him. This man had a dual problem: he could neither speak nor hear. No mention is made of who brought the man, or whether or not he had been following Jesus. Moreover, we are not told whether he recognized Jesus to be the Messiah.

There was no conversation; nothing was said about the man's faith or the faith of those who brought him to Jesus. It is apparent that the people who brought the man to Jesus felt that only He could help his situation. He need not ask for help, nor did Jesus ask him what he wanted. That he was brought to Jesus indicated

that he was there to have the demon cast out of him. The Greek word used in this miracle is *ek-ballo* and it means "to drive out with force, to expel, or to cast clean out." The same word is used in 8:16, 31; 10:1. Satan will not easily give up and must be driven out by force.

After the demon was driven out, the man spoke. He had been excluded from the community because of his condition. Jesus gave him back his life. There were two different responses to the miracle. The multitudes marveled and declared that they had never seen anything so spectacular in Israel. Darrell Bock notes that "The remark is not that the miracles were unique, for many of the greats of old, such as Moses, Joshua, Elijah, and Elisha, had performed miracles." What was unprecedented was that Jesus was actively engaged in the performance of miracles almost daily.

In contrast to the multitudes, the Pharisees said, "He casts out the demons by the ruler of the demons" (Matthew 9:34, NKJV). The remark of the Pharisees makes it clear that they did not deny that something supernatural was happening; they simply did not believe God had anything to do with it. Who were the Pharisees? The Pharisees were the largest and most influential religious party in Israel. They are said to have numbered more than six thousand. The Pharisees had their origin during the time of the Maccabean Revolt (ca. 168-165 BC). They were primarily concerned with protecting Israel from the influence and presence of Hellenism. The Pharisees were among the most vocal opponents of Jesus for a variety of reasons. All of their opposition stemmed from religious differences between themselves and Jesus. The conflicts between Jesus and the Pharisees provided an opportunity for Him to teach some of His most important lessons about righteousness and religious hypocrisy. The people received and were excited about Jesus; their leaders, on the other hand, rejected Him.

C. John Sends a Message and Jesus Responds (Matthew 11:2-6)

Now when John had heard in the prison the works of Christ, he sent two of his disciples, And said unto him, Art thou he that should come, or do we look for another? Jesus answered and said unto them, Go and shew John again those things which ye do hear and see: The blind receive their sight, and the lame walk, the lepers are cleansed, and the deaf hear, the dead are raised up, and the poor have the gospel preached to them. And blessed is he, whosoever shall not be offended in me.

John's ministry ended with his imprisonment for preaching against Herod Antipas taking Philip's wife (see Matthew 14:1-12). Josephus reported that John was imprisoned at the fortress Machaerus, which was situated east of the Dead Sea. Matthew reported that the popularity and magnetic persona of Jesus' ministry had reached John's ears in prison. Now when John in prison heard of the works of Christ, he sent *word* by his disciples, and said to Him, "Are you the Expected One, or do we look for someone else?" (Luke 7:19, NASB). John had heard of the works of Jesus—which are more than likely those ministry activities which Jesus listed in His response to John. John's question is puzzling to some New Testament scholars. Some scholars have doubted the historicity of the question, given how close John and Jesus were. However, there is a possible reason for John's question. (John had already perceived the Messianic nature of Jesus' mission.) Davies and Allison state, "If,

however, the query be judged historical, it must have sprung from rising hope or genuine bewilderment." Is it possible that John was just simply confused regarding who and what the Messiah's ministry would be like? It is quite possible that John's expectation of a Hero/King was in his mind as well—and that Jesus fit neither description. Hence, this could be the reason for the question, "Are you the One or do we look for another?"

Each of the Gospels is an attestation to the magnetic persona and preaching power of John the Baptist. In the days immediately preceding the ministry of Jesus Christ, John the Baptist was the most prominent religious person in Israel. There were reasons for this.

First, he was highly regarded and respected among the people of his day. Josephus wrote glowingly of him and kings feared his presence. He was not just another preacher in Judea. Even since before his birth, John was set apart by God to be the forerunner for the coming Messiah (see Luke 1:5-25; 39-44; 57-80). In Isaiah 40:3, the prophet foretold of John's coming over five hundred years before his birth. Second, God used John's preaching to specifically set the stage for the coming of Jesus. His preaching and baptizing aroused a deep desire in the hearts of men and women for God—and they flocked to where he was. Prior to John's ministry of baptism, Jews practiced ritual bathing—which was a custom that went back to the time of the Exodus and involved physical washing with water as a sign of consecration and spiritual cleansing. Third, John's ministry transitioned humanity from a time of preparation to the beginning of God's decisive entrance into human history in the person of His Son Jesus Christ. John represented the old wine of the Law, while Jesus represented the new wine of grace. In John, God prepared Israel for a time when something entirely new would break forth. Every time God does something new it is to advance His purposes.

III. CONCLUDING REFLECTION

Jesus heard the cry of the two blind men, but He did not respond immediately. He waited to see if they had faith. It helps to know that not everybody who says he or she wants help really believes God can help. The waiting of Jesus was to elevate their faith in Him. We may be asking God for something and the waiting period should be regarded as a time of elevating our faith.

The Pharisees faulted Jesus because He bypassed their authority. They accused Him of serving Satan. We must be careful not to arrogate the move of God to Satan. God is still healing today in different ways and manners. John sent for Jesus to ascertain whether or not He was the Messiah. When we are in doubt, we should not turn away from God. We should hold on to our faith in Him.

PRAYER

Father, help us to see Your work in Christ and to strive to be like Him. In Jesus' name we pray. Amen.

WORD POWER

Pharisee (Greek: *pharisaios* [pha-ri-sai-os])—means "a Jewish sect which started after the Exile." They recognized only the Old Testament. They craved for outward show, and always looked for front rows. They loved religious externalities such as: washing of hands and feet, prayer and fasting, and giving of alms. They believed in the existence of good and bad angels. They were bitter enemies of Jesus Christ and His cause. We should be careful not to be like them.

HOME DAILY BIBLE READINGS
(January 11–17, 2010)

Demonstrated in Acts of Healing

MONDAY, January 11: "A Physician Is Needed" (Luke 5:27-32)

TUESDAY, January 12: "A Cry for Healing" (Psalm 107:17-22)

WEDNESDAY, January 13: "A Prayer for Healing" (2 Kings 20:1-7)

THURSDAY, January 14: "An Amazing Faith" (Matthew 8:5-13)

FRIDAY, January 15: "The Father's Loving Care" (Hosea 11:1-4)

SATURDAY, January 16: "Sent Out to Heal" (Matthew 10:1-8)

SUNDAY, January 17: "Jesus' Healing Ministry" (Matthew 9:27-34; 11:2-6)

LESSON 8   January 24, 2010

DECLARED IN PRAYER

DEVOTIONAL READING: **John 11:38-44**
PRINT PASSAGE: **Matthew 11:25-30**

BACKGROUND SCRIPTURE: **Matthew 11:25-30**
KEY VERSE: **Matthew 11:28**

Matthew 11:25-30—KJV

25 At that time Jesus answered and said, I thank thee, O Father, Lord of heaven and earth, because thou hast hid these things from the wise and prudent, and hast revealed them unto babes.

26 Even so, Father: for so it seemed good in thy sight.

27 All things are delivered unto me of my Father: and no man knoweth the Son, but the Father; neither knoweth any man the Father, save the Son, and he to whomsoever the Son will reveal him.

28 Come unto me, all ye that labour and are heavy laden, and I will give you rest.

29 Take my yoke upon you, and learn of me; for I am meek and lowly in heart: and ye shall find rest unto your souls.

30 For my yoke is easy, and my burden is light.

Matthew 11:25-30—NRSV

25 At that time Jesus said, "I thank you, Father, Lord of heaven and earth, because you have hidden these things from the wise and the intelligent and have revealed them to infants;

26 yes, Father, for such was your gracious will.

27 All things have been handed over to me by my Father; and no one knows the Son except the Father, and no one knows the Father except the Son and anyone to whom the Son chooses to reveal him.

28 "Come to me, all you that are weary and are carrying heavy burdens, and I will give you rest.

29 Take my yoke upon you, and learn from me; for I am gentle and humble in heart, and you will find rest for your souls.

30 For my yoke is easy, and my burden is light."

BIBLE FACT

Christians are called upon to call on God at all times. However, there are moments in our lives when we have to take a step closer to Him. The invitation found in Matthew 11:28 is a general one in nature. Even though the word *Ye* means "You all," an individual can take a step of faith by going to God in prayer. Jesus says to those who come to Him: "I will in no wise cast out" (John 6:37, ASV). Prayer is a battle and that is why Satan will do everything to prevent us from praying. We can fill our day with activities—even religious activities—but when it is time to pray, that is when Satan rises up and begins to subtly attack us. Have you heard Christians say at the time of prayer, "Make it short"? Why do they make that statement? Think about it.

We admire those who are knowledgeable and seem to have all the answers to life. Where does that leave those who don't have everything all figured out? Jesus promised the truth and empowerment to those who follow and learn.

TOPICAL OUTLINE OF THE LESSON

I. **Introduction**
   A. Jesus' Prayer Life
   B. Biblical Background

II. **Exposition and Application of the Scripture**
   A. Jesus' Prayer to the Father (Matthew 11:25-27)
   B. The Great Invitation (Matthew 11:28-30)

III. **Concluding Reflection**

LESSON OBJECTIVES

Upon completion of this lesson, the students will know that:

1. Prayer played an important role in the life of Jesus;
2. Christians should devote more time to seeking the face of God in prayer; and,
3. Prayerless Christians are powerless Christians and they are being cheated by Satan.

POINTS TO BE EMPHASIZED
ADULT/YOUTH

Adult Topic: Inviting the Weary
Youth Topic: I Don't Get It!
Adult Key Verse: Matthew 11:28
Youth Key Verse: Matthew 11:29
Print Passage: Matthew 11:25-30

—While God and Jesus were "revealed" (verse 25) to certain humans, the same term is not used of what God entrusts to the Son. Jesus did not need to have God "revealed" to Him.
—Jesus offers those who are burdened and would follow Him an opportunity to exchange the yoke of the Law for His yoke of love.
—Jesus talks of godly wisdom and He taught His disciples to pray to God.
—Jesus saw God as the eternal Creator of humanity who sought to provide it with blessings of love.
—Jesus made it clear that prayer is a necessity to living a purposeful life.
—God reveals His will to those who seek Him.
—Jesus invites all people to come to Him with their burdens and learn how to please God.

CHILDREN

Children Topic: Giving Thanks
Key Verse: Matthew 11:25
Print Passage: Matthew 11:25-30

—Jesus' prayer was one of thanksgiving to God.
—Jesus joyfully recognized that great truths were being revealed to those who were open to them.
—Jesus expressed His desire to reveal God's truths to those who would come to Him in humility.
—Learning from Jesus brings rest from weariness and heaviness.

I. INTRODUCTION

A. Jesus' Prayer Life

Today's lesson is divided into two parts. The first is a focus on the prayer life of Jesus, and the second part contains His invitation that the heavy-laden and burdened seek refuge in Him. Jesus practiced one of the most important spiritual disciplines (which is prayer), and we hear Him calling the heavy-laden and burdened. Jesus practiced intensively the discipline of prayer. Prayer was the spark that ignited the activities of each new day: "And in the early morning, while it was still dark, He arose and went out and departed to a lonely place, and was praying there" (Mark 1:35, NASB). Jesus spent many hours alone in prayer. It was in those precious moments of prayer that He communed with God the Father, coming to a clear understanding of His work and ministry (see John 6:15).

B. Biblical Background

Jesus was very popular in the early days of His ministry. Jesus spent all of His time in Galilee with the exception of the times that He visited Jerusalem for observance of the annual Jewish festivals (see John 2:22-23; 5:1; 10:22-23; 13:1). Today's lesson does not take place in a particular city. More than likely Jesus was visiting each of these cities, given their close proximity to each other. During the early days of the mission His teachings were filled with power and authority (see Matthew 7:29; Mark 1:27). Also, there developed speculation among the people of Galilee that He just might be the Promised One. Jesus never made any claims to be the Messiah. However, Jesus did things that the people had never seen before—the miracles, healings, and raising people from the dead were just unheard of in that region (see Luke 5:26). All of these were signs that the Jews believed would accompany the coming of the Messiah.

Jesus had neared the halfway mark in His three-year earthly ministry. He had sent the twelve disciples out on their first preaching and healing mission (see Matthew 10:1ff.). Then He departed and went alone to preach and teach in the cities surrounding the Sea of Galilee. Chapter 11 is a pivotal point during the Galilean ministry of Jesus. First, there were questions raised by John the Baptist as to whether or not Jesus was in fact the Messiah. John sent two of his disciples to inquire about whether Jesus was the One or if they should look for someone else. Jesus sent word back to John about what was going on. Afterward, Jesus told the people gathered around Him that none of the prophets had come close to the stature of John, yet the least in the kingdom of heaven was greater than John.

Second, there appeared to be a growing rejection of Jesus' ministry and mission. Jesus was no longer being received and welcomed as in the earlier days.

II. EXPOSITION AND APPLICATION OF THE SCRIPTURE

A. Jesus' Prayer to the Father
(Matthew 11:25-27)

At that time Jesus answered and said, I thank thee, O Father, Lord of heaven and earth, because thou hast hid these things from the wise and prudent, and hast revealed them unto babes. Even so, Father: for so it seemed good in thy sight. All things are delivered unto me of my Father: and no man knoweth the Son, but the Father; neither knoweth any man the Father, save the Son, and he to whomsoever the Son will reveal him.

In these verses is described a very special moment in the ministry of Jesus. The phrase "At that time" denotes a close proximity to the reproach that had recently been given against the cities of Chorazin, Bethsaida, and Capernaum. Living within the borders of these three cities were people who were among the wealthiest in Galilee, yet they refused to accept Him as Messiah. Think for a moment of the magnitude of what Jesus did. When He could have resigned Himself to defeat and discouragement, He praised the Father for the positive results that had been achieved. Remember, the cities that Jesus condemned were not off in some distant place; rather, these cities were within a few miles of each other. Bethsaida was the greatest distance from Capernaum, which was the city where Jesus had His headquarters.

Jesus openly began to pray and thank God for the revelation of truth to those who were considered to be outsiders and nobodies (see verse 25). Jesus praised and thanked the Father that His work was not in vain and His words did not return void (see Isaiah 55:11).

Who were the wise? The wise were Jewish teachers, lawyers, and religious professionals (see 1 Corinthians 1:19-20). The intelligent were those with understanding of the Scriptures, yet they lacked revelation of the truth. The babes were not those measured by age but by humility and an absence of pride. Verse 26 is a reaffirmation of Jesus' statement of praise in verse 25.

Verse 27 sounds as though it could very well have come from the gospel of John and could very well be how Jesus spoke and taught at times: "All things have been handed over to Me by My Father; and no one knows the Son, except the Father; nor does anyone know the Father, except the Son, and anyone to whom the Son wills to reveal Him" (NASB). *All things have been handed over to me by My Father* has reference to knowledge, which Jesus possesses. Jesus has perfect understanding and knowledge of the Father and He likewise of Jesus. Here we have a picture of the perfect unity between Father and Son (see John 8:28; 10:30; 17:11, 21-22).

B. The Great Invitation
(Matthew 11:28-30)

Come unto me, all ye that labour and are heavy laden, and I will give you rest. Take my yoke upon you, and learn of me; for I am meek and lowly in heart: and ye shall find rest unto your souls. For my yoke is easy, and my burden is light.

These verses are found only in the book of Matthew. They follow right on the heels of His having offered praise to the Father for using His life and ministry to bring men and women to the knowledge of the truth. Jesus' words have meant much to countless numbers of believers who have found themselves laboring under the burdens of life. "Come to Me, all who are weary and heavy-laden, and I will give you rest" (verse 28, NASB). Unlike those who earlier were reproached for being self-sufficient and arrogant, there were and are people who are beaten and battered by life. Jesus said "Come to Me." This is a gracious invitation that is open to all—an invitation to all who are *weary*, which literally means "to be tired, worn out, and exhausted"; it can also denote "one who is filled with grief." Jesus extends an open invitation to all who have been bruised by life's heavy burdens. He says that He is able to give rest, or a cessation from the heaviness of life.

The invitation is to take up the yoke of Jesus Christ. In the New Testament, *yoke* is always used metaphorically and signifies bondage or submission to authority of some kind. In Matthew 23:4, Jesus pronounced woe upon the scribes and Pharisees because they were always placing heavy burdens of religious legalism upon the people's backs. He would not burden them with the endless laws and meticulous rules that had to be followed if one wanted to even have a chance of being righteous. It was impossible for the average person to keep the Law. The religious leaders made it difficult by their traditions (see Matthew 15:6; Galatians 1:14; Colossians 2:8).

This sort of weightiness with traditions and practices which are evident even in our generation can often get in the way of people being able to see God and then reach Him. Now there is a need to distinguish between what is the tradition of the Christian faith and the rise of traditionalism, which is what Jesus found repulsive. Among our most cherished Christian traditions are the celebration of the observance of the Lord's Supper, baptism, the birth of Christ, Easter, Pentecost, and Palm Sunday. Humanly developed traditions are those things that we invent and then seek to pass along as being holy and sacred.

"Take My yoke upon you, and learn from Me, for I am gentle and humble in heart; and you shall find rest for your souls" (Matthew 11:29, NASB). Jesus is always calling men and women to discipleship. It is not enough to indicate that one would like to be a follower of Jesus; to commit oneself to Him means to commit oneself to a learning process. In Him one finds rest from the burdens of life. Jesus was not against Judaism and the Torah. He was simply not for what the religionists had done with the covenant relationship. They had made it hard to follow God. Jesus says to take upon ourselves all that is necessary to be one of His disciples.

The *yoke* was a wooden bar or frame that was used to join animals together to enable them to pull a load. Biblically speaking, the yoke is an image of two things. First, it is the image of subjection or service. It is stated in Galatians 5:1 that "It was for freedom that Christ set us free"—and therefore we must "keep standing firm and do not be subject again to a yoke of slavery" (NASB). When Jesus sets you free from something, do not entangle yourself in that situation or habit again.

Second in the meaning of *yoke* is the image of being "joined together." In Paul's letter he expressed in a negative way what every believer must give serious consideration to in developing relationships and friendships. Paul wrote in 2 Corinthians 6:14, "Be ye not unequally yoked together with unbelievers: for what fellowship hath righteousness with unrighteousness? and what communion hath light with darkness?" Metaphorically speaking, the word *yoke* is used of "troublesome laws imposed on one," especially of the Mosaic Law.

III. CONCLUDING REFLECTION

I have been a pastor for nearly thirty years. During all of those years, I have witnessed more people leave and abandon the Christian church than stay and persevere. I often ask: "Why is this the case?" The answer is not far-fetched: it is the absence of a serious commitment to the inner life of prayer, fellowship, and communion with the Father. This is one of the most important lessons we learn from the life of Jesus Christ. In the midst of a time of great challenge and rising expectations, Jesus knew the power of prayer and praise. When we fail to practice the disciplines that bring us through the long nights of pain, suffering, and disappointment, we are not far from the realm of discouragement.

Second, many Christians do not appreciate the challenge of being followers of Jesus Christ in this age of secular post-modernism. The times have been dramatized by the most materialistic generation to have ever lived. Hence, many are taught to expect that God will bless one materially and with more and greater possessions. When that fails to come to pass, they falter and move on to the next big thing to come along (see Deuteronomy 18:15ff.).

Finally, it may be that people come to Christ with the wrong intention. The latter verses of the lesson clearly point us to a Christ who comforts us and leads us to embrace Him as the source of our comfort and strength. Spend a few moments thinking about how God has been the source of your strength and power.

PRAYER

Lord God, Creator and Redeemer, teach us to trust You more and to rely more readily on Your presence and power in our lives. In Jesus' name we pray. Amen.

WORD POWER

Labour (Greek: *kopiao* [ko-pi-a-o])—means "to grow weary, tired, exhausted with toil or burdens of grief." This word in content is a participle, which means "burden of heart combined with physical toiling." Jesus extends His hand of love to anyone to come and get relief.

HOME DAILY BIBLE READINGS
(January 18–24, 2010)
Declared in Prayer

MONDAY, January 18: "A Listening Father" (John 11:38-44)
TUESDAY, January 19: "Whenever You Pray" (Matthew 6:5-8)
WEDNESDAY, January 20: "Praying Alone" (Matthew 14:22-33)
THURSDAY, January 21: "Prayer and Blessing on Children" (Matthew 19:13-15)
FRIDAY, January 22: "Pray for Your Persecutors" (Matthew 5:43-48)
SATURDAY, January 23: "Prayer and Faith" (Matthew 21:18-22)
SUNDAY, January 24: "The Father's Gracious Will" (Matthew 11:25-30)

REVEALED IN REJECTION

DEVOTIONAL READING: Isaiah 53:1-9
PRINT PASSAGE: Matthew 13:54-58
KEY VERSE: Matthew 13:58

BACKGROUND SCRIPTURE: Matthew 13:54-58;
Luke 4:16-30

Matthew 13:54-58—KJV

54 And when he was come into his own country, he taught them in their synagogue, insomuch that they were astonished, and said, Whence hath this man this wisdom, and these mighty works?

55 Is not this the carpenter's son? is not his mother called Mary? and his brethren, James, and Joses, and Simon, and Judas?

56 And his sisters, are they not all with us? Whence then hath this man all these things?

57 And they were offended in him. But Jesus said unto them, A prophet is not without honour, save in his own country, and in his own house.

58 And he did not many mighty works there because of their unbelief.

Matthew 13:54-58—NRSV

54 He came to his hometown and began to teach the people in their synagogue, so that they were astounded and said, "Where did this man get this wisdom and these deeds of power?

55 Is not this the carpenter's son? Is not his mother called Mary? And are not his brothers James and Joseph and Simon and Judas?

56 And are not all his sisters with us? Where then did this man get all this?"

57 And they took offense at him. But Jesus said to them, "Prophets are not without honor except in their own country and in their own house."

58 And he did not do many deeds of power there, because of their unbelief.

BIBLE FACT

Reject simply means "to refuse to accept." Rejection happens in all facets of life. In many parts of the world there is fighting among tribes; one tribe rejects another tribe in order to gain supremacy. We reject candidates during election time. Churches reject one pastor in preference for another one. There are instances when children and adults reject one another because of color pigmentation. Jesus, the Savior of the world, was rejected by His own people and He moved on with His mission. Rejection is painful, but we can overcome it by trusting God to open doors for better opportunities.

TOPICAL OUTLINE OF THE LESSON

I. Introduction
A. Rejection
B. Biblical Background

II. Exposition and Application of the Scripture
A. The Home Scene (Matthew 13:54)
B. The Hostile Setting (Matthew 13:55-58)

III. Concluding Reflection

LESSON OBJECTIVES

Upon completion of this lesson, the students should know that:

1. Rejection should not deter a Christian from focusing on mission;
2. Challenges come from familiar people; and,
3. Unbelief is a deterrent to experiencing the power of God in action.

POINTS TO BE EMPHASIZED

ADULT/YOUTH

Adult Topic: Overcoming Rejection
Youth Topic: Coming Home …
Adult Key Verse: Matthew 13:58
Youth Key Verse: Matthew 13:57
Print Passage: Matthew 13:54-58

—The accounts of Jesus teaching in the synagogue and being rejected are also found in Mark 6:1-6 and Luke 4:16-30.
—Jesus made a habit of attending the synagogue on the Sabbath (see Luke 4:16). He taught there when He had an opportunity.
—Jesus was not surprised that prophets were without honor in their own country and in their own houses.
—Jesus' hometown people did not witness His deeds of power because of their unbelief.
—Jesus interpreted the Word of God much differently from His Jewish counterparts.
—Jesus told the people that they would not be the recipients of His miracles; instead, the miracles would be provided to others who had faith in Him, so they rejected Jesus and sought to kill Him (see Luke 4:29).

CHILDREN

Children Topic: Dealing with Rejection
Key Verse: Matthew 13:57
Print Passage: Matthew 13:54-58

—People in Jesus' hometown thought they knew Him.
—The people's limited knowledge of Jesus as the Son of God led them to be skeptical of His teachings and deeds of power.
—Although the name of the hometown is not mentioned, a similar passage in Luke's gospel links it to Nazareth.
—The people's rejection of Jesus hampered Jesus from continuing His ministry in His hometown.

I. INTRODUCTION

A. Rejection

Abraham Maslow (1908–1970) was a noted Jewish psychologist who developed what has come to be known as Maslow's Hierarchy of Needs. Essentially, this theory holds that all human beings have the same basic needs. The most basic of these needs is physiological (food, water, rest, etc.). These are followed by the need for safety, belonging, self-esteem, and self-actualization. Unless the lower tier of needs is satisfied, we will never reach our fullest potential. One of the needs that is central to human self-actualization is the need to belong—to be loved, appreciated, and accepted. When this need is not met, we are left vulnerable to social isolation, depression, loneliness, and a host of other negative emotions.

Every human is born with the need to be in community and to feel loved and accepted. We want to win the approval of those whom we are closest to and who are our closest companions.

What happens when we make a decision to follow the Lord Jesus Christ and honor Him as Savior? Persons who live in families where Christianity is ridiculed and rejected may experience the same type of response from family members. This makes today's lesson very valuable because in it we see Jesus Christ facing and dealing with community rejection. Jesus was not only rejected by the religious leaders of Israel, but He was also rejected by the very people with whom He grew up. As you study this lesson today, consider how you would have responded had you been in Jesus' position.

B. Biblical Background

One of the unique features of the gospel of Matthew is its structure. Matthew organized his account of the life and ministry of Jesus around five major discourses: 5:1–7:29; 10:1-42; 13:1-52; 18:1–19:2; and 23:1–25:46. Throughout the Gospels there are other occasions where Jesus taught and provided instruction for the people who had come to hear Him. Contained in chapter 13 is the third major discourse in the gospel of Matthew. The scene followed immediately after Jesus had completed His conversation with His mother, brothers, and sister (see Matthew 12:46-50; 13:1). They may have come to try to persuade Him to give up His ministry of preaching and teaching because of the concern being raised by prominent people and the religious elite.

The events described in the lesson have parallels in Mark 6:1-6 and Luke 4:16-30. Each of the writers recorded Jesus' visit to Nazareth. Jesus experienced the worst sort of rejection, which came from the people who personally knew Him and His family. Neither Matthew nor Mark provided any of the details of what Jesus said the day He visited the synagogue in Nazareth. Luke, however, recorded that Jesus read from the book of the prophet Isaiah 61, and stated that He was the living fulfillment of those verses. This may explain the negative reaction of the people toward Jesus in Nazareth. Luke also had this event occurring at the very beginning of the ministry of Jesus, shortly after the baptism and temptation narratives.

Chapter 13 contains much of the parabolic teachings of Jesus. In this chapter, Jesus began to teach His disciples in private, away from the Jewish population centers and their houses of worship. Here we see Him teaching along the seashore, as He began to face stiffer opposition from the scribes, Pharisees, and Sadducees. The content of His preaching and teaching had generated much debate among the religionists. The demonstrations of power (i.e., the casting out of demons) had led to accusations that He was being used by Beelzebub. Furthermore, they had questioned His authority.

II. EXPOSITION AND APPLICATION OF THE SCRIPTURE

A. The Home Scene
(Matthew 13:54)

And when he was come into his own country, he taught them in their synagogue, insomuch that they were astonished, and said, Whence hath this man this wisdom, and these mighty works?

Upon completing His parabolic teachings, Jesus headed south toward the hill country to Nazareth, which is located about twenty-five miles southeast of the Sea of Galilee. The city is situated in the hill country of Lower Galilee. (Today there is nothing that remains of this small village that existed during the time of Jesus. Nazareth is a thriving Christian city today.) The ancient town of Nazareth was about four miles southeast of Sepphoris, the city that Herod Antipas used as his capital before moving to Tiberias in Galilee. Nazareth was such an insignificant place that one of Jesus' own disciples asked if there was anything good that could come out of Nazareth (see John 1:45-46). The small town of Nazareth was not mentioned in the Old Testament, which attests to its relative obscurity. During the time of Jesus, it was a small village, occupied mostly by carpenters, tanners, shepherds, and small farmers. The village did have a synagogue, which is where Jesus paid His final visit.

Synagogues served multiple community purposes—they were houses of public prayer, places for instruction in the Torah, community meeting places, and very often served as the schools for children.

Jesus went home and entered the local synagogue. Synagogues were in wide use during the time of Jesus' ministry. In the Gospels Jesus often attended the religious meetings held in the synagogues, taught in them, healed the sick, and generally participated in the life of the local synagogues—particularly on the Sabbath (see Matthew 4:23; Mark 6:2; Luke 4:16-21). He received some of His harshest criticisms from members of the local synagogues (see Mark 6:1-4; Luke 4:28-29). Mark wrote that the event took place on the Sabbath. Jesus went into the synagogue and began to teach. All synagogues had a local rabbi or teacher who would share the Word of God weekly or as often as the people met. It was not uncommon for the leader of the synagogue to invite a teacher who was visiting to stand and teach.

We do not know if Mary and her other children were present. We are not told what Jesus taught; hence, the reference in Luke 4:18-21 may give some indication about what

Jesus taught. Anything else that we could say at this point would be more speculation than fact. We know that whatever Jesus taught, which was probably not far from the things He taught in Galilee, amazed and astounded the people present.

They began to ask among themselves, "Where did this man get this wisdom and these mighty works?" There were two things that amazed the people about Jesus.

First, they were astounded over His wisdom. The Greek word for "wisdom" is *sophia*, and it refers to a wide range of intellectual understandings about life. Jesus was obviously a man of wisdom well beyond His years. The astonishment may have been driven by the fact that Jesus was not formerly trained in any of the rabbinical schools of that day. It was probably not more than a few weeks or months prior to this event that He had been in their very midst living among them.

Second, they were amazed by the mighty demonstrations of power. We are not told what Jesus did in verse 58, but we are told that He did not do many mighty works in that place because of their unbelief. It is possible that this part of the response was based upon the news that may have been circulating in Galilee about the prophet from Nazareth. Capernaum was the main trade center in the area, and people from across Galilee came to the city to conduct business to buy and sell goods. It is highly conceivable that the people of Nazareth knew of His fame when He arrived. They appeared not to be questioning what He said or did; they simply wanted to know where He learned these things. "Where did this man get this wisdom and power?"

B. The Hostile Setting
(Matthew 13:55-58)

Is not this the carpenter's son? is not his mother called Mary? and his brethren, James, and Joses, and Simon, and Judas? And his sisters, are they not all with us? Whence then hath this man all these things? And they were offended in him. But Jesus said unto them, A prophet is not without honour, save in his own country, and in his own house. And he did not many mighty works there because of their unbelief.

As the scene unfolded they began to raise questions about Jesus' background. "Is not this the carpenter's son?" they asked. This was an obvious reference to Joseph. They were intimately acquainted with Jesus' entire family. "Is not his mother called Mary? and his brethren, James, and Joses, and Simon, and Judas?" (verse 55). The questions were raised in such a way as to say, "Who is this man, thinking that He can come here and speak this way?" The people gathered in the synagogue were outraged that someone from among them would come and try to show them up. The use of the personal names of Jesus' mother and brothers pointed to the intimacy they had with His background. Not only did they know His mother and brothers—they knew His sisters, although their names were never mentioned. We have no idea why Matthew did not include the names of the sisters of Jesus or why he did not mention Joseph by name. Some scholars have speculated that maybe Joseph was deceased at this point. We don't know. The response of the locals to Jesus is further evidence that Nazareth was not a very large place. The people knew too much about Him and were too familiar with His family.

It is stated in verse 57 that they were "offended in him." The Greek word for "offended" is *skandalizo (scan-dal-dzo)* and it gives us the

English word *scandal*. It literally means "to fall over, to judge unfavorably, impediment, or to be a stumbling block." Jesus' background and the fact that He grew up among them became a personal hindrance to their receiving His words.

The second part of verse 57 contains the only words spoken by Jesus during this entire episode.

In response to their hostility and rejection, Jesus announced that He was like all of the other prophets of ancient Israel. Jesus stated that a prophet had honor everywhere but in his own hometown and especially among his own people. In Deuteronomy 18:15, Moses stated that God would raise up a prophet from among His own people who would point them in the direction of God and share the Word of God with them.

What is a prophet? The *prophet* in ancient Israel was someone who spoke for God. This same definition can be applied today to preachers of the Gospel who carry a prophetic message to God's people from God. The word "prophet" comes from the Hebrew word *nabi*, which means "to call." Within ancient Hebrew tradition a prophet was someone who was called to deliver a message from and for the Lord God. The prophets were not necessarily men and women who had been called by God to predict the future. This is one of the primary misunderstandings that many people have regarding Hebrew prophetic preaching. God did use the prophets to tell Israel what would come if they continued to live in disobedience. They were primarily preachers on a mission from God.

The idea of *prophet* has within it two basic thoughts: calling out the Word of God and being called by God. The prophet was someone who sounded out the Word of God and who had been called by God. According to Isaiah 6:9, the man of God was called by God to "Go, and tell this people." The prophet was sent by God to tell the people what the Lord had to say.

The final visit of Jesus to Nazareth ended with a sad postscript. He did not do many mighty works there because of their unbelief. There is a variant rendering of this text in the book of Mark, in which is stated that Jesus did not do any miracles, except He laid hands on a few sick people. There is no contradiction between the two accounts. Remember, the people in Upper Galilee around Capernaum had seen some of the most spectacular demonstrations of power. They saw lepers cleansed, the lame walk, the blind made to see, and demons cast out. The power of faith was stronger around the Sea of Galilee, but in Nazareth the people simply could not get over the local boy coming home acting like He may have been bigger and better than them. Hence, Jesus was not able to do the mighty works there because of their lack of faith. What would have happened had the people been more open to the power of God and the ministry of Jesus?

III. CONCLUDING REFLECTION

Today's lesson has been a profile in courage, for the following reasons: first, because Jesus went to the very place He had been raised to preach and teach them about the kingdom of God. His desire was to lead those who were closest to Him into a new relationship with the Father. Many times we find it more convenient and easier to talk to people we don't know about faith than those who are most familiar with us. Why? Maybe it is because of the very thing that Jesus experienced—and rejection is a powerful deterrent to witnessing.

Second, it was a courageous move on the part of Jesus because even after the people rejected Him and were offended by His words, we are not told that He immediately left or reacted in anger. He must have stayed around to continue to preach, teach, and lay hands on those who would receive His presence.

These are two very powerful and important lessons for us. In this life we will come to know rejection and the possibility that people will not receive our witness. Yet we are commanded to stay focused and true to what God has called us to do. How would you have handled this situation if you were in Jesus' place? Maybe you have found yourself in the same situation; if so, what did you do?

PRAYER

Heavenly Father, teach us to be strong and then empower us for the days when men and women will not receive our words. Give us grace to minister to those who will listen and follow. In Jesus' name we pray. Amen.

WORD POWER

Unbelief (Greek: *apistia* [a-pis-tia])—means "faithlessness, disbelief, disobedience, want of faith in withholding belief in a divine thing." The people in Nazareth viewed Jesus as a village boy who had no authority or power. Their familiarity with Him caused Jesus not to do mighty works among them.

HOME DAILY BIBLE READINGS
(January 25–31, 2010)

Revealed in Rejection

MONDAY, January 25: "A Man of Suffering" (Isaiah 53:1-9)

TUESDAY, January 26: "No Knowledge of God" (Hosea 4:1-6)

WEDNESDAY, January 27: "Rejecting God's Command" (Mark 7:5-13)

THURSDAY, January 28: "The Lord Disciplines Those He Loves" (Proverbs 3:5-12)

FRIDAY, January 29: "Is Not This Joseph's Son?" (Luke 4:16-22)

SATURDAY, January 30: "Rejected at Home" (Luke 4:23-30)

SUNDAY, January 31: "Thwarting God's Power by Unbelief" (Matthew 13:54-58)

LESSON 10   February 7, 2010

RECOGNIZED BY A CANAANITE WOMAN

DEVOTIONAL READING: **Isaiah 42:1-9**
PRINT PASSAGE: **Matthew 15:21-28**

BACKGROUND SCRIPTURE: **Matthew 15:21-28**
KEY VERSE: **Matthew 15:28**

Matthew 15:21-28—KJV

21 Then Jesus went thence, and departed into the coasts of Tyre and Sidon.
22 And, behold, a woman of Canaan came out of the same coasts, and cried unto him, saying, Have mercy on me, O Lord, thou Son of David; my daughter is grievously vexed with a devil.
23 But he answered her not a word. And his disciples came and besought him, saying, Send her away; for she crieth after us.
24 But he answered and said, I am not sent but unto the lost sheep of the house of Israel.
25 Then came she and worshipped him, saying, Lord, help me.
26 But he answered and said, It is not meet to take the children's bread, and to cast it to dogs.
27 And she said, Truth, Lord: yet the dogs eat of the crumbs which fall from their masters' table.
28 Then Jesus answered and said unto her, O woman, great is thy faith: be it unto thee even as thou wilt. And her daughter was made whole from that very hour.

Matthew 15:21-28—NRSV

21 Jesus left that place and went away to the district of Tyre and Sidon.
22 Just then a Canaanite woman from that region came out and started shouting, "Have mercy on me, Lord, Son of David; my daughter is tormented by a demon."
23 But he did not answer her at all. And his disciples came and urged him, saying, "Send her away, for she keeps shouting after us."
24 He answered, "I was sent only to the lost sheep of the house of Israel."
25 But she came and knelt before him, saying, "Lord, help me."
26 He answered, "It is not fair to take the children's food and throw it to the dogs."
27 She said, "Yes, Lord, yet even the dogs eat the crumbs that fall from their masters' table."
28 Then Jesus answered her, "Woman, great is your faith! Let it be done for you as you wish." And her daughter was healed instantly.

BIBLE FACT

Christians have thoroughly examined the purpose and mission of Jesus as stated in Luke 4:18. When Jesus was in the Temple and He read the scroll, He re-emphasized His mission. We may argue that a lot of books have been written and sermons preached on His mission. However, a closer look at the way many Christians live today reveals no fulfillment of Jesus' mission. The woman in our text refused to accept the condition of her child's insanity. The irony of this situation is that this woman was not a Christian, but Jesus commended her for her faith. Help is always available if we go to Him.

Family members face issues and often cannot find help. Where can we find resources to help? A Gentile woman came to Jesus with persistence, seeking healing for her daughter, and Jesus healed the daughter.

TOPICAL OUTLINE OF THE LESSON

I. **Introduction**
   A. Encouragement
   B. Biblical Background

II. **Exposition and Application of the Scripture**
   A. A Desperate Mother's Plea (Matthew 15:21-23a)
   B. An Example of Determination (Matthew 15:23b-27)
   C. A Distinguished Woman (Matthew 15:28)

III. **Concluding Reflection**

LESSON OBJECTIVES

Upon completion of this lesson, the students will know that:

1. Jesus was not insulting the woman; rather, He was elevating her faith;
2. The healing of this woman's daughter testified to the universal love of Christ; and,
3. When Jesus heals, He does it wholly.

POINTS TO BE EMPHASIZED
ADULT/YOUTH

Adult Topic: **Hope for Healing**
Youth Topic: **Hope for Healing**
Adult/Youth Key Verse: **Matthew 15:28**
Print Passage: **Matthew 15:21-28**

—A woman of Canaan approached Jesus about healing her daughter.
—Jesus initially ignored the woman. When the disciples urged Him to send her away, He responded that His mission was only to the lost sheep of the house of Israel.
—The woman was undeterred by Jesus' initial rejection and persisted to plead her case.
—Jesus recognized the woman's great faith and immediately healed her daughter.
—Matthew set this story within the historical struggle between Jews (the chosen) and Gentiles (everyone else).
—This is an example in the book of Matthew of Jesus' ministering to non-Jews.
—Jesus repudiated discrimination based on gender and race.

CHILDREN

Children Topic: **Believe and Receive**
Key Verse: **Matthew 15:28**
Print Passage: **Matthew 15:21-28**

—Jesus' power was so well-known that even foreigners sought Him.
—Jesus explained that He was sent to the lost sheep of Israel.
—Jesus hears you even when you think He does not.
—Jesus will give you what you need.
—Jesus did not listen to His disciples; He did what He knew was right.
—Jesus taught that all who believe will receive.

I. INTRODUCTION

A. Encouragement

In his book, *Climbing Jacob's Ladder,* Dr. Andrew Billingsley, a highly regarded sociologist, tells several true stories of young black women who overcame tremendous odds to reach their personal pinnacles of success. He tells of a Charlene Carroll, who grew up in a family headed by a female. Her mother and father were divorced when she was a year old. Her mother became disabled, and she was eventually placed in foster care. She moved from one home to the next until she was eighteen, at which time she dropped out of high school and became pregnant. At that point she could have ended up living in poverty and on welfare.

However, Charlene had an aunt who was poor and lived in a public housing project and reached out to her and took her in. This aunt, who was poor in this world's riches, was rich in faith and encouragement. She gave Charlene her faith and courage. By the time Charlene was thirty-five, she was an entrepreneur with her own business, earning more than $100,000 a year.

Billingsley cited several reasons for Charlene's rise: (1) the strong work ethic instilled in her by her mother; (2) her own personal ambition and desire to rise above her situation; and (3) the loving care and support given by her aunt, who became a mother for her. This true story and thousands like it are vivid reminders that life does not have to terminate on a dead-end street.

B. Biblical Background

Jesus departed from Galilee and traveled northwest toward the coasts of Tyre and Sidon, the two major cities in Phoenicia. These were major seaport cities noted for their commerce and trade. The coastal region was approximately forty miles from Galilee. The two cities were primarily Gentile cities which had been heavily influenced by the Greek and Roman cultures. Tyre had a rich biblical history and is often mentioned in the Old Testament as being the home of many skilled artisans and carpenters (see 2 Samuel 5:11; 1 Kings 5:18; 7:13-47; 2 Chronicles 2:13-14; 4:11-17). We are not told why Jesus went to Phoenicia. It may have been because of the growing opposition of the Jewish religious leaders, who began to send investigators from Jerusalem to inquire about His teachings (see Matthew 15:1-19). Or it may have been to calm the fears of His disciples who became concerned about the charges Jesus leveled against the scribes and Pharisees (see Matthew 15:12). It may just have been that Jesus needed to get away from the demands of the large crowds of people who followed Him wherever He went (see 14:34-36).

II. EXPOSITION AND APPLICATION OF THE SCRIPTURE

A. A Desperate Mother's Plea
(Matthew 15:21-23a)

Then Jesus went thence, and departed into the coasts of Tyre and Sidon. And, behold, a woman of Canaan came out of the same coasts, and cried unto him, saying, Have mercy on me, O Lord, thou Son of David; my daughter is grievously vexed with a devil. But he answered her not a word.

Jesus departed from the area of Galilee and headed toward the Mediterranean seacoast cities of Phoenicia. Today this area is part of the nations of Lebanon and Syria. According to Matthew, the most recent location was Gennesaret, which was an area of plains and rolling hills just west of Capernaum (see Matthew 14:34; Mark 6:53). There is no archaeological evidence that a town of any size existed in the area where it is believed that Gennesaret was located. The reference could have been to the Sea of Galilee, which is sometimes referred to as the Lake of Gennesaret (see Luke 5:1). We do not know how long it took Jesus and His disciples to reach the area near Tyre and Sidon. This is a very tedious journey because the road winds west across a series of steep hills and mountains. Therefore, it may have taken several days to walk the forty-mile distance to the coastal region. This area was purely Gentile. With few exceptions, this being one, Jesus rarely entered areas occupied by Gentiles. It may be that Jesus went to a region where He knew that the Jewish religious leaders would not dare enter for fear of defilement (see John 18:28). We can only speculate what may have been the reason for the trip to the coast; some have been cited in the previous section of the lesson.

As they neared the area, a Canaanite woman met them and cried out to Jesus, saying, "Have mercy on me, O Lord, thou son of David..." (verse 22). The Canaanites had historically been enemies of the Jews for hundreds of years. They were descendants of the Philistines who were among the thorns in the sides of Saul and David. How the woman knew that Jesus was coming to the area where she lived is not stated. It was not important—for a miracle was about to take place. She cried out, literally crying or calling out with a loud voice. The tone of the word suggests that she refused to be silent, but continued to call out to Jesus. Her first request was for Jesus to have mercy on her. Never mind what her daughter was facing—she personally wanted and needed the gracious favor of Jesus Christ. The mother was not physically afflicted, but emotionally she was just as tormented, watching her child suffer so severely. Was this her only child? We do not know. Every mother grieves when her child is suffering.

In her desperation she called Jesus the Son of David, which was Jewish idiomatic phrasing for the *Messiah* (see Matthew 1:1; 9:27; 12:23). The words are also reminiscent of the life of David when God made a promise to him about an everlasting throne and perpetual kingdom. The woman wanted help for her daughter's condition; she was very grievously sick. This literally meant she was in misery or in a miserable condition. The girl had a devil. We don't know anything about the scope and severity of the demon's affliction, but such knowledge is not necessary. Demon possession is horrific, no matter the severity.

Jesus did not respond to anything the woman said. One wonders whether Jesus even heard the woman's screams for help. Why would Jesus look at this woman's plight and not say anything? Here Jesus was faced with a Gentile woman who was ethnically from the nation of people that Israel hated most. This is not to say that Jesus hated the woman or showed contempt for her. Jesus could not hate anyone and be who He was and is. Jesus heard the cry and sensed the deep respect that filled the woman's voice. Her use of the word *Lord* indicated that she saw in Him her only hope for help.

B. An Example of Determination
(Matthew 15:23b-27)

And his disciples came and besought him, saying, Send her away; for she crieth after us. But he answered and said, I am not sent but unto the lost sheep of the house of Israel. Then came she and worshipped him, saying, Lord, help me. But he answered and said, It is not meet to take the children's bread, and to cast it to dogs. And she said, Truth, Lord: yet the dogs eat of the crumbs which fall from their masters' table.

The disciples repeatedly demonstrated that their attitude toward people in trouble or who were hurting had not changed. As they did with the large multitude in Matthew 14:15, they wanted Jesus to send this woman away. They felt that this woman was intruding on their time with Jesus. By saying, "She is crying for us," the disciples revealed their insensitivity toward the woman's plight. They never even mentioned the condition of her daughter. They had seen scenes like this before and knew quite well that Jesus was more than able to help. Was it that this was a woman? Or could it have been her ethnicity? She was different and that can

sometimes separate the disciples of Jesus from the needs that people have for help. The woman showed deep respect, while the disciples had become so comfortable with Jesus that they never referred to Him as "Lord."

When Jesus did finally answer, He told her that His primary calling was to the house of Israel first. Israel was God's chosen people and the promise of the Messiah must first be realized among them. They must receive the Messiah and embrace His vision for global redemption. Israel was the first and most important sphere of His mission. This was the same charge that He had given His disciples for their first missionary mission (see Matthew 10:5-6). Why would Jesus make this statement here when He had healed the servant of a Roman centurion (in Matthew 8:5ff)? It is possible that in the case of the centurion the one requesting the help was a Gentile, but the one needing the help may have been a Jew. In this case the woman and her daughter were Gentiles. Jesus was being asked to do something He had not done. He was in or near an area where He had not gone. He spoke and here again we are not told who He spoke to. Did He answer the woman, in which case she would have felt hope? Or did He speak to the disciples, who would have felt that they had succeeded in turning Jesus' attention away from a Gentile woman?

The woman did not give up; rather, she persisted and showed determination. She came and worshiped Him (see verse 25). This indicates that she bowed before Him. She may have even pulled upon the garments of Jesus or grabbed His legs. All these are signs of sheer desperation. She said, "Lord, help me." There was no other recourse. Should Jesus leave and not cast the demon out of her daughter she would have lost the one opportunity she had to help her daughter.

In verse 26, Jesus answered again in a rather strange way: "It is not meet to take the children's bread, and to cast it to dogs." How are we to interpret these words of Jesus? On the surface the statement seems very rude and harsh. Jesus stated that it was not a good thing to take what rightfully belonged to the children and give it to someone else. Clearly, to take the bread that would be used to feed children and give it away would be to demonstrate misplaced priorities. The children in a family must be taken care of first. If one were to take the food that the children were to eat and give it to house pets, it would clearly indicate that the pets were more valuable than the children. It is also likely that Jesus may have been using a statement that was in wide circulation in Israel at the time. He must have spoken in a manner that would not arouse pain and hurt in the heart of the woman. She never lost hope and continued to press her need for help.

The woman was quick and thoughtful. She had a quick response to Jesus' statement. Even the dogs liked to eat the crumbs that fell from the Master's table now and then. Her words suggested that she was not asking Jesus to do anything that He would not normally do. She fully understood the magnitude of what she was requesting. There was not a hint of disrespect or disgust, even when Jesus responded with the words He used.

During one trip to Turkey (ancient Asia Minor) our group stopped at a restaurant near the ancient city of Antioch to have lunch (present-day Antakaya). It was like many places in Turkey, open and accessible to house pets and birds. At this particular establishment there were a number of cats who hung around waiting for crumbs or food to fall from the table. When it did, they would swoop in, grab the morsel, and run to wait for more. The woman in this story knew she was not a Jew and had no right to expect Jesus to do anything for her or her daughter. But, if there was any hope of help, she desperately wanted it, even if it was in the form of a few crumbs from the table.

C. A Distinguished Woman (Matthew 15:28)

Then Jesus answered and said unto her, O woman, great is thy faith: be it unto thee even as thou wilt. And her daughter was made whole from that very hour.

Then is a common word in the book of Matthew and is often used to indicate Jesus' response to something or someone. In this case, Jesus responded to the woman's faith or belief that He was the only person able to help her daughter. Jesus spoke directly to the woman. Two things are to be noted here. First, Jesus recognized the woman's faith as being great (Greek: *mega*—literally "very large"). It was the woman's faith in Jesus that led to the healing of her daughter. Great faith is not a measurement of size, but the absolute confidence that regardless of the circumstances and odds God can always be trusted (see Exodus 14:13; 1 Samuel 17:47; Daniel 3:16-19; Hebrews 11).

Second, the act of healing was immediate. Her daughter was made whole at that very hour. The word *whole* suggests that the healing was complete. It was used to denote healing of every sort: physical, emotional, and spiritual. There is no record of the woman's response. But there need not be—for she had already demonstrated her complete confidence and faith in the Lord Jesus Christ and her faith was justly rewarded.

III. CONCLUDING REFLECTION

It is very difficult for the average American Christian to understand hopelessness and real desperation. I don't imply that we have not faced trying times. Rather, I am implying that when one lives in a country where the options are practically non-existent, anyone who offers a glimmer of hope is like a messiah. It has been my privilege and blessing to lead several short-term mission trips to Nigeria and Kenya, and the reality of this story rings true in my spirit every time I read it. The woman who approached Jesus was a woman who had no options for help. Her only hope was Jesus Christ. We live in a country brimming with great privilege and tremendous opportunities. One day God will hold each of us accountable for what we have done with our time, spiritual gifts, and resources. The greatest action any believer can take is to share his or her faith in Jesus Christ with someone who may be lost in hopelessness. Jesus has taught us by precept and example that when we give away what the Father has given us, we give Him to others who are lost and in need of hope.

PRAYER

Heavenly Father, teach us to trust You in the good times and during the days when times are hard. May we learn the lesson of cultivating great faith in You. May the example of this mother reside in our hearts. In Jesus' name we pray. Amen.

WORD POWER

Answered (*apokrinomai* [a-po-kri-no-mai])—means "to give an answer to a question that has been proposed." Jesus looked at this woman eyeball to eyeball and began to speak. The woman was not disturbed by the reference Jesus made. She wanted an answer and she got it!

HOME DAILY BIBLE READINGS
(February 1–7, 2010)

Recognized by a Canaanite Woman

MONDAY, February 1: "Revelation to the Gentiles" (Luke 2:25-35)

TUESDAY, February 2: "God Shows No Partiality" (Romans 2:1-11)

WEDNESDAY, February 3: "A Light for the Gentiles" (Acts 13:44-49)

THURSDAY, February 4: "Nations Come to Your Light" (Isaiah 60:1-5)

FRIDAY, February 5: "Nations Walk by God's Light" (Revelation 21:22-27)

SATURDAY, February 6: "In Him the Gentiles Hope" (Romans 15:7-13)

SUNDAY, February 7: "Great Is Your Faith!" (Matthew 15:21-28)

LESSON 11   February 14, 2010

DECLARED BY PETER

DEVOTIONAL READING: **John 10:22-30**
PRINT PASSAGE: **Matthew 16:13-27**

BACKGROUND SCRIPTURE: **Matthew 16:13-27**
KEY VERSE: **Matthew 16:16**

Matthew 16:13-27—KJV

13 When Jesus came into the coasts of Caesarea Philippi, he asked his disciples, saying, Whom do men say that I the Son of man am?

14 And they said, Some say that thou art John the Baptist: some, Elias; and others, Jeremias, or one of the prophets.

15 He saith unto them, But whom say ye that I am?

16 And Simon Peter answered and said, Thou art the Christ, the Son of the living God.

17 And Jesus answered and said unto him, Blessed art thou, Simon Bar-jona: for flesh and blood hath not revealed it unto thee, but my Father which is in heaven.

18 And I say also unto thee, That thou art Peter, and upon this rock I will build my church; and the gates of hell shall not prevail against it.

19 And I will give unto thee the keys of the kingdom of heaven: and whatsoever thou shalt bind on earth shall be bound in heaven: and whatsoever thou shalt loose on earth shall be loosed in heaven.

20 Then charged he his disciples that they should tell no man that he was Jesus the Christ.

21 From that time forth began Jesus to shew unto his disciples, how that he must go unto Jerusalem, and suffer many things of the elders and chief priests and scribes, and be killed, and be raised again the third day.

22 Then Peter took him, and began to rebuke him, saying, Be it far from thee, Lord: this shall not be unto thee.

23 But he turned, and said unto Peter, Get thee behind me, Satan: thou art an offence unto me: for thou savourest not the things that be of God, but those that be of men.

24 Then said Jesus unto his disciples, If any man will come after me, let him deny himself, and take up his

Matthew 16:13-27—NRSV

13 Now when Jesus came into the district of Caesarea Philippi, he asked his disciples, "Who do people say that the Son of Man is?"

14 And they said, "Some say John the Baptist, but others Elijah, and still others Jeremiah or one of the prophets."

15 He said to them, "But who do you say that I am?"

16 Simon Peter answered, "You are the Messiah, the Son of the living God."

17 And Jesus answered him, "Blessed are you, Simon son of Jonah! For flesh and blood has not revealed this to you, but my Father in heaven.

18 And I tell you, you are Peter, and on this rock I will build my church, and the gates of Hades will not prevail against it.

19 I will give you the keys of the kingdom of heaven, and whatever you bind on earth will be bound in heaven, and whatever you loose on earth will be loosed in heaven."

20 Then he sternly ordered the disciples not to tell anyone that he was the Messiah.

21 From that time on, Jesus began to show his disciples that he must go to Jerusalem and undergo great suffering at the hands of the elders and chief priests and scribes, and be killed, and on the third day be raised.

22 And Peter took him aside and began to rebuke him, saying, "God forbid it, Lord! This must never happen to you."

23 But he turned and said to Peter, "Get behind me, Satan! You are a stumbling block to me; for you are setting your mind not on divine things but on human things."

24 Then Jesus told his disciples, "If any want to become my followers, let them deny themselves and

UNIFYING LESSON PRINCIPLE

Many people are curious about the Jesus of history. Who is Jesus really? Jesus affirmed that Peter's declaration of Jesus as the Christ, the Son of God, was a revelation by God.

cross, and follow me.

25 For whosoever will save his life shall lose it: and whosoever will lose his life for my sake shall find it.

26 For what is a man profited, if he shall gain the whole world, and lose his own soul? or what shall a man give in exchange for his soul?

27 For the Son of man shall come in the glory of his Father with his angels; and then he shall reward every man according to his works.

take up their cross and follow me.

25 For those who want to save their life will lose it, and those who lose their life for my sake will find it.

26 For what will it profit them if they gain the whole world but forfeit their life? Or what will they give in return for their life?

27 "For the Son of Man is to come with his angels in the glory of his Father, and then he will repay everyone for what has been done."

TOPICAL OUTLINE OF THE LESSON

I. **Introduction**
    A. The Church
    B. Biblical Background

II. **Exposition and Application of the Scripture**
    A. Jesus' Fundamental Question (Matthew 16:13-16)
    B. Jesus' Prophetic Pronouncement (Matthew 16:17-19)
    C. Requirements for Authentic Followers (Matthew 16:20-27)

III. **Concluding Reflection**

LESSON OBJECTIVES

Upon completion of this lesson, the students will know:

1. Jesus is the chief cornerstone of the church;

2. True followers of Jesus must understand what "denial of self" means; and,

3. Authority has been given to true followers of Christ.

POINTS TO BE EMPHASIZED

ADULT/YOUTH

Adult Topic: Declaring Allegiance

Youth Topic: I Know Who You Are!

Adult/Youth Key Verse: Matthew 16:16

Print Passage: Matthew 16:13-27

—People identified Jesus with the prophets Elijah and Jeremiah.

—People in the first century misunderstood who Jesus was, despite miraculous evidence.

—Peter affirmed Jesus as Messiah, then immediately scolded Him for predicting His suffering.

—This is one of the earliest declarations of Jesus' messiahship by a disciple.

—Jesus declared that Peter's declaration would be the foundation of the church.

—Jesus foretold His suffering, death, and resurrection in Jerusalem.

—After Peter objected, Jesus rebuked Peter and explained the cost of discipleship.

CHILDREN

Children Topic: Who Am I?

Key Verse: Matthew 16:16

Print Passage: Matthew 16:13-20

—Jesus asked His disciples, "Who do people say that the Son of Man is?"

—The disciples mentioned different names that people gave for Jesus.

—Jesus wanted to know who the disciples said He was.

—Jesus acknowledged Peter for his response, "You are the Messiah, the Son of the living God."

—God revealed to Simon Peter who Jesus was.

—Jesus said that His church would withstand assaults by evil forces.

I. INTRODUCTION

A. The Church

If there is one thing that Christians cannot agree upon, it is how to define and understand the Christian church in today's world. Some Christians define the church by its theological leanings, which are: conservative, fundamental, evangelical, orthodox, or liberal; some by its politics—it is Democratic or Republican. Then others define the church by its ethnicity: Is it African-American, Caucasian, African, Chinese, or multicultural? If you read the work of ten different theologians or Bible scholars, you would encounter ten different ways of thinking about the church. There would be very different views about everything from authority and worship to mission and church structure.

In recent years, the Christian church has undergone some very radical changes. Some of the changes have been for the best and others have been very divisive and destructive. They are just too numerous to even consider at this point. This has prompted some Christians to believe that the church has lost its way in the world. Regardless of one's theological or biblical perspective, one thing is clear: the church is the living embodiment of Jesus Christ in the world. The church is the product of God's purpose and the means by which global redemption will be achieved.

In Matthew 16:18, we have the first mention of the word *church* in the New Testament. The Christian church was historically founded and commissioned by Jesus Christ. The original marching orders of the church have not changed. Among the questions implicit in today's lesson are: Does the church mirror the image that we see in the New Testament? Is the church true to the biblical purpose of Jesus Christ?

B. Biblical Background

Today's lesson can be divided into two parts. The first part is contained in verses 13-20 and is Peter's confession in Caesarea Philippi. The second part, verses 21-27, is Jesus' first prediction of His passion.

Each of the Synoptic Gospels is a record of this event in Caesarea Philippi (see Mark 8:27-33; Luke 9:18-22). Peter's confession of Jesus as the Christ in Caesarea Philippi marked a major turning point in the ministry of Jesus. Caesarea Philippi was a major Greco-Roman city about fifty miles north of the Sea of Galilee.

As they walked, two important proclamations were made by Jesus. First, in response to Peter's confession, He gave His first prediction of His passion (verses 13-20). Second, Jesus issued a call to radical discipleship which involves complete obedience and submission to the Father's will (verses 21-27).

II. EXPOSITION AND APPLICATION OF THE SCRIPTURE

A. Jesus' Fundamental Question
(Matthew 16:13-16)

When Jesus came into the coasts of Caesarea Philippi, he asked his disciples, saying, Whom do men say that I the Son of man am? And they said, Some say that thou art John the Baptist: some, Elias; and others, Jeremias, or one of the prophets. He saith unto them, But whom say ye that I am? And Simon Peter answered and said, Thou art the Christ, the Son of the living God.

As they neared the environs of Caesarea Philippi Jesus asked His disciples a question. "Whom do men say that I the Son of man am?" (verse 13). The disciples responded by telling Jesus what the prevailing beliefs were about His identity. The ministry of Jesus had been so powerful that people were not quite sure of who He was. Their opinions ranged from John the Baptist to Elijah, Jeremiah, or one of the other prophets. The Jews believed the Messiah's appearance would be preceded by the appearance of one of these prophets.

During the Inter-Testamental Period, there developed the belief that the coming of the Messiah would be preceded by one of the great prophets of ancient Israel. One of the persons believed to be part of the coming eschatological age was Moses. In Deuteronomy 18:18, there is the mention of the Lord raising up a prophet from among the people. We see in Matthew's gospel that just as Moses was the lawgiver, Jesus was a greater lawgiver who reinterpreted and defined in a deeper spiritual way the true meaning of God's Law (see Matthew 5–7). The name of the prophet Elijah also figured prominently in some Jewish messianic expectations. One reason had to do with his being carried to heaven in a whirlwind (see 2 Kings 2:1-11). Based on Malachi 4:5-6, some Jews believed that Elijah would be the forerunner of the Messiah. There was also belief that he might even be the Messiah. These beliefs help us to understand more clearly the response of the disciples to the question of Jesus when they visited Caesarea Philippi.

In verse 15, Jesus raised a second question with His disciples: "But whom say ye that I am?" They had witnessed the greatest miracles and heard the most profound teachings by anyone. Peter spoke and said, "You are the Christ, the Son of the living God." Peter not only spoke for himself, but for the rest of the disciples as well.

B. Jesus' Prophetic Pronouncement
(Matthew 16:17-19)

And Jesus answered and said unto him, Blessed art thou, Simon Bar-jona: for flesh and blood hath not revealed it unto thee, but my Father which is in heaven. And I say

also unto thee, That thou art Peter, and upon this rock I will build my church; and the gates of hell shall not prevail against it. And I will give unto thee the keys of the kingdom of heaven: and whatsoever thou shalt bind on earth shall be bound in heaven: and whatsoever thou shalt loose on earth shall be loosed in heaven.

In verse 17, Jesus pronounced a blessing upon Peter. He called him by his full name—Simon Bar-jona. Peter's declaration of the messiahship of Jesus was not from his own reasoning, nor did it come from consultation with the other disciples. "Flesh and blood" did not reveal this information to Peter. Flesh and blood could be interpreted as human reasoning and wisdom. Jesus stated that His Father in heaven had given to Peter the revelation of His divine personhood.

Verse 18 has been the source of numerous volumes of books and the cause of endless debates. What is clear is that Jesus spoke directly to Peter and said that "upon this rock I will build my church." At the heart of the debate has been the question of whether Jesus referred to Peter as the rock or his faith statement as the rock. First, it would be difficult to maintain that Peter was the rock upon which the church was built because Paul also planted numerous churches as did many other early pioneering missionaries and evangelists. Second, Peter was not the Messiah, hence he was in no position to be the foundation upon which God would stake the redemption of the entire world. It is apparent that Jesus could have only been referring to Himself: "Upon my life, sacrifice, and obedience I will build my church." Third, Peter has never been thought of or referred to as the rock in the New Testament. That honor and position has always gone to Jesus Christ (see 1 Corinthians 10:4; 1 Peter 2:6-8, especially the reference to the "Chief Cornerstone").

The "gates of hell" referred to the power of death and destruction. Gates were symbols of security and strength. When Jesus said that the gates of hell would not prevail against the church, He meant that not even death would be strong enough to kill, stop, or hinder the progress and growth of the church.

Jesus promised to give Peter the keys to the kingdom of heaven. Keys provided access. The kingdom of heaven is not a spatial location. It is not a physical city. It is not a specific place; rather, it refers to the rule of God in the hearts and lives of men and women. Peter was to be given the right to lead people to Jesus Christ (see John 21:15-17). He could bind and loose. These words have been understood in a variety of ways. The most likely meaning had to do with opening the Scriptures and releasing people to serve God in freedom and obedience (see Matthew 23:13). The church of this generation has also been given the keys to the kingdom, wherein we can lead men and women to saving faith in the Lord Jesus Christ.

C. Requirements for Authentic Followers (Matthew 16:20-27)

Then charged he his disciples that they should tell no man that he was Jesus the Christ. From that time forth began Jesus to shew unto his disciples, how that he must go unto Jerusalem, and suffer many things of the elders and chief priests and scribes, and be killed, and be raised again the third day. Then Peter took him, and began to rebuke him, saying, Be it far from thee, Lord: this shall not be unto thee. But he turned, and said unto Peter, Get thee behind me, Satan: thou art an offence unto me: for thou savourest not the things that be of God, but those that be of men. Then said Jesus unto his disciples, If any man will come after me, let him deny himself, and take up his cross, and follow me. For whosoever will save his life shall lose it: and whosoever will lose his life for my

sake shall find it. For what is a man profited, if he shall gain the whole world, and lose his own soul? or what shall a man give in exchange for his soul? For the Son of man shall come in the glory of his Father with his angels; and then he shall reward every man according to his works.

Beginning at that point, everything began to change. For the first time Jesus told His disciples that the Messiah would suffer many things, and be killed and then raised on the third day. Peter wanted to rebuke Jesus and told Him that what He was saying would never happen (verse 22). The implication of his statement was that whatever it took to keep this from happening, he, along with the others, would not permit it to be so. Jesus rebuked Peter, calling him Satan. A few minutes earlier Peter was receiving revelations from God. Now He appeared to be on the side of the devil. Jesus told him that he was not thinking about the things of God, but that his mind was entirely focused on the wrong things. He was thinking about things that occupied the minds of men (verse 23).

Then the conversation shifted from Peter and his misguided notions of saving Jesus from the mission that the Father sent Him to do to addressing all of the disciples. Verse 24 contains Jesus' call to radical discipleship. There are two points that are critical to our understanding of His words. First, this was an open invitation from Jesus. He did not and does not call a certain kind of person. His invitation is to *whosoever will*. The men and women who first followed Him were fishermen, tax collectors, prostitutes, radicals, rascals, and revolutionaries. They were the common people, who heard His message and gladly received it. Second, let no man or woman ever say that he or she was tricked into following Jesus. Jesus

did not compel the men who followed Him from Galilee to do so. He made them no false or veiled promises of greatness and grandeur. He did not offer an easy way—in fact, He told them that the road would be rough.

What did Jesus mean when He called upon the crowd to deny self? It does not mean that when we give up something, someone, some idea, some goal, or some dream or aspiration that we have denied ourselves in the sense of what Jesus meant. *To deny oneself* is "to give up, relinquish any and all claims to ourselves." It is to give up the right to ourselves. It means that we shift the center of our lives away from ourselves to God and His purposes. We move out of the center, and He becomes the center of our lives, and not just our joys.

To Jews, the idea of a cross was repugnant—after all, it was not a Jewish form of punishment, but a Roman form of punishment. Jews would stone a person to death. Romans would crucify a man. The cross meant certain death. When a man took up that crossbeam to carry it, he knew that he was on the way to dying. But what does it mean to "bear one's cross"? The first understanding is expressed in the idea of humble obedience. In other words, we are called upon to submit our wills to the divine will of God. It is about being obedient to the heavenly voice. The second has to do with the idea of death. On one hand, the cross meant actual death for Jesus and His first disciples. Christians, however, must understand this death symbolically—that is, we are called upon to die to ourselves.

Jesus said that the things that men and women seek the most can be the very things that cause them to lose their eternal rewards. Humankind's quest for money, possessions, and power were at the heart of the great global financial collapse of 2008. Many people made billions of dollars but lost their way and compromised their values of honesty and integrity. One's soul is so valuable that no amount of money can be exchanged for it (verse 26).

III. CONCLUDING REFLECTION

One of the biggest causes of conflict and confusion in so many churches has to do with authority and power. Men and women jostle and seek to exert unauthorized and illegitimate authority over the house of God and the people of God. Jesus told Peter and the other disciples that the church belonged to Him, and His words removed any doubt about ownership (see Acts 20:28; 1 Corinthians 1:1-2). He is the Head of the body and it was His blood that was shed that redeems all men and women (see Ephesians 1:7, 22; 4:15; Colossians 1:18; 2:10; 1 Peter 2:7). We are all members of His body called into existence to do His will and bidding in the world (see 2 Corinthians 5:19-20).

The call to service still rings loud and clear. Jesus has given us a clarion call to go forth and make disciples of others. But, before we can and will accept, there must be a humbling of ourselves and a deep commitment to His purpose. Take a few minutes to reflect over your life and ask yourself if your personal ministry mirrors anything like what you find in the Gospels.

PRAYER

Heavenly Father, there are so many challenges to committed service that we face. Teach us how to love You by obediently following You. In Jesus' name we pray. Amen.

WORD POWER

Thou Art the Christ (*Su-ei-o Chri-stos*)—**The first word, *thou*, is an emphatic pronoun; plus the definite article (*the*) makes it crystal clear that no other is the Savior, the anointed of God. Only Jesus Christ is *the* Son of God. Any debate as to whether Jesus is the Son of God collapses in the presence of the emphatic position of the pronoun (Thou).**

HOME DAILY BIBLE READINGS
(February 8–14, 2010)

Declared by Peter

MONDAY, February 8: "My Sheep Hear My Voice" (John 10:22-30)
TUESDAY, February 9: "Believe in the Good News" (Mark 1:9-15)
WEDNESDAY, February 10: "Only Believe" (Mark 6:34-44)
THURSDAY, February 11: "Help My Unbelief" (Mark 9:14-27)
FRIDAY, February 12: "Ask and Believe" (Mark 11:20-25)
SATURDAY, February 13: "Both Lord and Messiah" (Acts 2:29-36)
SUNDAY, February 14: "You Are the Messiah" (Matthew 16:13-27)

WITNESSED BY DISCIPLES

DEVOTIONAL READING: 2 Peter 1:16-21
PRINT PASSAGE: Matthew 17:1-12

BACKGROUND SCRIPTURE: Matthew 17:1-12
KEY VERSE: Matthew 17:2

Matthew 17:1-12—KJV

AND AFTER six days Jesus taketh Peter, James, and John his brother, and bringeth them up into an high mountain apart,

2 And was transfigured before them: and his face did shine as the sun, and his raiment was white as the light.

3 And, behold, there appeared unto them Moses and Elias talking with him.

4 Then answered Peter, and said unto Jesus, Lord, it is good for us to be here: if thou wilt, let us make here three tabernacles; one for thee, and one for Moses, and one for Elias.

5 While he yet spake, behold, a bright cloud overshadowed them: and behold a voice out of the cloud, which said, This is my beloved Son, in whom I am well pleased; hear ye him.

6 And when the disciples heard it, they fell on their face, and were sore afraid.

7 And Jesus came and touched them, and said, Arise, and be not afraid.

8 And when they had lifted up their eyes, they saw no man, save Jesus only.

9 And as they came down from the mountain, Jesus charged them, saying, Tell the vision to no man, until the Son of man be risen again from the dead.

10 And his disciples asked him, saying, Why then say the scribes that Elias must first come?

11 And Jesus answered and said unto them, Elias truly shall first come, and restore all things.

12 But I say unto you, That Elias is come already, and they knew him not, but have done unto him whatsoever they listed. Likewise shall also the Son of man suffer of them.

Matthew 17:1-12—NRSV

SIX DAYS later, Jesus took with him Peter and James and his brother John and led them up a high mountain, by themselves.

2 And he was transfigured before them, and his face shone like the sun, and his clothes became dazzling white.

3 Suddenly there appeared to them Moses and Elijah, talking with him.

4 Then Peter said to Jesus, "Lord, it is good for us to be here; if you wish, I will make three dwellings here, one for you, one for Moses, and one for Elijah."

5 While he was still speaking, suddenly a bright cloud overshadowed them, and from the cloud a voice said, "This is my Son, the Beloved; with him I am well pleased; listen to him!"

6 When the disciples heard this, they fell to the ground and were overcome by fear.

7 But Jesus came and touched them, saying, "Get up and do not be afraid."

8 And when they looked up, they saw no one except Jesus himself alone.

9 As they were coming down the mountain, Jesus ordered them, "Tell no one about the vision until after the Son of Man has been raised from the dead."

10 And the disciples asked him, "Why, then, do the scribes say that Elijah must come first?"

11 He replied, "Elijah is indeed coming and will restore all things;

12 but I tell you that Elijah has already come, and they did not recognize him, but they did to him whatever they pleased. So also the Son of Man is about to suffer at their hands."

UNIFYING LESSON PRINCIPLE

People sometimes seek special spiritual experiences. Which experiences are authentic? Three disciples experienced a spiritual encounter that confirmed Jesus as the Son of God.

TOPICAL OUTLINE OF THE LESSON

I. Introduction
  A. An Unusual Experience
  B. Biblical Background

II. Exposition and Application of the Scripture
  A. The Transfiguration Experience
     (Matthew 17:1-4)
  B. The Voice of God's Approval
     (Matthew 17:5-8)
  C. The Great Rejection
     (Matthew 17:9-12)

III. Concluding Reflection

LESSON OBJECTIVES

Upon completion of this lesson, the students will know that:

1. Jesus was physically transfigured in the presence of Peter, James, and John;
2. God sent a message of authentication to enable the witnesses to believe in Jesus; and,
3. Jesus was fully aware of His impending total rejection and death.

POINTS TO BE EMPHASIZED

ADULT/YOUTH
Adult Topic: **Mountaintop Experiences**
Youth Topic: **I See You!**
Adult/Youth Key Verse: **Matthew 17:2**
Print Passage: **Matthew 17:1-12**

—The presence of Moses and Elijah confirmed that Jesus was the fulfillment of God's covenant.
—Jesus used typology to explain the identity of John the Baptist.
—The Mount of Transfiguration was for Jesus a spiritual mountain peak. He was empowered to take the way of the Cross.
—Jesus' changed form prefigured His resurrection.
—Matthew 17:5 is a reiteration of God's affirmation of Jesus as "the Beloved" at Jesus' baptism (3:17).
—Jesus took Peter, James, and John to the top of the mountain where He was transfigured.
—As He was transfigured, a voice from heaven spoke saying, "This is my Son."

CHILDREN
Children Topic: **A Special Appearance**
Key Verse: **Matthew 17:5**
Print Passage: **Matthew 17:1-8**

—Peter, James, and John were with Jesus when Moses and Elijah appeared.
—Jesus talked to Moses and Elijah in the presence of the disciples.
—A voice from the cloud said, "This is my Son, the Beloved; with him I am well pleased; listen to him!"
—Sometimes God wants us to be quiet and not tell everything.

I. INTRODUCTION

A. An Unusual Experience

The one place I enjoy most when I travel to Israel is the Mount of Olives. From the Mount of Olives one can see the Old City of Jerusalem with its bustling activity. And one can sense the pain and hear the words of Jesus as He wept over Jerusalem and pleaded with her to accept the day of her visitation (see Luke 19:41-44). These have been truly mountaintop experiences for me and the people who have traveled with me.

Today's lesson is a record of another grand and glorious mountaintop experience. From the lesson, we will learn about the Transfiguration and its lasting impact on the lives of Peter, James, and John. We will see that there are moments in life when God speaks to us to confirm His presence, give us a new assignment, or empower us for periods of greater spiritual growth. These are some of the results that Peter, James, and John may have experienced on the Mount of Transfiguration.

B. Biblical Background

All three of the Synoptic Gospels are records of the Transfiguration. Matthew and Mark (Mark 9:2-8) cited that it took place six days after the events described in chapter 16, while Luke stated that the Transfiguration took place eight days later (see Luke 9:28-36). The fact that each of the Gospel writers reported this event lends credence to its importance in the life of Jesus and to the early Christian church. The Transfiguration occurred at a point when the ministry of Jesus was nearing its climax in Galilee. We do not know the time of year that this took place; more than likely it could have been early fall or mid-winter. Within a few weeks or months of the Transfiguration, Jesus would begin the journey to Jerusalem to face the final chapter in the three-year journey of His ministry and mission (see Matthew 19:1; Luke 9:51-52).

We raise many questions in trying to understand the passage. Why would Jesus take Peter, James, and John with Him? What was the meaning of the Transfiguration for Jesus? How does this passage speak to believers today? At the conclusion of this lesson, we hope to answer some of the questions raised.

II. EXPOSITION AND APPLICATION OF THE SCRIPTURE

A. The Transfiguration Experience (Matthew 17:1-4)

AND AFTER six days Jesus taketh Peter, James, and John his brother, and bringeth them up into an high mountain apart, And was transfigured before them: and his face did shine as the sun, and his raiment was white as the light. And, behold, there appeared unto them Moses and Elias talking with him. Then answered Peter, and said unto Jesus, Lord, it is good for us to be here: if thou wilt, let us make here three tabernacles; one for thee, and one for Moses, and one for Elias.

Six days after the visit to Caesarea Philippi, Jesus took Peter, James, and John to a high mountain. The selection of these three disciples is an indication that Jesus considered them to be among His most trusted and valued companions. Some refer to them as the "inner circle," though Jesus never used this term. These same three men were with Jesus during very important events (see Matthew 26:37; Mark 5:37). It was not that Jesus loved these men more than the others; it may be that they would become the foundational leaders of the early Christian movement and it was crucial for them to have a broader and more powerful witness of the life and ministry of Jesus.

There has been a great deal of discussion and speculation about the exact mountain referred to in these passages. Some interpreters have suggested Mount Tabor, which is located in the Jezreel Valley. This location has been rejected because at the time, archaeologists say that there was a Roman garrison occupying the mountain because of its strategic location. And besides, it is quite a distance from Caesarea Philippi and the journey would have required Jesus to pass through Capernaum. There is no mention of that having occurred.

A second suggestion has been Mount Hermon, but this also seems highly unlikely as the place of the Transfiguration because of the distance from Caesarea Philippi, and the fact that the mountaintop is covered with snow year-round. It is highly unlikely that Jesus would have chosen such a spot, and there is no record of Jesus ever having visited Mount Hermon. The most likely location is Mount Meron, which is approximately four thousand feet high and clearly fits the description given by Matthew. Furthermore, it is within easy walking distance of Caesarea Philippi and would accord well with the account of the events that immediately followed the Transfiguration.

While they were on the mountain, Jesus was transfigured before the three disciples. The Greek word for "transfigured" is *metamorphoo* and it literally means "to be transformed, to change in form." This word is used by Paul in his letter to the Romans to talk about the transformation that takes place in believers' lives when they submit to the lordship of Jesus Christ (see Romans 12:2). While the disciples were talking and walking with Jesus, this miraculous change took place instantly. Everything about Jesus changed and began to glow and radiate like the brightness of the sun. His skin, clothes, and face shone as the brightest light. There is no record of a conversation or any words of warning by Jesus that this was about to take place.

Suddenly, out of nowhere, there appeared Moses and Elijah, both of whom were talking to Jesus. Why Moses and Elijah? The answer may lie in an earlier statement made by Jesus in Matthew 5:17 where Jesus said that He had not come to destroy the Law or the prophets but to fulfill. This meeting with Moses and Elijah may have served as confirmation that Jesus was indeed the Messiah. Moses was the great lawgiver and Elijah was the first of the great prophets of ancient Israel. We know that Elijah never died (see 2 Kings 2:11-12). Furthermore, there was a belief that the appearing of the Messiah would be preceded by Elijah (see Malachi 4:5). There was a tradition that developed during the Intertestamental Period that Moses may have never died, since no one ever found the site of his burial. Josephus, the Jewish historian, wrote that Moses was taken directly to heaven. We have no record of the conversation between Jesus and Moses and Elijah. Therefore, anything that we would say in that regard would be mere speculation. Luke, however, did add that the two men were speaking to Jesus about what He was to accomplish in Jerusalem (see Luke 9:31).

B. The Voice of God's Approval (Matthew 17:5-8)

While he yet spake, behold, a bright cloud overshadowed them: and behold a voice out of the cloud, which said, This is my beloved Son, in whom I am well pleased; hear ye him. And when the disciples heard it, they fell on their face, and were sore afraid. And Jesus came and touched them, and said, Arise, and be not afraid. And when they had lifted up their eyes, they saw no man, save Jesus only.

Was the Transfiguration for Jesus and confirmation by the Father of His divine sonship, or was it for Peter, James, and John? It could be that God used this moment to validate before them the Personhood of Jesus as the Christ. Their sojourn with Jesus may have brought them to the place of over-familiarity with Jesus to the extent that He was not seen for who He really was. Such is the reality with us as well. We can become so familiar with the trappings and rituals of religion that we forget that Christianity is all about Christ and His purpose of ministry and mission.

As on several other occasions, Peter spoke first. Mark stated that initially Peter did not know what to say (see Mark 9:6). Peter may not have known what to say, but he recognized that where they were was unlike any other place they had been with Jesus. "Lord, it is good for us to be here." Peter used the title *Lord,* which indicated respect and submission to the deity of Christ. He wanted to build three tabernacles to commemorate the site and the presence of the three men together in the same place.

While they were speaking, the four of them were suddenly enveloped in a cloud and a voice thundered from the cloud saying, "This is my beloved Son, in whom I am well pleased; hear ye him." The immediate response of the disciples was to fall down out of fear. They had neither been in nor known such an event to happen in their lives. Jesus reassured them that they had nothing to be afraid of. When they finally opened their eyes, they saw only Jesus.

These verses contain several allusions that reflect the life of ancient Israel. It would have been very difficult for a Jewish reader of the book of Matthew to miss the significance of what he or she had just heard or read. The three men clearly look back to the time of the Exodus and remind us of the institution of the Feast of Booths (see Leviticus 16:34; Deuteronomy 16:13; compare also with Zechariah 14:16). The presence of the cloud that enveloped Jesus and the disciples would remind Jewish readers of the cloud that settled over the Tabernacle (see Exodus 40:34-38). The presence of the cloud and pillar of fire was representative of God's continuing presence with Israel.

The voice that spoke looked back to the time of Jesus' baptism when the voice of God spoke from the heavens and announced to Him that the Father was well-pleased with Him. First, God said to them that Jesus was His beloved Son. Here we see the affirmation of the person of Jesus. He was not just another prophet; rather, He was the Son of the Most High. Second, God announced to them that

He was well-pleased with Jesus. This clearly ran counter to the brewing storm of hostility from the Jewish religious leaders and maybe even some of the local people. Jesus had become the poster child for trouble in Israel. Yet, the Father was well-pleased with His life. Third, they were instructed to hear Him. The Transfiguration confirmed the miracles, the exorcisms, the teachings, and the preaching of Jesus. The disciples may have not known fully and truly who Jesus was, but this was clearly an event and day that Peter never forgot. He later wrote about the experience in his second letter (see 2 Peter 1:16-18). Although it would be several months before they would come to the fullness of the knowledge of the Son of God, the day of Transfiguration was etched forever in their memories.

C. The Great Rejection
(Matthew 17:9-12)

And as they came down from the mountain, Jesus charged them, saying, Tell the vision to no man, until the Son of man be risen again from the dead. And his disciples asked him, saying, Why then say the scribes that Elias must first come? And Jesus answered and said unto them, Elias truly shall first come, and restore all things. But I say unto you, That Elias is come already, and they knew him not, but have done unto him whatsoever they listed. Likewise shall also the Son of man suffer of them.

The disciples were probably still in a state of shock, awe, and amazement at having just lived through the experience of the Transfiguration. Maybe they were talking to Jesus about what they had just seen and heard and wanted to know more about the vision. Jesus did not entertain discussion about it but gave emphatic instructions that they were to tell no one about the vision (see verse 9). The disciples were to keep silent until the Son of Man had been raised again from the dead. "Son of Man" is a title that Jesus used exclusively to refer to Himself. Its roots date back to the prophetic ministry of Ezekiel (see Ezekiel 3:17; 6:2), and it appeared in Daniel 7:13, where there was the image of a figure like a Son of Man descending with the clouds. Scholars are not sure how Jesus understood this title, nor can we be sure if the understanding of Jesus was the same as that of Daniel.

There was no reaction by the disciples to the statement of Jesus that He would be raised again from the dead. Rather than discuss the statement Jesus had just made, they wanted to know when Elijah would appear (verse 10). They referred to the teaching of the scribes who taught that Elijah must first appear before the Messiah came. This belief was grounded in Malachi 4:4-5 and in the Apocrypha book of Sirach 48:10 where there is a reference to Elijah coming and restoring Israel. Maybe the disciples were thinking that the appearance of Elijah on the mountain was the sign that the messianic age had begun.

Jesus answered their question by telling them that Elijah would come first and restore all things (verse 11). In fact, Elijah had already come and when he appeared there was no recognition of him by the people or the religious leaders. They did to him what they had done to all of the other prophets. Jesus here was making reference to John the Baptist (see Matthew 11:11-12; 14:2; 16:14; compare with Mark 6:14; Luke 7:33). Jesus said that eventually the religious leaders would do to the Son of Man what had been done to the messianic forerunner. In the words and actions of Jesus we see Him preparing His disciples for what was rapidly approaching—the agony of the Cross.

III. CONCLUDING REFLECTION

The Transfiguration provides us with an excellent opportunity for an assessment to understand who Jesus was and is today. Just as the disciples were not always sure of who He was, so among His followers today there are those of us whose understanding may be fuzzy. We are provided with the opportunity for re-commitment to the purposes of the Lord Jesus Christ. The closer one draws to the Christ, the greater and clearer becomes the vision of His purpose in the world and the church's mission. Just as Jesus called His first disciples to radical commitment to mission and ministry, He also calls this generation to commitment to the redemptive purpose of God. One of the key challenges that today's church leaders face is with the church becoming overly familiar with Jesus to the extent that we lose our edge and drive to reach the world with the Gospel. The Transfiguration serves as a reminder that in spite of the growing number of religious voices in the world today, we are still summoned to hear Him.

PRAYER

Heavenly Father, in whose hands we rest, grant that we may walk more worthy of the vocation to which You have called us. May we in this moment recognize that the closer we draw to Jesus Christ, the greater become the expectations You have of us. In Jesus' name we pray. Amen.

WORD POWER

Transfigured (*metamorphoo* [me-ta-mor-phoo])—means "to change into another form." At the Mount of Transfiguration, Jesus' appearance was changed and He was engulfed by divine brightness. Paul used the same word in 2 Corinthians 3:18—that Christians also are being transformed when we focus on Christ.

HOME DAILY BIBLE READINGS
(February 15–21, 2010)

Witnessed by Disciples

MONDAY, February 15: "Eyewitnesses of Jesus' Majesty" (2 Peter 1:16-21)

TUESDAY, February 16: "Witness of the True Light" (John 1:6-13)

WEDNESDAY, February 17: "The Kingdom Has Come" (Matthew 12:22-28)

THURSDAY, February 18: "Beseeched the Lord, David's Son" (Matthew 20:29-34)

FRIDAY, February 19: "Hailed as the Son of David" (Matthew 21:1-11)

SATURDAY, February 20: "To This We Are Witnesses" (Acts 3:11-16)

SUNDAY, February 21: "Listen to Him" (Matthew 17:1-12)

LESSON 13   February 28, 2010

ANOINTED BY A WOMAN IN BETHANY

DEVOTIONAL READING: **Deuteronomy 15:7-11**   BACKGROUND SCRIPTURE: **Matthew 26:6-13**
PRINT PASSAGE: **Matthew 26:6-13**   KEY VERSE: **Matthew 26:13**

Matthew 26:6-13—KJV

6 Now when Jesus was in Bethany, in the house of Simon the leper,

7 There came unto him a woman having an alabaster box of very precious ointment, and poured it on his head, as he sat at meat.

8 But when his disciples saw it, they had indignation, saying, To what purpose is this waste?

9 For this ointment might have been sold for much, and given to the poor.

10 When Jesus understood it, he said unto them, Why trouble ye the woman? for she hath wrought a good work upon me.

11 For ye have the poor always with you; but me ye have not always.

12 For in that she hath poured this ointment on my body, she did it for my burial.

13 Verily I say unto you, Wheresoever this gospel shall be preached in the whole world, there shall also this, that this woman hath done, be told for a memorial of her.

Matthew 26:6-13—NRSV

6 Now while Jesus was at Bethany in the house of Simon the leper,

7 a woman came to him with an alabaster jar of very costly ointment, and she poured it on his head as he sat at the table.

8 But when the disciples saw it, they were angry and said, "Why this waste?

9 For this ointment could have been sold for a large sum, and the money given to the poor."

10 But Jesus, aware of this, said to them, "Why do you trouble the woman? She has performed a good service for me.

11 For you always have the poor with you, but you will not always have me.

12 By pouring this ointment on my body she has prepared me for burial.

13 Truly I tell you, wherever this good news is proclaimed in the whole world, what she has done will be told in remembrance of her."

BIBLE FACT

The word *love* has suffered and continues to suffer misuse among Christians. We use the word *love* for all kinds of things. Christians say: "I *love* my dog; I *love* my house; I *love* my car; I *love* my church; I *love* my husband [or wife]." We use the word *love* flippantly and it has lost its real meaning. The woman in our text demonstrated real and deep love when she poured her expensive perfume on Jesus' feet and wiped it with her hair. When was the last time you displayed concrete love to anybody in the name of God?

Persons who truly love find ways to demonstrate that love. Can we ever give too much love? Jesus commended a woman who gave extravagantly out of her love for Jesus as Messiah.

TOPICAL OUTLINE OF THE LESSON

I. Introduction
A. Poor, but Gives
B. Biblical Background

II. Exposition and Application of the Scripture
A. The Gratuitous Giving (Matthew 26:6-7)
B. The Disciples' Reaction (Matthew 26:8-9)
C. The Woman's Commendation (Matthew 26:10-11)
D. The Woman's Commemoration (Matthew 26:12-13)

III. Concluding Reflection

LESSON OBJECTIVES

Upon completion of this lesson, the students will know that:

1. Everyone is capable of giving to the Lord's work;
2. Jesus honored and still honors those who give with all their hearts; and,
3. The spirit of giving is God's Spirit, and we should give without grumbling.

POINTS TO BE EMPHASIZED
ADULT/YOUTH

Adult Topic: Extravagant Love
Youth Topic: I Kneel before You
Adult Key Verse: Matthew 26:13
Youth Key Verse: Matthew 26:7
Print Passage: Matthew 26:6-13

—The value of the alabaster jar of perfume was three hundred denarii, or about a year's wage (Mark 14:3-9; John 12:1-8).
—The woman's extravagant act stands in stark contrast with the religious leaders' non-recognition of Jesus and with the disciples' attitudes.
—Jesus' statement about the poor was not demeaning, but a statement of fact (verse 11).
—The extravagant gift symbolized the woman's total devotion to Jesus.
—Jesus went to the home of Simon the leper in Bethany.
—A woman anointed Jesus with costly ointment.
—Jesus continued to prepare His disciples for His death.

CHILDREN

Children Topic: A Special Act of Love
Key Verse: Matthew 26:13
Print Passage: Matthew 26:6-13

—Jesus had expensive oil poured on His head.
—Jesus declared that the woman had not wasted the oil but rather had prepared Him for His burial.
—Jesus does not place monetary value on people or things.
—Jesus let the disciples know that He would not always be with them in the flesh, but the poor would always be with them.
—Jesus said that the woman who poured the perfume on His head would always be remembered for her sacrificial act of love.

I. INTRODUCTION

A. Poor, but Gives

Poverty is the number-one economic problem in the world today. It is estimated by the World Bank and other United Nations agencies that nearly 1.8 billion people live in abject poverty. These are people whose lives are best described as inhumanly deplorable. If you ever see poverty through the eyes of Jesus Christ, it will change forever the way you look at life. The many short-term mission trips I have taken to Kenya and Nigeria have given me a very different perspective from which to view and understand abject poverty. I have been places where people have never seen a doctor nor ever received any medication of any sort, yet many of them know how to give to God.

In today's lesson, Jesus commended a poor woman for her act of extravagant love. The disciples became indignant that such priceless oil was seemingly wasted. Yet, Jesus commended her because she had done a good work. In this final lesson in the quarter, we want to see the extent of this woman's sacrificial love gift through the eyes of someone who had the least to give, but gave more than all of the disciples combined.

B. Biblical Background

In today's lesson, we find Jesus in the final days of His ministry. This is the first major passage in the Passion narrative. It is situated between the plot of the religious leaders and the institution of the Lord's Supper. It is recorded in Matthew 26:2 that it was exactly two days before the traditional Jewish Passover celebration. Jesus was staying in the small village of Bethany, which also was the home of Mary, Martha, and Lazarus (see John 11:1). He probably spent a lot of His time in Bethany whenever He would come to Jerusalem for annual Jewish feasts. This particular evening, He was having dinner in the home of Simon the leper. During the dinner a woman entered the room where they were seated and anointed Jesus with some very expensive oil. The disciples showed that they were totally unaware of the significance of the woman's act of love. Rather than rebuke the woman for wasting precious oil, Jesus commended her actions and declared that she would be spoken about wherever the Gospel was preached. During the conversation, He shared with them that the days of His ministry on the earth were drawing to a swift conclusion. He knew that His time had come to be delivered up into the hands of the chief priests and elders of the people.

At the same time when Jesus was staying in Bethany, the chief priests and the elders of the people had gathered in the home of Caiaphas to finalize their plot to kill Jesus (Matthew 26:3). There was only one problem with their wicked scheme: they were afraid that if they seized Jesus at the wrong time they might set off a revolt (Matthew 26:5). This idea was quickly dismissed because they knew that the Romans were very intolerant of riots and the very appearance of disorder. The Romans would not hesitate to deal swiftly, decisively, and viciously with insurgents.

II. EXPOSITION AND APPLICATION OF THE SCRIPTURE

A. The Gratuitous Giving
(Matthew 26:6-7)

Now when Jesus was in Bethany, in the house of Simon the leper, There came unto him a woman having an alabaster box of very precious ointment, and poured it on his head, as he sat at meat.

The book of Matthew set the final day of Jesus' ministry in the small village of Bethany. It was two miles from Jerusalem, situated on the eastern slope of the Mount of Olives. The name *Bethany* means "House of fig." As previously mentioned, it was the home of Martha, Mary, and Lazarus. The village is mentioned at least four times in the Gospels (see Matthew 26:6; Luke 10:38-42; John 11:1-44; 12:1-11). Jesus was visiting in the home of a man named Simon who was a leper. Jesus healed many lepers during His ministry (Matthew 8:1-4; 10:8; Mark 1:40; Luke 4:27; 17:12). It is possible that Simon—in whose home Jesus was having dinner—may have been one of the lepers Jesus healed. Again, we see Jesus doing things that the religious leaders would never do: associating with sinners, lepers, and tax collectors. The Law strictly forbade anyone from having dinner with or being in the house of a leper (see Leviticus 13:42-47). Leprosy or no leprosy, Jesus was and is above all kinds of sicknesses. Jesus did not allow the condition of His host to deter Him from lodging there.

While they were having dinner a woman entered the room with an alabaster box of very precious ointment. *Alabaster* was a very precious stone and was often used as a container for very expensive perfumes and oils. The woman came into the room unannounced and uninvited and began to pour the oil on the head of Jesus. Some traditions hold that the woman was Mary (see John 12:3). We cannot be certain because Matthew did not name her. One can only imagine the shock, surprise, and stunned stares that may have greeted this woman's act of love.

In these verses we clearly learn some very powerful lessons about Jesus. For one thing, He never shied away from people who were considered to be less than desirable. The Law forbade such associations, but these were just the people Jesus would take into His presence. Simon could not escape the label. He more than likely carried it with him until the day he died.

B. The Disciples' Reaction
(Matthew 26:8-9)

But when his disciples saw it, they had indignation, saying, To what purpose is this waste? For this ointment might have been sold for much, and given to the poor.

The reaction of the disciples was immediate and excessive. First, they may have been incensed that a woman would dare enter the room when men were having a fellowship meal. Second, they may have been irritated that she would dare impose herself upon the Master without permission. Third, they were outraged that she seemingly wasted a very precious ointment by pouring it over the head of Jesus. *Indignation* is a very strong word and has in it the idea of a damnable act. The very use of the word by Matthew is an indication of the strong reactions of the disciples. Matthew did not say that it was one or two of the disciples; he used the plural, which means that all of them took part in voicing their objections to what this woman had done.

In verse 8, they stated that this was a waste. The oil could have been sold for a sizeable profit and the money used to help the poor. One could argue that the points the disciples made were commendable and certainly in line with the teachings and ministry of Jesus. He had spent a lot of time with poor people, the disenfranchised, and those who lived on the margins (see Luke 7:36-40; 15:1). Earlier in the week Jesus taught the disciples that they were to be committed to serving the poor. In Mark 14:5 we get a sense of the value of the oil. It was worth three hundred denarii, the equivalent of a year's wage. This was a lot of money that could have been used for a more noble and meaningful purpose, at least in the minds of the disciples. Is it possible that the perspective of the disciples was much distorted when it came to money and how it was to be used in ministry? Their attitudes are often reflected in the attitudes of church leaders today, whose perspectives and priorities for using money may not reflect the mind of Jesus Christ.

C. The Woman's Commendation (Matthew 26:10-11)

When Jesus understood it, he said unto them, Why trouble ye the woman? for she hath wrought a good work upon me. For ye have the poor always with you; but me ye have not always.

The response of Jesus to the act of the woman and the actions of His disciples was very revealing. First, it was an indication that Jesus cared deeply about the individual. He wanted to know why the disciples were bashing and beating up on this woman. Imagine being ganged up on by a group of hardcore fishermen, tax collectors, and zealots. This was a very tough position for this woman to be in. Had Jesus not come to her defense, there is no telling what could have happened. Jesus defended her and said that she had done a very good work. "Her actions were directed to Me."

As the Gospel of the church, this story and the response of Jesus reveal how differently the followers of Jesus thought about some matters than their Master. Christians can be very insensitive at times to the poor and the hurting. We can see them and not be moved because we see so much brokenness. Another aspect of this story is the interpersonal dimension. How often have Christians hurt others and belittled their service because it does not fit their perspectives or ideas? Many well-meaning people have been driven from the church by misguided Christians whose intentions may have been honorable, but they misrepresented the teachings of the Lord Jesus Christ.

Jesus took the opportunity to address their concerns about the poor. He quoted Deuteronomy 15:11 (compare verses 1-11, especially verse 4). This verse has often been misinterpreted to support the failure to end poverty in the world today. The reasoning goes like this: "Surely if Jesus said that the poor would always be with us, there is virtually no reason to even think that we can eliminate poverty." Jesus knows the hearts of human beings, and He knew that selfishness, greed, and covetousness were among the central reasons that poverty would thrive in the world today. Interpreters who use these verses to discount the mandate for social action and social ministry leave out of their thinking Deuteronomy 15:4, wherein God declared that because of His blessings upon His people there must not and should not be any poor among them. Jesus defended the woman on the grounds that the disciples could always serve the needs of the poor. They could always do kind and charitable alms to the poor, but He would not always be with them.

D. The Woman's Commemoration
(Matthew 26:12-13)

For in that she hath poured this ointment on my body, she did it for my burial. Verily I say unto you, Wheresoever this gospel shall be preached in the whole world, there shall also this, that this woman hath done, be told for a memorial of her.

Jesus was very clear about the significance of this woman's actions. She had anointed Him in anticipation of His death. Here was another direct reference to His death and burial. The disciples were still not catching the Master's thoughts. Maybe they thought He was speaking metaphorically or in some veiled language. Jesus established this woman's act as an everlasting tribute to her. Wherever the Gospel is preached and we recite the passion story, the account of this woman's abundant love for Jesus will also be told.

Several thoughts are relevant for today's believers. First, our love for Jesus should be without boundaries or limitations. This woman was willing to give up the most expensive possession she had for Jesus. Second, we must be willing to face and endure the harshest criticism when it comes to surrender and service to the Lord Jesus Christ. Finally, Jesus will recognize and remember our acts of service.

Hebrews 6:10 is a reminder to us that God is not unrighteous to forget our work and labor of love. What we have done in the name of the Lord Jesus Christ—down to the smallest of details—will never go unnoticed. This woman received a personal "well done" from the Lord Jesus Christ in her lifetime.

III. CONCLUDING REFLECTION

As we bring this quarter to a close, it is apparent from our study that Jesus was determined to face the agony of the Cross undeterred. There were occasions along the journey when it would have been easy for Him to be swayed by His popular appeal or by the certain fear of facing such an agonizing and excruciating death. Yet, He steadfastly went forward to face the pain of Calvary so that we might live. Today's lesson has been a profile in courage and generosity. The woman stands juxtaposed to the disciples who, although having witnessed some of the spectacular events in history, still never caught what God had revealed to the heart and spirit of this woman. She prepared Him for the day when He would be buried in death so that we might be made the righteousness of God in Him.

Regarding poverty in and around us, we must be willing to give our best to relieve others who are suffering. One visit to a developing nation will convince you that there are "haves and have nots." There is another side to Jamaica, Haiti, Bermuda, and other Caribbean islands—and that is the poverty of many of the people of African descent in that region of the world. Worldwide poverty must clearly become the most pressing concern of the developed nations of the world. There is a clear mandate in the Scriptures that the followers of Jesus are expected to be concerned about the poor and helpless (see Matthew 25:31-46; Luke 4:18-20). By conservative estimates, nearly 1.5 billion people go to bed hungry each night. Nearly two billion people do not have fresh water to drink. Nearly two billion of the world's people can neither read nor write. The poor that I speak of have no running water in their homes and they live in makeshift shanties with thatched roofs. They have never had electricity, and most live off of less than $200 per family per year.

Poverty is just as real in America as it is in the developing nations of the world. It merely looks a little different. In America, it manifests itself as homelessness, economic dislocation, and isolation. It is seen as the producer of a massive drug trade in poor communities, with its by-products of crime, violence, abuse, child neglect, and child exploitation. In America, poverty has no particular racial identity and it is not gender-conscious. There are more men living in poverty than women. Children are its worst victims. Poverty is an American nightmare that will not vanish in this the richest, most powerful nation in the whole world.

PRAYER

Lord, teach us to trust You in every area of our lives. May we be willing to make whatever sacrifice is necessary for the work of Your kingdom. In Jesus' name we pray. Amen.

WORD POWER

Memorial (Greek: *mnemosunon* [ne-mo-su-non])—means "something by which the memory of any person or thing is preserved for posterity's sake; to perpetuate one's memory." The woman was not looking for her name to be known, but Jesus elevated her kindness to instruct us to give anonymously. Whatever we do to advance the kingdom of God is known to our Father in heaven.

HOME DAILY BIBLE READINGS
(February 22–28, 2010)

Anointed by a Woman in Bethany

MONDAY, February 22: "Give Liberally" (Deuteronomy 15:7-11)

TUESDAY, February 23: "Women Devoted to Prayer" (Acts 1:12-14)

WEDNESDAY, February 24: "Women Facing Persecution" (Acts 8:1-3; 9:1-2)

THURSDAY, February 25: "Female Believers Baptized" (Acts 8:4-13)

FRIDAY, February 26: "Leading Women Accept Christ" (Acts 17:1-4)

SATURDAY, February 27: "A Hospitable Woman" (Acts 16:11-15)

SUNDAY, February 28: "A Good Service for Jesus" (Matthew 26:6-13)

Teachings on Community

GENERAL INTRODUCTION

The three units in this quarter are explorations of teachings on community through the Old Testament books of Jonah and Ruth and through the teachings of Jesus and the early church. The coming together of faithful people in response to God's call and how they decided with God's help to relate to one another becomes the focus.

Unit I, *Community with a Mission,* is a four-lesson unit that is an examination of two books of the Old Testament, Jonah and Ruth. The two lessons from the book of Jonah deal with Jonah's mission to the community and the redemption of that community. The two lessons from the book of Ruth are focuses on the family as a community with the need to survive and be accepted in the larger community.

Unit II is a look at only four of many passages that could be chosen to illustrate *Teachings of Jesus* related to community. The themes deal with light, love, connectedness, and a feast.

Unit III is drawn from three teachings from the book of Colossians and one each from the books of Philemon and Jude that relate *Teachings of the Church* on community. In the book of Colossians, the learners will study the faithfulness of the community and how the community was established and chosen. The letter to Philemon helps us look at welcoming in the community, and the letter of Jude is an examination of a community at risk.

*This quarter's lessons have been adapted for the children's section to facilitate their easier absorption of the content.

LESSON 1	March 7, 2010

MISSION TO THE COMMUNITY

DEVOTIONAL READING: Matthew 21:28-32
PRINT PASSAGE: Jonah 1:1-3; 3:1-9

BACKGROUND SCRIPTURE: Jonah 1:1-3; 3:1-9
KEY VERSE: Jonah 3:5

Jonah 1:1-3; 3:1-9—KJV

NOW THE word of the LORD came unto Jonah the son of Amittai, saying,

2 Arise, go to Nineveh, that great city, and cry against it; for their wickedness is come up before me.

3 But Jonah rose up to flee unto Tarshish from the presence of the LORD, and went down to Joppa; and he found a ship going to Tarshish: so he paid the fare thereof, and went down into it, to go with them unto Tarshish from the presence of the LORD.

.....

AND THE word of the LORD came unto Jonah the second time, saying,

2 Arise, go unto Nineveh, that great city, and preach unto it the preaching that I bid thee.

3 So Jonah arose, and went unto Nineveh, according to the word of the LORD. Now Nineveh was an exceeding great city of three days' journey.

4 And Jonah began to enter into the city a day's journey, and he cried, and said, Yet forty days, and Nineveh shall be overthrown.

5 So the people of Nineveh believed God, and proclaimed a fast, and put on sackcloth, from the greatest of them even to the least of them.

6 For word came unto the king of Nineveh, and he arose from his throne, and he laid his robe from him, and covered him with sackcloth, and sat in ashes.

7 And he caused it to be proclaimed and published through Nineveh by the decree of the king and his nobles, saying, Let neither man nor beast, herd nor flock, taste any thing: let them not feed, nor drink water:

8 But let man and beast be covered with sackcloth, and cry mightily unto God: yea, let them turn every one from his evil way, and from the violence that is in their hands.

9 Who can tell if God will turn and repent, and turn away from his fierce anger, that we perish not?

Jonah 1:1-3; 3:1-9—NRSV

NOW THE word of the LORD came to Jonah son of Amittai, saying,

2 "Go at once to Nineveh, that great city, and cry out against it; for their wickedness has come up before me."

3 But Jonah set out to flee to Tarshish from the presence of the LORD. He went down to Joppa and found a ship going to Tarshish; so he paid his fare and went on board, to go with them to Tarshish, away from the presence of the LORD.

.....

THE WORD of the LORD came to Jonah a second time, saying,

2 "Get up, go to Nineveh, that great city, and proclaim to it the message that I tell you."

3 So Jonah set out and went to Nineveh, according to the word of the LORD. Now Nineveh was an exceedingly large city, a three days' walk across.

4 Jonah began to go into the city, going a day's walk. And he cried out, "Forty days more, and Nineveh shall be overthrown!"

5 And the people of Nineveh believed God; they proclaimed a fast, and everyone, great and small, put on sackcloth.

6 When the news reached the king of Nineveh, he rose from his throne, removed his robe, covered himself with sackcloth, and sat in ashes.

7 Then he had a proclamation made in Nineveh: "By the decree of the king and his nobles: No human being or animal, no herd or flock, shall taste anything. They shall not feed, nor shall they drink water.

8 Human beings and animals shall be covered with sackcloth, and they shall cry mightily to God. All shall turn from their evil ways and from the violence that is in their hands.

9 Who knows? God may relent and change his mind; he may turn from his fierce anger, so that we do not perish."

UNIFYING LESSON PRINCIPLE

In a world filled with good and evil, persons are forced to choose between good and evil. What happens to people who turn from their wicked ways in sorrow? Jonah's plea to the people of Nineveh caused them to believe in God and fast, trusting that God would forgive them.

TOPICAL OUTLINE OF THE LESSON

I. **Introduction**
   A. The Centrality of Community
   B. Biblical Background

II. **Exposition and Application of the Scripture**
   A. Divine Command and Attempted Escape (Jonah 1:1-3)
   B. Jonah's Renewed Commission (Jonah 3:1-4)
   C. An Entire Community Repents (Jonah 3:5-9)

III. **Concluding Reflection**

LESSON OBJECTIVES

Upon completion of this lesson, the students will know that:

1. Obedience is important and there are ramifications contingent on the lack of it;

2. The entire city of Nineveh repented and God had mercy on them; and,

3. If we as individuals and a community repent, God can also pardon us.

POINTS TO BE EMPHASIZED

ADULT/YOUTH

Adult Topic: Influencing Community Change
Youth Topic: Mission Unwanted!
Adult Key Verse: Jonah 3:5
Youth Key Verse: Jonah 1:2
Print Passage: Jonah 1:1-3; 3:1-9

—Jonah disobeyed a clear instruction from God.

—Jonah was unwilling to help a community that God wanted to save.

—When told of their impending destruction, the community of Nineveh mourned their sin and repented.

—The people acted individually and as a community.

—Jonah reluctantly obeyed and the king of Nineveh responded to Jonah's preaching, declaring a fast, and calling everyone to repentance.

CHILDREN

Children Topic: Jonah Obeyed
Key Verse: Jonah 3:3
Print Passage: Jonah 1:1-3; 3:1-9

—Jonah disobeyed God's command, which caused calamity aboard the ship.

—The men aboard the ship pleaded for relief from the violent storm.

—Even though Jonah was disobedient, God provided a safe haven for him.

—Jonah's deep-sea experience opened his understanding of God's ways.

—After being ejected from his fishy grave, Jonah took God's message to the Ninevites.

—The Ninevites received God's message and prayed they would not perish.

I. INTRODUCTION

A. The Centrality of Community

This quarter's lessons center upon the importance of community. As we study various passages in the Bible, we will focus on the development of communities in biblical times. How did they begin and grow? What were the primary values? What structures of government, family, economy, and religion did they implement? What role did allegiance to God play in their lives, individually and collectively? How do those societies and their understanding of "community" differ from ours?

Today, we evaluate the community of Nineveh where the resistant prophet, Jonah, went to declare the fierce Word of the Lord. Surpassing the actions of the Israelites, the Ninevites actually repented upon hearing the straightforward message of potential doom because of their wickedness. The wholesale humility to put on sackcloth and appeal to almighty God for His grace and mercy singularly characterized the people of Nineveh. No other tribe or nation in the Scriptures responded to God's Word as they did. In fact, the Lord Jesus commended them for their repentance (see Matthew 12:41). What enabled the people who lived in this Assyrian capital city to reverse the way in which they were living? How were they able as a nation to understand that they could no longer trample recklessly upon God's holiness and squander His grace?

B. Biblical Background

We have another opportunity to consider the quirkiness of Jonah, who did not care to become a member of the Ninevite community. Actually, he relegated God's first instruction to being an absolute waste of time. Thinking of himself as "the captain of his own soul and the master of his fate," Jonah proudly ignored God's direction and left for Tarshish. Immediately, our minds fill with our childhood images of Jonah's voyage and imprisonment in the belly of the whale. Perhaps, we now think, Jonah rightly deserved the three days and nights in the darkness of confusion, inertia, and failure to reach his destination because of his categorical refusal to obey God's instructions. Yet, concentrating upon the frightening consequences of Jonah's defiance eclipses God's persistent kindness and mercy. After the whale vomited Jonah out of his mouth and Jonah landed on dry land, the Lord condescended and gave the prophet a second chance "to get it right."

II. EXPOSITION AND APPLICATION OF THE SCRIPTURE

A. Divine Command and Attempted Escape (Jonah 1:1-3)

NOW THE word of the LORD came unto Jonah the son of Amittai, saying, Arise, go to Nineveh, that great city, and cry against it; for their wickedness is come up before me. But Jonah rose up to flee unto Tarshish from the presence of the LORD, and went down to Joppa; and he found a ship going to Tarshish: so he paid the fare thereof, and went down into it, to go with them unto Tarshish from the presence of the LORD.

The phrase "The word of the Lord" affirms the divine source of the message to Jonah (see Joel 1:1). God was concerned about the wickedness of the Ninevites and sent His Word to Jonah to go to Nineveh, the great city. Nineveh was the capital city of the Assyrian Empire. It was a cosmopolitan city in those days. Verse 2 is an emphasis on the wickedness of the people, but God did not want to punish them without warning them of their impending doom. The love of God to human beings is beyond our comprehension. God finds His own messenger in every generation; whether or not His messengers will do His ultimate will is another question.

Jonah demonstrated the mysterious ways in which opposite characteristics can exist in the same personality. He possessed the strength of self-will as he proactively chose to disregard the divine order to go to Nineveh and proclaim the Word of the Lord. On the contrary, the prophet displayed a weakness as he used an avoidance method of ignoring God by plotting an escape to Tarshish. Nevertheless, God had set apart this "reluctant missionary" for the distinct purpose of preaching to the Ninevites. Battling these warring characteristics of self-determination and divine command, Jonah evaded the situation initially. Soon he fell into the hands of a God who would not tolerate humankind's insult to His character and will.

B. Jonah's Renewed Commission
(Jonah 3:1-4)

AND THE word of the LORD came unto Jonah the second time, saying, Arise, go unto Nineveh, that great city, and preach unto it the preaching that I bid thee. So Jonah arose, and went unto Nineveh, according to the word of the LORD. Now Nineveh was an exceeding great city of three days' journey. And Jonah began to enter into the city a day's journey, and he cried, and said, Yet forty days, and Nineveh shall be overthrown.

Jonah's new commission was essentially the same as the one he had received in chapters 1 and 2. In contrast to chapter 1, Jonah obeyed the command of the Lord the second time. The plan of God is forever the same, which is to bring us back to Himself. God's message had not changed—the problem was the messenger. Revealed in the second portion of the printed Scripture is the obedience of the Ninevites, who had the same acquaintance with God as Jonah. Prior to their remarkable feat of repentance and humility, the disgruntled and disobedient prophet finally found the willingness to obey. Conceivably, Jonah now obeyed God in gratitude for the Lord's mercy and grace in releasing him from the depths of darkness. The text states plainly, "Then the word of the Lord came to Jonah a second time" (verse 1, NIV). I imagine that Jonah's imprisonment in the belly of the whale afforded him the time to reconsider his stubbornness. He probably did not change his outlook on the worth of the Ninevites. Yet, in appreciation for God's gracious offer of a second chance, Jonah ended his internal strife and balanced his self-centered motives with the necessity of following a loving God who was kind enough to free him from perpetual darkness and allow him to see the light of day again.

Jonah's experience models the power of redemption for us. It is never too late to begin serving God with our hearts, minds, souls, and strength. We can begin today to reverse the course of our lives. We can change our focus and priorities. We can start each day with the intent of making almighty God our ultimate concern. Everything else pales in comparison to the majesty and magnificence of living peacefully and joyously in the direct will of God.

Look at Jonah's instantaneous success! On the first day of adhering to God's call, he achieved a national revival. Interestingly, Jonah preached one of the shortest sermons in the Bible and perhaps in the history of preaching. In response to the warning of annihilation within the next forty days, "the Ninevites believed God" (verse 5). "From the greatest to the least," the whole nation put on sackcloth and participated in a fast. They grieved over their sins and denied their worldly appetites. Essentially, the spiritual practice of self-denial enables us to more clearly receive divine revelation. When we are chomping on double cheeseburgers, fries, and apple turnovers while drinking sodas, rarely are we thinking about our spiritual condition. Remarkably, Jonah's message awakened the entire country, despite their socio-economic status; the rich as well as the poor demonstrated faith in God by mourning, contrition, repentance, and self-restraint. Imagine a revival in contemporary America when the wealthiest one percent of citizens would join in solidarity with the underclasses. God's Word is for everyone. Despite the wickedness of the Ninevites, they were open to God's message and repented immediately. If our message is simple and direct, we may be shocked at people's responses.

C. An Entire Community Repents
(Jonah 3:5-9)

So the people of Nineveh believed God, and proclaimed a fast, and put on sackcloth, from the greatest of them even to the least of them. For word came unto the king of Nineveh, and he arose from his throne, and he laid his robe from him, and covered him with sackcloth, and sat in ashes. And he caused it to be proclaimed and published through Nineveh by the decree of the king and his nobles, saying, Let neither man nor beast, herd nor flock, taste any thing: let them not feed, nor drink water: But let man and beast be covered with sackcloth, and cry mightily unto God: yea, let them turn every one from his evil way, and from the violence that is in their hands. Who can tell if God will turn and repent, and turn away from his fierce anger, that we perish not?

The king's humility and the immediate obedience of the people starkly represented the seriousness with which the Ninevites heeded the Word of the Lord. The king rose from the Assyrian throne, discarded his royal robes, covered himself with sackcloth like his subjects, and sat down in the dust. The king's action is reminiscent of the lowly origins of humankind in contrast with the infinite and holy attributes of almighty God. We are dust! God can blow upon our lives like a candle's flame in the wind. Who are we to think that we can trespass on the holiness and righteousness of God? What an incredible depiction of the utter limitations of human beings.

Then, the king utilized his royal power to legally compel the nation to adhere strictly to his proclamation (demanding the continuance of the fast in sackcloth) until God responded mercifully. The king himself led his people in this communal repentance. We learn from verse 6 that the king abandoned his royal position, laid aside his robe, and covered himself with ashes; furthermore, Ninevites were to cease and desist from "their evil ways and their violence" (NIV). Prayer for divine relief was the basis of the proclamation. The king evidently hoped that national unity and solidarity in this effort would cause almighty God "to relent and with compassion turn from his fierce anger so that we will not perish" (verse 9, NIV).

Anthropologists and archeologists can tell us very little about the distinctive and unique character of the Ninevites. The biblical record remains one of the most reliable sources. Accordingly, we can extract a few informative and instructive attributes about their collective personality. First, notwithstanding their excessive evil and violence, they possessed the humility to repent upon hearing the terrible Word of the Lord. Second, they had the capacity to obey higher authority—they followed the king's proclamation. Third, although they greatly indulged their self-seeking desires and myriad lusts, they steadfastly turned to God when they heard His messenger. Jonah's preaching had a positive impact on their lives. They turned from their old ways with fasting, confession, repentance, and fervent prayer. Fourth, they adhered to the practice of egalitarianism in which they valued each person regardless of his or her wealth, education, religion, and social position. From the king to the keeper of the cows, the entire nation appealed to God for relief and mercy.

The foregoing collective personality of the Ninevites offers instruction on the type of community that churches should strive to be. If confronted with a similar spiritual challenge, would a church, congregationally and individually, muster the humility, obedience, faith, and personal commitment to seek the Lord's face for wisdom and resolution? What if nuclear families mimicked the actions of the Ninevites when turmoil afflicted one of their members? Could a solution to drug-infested neighborhoods and crime-ridden municipalities be found in these spiritual responses to overwhelming dilemmas?

Although they were Assyrians and not Israelites, the Ninevites demonstrated the power of a community with a mission. They turned from wholesale self-indulgence to living to the honor and glory of almighty God.

III. CONCLUDING REFLECTION

Jonah's stubborn refusal to follow the will of God rightly landed him in the belly of the whale. Our daily resistance to the urging of the Holy Spirit enables us to empathize with Jonah. Over time, the cumulative sum of our negative responses equate to a spiritual vacuum equal to the darkness of the three days and three nights in the abyss. Yet, Jonah's example encourages us to look beyond our human frailties, failures, and incapacities and see the goodness and mercy of a "God of the second chance." He continually gives us the chance to "get it right" by finally heeding His good, pleasing, and perfect will. When we do so, we find possibly immediate success and perhaps even excellence as Jonah did when he eventually preached in Nineveh. Surprisingly and favorably, Jonah discovered a community, with a mission of serving the Lord, as the Ninevites repented and exchanged their self-centered lives for lives devoted to the Lord.

Often, God affords us the gracious opportunity to correct our mistakes after we have made wrong decisions. Many believers popularly refer to our heavenly Father as "the God of a second chance." Out of His infinite knowledge, wisdom, and patience, He kindly grants us another possibility to complete a divine mission. Jonah received another chance to preach to the people of Nineveh and thereby assist them in establishing a genuinely spiritual, loving, honest, and caring community that worshiped almighty God above anyone and anything else.

Quite possibly, Jonah's actions mirror our own resistance to following the Lord's guidance. Is there any divine directive that you are presently postponing? Has God put a call upon your life and do you selectively choose to disobey Him with the excuse that you are busy doing other worthwhile things? Have you purchased a "ticket to Tarshish" by conveniently making yourself unavailable to God? Does devoting the lion's share of your time, energy, abilities, and talents to your spouse, children, extended family, and job prevent you from answering the Lord's call? In your heart of hearts, do you really desire to do so and fully intend to do so when things let up? Jonah's example encourages us to define clearly the components of our resistance to the divine call upon our lives. Incidentally, as Baptists, we believe in the priesthood of all believers; practically speaking, that means all disciples, whether clergypersons or laity, are ministers with a calling upon their lives. God expects each of us to seek His guidance to discern the exact nature of His calling and to devote the bulk of our lives to fulfilling that purpose and mission. The biblical writer recorded the vivid illustration of Jonah to portray the considerable waste of time and talent when we brush aside the will of almighty God. Moreover and most fortunately, the prophet's life is an illustration of the possibility of redemption when we finally accede to the voice of God.

PRAYER

Heavenly Father, for the beauty of this day, we thank You. Teach us how to be a community with the mission of living to Thy honor, glory, and praise. In Jesus' name we pray. Amen.

WORD POWER

Believe (Hebrew: `aman [a-man])—this word means "to stand firm, to believe absolutely, to be sure or certain." The word is in the imperfect tense, which carries the idea of continuous action. The people of Nineveh believed the message of God. They did not allow their wickedness to bring down God's wrath. Their belief in God's warning was not passive action; rather, what they heard caused them to first believe and they repented.

HOME DAILY BIBLE READINGS
(March 1-7, 2010)

Mission to the Community

MONDAY, March 1: "Obedience to God's Call" (Matthew 21:28-32)

TUESDAY, March 2: "No Prophet among Us" (Psalm 74)

WEDNESDAY, March 3: "A Trustworthy Prophet" (1 Samuel 3:10-21)

THURSDAY, March 4: "A Prophet's Visions" (Numbers 12:3-9)

FRIDAY, March 5: "A Prophet's Words" (Deuteronomy 18:15-22)

SATURDAY, March 6: "A Prophet's Prayer" (Jonah 2:1-9)

SUNDAY, March 7: "A Prophet's Commission" (Jonah 1:1-3; 3:1-9)

LESSON 2

March 14, 2010

A COMMUNITY TO REDEEM

DEVOTIONAL READING: **Matthew 9:9-13**
PRINT PASSAGE: **Jonah 3:10; 4:1-5**

BACKGROUND SCRIPTURE: **Jonah 3:10; 4:1-11**
KEY VERSE: **Jonah 4:2**

Jonah 3:10; 4:1-5—KJV

10 And God saw their works, that they turned from their evil way; and God repented of the evil, that he had said that he would do unto them; and he did it not.

....

BUT IT displeased Jonah exceedingly, and he was very angry.

2 And he prayed unto the LORD, and said, I pray thee, O LORD, was not this my saying, when I was yet in my country? Therefore I fled before unto Tarshish: for I knew that thou art a gracious God, and merciful, slow to anger, and of great kindness, and repentest thee of the evil.

3 Therefore now, O LORD, take, I beseech thee, my life from me; for it is better for me to die than to live.

4 Then said the LORD, Doest thou well to be angry?

5 So Jonah went out of the city, and sat on the east side of the city, and there made him a booth, and sat under it in the shadow, till he might see what would become of the city.

Jonah 3:10; 4:1-5—NRSV

10 When God saw what they did, how they turned from their evil ways, God changed his mind about the calamity that he had said he would bring upon them; and he did not do it.

.....

BUT THIS was very displeasing to Jonah, and he became angry.

2 He prayed to the LORD and said, "O LORD! Is not this what I said while I was still in my own country? That is why I fled to Tarshish at the beginning; for I knew that you are a gracious God and merciful, slow to anger, and abounding in steadfast love, and ready to relent from punishing.

3 And now, O LORD, please take my life from me, for it is better for me to die than to live."

4 And the LORD said, "Is it right for you to be angry?"

5 Then Jonah went out of the city and sat down east of the city, and made a booth for himself there. He sat under it in the shade, waiting to see what would become of the city.

BIBLE FACT

Jonah—the prophet who was swallowed by a great fish—was not always a reluctant spokesman for the Lord. During the reign of Jeroboam II (AD 793-753), he predicted the remarkable expansion of Israel's territory (see 2 Kings 14:25). Some Bible scholars do not believe in a literal Jonah; they relegate his story to allegory. But we believe the story of Jonah is true. Even Jesus Christ made an allusion to Jonah (see Matthew 12:38-41; Luke 11:29-32). God asked him to go and preach repentance to the Ninevites, but he went in the opposite direction. But God prevailed by letting a big fish swallow Jonah. When God freed him, Jonah went to Nineveh and preached the shortest sermon ever recorded, "Yet forty days and Nineveh shall be overthrown."

Every Christian who is wise in heart should take heed. We may not be swallowed up by a big fish, but God can use anything to take us to where His name will be glorified.

UNIFYING LESSON PRINCIPLE

When others receive some sort of benefit, deserved or undeserved, we can experience jealousy and anger and say, "Why them?" Is there another way to respond? Jonah came to realize that God was in control of things in the world and God's way of dealing with others differs from that of humankind, but God's steadfast love abounds to all.

TOPICAL OUTLINE OF THE LESSON

I. **Introduction**
   A. The Infinite Love of God for Humankind
   B. Biblical Background

II. **Exposition and Application of the Scripture**
   A. God's Anger Subsides (Jonah 3:10)
   B. Jonah's Disappointment (Jonah 4:1)
   C. Jonah, an Ambiguous Prophet (Jonah 4:2-5)

III. **Concluding Reflection**

LESSON OBJECTIVES

Upon completion of this lesson, the students will know that:

1. After we receive pardon, there is a mission to be accomplished;
2. Jonah was disappointed because God pardoned Nineveh;
3. God's disappointment of Jonah did not stop God from caring for him; and,
4. God cares for us even when we are careless.

POINTS TO BE EMPHASIZED
ADULT/YOUTH

Adult Topic: Jealousy of Others
Youth Topic: Redeem Them?
Adult Key Verse: Jonah 4:2
Youth Key Verse: Jonah 3:10
Print Passage: Jonah 3:10; 4:1-5

—God responded positively to the repentance of the Ninevites.
—Jonah responded to God's forgiveness of Nineveh with anger.
—Jonah decided he would rather die than accept God's will.
—Jonah wanted the wicked city to receive punishment due them and not be forgiven.
—Jonah knew he would be embarrassed if none of his warnings to the people in Nineveh came true, so he wanted to die.
—God's answer to Jonah's anger is a statement of both God's sovereignty and God's redemptive heart.
—Jonah left the city in a huff and built a booth for himself outside the city where he sat and pouted.

CHILDREN

Children Topic: All People Are Valued
Key Verse: Jonah 4:2
Print Passage: Jonah 3:10; 4:1-5

—God's words had a miraculous effect on the Ninevites.
—Why did Jonah become angry when God saved Nineveh?
—Jonah was so angry about God's compassion for the Ninevites that he prayed for death.
—God showed Jonah His power with a vine, a worm, a scorching east wind, and a blazing sun.
—God showed Jonah that all humans have value regardless of their past.
—Angry words to God can bring us closer to God if we are willing to listen and learn.

I. INTRODUCTION

A. The Infinite Love of God for Humankind

What an awesome, amazing, and incredible God we serve! God's infinite character extends to His unconditional and limitless love of humankind. His heart is big enough to love each and every single one of the six billion (6,000,000,000) people on earth. His love extends freely to every person regardless of race, creed, color, ethnicity, culture, language, religion, and politics. Unfortunately, many well-meaning believers confuse God's love with their personal preferences. They tend to think that God loves the people whom they love. Falsely, they assume that God's judgment extends more to people who are not like them. Other misguided believers choose to love people whose values and mannerisms are most similar to their own. They mistakenly suspect that God mimics their behavior as it relates to loving others. In contrast, multiple biblical writers reveal an ever-present, all-kind, all-knowing, all-powerful, and all-loving God whose affection for humankind does not adjust to the limited and often erroneous ways in which we relate to each other.

B. Biblical Background

In today's lesson, we observe the prophet, Jonah, who insisted that God should reserve His love for the people who were most deserving of it. Jonah actually became very angry toward God for squandering His compassion upon the Ninevites. Although he eventually relented and obeyed God's call, Jonah harbored a twisted and gleeful expectation in his heart that God would destroy the city of Nineveh. Imagine Jonah's disdain and disregard for a city of 120,000 people, plus livestock! Consider further the fact that Jonah was an anointed and sent prophet of God. How do we balance his divine office with the utter indifference that Jonah held in his heart for the Ninevites?

II. EXPOSITION AND APPLICATION OF THE SCRIPTURE

A. God's Anger Subsides
(Jonah 3:10)

And God saw their works, that they turned from their evil way; and God repented of the evil, that he had said that he would do unto them; and he did it not.

This lesson's passage contains two central themes. It divides evenly between Jonah's fury over the Lord's forgiveness of the Ninevites and our heavenly Father's enduring desire to teach humankind to love each other as He does. The final verse of the third chapter is a detailed account of the success of Jonah's preaching and the subsequent repentance and revival. The entire pagan city of Nineveh believed Jonah's message and repented. The Word of God had a spectacular influence and the Ninevites did not suffer the consequences of their wickedness—unlike Sodom and Gomorrah, which perished because there were not found five righteous people living there.

We are serving a God who is full of mercy who does not willingly afflict His children (see Lamentations 3:3). He is always ready to receive us when we truly come to Him in full repentance. God's desire is always toward us. The Ninevites were on the way to destruction, but God sent a messenger to them to warn them of the impending doom. The Ninevites' repentant attitude engendered the mercy of the almighty God.

B. Jonah's Disappointment
(Jonah 4:1)

BUT IT displeased Jonah exceedingly, and he was very angry.

Why did Jonah, a prophet of God, become angry when God chose to suspend His anger against His creatures? The Jews in Jonah's day were prejudiced. They did not want Gentiles to enjoy the mercy of God like they did. The Jews had forgotten their original purpose: to be a blessing to other nations. Surprisingly, Jonah was not pleased with the results of his preaching or God's responses to the Ninevites. Rather than relishing this monumental and unparalleled spiritual success, Jonah ignited his anger which represented his maniacal thirst for the annihilation of the city of Nineveh.

Jonah became very angry, or very *grieved.* The problem with Jonah was that he could not afford to see God's glory among the Gentiles.

Sometimes we find ourselves in situations where we feel justified and we want God to at least recompense our perceived enemies with one kind of judgment or the other. What we are looking for is justification of ourselves. However, in the story of Jonah, we are forced to rethink our narrow understanding of God, particularly God's universal love for all humankind.

C. Jonah, an Ambiguous Prophet
(Jonah 4:2-5)

And he prayed unto the LORD, and said, I pray thee, O LORD, was not this my saying, when I was yet in my country? Therefore I fled before unto Tarshish: for I knew that thou art a gracious God, and merciful, slow to anger, and of great kindness, and repentest thee of the evil. Therefore now, O LORD, take, I beseech thee, my life from me; for it is better for me to die than to live. Then said the LORD, Doest thou well to be angry? So Jonah went out of the city, and sat on the east side of the city, and there made him a booth, and sat under it in the shadow, till he might see what would become of the city.

We must pay attention to the mindset of Jonah. Jonah did not murmur or complain of God. He complained to God of himself. We still see the love of God even to Jonah. God took time to listen to him without punishing him for his disobedience. Jonah had a good understanding of God, when he said, "I knew that thou art a gracious God." The graciousness of God caused him to flee from God's presence. The graciousness of God causes us to pause and think about the way we evangelize. Do we evangelize because God loves people? Or do we do it because we feel that God is one day going to rain down fire and punishment upon people? The prophet could not hide his prejudice against the Gentile nation. Jonah did not understand the infinite love of God. Jonah revealed his heartfelt thoughts when he frankly disclosed to God in prayer his contempt for the Ninevites. He said, "O LORD, is this not what I said when I was still at home? That is why I was so quick to flee to Tarshish" (verse 2, NIV). More significantly, Jonah did not want to travel to Nineveh to announce gloom and doom because he correctly suspected that in the final analysis the Lord's heart would be moved by the confession, repentance, and humility of the people. If God were going to destroy the Ninevites, He did not need Jonah to travel to the city and preach a very bleak sermon. Also, if their repentance would stay the mighty and avenging hand of God, then the trip was equally unnecessary. Essentially, the missionary expedition was appropriate, according to Jonah's only logic, if the Ninevites received their due punishment and the Lord lifted Jonah out of the city before the onslaught of the hellfire and brimstone.

Startlingly enough, Jonah became dejected because God was "a gracious and compassionate God, slow to anger and abounding in love, a God who relents from sending calamity" (verse 2, NIV). In seeking to denigrate God's attributes of love, mercy, and kindness, Jonah ironically described a wonderful and majestic heavenly Father whose infinite grace and compassion extends to a thousand generations forevermore.

After defining those magnificent divine characteristics, Jonah prayed for his death. He determined that he would be better off dead than alive. The Ninevite revival disgusted the prophet to the degree that he actually pled with the Lord to take his own life. Notice that Jonah's self-deception grew to the point that he persuaded himself that his one life held greater worth than the collective lives of the citizens of Nineveh. See how deeply racial and religious discrimination can seep into the minds and hearts of otherwise well-meaning believers?

The Lord asked Jonah about the prophet's righteous indignation. "Have you any right to be angry?" (verse 4, NIV). It seems logical to assume that Jonah had experienced previously the grace, mercy, and love of God. In the preceding chapter, he received a blessed second chance after his stint in the belly of a whale. Should not Jonah's thankfulness have motivated him to appreciate the revival in Nineveh? Did he only believe that the Israelites were the only people to whom God should show His compassion? Jonah cloaked his cultural and religious chauvinism under the socially and theologically respectable garments of holy anger. He posited that God was wasting His divine self upon people who could not appreciate such an incalculable gift. However, God's question reminded and exhorted Jonah that the same God who had sympathy upon him loved the Ninevites enough to show them a similar kindness. How could the prophet justify his fury given his recent escape from the eternal abyss of darkness and separation from almighty God? What right did Jonah have to be angry?

III. CONCLUDING REFLECTION

What is your reaction when a hard-core criminal turns to the Lord? Is it possible that your view is as narrow as Jonah's? We must constantly be conscious that we do not deserve God's mercy. God saved us based on His own initiative. The church, *ecclesia,* is the called-out community of God's people who uniquely and particularly dedicate their lives for God's especial purpose. One connecting link between each member of the church is the experience of God's redemptive love. Although we came from very different walks of life, each of us stood in need of redemption before we came to Christ. Together, we were a community to redeem.

As we walk progressively with the Lord and fellowship with each other, in order to fulfill the "Great Commission" (see Matthew 28:18-20), we must reach back and live the love. We are called to look for communities to redeem just as we were redeemed. Rather than pegging people as pathological statistics, we are commanded to look at them with the eyes of the heart and spirit. When we do so, we see them as communities to redeem.

Jonah's disposition affords us an opportunity to examine our understanding of God's love. Spiritual maturity equips us with the skills and tools of showing God's love, pardon, and compassion to all people. Nevertheless, Jonah pitifully determined that a withering vine which provided him shade possessed a greater worth than the entire population of a small city. Perhaps we, like Jonah, only assign value to people who directly enhance our lives. Usually, they are people who look, act, speak, dress, and live just like us. But, people whose standards of living differ from ours are children of God, too. Our second lesson from this disgruntled prophet provides another chance to consider the many ways, intentionally and unintentionally, that we regrettably imitate Jonah's loveless behavior.

The relevant question is this: who takes the glory in all that we are doing in the name of the Lord? In Jonah's case, he may have been more concerned about his own reputation than God's. He was fully aware that if the Ninevites repented, none of his preachings would come to fruition. Are you more concerned about your glory or God's?

PRAYER

Father in heaven, we thank You for the gift of Your redeeming love in our Lord and Savior, Jesus Christ. Teach us to recall always that we are in need of Your gracious and loving redemption. In Jesus' name we pray. Amen.

WORD POWER

Gracious (Hebrew: *channuwn* [khan-nun])—means "to be gracious, merciful (mercy full, or full of mercy; benignant)." This word, *gracious,* has lost its meaning in the modern world. It is difficult for us to fathom its depth. We talk about being gracious but we are not patient. We talk about mercy, but we cannot stand a little insult. God is merciful toward sinners.

HOME DAILY BIBLE READINGS
(March 8-14, 2010)

A Community to Redeem
MONDAY, March 8: "Great Power to Redeem" (Psalm 130)
TUESDAY, March 9: "The Need for Redemption" (Isaiah 59:9-15)
WEDNESDAY, March 10: "The Lord, Your Redeemer" (Isaiah 44:21-28)
THURSDAY, March 11: "The Lord Has Redeemed" (Isaiah 48:17-22)
FRIDAY, March 12: "In Christ We Have Redemption" (Ephesians 1:3-12)
SATURDAY, March 13: "The Forgiveness of Sins" (Acts 26:12-18)
SUNDAY, March 14: "Being Right or Being Gracious" (Jonah 3:10–4:5)

FAMILY AS COMMUNITY

DEVOTIONAL READING: John 20:24-29
PRINT PASSAGE: Ruth 1:1-9, 14b, 16

BACKGROUND SCRIPTURE: Ruth 1:1-16
KEY VERSE: Ruth 1:16

Ruth 1:1-9, 14b, 16—KJV

NOW IT came to pass in the days when the judges ruled, that there was a famine in the land. And a certain man of Bethlehem-judah went to sojourn in the country of Moab, he, and his wife, and his two sons.

2 And the name of the man was Elimelech, and the name of his wife Naomi, and the name of his two sons Mahlon and Chilion, Ephrathites of Bethlehem-judah. And they came into the country of Moab, and continued there.

3 And Elimelech Naomi's husband died; and she was left, and her two sons.

4 And they took them wives of the women of Moab; the name of the one was Orpah, and the name of the other Ruth: and they dwelled there about ten years.

5 And Mahlon and Chilion died also both of them; and the woman was left of her two sons and her husband.

6 Then she arose with her daughters in law, that she might return from the country of Moab: for she had heard in the country of Moab how that the LORD had visited his people in giving them bread.

7 Wherefore she went forth out of the place where she was, and her two daughters in law with her; and they went on the way to return unto the land of Judah.

8 And Naomi said unto her two daughters in law, Go, return each to her mother's house: the LORD deal kindly with you, as ye have dealt with the dead, and with me.

9 The LORD grant you that ye may find rest, each of you in the house of her husband. Then she kissed them; and they lifted up their voice, and wept.

.....

14 Orpah kissed her mother in law; but Ruth clave unto her.

Ruth 1:1-9, 14b, 16—NRSV

IN THE days when the judges ruled, there was a famine in the land, and a certain man of Bethlehem in Judah went to live in the country of Moab, he and his wife and two sons.

2 The name of the man was Elimelech and the name of his wife Naomi, and the names of his two sons were Mahlon and Chilion; they were Ephrathites from Bethlehem in Judah. They went into the country of Moab and remained there.

3 But Elimelech, the husband of Naomi, died, and she was left with her two sons.

4 These took Moabite wives; the name of the one was Orpah and the name of the other Ruth. When they had lived there about ten years,

5 both Mahlon and Chilion also died, so that the woman was left without her two sons and her husband.

6 Then she started to return with her daughters-in-law from the country of Moab, for she had heard in the country of Moab that the LORD had considered his people and given them food.

7 So she set out from the place where she had been living, she and her two daughters-in-law, and they went on their way to go back to the land of Judah.

8 But Naomi said to her two daughters-in-law, "Go back each of you to your mother's house. May the LORD deal kindly with you, as you have dealt with the dead and with me.

9 The LORD grant that you may find security, each of you in the house of your husband." Then she kissed them, and they wept aloud.

.....

14 Orpah kissed her mother-in-law, but Ruth clung to her.

…..

16 And Ruth said, Intreat me not to leave thee, or to return from following after thee: for whither thou goest, I will go; and where thou lodgest, I will lodge: thy people shall be my people, and thy God my God.

…..

16 But Ruth said, "Do not press me to leave you or to turn back from following you! Where you go, I will go; where you lodge, I will lodge; your people shall be my people, and your God my God."

TOPICAL OUTLINE OF THE LESSON

I. **Introduction**
   A. The Power of Commitment
   B. Biblical Background

II. **Exposition and Application of the Scripture**
   A. Provision in the Midst of Famine (Ruth 1:1-6)
   B. An Act of Selfless Love (Ruth 1:7-9)
   C. The Vow of Commitment (Ruth 1:14b, 16)

III. **Concluding Reflection**

LESSON OBJECTIVES

Upon completion of this lesson, the students will know that:

1. Ruth demonstrated unequal family commitment to a foreign woman;
2. God rewarded Naomi with a faithful daughter-in-law; and,
3. Faithfulness in the family leads to a strong community.

POINTS TO BE EMPHASIZED

ADULT/YOUTH

Adult Topic: Commitment to a New Community
Youth Topic: Who's in the Family?
Adult Key Verse: Ruth 1:16
Youth Key Verses: Ruth 1:14, 16
Print Passage: Ruth 1:1-9, 14b, 16

—Without the support of her husband and sons who had died, Naomi decided to return to her original community for support.

—Orpah decided to return to her mother's house and remain in her community.

—Moab was the country settled by the descendants of Lot's child by his oldest daughter (Genesis 19:37).

—During the time of the Judges, Elimelech, his wife Naomi, and their two sons left Judah because of famine and settled in Moab.

—After the deaths of her husband and sons, Naomi encouraged her daughters-in-law to go back to stay with their own families, but Ruth insisted on remaining loyal and committed to her mother-in-law.

—Ruth's primary concern was not her own well-being, but rather for that of her mother-in-law.

CHILDREN

Children Topic: Bonding with Relatives
Key Verse: Ruth 1:16
Print Passage: Ruth 1:1-9, 14b, 16

—A family had to relocate because of a famine.

—The women lost their sources of support.

—As Naomi prepared to return home after hearing the famine was over, she expressed concern for Orpah and Ruth.

—Her daughter-in-law Ruth prevailed upon Naomi to allow her to return home with her.

—Ruth accepted Naomi's God as her God.

—Ruth made a commitment to support and protect Naomi, her mother-in-law.

I. INTRODUCTION

A. The Power of Commitment

As a pastor officiating at the exchange of vows during holy matrimony, I always encourage engaged couples to include the "Vow of Commitment" found in today's background Scripture. Contrary to the direct benefits that she stood to gain by returning to her family in the midst of a famine, Ruth made an everlasting commitment with her mother-in-law, Naomi, a widow who had recently lost both of her sons. In biblical times, the death of a woman's husband and sons meant that she would be destitute for the rest of her life; such a woman would be dependent upon relatives, friends, and the extended community for subsistence. Receiving the news in Moab that the famine in Israel had decreased in its intensity and that the Lord graciously provided food for His people, Naomi decided to return home. Initially, her daughters-in-law, Orpah and Ruth, departed with her enroute to Judah. Naomi thanked them for their kindness to her deceased sons and to her. But she greatly desired that they stay in Moab and find new husbands and in this way enjoy the fulfilling lives that their husbands' untimely deaths temporarily stole from them. After much prodding, Orpah accepted Naomi's directive to remain in Moab. In an opposite reaction, Ruth absolutely refused to heed Naomi's pleas. From a different nationality, religion, culture, creed, language, and ethnicity, Ruth pledged never to leave Naomi, to adopt her people as family, to worship their God, and to abide with her until death separated them.

B. Biblical Background

It is easy to dwell primarily upon the favorable ending of this story. However, taking that approach overshadows the tremendous amount of loss and the dire circumstances in which Ruth and Naomi lived. Elimelech, Naomi's husband, and their two sons, Mahlon and Chilion, originally traveled and temporarily settled in Moab to escape the brutal famine in Judah. The Old Testament records approximately twelve different occurrences of famine. Because the land (in any given year) produced just enough food to feed the population of the Ancient Near East, a famine inevitably meant the threat of starvation for the weak, widowed, and otherwise powerless people. Suffice it to say, the mention of a famine was not an illustrative literary technique. The very mention of one meant that countless lives of children and women hung in the balance. Again, Naomi, in a greater set of dire circumstances, became a widow and was childless in a foreign land. Her daughters-in-law and their natural families were under no obligation to care for Naomi. Practically speaking, she had to fend for herself. Hearing that the famine in Judah was lessening, Naomi prepared to return to her native land. Remarkably, Orpah and Ruth left with her. In a most gracious act, Naomi looked beyond her personal situation and encouraged her daughters-in-law to pursue lives in Moab that would yield marriage, love, family, and fulfillment. She selflessly released them from any obligation that they thought they had toward her and the memory of her dead sons, their former husbands. Essentially, three widows—one elderly and the other two young—were left trying to journey forward in life with meager resources in the midst of a famine. Notwithstanding those desperate conditions, they decided to forge a bond that surpassed law, religion, and social custom.

It is significant to consider the reasons why Orpah actually accepted Naomi's blessing and returned to her family and home. As a young widow at the time, marriage to a gainfully employed husband would be her most obvious means of provision and survival. There was also the issue of children and continuing a lineage. Women without children were considered barren and thus cursed by God. In going with Naomi, Orpah conceivably would have surrendered her opportunity and desire to be married and have a family. As a consequence, Naomi understood Orpah's decision and probably did not judge her because of it.

II. EXPOSITION AND APPLICATION OF THE SCRIPTURE

A. Provision in the Midst of Famine (Ruth 1:1-6)

NOW IT came to pass in the days when the judges ruled, that there was a famine in the land. And a certain man of Bethlehem-judah went to sojourn in the country of Moab, he, and his wife, and his two sons. And the name of the man was Elimelech, and the name of his wife Naomi, and the name of his two sons Mahlon and Chilion, Ephrathites of Bethlehem-judah. And they came into the country of Moab, and continued there. And Elimelech Naomi's husband died; and she was left, and her two sons. And they took them wives of the women of Moab; the name of the one was Orpah, and the name of the other Ruth: and they dwelled there about ten years. And Mahlon and Chilion died also both of them; and the woman was left of her two sons and her husband. Then she arose with her daughters in law, that she might return from the country of Moab: for she had heard in the country of Moab how that the LORD had visited his people in giving them bread.

Naomi received word in Moab that the Lord had come to the aid of His people by providing food. The severity of the famine lifted in Israel allowing Naomi and her daughters-in-law to return home. This journey would be bittersweet at best. It would occur after the deaths of their three husbands who died in the land of their temporary abode. It is amazing how death can bring people closer to each other. We do not know the nature of the relationship of these three women prior to their collective experience with bereavement and widowhood. We surmise that they joined together in a previously unparalleled bond. Whereas God supplied food in Israel, He also gave Naomi, Ruth, and Orpah food for the soul in the fellowship, love, and community of each other.

The bond of these women represents a

greater union in the family of God. The marriage of Ruth to Naomi's son forever joined Moab and Judah. Matthew's gospel contains one of the genealogies of our Lord. It comes as no surprise that it includes Ruth, a Moabite woman who traditionally would have been despised by the Israelites. Mystically and majestically, almighty God used the famine to create a connection between nations of people who had previously fought each other. By incorporating a Gentile woman into Christ's lineage, the Lord demonstrated His unconditional love for all people.

B. An Act of Selfless Love
(Ruth 1:7-9)

Wherefore she went forth out of the place where she was, and her two daughters in law with her; and they went on the way to return unto the land of Judah. And Naomi said unto her two daughters in law, Go, return each to her mother's house: the Lord deal kindly with you, as ye have dealt with the dead, and with me. The Lord grant you that ye may find rest, each of you in the house of her husband. Then she kissed them; and they lifted up their voice, and wept.

In response to the favorable word about the end of the famine, Naomi began the journey back to Judah with her daughters-in-law. After a period of reflection, she exhibited one of the most touching acts of selfless love recorded in the Bible. Naomi told Ruth and Orpah to return to their mothers and families. In so doing, Naomi released them from their commitment to live with her regardless of the hard circumstances and personal costs. Further, Orpah and Ruth pled with Naomi to continue the journey to Judah. But, this gracious and wise older woman detailed the stubborn facts for them. Should they return with her, they would be consigning themselves to living as widows for the rest of their lives. In fairness to these young women who had many years before them, Naomi lovingly and perhaps forcefully encouraged them to go back to their native land to find whatever life offered. Naomi's act foreshadowed the sacrificial and selfless love of God in Jesus Christ. The community that formed between the three of them transformed into a family in which the members' love for each other enabled them to consider what was best for the others. Because Naomi unconditionally surrendered her will and her care into the hands of almighty God, she affectionately sent her caring daughter-in-law back to her mother.

C. The Vow of Commitment
(Ruth 1:14b, 16)

Orpah kissed her mother in law; but Ruth clave unto her. ... And Ruth said, Intreat me not to leave thee, or to return from following after thee: for whither thou goest, I will go; and where thou lodgest, I will lodge: thy people shall be my people, and thy God my God.

Ruth's reply to Naomi's urgings surpassed her selfless love. For the rest of human history, these two women would teach generations what community and family really are. Immediately, we assume that communities develop around people who share many commonalities. Usually, we associate communities with people from similar backgrounds, education, values, economic status, and aspirations. We define families with strict biological, genealogical, and genetic connections. In disagreement, Ruth and Naomi established familial and communal bonds that merged faith, commitment, and a willingness to grow in relationship with someone. I suspect that observing Naomi's character and genuine faith in God motivated Ruth to offer her immortal words of commitment.

Plausibly, Ruth admired Naomi's steadfast faith in God despite the famine that led to her stay in Moab, the deaths of her husband and sons, and her words "the Lord's hand has gone out against me!" (Ruth 1:13, NIV). In addition, Naomi decided to leave in response to learning of the Lord's provision.

Let's examine exactly what Ruth pledged. First, she appealed to Naomi to cease from urging her to leave or return to Moab. Second, Ruth promised to go wherever Naomi went. This component of the vow is reminiscent of God's directive to Abram to go to the place where He sent him. Ruth agreed to follow God's instructions as He revealed them to Naomi. Third, Ruth pledged to assume Naomi's family as her very own. That is a critical commitment considering the racial, cultural, and national tensions between the Israelites and Moabites. Plus, Ruth had no assurance that Naomi's family would receive her as favorably as her mother-in-law had. Yet, Ruth agreed to overcome all of the necessary human, relational, and social barriers to ensure the fidelity, strength, and growth of her relationship with Naomi. Furthermore, Ruth swore to change her religion; she would begin serving the God of Israel instead of the deities of Moab with whom she had grown up. Essentially, Ruth vowed to become a Jewish convert; she would begin to follow the Law of Moses with its many legal dictates revealing the holy character and name of almighty God. Ruth sealed her vow of commitment by requesting severe divine judgment should she fail to keep her commitment.

Ruth and Naomi's dedication to each other exemplifies the commitment that disciples of our Lord are to have toward Him and each other in the church. More specifically, their relationship and vow illustrate the undying covenant that a husband and a wife are to share in marriage. God perfectly intends that only death should separate a man and woman who share Ruth's vow of commitment. Undergirded by God's love in Christ, this type of vow is the defining and distinguishing characteristic of Christian men and women, whether in marriage or within the body of Christ. The Lord says that the love that we show toward each other will demonstrate to the world that we are His disciples (see John 13:34-35).

III. CONCLUDING REFLECTION

Families are the primary communities to which we belong. In the nuclear family unit, we receive our first lessons of life relating to faith, education, commitment, values, work, and ambition. We learn to love God and neighbor because our parents or primary caretakers teach us the importance of genuine spirituality. In fact, we learn to love ourselves because our mothers and fathers teach us about our uniqueness as children of God. Additionally, as members of families, we learn how to care about others and share our resources of time, talent, treasure, and temperament with them. The lessons in the family community extend to the church and larger society. Interestingly, the Lord Jesus Christ redefined the family and in so doing He revised the traditional notions of the purpose and composition of a community.

We must reflect and ask: On what basis did Ruth make this astonishing vow of commitment to a mother-in-law with whom she no longer shared any legal, moral, ethical, or spiritual obligation? It is often said, "Blood is thicker than water." That saying elevates familial relationships over all others—whether they are business, school, friends, or church. However, the compelling story of today's text counteracts this age-old wisdom about the values and importance of relationships. The interaction and shared principles of Ruth and Naomi teach us that there are relationships in which people do not share genealogy, a legacy, or genetics, but have a love for each other that supercedes the traditional notions of family bonds and commitments. Usually, a person's understanding and integration of God's unconditional love are the foundation upon which he or she is able to make a lifelong commitment without the communal expectation of the family structure. More specifically, in the church, the shared brotherhood and sisterhood of the blood of Jesus Christ—our Lord and Savior—often exceeds the significance of biology and lineage. The fact that you can become closer to your Christian family than your natural one demonstrates the power of commitment to Christ and its ability to extend to other relationships.

PRAYER

Heavenly Father, help us to remain faithful to the end. We have seen commitment in the life of Ruth; help us to be so committed. In Jesus' name we pray. Amen.

WORD POWER

Intreat (*paga* [pa-gah]): means "to strike upon something whether in a good or bad sense; keep pushing, to assail anyone with petitions, to urge." The word is cast in the imperfect tense, which means a continuous action. However, Ruth emphatically rejected the entreatment of Naomi.

HOME DAILY BIBLE READINGS
(March 15-21, 2010)

Family as Community

MONDAY, March 15: "A Shared Experience" (John 20:24-29)

TUESDAY, March 16: "A Shared Reward" (1 Samuel 30:21-31)

WEDNESDAY, March 17: "A Shared Advantage" (Luke 3:10-14)

THURSDAY, March 18: "A Shared Oath" (1 Samuel 20:30-42)

FRIDAY, March 19: "A Shared Responsibility" (Romans 14:13-21)

SATURDAY, March 20: "A Shared Love" (John 15:9-17)

SUNDAY, March 21: "A Shared Faith" (Ruth 1:1-9, 14b, 16)

LESSON 4   March 28, 2010

ACCEPTANCE IN COMMUNITY

DEVOTIONAL READING: Romans 12:9-18
PRINT PASSAGE: Ruth 2:5-12; 3:9-11

BACKGROUND SCRIPTURE: Ruth 2–3
KEY VERSE: Ruth 3:11

Ruth 2:5-12; 3:9-11—KJV

5 Then said Boaz unto his servant that was set over the reapers, Whose damsel is this?

6 And the servant that was set over the reapers answered and said, It is the Moabitish damsel that came back with Naomi out of the country of Moab:

7 And she said, I pray you, let me glean and gather after the reapers among the sheaves: so she came, and hath continued even from the morning until now, that she tarried a little in the house.

8 Then said Boaz unto Ruth, Hearest thou not, my daughter? Go not to glean in another field, neither go from hence, but abide here fast by my maidens:

9 Let thine eyes be on the field that they do reap, and go thou after them: have I not charged the young men that they shall not touch thee? and when thou art athirst, go unto the vessels, and drink of that which the young men have drawn.

10 Then she fell on her face, and bowed herself to the ground, and said unto him, Why have I found grace in thine eyes, that thou shouldest take knowledge of me, seeing I am a stranger?

11 And Boaz answered and said unto her, It hath fully been shewed me, all that thou hast done unto thy mother in law since the death of thine husband: and how thou hast left thy father and thy mother, and the land of thy nativity, and art come unto a people which thou knewest not heretofore.

12 The LORD recompense thy work, and a full reward be given thee of the LORD God of Israel, under whose wings thou art come to trust.

…..

9 And he said, Who art thou? And she answered, I am Ruth thine handmaid: spread therefore thy skirt over thine handmaid; for thou art a near kinsman.

10 And he said, Blessed be thou of the LORD, my daughter: for thou hast shewed more kindness in the latter end than at the beginning, inasmuch as thou

Ruth 2:5-12; 3:9-11—NRSV

5 Then Boaz said to his servant who was in charge of the reapers, "To whom does this young woman belong?"

6 The servant who was in charge of the reapers answered, "She is the Moabite who came back with Naomi from the country of Moab.

7 She said, 'Please, let me glean and gather among the sheaves behind the reapers.' So she came, and she has been on her feet from early this morning until now, without resting even for a moment."

8 Then Boaz said to Ruth, "Now listen, my daughter, do not go to glean in another field or leave this one, but keep close to my young women.

9 Keep your eyes on the field that is being reaped, and follow behind them. I have ordered the young men not to bother you. If you get thirsty, go to the vessels and drink from what the young men have drawn."

10 Then she fell prostrate, with her face to the ground, and said to him, "Why have I found favor in your sight, that you should take notice of me, when I am a foreigner?"

11 But Boaz answered her, "All that you have done for your mother-in-law since the death of your husband has been fully told me, and how you left your father and mother and your native land and came to a people that you did not know before.

12 May the LORD reward you for your deeds, and may you have a full reward from the LORD, the God of Israel, under whose wings you have come for refuge!"

…..

9 He said, "Who are you?" And she answered, "I am Ruth, your servant; spread your cloak over your servant, for you are next-of-kin."

10 He said, "May you be blessed by the LORD, my daughter; this last instance of your loyalty is better than the first; you have not gone after young men,

followedst not young men, whether poor or rich.

11 And now, my daughter, fear not; I will do to thee all that thou requirest: for all the city of my people doth know that thou art a virtuous woman.

whether poor or rich.

11 And now, my daughter, do not be afraid, I will do for you all that you ask, for all the assembly of my people know that you are a worthy woman."

TOPICAL OUTLINE OF THE LESSON

I. **Introduction**
    A. The Fear of Rejection
    B. Biblical Background

II. **Exposition and Application of the Scripture**
    A. Ruth Appears in the Field (Ruth 2:5-7)
    B. Ruth Receives Favor (Ruth 2:8-12)
    C. Ruth Reveals Her Identity (Ruth 3:9-11)

III. **Concluding Reflection**

LESSON OBJECTIVES

Upon completion of this lesson, the students will know that:

1. God favored Ruth for her unflinching love;
2. Longing for acceptance should be done in a way that glorifies God; and,
3. Assimilation rather than isolation leads to community approval.

POINTS TO BE EMPHASIZED

ADULT/YOUTH

Adult Topic: Gaining Acceptance
Youth Topic: We Welcome You
Adult Key Verse: Ruth 3:11
Youth Key Verse: Ruth 2:10b
Print Passage: Ruth 2:5-12; 3:9-11

—Permission to allow one to glean his field was part of the holiness code (see Leviticus 19:9-10).

—Boaz offered work and protection to Ruth in his household, clan, and community.

—Boaz welcomed Ruth to his household because he admired her loyalty to Naomi.

—Boaz revealed his willingness to accept kinsman-redeemer responsibility for Ruth by expressing care for her.

—God honored Ruth's commitment to her mother-in-law by guiding her to the field of Boaz.

—Boaz was a wealthy and influential relative of Naomi's husband, a man who took great care to follow the Mosaic law, was sensitive to those in need, and cared for his workers.

—Ruth gained a good reputation through her hard work, kindness, faithfulness, loving behavior, bravery, and positive attitude.

CHILDREN

Children Topic: Welcome to the Community
Key Verse: Ruth 2:12
Print Passage: Ruth 2:1-12

—To provide food for Naomi and herself, Ruth took the initiative to glean in a field of grain.

—By the leading of the Spirit, Ruth gleaned in a field owned by a rich kinsman of Naomi's deceased husband.

—Ruth found favor with Boaz who invited her into his community.

—Boaz revealed to Ruth why he found favor with her.

—Boaz and Ruth found their future in each other.

—When we do for others, we may be rewarded beyond our wildest imagination.

I. INTRODUCTION

A. The Fear of Rejection

Our previous lesson concluded with Ruth's eternal vow of commitment to Naomi. Ruth would travel back to Judah with Naomi and live as an Israelite woman instead of the Moabite whom she was. Ruth pledged that only death would separate her from Naomi. What about Naomi's family and friends? Would Naomi's recitation of Ruth's vow and loyalty suffice to convince Naomi's family that Ruth should become a bona fide member of the family?

Often we hear the saying, "Blood is thicker than water." This adage exhorts people to remember the importance of their relationships with family members. In fact, they should value these ties more greatly than they should value relationships with friends, fellow church members, and others. If confronted with a choice between family and friends, this maxim states clearly that one favors relatives at all costs. Loyalty belongs to them above all others. Had Naomi's family taken this attitude with Ruth, they would have ignored her. The combination of the religious, cultural, and tribal differences would suffice to justify their actions. In addition, taking on another person to feed during a protracted famine would have been reason enough for some members of Naomi's family to reject Ruth. With "benign neglect" toward Ruth, they would have rejoiced over Naomi's return but would have insisted that Ruth return—as she was not a member of the family.

B. Biblical Background

The book of Ruth is a beautiful love story. There are three major characters in this story—namely: Ruth, Naomi, and Boaz. The events in the book transpired during the time between 1400–1050 BC. The author of this book is unknown. The story of Ruth commands our respect. After the death of her husband, Ruth decided to follow Naomi to Judah. Ruth, a Gentile among the Jews, dared to break cultural barriers. On arrival in Judah during harvest season, she (at the encouragement of Naomi) went to the field of Boaz to glean leftovers behind the reapers. The gleaning in Boaz's field led Ruth to find grace in an uncommon place.

The exceedingly gracious and respectful actions of Boaz demonstrate the power of God's love to transcend human customs and limitations. The humility of Ruth led to a marriage with Boaz, who became a kinsman-redeemer. The daring action of Ruth led her to become a mother to be remembered in sacred history.

II. EXPOSITION AND APPLICATION OF THE SCRIPTURE

A. Ruth Appears in the Field
(Ruth 2:5-7)

Then said Boaz unto his servant that was set over the reapers, Whose damsel is this? And the servant that was set over the reapers answered and said, It is the Moabitish damsel that came back with Naomi out of the country of Moab: And she said, I pray you, let me glean and gather after the reapers among the sheaves: so she came, and hath continued even from the morning until now, that she tarried a little in the house.

Amazingly, Ruth fulfilled her vow of commitment to Naomi in this strange land. In today's passage, we find Ruth faithfully caring for the needs of her mother-in-law. Ruth set out, with Naomi's permission, to glean the leftover grain in the fields. You will recall that the Law instructed harvesters to leave some grain and produce for the poor who would be hungry and in need (see Leviticus 19:10). They were not to gather every single bit of grain. Israel was told to remember the days when they wandered hungry, thirsty, and in need in the wilderness. God gave some of the people whom they encountered a favorable heart toward Israel. Accordingly, they should demonstrate their gratitude by helping other hungry and thirsty strangers via leaving grain and produce, and water in the wells. Ruth set out to find food and water for Naomi and herself.

As Ruth was gleaning, Boaz arrived in the field. He took notice of her and he inquired of his foreman, "Whose young woman is that?"

(verse 5, NIV). The foreman replied, "It is the young Moabite woman who came back with Naomi" (see verse 6). Ruth was very industrious, because it is stated in the text, "She…has continued from morning until now" (verse 7, NKJV). Even though her task was tiring and menial, yet she walked tirelessly and faithfully. The question we need to ask is, "What is your attitude when the task you have been given is not up to your true potential?" Ruth demonstrated industriousness by working from morning until evening except for occasional rest. We should not forget that God was working behind the scenes in the life of Ruth. As Christians, we believe in the sovereignty of God and, therefore, even in our own lives God is working. The problem with modern Christians is that the degree of sensitivity to God's presence is at an all-time low. We are drawn to the latest news, breaking news, developing news, cell phones, e-mail, and I-pod—to mention a few of the things that make us less sensitive.

B. Ruth Receives Favor
(Ruth 2:8-12)

Then said Boaz unto Ruth, Hearest thou not, my daughter? Go not to glean in another field, neither go from hence, but abide here fast by my maidens: Let thine eyes be on the field that they do reap, and go thou after them: have I not charged the young men that they shall not touch thee? and when thou art athirst, go unto the vessels, and drink of that which the young men have

drawn. Then she fell on her face, and bowed herself to the ground, and said unto him, Why have I found grace in thine eyes, that thou shouldest take knowledge of me, seeing I am a stranger? And Boaz answered and said unto her, It hath fully been shewed me, all that thou hast done unto thy mother in law since the death of thine husband: and how thou hast left thy father and thy mother, and the land of thy nativity, and art come unto a people which thou knewest not heretofore. The Lord recompense thy work, and a full reward be given thee of the Lord God of Israel, under whose wings thou art come to trust.

Moved by Ruth's humility as a stranger in a foreign land, Boaz told Ruth, "Do not go to glean in another field" (verse 8, NKJV). She was to stay with other young women in the field. We have no reason to doubt the integrity of Boaz; he did what he did with respect for a foreigner. Ruth must follow the reapers instead of harvesting from the leftovers. Boaz demonstrated extraordinary concern for Ruth's provision and protection. He even offered water to Ruth.

In verses 11 and 12, Boaz explained that he favored Ruth because she had shown loyal love to her mother-in-law. Unlike many women in our day who have no attachment to their mothers-in-law, Ruth was highly favored because of her respect and caring attitude for Naomi. Boaz gave an unexpected blessing, asking that God would abundantly reward Ruth for her remarkable loyalty. On many occasions, the way God's blessing comes is not through channels we consider likely sources. Ruth started to glean around the field, and Boaz showed up in the field. From that encounter, Ruth—a poor widow who had lost hope—was blessed beyond her expectations. We miss the blessing of God when we become selfish and self-centered. Boaz invoked the blessing of God on Ruth by saying that God would abundantly reward her. Boaz's

belief in Ruth's genuineness enabled the others to accept her as one of their very own. Spiritually speaking, Boaz personified the love of God who freely and faithfully accepted anyone who humbly and sincerely responded to God's love with genuine repentance and a lifelong desire to live in accordance with the teachings and commands of the Lord.

In verse 12, Boaz said, "and a full reward be given thee." The integrity of Boaz is revealed in this statement. In essence, the kindness Boaz exhibited was little in comparison to Ruth's faithfulness. God alone could give her a full reward of her kindness to her husband and her mother-in-law. Why this bestowal of blessing? Because Ruth had come to dwell under the wings of the Most High God (see Deuteronomy 32:11).

As members of the church, the family of God on the earth, we should equally be willing to receive persons who desire to become genuine disciples of our Lord. We should not put them through any pedigree or litmus test to determine whether they are worthy of admission. In gratitude for God's unconditional acceptance of us when we responded to His appeals, we must receive our brothers and sisters with the same redemptive and unbiased love with which we were admitted to the household of faith.

Boaz's willingness and graciousness in meeting Ruth's physical needs in the midst of a longstanding famine resembles God's limitless love and unmerited favor toward those persons who, like Ruth, humbly come to Him. He meets their spiritual, emotional, mental, and psychological needs in the famine of human existence.

Ruth's life exhibited admirable qualities.

She was a hardworking lady. These qualities gained her an unparalleled reputation.

C. Ruth Reveals Her Identity
(Ruth 3:9-11)

And he said, Who art thou? And she answered, I am Ruth thine handmaid: spread therefore thy skirt over thine handmaid; for thou art a near kinsman. And he said, Blessed be thou of the LORD, my daughter: for thou hast shewed more kindness in the latter end than at the beginning, inasmuch as thou followedst not young men, whether poor or rich. And now, my daughter, fear not; I will do to thee all that thou requirest: for all the city of my people doth know that thou art a virtuous woman.

The phrase "Who art thou?" (verse 9) signified that Boaz felt a strange woman was close by. Ruth revealed her identity by saying, "I am Ruth, your maidservant. Take your maidservant under your wing" (verse 9). The "wing" is an emblem of protection, and is a metaphor taken from young chickens running under the wing of their mother for protection from predators. The request here was for Boaz to take her to be his wife, because he was the kinsman-redeemer. In other words, as a kinsman, Boaz was the redeemer to whom the right of redemption belonged. According to Adam Clark, even to the present day, when a Jewish man gets married, he throws the skirt over her, which symbolizes that he has taken her under his protection.

Without mincing words, Boaz blessed Ruth again for her faithfulness and chastity. Recalling how Ruth had carried herself in Bethlehem, Boaz said, "Thou hast shewed more kindness" (verse 10). In other words, Ruth had proven beyond any shadow of doubt that she was a reliable woman. Ruth could have run after young men in the village, but she cleaved to Naomi and was hoping against hope. Ruth's desire was to perpetuate the memory of her deceased husband so that his name would not be forgotten in Israel (see Deuteronomy 25:5-10). The latter act of Ruth brought shock to Boaz. In the ancient Middle East, not having an heir was considered a tragedy for the family. The elaborate praise of Boaz showed that Ruth (as a godly woman) had not compromised herself. Boaz's prayer and words revealed that Ruth, the Moabite woman who now dwelled in Israel, had actually found favor in the eyes of the Lord, more so than in the eyes of Boaz.

It is significant to note that Ruth's actions did not in and of themselves yield God's kindnesses. Most probably unaware of the Abrahamic covenant, Ruth acted kindly toward Naomi out of Ruth's inner beliefs, culture, and character. Yet, her generosity was consistent with the covenant. God faithfully adhered to this covenant which He established on the basis of His name, the only basis by which God can swear. As a consequence, God mercifully moved the heart of Boaz to be kind to Ruth. This repayment was not the just recompense for an act of righteousness in which a nice, giving, and kind person expected remuneration from almighty God for her commendable deeds.

III. CONCLUDING REFLECTION

As we come to the conclusion of this lesson, it is important to know that your decision may lead you to a position of prominence or demotion. No matter the angle from which you view this story, there are bright lights that illuminate the mind. Ruth became a widow very early in life. She was a Moabite who married a Jew. Naomi, her mother-in-law, became a widow and was childless, yet Ruth decided to follow her mother-in-law to a strange country. How could a young widow see apparent failure and yet decide to follow? We could surmise that the unseen hand of God was leading her in a perplexing time.

From Boaz's example, we learn the importance of learning to create communities of hospitality. The fundamental example is the church—which is a community "called out" from the values, manners, and behavior of the wider secular world. Disciples liberally share the love of Christ with new believers, foreigners to a new way of life. We do so in appreciation of the acceptance that we obtained when we first believed in the Lord and were saved. Each disciple endeavors to emulate the actions of Boaz as we allow the Lord to transform our thinking and hearts so that we unreservedly and heartily share His love by giving our resources to people in need. Most practically, Boaz's example reveals one of the most effective means to serve our Lord. We actually serve Him by serving people. Tending to their needs is the most direct method of fulfilling the Great Commandment and the Great Commission.

PRAYER

Father in heaven, we thank You for the beauty of this day. For Your lovingkindness toward us, we thank You, O Lord. Teach us to serve You by meeting the needs of Your children around us. In Jesus' name we pray. Amen.

WORD POWER

Virtuous (Hebrew: *khay`yil* [khah`-yil])—means "strength, might, power, upright, an honest person, or a person of substance." This word, *virtuous,* has the same meaning as *valor.* Naomi described Ruth using a lovely word because of Ruth's insistence on following Naomi to Bethlehem. Every child of God is called to demonstrate such magnanimity in the face of apparent failure.

HOME DAILY BIBLE READINGS
(March 22-28, 2010)

Acceptance in Community
MONDAY, March 22: "Live Peaceably with All" (Romans 12:9-18)

TUESDAY, March 23: "A Debtor to Others" (Romans 1:8-15)

WEDNESDAY, March 24: "Mercy Triumphs" (James 2:8-13)

THURSDAY, March 25: "Wisdom from Above" (James 3:13-18)

FRIDAY, March 26: "For All Peoples" (Isaiah 56:3-8)

SATURDAY, March 27: "Members of God's Household" (Ephesians 2:11-20)

SUNDAY, March 28: "Blessed with Acceptance" (Ruth 2:5-12; 3:9-11)

LESSON 5   April 4, 2010 (Easter)

THE COMMUNITY FACES PAIN AND JOY

DEVOTIONAL READING: **Psalm 5**
PRINT PASSAGE: **John 16:16-24; 20:11-16**
KEY VERSE: **John 16:16**

BACKGROUND SCRIPTURE: **John 13:21-30;**
16:16-24; 20:11-16

John 16:16-24; 20:11-16—KJV

16 A little while, and ye shall not see me: and again, a little while, and ye shall see me, because I go to the Father.

17 Then said some of his disciples among themselves, What is this that he saith unto us, A little while, and ye shall not see me: and again, a little while, and ye shall see me: and, Because I go to the Father?

18 They said therefore, What is this that he saith, A little while? we cannot tell what he saith.

19 Now Jesus knew that they were desirous to ask him, and said unto them, Do ye enquire among yourselves of that I said, A little while, and ye shall not see me: and again, a little while, and ye shall see me?

20 Verily, verily, I say unto you, That ye shall weep and lament, but the world shall rejoice: and ye shall be sorrowful, but your sorrow shall be turned into joy.

21 A woman when she is in travail hath sorrow, because her hour is come: but as soon as she is delivered of the child, she remembereth no more the anguish, for joy that a man is born into the world.

22 And ye now therefore have sorrow: but I will see you again, and your heart shall rejoice, and your joy no man taketh from you.

23 And in that day ye shall ask me nothing. Verily, verily, I say unto you, Whatsoever ye shall ask the Father in my name, he will give it you.

24 Hitherto have ye asked nothing in my name: ask, and ye shall receive, that your joy may be full.

.....

11 But Mary stood without at the sepulchre weeping: and as she wept, she stooped down, and looked into the sepulchre,

12 And seeth two angels in white sitting, the one at the head, and the other at the feet, where the body of Jesus had lain.

John 16:16-24; 20:11-16—NRSV

16 "A little while, and you will no longer see me, and again a little while, and you will see me."

17 Then some of his disciples said to one another, "What does he mean by saying to us, 'A little while, and you will no longer see me, and again a little while, and you will see me'; and 'Because I am going to the Father'?"

18 They said, "What does he mean by this 'a little while'? We do not know what he is talking about."

19 Jesus knew that they wanted to ask him, so he said to them, "Are you discussing among yourselves what I meant when I said, 'A little while, and you will no longer see me, and again a little while, and you will see me'?

20 Very truly, I tell you, you will weep and mourn, but the world will rejoice; you will have pain, but your pain will turn into joy.

21 When a woman is in labor, she has pain, because her hour has come. But when her child is born, she no longer remembers the anguish because of the joy of having brought a human being into the world.

22 So you have pain now; but I will see you again, and your hearts will rejoice, and no one will take your joy from you.

23 On that day you will ask nothing of me. Very truly, I tell you, if you ask anything of the Father in my name, he will give it to you.

24 Until now you have not asked for anything in my name. Ask and you will receive, so that your joy may be complete.

.....

11 But Mary stood weeping outside the tomb. As she wept, she bent over to look into the tomb;

12 and she saw two angels in white, sitting where the body of Jesus had been lying, one at the head and the other at the feet.

Communities experience not only great pain and sorrow but also great relief and joy. Why should communities have hope? Jesus foretold His betrayal, death, and resurrection, and He taught that pain and sorrow would be replaced by relief and joy.

13 And they say unto her, Woman, why weepest thou? She saith unto them, Because they have taken away my Lord, and I know not where they have laid him.
14 And when she had thus said, she turned herself back, and saw Jesus standing, and knew not that it was Jesus.
15 Jesus saith unto her, Woman, why weepest thou? whom seekest thou? She, supposing him to be the gardener, saith unto him, Sir, if thou have borne him hence, tell me where thou hast laid him, and I will take him away.
16 Jesus saith unto her, Mary. She turned herself, and saith unto him, Rabboni; which is to say, Master.

13 They said to her, "Woman, why are you weeping?" She said to them, "They have taken away my Lord, and I do not know where they have laid him."
14 When she had said this, she turned around and saw Jesus standing there, but she did not know that it was Jesus.
15 Jesus said to her, "Woman, why are you weeping? Whom are you looking for?" Supposing him to be the gardener, she said to him, "Sir, if you have carried him away, tell me where you have laid him, and I will take him away."
16 Jesus said to her, "Mary!" She turned and said to him in Hebrew, "Rabbouni!" (which means Teacher).

TOPICAL OUTLINE OF THE LESSON

I. **Introduction**
   A. A Somber Mood
   B. Biblical Background

II. **Exposition and Application of the Scripture**
   A. Sorrow Mixed with Joy (John 16:16-18)
   B. The Blessing of Resurrection (John 16:19-24)
   C. Mary Magdalene's Post-Resurrection Encounter (John 20:11-16)

III. **Concluding Reflection**

LESSON OBJECTIVES

Upon completion of this lesson, the students will know that:

1. The sorrow and pain of the disciples vanished when they saw the empty grave;
2. Mary Magdalene demonstrated true faith by waiting until she heard the news of the risen Lord; and,
3. Our believing in the risen Lord is not in vain.

POINTS TO BE EMPHASIZED

ADULT/YOUTH
Adult Topic: Loss and Life
Youth Topic: Double Whammy: Pain and Joy!
Adult Key Verse: John 16:16
Youth Key Verse: John 16:22
Print Passage: John 16:16-24; 20:11-16
—Jesus' statement in John 16:16 was not understood by His disciples but evidently refers to His death and resurrection.
—Burial in first-century Palestine was typically not in the

ground, but on a ledge in a hollowed-out cave, similar today to a mausoleum.

—The "two angels" mentioned in the book of John (20:12) are "two men" in Luke 24:4, a "young man" in Mark 16:5, and an "angel" in Matthew 28:2.

—"Rabboni" (John 20:16) is evidently the familiar term by which Mary referred to Jesus.

—Jesus' first resurrection appearance was to a woman.

—Jesus knew the path He walked led to His death.

—Jesus was speaking to His disciples after the Last Supper, preparing them for the things to come.

—Jesus told His disciples to ask God the Father in His name and the request would be granted.

CHILDREN

Children Topic: From Sorrow to Joy
Key Verse: John 20:18
Print Passage: John 13:21-30; 20:11-16

—Jesus announced His betrayal.

—Jesus identified His betrayer by offering him a piece of bread.

—The disciples did not understand what Jesus was telling them.

—Jesus appeared first to Mary Magdalene as she went to the tomb.

—When Mary Magdalene heard her name, she realized she was speaking to Jesus.

—Just as Mary Magdalene told the disciples about Jesus' resurrection, children can tell others about Jesus.

I. INTRODUCTION

A. A Somber Mood

Imagine that you are an invisible witness in a hotel suite occupied by the eleven apostles on the day following the Crucifixion. Chances are you would witness an incredible amount of grief, disappointment, anger, hopelessness, and regret. All the languages of the world fail to convey the utter confusion, extreme pain, and overall bewilderment that the apostles shared.

B. Biblical Background

The collective grief and pain of the disciples blinded them to seeing the purpose of Jesus' teachings and actions. As they nursed their emotional and spiritual pain, they failed to recall anything that He taught them during the three and one-half years of His public ministry. During that time, He specifically tutored them about the nature, principles, and purposes of the kingdom of God which He came to establish on the earth. Imprisoned by their self-seeking ambitions and self-centered fears about the fate of Israel, they did not comprehend these lessons. Instead, they harbored grand ideas about the forthcoming rebellion and the lofty positions of power that they would hold upon its successful conclusion.

The second thing in today's Scripture passage is a record of the disciples' ignorance concerning the Lord's purposes. Approximately forty-eight hours prior to their sorrowful Saturday afternoon, He had foretold His crucifixion, death, and ascension to His Father. Furthermore, He stated clearly that they would weep and mourn while the world rejoiced. He prophesied that they would experience tremendous grief and pain. Yet He also encouraged them with the assurance that their pain would possess their eternal purpose, their lament would become laughter, and their hopelessness would yield to joy because of His eventual resurrection—and their meeting again.

II. EXPOSITION AND APPLICATION OF THE SCRIPTURE

A. Sorrow Mixed with Joy
(John 16:16-18)

A little while, and ye shall not see me: and again, a little while, and ye shall see me, because I go to the Father. Then said some of his disciples among themselves, What is this that he saith unto us, A little while, and ye shall not see me: and again, a little while, and ye shall see me: and, Because I go to the Father? They said therefore, What is this that he saith, A little while? we cannot tell what he saith.

"In a little while…"; here, Jesus was telling His disciples what was going to take place very shortly. The trip to Calvary, the death on the cross, and the Resurrection were going to take place. The phrase "you will see me" is a highlight of the post-Resurrection appearances. The disciples were not ready for this type of news. But Jesus did not hide from them what was about to take place. The phrase "you will see me" has been variously interpreted to mean: (1) the disciples would literally see Jesus; and (2) the disciples would spiritually see Jesus after the Ascension because of the work of the Holy Spirit. These two interpretations are one. The disciples would literally see Jesus. They saw Him at His resurrection when He came out of the grave and appeared to so many of His disciples. Also, on the Day of Pentecost, He came in the form of the Holy Spirit.

Jesus' ascension would cause the disciples to weep, but the world would laugh. Truly when Jesus was going to Calvary, the people who saw Him that day were laughing. They laughed because Jesus could not fend off the ones who were inflicting pain on Him. On the other hand, the disciples were bewildered. However, Jesus assured the disciples that their sorrow would turn into joy. Please note this is not merely a case of sorrow being followed by joy. The fact is that the sorrow itself would be transformed. In essence, the death of Jesus would be first a sorrow and then unspeakable joy.

B. The Blessing of Resurrection
(John 16:19-24)

Now Jesus knew that they were desirous to ask him, and said unto them, Do ye enquire among yourselves of that I said, A little while, and ye shall not see me: and again, a little while, and ye shall see me? Verily, verily, I say unto you, That ye shall weep and lament, but the world shall rejoice: and ye shall be sorrowful, but your sorrow shall be turned into joy. A woman when she is in travail hath sorrow, because her hour is come: but as soon as she is delivered of the child, she remembereth no more the anguish, for joy that a man is born into the world. And ye now therefore have sorrow: but I will see you again,

and your heart shall rejoice, and your joy no man taketh from you. And in that day ye shall ask me nothing. Verily, verily, I say unto you, Whatsoever ye shall ask the Father in my name, he will give it you. Hitherto have ye asked nothing in my name: ask, and ye shall receive, that your joy may be full.

To further explain His Word, Jesus used the example of a pregnant mother. The moment of delivery involves excruciating pain, but the woman would continue to endure because a child was coming into the world. But no sooner would the child be born that sorrow would be transformed into joy in the birth of the child.

Let us note the contrast between the disciples and the world. The world rejoiced as the disciples wept, but the disciples would see Jesus again, meaning that it was not over until it was *all* over. The world's joy was temporary while the disciples' joy would last forever. The world's values are often the opposite of God's values. Our situations as Christians can make us feel inadequate, particularly when things are not going the way of our expectation; this can cause us to feel like misfits. We must always remember that even if life is difficult now, one day we will rejoice. We must focus on Christ and not our situation.

In verse 22, Jesus said, "I will see you again." This statement confuses other so-called religious leaders. None among the religious leaders ever boasted of a post-Resurrection appearance. Again Jesus said, "Your joy no one will take" (verse 22, NKJV). Jesus was the source of their joy and ours as well. We cannot succumb to any intimidation or threat because the One who conquered death will appear again as our Savior.

The phrase "Until now you have asked for nothing" (verse 24, NASB) should grab our attention. The disciples had performed miracles on their own; they had gone through some villages preaching about the Lord Jesus Christ with miracles following their work, but Jesus said, "You have asked for nothing." Jesus' ascension to the Father would make access to the Father more direct. No one would need to serve as an intermediary. Through Jesus Christ, we have been consecrated as the priests of God.

Many have been petitioning God in Jesus' name. Why is it that their prayers are not answered? The phrase "In Jesus' name" means that anyone who wants his or her prayer to be answered must also have the nature of Christ dwelling on the inside. It is one thing to confess Jesus as the Lord and Savior, but it is quite another thing to be in alignment with the nature of Christ. Christ must richly dwell in the believer if the believer receives answers to prayers. Asking presupposes a need or needs. It is the desire of the fathers to answer when children call. The heavenly Father wants to grant the petitions of His children, if His children are in line with Him. The honor of the Father lies in the joy of His children.

C. Mary Magdalene's Post-Resurrection Encounter (John 20:11-16)

But Mary stood without at the sepulchre weeping: and as she wept, she stooped down, and looked into the sepulchre, And seeth two angels in white sitting, the one at the head, and the other at the feet, where the body of Jesus had lain. And they say unto her, Woman, why weepest thou? She saith unto them, Because they have taken away my Lord, and I know not where they have laid him. And when she had thus said, she turned herself back, and saw Jesus standing, and knew not that it was Jesus. Jesus saith unto her, Woman, why weepest thou? whom seekest thou? She, supposing him to be the gardener, saith unto him, Sir, if thou have borne him hence, tell

me where thou hast laid him, and I will take him away. Jesus saith unto her, Mary. She turned herself, and saith unto him, Rabboni; which is to say, Master.

Each of the Resurrection accounts is eternally fascinating because of the different details that each of the four evangelists chose to include. John recorded an exciting sprinting contest between Peter and the beloved disciple. The latter, who was years younger, outran Peter and arrived at the tomb first. He instantly believed in the Resurrection account that the woman had given earlier. Peter left the tomb in amazement but not necessarily with unrelenting faith. These two left the scene and returned to their homes.

In contrast, Mary Magdalene remained outside of the empty tomb; she stood there crying. As she grieved, she bent down and looked again into the tomb. She saw two angels seated at the head and foot of where Jesus had lain. They asked her, "Woman, why are you crying?" (verse 13, NIV). She responded by detailing the depth of her pain and plausibly stating her bewilderment as to how she would live without her Lord. Mary's personal grief represented that of the community of seventy-plus persons who had followed. They willingly gave up their former lives to follow Him as He taught with authority, healed with divine and miraculous power, and preached the Good News of the kingdom of God to the poor. But it all came to a crashing, inexplicable, and hopeless end over the course of the weekend. Being astonished, Mary and her compatriots had no idea how they would pick up the pieces and journey forward without Jesus.

Then, incredibly, Mary heard her name. Looking at a man whom she mistook for the gardener, Mary's deep grief and flowing tears blinded her to the fact that she was in the presence of the risen Lord. Wholly bereaved, she pled for the return of Jesus' body. Upon hearing her name, Mary realized that the man was the Lord Jesus. She said, "Rabboni!" (verse 16, NIV). Instantly, her grief turned to joy as she realized that death did not conquer her Lord. He lived and lives eternally. Like a new mother who exalts over the new life of her baby, Mary delighted in the new life that the Lord offered to those who follow and believe in Him. It was after He called her by name that she accepted that He was alive. In Mary's attempting to touch Him and never lose Him again, the risen Lord charged her not to touch Him, but to go to the disciples with the good news of His resurrection from the dead. Obediently, Mary went to the disciples with the news, "I have seen the Lord!" (verse 18, NIV).

Mary's action is an illustration of the difference that one genuine person of faith can make in the midst of the anguish and despair of pain and loss. One person who truly believes in the power of the Resurrection can positively affect an entire community who may fall prey to the temptation of believing that all is lost permanently. Mary probably shared some of her disappointment and confusion in their initial sorrow and bereavement. Nonetheless, she encouraged the disciples with the truth and good news of her direct encounter with the risen Lord.

III. CONCLUDING REFLECTION

In today's lesson, we consider three penetrating passages of Scripture. The first is a record of John's version of "The Last Supper" in which the Lord rose from the table and washed the disciples' feet during a meal. In so doing, He taught them the significance of humility, service, and love. This triad of interrelated characteristics also comprised practical means for sharing God's love with people who were hurting. Second, the Lord taught the disciples about the imminent grief and despair that they would soon feel. Yet, He reassured them that it would not last permanently but would change to joy. Moreover, because the world did not give them the forthcoming joy, the world would not be able to take it away. Third, John uniquely recorded a resurrection account that prominently featured Mary Magdalene, who instantly overcame her pain and grief upon beholding the risen Lord.

Combined, these passages serve as reminders that there is always a divine purpose to our pain. Essentially, pain is the most practical means for personal growth and communal transformation. However, we must always recall the good news of Easter on a daily basis. No matter how dismal and full with despair life becomes, God (in the act of the Resurrection) reminds us that new life is always the outcome.

Using the analogy of childbirth, Jesus defined the immediate time as one of anguish. Like a mother in labor, they would hurt fiercely as they experienced the events of the next day. Also, similar to a mother who delivers a healthy baby, their pain would dissipate as they rejoiced over the outcome of their heartache. However, they totally missed the value of this metaphor and its enduring lesson. They remained focused upon their predetermined ideas about the ministry and mission of Jesus of Nazareth. Moreover, their communal grief on this Saturday impeded their recollection of the promise that God would transform their grief into joy.

PRAYER

Heavenly Father, we thank You that Your faithfulness culminated in the Resurrection. Help us, by the power and might of the Holy Spirit, to recall this gift of abundant and eternal life as we experience pain, grief, and loss. In Jesus' name we pray. Amen.

WORD POWER

See (*thereo; optanommai*)—"See" appears two times in the Key Verse. The first one, *thereo*, means "to see like a spectator, who watches a game without involvement." The second *(optanomai)* is "to see subjectively (inwardly and objectively; outwardly)." The two words are important to understand if one wants a deeper relationship with God.

HOME DAILY BIBLE READINGS
(March 29–April 4, 2010)

The Community Faces Pain and Joy
MONDAY, March 29: "Take Refuge in God" (Psalm 5)
TUESDAY, March 30: "The Persecuted's Endurance" (Luke 21:12-19)
WEDNESDAY, March 31: "The Persecuted's Reward" (Matthew 5:11-16)
THURSDAY, April 1: "Distress Turns to Praise" (Psalm 69:16-20, 29-33)
FRIDAY, April 2: "One of You Will Betray Me" (John 13:21-30)
SATURDAY, April 3: "The Joy of Seeing the Lord" (John 20:11-18)
SUNDAY, April 4: "Your Pain Will Turn into Joy" (John 16:16-20)

LESSON 6   April 11, 2010

LOVE WITHIN THE COMMUNITY

DEVOTIONAL READING: John 13:31-35
PRINT PASSAGE: 1 John 2:9-11, 15-17

BACKGROUND SCRIPTURE: 1 John 2:7-17
KEY VERSE: 1 John 2:10

1 John 2:9-11, 15-17—KJV

9 He that saith he is in the light, and hateth his brother, is in darkness even until now.

10 He that loveth his brother abideth in the light, and there is none occasion of stumbling in him.

11 But he that hateth his brother is in darkness, and walketh in darkness, and knoweth not whither he goeth, because that darkness hath blinded his eyes.

.....

15 Love not the world, neither the things that are in the world. If any man love the world, the love of the Father is not in him.

16 For all that is in the world, the lust of the flesh, and the lust of the eyes, and the pride of life, is not of the Father, but is of the world.

17 And the world passeth away, and the lust thereof: but he that doeth the will of God abideth for ever.

1 John 2:9-11, 15-17—NRSV

9 Whoever says, "I am in the light," while hating a brother or sister, is still in the darkness.

10 Whoever loves a brother or sister lives in the light, and in such a person there is no cause for stumbling.

11 But whoever hates another believer is in the darkness, walks in the darkness, and does not know the way to go, because the darkness has brought on blindness.

.....

15 Do not love the world or the things in the world. The love of the Father is not in those who love the world;

16 for all that is in the world—the desire of the flesh, the desire of the eyes, the pride in riches—comes not from the Father but from the world.

17 And the world and its desire are passing away, but those who do the will of God live forever.

BIBLE FACT

The unbroken common thread that weaves the book of the apostle John together is "love." In the gospel of John, the word *love* appears twenty-two times; in John's epistle, it appears forty-two times. The sustainability of any community depends on love. Family as a nucleus can do nothing without love. This is the reason why Jesus emphasized the importance of love. From the book of Genesis to Revelation, the love of God has shone toward His creatures. John underscored the importance of love when he said, "He who . . . hates his brother, is in darkness until now" (1 John 2:9, NKJV).

Hidden hatred and private animosity are litmus tests for the presence of hatred. Christians should take note of their hearts. Is the love of God truly in us?

Hate is rampant in our world, and we see evidence of that daily. Is there another way to live? John reiterated Jesus' teaching about love and exhorted believers to walk in the light of love.

TOPICAL OUTLINE OF THE LESSON

I. **Introduction**
   A. The Culture of Narcissism
   B. Biblical Background

II. **Exposition and Application of the Scripture**
   A. Love and Hate Are Unequal (1 John 2:9-11)
   B. Worldly Elements (1 John 2:15-16)
   C. A Solemn Warning (1 John 2:17)

III. **Concluding Reflection**

LESSON OBJECTIVES

Upon completion of this lesson, the students will:

1. See love as a Christian way of life;
2. Have less of an appetite for worldly things;
3. Embrace love as commanded by Jesus Christ; and,
4. Focus more on eternal matters.

POINTS TO BE EMPHASIZED

ADULT/YOUTH

Adult Topic: Living in the Light of Love
Youth Topic: Love Rules!
Adult/Youth Key Verse: 1 John 2:10
Print Passage: 1 John 2:9-11, 15-17

—This passage is a reminder of the new commandment of Jesus in John 13:34.
—Obedience to the law of love is necessary to live in the light (see 1 John 2:3-6).
—"Love" in the book of John defines the nature and activity of God (see 1 John 4:8-9) and describes the way in which human beings turn to God (1 John 4:16).
—"Lives" (see 1 John 2:10) is the same word translated in John 15 as "abid[ing]" in the vine.
—When used by Jesus (see Mark 1:11), "beloved" is equivalent to "only" (see John 3:16).
—John taught us that if you love someone, you would not cause that person to stumble.
—A believer cannot practice love for another believer and love for the world at the same time.

CHILDREN

Children Topic: Love Binds Us Together
Key Verse: 1 Corinthians 13:13
Print Passage: 1 John 2:9-11, 15-17

—Our behavior marks us as Christians.
—Loving like Christ Jesus identifies us as one of His followers.
—John encouraged the people to follow Jesus' commandments.
—*Love* has a broad meaning as Jesus lived and expressed it.
—*Love* is the key to walking in the light.
—Christian love is not just a feeling but includes sacrificial actions, if one follows Jesus.

I. INTRODUCTION

A. The Culture of Narcissism

The late Professor Christopher Lasch, a prominent social critic at the time of his death, wrote a memorable book by the title of this section. In *The Culture of Narcissism,* Lasch excoriated the American media for glamorizing selfishness and hedonism. He cautioned the public about excessive selfishness and ignoring the needs of others. At the time of publication, the book was a response to glorified narcissism on many college and university campuses in which few students aspired to graduate from school or professions of service. Many wanted to pursue legal, business, and medical careers with the ambition of making lots of money and buying material things. The prevalence of this way of thinking eroded love and community service and emphasized selfishness and the unbridled appetite for worldly things.

Jesus established a new law of love which called disciples to a standard of caring for the poor and others that surpassed the letter of the law. In John 13:32-35, the Lord says that the world will know that we are His disciples by the love that we show to each other. Love for people to whom we are not related biologically is a distinction of the family of God. It does not matter what a person's legacy, pedigree, or genealogy are. We love the person because he or she is a child of God, and for no other reason. We love because the Lord first loved us. We love in gratitude for the love that we receive. We love without expecting anything in return. We love without wanting to receive recognition for our deeds, words, and sharing. We love, finally, in obedience to the command of our Lord.

Today's lesson affords us an opportunity to assess how well we are obeying the Lord's command to love. Assuredly, the Lord is not directing us to love with words only. We demonstrate our love by sharing the resources of our time, talents, tithes, and temperament. In essence, rhetoric and reality must fit like a hand in a tailored glove. Nonetheless, the question remains whether the church practically and commendably follows this command of the Lord. Does the larger society look at the church, worldwide or local, and marvel at our selfless sharing of our resources to the honor and glory of Christ? Are we the first ones to respond to natural disasters with food, clothing, shelter, and programs for long-term recovery and restoration? Do we sit idly by and wait for the governments of the world to handle the needs of God's children? As a member of your local church, do you feel the unconditional love of Christ from your fellow brothers and sisters? Can someone reliably characterize your church as a place of love for all persons who enter?

B. Biblical Background

The gospel and epistles of John emerge out of the beloved community. This gathering of disciples, as biblical tradition holds, centered on the apostle John, the youngest of the original eleven apostles and the "beloved disciple." Geographically, they were located in the region that included the city of Ephesus. However, it is not thought that they comprised the church of Ephesus to whom the apostle Paul wrote the New Testament canonical letter. A vibrant metropolitan area at the time—with major commerce, diverse people because of the trade routes, and plurality of religion, philosophy, and ideology (not to mention myriad cultural customs)—this region presented a formidable challenge to the believers there. How would they handle the inherent clashes between Christ and culture? How would they follow the dictates to love unconditionally and selflessly, given the predominant selfishness of the surrounding society?

These are not rhetorical questions. They were major challenges for members of the beloved community, some of whom struggled with fidelity to the teachings of Christ. The apostle John wrote the epistle from which today's text comes to clarify this issue for the young disciples of Christ who wanted the benefit of his direct experience with the Lord. Regrettably, he addressed the incidences of persons who left the beloved community because they did not fully subscribe wholeheartedly to Christ's commands to love. He said that they left because in their hearts they did not really belong.

Their first-century dilemma mirrors a pressing challenge for the contemporary American church: Do average disciples love Christ enough to give liberally of their resources so that the church can obey this command with integrity?

II. EXPOSITION AND APPLICATION OF THE SCRIPTURE

A. Love and Hate Are Unequal (1 John 2:9-11)

He that saith he is in the light, and hateth his brother, is in darkness even until now. He that loveth his brother abideth in the light, and there is none occasion of stumbling in him. But he that hateth his brother is in darkness, and walketh in darkness, and knoweth not whither he goeth, because that darkness hath blinded his eyes.

Throughout his writings, John maintained a duality between light and darkness, love and hate, and life and death. Often, we think we live in the first halves of these couplets if we are financially prosperous, physically well, morally correct, and ethically righteous. We reason that we live in the second halves when we experience moral lapses and the consequences of personal sins. However, the great apostle of love exhorted us to consider that we live in darkness, hatred, and death when we fail to love our brothers and sisters. Fundamentally, obedience to the law of love is a requirement to living in the light.

In this section, he began by saying, "He who says he is in the light..." (1 John 2:9, NKJV). The word *light* here refers to the one who has encountered Jesus Christ as Lord and Savior and has formed a relationship with Jesus. Such a one is already in the light. If anyone who is in the light hates another Christian, that one is a staunch liar. That one has not truly encountered the light, which is Jesus.

Darkness and light do not co-exist. And as long as darkness and light do not co-exist in the physical, it stands to reason in the spiritual that whoever has encountered Christ cannot continue to live with a hateful mind.

Who is a brother or sister here? Is he or she any human being, or is he or she a member of the Christian church? In this context of the lesson, the brother or sister is another Christian in the body of Christ. The one who hates is in the darkness. "Darkness" here means the one without Christ. Jesus Christ Himself said, "Not every one that saith unto me, Lord, Lord, shall enter into the kingdom of heaven" (see Matthew 7:21). The one who continues in a hateful mind is not a Christian; this is the reason why John used the word *darkness* to underscore the importance of being a Christian. Hating any person and walking in the light are mutually exclusive. It is those who love fellow believers who abide in the light (see verse 10). As Christians, love and hatred cannot remain active together in the same person.

In verse 11, John reminded Christians that hatred leads to darkness. The ones who remain in darkness are lost and have no clue as to their destination. In the physical experience, blindness is a challenge. In the spiritual, the spiritually blind are heading in the opposite direction, where there is no heaven.

B. Worldly Elements
(1 John 2:15-16)

Love not the world, neither the things that are in the world. If any man love the world, the love of the Father is not in him. For all that is in the world, the lust of the flesh, and the lust of the eyes, and the pride of life, is not of the Father, but is of the world.

John now turned to exhortation. There were temptations outside that appealed to Christians. He warned, "Do not love the world or the things in the world" (verse 15, NKJV).

As one who had tasted the love of God, he enumerated important pitfalls for every Christian to take note of. The word *love* here is *agapao*, and it is a verb—an action word. The word *love* as it is used here expresses "choice" and "esteem." However, the word *love* is preceded by an emphatic negative—"do not." This is a serious warning for Christians.

Another important word in this section is *world*. This does not refer to the planet earth. Rather, it refers to "that part of humanity, traditions, customs, and thoughts that belong to the darkness or philosophies that shape human thinking and alienate the creature from the Creator." In order to help his readers, John named some of the elements of the world as: (1) the lust of the flesh; (2) the lust of the eyes; and (3) the pride of life.

What is the "lust of the flesh"? The *lust of the flesh* refers to "desire for sinful sensual pleasure." It is preoccupation with gratifying physical desires. This lust has led many to untold sorrows. Some have been hooked by drugs, sexual addiction, and drunkenness. The lust of the flesh has led many to pornographic magazines and X-rated movies. Some have private television channels which they prefer to watch alone. The lust of the flesh has led to many broken homes; many of those were Christian homes. Many children are also hooked in different ways as a result of parents who are unable to control their own inordinate desires.

What is the "lust of the eyes"? This is the craving and accumulating of *things*, bowing to the gods of materialism and consumerism. We are saturated with all kinds of materials through television advertisements. New products are coming to stores in droves. Car manufacturers come out with the latest models. Cell phone manufacturers know how to package their deals in order to appeal to the eyes. New homes are given different names to appeal to our insatiable appetites. One man said that human beings, apart from being called homo sapiens, should be called "homo-junketees." We flood our homes with all kinds of things, to the point that we have to go and rent outside space in which to keep these things.

The third element here is particularly interesting. The Greek term for *pride* here is *alazoneia*. The verb form of this word means "to act the alazon: a boaster, a braggart, and an empty pretender." *Pride* here is empty talk, or words without substance. Above all, the one who is full of the pride of life trusts in his or her own resources and disdains the power of God and the rights of others.

All of this, declared John, is of the world. Whoever loves God must restrain himself or herself from these elements. To truly serve God, one must "gather up the loins of one's heart." The world system has a way of diverting our attention from the real purpose of our existence, which is living to please God.

C. A Solemn Warning
(1 John 2:17)

And the world passeth away, and the lust thereof: but he that doeth the will of God abideth for ever.

In this verse, John highlighted the brevity of life. To be consumed with earthly life is to be totally oblivious to the things of God. To be consumed with this present life is to be unprepared for the next one, which is eternity with God. It is tragic to have everything here on earth but fail to attain eternal life. When we have a strong desire to possess earthly goods at the expense of heaven, it indicates that we have

no idea of who our Savior is. Jesus said, "What shall it profit a man, if he shall gain the whole world, and lose his own soul?" (Mark 8:36). Knowing that this sinful world and our desires for its pleasures will end can give us courage to control our greedy, self-indulgent behavior and to do and continue doing God's will.

III. CONCLUDING REFLECTION

The world needs a greater supply of love than oil. Seemingly, there is so little love in the world that people should secure it wherever and however they find it. Their pursuit and obtainment of love may cross traditional boundaries and conventional relationships. Many people fight to share loving relationships with another person and other people. As a pastor, I constantly counseled people who were the victims of unrequited love, even persons in marriages. Broken relationships are a norm for many adults. However, the great apostle of love reminded us that the church, in total obedience to Christ, must be a community of love. Christ's sacrificial and supreme love is the foundation for relationships in the church. In appreciation of His perfect example, disciples emulate His love in contrast to the values of the world.

John concluded today's passage with a warning to resist the temptation to love the world and the things that it offers. The wizards of Madison Avenue, the lobbyists of K Street, the moguls of Hollywood, and the tycoons of multimedia all lure believers into the world with their colorful depictions of the things of the world. Slick and glossy advertisements tempt one to believe that happiness is found in clothing, perfume, shoes, and other material possessions. Political lobbyists in Washington,

D.C. make us think that power is the only means of security. Daily, we are bombarded with the shiny images of movie and entertainment celebrities through whom many people live vicariously. But beneath the surface of these glitzy façades is the hopelessness in which many of these people live. They may actually desire the stability of average loving and spiritually committed people. Still, countless disciples split their hearts by continuing to pursue these temporal things to the detriment of loving their brothers and sisters by sharing the Lord's blessings with them.

Forcefully, John extended his use of the duality to affirm the spiritual principle that the love of God cannot dwell simultaneously in the heart of someone who loves the world.

In addition, he submitted unequivocally that the love of the world does not come from the Father. It contradicts the love of God, which seeks healing and wholeness of each child of God. Remarkably, John considered the love of the world and its pursuit of selfish and material aims as hatred of the Creator—God. He undercut the prevailing notion that one loves everyone if one has a warm fuzzy feeling in one's heart.

PRAYER

Our loving Father and Lord, help us to better understand Your love. Imbue us with a greater appreciation for the gift of Your life on the Cross. In Jesus' name we pray. Amen.

WORD POWER

Love (Greek: *agapao* [a-ga-pa-o])—this means "to have preference for, wish well, or regard the welfare of someone." It is the love of Christians toward one another, regardless of gender, race, or color. It is the love of God which provides salvation for human beings through the death of Jesus on the cross.

HOME DAILY BIBLE READINGS
(April 5-11, 2010)

Love within the Community

MONDAY, April 5: "A New Commandment to Love" (John 13:31-35)

TUESDAY, April 6: "Your Treasure and Your Heart" (Matthew 6:19-24)

WEDNESDAY, April 7: "Love Your Neighbor" (Romans 13:8-10)

THURSDAY, April 8: "Who Is My Neighbor?" (Luke 10:29-37)

FRIDAY, April 9: "Love Your Enemies" (Luke 6:27-36)

SATURDAY, April 10: "Love and Obedience to the Commandments" (John 14:15-17)

SUNDAY, April 11: "Living in the Light of Love" (1 John 2:9-11, 15-17)

LESSON 7   April 18, 2010

CONNECTING IN COMMUNITY

DEVOTIONAL READING: Romans 5:1-11
PRINT PASSAGE: Matthew 22:34-40
KEY VERSE: Matthew 22:37

BACKGROUND SCRIPTURE: Matthew 5:17-20; 22:34-40

Matthew 22:34-40—KJV

34 But when the Pharisees had heard that he had put the Sadducees to silence, they were gathered together.

35 Then one of them, which was a lawyer, asked him a question, tempting him, and saying,

36 Master, which is the great commandment in the law?

37 Jesus said unto him, Thou shalt love the Lord thy God with all thy heart, and with all thy soul, and with all thy mind.

38 This is the first and great commandment.

39 And the second is like unto it, Thou shalt love thy neighbour as thyself.

40 On these two commandments hang all the law and the prophets.

Matthew 22:34-40—NRSV

34 When the Pharisees heard that he had silenced the Sadducees, they gathered together,

35 and one of them, a lawyer, asked him a question to test him.

36 "Teacher, which commandment in the law is the greatest?"

37 He said to him, "'You shall love the Lord your God with all your heart, and with all your soul, and with all your mind.'

38 This is the greatest and first commandment.

39 And a second is like it: 'You shall love your neighbor as yourself.'

40 On these two commandments hang all the law and the prophets."

BIBLE FACT

THE PHARISEES: The origin of the name *Pharisee* comes from Aramaic, *perashiym,* meaning "separated." Paul used the same word (perashiym) to distinguish his calling (see Romans 1:1; Galatians 1:15). In the case of the Pharisees, they were separated for their legal righteousness. The Pharisees as a religious group and political party had their roots in Hasidim. The Hasidim came into existence in the second century BC. The influence of Hellenism was bearing on Jewish religion, and in order to purify the Jewish religion, the Hasidim opted for strict observance of Jewish ritual laws. The Pharisees succeeded the Hasidim.

Jesus recognized their ardent devotion to the Law of God when He said, "unless your righteousness exceeds the righteousness of the scribes and Pharisees, you will by no means enter the kingdom of heaven" (Matthew 5:20, NKJV). We can conclude that the springing up of the Pharisees involved patriotism and fidelity to the covenant.

TOPICAL OUTLINE OF THE LESSON

I. Introduction

   A. The Bookends of the Christian Life

   B. Biblical Background

II. Exposition and Application of the Scripture

   A. A Lawyer Poses a Question (Matthew 22:34-36)

   B. The First Great Commandment (Matthew 22:37-38)

   C. The Second Great Commandment (Matthew 22:39-40)

III. Concluding Reflection

LESSON OBJECTIVES

Upon completion of this lesson, the students will know that:

1. Jesus silenced the Sadducees but the Pharisees became His archenemies;

2. The love for God should be the pursuit of every Christian;

3. The love for neighbor and for self is equally required; and,

4. We must demonstrate love for God and our neighbors.

POINTS TO BE EMPHASIZED

ADULT/YOUTH

Adult Topic: The Necessity of Love

Youth Topic: Let's Be Connected

Adult Key Verse: Matthew 22:37

Youth Key Verse: Matthew 22:39

Print Passage: Matthew 22:34-40

—Jesus denied that He had come "to abolish the law or the prophets" (Matthew 5:17, NRSV).

—Jesus expressed His commitment to fulfill the Law in the sense of "to complete" it.

—Jesus drew His answer from the Shema (see Deuteronomy 6:5), which was recited twice daily by the Jews, but He added a second companion commandment from Leviticus 19:18.

—"Enter the kingdom of heaven" (Matthew 5:20, NRSV) does not mean "go to heaven" but "become one of God's people."

—Jesus taught that the test of true greatness is in doing the will of God.

—The Pharisee asked Jesus which of all the laws in the Torah was most important.

—Jesus was teaching within the biblical tradition of care for the stranger and the neighbor.

CHILDREN

Children Topic: Love One Another!

Key Verses: Matthew 22:37, 39

Print Passage: Matthew 22:34-40

—Jesus accepted and used the Old Testament as the authority for His ministry.

—God's laws were given to help people love God and others.

—The Pharisees knew and obeyed the Ten Commandments.
—The Pharisees questioned Jesus about the greatest commandment.
—Jesus summarized the Ten Commandments in two commands.

I. INTRODUCTION

A. The Bookends of the Christian Life

"The Great Commandment" and "The Great Commission" are the bookends of the Christian life. Discipleship development, which is one's striving to make God his or her ultimate concern, is the primary purpose for which a disciple lives. As theological tradition holds, we are created to glorify God and enjoy Him forevermore. "The Great Commandment" dictates that we are to love the Lord with all of our hearts, minds, souls, and strength. Additionally, we are to love our neighbors as we love ourselves. Central to the second half of "The Great Commandment" is the fulfillment of "The Great Commission." We must prioritize sharing the love of God in Jesus Christ with all the people we encounter. Unwavering love of God and evangelism are the two major pillars of a Christian's life.

All the same, disciples do not fulfill these grand aims in isolation. There are no "Lone Ranger" Christians. All believers ought to belong to a Bible-believing church. We practice God's love in community. Anyone who has belonged to a local church for any length of time realizes the difficulty of living God's love in a communal setting. Shameless power plays undermine this spiritual objective. Large numbers of members with personal problems and character incapacities severely limit the church's abilities to live the Gospel. Then, there are those who insist upon the fulfillment of their personal preferences or they will "take their marbles and go home." Lingering low self-esteem greatly impedes progress toward missions and outreach. There are those persons who will only work if they will get credit publicly for their efforts. The sum of these unfortunate characterizations is a vivid portrayal of the extreme difficulty of living the love of God in a collective gathering of believers. Nonetheless, the Bible mandates that we strive to do so.

B. Biblical Background

In this narrative, we encounter the Sadducees and the Pharisees interacting with Jesus on the question of love. During Jesus' time on earth, He often clashed with the Pharisees and the Sadducees. These two groups pretended to be religious, but they were very unloving and unmerciful to people. The Pharisees were very proud of the fact that they were observant of the Law of Moses. Jesus compared them to "whitewashed tombs." They appeared to be holy from the outside, but in reality they were like graves full of dead people's bones. The Sadducees were another sect of religious leaders. They came from wealthy backgrounds. They did not believe in an afterlife, because they did not see it mentioned in the Law of Moses. These two groups were religiously incongruent.

The new law of love interestingly places a greater burden on believers than the letter of the Law. Love requires us to go to any length to demonstrate God's will. Giving exceeds the ten percent of the tithe. Elsewhere, we are told to give generously, not out of necessity and duty. Forgiveness demands that we extend mercy and grace as many times as necessary to yield resolution and reconciliation. This absolves those who do bad things of our demands for restitution, although they may adhere to the urging of the Holy Spirit to restore. The law of love definitely removes any claims that we may have for punishment of perpetrators who do wrong. Leadership in the church emerges from faithful service to Christ. The assurance of salvation is given to those persons who persevere until the end. Suffice it to conclude that Christ's standard for love surpasses the legalisms of the Old Testament and its rituals.

Instead, Christ calls us into a vibrant relationship that demands that we share His love with everyone. Cultivating the spiritual discipline of self-denial is the first step toward loving God wholeheartedly and one's neighbor selflessly. Christ teaches us that love is not a feeling, but a lifestyle of commitment and action. As the model of love, Jesus shows us how to love others as we love ourselves. The new law of selfless and sacrificial love fulfills the thousands of variables of the Old Testament Law. Again, disciples obey this mandate in the context of community rather than in isolation.

II. EXPOSITION AND APPLICATION OF THE SCRIPTURE

A. A Lawyer Poses a Question
(Matthew 22:34-36)

But when the Pharisees had heard that he had put the Sadducees to silence, they were gathered together. Then one of them, which was a lawyer, asked him a question, tempting him, and saying, Master, which is the great commandment in the law?

As a precursor to this section, the text is a record of the Lord's denial that He came "to abolish the Law or the Prophets" (Matthew 5:17, NIV). Our heavenly Father is a loving and most merciful God, but He is also a holy God whose perfect character cannot be tempted by evil. The Law was given to help us relate to His holiness. The prophets were sent to preach about God's desire that we live as just, righteous, and merciful people. Jesus came to show us how to do so. He is the human fulfillment of the Law and the prophets, living a perfect, sinless, and righteous life. To solidify His point, the Lord says that not even a comma will fall from the Law before it is fulfilled (see verse 18). In fact, He predicts that heaven and earth would cease before the Law would. In Matthew 5:17, Jesus expressed His commitment "to complete" the Law and the prophets by establishing the new covenant of love through the gift of His shed blood and broken body.

The Pharisees took the occasion of the silence of the Sadducees to confront Jesus about the issue of the Law of Moses. The Sadducees were silenced because they could not stand the knowledge of Jesus Christ; it was too advanced and divine in origin. The Pharisees were more concerned about the rigidity of the Law, and they were not satisfied until they laid heavy burdens on the community. They opposed Jesus because of the way He interpreted the Law. This time around in our text, the intent of the Pharisees was not pure; rather, they were looking for an occasion to trap Jesus (see Matthew 22:15). In the second portion, an expert in the Law—the Jewish Torah (the first five books of the canonical Old Testament)—tested Jesus by asking Him to state the greatest commandment of God.

One of the Pharisees put a question to Jesus to tempt Him. The word *tempt* is interesting. It carries the idea "to attempt to test one maliciously or craftily in order to prove one's feeling or judgment." The Pharisees were as crafty as the devil. When Jesus completed His forty days of fasting, Satan came to tempt Him. The same word used by the Pharisees on this occasion was used in reference to Satan. But Jesus said, "Thou shalt not tempt" (Matthew 4:7). When the Pharisees asked about which commandment is the greatest they intended to trap Jesus, but Jesus put an end to their foolishness.

The Pharisees, in their attempt to keep the laws of God, came up with six hundred laws a person must keep in order to be a faithful follower of God. If we go by simple arithmetic, in order to keep one law, one had to pay close attention to sixty. This is why one of them came to Jesus to tempt Him. However, the Pharisees met more than their match in the person of Jesus Christ. Today, there are so-called scholars who find fault with the Bible, but as Jesus and His ministry outlived the Pharisees, in the same manner the truth of the Word continues to outlive its detractors. Many of them are in the grave, but the Word of God continues to spread like wildfire.

B. The First Great Commandment (Matthew 22:37-38)

Jesus said unto him, Thou shalt love the Lord thy God with all thy heart, and with all thy soul, and with all thy mind. This is the first and great commandment.

Jesus replied by first citing the Shema (see Deuteronomy 6:5), which the Jews said aloud twice daily. The Shema was the Jewish confession of faith. The confession was called "Shema" because it began with the Hebrew word *shema,* meaning, "Hear, O Israel: The Lord our God, the Lord is one. Love the Lord your God with all your heart and with all your soul and with all your strength" (Deuteronomy 6:4-5, NIV). Matthew's gospel adds the dimension of *mind.* Thereby, he includes the major components of human existence.

The phrase "Love the Lord your God" is an important phrase. The first and foremost law is to love God. The Greek word used is *agapao,* meaning "to have total affection for an object." This love is an undiluted type of love. This love did not begin with the Pharisees, and that is why Jesus predicated the word *love* with "shalt" in the *King James Version.* The love which the Pharisees claimed to have was a shallow love. It was rooted and loaded with penal codes; such love would be a forced love at best and hypocritical at worst. Matthew Henry said, "Love is the leading affection. God created us in love and He expects us to love Him in return."

The first commandment reads, "Thou shalt have no other gods before me" (Exodus 20:3). In other words, God expects us to genuinely love Him. The love we have for God should have no rival, no competing love. It must be a wholehearted love, which leaves no room for lesser things. *Love* is the first and the greatest thing that God requires from us, and it is the first order of our response to Him. God showed His love by putting other creatures under us; therefore, those things should not take the place of God in our hearts.

C. The Second Great Commandment
(Matthew 22:39-40)

And the second is like unto it, Thou shalt love thy neighbour as thyself. On these two commandments hang all the law and the prophets.

Furthermore, Jesus added as a companion commandment the one found in Leviticus 19:18 (NKJV), which reads, "You shall not take vengeance, nor bear any grudge…but you shall love your neighbor as yourself." The commandment stated here is not an imperative; rather, it is cast in the imperfect tense, which by interpretation means "to do things in a continuous manner." The love of neighbor must not stop; it must continue. This Old Testament law is advice against revenge or bearing grudges. Instead, it is a command to us to love our neighbors as ourselves. If we were to follow this command, we would relinquish immediately our thirst for retaliation, because we would not want to punish someone we love. Together, these companion commandments contain the essence of the thousands of principles and corollaries of the Old Testament law.

Put forth by an expert in the Law, the question about the greatest commandment arose because Jesus had silenced the Sadducees. In response, the Pharisees, who believed in the Resurrection and represented the other half of the ruling religious council, the Sanhedrin, sought to demonstrate that this carpenter, the Son, could not best their years of training in the Law. With this test, they resorted to religious tradition and conventional wisdom. They relied upon rituals, religiosity, and righteousness as found in the study of the black letter of the Law. In contrast, Jesus emphasized the importance of relationship with God and people. As one strives to live in love and with integrity with almighty God and one's neighbor, one inevitably fulfills the Law.

The essence of what Jesus was saying is that if we truly love God and our neighbors, we will naturally keep the commandments. This is looking at God's law positively. In order to satisfy the demands of the Law, we should focus on Jesus and His teachings. Even though the Pharisees were His staunch enemies, yet He took the time to listen and to teach them. So instead of worrying about all we should not do, we should do all we can do to show our love for God and others.

III. CONCLUDING REFLECTION

Laws are necessary for the preservation of justice, order, and quality of life in any society. Indifference toward the laws results in chaos and lawlessness. Accordingly, the loss of freedom and the payment of fines are possible consequences of violating the laws. The absence of law enforcement allows the commission of countless crimes of monumental proportions. In New Orleans following Hurricane Katrina and in Bosnia and Yugoslavia following the dismantling of the former Communist regimes, unprecedented lawlessness occurred. Women, children, and many other undeserving adults were the victims of unspeakable crimes. Regrettably, the presence of armed peace officers and criminal courts are necessary to coerce people to treat their fellow citizens with dignity and respect.

God in Christ established a new law of love. If every person followed the companion laws of loving God with all of our being and loving our neighbors as we love ourselves, then we would need less law enforcement. Crimes would decrease. We would be able to use society's resources and tax dollars for other social challenges. We could concentrate upon curing longstanding diseases and providing quality and equal education to all of our children. Essentially, practicing love towards everyone would result in a more just and equitable society. Achieving that grand aim most definitely accomplishes the message of the Law and prophets.

Unbelievably, many Christians do not read the Old Testament seriously. They do not, in their opinion, serve the vengeful, bloodthirsty "God of the Old Testament" who dealt harshly with Israel. Other believers ascribe to the notion that modern disciples are no longer bound to the requirements of the old covenant. Christ issued a new covenant which releases disciples from the burdens of the letter of the Law. "The letter kills but the Spirit gives life." In challenge to this prominent yet fallacious idea, Matthew's gospel contains "The Sermon on the Mount" in which the Lord established a new law of love. In this sermon, Jesus plainly says that He did not come to abolish the Law and the prophets. Rather, He came to fulfill them.

PRAYER

O God of love who freely and generously loves us with the gift of Your one and only begotten Son, teach us to love as You do. Make us ever mindful that You are love. In Jesus' name we pray. Amen.

WORD POWER

Love (Greek: *agapao* [a-ga-pa-o])—means "to be full of goodwill and exhibit the same, and to have a preference for something." The word *love* is cast in the future tense, which means an action which has not yet occurred, and must start and be kept going. Love is a Christian trait which must not diminish.

HOME DAILY BIBLE READINGS
(April 12-18, 2010)

Connecting in Community

MONDAY, April 12: "Reconciled with God" (Romans 5:1-11)

TUESDAY, April 13: "Refusing Christ" (John 5:39-47)

WEDNESDAY, April 14: "Fulfilling the Law" (Matthew 5:17-20)

THURSDAY, April 15: "Neglecting the Love of God" (Luke 11:42-44)

FRIDAY, April 16: "Hearing and Accepting the Word" (John 8:39-47)

SATURDAY, April 17: "Rooted and Grounded in Love" (Ephesians 3:14-19)

SUNDAY, April 18: "The Great Commandment" (Matthew 22:34-40)

LESSON 8   April 25, 2010

INCLUSION IN COMMUNITY

DEVOTIONAL READING: Psalm 65:1-8
PRINT PASSAGE: Luke 14:15-24

BACKGROUND SCRIPTURE: Luke 14:7-24
KEY VERSE: Luke 14:21

Luke 14:15-24—KJV

15 And when one of them that sat at meat with him heard these things, he said unto him, Blessed is he that shall eat bread in the kingdom of God.

16 Then said he unto him, A certain man made a great supper, and bade many:

17 And sent his servant at supper time to say to them that were bidden, Come; for all things are now ready.

18 And they all with one consent began to make excuse. The first said unto him, I have bought a piece of ground, and I must needs go and see it: I pray thee have me excused.

19 And another said, I have bought five yoke of oxen, and I go to prove them: I pray thee have me excused.

20 And another said, I have married a wife, and therefore I cannot come.

21 So that servant came, and shewed his lord these things. Then the master of the house being angry said to his servant, Go out quickly into the streets and lanes of the city, and bring in hither the poor, and the maimed, and the halt, and the blind.

22 And the servant said, Lord, it is done as thou hast commanded, and yet there is room.

23 And the lord said unto the servant, Go out into the highways and hedges, and compel them to come in, that my house may be filled.

24 For I say unto you, That none of those men which were bidden shall taste of my supper.

Luke 14:15-24—NRSV

15 One of the dinner guests, on hearing this, said to him, "Blessed is anyone who will eat bread in the kingdom of God!"

16 Then Jesus said to him, "Someone gave a great dinner and invited many.

17 At the time for the dinner he sent his slave to say to those who had been invited, 'Come; for everything is ready now.'

18 But they all alike began to make excuses. The first said to him, 'I have bought a piece of land, and I must go out and see it; please accept my regrets.'

19 Another said, 'I have bought five yoke of oxen, and I am going to try them out; please accept my regrets.'

20 Another said, 'I have just been married, and therefore I cannot come.'

21 So the slave returned and reported this to his master. Then the owner of the house became angry and said to his slave, 'Go out at once into the streets and lanes of the town and bring in the poor, the crippled, the blind, and the lame.'

22 And the slave said, 'Sir, what you ordered has been done, and there is still room.'

23 Then the master said to the slave, 'Go out into the roads and lanes, and compel people to come in, so that my house may be filled.

24 For I tell you, none of those who were invited will taste my dinner.'"

BIBLE FACT

The condition for participating in Jesus' Supper: the parable in this lesson is a lucid description of the people who will not participate in the supper. The supper was ready and people were invited, but they were full of flimsy excuses. What excuses are you making when you are called to do something for God? Little excuses are an indication of a lack of familiarity with the risen Savior.

TOPICAL OUTLINE OF THE LESSON

I. Introduction
A. An Ideal Dinner Party
B. Biblical Background

II. Exposition and Application of the Scripture
A. Invitation to the Supper (Luke 14:15-17)
B. Excuses! Excuses!! Excuses!!! (Luke 14:18-20)
C. Invitation Extended to the Invalids (Luke 14:21-23)
D. Original Invitees Excluded (Luke 14:24)

III. Concluding Reflection

LESSON OBJECTIVES

Upon completion of this lesson, the students will know:

1. How to live in humility;
2. The consequences of disobeying God's invitation;
3. That the Gospel is a universal invitation to an eternal banquet; and,
4. How to invite others from all walks of life to God's banquet.

POINTS TO BE EMPHASIZED

ADULT/YOUTH

Adult Topic: All Are Invited
Youth Topic: A Beggar's Banquet
Adult Key Verse: Luke 14:21
Youth Key Verse: Luke 14:21b
Print Passage: Luke 14:15-24

—Luke 14:1-6 is the last of four Sabbath controversies in the gospel of Luke (see 6:1-11; 13:10-17).
—In Luke 14:12-14 is provided very similar counsel to Jesus' words in Matthew 6:1-6, 16-18.
—The "crippled, blind, and lame" were traditionally rejected as impure outsiders (see Leviticus 21:17-23).
—Jesus told the guests not to seek places of honor, but to be humble when they were invited to a feast or banquet.
—Luke placed this reading in the context of the kingdom of God.
—Jesus taught about the connection between humility and hospitality.
—Jesus was at a banquet thrown by an important Pharisee when He told this parable of the great banquet.
—The parable was certainly aimed at the Pharisees and others who took and take their salvation for granted.

CHILDREN

Children Topic: Everyone Is Included
Key Verses: Luke 14:11, 14a
Print Passage: Luke 14:7-14

—Jesus advised people not to rush for the best seats at a feast.
—Jesus taught that service is more important than status.
—Jesus taught that invitations to a feast should not be exclusive.
—Jesus taught that the kingdom is for everyone, especially for those who cannot repay the invitation.

I. INTRODUCTION

A. An Ideal Dinner Party

If you were to host the ideal dinner party, whom would you invite? Chances are the average person would invite his or her favorites from the worlds of entertainment and athletics. With regard to your profession, would you invite the most significant people in your field? Assuredly, you would invite your boss to impress him or her. Would you include any political, business, or educational leaders? How many and what type of people would you include in your dinner party community?

Would your guest list include any marginalized people? What about recovering alcoholics and drug addicts who live in halfway houses? Chances are that these people may not have had a formal meal in a long time, if ever. What about illegal immigrants, who fear for their physical safety and the stability of their families? There are many poor senior citizens who daily choose between medications, food, and gasoline. Would any of them make your list? Last, what about the tens of thousands of children in foster care who have never known what it means to have their own bedrooms? Would you give them an opportunity to experience a formal meal setting?

B. Biblical Background

Luke, a Gentile, wrote his gospel with the purpose of reassuring his readers that the kingdom of God as revealed in our Lord Jesus Christ was unconditionally available to Gentile communities worldwide. He included the parable told by Jesus in today's passage to support this position. Persons on the original invitation list found flimsy excuses to deny God's appeal through the covenant, Law, and prophets. In Christ, the Father implemented a new covenant which extends to everyone who believes, regardless of his or her background, culture, nation, or previous creed. In so doing, God opens the doors of the spiritual banquet hall and lets anyone in who wants to attend the feast.

A major theme of Luke's gospel is God's love toward the poor, crippled, lame, and blind. The Lord, in bringing them to the banquet and issuing an invitation to those on the highways, exercised a preferential option toward these marginalized and disenfranchised persons. Mostly, these people responded favorably to the Lord's love, because they were happy to be noticed at all. In comparison, the evangelist warned against people who practiced self-importance and self-promotion because they were busy with business, property, and marital affairs. In opposition to this worldly concept, God makes room for everyone and provides a seat at the banquet table for anyone who comes. He does so out of the limitless love that fills His infinite heart.

II. EXPOSITION AND APPLICATION OF THE SCRIPTURE

A. Invitation to the Supper
(Luke 14:15-17)

And when one of them that sat at meat with him heard these things, he said unto him, Blessed is he that shall eat bread in the kingdom of God. Then said he unto him, A certain man made a great supper, and bade many: And sent his servant at supper time to say to them that were bidden, Come; for all things are now ready.

Prior to this event, Jesus discussed the importance of not seeking a higher position when attending a banquet. He gave His listeners a lesson by advising that they should always look for a lowly place, and an unrecognized position (see Luke 14:7-11). Jesus gave advice to those to be invited to a dinner or supper. Upon hearing this sobering teaching, one of the men sitting across the table from Jesus was touched. Then Jesus said, "Blessed is he that shall eat bread in the kingdom of God" (Luke 14:15). The *kingdom of God* here refers to the coming kingdom of God. In some contexts, the kingdom of God is the rule of Christ through the Holy Spirit in the hearts of people.

We do not have the record of the exchange that went on between Jesus and this man, except for the above-mentioned statement. The verse was pointing to the coming feast which all believers will partake of at the coming of Jesus. The man was astounded at the glory of the kingdom's feast, but he was not among the partakers. We are not sure whether this man at this point accepted Christ into his life.

In order to enlighten this man's understanding and that of those who were with Him, Jesus presented another parable. A *parable* is an imaginary story to illustrate an important concept. In the classic way, a parable is comparing earthly truths with heavenly truths in order to give clearer and more effective understanding. In this text, Jesus gave a parable about a certain man who planned a great supper and invited many people. In the ancient world, invitations to a feast were sent out well in advance of the meal. Then on the day of the feast, servants or town criers would announce the start of the meal. The message was simple: "Come, for all things are now ready" (verse 17).

The parable at this point is an illustration of the generosity of the man who invited friends to come and dine with him; he did not solicit for their food. It was not a potluck, where they were supposed to bring their own food. It was free, and all they needed to bring were their empty stomachs.

B. Excuses! Excuses!! Excuses!!!
(Luke 14:18-20)

And they all with one consent began to make excuse. The first said unto him, I have bought a piece of ground, and I must needs go and see it: I pray thee have me excused. And another said, I have bought five yoke of oxen, and I go to prove them: I pray thee have me excused. And another said, I have married a wife, and therefore I cannot come.

It was as if the invitees conspired to reject the invitation. The text reads, "But they all with one accord" (verse 18, NKJV). The phrase *one accord* suggests prior agreement between people. The first responder said, "I have bought a piece of ground" (verse 18, NKJV); another said, "I have bought five yoke of oxen" (verse 19). A closer look at these two excuses shows that these men were bogged down with material things. The man had bought the land; it was his, and there was no reason for him to refuse to go to the party. His excuses were lame. What kind of man buys a piece of land and goes to check it? If you have already bought ten oxen, what is the need of testing them after you have already purchased them? This man's excuses were also flimsy. But before we judge this man for the excuse he gave, we need to critically examine our society in the twenty-first century. We are consumed with so many modern things ranging from the cars we drive to the houses we live in, the type of dishwasher in our kitchens, the brand-name clothes we wear, tennis shoes, and so forth. When we buy new things we are preoccupied with them. We become like little children when idolizing our new "stuff." Many people in our day prefer detailing cars instead of washing them. Some even take the time allotted for fellowshipping on Sunday to do menial things at home.

As individuals, the question is: what excuse do you give when you are invited to any occasion? What excuse do you give on Sundays and about other church activities? What excuse do you give for not following Jesus? Another invitee said, "I have married a wife" (verse 20). This man could have asked his wife to accompany him to the dinner. While the Old Testament exempted a man from military duty (see Deuteronomy 20:7), marriage was not an excuse for avoiding social duties. The crux of the matter was that the man regarded his own affairs as more important than the feast to which he was invited. This excuse was about a man who put his family before the Lord.

These excuse makers condemned themselves; their excuses revealed their inner lives. In this parable, the guests insulted the host by making excuses which had no foundation. God's first invitation came through Moses and the prophets; the second came from His Son, Jesus Christ. Even in the present, the Holy Spirit is still knocking on people's hearts, urging them to come to God's banquet. We must bear in mind that God never asks us to give up something good unless He plans to replace it with something far better. Jesus is not calling us to become ambassadors for nothing. This parable serves to illuminate our minds and get us prepared for the wedding supper of the Lamb (see Revelation 19:6-9).

C. Invitation Extended to the Invalids (Luke 14:21-23)

So that servant came, and shewed his lord these things. Then the master of the house being angry said to his servant, Go out quickly into the streets and lanes of the city, and bring in hither the poor, and the maimed, and the halt, and the blind. And the servant said, Lord, it is done as thou hast commanded, and yet there is room. And the lord said unto the servant, Go out into the highways and hedges, and compel them to come in, that my house may be filled.

The fourteenth chapter of the book of Luke opens with the last of four Sabbath controversies. In these dilemmas, Jesus redefined the purpose of the Sabbath and obeying it to the detriment of leaving a broken person in the same predicament because it was the day of worship. These disputes afforded the Lord the setting and occasion to share wisdom about worthwhile honor in the sight of God and people. Then, He finished this teaching by encouraging His listeners to consider the poor, crippled, lame, and blind in their lives. The poor, the maimed, the lame, and the blind match the list in verse 13. The word *compel* means "to prevail on someone by the most earnest entreaties." The servant had to use wisdom and persuasive words to bring people in. Jesus used this word in Matthew 14:22 and in Mark 6:45. In those two places, Jesus constrained His disciples to get into the vessel. Traditionally, such persons were shunned as impure because of the prevalent belief that their infirmities manifested sin.

The fact that the master asked his servants to go out into the highways and hedges signified that there was still room in the house. The master said, "Go out quickly" (verse 21). This invitation was urgent—because the banquet was ready. Similarly, the Gospel is ready and there is little time to waste. The master of the ceremony's second invitation extended the scope of the offer to those who were considered to be socially unfit. Jesus concluded this ongoing religious argument by stating that almighty God favors people over religious regulations.

D. Original Invitees Excluded
(Luke 14:24)

For I say unto you, That none of those men which were bidden shall taste of my supper.

In the concluding verses of this parable, the master instructed His servants to "compel them to come in" (verse 23) to the banquet. This was not a violent or otherwise coercive act. Rather, it referred to the power of love. Christ's love compels us to reply affirmatively to God's appeal. When we realistically understand the indescribable gift of Christ's sacrifice, we yield to God's appeal with humble submission. Jesus at this point revealed what mattered most. Jesus unveiled His mind in this parable. In His supper, which is to come, all those who refuse His invitation will one day blame themselves. There will be no opportunity for a second chance.

The preachers and teachers of the Word are encouraged to make the invitation to the Lord's final supper with urgency and love.

"Go out into the highways and hedges" (verse 23) reveals that preachers and teachers of the world must apply seriousness in appealing to all to come in. There should be no discrimination in the appeal to come to the Gospel. The final supper is the Lord's Supper; we are the servants who must compel people to come in as they are. We cannot determine who is fit for the Master's feast.

Punishment is also attached to this invitation: those who are prideful and reject the invitation of God will forever be lost. None who were originally invited would be there (see verse 24). The use of the word *none* in this verse informs us that the final Supper will be strictly for those who have prepared their hearts and accepted the offer of salvation. Those Christians also who are now in the fold must live in obedience. They too must invite others to the feast. It is not just for the preachers and teachers of the world to invite and compel people. In our day, we can use movies and special programs to bring outsiders to the saving knowledge of the Lord.

As Christians, we too can resist or delay responding to God's invitation, and our excuses may sound reasonable—work duties, family responsibilities, or whatever they may be. Nevertheless, God's invitation is the most important event in our lives. Our earthly and eternal peace depends on our response.

III. CONCLUDING REFLECTION

In creating a community, whether it comprises a dinner party, civic organization, or church, it is important to consider who is missing as well as who is present. Today's lesson is a challenge to us to examine our tendencies toward self-promotion. Few people associate with people who offer nothing in return. If you ever eavesdrop upon lunchtime restaurant conversations, you overhear invitations to play golf, socialize, and otherwise collaborate because in the end all parties involved can benefit materially and financially. Many annual awards ceremonies center upon likable people who cycle recognition among themselves and their acquaintances. Again, the question arises about who is left out.

Is there a community where everyone belongs? Is there a place where anyone will be included regardless of who that one is and what he or she has or has not done? Is there a community with an open admission policy? The church is that community! Everyone should be included in the church. Yet, local churches often struggle with their practice of this Christ-like principle of including everyone.

In Christ's stead, believers have the responsibility of inviting unbelievers to become part of the kingdom of God. We are the ones who are to travel near and far and proclaim to everyone that a community exists in which everyone is welcomed without any preconditions. The church is a community that includes everybody. This invitation will be a life-changing event, as the respondents will find food for their souls. Moreover, they will receive the greater blessing of learning about the majesty of God as they learn from the different types of people who belong to the kingdom of God.

As an individual, are you making excuses to avoid responding to God's call? Jesus reminds us in this parable that the time will come when God will pull His invitation and offer it to others; then it will be too late to get into His eternal banquet. There is no room for excuses. We must make up our minds whether to obey Him or disobey Him.

PRAYER

Our gracious, loving, and merciful Father, thank You for loving us unconditionally. We appreciate Your incredible gift. Move our hearts and minds to action as we share Your unfailing love with all of Your children. In Jesus' name we pray. Amen.

WORD POWER

Compel (Greek: *anagkazo* [a-nag-ka-zo])—this means that the word comes from *anank*—necessity; it is "to constrain, whether by threat or persuasion," or to "entreat with the sense of urgency." The servant in this lesson was asked to persuade others to come.

HOME DAILY BIBLE READINGS
(April 19-25, 2010)

Inclusion in Community

MONDAY, April 19: "God Is the Hope for All" (Psalm 65:1-8)
TUESDAY, April 20: "All Nations Shall Come" (Psalm 86:8-13)
WEDNESDAY, April 21: "Come and Learn God's Ways" (Isaiah 2:1-4)
THURSDAY, April 22: "King of the Nations" (Revelation 15:3-4)
FRIDAY, April 23: "Ministry to All" (Matthew 25:31-40)
SATURDAY, April 24: "Humility and Hospitality" (Luke 14:7-14)
SUNDAY, April 25: "Invite All to Come" (Luke 14:15-24)

A FAITHFUL COMMUNITY

DEVOTIONAL READING: **Jeremiah 29:10-14**
PRINT PASSAGE: **Colossians 1:1-14**

BACKGROUND SCRIPTURE: **Colossians 1**
KEY VERSE: **Colossians 1:9**

Colossians 1:1-14—KJV

PAUL, AN apostle of Jesus Christ by the will of God, and Timotheus our brother,

2 To the saints and faithful brethren in Christ which are at Colosse: Grace be unto you, and peace, from God our Father and the Lord Jesus Christ.

3 We give thanks to God and the Father of our Lord Jesus Christ, praying always for you,

4 Since we heard of your faith in Christ Jesus, and of the love which ye have to all the saints,

5 For the hope which is laid up for you in heaven, whereof ye heard before in the word of the truth of the gospel;

6 Which is come unto you, as it is in all the world; and bringeth forth fruit, as it doth also in you, since the day ye heard of it, and knew the grace of God in truth:

7 As ye also learned of Epaphras our dear fellowservant, who is for you a faithful minister of Christ;

8 Who also declared unto us your love in the Spirit.

9 For this cause we also, since the day we heard it, do not cease to pray for you, and to desire that ye might be filled with the knowledge of his will in all wisdom and spiritual understanding;

10 That ye might walk worthy of the Lord unto all pleasing, being fruitful in every good work, and increasing in the knowledge of God;

11 Strengthened with all might, according to his glorious power, unto all patience and longsuffering with joyfulness;

12 Giving thanks unto the Father, which hath made us meet to be partakers of the inheritance of the saints in light:

13 Who hath delivered us from the power of darkness, and hath translated us into the kingdom of his dear Son:

Colossians 1:1-14—NRSV

PAUL, AN apostle of Christ Jesus by the will of God, and Timothy our brother,

2 To the saints and faithful brothers and sisters in Christ in Colossae: Grace to you and peace from God our Father.

3 In our prayers for you we always thank God, the Father of our Lord Jesus Christ,

4 for we have heard of your faith in Christ Jesus and of the love that you have for all the saints,

5 because of the hope laid up for you in heaven. You have heard of this hope before in the word of the truth, the gospel

6 that has come to you. Just as it is bearing fruit and growing in the whole world, so it has been bearing fruit among yourselves from the day you heard it and truly comprehended the grace of God.

7 This you learned from Epaphras, our beloved fellow servant. He is a faithful minister of Christ on your behalf,

8 and he has made known to us your love in the Spirit.

9 For this reason, since the day we heard it, we have not ceased praying for you and asking that you may be filled with the knowledge of God's will in all spiritual wisdom and understanding,

10 so that you may lead lives worthy of the Lord, fully pleasing to him, as you bear fruit in every good work and as you grow in the knowledge of God.

11 May you be made strong with all the strength that comes from his glorious power, and may you be prepared to endure everything with patience, while joyfully

12 giving thanks to the Father, who has enabled you to share in the inheritance of the saints in the light.

13 He has rescued us from the power of darkness and transferred us into the kingdom of his beloved Son,

There are people in communities of faith who lack the power to lead worthy lives. Where and how can we connect with God's strength and glorious power? Paul told the Colossians that their power as a congregation of hope and faith had come to them by their acceptance of the Word of Truth, the Gospel.

14 In whom we have redemption through his blood, even the forgiveness of sins.

14 in whom we have redemption, the forgiveness of sins.

TOPICAL OUTLINE OF THE LESSON

I. **Introduction**
   A. Faithfulness
   B. Biblical Background

II. **Exposition and Application of the Scripture**
   A. Paul: Apostle by God's Will (Colossians 1:1-2)
   B. Reasons for Thanksgiving and Prayer (Colossians 1:3-8)
   C. Paul's Intercessory Prayer (Colossians 1:9-14)

III. **Concluding Reflection**

LESSON OBJECTIVES

Upon completion of this lesson, the students will:
1. Discover the incredible power of intercessory prayer in the lives of believers;
2. Glean petitions from Paul's prayer to use in praying for others; and,
3. Be able to employ the rules for Christian living.

POINTS TO BE EMPHASIZED

ADULT/YOUTH

Adult Topic: **Understanding and Living Truth**
Youth Topic: **Living Faithfully—Together**
Adult Key Verse: **Colossians 1:9**
Youth Key Verses: **Colossians 1:3-4**
Print Passage: **Colossians 1:1-14**

—Paul opened this letter with a prayer of thanksgiving and intercession for the Colossians.
—The prominent theme of hope in Paul's prayer was meant to assure the Colossians of the salvation promised to them in Christ.
—These verses model intercessory prayer that goes beyond petitions for physical healing and they encourage prayer that includes petitions for spiritual growth and well-being.
—Paul used a common literary contrast of the day, conveying the idea of darkness as having negative qualities and light as having positive qualities.
—Paul prayed that the Colossians be made strong in the strength of Christ, and he reminded them that God the Father had transferred them into the kingdom of Jesus and they had received forgiveness for their sins.
—God reconciled us to Himself through the death of Jesus, who is the central and ultimate "Empowerer" of the Christian life and community.

CHILDREN

Children Topic: **Learn Together**
Key Verse: **Colossians 1:4**
Print Passage: **Colossians 1:1-14**

—Paul wrote letters of encouragement and instruction to the new churches.

—Paul probably did not establish the church himself, but sent his colleague Epaphras to preach and serve there.

—Paul prayed and gave thanks for the church at Colossae and for other churches as well.

—Paul acknowledged that the community of believers in Colossae had grown because of their acceptance of the Gospel.

I. INTRODUCTION

A. Faithfulness

Faithfulness to Christ is a challenge that Christians have faced since the beginning of the church. The teachings of Christ inherently clash with the secular, humanistic, and dominant cultures in which believers live. How can disciples balance the tension between faith and citizenship? When forced to choose, will our allegiance go to Christ or to the state? "Let the average man be put to the proof on the question of who is above...Let him be forced into making a choice between God and money, between God and personal ambition...and God will take second place every time" (A. Tozer). Are we Americans who happen to be Christians or Christians who happen to be Americans? The choices we make reveal the God we claim to know.

In many instances, people in the church lack the character and will to lead lives of Christian integrity. Spiritual immaturity, insincerity, divided loyalties, and incomplete faith suffice to explain this regrettable occurrence in many disciples' lives. Still, the question remains, "How does a genuine believer practice the Christian life on a daily basis?" More practically, how do we obtain the spiritual power and mental will to align our professions of faith with daily behavior?

B. Biblical Background

The epistle of Paul to the church of Colossae was written for two main reasons: (1) to combat two doctrinal errors that were threatening to destroy the church (see Colossians 2:14-17); and (2) there was a type of mysticism (see Colossians 2:18-23). From Paul's letter to the Colossians we learn about the rules for Christian living. He informed them that the power they sought emerged from their unqualified acceptance of the Gospel and teachings of Christ. Their town was populated with diverse people who adhered to many different religious and ideological beliefs. Understandably, some new and young believers would fall prey to the temptation to blend Christianity with their former patterns of thinking. This type of syncretism inevitably led to moral compromise. Paul wrote to instruct them that they could no longer recklessly indulge their physical instincts to the detriment of their Christian witness. Instead, they must make an irreversible commitment to Christ and live in accordance with His teachings. When they did this, they would discover pleasantly the power of the Holy Spirit, who would equip them with integrity.

II. EXPOSITION AND APPLICATION OF THE SCRIPTURE

A. Paul: Apostle by God's Will
(Colossians 1:1-2)

PAUL, AN apostle of Jesus Christ by the will of God, and Timotheus our brother, To the saints and faithful brethren in Christ which are at Colosse: Grace be unto you, and peace, from God our Father and the Lord Jesus Christ.

Paul called himself an apostle of Jesus Christ. The word *apostle* in the original language means "envoy" or "messenger." It also denotes an approved spokesperson, one who is sent as a personal representative. Paul's apostleship was not based on personal choice. He was chosen by the will of God. The phrase "By the will of God" means that he was appointed; this was not just a matter of his having achieved personal goals. Paul made his credentials known in order for the recipients of his epistle to gain approval. Paul was conscious that he was not among the original twelve, but nonetheless he too was an apostle of great repute. It must be emphasized that all Christians are called to be God's spokespersons. We may not go beyond our cities and towns, but we must consciously remind ourselves of our identity in Christ. This epistle, along with the books of Philippians and Philemon, are known as his prison epistles.

Paul, in this epistle, mentioned Timothy as his brother in Christ. In some of his other epistles, he referred to him as "son in the Lord." We also note the word *saint* in his opening greetings. The word *saint* means "holy people." It means "one who is set apart to do God's will." It was a common word for the apostle and he used it at least eighty times in his epistles. Roman Catholics still believe that only the dead among them can be called saints. But as Baptists, we believe that we are saints the moment we place our trust in Jesus Christ as our Savior and Lord. We may not call ourselves saints, but in essence we are saints by the will of God.

The city of Colossae was a hundred miles east of Ephesus on the Lycus River. Colossae was not as influential as the city of Laodicea; however, it was a crossroads for ideas and religions. There was a large concentration of Jews who fled there during the reigns of Antiochus III and IV, almost four hundred years before Christ. The founder of the church was Ephapras (see Colossians 1:7).

B. Reasons for Thanksgiving and Prayer
(Colossians 1:3-8)

We give thanks to God and the Father of our Lord Jesus Christ, praying always for you, Since we heard of your faith in Christ Jesus, and of the love which ye have to all the saints, For the hope which is laid up for you in heaven, whereof ye heard before in the word of the truth of the gospel; Which is come unto you, as it is in all the world; and bringeth forth fruit, as it doth also in you, since the day ye heard of it, and knew the grace of God in truth: As ye also learned of Epaphras our dear fellowservant, who is for you a faithful minister of Christ; Who also declared unto us your love in the Spirit.

The apostle Paul showed his tender concern that he had for the church in Colossae. Paul was praying for them always because he was impressed with their faith in Christ. The duty of called people of God is to pray ceaselessly for the ones God has put under their spiritual care. Verse 4 reads: "Since we heard of your faith in Christ Jesus." Paul often used these three terms—faith, love, and hope—together (see Romans 5:2-5; 1 Corinthians 13:13; 1 Thessalonians 5:8). This church had placed their *faith* in Christ and Paul commended them in this epistle. *Love* comes from faith and it is an evidence of genuine faith (see James 2:14-26). *Hope* refers to the result of faith, the treasure laid up in heaven where our faith will ultimately find its fulfillment in the presence of our Savior.

Although this passage is a record of an eloquent prayer, it contains several major theological and practical matters for daily Christian living. Beyond their newfound faith, love for the saints, and hope "stored up for you in heaven" (verse 5, NIV), Paul reveled in "the word of truth, the gospel that has come to you" (see verses 5-6). He implied that they had heard the orthodox message concerning the life, ministry, teachings, death, and resurrection of the Lord Jesus Christ. In the sixth verse, he also mentioned that the Gospel was "bearing fruit and growing" all over the then-known world. As a consequence, it was most necessary that the saints parallel their lives with their witness. More specifically, Paul meant the whole Roman Empire by "the whole world." His reference reflected the rapid-fire spread of the Gospel. Lest the message become tainted with hypocrisy and indifference, the apostle prayed that the church of Colossae would accept the moral requirements and ethical duties of Christians.

C. Paul's Intercessory Prayer
(Colossians 1:9-14)

For this cause we also, since the day we heard it, do not cease to pray for you, and to desire that ye might be filled with the knowledge of his will in all wisdom and spiritual understanding; That ye might walk worthy of the Lord unto all pleasing, being fruitful in every good work, and increasing in the knowledge of God; Strengthened with all might, according to his glorious power, unto all patience and longsuffering with joyfulness; Giving thanks unto the Father, which hath made us meet to be partakers of the inheritance of the saints in light: Who hath delivered us from the power of darkness, and hath translated us into the kingdom of his dear Son: In whom we have redemption through his blood, even the forgiveness of sins.

In the ninth verse, Paul defined more straightforwardly his themes of persistent intercessory prayer, living a Christlike life, and receiving the empowerment of the Holy Spirit to do so. Paul's prayer was directed to God, who was said to have qualified believers to share the portion which is the inheritance of the saints who dwell in the realm of light. Paul did not stop asking God to reveal to the Colossians His will, give them spiritual wisdom, and yield practical understanding (see verse 10). These three objectives of prayer suffice for us, just as they did for the Colossians. We need those spiritual attributes as we strive to honor the Lord in each sphere of life. Then, Paul detailed the purpose of "a life worthy of the Lord and may please him in every way" (see verse 10, NIV). Such generates fruit for the kingdom, good works that glorify the Lord, and growth in the knowledge of God. A genuinely yielded and obedient life offered to the honor of Christ will bring more people into the kingdom of God than any grandiloquent sermon. A faithful disciple would do the work of Christ to please Him. He or she would not worry about whether anyone was looking. Through good deeds, he or she would share the love of Christ, which touches the hearts of unbelievers and compels their belief in due time. Today, it stands to reason that committed believers develop personally and grow spiritually. They obtain a greater revelation of their uniqueness and calling as Christians and they receive deeper spiritual insights as they make Christ their ultimate concern.

Next, Paul prayed that the Colossians would lead lives "worthy of the Lord," seeking to please Him in every way. It has been said that "The spiritual life is not a theory." Also, it is more than mere verbal affirmation of a confession of faith or an articulate recitation of proper doctrine. God intends for disciples to conduct themselves in a manner that honors and glorifies His name in all circumstances. I disdain the prevalent and prominent appeal to being "spiritual and not religious" by many celebrities whose spirituality does not appear to require any type of moral or ethical behavior. Many of these "spiritual" people have been married multiple times by mid-life; they exchange partners and lovers in live-in situations with the frequency with which other people change cars. New believers must accept that they cannot live with divided loyalties. They cannot have one foot in the muck and mire of the world and the other in the kingdom of God hoping for eternal salvation. Essentially, Paul desired that the Colossians begin to ask God for the daily grace to align their profession of faith in Christ with a lifestyle that possessed the integrity necessary to lead other people to the Lord.

Paul proceeded to list specific petitions with a grand purpose. He desired that the Colossians: (1) bear fruit in every good work; (2) grow in the knowledge of God, and be given power "according to His glorious might" (verse 11, NIV); (3) please and honor God in everyday living; (4) bear good fruit; (5) understand God's will; (6) be filled with God's strength; (7) be endowed with grace and strength; (8) be full of Christ's joy; and (9) give thanks always. Note the specific nature of these requests. Even as new believers, Paul wanted the Colossians to produce a harvest of other souls for the kingdom of God. He greatly hoped that they would establish a vibrant relationship with God, getting to know Him as spouses come to know each other over time. Paul also asked that these new saints experience the incredible power of the Holy Spirit. Literally, this petition translates into a request that they be given "spiritual dynamite" to blow up the former sin that entangled them and the prisons of temptation that would incarcerate them again. The purpose of these specific requests was to develop endurance, patience, and joy in the character of the Colossian Christians. Many Christians today are unaware of how to pray for other Christians. The list above could serve as a model of prayer for others, particularly the growing Christians.

Three attributes were named—*endurance, patience,* and *joy*—that are essential for spiritual growth. These attributes are essential to the long-range growth and development of any disciple, then and now. Inevitably, the pink cloud of neophyte (new convert) fever will dissipate. A new believer's feet will feel the force of gravity again; he or she will return to the soil of the earth to deal with life's daily adversities and challenges. When that reality recommenced, Paul hoped that the Colossian Christians would have begun sincerely the process of formulating the Christian character and maturity to face life's situations with confidence.

III. CONCLUDING REFLECTION

Intercessory prayer strengthens believers with the power of the Holy Spirit. Literally, it translates into divine dynamite, which in turn blows out the hindrances to a faithful life. This power emerges from God's "glorious might."

Furthermore, this divine grace equips believers with endurance, patience, joy, and thanksgiving. All of these traits combine to allow the average believer to live to the honor and glory of Christ with integrity.

Gathering for intercessory prayer in a church equates with athletic teams attending practice sessions. Regardless of their talent and abilities, sports teams must drill themselves, memorize their plays, and rehearse defenses and perfect offenses with the goal of refining their skills. They do so with the intent of ensuring that they win each game.

In the same way, the church ought to gather for intercessory prayer so that they might experience the unfathomable power and grace of the almighty God. I believe that each member of a church can know confidently his or her purpose in life, discern the spiritual gifts with which he or she has been divinely empowered, discover the daily grace of God to utilize these gifts, and actualize his or her potential to the honor and glory of our Lord. However, such monumental feats will not occur in a church that does not prioritize prayer. Very unfortunately, prayer meeting and Bible study are the least-attended services in any church. Not surprisingly, the church maintains a losing streak in trying to defeat sin, sickness, fear, and myriad adversities that befall disciples. The failure to gather to cultivate the practice of intercessory prayer simply and most reliably clarifies the church's impotence in response to its many challenges.

PRAYER

Our Father, thank You for Your unfailing love and grace. Give us Your Holy Spirit, so that we may lead lives that truly honor and glorify You. In Jesus' name we pray. Amen.

WORD POWER

Knowledge (Greek: *epignosis* [e-pig-no-sis])—this word means "precise and correct knowledge in things ethical and divine." It carries the idea of full experiential knowledge, full discernment or acknowledgement. The Colossians had shown by their faith and love that they were disposed to do God's will, and this was all the more reason why Paul prayed for them. We should pray this prayer for ourselves so that we and others can have full knowledge of God.

HOME DAILY BIBLE READINGS
(April 26–May 2, 2010)

A Faithful Community
> **MONDAY, April 26:** "A Future with Hope" (Jeremiah 29:10-14)
> **TUESDAY, April 27:** "A Faithful Servant" (Matthew 25:14-21)
> **WEDNESDAY, April 28:** "Faithful in a Very Little" (Luke 16:10-12)
> **THURSDAY, April 29:** "Trustworthy Stewards" (1 Corinthians 4:1-5)
> **FRIDAY, April 30:** "Steadfast in the Faith" (Colossians 1:15-23)
> **SATURDAY, May 1:** "Paul's Faithful Service" (Colossians 1:24-29)
> **SUNDAY, May 2:** "The Gospel Bearing Fruit" (Colossians 1:1-14)

LESSON 10   May 9, 2010

AN ESTABLISHED COMMUNITY

DEVOTIONAL READING: Ephesians 3:14-21   **BACKGROUND SCRIPTURE: Colossians 2:1-19**
PRINT PASSAGE: Colossians 2:1-10   **KEY VERSE: Colossians 2:8**

Colossians 2:1-10—KJV

FOR I would that ye knew what great conflict I have for you, and for them at Laodicea, and for as many as have not seen my face in the flesh;

2 That their hearts might be comforted, being knit together in love, and unto all riches of the full assurance of understanding, to the acknowledgement of the mystery of God, and of the Father, and of Christ;

3 In whom are hid all the treasures of wisdom and knowledge.

4 And this I say, lest any man should beguile you with enticing words.

5 For though I be absent in the flesh, yet am I with you in the spirit, joying and beholding your order, and the stedfastness of your faith in Christ.

6 As ye have therefore received Christ Jesus the Lord, so walk ye in him:

7 Rooted and built up in him, and stablished in the faith, as ye have been taught, abounding therein with thanksgiving.

8 Beware lest any man spoil you through philosophy and vain deceit, after the tradition of men, after the rudiments of the world, and not after Christ.

9 For in him dwelleth all the fulness of the Godhead bodily.

10 And ye are complete in him, which is the head of all principality and power.

Colossians 2:1-10—NRSV

FOR I want you to know how much I am struggling for you, and for those in Laodicea, and for all who have not seen me face to face.

2 I want their hearts to be encouraged and united in love, so that they may have all the riches of assured understanding and have the knowledge of God's mystery, that is, Christ himself,

3 in whom are hidden all the treasures of wisdom and knowledge.

4 I am saying this so that no one may deceive you with plausible arguments.

5 For though I am absent in body, yet I am with you in spirit, and I rejoice to see your morale and the firmness of your faith in Christ.

6 As you therefore have received Christ Jesus the Lord, continue to live your lives in him,

7 rooted and built up in him and established in the faith, just as you were taught, abounding in thanksgiving.

8 See to it that no one takes you captive through philosophy and empty deceit, according to human tradition, according to the elemental spirits of the universe, and not according to Christ.

9 For in him the whole fullness of deity dwells bodily,

10 and you have come to fullness in him, who is the head of every ruler and authority.

BIBLE FACT

THE MYSTERY OF GOD: In his epistle to the Galatians, Paul believed that God had opened the door of eternity to the Gentiles. Not only did the door to eternity open, but God also bestowed the blessing of Abraham upon the Gentiles. In the same vein, Paul, in his epistle to the Colossians, affirmed that the Colossians should walk worthy of their profession of faith in Christ. We contemporary Christians should walk worthy as well.

UNIFYING LESSON PRINCIPLE

People are deceived by all kinds of philosophies and human traditions that lead them away from the hidden treasures of knowledge and wisdom. Where can we find those hidden treasures? Paul told the Colossians that knowledge and wisdom are in Christ Jesus and in the lives of those who are growing in Christ.

TOPICAL OUTLINE OF THE LESSON

I. Introduction
   A. A First-Century Theological Buffet
   B. Biblical Background

II. Exposition and Application of the Scripture
   A. Remain in Love (Colossians 2:1-3)
   B. Stay in Christ (Colossians 2:4-7)
   C. Watch Out for Empty Philosophy (Colossians 2:8-10)

III. Concluding Reflection

LESSON OBJECTIVES

Upon completion of this lesson, the students will know that:

1. The epistle to the Colossians is relevant to us today;
2. There are different kinds of teachers with strange philosophies who disguise themselves as Christians; and,
3. Standing firm and ready to defend your faith is a call to all Christians.

POINTS TO BE EMPHASIZED

ADULT/YOUTH

Adult Topic: Distinguishing Truth from Deceit
Youth Topic: Stand Firm
Adult Key Verse: Colossians 2:8
Youth Key Verses: Colossians 2:6-7
Print Passage: Colossians 2:1-10

—Paul's pastoral objective in this letter was to help the Colossians understand the mystery of God's reconciling work made known in Christ.
—Many of the members in the church of Colossae did not know Paul personally.
—Paul encouraged an approach to Christian living that was rooted in Christ.
—Paul warned the church about false prophets and false knowledge that would woo them from Christ.
—The church in Colossae was confused by "philosophies" and its members were in danger of losing sight of Christ.
—This letter asserts both the centrality and superiority of Christ and His power underlying true faithful living.
—Paul told the Colossians that he struggled to help those whom he had never met, like them and the Laodiceans.

CHILDREN

Children Topic: Grow Strong Together
Key Verses: Colossians 2:6-7
Print Passage: Colossians 2:1-10

—Paul was writing to believers in Colossae and Laodicea, many of whom he did not know personally because he had not visited them.
—Paul encouraged the believers to grow in their understanding and wisdom.

—Paul encouraged the believers to continue to grow in their faith and lives in Christ.

—Paul taught them that treasures of wisdom and knowledge were in Christ Jesus.

—Paul was concerned that false teachings might sway them from their faith.

I. INTRODUCTION

A. A First-Century Theological Buffet

In this second chapter of the book of Colossians, Paul urged the new Christians in Colossae to persevere in their knowledge of and relationship with the Lord Jesus Christ. He encouraged them to grow in Christ so that the "hollow and deceptive philosophy, which depends on human tradition and the basic principles of this world rather than on Christ" (Colossians 2:8, NIV) would not imprison them. Myriad religions and ideologies permeated Roman society. The average person in the Roman Empire could choose from a theological smorgasbord. Mostly, these options clashed with the teachings of Christ, as did the principles of the dominant culture. Concerned that the new believers in the Colossian church would submit to the misleading practice of blending the Gospel with secular philosophy, Paul developed his theme relating to the necessity of maintaining sole allegiance to Christ. Parenthetically, the notion of mixing religions that do not correlate logically is called *syncretism*. Nonetheless, Paul severely cautioned the Colossians against this temptation. Rather than sampling the myriad philosophies of the surrounding culture, Paul said that Christians should delve into the richness of the knowledge of Christ, who was and is the long-awaited mystery that God revealed in the Incarnation.

This portion of the letter is a reminder to us of the importance of correct doctrine. A pervasive notion at the time stipulated that Christ did not actually die on the cross—an image of Him did. Painstakingly, Paul asserted the truth of the Gospel. Many "mystery" religions and secret societies attempted to co-opt the spreading message of Christ. Paul clarified that the mystery of Christ was the bodily revelation of the Triune God in Him. In the paradox of eternity assuming a human form, God forever reconciles humankind to Himself and restores the original relationship He intended in the Garden of Eden. Paul insisted that Christian living could only be based upon the teachings and saving work of Jesus Christ.

B. Biblical Background

Responding to God's love in Christ cannot be just an emotional experience. Formulaic testimonies of dramatic and perhaps even melodramatic conversion experiences abound in the church. Unfortunately, many believers consider the recitation of the date, time, place, and details of their conversion experience as the culminating event in the life of a disciple. Others unwisely assume that copies of their baptism certificates are recorded in heaven. These two things suffice to ensure them of eternal salvation and admittance to heaven upon their physical expiration. This predominant notion of "once saved, always saved" robs believers of the limitless riches and infinite discoveries of growing in a relationship with and under the lordship of Jesus Christ. Paul's admonition to the Colossians to develop their intellectual commitment as Christians, as well as their devotion of the heart, speaks to contemporary disciples as forcefully as it did in the first century.

II. EXPOSITION AND APPLICATION OF THE SCRIPTURE

A. Remain in Love
(Colossians 2:1-3)

FOR I would that ye knew what great conflict I have for you, and for them at Laodicea, and for as many as have not seen my face in the flesh; That their hearts might be comforted, being knit together in love, and unto all riches of the full assurance of understanding, to the acknowledgement of the mystery of God, and of the Father, and of Christ; In whom are hid all the treasures of wisdom and knowledge.

Even though this epistle bears the name of Colossae, it was intended to be read in the church in Laodicea. Laodicea was a sister city of Colossae, about eleven miles away. The aim of Paul was to reach as many as possible for the Gospel of Jesus Christ. The religious peddlers in this region were wreaking serious havoc on the body of Christ. It was Paul's intention to encourage them in the midst of oppositions. Paul wanted them to remain in their love for Christ and one another. The only way to quench the venom of religious counterfeits is to remain in our love for each other, and Jesus Christ as the Head of the church. Paul was counting on unity and brotherly love as an antidote against the heresy that was going around.

Our churches should be encouraged to work together with likeminded churches to carry out the mandate of Christ. Church leaders should bear in mind that no matter the size of their budget for outreach, on Judgment Day the message will be, "Thou has been faithful over a few things" (see Matthew 25:21). This message should encourage us to work together in reaching the masses who are lost in sin (see Luke 19:17).

Though the false teachers in Colossae spoke of initiating newcomers into a superior knowledge, Paul encouraged his readers that they had the capacity to understand the mystery of God without the help of false philosophers (see Colossians 1:26-27). These philosophers were known as Gnostics; they were the group of teachers who claimed superiority over others. The Gnostics believed that knowledge was the way to salvation. Three principal teachings of the Gnostics were: (1) that important secret knowledge was hidden from believers; (2) that the body was evil; and (3) that Christ only *appeared* to be human. For this reason, Gnosticism was condemned as false and heretical by several writers of the New Testament.

B. Stay in Christ
(Colossians 2:4-7)

And this I say, lest any man should beguile you with enticing words. For though I be absent in the flesh, yet am I with you in the spirit, joying and beholding your order, and the stedfastness of your faith in Christ. As ye have therefore received Christ Jesus the Lord, so walk ye in him: Rooted and built up in him, and stablished in the faith, as ye have been taught, abounding therein with thanksgiving.

In this pericope Paul said, "I tell you this" (verse 4, NIV). In other words, Paul was emphasizing the importance of the doctrine of Christ. The arguments of the false teachers as summarized above seemed to be good to people who were not sound in faith, but they were like a cankerworm that can destroy the foundation of faith. Paul warned his readers against teachers who were smooth talkers with persuasive words. The Greek word *paralogizeeta* that Paul used means "to deceive by subtle reasoning." Verse 5 helps us to understand that Paul was not physically present, but nonetheless he would not allow the Gnostics to destroy the faith of his readers. We notice here that Paul had a tender, shepherding heart. Only an individual with such a heart could do what Paul was doing. With what we see here, we can deduce that Paul was also a great apologist (defender of the faith). Contrary to Paul's statement that we are saved by grace, the Gnostics believed that only certain "knowledgeable" people could join their elite group. This was all the more reason why Paul encouraged his readers to stay together in love and in Christ. Paul's readers were not at this point flagging in their dedication to Christ, but he needed to warn them to not allow the false teachers to overthrow their faith. He wrote to combat the possibility that the Colossians would lapse into mixing and matching faiths and loyalties.

Undoubtedly, this tendency spread confusion, weakened the value of the Gospel, and resulted in moral and ethical compromises. He exceedingly desired that the new and young believers, many of whom Paul had not met personally, "may have the full riches of complete understanding" (2:2, NIV). In essence, he submitted that coming to know Christ and being baptized in His name were only the beginning of a lifelong journey. He earnestly prayed that they would comprehend the intricate mysteries that God reveals in Christ, who possesses the hidden treasures of godly counsel and teaching.

Just as the Colossian believers had begun their walk with Christ, so Paul encouraged them to continue in their walk with Him. Paul used four words to describe the Colossian believers' walk with Christ. The tense of the word translated *rooted* denotes a complete action; the believers had been "rooted in Christ." The next three terms—*built up, established,* and *abounding*—are all in the present tense, indicating the continual growth that should characterize every Christian's walk with Christ.

C. Watch Out for Empty Philosophy (Colossians 2:8-10)

Beware lest any man spoil you through philosophy and vain deceit, after the tradition of men, after the rudiments of the world, and not after Christ. For in him dwelleth all the fulness of the Godhead bodily. And ye are complete in him, which is the head of all principality and power.

This is one of the famous verses which many are using to discourage people from studying or reading philosophy. This was not Paul's position. Paul was a great philosopher. The interaction of Paul with the Stoic and Epicurean philosophers in Athens revealed his depth of thought (see Acts 17:1-34). Paul was warning his readers, including us, not to be taken in by any philosophy that did and does not align to a proper knowledge of Christ. In our contemporary world, we are seeing eastern religions taking root and expanding at an alarming rate. Many Christians are falling prey to yoga under the name of *meditation*.

The false teachers in Colossae had combined worldly philosophies with the Gospel. These philosophies were spoken of by Paul as the basic principles of the world, which some had interpreted as "spirits" or "angels" who supposedly controlled a person's life (see Galatians 4:3, 9). These teachers were very subtle in the way they presented their doctrines. They employed the power of persuasion to indoctrinate their pupils. Paul's strongest indictment against the heretics was that their teaching was not according to Christ, and as a result they were not walking with Christ.

Warning! In contemporary halls of academic endeavor and departments of religion, the paradigm of "Higher Biblical Criticism" posits that a learned, reasonable person cannot accept the Bible at face value. Rather, he or she must study the ancient languages and the cultural origins that produced the text to determine its most legitimate meaning. We cannot assume that it means what it says. We must allow for the fallibility of the human agents who wrote the books of the Bible. Actually, the Scriptures contain the record of the history, religion, and literature of the Hebrew Bible and the New Testament writings. This construct—which mimics the scientific method and thereby subscribes to its criteria for determining validity—undercuts the worth of revelation, propositional truth, and biblical claims of divine inspiration. Seductively, this way of thinking appears to empower its adherents by freeing them from allegiance to a "parrot religion." However, it is essentially powerless when its followers face life-threatening health challenges, the failures of marriages, broken homes, and the other adversities and circumstances of life that average believers confront daily.

Paul appealed to the Colossians to be orderly and firm in their faith in Christ. Practically speaking, he first recommended a systematic and disciplined study of the Gospel. Second, he suggested that his hearers resist the temptation of wavering. If they heeded this advice, they would continue in Christ, being "rooted and built up in him, strengthened in the faith as you were taught, and overflowing with thankfulness" (verse 7, NIV). Paul assured the Colossians of the worth of investing their time, talent, tithes, and temperament as they deepened their relationships with Christ.

Consider what they would have missed if they had remained young in the faith. They would never have known the genuine faithfulness of Christ. They would not have experienced the enduring power and wisdom of the Gospel to redress each and every human challenge. They would not have progressed to the point of trusting almighty God when one does not have any other options or resources upon which to rely. If they failed to deepen their commitment to Christ, they would not be able to genuinely rely upon Him and trust the truth of His teachings. The mere fact that they would entertain alternative philosophies demonstrated a lack of trust in the Gospel. Paul wanted them to rest assuredly upon the claims of Christ of who He is—the embodiment of the fullness of the Deity.

III. CONCLUDING REFLECTION

We face the same challenge of unconditional commitment. Science, technology, demographers, futurists, and other public policy and researchers claim to have the truth about the worth of human life. Many Christians lamentably compartmentalize their theology, politics, economics, and sociology. They do not strive for intellectual coherence and personal integrity in all areas of their lives. In matters of faith, they settle for fleeting feelings and heightened emotions to resolve any inconsistencies. In so doing, they miss the opportunity to delve more richly and deeply into their faith and see the ways in which it possesses divine and eternal wisdom to meet any human need.

The entry point to a fellowship with God is receiving Christ as Lord of your life. But you must continue to grow through personal devotion—reading the Word of God and thinking through what you have read. You align yourself with a Bible-believing church where the Bible is being preached in its fullness. You make yourself available to serve God in whatever capacity God has gifted you. To be rooted in Christ is not just going to church; there must be daily cleansing and asking the Holy Spirit to reveal to you areas of your life that need improvement. You can live for Christ if you determine to do so (see Romans 12:1-2).

Always be on the alert because there are many forms of religion and their teachers are very smart. They can quote the Bible with accuracy, but they deny the power of the Resurrection. Many so-called Christians today have denied the virgin birth of Jesus; if you are not careful, they will persuade you to believe their heresy.

PRAYER

Most gracious, holy, and loving Father, look kindly upon the needs of Your children. Help us to be alert when we are about to be drawn away from You by smooth talkers. Make us strong and able to devote ourselves wholeheartedly to loving and serving You. In Jesus' name we pray. Amen.

WORD POWER

Philosophy (Greek: *philosophia* [phi-lo-so-phia])—means "the love of wisdom, or skill in any branch of knowledge." The word *philosophy* as used here means "speculative inquiries into the nature and classes of angels." It can also refer to a method used in regulating Mosaic Law respecting practical religion.

HOME DAILY BIBLE READINGS
(May 3-9, 2010)

An Established Community
MONDAY, May 3: "The Power and Wisdom of God" (1 Corinthians 1:20-25)
TUESDAY, May 4: "The Glory of God in Christ" (2 Corinthians 4:1-6)
WEDNESDAY, May 5: "The Full Stature of Christ" (Ephesians 4:11-16)
THURSDAY, May 6: "One Body in Christ" (Romans 12:3-8)
FRIDAY, May 7: "Grow in Grace and Knowledge" (2 Peter 3:14-18)
SATURDAY, May 8: "Hold Fast to Christ" (Colossians 2:11-19)
SUNDAY, May 9: "Fullness in Christ" (Colossians 2:1-10)

LESSON 11   May 16, 2010

A CHOSEN COMMUNITY

DEVOTIONAL READING: Isaiah 41:4-10
PRINT PASSAGE: Colossians 3:12-17

BACKGROUND SCRIPTURE: Colossians 3
KEY VERSE: Colossians 3:12

Colossians 3:12-17—KJV

12 Put on therefore, as the elect of God, holy and beloved, bowels of mercies, kindness, humbleness of mind, meekness, longsuffering;

13 Forbearing one another, and forgiving one another, if any man have a quarrel against any: even as Christ forgave you, so also do ye.

14 And above all these things put on charity, which is the bond of perfectness.

15 And let the peace of God rule in your hearts, to the which also ye are called in one body; and be ye thankful.

16 Let the word of Christ dwell in you richly in all wisdom; teaching and admonishing one another in psalms and hymns and spiritual songs, singing with grace in your hearts to the Lord.

17 And whatsoever ye do in word or deed, do all in the name of the Lord Jesus, giving thanks to God and the Father by him.

Colossians 3:12-17—NRSV

12 As God's chosen ones, holy and beloved, clothe yourselves with compassion, kindness, humility, meekness, and patience.

13 Bear with one another and, if anyone has a complaint against another, forgive each other; just as the Lord has forgiven you, so you also must forgive.

14 Above all, clothe yourselves with love, which binds everything together in perfect harmony.

15 And let the peace of Christ rule in your hearts, to which indeed you were called in the one body. And be thankful.

16 Let the word of Christ dwell in you richly; teach and admonish one another in all wisdom; and with gratitude in your hearts sing psalms, hymns, and spiritual songs to God.

17 And whatever you do, in word or deed, do everything in the name of the Lord Jesus, giving thanks to God the Father through him.

BIBLE FACT

CHOSEN COMMUNITY: In this epistle, one thing that stands out is the admonition to Christians to put into practice behavior that evidenced their encounter with the risen Savior. The Colossian community was experiencing some tension in the body of Christ. Implied in Paul's admonition was the fact that some members could not stand other members. There was no love among brethren. The only way by which Christians stand out is the love that binds them together, and they must display it in concrete ways.

As a chosen community, we must realize that we did not choose ourselves; it was the love of God that gave us access to the Father's throne, and therefore we must at all times behave as "a chosen community."

UNIFYING LESSON PRINCIPLE

Sometimes people are confused about what it means to be chosen. What does it mean to be chosen by God? Paul taught that our calling includes kindness and humility, forgiveness, love, the peace of Christ, thankfulness, and worship.

TOPICAL OUTLINE OF THE LESSON

I. Introduction

    A. What Does It Mean to Be Chosen?

    B. Biblical Background

II. Exposition and Application of the Scripture

    A. The "Elect of God" Qualities (Colossians 3:12-13)

    B. Higher Christian Qualities (Colossians 3:14)

    C. Christian "Daily Basis" Traits (Colossians 3:15-17)

III. Concluding Reflection

LESSON OBJECTIVES

Upon completion of this lesson, the students will know:

1. What it means to be a chosen community in Christ;

2. The characteristics of a chosen community; and,

3. The Christian's list of virtues, and how to assess their progress, individually and corporately, in obtaining them.

POINTS TO BE EMPHASIZED

ADULT/YOUTH

Adult Topic: A Sense of True Belonging

Youth Topic: Hey, I've Been Chosen!

Adult/Youth Key Verse: Colossians 3:12

Print Passage: Colossians 3:12-17

—The thrust of this passage suggests that learning to live the Christian life both individually and corporately is what brings greatest honor to the name of Christ.

—Love is a crucial component of forgiveness.

—This passage contains a list of vices (verses 5-11) and a list of virtues (verses 12-17). Greek teachers commonly used such lists to challenge students.

—Paul encouraged the church to bring their thoughts, desires, and attitudes under the governance of the Word of God.

—The Holy Spirit will aid the believer to remove anything that supports or feeds sexual immorality, impurity, lust, evil desires, and greed.

—If you are a Christian, then live as Christ did: be compassionate, kind, humble, gentle, patient, and forgiving—and, finally, do everything in the name of the Lord Jesus.

—Paul provided definitions of Christian community and Christian freedom.

CHILDREN

Children Topic: Act in Love Together

Key Verse: Colossians 3:12

Print Passage: Colossians 3:12-17

—This Scripture includes characteristics of the life of God's chosen ones.

—Love binds all other characteristics in a harmonious way.

—We must teach one another as we live as God's chosen ones.

—Everything is to be done out of gratitude and honor to God and in Jesus' name.

I. INTRODUCTION

A. What Does It Mean to Be Chosen?

The question for this section is one that Christians must ask on a daily basis. Some Christians equate God's blessing and bestowal of chosen status upon us with financial and material well-being. Moreover, they insist that discipleship exempts them from physical illness and the twists and turns of the volatile and declining global markets and economy. What a pity that we would reduce God's blessing to temporal and earthly items that thieves can take and moth and rust corrupt (see Matthew 6:19).

The Christian life is not a system of moral "dos" and don'ts." It is not possible to establish a list of ethical regulations, positive and negative, and then quantify one's righteousness according to the percentages of the time that one adheres to these rules. The Christian life is not a process of demanding things from God and pointing to them as evidence of being "highly blessed and favored of the Lord." Instead, the Christian life is a relationship with God through the person of our Lord and Savior, Jesus Christ. It is a matter of realizing that one is chosen as an instrument of the Lord to spread His Gospel and build His kingdom on the earth. It is the joy of knowing one's uniqueness as a child of God. It is a process of discovering the singular talents, abilities, and gifts that God graciously gives us at birth and illuminates when we respond positively to His loving appeals. It is progressing to the spiritual awakening of living in total faith and genuine reliance upon Christ. This way of life enables us to live completely free of fear, doubt, anger, and hopelessness. More significantly, it is a lifelong process of acquiring the mind, heart, and character of Christ.

B. Biblical Background

The word *church* in Greek is *ecclesia,* or "the called-out and chosen community." As a consequence, members of the church have been called out of the world's darkness and into the marvelous light of the presence and wisdom of Christ. We are chosen for the express divine purpose to be instruments of God's love, messengers of His grace, and channels of His peace.

In the midst of the societal insanity of Rome, the Lord called out the Colossians and chose them to do His bidding in their region of the Roman Empire. What an amazing privilege for them! However, with privilege comes responsibility. They were not chosen by God to do whatever they wanted to do. They had to adhere to a higher standard of living as disciples. While they could not violate moral imperatives, they must meet the ethical principles of love, compassion, and integrity in *deed* more than *words.* They would have to adhere to the new law of love which Christ implemented in His preaching, teaching, and healing. They must cultivate the virtues of kindness, meekness, patience, and forgiveness. Being chosen by Christ is more than a self-congratulatory occurrence because of a few material possessions. In gratitude for one's "belovedness" as a child of God, one relays His love and forgiveness to others.

II. EXPOSITION AND APPLICATION OF THE SCRIPTURE

A. The "Elect of God" Qualities (Colossians 3:12-13)

Put on therefore, as the elect of God, holy and beloved, bowels of mercies, kindness, humbleness of mind, meekness, longsuffering; Forbearing one another, and forgiving one another, if any man have a quarrel against any: even as Christ forgave you, so also do ye.

Christlike virtues are the clearest indication that believers accept their chosen status. Interestingly, the power of the previously listed intrinsic qualities surpasses the righteousness that results from avoiding the vices listed in the first part of this chapter. Still, Paul concentrated upon the individual and corporate dimensions of living as a chosen son or daughter of the Lord. On both levels, people were and are to achieve great glory for the Lord.

How does a chosen community define itself? What will be its underlying virtues and unifying principles? How will outsiders know that this chosen community exists? A chosen community distinguishes itself with its principles and practices. What does it offer that other groups do not? For the church of Colossae, Paul offered a strategy to help believers live for God on a daily basis.

Paul began by addressing the Colossians with their new identity, which was "chosen one." To be chosen by God was a privileged position. It meant there was no more enmity between God and the chosen ones. Rather than them choosing God, God chose them. God paid the penalty for their sins by allowing Jesus to die on the cross. The phrase "as the elect of God" (verse 12) means that God chose the Christians, and chose them to be special in His plan. Some Christians are frightened by the word *elect*, but it should be taken as a comfort and a destiny to fulfill.

The elect are also called *holy*. This is an imputed holiness. None of us can be holy to the satisfaction of the holy God. However, through the vicarious death of Christ on the cross, we are made holy and acceptable to God. Paul added another virtue—"beloved." To be beloved of God is to be totally forgiven, and possessing a right standing in the presence of God. Such a position leads to serving God with hilarious joy.

When Christians realize their privileged position, which they did not and do not deserve, then they must put on "tender mercies." This word expresses yearning compassion, which has its seat in the heart, and which we feel to act on our inward parts (see Genesis 43:30; Jeremiah 31:20; Luke 1:78). Christians must also put on kindness, which is the spirit of sharing one's love with the undeserving brother or sister. Paul mentioned humility. *Meekness* is an important Christian characteristic; it means "to have a teachable spirit." Jesus, while preaching on the Mount, said, "Blessed are the meek: for they shall inherit the earth" (Matthew 5:5). At the end of this verse, Paul used *longsuffering*, a word seldom used in our generation. Many of the elderly among us possess this virtue, but many of the younger ones have no understanding of this virtue. We want something now. We do not know how to wait in line. We are easily offended and constantly irritated. We want to become CEO of our own company overnight.

In verse 13, Paul used two words: *forbearing* and *forgiving*. *Forbearing* has the connotation of our attitude toward present offences. If we have forgiven someone and the same person offends again, Paul said to *forbear*—in other words, hold on to Christ's virtue, which constantly forbears us. We must also keep on *forgiving*. Paul exhorted the Colossians to forgive as Christ forgave them. Certainly, genuine forgiveness is a distinct virtue in a revengeful society. The Romans prided themselves on the strength and logic of their law to adjudicate offenses and crimes. In fact, American constitutional and criminal law, specifically, and the Anglo-American legal tradition, are indebted substantially to the Roman system of law. Both the Romans and our own society have marveled at the Christian practice of forgiveness, which relinquishes the right to punish. The larger society does not understand how Christian victims of violent crimes genuinely forgive those who have harmed them. Their amazement stems from their ignorance of the radicalism of God's grace and the atoning nature of Christ's love. As a consequence, Paul encouraged the Colossians to understand their chosen status in terms of the spiritual requirements to love and forgive as Christ did. David said, "If you, O Lord, kept a record of sins, O Lord, who could stand?" (Psalm 130:3, NIV). It is imperative for Christians to forgive and keep on forgiving.

B. Higher Christian Qualities
(Colossians 3:14)

And above all these things put on charity, which is the bond of perfectness.

Is there any virtue that is higher than other Christian virtues? The answer is an unequivocal yes! Of all the virtues, love is the supreme. It covers a lot of sins (see 1 Peter 4:8). Love is the foundation for all the virtues. Without an appreciation of Christ's sacrificial love, one would not be motivated to extend these virtues to others. Yet, in so doing, the epistle to the Colossians appealed to unbelievers on Christ's behalf and drew them to the kingdom with His love. Love completed and completes the Christian's social and spiritual existence. Paul said "Above all," meaning that of all the virtues described thus far, love superseded them all. Paul was appealing to his readers to realize that love was the law of Christ (see Matthew 22:37; Galatians 6:2). The heretics were trying to destroy the fellowship of the Christians, and Paul quickly pointed out that if the Christians truly loved God, they could not be moved. Love is the bond of perfection. Love perfectly fulfills what God requires of us in relationship.

In 1 Corinthians 13, as Paul came to the end of the chapter, he said, "Now these three remain: faith, hope and love. But the greatest of these is love" (1 Corinthians 13:13, NIV). The church in Corinth, during the time of Paul, was morally corrupt. Love had become a mixed-up term. Love was and is the greatest of all human qualities, and most importantly, it is an attribute of God Himself (see 1 John 4:8). Love involves unselfish service to others, and for this reason Paul said in our text, "Above all"—meaning above all other virtues, love is supreme.

C. Christian "Daily Basis" Traits
(Colossians 3:15-17)

And let the peace of God rule in your hearts, to the which

also ye are called in one body; and be ye thankful. Let the word of Christ dwell in you richly in all wisdom; teaching and admonishing one another in psalms and hymns and spiritual songs, singing with grace in your hearts to the Lord. And whatsoever ye do in word or deed, do all in the name of the Lord Jesus, giving thanks to God and the Father by him.

The word *let* was an exhortation to keep doing what was yet to exist among the Colossians. "Let the peace of God rule in your hearts" (verse 15). This statement means that peace should characterize the community of God's people, and that peace was a standard for discerning God's will. Another way to understand the phrase "let the peace of God rule in your hearts" is to let the peace of God be the referee of your life. The false teachers in the Colossian church had made themselves out to be referees, trying to impose certain ways of living. However, Paul exhorted them to allow the peace which comes from Christ to rule their hearts, or to umpire their hearts. There would be times when anger, envy, and other passions arose, but the Colossians should always remember the peace of God. Do not let those passions rule your life, so that you are swayed by them, but let the peace of Christ be the decider of everything.

The phrase "To which also ye are called" is a reminder to Paul's readers to constantly remember their privileged position. Their calling came from the God of peace, who had reconciled them to Himself. Therefore it was imperative for them to extend peace to others as well. We too must also emphasize the significance of being "in one body." The unity of the body was and is a strong argument for peace among the members. Paul also exhorted them to be thankful for their calling. They should remember who they were before they became followers of Christ. Therefore, they must be thankful to God who chose them. Failure to have peace in their hearts would be inconsistent with the phrase "in one body."

This lesson concludes with a few practical suggestions for growing and flourishing in a chosen community. First, be thankful. Second, saturate your mind and heart in the Word of Christ. Third, teach and challenge each other with Christ's wisdom in worship and Bible study. Fourth, let every deed be done to the honor, glory, and praise of Christ Jesus, the Lord and Savior of humankind. Weekly fellowship with likeminded believers solidifies one's assurances as a member of the chosen community. These practices result in personal growth and spiritual development. They guard against indifference and atrophy.

III. CONCLUDING REFLECTION

The proliferation of new civic organizations and social clubs demonstrates the pervasive hunger that many people have to belong to something. Some of them join these groups because they believe that they can obtain identity, authority, and benefits that they could not acquire otherwise. They want to be accepted by peers, colleagues, neighbors, and friends. Each year on the nation's college and university campuses, millions of students submit to insidious actions as they rush to join fraternities and sororities. Their desire to belong to these groups and receive the privileges of membership leads them to commit ridiculous deeds in which they demean themselves and possibly risk their lives. The thirst to belong fuels this acquiescence of superficiality.

Then there are the people who do not join

any groups because of their fear of rejection. These types of persons also find it difficult to believe that they will be included wholly in the community. In sum, whether groveling in a self-effacing manner or pretending to prefer isolation, people have a tremendous need to belong to a community.

In my mind, I hear the lyrics of the theme song to the *Cheers* sitcom which took place in a bar in Boston: "Sometimes you want to go where everybody knows your name, and they're always glad you came. You want to be where everybody knows your name." The bar community of "Cheers" afforded each character a place where he or she was valued for simply showing up. Although they fought with each other, they always found a way to forgive and move on. They shared each other's successes and they hurt in the midst of each other's pain. Seemingly, they loved each other unconditionally. Would it not be great if each local church could have the same attitude toward its group of disciples?

PRAYER

Gracious God, our Father, we are Your children and we are members of Your family. Daily, let us recall the inheritance that we enjoy as members of the household of faith. Grant us grace to sustain us. In Jesus' name we pray. Amen.

WORD POWER

Put On (Greek: *Enduo* [en-du-o])—means "to envelop in," or "to hide in." It could refer to putting on clothes. The essence of what Paul was saying is that Christians should always clothe themselves with kindness, just as in the way they put on clothes. If a Christian fails to be kind, then he or she has yet to understand his or her new position in Christ.

HOME DAILY BIBLE READINGS
(May 10-16, 2010)

A Chosen Community

MONDAY, May 10: "I Am Your God" (Isaiah 41:4-10)

TUESDAY, May 11: "You Are My Witnesses" (Isaiah 43:10-13)

WEDNESDAY, May 12: "You Must Forgive" (Luke 17:1-6)

THURSDAY, May 13: "Fruit of the Spirit" (Galatians 5:22-26)

FRIDAY, May 14: "Seek the Things Above" (Colossians 3:1-11)

SATURDAY, May 15: "Serve the Lord" (Colossians 3:18-25)

SUNDAY, May 16: "Live as God's Chosen Ones" (Colossians 3:12-17)

LESSON 12   May 23, 2010

AT HOME IN THE COMMUNITY

DEVOTIONAL READING: Colossians 4:2-9
PRINT PASSAGE: Philemon 8-18

BACKGROUND SCRIPTURE: Philemon
KEY VERSE: Philemon 21

Philemon 8-18—KJV

8 Wherefore, though I might be much bold in Christ to enjoin thee that which is convenient,

9 Yet for love's sake I rather beseech thee, being such an one as Paul the aged, and now also a prisoner of Jesus Christ.

10 I beseech thee for my son Onesimus, whom I have begotten in my bonds:

11 Which in time past was to thee unprofitable, but now profitable to thee and to me:

12 Whom I have sent again: thou therefore receive him, that is, mine own bowels:

13 Whom I would have retained with me, that in thy stead he might have ministered unto me in the bonds of the gospel:

14 But without thy mind would I do nothing; that thy benefit should not be as it were of necessity, but willingly.

15 For perhaps he therefore departed for a season, that thou shouldest receive him for ever;

16 Not now as a servant, but above a servant, a brother beloved, specially to me, but how much more unto thee, both in the flesh, and in the Lord?

17 If thou count me therefore a partner, receive him as myself.

18 If he hath wronged thee, or oweth thee ought, put that on mine account.

Philemon 8-18—NRSV

8 For this reason, though I am bold enough in Christ to command you to do your duty,

9 yet I would rather appeal to you on the basis of love—and I, Paul, do this as an old man, and now also as a prisoner of Christ Jesus.

10 I am appealing to you for my child, Onesimus, whose father I have become during my imprisonment.

11 Formerly he was useless to you, but now he is indeed useful both to you and to me.

12 I am sending him, that is, my own heart, back to you.

13 I wanted to keep him with me, so that he might be of service to me in your place during my imprisonment for the gospel;

14 but I preferred to do nothing without your consent, in order that your good deed might be voluntary and not something forced.

15 Perhaps this is the reason he was separated from you for a while, so that you might have him back forever,

16 no longer as a slave but more than a slave, a beloved brother—especially to me but how much more to you, both in the flesh and in the Lord.

17 So if you consider me your partner, welcome him as you would welcome me.

18 If he has wronged you in any way, or owes you anything, charge that to my account.

BIBLE FACT

From uselessness to usefulness—this is a heartfelt epistle to Philemon, to take back Onesimus. Onesimus encountered Christ through the ministry of Paul, but there was a wall between Philemon and Onesimus. Onesimus was a slave who wronged Philemon, but Christ had taken over Onesimus's life. This epistle is an admonishment for all Christians not to discount the power of the Gospel.

TOPICAL OUTLINE OF THE LESSON

I. Introduction
   A. A Real Friend
   B. Biblical Background

II. Exposition and Application of the Scripture
   A. An Appeal for Love's Sake (Philemon 8-11)
   B. Paul Sends Onesimus Back (Philemon 12-14)
   C. Onesimus, a Brother in Christ (Philemon 15-18)

III. Concluding Reflection

LESSON OBJECTIVES

Upon completion of this lesson, the students will be able to:

1. Discard the conventional notions of friendship and develop biblically based friendships;
2. Understand how Paul's relationships affected Onesimus's conversion to Christianity; and,
3. Understand the importance of total forgiveness as a means of developing strong Christian bonds.

POINTS TO BE EMPHASIZED

ADULT/YOUTH

Adult Topic: Doing the Right Thing
Youth Topic: Homeward Bound
Adult Key Verse: Philemon 21
Youth Key Verses: Philemon 15-16
Print Passage: Philemon 8-18

—The book of Philemon was one of Paul's "prison epistles" that was addressed to an individual person rather than to a church.
—Paul wrote this letter to facilitate a new relationship between Philemon, a slave master, and Onesimus, his runaway slave.
—Onesimus is mentioned in Colossians 4:9 as a traveling companion of Tychicus.
—Paul used a play on words when he contrasted Onesimus, whose name means "useful," as being formerly useless but now useful (Philemon 11).
—In the letter, Paul, who could have ordered Philemon to do what is right, appealed to him for love's sake for a new convert to Christ, who was now more than a slave.
—He also made a personal plea to Philemon to accept Onesimus as he would Paul himself, "If you consider me a partner [a close friend]" (Philemon 17).
—Paul promised to repay personally any loss suffered by Philemon because of Onesimus.

CHILDREN

Children Topic: Act as Friends
Key Verse: Philemon 17
Print Passage: Philemon 8-18

—Paul wrote a personal letter from prison to Philemon, a valued friend.

—Paul wrote on behalf of Onesimus, Philemon's runaway slave, who was a new believer.
—Paul offered to pay Philemon for anything that Onesimus owed Philemon.
—Paul asked Philemon to accept Onesimus back as a brother rather than as a slave.

I. INTRODUCTION
A. A Real Friend

Friendship is one word that means different things to different people. It is a term that we use rather loosely. People refer to people with whom they have not spoken for decades as friends. Others may insist that they are friends to a certain person, but have never sacrificed anything to enrich the person's life. Who are the people in your life who genuinely wish you well and desire your happiness to the same extent as their own? Who are the few people upon whom you can rely in the midst of adversity and great loss? Who are the people who love and respect your spouse and children as you do? Who are the people who will use their power, influence, and resources to help you in bettering your standard of living? I reason that the people whose names come to mind as you answer these questions are your real and true friends.

Through the prism of one of the most troubling books in the New Testament, we glean some lessons about friendship. Paul addressed this letter to Philemon with the goal of brokering reconciliation between this slave master and his runaway slave, Onesimus. Parallel to Paul's primary purpose was his secondary but serious concern for the well-being of Onesimus. In essence, Paul advocated for Onesimus by asking Philemon to receive him with impunity. Paul informed Philemon that he vouched for Onesimus, because they shared the bond of relationship in Christ. What an amazing progression—from human slavery to lifelong servitude to Christ! As believers of any social standing, economic rank, or political persuasion, we enjoy the assurance that we are at home in the community of faith.

B. Biblical Background

It is important to note that historical parallels are not helpful. Two historical eras are fundamentally different as the details of causes and the specifics of effects will never match as the chronology remains incongruent. Therefore, as we examine the practice of slavery in the Roman Empire, we cannot draw comparisons, nor can we equate it with the practice of chattel slavery in the United States. We know that the apostle Paul, as a Roman citizen who had the benefits of education and the privileges of being a Pharisee, held no opposition to slavery. Some biblical scholars minimize the effect of the system in Rome. They stipulate that it was not that bad, since the Roman slaves were servants and possessed control of their talents, work, bodies, and movement. They characterize the Roman practice of slavery as similar to the system of indentured servitude in Europe and the North American colonies for non-Africans. Moreover, some Bible scholars posit that Roman slaves were professionals in medicine, business, and other trades. Within that cultural and political context, Paul requested forbearance for Onesimus from Philemon.

II. EXPOSITION AND APPLICATION OF THE SCRIPTURE

A. An Appeal for Love's Sake (Philemon 8-11)

Wherefore, though I might be much bold in Christ to enjoin thee that which is convenient, Yet for love's sake I rather beseech thee, being such an one as Paul the aged, and now also a prisoner of Jesus Christ. I beseech thee for my son Onesimus, whom I have begotten in my bonds: Which in time past was to thee unprofitable, but now profitable to thee and to me.

Interestingly, Paul's letter to Philemon was written during one of his periods of imprisonment. Evidently, he minimally considered the mental anguish that the rift in the relationship between the slave master and slave caused. One imagines that Paul had to consider the practical effects of facilitating Onesimus's return to Philemon. Nonetheless, Paul penned this personal letter with the objective of establishing a new relationship between the two men. Again, one imagines Paul's ruminating upon the idea of new creation in which the past faded away completely and the dawn of a new existence emerged. He desired this for Onesimus.

Paul continued his plea for Onesimus in verse 8 (NIV) by using the word *therefore*. In other words, in light of the foundation that had been laid (see verses 4-7), Paul made his request known. What Philemon had experienced from God he must now be ready to offer to Onesimus. The phrase "I might be very bold" (verse 8, NKJV) refers to free and open speaking. The phrase is also an indication that since Paul was older and an apostle, he could have used his authority with Philemon to show him how to treat his runaway slave. But Paul based his request not on his own apostolic authority, but on Philemon's Christian commitment. This also shows that the ground is level at the Cross. The old and the new converts had the same access to the throne of grace. God was and is no respecter of persons. Paul wanted Philemon's heartfelt, not grudging, obedience.

We see that Paul was a humble apostle. He chose not to impose a demand on a new convert, but treated him as equal in the presence of God. When you know something is right and you have the power to demand it, do you appeal to your own authority or do you consider the relationship of the other person with Jesus Christ? Here Paul provided a classic example of how to deal with a possible conflict between Christian brethren. Paul appealed to Philemon to cooperate in this process. Rather than give a harsh treatise in which a runaway slave would be returned indifferently to the horrors of slavery, the letter to Philemon is a mediation document. Paul attempted to restore this slave within the dignity of Christ, since Onesimus was Paul's brother in the Lord. Without addressing the justice and equity of the practice of slavery in Rome, Paul attempted to ensure that his fellow brother in the Lord was treated as he ought to be as a child of God.

In verse 11 (NIV), Paul rhetorically played upon words. He noted that Onesimus's name meant "useful." He acknowledged that he had become useless, due to various circumstances.

However, since becoming a Christian, Onesimus had discovered a new purpose for work and service. He would work as if he worked for the Lord, and not for another human being. He would seek to honor and glorify the Lord in his service. He would forever be useful to any master as he really served the Master. Paul used this linguistic technique to allay any remaining fears that Philemon might have had about Onesimus's work ethic.

B. Paul Sends Onesimus Back
(Philemon 12-14)

Whom I have sent again: thou therefore receive him, that is, mine own bowels: Whom I would have retained with me, that in thy stead he might have ministered unto me in the bonds of the gospel: But without thy mind would I do nothing; that thy benefit should not be as it were of necessity, but willingly.

Onesimus had been converted to the Christian faith; he was no longer a slave in the Roman understanding of the word, but was now a slave of Christ. Onesimus had done something wrong in that he escaped from his master. Paul was aware of the traditional punishment for a runaway slave; hence, he appealed to Philemon to treat Onesimus as a brother. Paul was appealing to Philemon to forget the lifestyle of Onesimus. He was formerly useless, but now was useful. Under Roman law, the slave owner had complete and total control over a slave. It was not unusual for slaves to be crucified for lesser offenses than escape. According to Dr. Lightfoot, "Roman law...practically imposed no limits to the power of the master over his slave." The alternative of life or death rested solely with Philemon. Why did Rome enact harsh penalties against slaves? There were as many as sixty million slaves, so they were capable of staging riots. This is why the Roman

authorities imposed deadly consequences on slaves for violating the law.

Paul wished to keep Onesimus to minister to him in three areas: first, if Onesimus stayed with Paul, it would be like him (Philemon) serving Paul; Onesimus would serve Paul on Philemon's behalf. Such a statement appealed to the law of respect and affection. Second, if Onesimus stayed, he would be helping a man in chains. In other words, Paul was saying, "Philemon, I know Onesimus might be of some use to you. Yet I am in chains, and need all the help I can get." Third, if Onesimus stayed, he would be helping Paul spread the Gospel. Onesimus would become a messenger from Paul to local Christian assemblies. Paul expressed his desire to have Philemon involved in the decision of whether or not Onesimus could remain with him. Therefore, he would act only with Philemon's consent.

Paul had every reason to hold on to his new convert (Onesimus.) But out of respect, Paul would do nothing to hinder Onesimus from going back to his former boss. Sending Onesimus back to his master showed how Paul viewed Philemon, a Christian. Philemon would become an example to other Christian slave owners to forgive their runaway slaves in the name of the Lord. Philemon was a different sort of Christian. He was a Christian full of good deeds. On account of that, Paul was protecting the reputation of Philemon in the midst of ungodly people. In his epistle to the Romans, Paul stated, "Do not let your good be spoken of as evil" (Romans 14:16, NKJV). Philemon's willingness to receive Onesimus back would add more to his reputation as a Christian. Paul gave Philemon the freedom to receive Onesimus of his own choice, not out of Paul's compulsion.

C. Onesimus, a Brother in Christ
(Philemon 15-18)

For perhaps he therefore departed for a season, that thou shouldest receive him for ever; Not now as a servant, but above a servant, a brother beloved, specially to me, but how much more unto thee, both in the flesh, and in the Lord? If thou count me therefore a partner, receive him as myself. If he hath wronged thee, or oweth thee ought, put that on mine account.

Paul explained the providential hand of God at work in Onesimus's escape. Onesimus ran away and the Lord guided him to meet Paul. Paul said, "He departed for a while for this purpose, that you might receive him forever, no longer as a slave but more than a slave—a beloved brother" (see verses 15-16, NKJV). We see how the power of the Gospel can change the foulest sinner into a saint. Paul himself had been an archenemy of Jesus Christ and those who were His followers. But when he encountered Christ, his life was never again the same. The transformation which Paul experienced helped him to vouch for Onesimus. It was true that Philemon had *departed* for a while; the word *departed* does not sound nearly as bad as *escape* or *jump bail*. It was God's plan that Onesimus would run away. There are divine designs that are beyond human understanding, and here was one of them. How would an escaped slave come in contact with a man of God (Paul) and the slave then become a brother in Christ? Paul contrasted the temporary separation of Onesimus's running away to the eternal benefit of his salvation.

Onesimus was on equal footing in God's view with his former boss and Paul. This is expressed in the statement, "no longer as a slave...a beloved brother." The phrase "no longer" expresses the cessation of formal sins and assuming a new life in Christ. God was no longer holding the past against Onesimus. He was now a new creature; old things had passed away. The Greek word used suggests that no one ought to hold the past against Onesimus. God had forgiven him when he encountered Christ through Paul. His forgiveness was as sound as Paul was.

The phrase "both in the flesh and in the Lord" (verse 16, NKJV) suggests that not only would Onesimus be useful in the flesh, but also he would be useful in the work of the Lord. Even though Paul did not categorically denounce slavery, one may deduce that he worked in restoring relationships between slaves and their owners. If Philemon could take Onesimus back as a Christian brother, then the entire Roman Empire had a case to look up to as a reference.

Paul genuinely loved Onesimus and he was ready to pay for his failures. Paul promised to pay whatever Onesimus owed Philemon in full. The use of the phrase "put that on my account" (verse 18, NKJV) is proof of the seriousness with which Paul vouched for Onesimus. The phrase is also a reminder to us of the theological truth that our sins were charged over to Christ, even though He had not earned them. Paul knew that Philemon would accord him the greatest respect and he would want Philemon to extend such to a slave who had come to know Christ as his Lord and Savior. Paul was an authentic Christian. He practiced what he preached. In Christ there is neither Jew nor Gentile, male nor female—we are all heirs of God and joint-heirs with the Lord Jesus Christ.

III. CONCLUDING REFLECTION

If we can see beyond the surface offenses of a human being returning to slavery, we will discover a touching story of Christian friendship. Paul taught us the example of loyalty and advocacy. Surprisingly, the ties of friendship and relationships in the church exceeded the strength of familial connections. Contrary to popular belief, blood was and is not always thicker than water. Paul's courage in standing up for Onesimus eventually transformed his life as he became one of the Christian giants following the apostolic era. Paul's consideration in turn gave Onesimus the strength to change his character. More than being a political and social blight on the pages of the New Testament, Paul's letter to Philemon is a reflection of the potential of the Gospel to renew relationships and change lives, regardless of social position. Quite possibly, it reoriented the destiny of a runaway slave and providentially put him on a path toward the ultimate liberty of unconditional service to Christ.

Are there people who need you to demonstrate such self-sacrifice toward them? Each of us has received forgiveness from God, and we must be willing to forgive others who have wronged us. One writer said, "Forgiveness is hard but it is sweeter than revenge." We must forgive for Jesus' sake.

PRAYER

Our heavenly Father, grant us the grace to understand Your love for us. Help us to forgive as You forgave us. In Jesus' name we pray. Amen.

WORD POWER

Obedience (Greek: *hypakoe* [hypa-ko-e])—means "compliance, submission, or an obedience shown in observing the requirements of Christianity." The etymology of the word suggests hearing through an agency and being ready to comply.

HOME DAILY BIBLE READINGS
(May 17-23, 2010)

At Home in the Community

MONDAY, May 17: "A Faithful and Beloved Brother" (Colossians 4:2-9)

TUESDAY, May 18: "Those Who Love Christ" (John 14:21-24)

WEDNESDAY, May 19: "Love and Service" (John 21:15-19)

THURSDAY, May 20: "Conformed to Christ's Image" (Romans 8:28-39)

FRIDAY, May 21: "An Example of Love" (Philemon 1-7)

SATURDAY, May 22: "A Confidence Based on Love" (Philemon 19-25)

SUNDAY, May 23: "An Appeal to Love" (Philemon 8-18)

LESSON 13   May 30, 2010

AT RISK IN THE COMMUNITY

DEVOTIONAL READING: 1 Timothy 6:3-10
PRINT PASSAGE: Jude 3-7, 19-21, 24-25

BACKGROUND SCRIPTURE: Jude
KEY VERSES: Jude 22-23

Jude 3-7, 19-21, 24-25—KJV

3 Beloved, when I gave all diligence to write unto you of the common salvation, it was needful for me to write unto you, and exhort you that ye should earnestly contend for the faith which was once delivered unto the saints.

4 For there are certain men crept in unawares, who were before of old ordained to this condemnation, ungodly men, turning the grace of our God into lasciviousness, and denying the only Lord God, and our Lord Jesus Christ.

5 I will therefore put you in remembrance, though ye once knew this, how that the Lord, having saved the people out of the land of Egypt, afterward destroyed them that believed not.

6 And the angels which kept not their first estate, but left their own habitation, he hath reserved in everlasting chains under darkness unto the judgment of the great day.

7 Even as Sodom and Gomorrha, and the cities about them in like manner, giving themselves over to fornication, and going after strange flesh, are set forth for an example, suffering the vengeance of eternal fire.

        …..

19 These be they who separate themselves, sensual, having not the Spirit.

20 But ye, beloved, building up yourselves on your most holy faith, praying in the Holy Ghost,

21 Keep yourselves in the love of God, looking for the mercy of our Lord Jesus Christ unto eternal life.

        …..

24 Now unto him that is able to keep you from falling, and to present you faultless before the presence of his glory with exceeding joy,

25 To the only wise God our Saviour, be glory and majesty, dominion and power, both now and ever. Amen.

Jude 3-7, 19-21, 24-25—NRSV

3 Beloved, while eagerly preparing to write to you about the salvation we share, I find it necessary to write and appeal to you to contend for the faith that was once for all entrusted to the saints.

4 For certain intruders have stolen in among you, people who long ago were designated for this condemnation as ungodly, who pervert the grace of our God into licentiousness and deny our only Master and Lord, Jesus Christ.

5 Now I desire to remind you, though you are fully informed, that the Lord, who once for all saved a people out of the land of Egypt, afterward destroyed those who did not believe.

6 And the angels who did not keep their own position, but left their proper dwelling, he has kept in eternal chains in deepest darkness for the judgment of the great Day.

7 Likewise, Sodom and Gomorrah and the surrounding cities, which, in the same manner as they, indulged in sexual immorality and pursued unnatural lust, serve as an example by undergoing a punishment of eternal fire.

        …..

19 It is these worldly people, devoid of the Spirit, who are causing divisions.

20 But you, beloved, build yourselves up on your most holy faith; pray in the Holy Spirit;

21 keep yourselves in the love of God; look forward to the mercy of our Lord Jesus Christ that leads to eternal life.

        …..

24 Now to him who is able to keep you from falling, and to make you stand without blemish in the presence of his glory with rejoicing,

25 to the only God our Savior, through Jesus Christ our Lord, be glory, majesty, power, and authority, before all time and now and forever. Amen.

TOPICAL OUTLINE OF THE LESSON

I. Introduction
A. A Lingering Danger in the Church
B. Biblical Background

II. Exposition and Application of the Scripture
A. Appeal to Contend for the True Faith (Jude 3-7)
B. Appeal for Personal Spiritual Growth (Jude 19-21)
C. Concluding Doxology (Jude 24-25)

III. Concluding Reflection

LESSON OBJECTIVES

Upon completion of this lesson, the students will be able to:

1. Distinguish between true and false teachings;
2. Withstand and stand for the truth of the Gospel; and,
3. Define ways in which we can assist at-risk believers in committing to disciplined study of the Bible.

POINTS TO BE EMPHASIZED

ADULT/YOUTH
Adult Topic: Tempering Judgment with Mercy
Youth Topic: Are You for Real?
Adult Key Verses: Jude 22-23
Youth Key Verses: Jude 24-25
Print Passage: Jude 3-7, 19-21, 24-25

—The letter was written in part to counter the idea that Jesus only seemed to be a human (Docetism).
—The letter encouraged the church to eradicate doctrines and practices that were contrary to apostolic doctrine.
—The author of the letter warned the church that wrong teaching led to wrong thinking and behaving.
—One specific area of concern in the letter of Jude was that denying Christ's return and coming judgment became a license for immorality.
—Jude reminded them that God condemned those who were rebellious and unfaithful.
—Jude specifically warned that some ungodly people masquerade as Christians.
—He implored the faithful to build their faith, have mercy on those who were lost but could be saved, and have mercy on those who could not.

CHILDREN
Children Topic: Hold On to Truth
Key Verse: Jude 3
Print Passage: Jude 3-7, 19-21, 24-25

—We are told little about Jude except that he was "A servant of Jesus Christ and brother of James" (verse 1, NRSV).
—Jude was alarmed by false teachings among the Christians.
—He pleaded for the Christians to resist false teaching and struggle for and hold on to the faith.

—Jude told the Christians some actions they could take in keeping the faith.

—The last two verses of the book of Jude are a benediction.

I. INTRODUCTION

A. A Lingering Danger in the Church

The inability to distinguish clearly between the principles and actions of the church and those of secular society depicts one of the church's greatest spiritual needs today. Debatably, there is no discernible difference between the behavior of believers and the average citizen. More regrettably, the church mimics the world rather than being the "called-out community" *(ecclesia)* whose existence is fundamentally grounded in the will and service of our Lord Jesus Christ. To resolve this intractable dilemma, the church must return to its basic purpose as a biblically based New Testament church, operating according to the teachings of our Lord.

Reaffirming the Bible as the rule of faith and practice resolves a number of attendant problems for the local church. Moral and ethical laxity in the pews arises from protracted biblical illiteracy. Plainly speaking, most congregants do not know the Bible well enough to follow it. They are not acquainted with the commands of Christ. They cannot explain adequately the reasons why obeying our Lord supercedes the moral relativism and ethical aimlessness of the dominant culture.

Ignorance of the Scriptures precludes the development of a wobbly relationship with the Lord. Evangelism inevitably suffers when believers do not understand the Great Commission. They fail to commit the resources of time, money, and service to actualize this crucial purpose of the church. It stands to reason then that countless lives remain untouched by Christ's love. Additionally, disregard for disciplined study of the Word of God creates vulnerability for the average believer who may be exploited by the crass commercialism practiced in several sectors of the church.

B. Biblical Background

The book of Jude came out of a context of protracted false teaching in the church. As the first century neared an end and the original apostles died, preserving the legitimacy of the primary Gospel message became a substantial challenge for the growing church. This reality produced a vacuum that many false teachers gladly occupied. For selfish, financial, social, and ecclesiastical gain, these men purposefully distorted the Gospel of Christ.

In response, Jude desired to help believers who were at-risk in discerning the content of true and false teachings. The book reminded disciples to cling steadfastly to the orthodox faith that the apostles bequeathed to them. Moreover, Jude encouraged believers to persevere in their belief in the divinity and saving work of

Jesus Christ. Interestingly, Christian heresy usually arises from a failure to acknowledge unwaveringly the divinity of Jesus of Nazareth. In conjunction with detailing the forthcoming judgment on false teachers, Jude offered strategies for reclaiming victims and other at-risk believers of these distortions of the Gospel.

II. EXPOSITION AND APPLICATION OF THE SCRIPTURE

A. Appeal to Contend for the True Faith (Jude 3-7)

Beloved, when I gave all diligence to write unto you of the common salvation, it was needful for me to write unto you, and exhort you that ye should earnestly contend for the faith which was once delivered unto the saints. For there are certain men crept in unawares, who were before of old ordained to this condemnation, ungodly men, turning the grace of our God into lasciviousness, and denying the only Lord God, and our Lord Jesus Christ. I will therefore put you in remembrance, though ye once knew this, how that the Lord, having saved the people out of the land of Egypt, afterward destroyed them that believed not. And the angels which kept not their first estate, but left their own habitation, he hath reserved in everlasting chains under darkness unto the judgment of the great day. Even as Sodom and Gomorrha, and the cities about them in like manner, giving themselves over to fornication, and going after strange flesh, are set forth for an example, suffering the vengeance of eternal fire.

Jude called his recipients *beloved,* a term that signified Christian brothers and sisters. The term *beloved* has gone out of fashion among Christians today; we prefer titles like reverend, apostle, bishop, the right reverend, and so forth. However, in Christ we are beloved. The word *beloved* also signifies saints. Through the death and resurrection of Christ, Christians are saints. The use of the phrase "I was very diligent to write to you" (Jude 3, NKJV), in the opening of this epistle, seems to indicate that Jude intended to write a more general doctrinal letter, but the crisis at hand necessitated this shorter epistle. There was doctrinal error going around that could overthrow the faith of many among the beloved, and Jude was ready to quickly nip it in the bud.

When Jude spoke of *common salvation,* he was referring to the unity that all believers have in Christ Jesus. Even though Jude used the words *common salvation,* it should be understood that our salvation is not common in the sense of being cheap. Our salvation came from only one source, and that is through Jesus Christ. Our salvation caused God to give His only Son, who died a painful death on the cross. Another way of understanding the commonality of our faith is that all believers—Jews or Gentiles, slaves or masters, men or women—come through the same door: Jesus Christ. The common faith in Jesus Christ places us all in the same community. To be a Christian means one belongs to millions of Christians who are present and those who have gone to their reward.

On the basis of the commonality of Christian faith, Jude appealed to his readers to contend earnestly for their faith. The heretics were subtle. Their primary tactics were to pervert God's grace and to deny the authority of the Lord (see Proverbs 1:29). There are many pseudo-religions claiming to know God and overthrowing the faith of many so-called Christians. The faith that was delivered to the saints of old is worth contending for. The phrase *the faith* means "the essential truths of the Gospel that all the Christians hold in common."

The word *once* is very important in this section. It means that faith was delivered one time and there will be no more repetition. We are distributing this faith from generation to generation. There is no other gospel and there will be none. Therefore we must continue to silence the heretics among us. The heretics are the ungodly men and women who in our day believe that Jesus is not the only way to God. They believe Christianity is one of the many ways to God. Many of these people are in our Bible colleges and seminaries and some are pastors in churches around the nation.

In verses 5-7, Jude gave three examples of rebellion—namely: 1) the children of Israel, who, although they were delivered from Egypt, refused to trust God and enter the Promised Land (see Numbers 14:26-39); 2) some of the angels, although they were once pure, holy, and living in God's presence, became prideful (see 2 Peter 2:4); and 3) the inhabitants of the cities of Sodom and Gomorrah were so sin-soaked that God wiped them out of existence (see Genesis 19:1-29). The conclusion is that if the chosen people, the angels, and sinful cities were wiped out because of sin, false teachers will also be severely punished.

B. Appeal for Personal Spiritual Growth (Jude 19-21)

These be they who separate themselves, sensual, having not the Spirit. But ye, beloved, building up yourselves on your most holy faith, praying in the Holy Ghost, Keep yourselves in the love of God, looking for the mercy of our Lord Jesus Christ unto eternal life.

Before this section, Jude described in detail the characteristics of these men (see verses 16-18). But in verse 19 (NIV), he called them "sensual persons." In other words, these people were not spiritual—they were carnal and insensitive to the Holy Spirit. *Sensual* in this context has nothing to do with sexual attractiveness. Rather, it describes the person who lives only by and for what he or she can get through the physical senses. These people are dead spiritually. Their lifestyles are what we call *hedonistic,* meaning, "If it feels good, do it," or, "How can it be wrong if it feels so good?" Jude said they caused division among believers. In many Bible colleges and seminaries, there are instructors whose theological point of view is diametrically opposed to that of the Word of God. They cause a lot of division in the body of Christ because of their lopsided theology. When Jude declared that the false teachers were without the Spirit, he left no doubt as to their eternal destiny. The false teachers of our day are also going to face the judgment of God at God's own time.

The phrase "not having the Spirit" could be written over many local bodies of believers, or church projects. In our day, we need men and women who fear the Lord and are ready to stand up for the truth. In verse 20, Jude told us how to keep ourselves in the love of God. Jude was advocating an inward-looking approach to Christian living. He wanted believers to keep themselves in harmony with God's ever-present love. Just as Paul reminded readers (in Romans 8:35-39) that nothing could separate us from the love of God, Jude warned about the same thing. Christians must cultivate a deep, spiritual walk with God. Christians must continue to nurture their spiritual growth through fervent prayers in the Spirit. Jude encouraged believers to be mindful of their spiritual condition. They must learn how to grow in the grace of God. Jude in essence was saying that evil teachers were here to stay and, therefore, it was imperative for individual Christians not to give in to their heresies. It stands to reason that defending the true and enduring Gospel of Christ necessitates a thorough knowledge of the same. This defense cannot merely be verbal and theoretical. It must also be evident in the way that believers live. Consequently, obedience in daily living to the teachings of Christ is as important as oral consent.

C. Concluding Doxology
(Jude 24-25)
Now unto him that is able to keep you from falling, and to present you faultless before the presence of his glory with exceeding joy, To the only wise God our Saviour, be glory and majesty, dominion and power, both now and ever. Amen.

Jude concluded his epistle with a famous doxology, a brief declaration of praise to God. This doxology is a reminder to us of God's care and of our destiny. The phrase "Now unto Him" (verse 24) is a heartfelt prayer to God. Having exposed the plan and plot of the evil teachers and their end, Jude now handed over the lives of his readers to God. Jude never met most of his readers, but he trusted in God, the Father of mercies. He believed that God was able to keep believers to the end. The evil teachers had corrupted so many lives that the concern was whether they would get to heaven or not. However, Jude said that God was able to keep one from the power of the evil one. Christians were and are not able to keep themselves, but God was and is able to keep them from falling into the trap of the evil one. God would keep His own spiritually safe to the end. Paul essentially said the same thing: "Being confident of this very thing, that He who has begun a good work in you will complete it until the day of Jesus Christ" (Philippians 1:6, NKJV).

The love of God never fails. Jude encouraged his readers to know that Jesus Christ will uphold believers to the end, and He will one day present them faultless before the Father. The presentation will be glorious; Jude was short of words in describing the scene. Because God is faithful, we will not appear before Him in shame. The word *faultless* is a Greek word used to describe "sacrificial animals that had no blemish"—thus fit to be offered to God. We are called to be holy and to a partnership with God, and He will not abandon us halfway. The phrase "Who alone is wise… Both now and forever" (verse 25, NKJV) is a reminder to us of God's wisdom, glory, majesty, and power. "Both now and forever" is a complete statement about eternity. Our victory and our triumph over the evil one and his followers are forever.

III. CONCLUDING REFLECTION

Primarily, the book of Jude combated the rising heresy of Docetism. This teaching relegated Jesus Christ to an incomparable moral philosopher. Its adherents stipulated that a divine Christ would not have submitted to crucifixion. They reasoned that God would not condescend to subject Himself to the whims and actions of finite humankind. Accordingly, they further reasoned that an image of Christ was crucified for those who believed that they saw the actual, physical body of Christ on the cross. Furthermore, they extended this teaching by denouncing the return of Christ and the subsequent judgment of the world and its inhabitants from time immemorial. Essentially, these teachings left their followers with license to interpret the Gospel as they pleased.

Jude forcefully warned the church to discard irretrievably any doctrines and practices that contradicted the original apostolic teachings. First, the apostles learned directly from the Lord for three and a half years—the course of His public ministry. Any teaching that did not correlate with their message and the writings directly linked to them should have been eradicated. Second, the author of the book of Jude cautioned the church that faulty teaching resulted in fallacious thinking and morally questionable behavior. Almost immediately, this confusion yielded a license for sin and indulgence for people of self-centered motives and physical instincts. Third, Jude suggested that the faithful offer mercy and compassion to the unfaithful, but exhorted them to do so without being unduly influenced by the unfaithful.

The book of Jude serves as a reminder to us to return to the basics of knowing the Word, so that we might rightly divide the sermons and teachings that we hear.

PRAYER

Lord, help us to hide Your Word in our hearts so that we might not sin against You. Embolden us with Your Spirit so that we may stand firm in defense of Your truth. In Jesus' name we pray. Amen.

WORD POWER

Difference (Greek: *diakrino* [di-a-kri-no])—means "to separate, make a distinction, and contend." The word *difference* is found in the Key Verse. In this context, it means there are Christians who are making distinctions in their witnessing. They are able to separate false statements from the truth. Basically, we must try to bring back those who have been seduced by evil teachers.

HOME DAILY BIBLE READINGS
(May 24-30, 2010)

At Risk in the Community

MONDAY, May 24: "Godliness and Contentment" (1 Timothy 6:3-10)

TUESDAY, May 25: "Seeking a Lost Sheep" (Luke 15:1-7)

WEDNESDAY, May 26: "Searching for a Lost Coin" (Luke 15:8-10)

THURSDAY, May 27: "Welcoming a Lost Son" (Luke 15:11-24)

FRIDAY, May 28: "Rebuke of the Unprincipled" (Jude 8-16)

SATURDAY, May 29: "Admonition to Faith and Mercy" (Jude 17-25)

SUNDAY, May 30: "Contend for the Faith" (Jude 3-7)

Christian Commitment in Today's World

GENERAL INTRODUCTION

The study this quarter is a focus on Christian commitment. Its three units are explorations of the nature, foundation, and marks of commitment as they apply to Christians in today's world.

Unit I, *The Naure of Christian Commitment,* has four lessons. The first is an affirmation that genuine commitment is visible to others. Lesson 2 sets Christian commitment within the context of the desire to please God. Lesson 3 is an exploration of how believers sustain one another in their commitment. Lesson 4 is a look at the way in which Christian commitment is both reinforced and strengthened by concrete actions that grow out of a desire to please God.

Unit II, *The Foundation of Christian Commitment,* includes lessons 5–8. Lesson 5 sets Christian commitment within the cosmic context of God's plan for all creation. Lesson 6 is a description of the aim of commitment as giving glory to Christ. Lesson 7 is an affirmation that Christian commitment grows from a response to being chosen by God and sanctified by the Spirit. Lesson 8 is an exploration of how the ability to stay committed is grounded in God's faithfulness.

Unit III, *The Marks of Christian Commitment,* embraces lessons 9–13. Lessons 9 and 10 are explorations of how God sustains the faithful in all circumstances and calls them, through Jesus' example, to claim life through serving others. Lesson 11 is a look at how Christian commitment draws believers into the future, preoccupied with God's mission in Christ. Lesson 12 is a description of the joy and peace of commitment, and lesson 13 is a focus on how human commitment is upheld by God's commitment and faithfulness.

*The lessons for the children flesh out the concepts from the books of Thessalonians, Philippians, and Jude, with stories from the book of Acts about Paul's later journeys.

DAVID PRAISING THE LORD

יהוה

Praise him with the sound of a trumpet,
Praise him with the Psaltery and Harp.
Psalm CL. v. 3.

Pub. by Hogg & C.º Paternoster row.

LESSON 1

June 6, 2010

VISIBLE TO GOD

DEVOTIONAL READING: **Titus 2:11-15**
PRINT PASSAGE: **1 Thessalonians 1:1-10**

BACKGROUND SCRIPTURE: **1 Thessalonians 1**
KEY VERSE: **1 Thessalonians 1:6**

1 Thessalonians 1:1-10—KJV

PAUL, AND Silvanus, and Timotheus, unto the church of the Thessalonians which is in God the Father and in the Lord Jesus Christ: Grace be unto you, and peace, from God our Father, and the Lord Jesus Christ.

2 We give thanks to God always for you all, making mention of you in our prayers;

3 Remembering without ceasing your work of faith, and labour of love, and patience of hope in our Lord Jesus Christ, in the sight of God and our Father;

4 Knowing, brethren beloved, your election of God.

5 For our gospel came not unto you in word only, but also in power, and in the Holy Ghost, and in much assurance; as ye know what manner of men we were among you for your sake.

6 And ye became followers of us, and of the Lord, having received the word in much affliction, with joy of the Holy Ghost:

7 So that ye were ensamples to all that believe in Macedonia and Achaia.

8 For from you sounded out the word of the Lord not only in Macedonia and Achaia, but also in every place your faith to God-ward is spread abroad; so that we need not to speak any thing.

9 For they themselves shew of us what manner of entering in we had unto you, and how ye turned to God from idols to serve the living and true God;

10 And to wait for his Son from heaven, whom he raised from the dead, even Jesus, which delivered us from the wrath to come.

1 Thessalonians 1:1-10—NRSV

PAUL, SILVANUS, and Timothy, To the church of the Thessalonians in God the Father and the Lord Jesus Christ: Grace to you and peace.

2 We always give thanks to God for all of you and mention you in our prayers, constantly

3 remembering before our God and Father your work of faith and labor of love and steadfastness of hope in our Lord Jesus Christ.

4 For we know, brothers and sisters beloved by God, that he has chosen you,

5 because our message of the gospel came to you not in word only, but also in power and in the Holy Spirit and with full conviction; just as you know what kind of persons we proved to be among you for your sake.

6 And you became imitators of us and of the Lord, for in spite of persecution you received the word with joy inspired by the Holy Spirit,

7 so that you became an example to all the believers in Macedonia and in Achaia.

8 For the word of the Lord has sounded forth from you not only in Macedonia and Achaia, but in every place your faith in God has become known, so that we have no need to speak about it.

9 For the people of those regions report about us what kind of welcome we had among you, and how you turned to God from idols, to serve a living and true God,

10 and to wait for his Son from heaven, whom he raised from the dead—Jesus, who rescues us from the wrath that is coming.

BIBLE FACT

THE THESSALONIANS: The church in Thessalonica was founded around AD 51, during Paul's second missionary journey. Some were envious of the success of this church and started to foment trouble. The epistle was written to encourage the young church to remain faithful in the face of opposition and give them the assurance of Christ's return.

TOPICAL OUTLINE OF THE LESSON

I. Introduction
    A. Congregational Effectiveness
    B. Biblical Background

II. Exposition and Application of the Scripture
    A. Paul's Words of Greeting (1 Thessalonians 1:1)
    B. Paul's Prayer of Thanksgiving (1 Thessalonians 1:2-5)
    C. Paul's Glowing Commendation (1 Thessalonians 1:6-10)

III. Concluding Reflection

LESSON OBJECTIVES

Upon completion of this lesson, the students will know that:

1. The church in Thessalonica exemplified a Christlike spirit;
2. Christians' congregational effectiveness comes from commitment to Christ; and,
3. Behind the spirit of commitment is love for fellow believers.

POINTS TO BE EMPHASIZED

ADULT/YOUTH

Adult Topic: Witness in Daily Life
Youth Topic: Seeing Is Believing
Adult/Youth Key Verse: 1 Thessalonians 1:6
Print Passage: 1 Thessalonians 1:1-10

—*Silvanus* is a variant of the name *Silas* in Greek.
—In Paul's time, Thessalonica was part of the vast Roman Empire and a commercial and cultic center of Greece.
—The first converts of Paul and Silas in Thessalonica were subjected to persecution.
—Paul praised the church for being an example to others.
—Paul told the Thessalonians how thankful he was for their strong faith and steady looking forward to Christ's return.
—The Thessalonians listened to and believed in Paul's witness to them about the truth of Jesus Christ.
—The Thessalonians became examples to others of what it means to have faith in God.
—The Thessalonians believed in the resurrection of Jesus Christ and that He is our only Savior from God's wrath.

CHILDREN

Children Topic: Be an Example to Others
Key Verse: 1 Thessalonians 1:7
Print Passage: Acts 17:1-9; 1 Thessalonians 1:8-10

—Paul's preaching about Christ converted Jews and Greeks, both men and women.
—Paul's proclamation of Christ also caused controversy in Thessalonica.
—Later Paul wrote to the Thessalonians, congratulating them on their steadfast faith and hope.

—The Thessalonians believed the good news and became examples to others.
—The faith of the Thessalonians became widely known, and it led many others to believe in God.

I. INTRODUCTION

A. Congregational Effectiveness

How do you measure a congregation's effectiveness? The drive to answer this question is one of the consuming quests of many church leaders. Conferences, seminars, and workshops are conducted annually and attended by thousands of church leaders, all seeking the same thing: the key to becoming an effective congregation. There is no shortage of published material on how to achieve every pastor's elusive dream—congregational effectiveness. I have attended conferences and workshops, but to no avail. There is but one way to become an effective congregation—that is to passionately, intentionally, and faithfully pursue the purposes of the Lord Jesus Christ. In the summer of 1983, I read a book by Joe S. Ellis entitled *The Church on Purpose: Keys to Effective Church Leadership*. His book energized my thinking about creating the climate for congregational effectiveness. The basic premise of the book is that "commitment to purpose is the key to a congregation's effectiveness." In effective congregations every effort is made to ensure that the congregation is focused on the larger strategic purpose of God—that the entire world should be saved. When the people of God have a clear sense of the purpose of Christ, embraced by all, the church will not only grow, but also will achieve great results in the name of the Lord Jesus Christ. This is one of the central lessons of today's study. The church in Thessalonica became a powerful and influential witness of the grace of God in Macedonia. Why? They remained true to the purpose of Jesus Christ.

B. Biblical Background

First Thessalonians is one of the epistles of Paul. It, like all of the epistles of Paul, was a really personal conversation that Paul had with the churches he founded. They were originally intended to be read by the people to whom he addressed them.

In order to understand the letter and the circumstances that gave rise to the contents of the letter, it will be helpful if we understand its historical, geographical, and cultural context by asking some relevant questions.

1. *When was the church in Thessalonica founded?*
   The church was established during Paul's second missionary journey. According to Acts 16:8-9, Paul had a vision that he was called by a Macedonian man to come over and help them.
2. *Why go to Thessalonica?*
   It was the most prominent city in the region. It was the major commercial, agricultural,

and political city in Macedonia. It was the Roman capital of Macedonia and was a free city. There was a large Jewish population living in Thessalonica.

3. *What were the circumstances surrounding the establishment of the church?*
   When Paul and his companions arrived in Thessalonica, they found lodging, and went to the Jewish synagogue on the Sabbath day. Paul always began his initial missionary work in cities that had Jewish synagogues.

4. *Why did Paul, Silas, and Timothy leave the city?*
   The Jews became jealous of their success and literally ran them out of town. They hired some thugs and caused a riot in the city (see Acts 17:5-10).

II. EXPOSITION AND APPLICATION OF THE SCRIPTURE

A. Paul's Words of Greeting
(1 Thessalonians 1:1)

PAUL, AND Silvanus, and Timotheus, unto the church of the Thessalonians which is in God the Father and in the Lord Jesus Christ: Grace be unto you, and peace, from God our Father, and the Lord Jesus Christ.

The discoveries of hundreds of ancient manuscripts and writings that go back to the first century have been an invaluable resource in understanding Paul's epistle. His epistles certainly fit the form and style of ancient letters of that day. Paul began by indicating that he and Silvanus (Silas) and Timotheus (Timothy) were all together. He did not refer to himself using the title of "apostle"; this would come in later letters. Silas and Timothy were two most well-known early Christian missionaries. Silas joined Paul after the split with Barnabas (see Acts 15:36-41; compare also to Acts 15:22, 32; 2 Corinthians 1:19). Timothy met Paul and joined him during his second missionary journey through Derbe and Lystra (see Acts 16:1-3; compare also to Acts 19:22; 1 Corinthians 4:17; Philippians 2:19; 2 Timothy 1:5; 3:14-15).

The letter was addressed to the entire church of Thessalonica. Paul used what came to be a customary greeting, extending peace and grace to the saints "from God our Father and the Lord Jesus Christ." Two important words in Paul's belief system were used in this greeting: *grace* and *peace*. *Grace* is the unmerited favor of God bestowed freely and without works. God is the source of our peace. *Peace* with God is the result of the finished work of Jesus Christ at Calvary (see Romans 5:18; Ephesians 2:14-15). Paul connected these two words time after time in later letters to other churches.

B. Paul's Prayer of Thanksgiving
(1 Thessalonians 1:2-5)

We give thanks to God always for you all, making mention of you in our prayers; Remembering without ceasing your work of faith, and labour of love, and patience of hope in our Lord Jesus Christ, in the sight of God and our Father; Knowing, brethren beloved, your election of God. For our gospel came not unto you in word only, but also in power, and in the Holy Ghost, and in much assurance; as ye know what manner of men we were among you for your sake.

The Thessalonians were very dear to Paul's heart. His words of thanksgiving convey three primary thoughts. First, he thanked God for them and he would tell them why later in the chapter. Second, he reminded them that he prayed constantly and consistently for them. Third, he prayed for them and he wanted the people to know it.

In verse 3, he wrote: "Remembering without ceasing." This was Paul's way of indicating what he was thankful to God for. The phrase "work of faith" means that when the Thessalonians were saved, good works resulted from their new lives in Jesus Christ. He was not saying that they were saved because they performed good works. We know from Scripture that religious works cannot save people (see Romans 3:28; Galatians 2:14). Here is the point of the phrase: *their faith led to work.* We are saved to become servants of God. In Ephesians 2:8-9 it is stated, "For by grace are ye saved through faith; and that not of yourselves: it is the gift of God: Not of works, lest any man should boast." God has called us to a level of Christian service into which we have not even begun to tap.

Second, Paul pointed to their labor of love. This is another interesting phrase; these words have come to be used to describe some work that we do for pleasure. Some people see gardening as a "labor of love." It is something that they get great enjoyment out of doing. In the passage, this is a powerful combination of two powerful words: *labor*—which means "to toil; to labor to the point of exhaustion; to arduously work"; when a person truly loves Christ, he or she is prompted and driven to arduously labor for Christ; and *love* (used here as *agape*—the highest and greatest manifestation of love for God and humans). Paul recalled their intense labor for God, which was prompted by their love for Him. The love expressed here was not simply an emotional response; rather, it speaks of intensive labors in the kingdom that is prompted by a zealous love for God the Father. Love stirs up the church to labor.

Third, Paul pointed to their patience and hope. *Hope* is the source of the believer's endurance. *Hope* is a word that is always future-oriented (see Psalm 39:7; Romans 8:24-25). Hope looks beyond the current situation and sees the other side of darkness. We endure because we know in our spirits that trouble will not always last. We press on because we know that awaiting us is a crown of righteousness. We suffer for the cause of Christ because we know that the Lord will not allow satanic powers to overwhelm or destroy us (see 2 Corinthians 4:7-10, 16).

The word *election* in verse 4 is a reference to God's having chosen the Thessalonians for salvation, as He has chosen all men and women to be saved. *Election* is a word that points to God's sovereign right to choose people and places for His own purpose. Abraham was chosen (see Genesis 12:1f.), Israel was chosen (see Deuteronomy 7:6), and Jerusalem is chosen to be the Holy City (see 2 Chronicles 6:2, 34). Believers are called and chosen according to God's purpose (see Romans 8:28). Paul referred to the Thessalonians as the people who were loved by God.

Verse 5 serves as a conclusion to the formal greeting by reminding them how they came to faith in Jesus Christ. Paul had made the Gospel his—not that he was the origin of it, but it had impacted his life to the extent that he made it his. He called it "Our gospel," the good news about the love of God demonstrated in Jesus Christ (see Romans 5:8-10). It was the message Paul was not ashamed to preach (see Romans 1:16).

This Gospel had come to the Thessalonians in four ways: first, it was through the use of words; second, these words were accompanied by preaching with power; third, the words were delivered through the agency of the Holy Spirit who brought conviction to the Thessalonians (see also Acts 2:1-4; 1 Corinthians 2:1-5); and fourth, the Word was preached with assurance. It was not just a Word to be delivered, but it was first believed and fully embraced by Paul (see 2 Timothy 1:12). Paul's faith was not just talk, but a practical demonstration and manifestation of the power of God. They could look at his life and discern the depth of his faith and confidence in God (see James 1:22-27).

C. Paul's Glowing Commendation (1 Thessalonians 1:6-10)

And ye became followers of us, and of the Lord, having received the word in much affliction, with joy of the Holy Ghost: So that ye were ensamples to all that believe in Macedonia and Achaia. For from you sounded out the word of the Lord not only in Macedonia and Achaia, but also in every place your faith to God-ward is spread abroad; so that we need not to speak any thing. For they themselves shew of us what manner of entering in we had unto you, and how ye turned to God from idols to serve the living and true God; And to wait for his Son from heaven, whom he raised from the dead, even Jesus, which delivered us from the wrath to come.

Paul commended the Thessalonians for several reasons. First, they had become imitators and followers of him and of the Lord. This seems a bit backwards at first, but the reality is that the first Bible that the unchurched and unconverted read was the lives of the disciples of Jesus Christ. Paul would use these words again in other letters (see 1 Corinthians 4:11; 11:1). The preaching of the Gospel in Thessalonica was not without challenge, opposition, and persecution (see Acts 17:5-9). Their afflictions did not temper their joy. They were filled with the joy of the Holy Spirit. Their joy in Christ pushed them to become even more active in the spread of the Gospel throughout Macedonia. They became an example for all of the believers in Macedonia and Achaia (verse 7). This was an area that practically covered all of Greece. Here was one church whose faith, witness, and example of faith under pressure served to encourage all of the other believers in the region. Their faith was known, but also they proclaimed the Gospel throughout the area. The phrase "For from you" meant that they were evangelistic in their focus. They were more concerned that people be brought to the reality of the saving faith in the Lord Jesus Christ. Their faith was spread abroad, evidently to the extent that everywhere he went people had already heard about the new church in Thessalonica. This is a very far cry from what we want our churches to be known for today. Congregations today seek to be known for their buildings, youth and children's ministries, women's ministries, social ministries, Christian education ministries, preaching ministries, and praise and worship ministries. But very few are known as evangelistic congregations that actively engage in soul winning.

In verses 9-10, Paul reported that everywhere he went the Word was the same. He made three specific statements that he had heard about the Thessalonians. First, they turned from idols. This clearly indicated that the majority of the converts in Thessalonica were Gentiles, who were worshipers of idols. Second, it was reported that they were serving the true and living God. This was one whom he called their Father as well as the Father of the Lord Jesus Christ. Third, he mentioned that they lived with expectant hope of the Lord's return.

They were waiting for the Son of God to come from heaven, a theme that Paul would examine more fully in chapter 4.

III. CONCLUDING REFLECTION

This epistle speaks out of a genuine spirit of love and compassion for other believers. Paul wrote because he was deeply concerned about how the believers in Thessalonica were doing. They had undergone intensive persecution, and he was not aware of how they were faring. He did not know if they were still a viable congregation. He did not know if they had given in to the attacks of persecution. He did not know whether or not any of them had been murdered for their beliefs. He simply did not know how they were doing. And this only increased his level of anxiety concerning their well-being.

In their efforts to become religious success stories, many churches have lost the sense of warmth and hospitality. We are extremely busy today, even in our houses of worship. And that gives an air of effectiveness in ministry—but being busy, hustling and bustling about are never the true marks of a Christian congregation. This simply says one is good at organizing activity. Unless we guard our hearts and spirits, we can become mechanical, a kind of auto-pilot religion moved by rote learning and customary practices. We can forget that Christianity is not just a religion of dogmas, doctrines, and disciplines, but is intensely relational and personal. We are at our best when we live out the ethic of love and mutual respect for one another.

PRAYER

Eternal God, grant us the will and minds to follow You. May our lives mirror the life of Jesus Christ in such a way that others will want to follow You. In Jesus' name we pray. Amen.

WORD POWER

Imitators (Greek: *mimites*)—the word means "followers." To be a follower in the context of this lesson means that the followers believed the same truths, walked in the same ways, and minded the same things. The manner of life of the follower is consistent with the declared truth. The Thessalonians were true imitators of Christ, who was preached to them by Paul.

HOME DAILY BIBLE READINGS
(May 31–June 6, 2010)

Visible to God

> MONDAY, May 31: "God Sees All" (Ezekiel 14:1-8)
> TUESDAY, June 1: "A Purified People" (Titus 2:11-15)
> WEDNESDAY, June 2: "Faith and Convictions" (Romans 14:22-23)
> THURSDAY, June 3: "Imitators of Christ" (1 Corinthians 10:23–11:1)
> FRIDAY, June 4: "The Outcomes of Faith" (Hebrews 13:1-7)
> SATURDAY, June 5: "Following Christ's Example" (John 13:3-15)
> SUNDAY, June 6: "An Exemplary Faith" (1 Thessalonians 1)

LESSON 2   **June 13, 2010**

PLEASING TO GOD

DEVOTIONAL READING: **Galatians 1:1-10**
PRINT PASSAGE: **1 Thessalonians 2:1-12**

BACKGROUND SCRIPTURE: **1 Thessalonians 2**
KEY VERSE: **1 Thessalonians 2:4**

1 Thessalonians 2:1-12—KJV

FOR YOURSELVES, brethren, know our entrance in unto you, that it was not in vain:

2 But even after that we had suffered before, and were shamefully entreated, as ye know, at Philippi, we were bold in our God to speak unto you the gospel of God with much contention.

3 For our exhortation was not of deceit, nor of uncleanness, nor in guile:

4 But as we were allowed of God to be put in trust with the gospel, even so we speak; not as pleasing men, but God, which trieth our hearts.

5 For neither at any time used we flattering words, as ye know, nor a cloke of covetousness; God is witness:

6 Nor of men sought we glory, neither of you, nor yet of others, when we might have been burdensome, as the apostles of Christ.

7 But we were gentle among you, even as a nurse cherisheth her children:

8 So being affectionately desirous of you, we were willing to have imparted unto you, not the gospel of God only, but also our own souls, because ye were dear unto us.

9 For ye remember, brethren, our labour and travail: for labouring night and day, because we would not be chargeable unto any of you, we preached unto you the gospel of God.

10 Ye are witnesses, and God also, how holily and justly and unblameably we behaved ourselves among you that believe:

11 As ye know how we exhorted and comforted and charged every one of you, as a father doth his children,

12 That ye would walk worthy of God, who hath called you unto his kingdom and glory.

1 Thessalonians 2:1-12—NRSV

YOU YOURSELVES know, brothers and sisters, that our coming to you was not in vain,

2 but though we had already suffered and been shamefully mistreated at Philippi, as you know, we had courage in our God to declare to you the gospel of God in spite of great opposition.

3 For our appeal does not spring from deceit or impure motives or trickery,

4 but just as we have been approved by God to be entrusted with the message of the gospel, even so we speak, not to please mortals, but to please God who tests our hearts.

5 As you know and as God is our witness, we never came with words of flattery or with a pretext for greed;

6 nor did we seek praise from mortals, whether from you or from others,

7 though we might have made demands as apostles of Christ. But we were gentle among you, like a nurse tenderly caring for her own children.

8 So deeply do we care for you that we are determined to share with you not only the gospel of God but also our own selves, because you have become very dear to us.

9 You remember our labor and toil, brothers and sisters; we worked night and day, so that we might not burden any of you while we proclaimed to you the gospel of God.

10 You are witnesses, and God also, how pure, upright, and blameless our conduct was toward you believers.

11 As you know, we dealt with each one of you like a father with his children,

12 urging and encouraging you and pleading that you lead a life worthy of God, who calls you into his own kingdom and glory.

TOPICAL OUTLINE OF THE LESSON

I. **Introduction**
   A. Religious Conviction
   B. Biblical Background

II. **Exposition and Application of the Scripture**
   A. Preachers that Made a Difference
      (1 Thessalonians 2:1-2)
   B. Preachers with Integrity and Character
      (1 Thessalonians 2:3-4)
   C. Preachers with Compassionate Hearts
      (1 Thessalonians 2:5-8)
   D. Preachers Walking Worthy
      (1 Thessalonians 2:9-12)

III. **Concluding Reflection**

LESSON OBJECTIVES

Upon completion of this lesson, the students will know that:

1. Paul was not just an apostle but a man with a true pastoral heart;
2. In the face of opposition and criticisms, Christians must not give up; and,
3. Living a holy life is imperative for every child of God.

POINTS TO BE EMPHASIZED

ADULT/YOUTH

Adult Topic: Motives for Commitment
Youth Topic: Setting Good Goals
Adult Key Verse: 1 Thessalonians 2:4
Youth Key Verse: 1 Thessalonians 2:2
Print Passage: 1 Thessalonians 2:1-12

—Paul referenced his experience in Philippi where he and Silas (Silvanus) suffered physical violence (see Acts 16:22-24).
—Paul used family terms to describe relationships among people to whom he had preached the Gospel.
—Paul understood that his mission was to communicate the truth and love of God through Jesus Christ.
—Commitment to God and love for the faith community motivated Paul's ministry.
—Paul reminded the Thessalonians that his teaching to them was to please God, who invited them into the kingdom.
—Paul told the Thessalonians that his preaching to them had no false motives or evil purposes.
—Paul reminded the Thessalonians of how hard he worked when he was with them.

CHILDREN

Children Topic: Living a Pleasing Life
Key Verse: 1 Thessalonians 2:4
Print Passage: Acts 17:10-14; 1 Thessalonians 2:1-4

—When Paul preached in Berea, many believed his message about Christ, even some Greeks of high standing.
—The Thessalonians continued to stir up trouble for Paul and caused him to leave Berea.
—Even though they were mistreated and opposed, Paul, Silas, and Timothy spoke courageously about God.

—Paul assured the Thessalonians that there was no deceit or trickery in his preaching.

—Paul, Silas, and Timothy preached not to please humans but to please God.

I. INTRODUCTION

A. Religious Conviction

In today's lesson, we learn positive lessons from Paul and his companions who wanted their motives and methods to be clearly understood. Paul made it clear that he did not preach for selfish gain or prestige, which was the case of some in Philippi (see Philippians 1:15; 2:3). Paul determined to preach the Gospel without fear and to live a life that pleased God.

B. Biblical Background

In the previous lesson, we began our study of 1 Thessalonians by understanding the historical background that gave rise to the Christian community in Thessalonica. Some interpreters of the book of 1 Thessalonians have thought that there may have been some opposition to the new Christian community after Paul, Silas, and Timothy left the city. We are not sure because Paul never mentioned this by name. It is possible, given the very overt hostility that they experienced in the city, that there were people who may have sought to discredit him and the work he had done.

Paul wanted there to be no doubt that he and the other disciples were men whose character was above reproach and without any hidden agendas or motives. According to Leon Morris, Paul had been the object of some sharp criticism, and this might well have led some of the Thessalonians to disregard what he wrote. This second chapter is rich and overflowing with spiritual nuggets that will encourage, enrich, and enlarge our understanding of the importance of spiritual leaders and how they make a difference in the lives of the people of God.

II. EXPOSITION AND APPLICATION OF THE SCRIPTURE

A. Preachers that Made a Difference
(1 Thessalonians 2:1-2)

FOR YOURSELVES, brethren, know our entrance in unto you, that it was not in vain: But even after that we had suffered before, and were shamefully entreated, as ye know, at Philippi, we were bold in our God to speak unto you the gospel of God with much contention.

In verse 1, Paul continued the line of thought he began in 1 Thessalonians 1:9—how the Thessalonians had turned from idols to serve the living and true God. "For yourselves, brethren, know our entrance in unto you, that it was not in vain" (verse 1). The word *vain* is derived from the Greek word *kenos*, which is a metaphor for "endeavors" and "labors." When they arrived, their preaching and teaching were purposeful and productive. Upon their arrival in Thessalonica, there were no believers in the Lord Jesus Christ; when they left, there was an infant Christian church. The very fact that there were believers who had formed the nucleus of a vibrant church after he and Silas were forced to leave hurriedly was evidence of an effective ministry. There may have been numerous critics that emerged when they left the city, but the work they did could not be denied.

In verse 2, Paul reminded the believers in Thessalonica how he had come to them with boldness. The Greek word that is used for *boldness* here means "to grow confident, have boldness, show assurance, or assume a posture of boldness." The more he preached, even facing opposition, the stronger he became. The more he taught the Word, the greater became the revelation of God's truth. The more he was witness to the power of God, the greater became the confidence that God was in fact with him and Silas.

How does one stand up under that kind of unrelenting opposition? How does one make full proof of one's ministry when the devil raises up opposition at every turn? One must rely not on one's own strength, but upon the power of God (see Ephesians 6:9-18). It was the power of God that gave Paul the courage to preach and teach with boldness. Therefore, if one is engaged in a ministry, whether it is a continuing ministry or a temporary assignment, the power of God will enable one to be successful in getting it done.

B. Preachers with Integrity and Character (1 Thessalonians 2:3-4)

For our exhortation was not of deceit, nor of uncleanness, nor in guile: But as we were allowed of God to be put in trust with the gospel, even so we speak; not as pleasing men, but God, which trieth our hearts.

The ancient world was full of roaming philosophers, preachers, and religious charlatans in every shade and color imaginable. It was not uncommon for them to move from city to city, peddling their wares and announcing new ideas and beliefs, or proclaiming to be the representatives of a god. Jesus warned His disciples to beware of false prophets and teachers who deceived and led men and women astray (see Matthew 7:15; 24:11, 24; 2 Timothy 3:13; Titus 1:10; 2 Peter 1).

Paul made it clear from the outset that there was no way that anyone would want to endure the persecution and stiff-necked opposition that they faced in Thessalonica without pure motives. Contrary to the common practices of that day their exhortation was filled neither with deceit nor with *uncleanness,* a word that could refer to either sexual immorality or impure motives. Last, it was not filled with "guile," probably indicating that his methods were not filled with tricks to fool people.

The word *allowed* is derived from a Greek word that means "to test" or "try." It has in it the idea of authenticating to prove the worth or value of a thing. Paul had already been tested on previous missions (see Acts 9:23; 13:48-50; 14:19-20). The preaching of the Gospel was a sacred trust and one wherein Paul saw himself as a steward of the manifold grace of God (see 1 Corinthians 4:2). God had called him and given him the assignment (see Galatians 1:11-12, 15). Paul wanted to please God, not human beings. The Greek word that is translated as "allowed" is the same word for "trieth." In the second use the present active tense suggested that the motives of Paul were continuously under examination by God. Paul wanted to make sure that the Thessalonians knew that they were without scandal and would never be in a position to be accused by anyone of any impropriety.

The year 2008 will be remembered as the

year of the scandal and birth of the "mega frauds." Trillions of dollars were lost and swindled out of the American people and others around the world by smooth-talking crooks. There is always the possibility of this kind of thievery occurring among the people of God. The church is not immune from financial, sexual, or doctrinal scandal. Therefore, it is critical that leaders of the people of God be ever aware of the image that they present to the public. In an age of instantaneous information, YouTube, and Internet video streaming, misconduct can be beamed around the world continuously. Paul reminded us that integrity and character are key traits for every leader to have.

C. Preachers with Compassionate Hearts
(1 Thessalonians 2:5-8)

For neither at any time used we flattering words, as ye know, nor a cloke of covetousness; God is witness: Nor of men sought we glory, neither of you, nor yet of others, when we might have been burdensome, as the apostles of Christ. But we were gentle among you, even as a nurse cherisheth her children: So being affectionately desirous of you, we were willing to have imparted unto you, not the gospel of God only, but also our own souls, because ye were dear unto us.

"For" introduces the next major section in the lesson wherein Paul expounded and further developed the thoughts expressed in verse 4. Paul drew real distinctions between what they could have been, which is stated in verse 3, and what they actually did. Again, we are not sure whether there were people in the church or community who wanted to label the apostle and his companions as charlatans who were greedy for money. He reminded them that when they went to Thessalonica, they did not go with flattering words. *Flattery* (Greek: *Kolakeia*, pronounced ko-la-ki-ah) was

commonly used to gain access to wealthy people and their fortunes. Paul stated that neither he nor his companions had used flattery in any way (see 1 Corinthians 2:1-5). According to Gene L. Green, "The ancients recognized that flattery was evidence of the bad character of the person who used it to persuade or move others to action." The ministry of Paul in Macedonia had not been conducted out of greed or the need to use flattering words for personal gain.

Paul did not need the affirmation of people, nor had he sought it from the Thessalonians (verse 6). The Macedonian Christians were poor (see 2 Corinthians 8:1-5). Rather than be a burden or request financial support from them, Paul reminded them that he had not been a burden to them. Although they could have requested support, they would not (see 1 Corinthians 9:1ff.). Rather than being a leader with harshness and demanding his right, Paul had been among them as a nurse. The image of a nurse was a picture of compassion and concern. Paul chose to be gentle and caring (verse 7). He was not content just to share the Gospel; he wanted to share *himself.* In these words, we sense the heart of a man who genuinely cared about the people in Thessalonica. This may be a reflection on the character of the people as well. The Thessalonians were not just people whom he preached to, but they were very dear to his heart. He had been the midwife of their faith and given birth to a courageous community of disciples who were unashamed and unafraid to declare the Gospel.

D. Preachers Walking Worthy
(1 Thessalonians 2:9-12)

For ye remember, brethren, our labour and travail:

for labouring night and day, because we would not be chargeable unto any of you, we preached unto you the gospel of God. Ye are witnesses, and God also, how holily and justly and unblameably we behaved ourselves among you that believe: As ye know how we exhorted and comforted and charged every one of you, as a father doth his children, That ye would walk worthy of God, who hath called you unto his kingdom and glory.

The phrase "For ye remember" called upon the Thessalonians to bring back to the forefront of their thoughts the time and circumstances under which Paul and his companions worked among them. They were not just there waiting to preach and teach in the evenings, but were actively engaged in hard work night and day. This probably means that they worked very long hours and in the midst of their work they would share the Gospel with others. It would be easy for Paul to find work because he was a tentmaker by trade and profession (see Acts 18:1-3). Paul would not be obligated to anyone, nor would he have it said that his sole purpose for preaching was for money. This was a practice that he followed throughout his missionary endeavors (see 1 Corinthians 9:7, 18; 2 Corinthians 11:9; 12:13-14; compare with Nehemiah 5:15-18). Preaching for money would make Paul a financial burden on the people and would have negated the work of the ministry.

Not only were they to remember, but they, along with God, were witnesses to how they had lived in the city. Ancient Thessalonica was a very large and busy city. It bustled with activity and one could have easily gotten lost in the crowd. The missionaries did not have secret lives that were not open for public scrutiny.

Paul reminded them again how they had lived *holily* (a reference to their piety), *justly* (which means "right living" or "righteously"), and *blamelessly* (verse 10). They lived the life they preached, and they lived it among the very people to whom they preached.

Again, in verse 11, Paul appealed to the memory of the Thessalonians to recall how the missionaries were among them as encouragers and comforters. The phrase "charged every one of you" pointed to his willingness to take time with individuals. In many congregations today, the members have to go through intermediaries to see their pastor. Many pastors have unlisted telephone numbers, private residences, and security details to keep the members from barging into their offices. Paul taught by his example that a pastor is first and foremost a spiritual father to the flock and leads best by caring for the flock.

Verse 12 concludes the section, with Paul calling upon the Thessalonians to "walk worthy of God." The Greek verb for the word *walk* conveys the idea of living or conducting one's life in accordance with biblical standards. We can best translate the word *walk* as "live as Christians." The Greek word for *worthy* is at its core the idea of "weight" or "value." Therefore, *walking worthy* means that we are going to live lives that are equal to the life of Jesus Christ (see Romans 6:4; Ephesians 4:1; Colossians 1:9-10). The present aim and goal is to live in this world so that God is glorified and pleased. The ultimate goal is to reach the kingdom, where God's fullness and glory will be manifested. It was to this that the Thessalonians and all believers had and have been called.

III. CONCLUDING REFLECTION

Lately, I have been reflecting over why the vast majority of congregations experience sporadic and spotty growth. We often describe this using the metaphor of the "front door–back door." New converts and disciples come in the front door, but it is not long before they have gone out the back door, never to return. Some of the more recent revelations and studies reveal that the problem of the back door has a lot to do with what happens as people enter the front door. Once people are in many churches, some people find them to be irrelevant and unable to meet their needs, or the things that really impact their lives. Churches can be cold, impersonal religious gatherings where real fellowship and community are found in the sermon, but are absent among the people. Paul's actions teach every pastor and congregational leader a lesson in leading with the heart. He taught us that the kingdom of God grows best when we display genuine care and concern for the things and people that God cares the most about.

PRAYER

Eternal God, forgive us our selfishness and self-centered ways. May our hearts be open to You and Your will and then to each other. Grant us the peace that surpasses all understanding that we may live in such a way that our lives glorify You in every way. In Jesus' name we pray. Amen.

WORD POWER

Nurse (Greek: *Trophos* [tro-phos])—in this context, the word *nurse* carries the idea of gentleness and kindness. It reveals the heart of Paul to the church in Thessalonica. Paul possessed a thoroughly pastoral heart. A Christian leader who is void of a nursing heart has not found his or her true calling.

HOME DAILY BIBLE READINGS
(June 7-13, 2010)

Pleasing to God

MONDAY, June 7: "Seeking God's Approval" (Galatians 1:1-10)

TUESDAY, June 8: "Examining the Scriptures" (Acts 17:10-14)

WEDNESDAY, June 9: "Faith that Pleases God" (Hebrews 11:4-7)

THURSDAY, June 10: "Doing What Pleases God" (1 John 3:18-24)

FRIDAY, June 11: "Imitators of the Faithful" (1 Thessalonians 2:13-16)

SATURDAY, June 12: "Paul's Glory and Joy" (1 Thessalonians 2:17-20)

SUNDAY, June 13: "A Life Worthy of God" (1 Thessalonians 2:1-12)

LESSON 3   June 20, 2010

SUSTAINED THROUGH ENCOURAGEMENT

DEVOTIONAL READING: **Acts 4:32-37**
PRINT PASSAGE: **1 Thessalonians 3:1-13**

BACKGROUND SCRIPTURE: **1 Thessalonians 3**
KEY VERSE: **1 Thessalonians 3:7**

1 Thessalonians 3:1-13—KJV

WHEREFORE WHEN we could no longer forbear, we thought it good to be left at Athens alone;

2 And sent Timotheus, our brother, and minister of God, and our fellowlabourer in the gospel of Christ, to establish you, and to comfort you concerning your faith:

3 That no man should be moved by these afflictions: for yourselves know that we are appointed thereunto.

4 For verily, when we were with you, we told you before that we should suffer tribulation; even as it came to pass, and ye know.

5 For this cause, when I could no longer forbear, I sent to know your faith, lest by some means the tempter have tempted you, and our labour be in vain.

6 But now when Timotheus came from you unto us, and brought us good tidings of your faith and charity, and that ye have good remembrance of us always, desiring greatly to see us, as we also to see you:

7 Therefore, brethren, we were comforted over you in all our affliction and distress by your faith:

8 For now we live, if ye stand fast in the Lord.

9 For what thanks can we render to God again for you, for all the joy wherewith we joy for your sakes before our God;

10 Night and day praying exceedingly that we might see your face, and might perfect that which is lacking in your faith?

11 Now God himself and our Father, and our Lord Jesus Christ, direct our way unto you.

12 And the Lord make you to increase and abound in love one toward another, and toward all men, even as we do toward you:

1 Thessalonians 3:1-13—NRSV

THEREFORE WHEN we could bear it no longer, we decided to be left alone in Athens;

2 and we sent Timothy, our brother and co-worker for God in proclaiming the gospel of Christ, to strengthen and encourage you for the sake of your faith,

3 so that no one would be shaken by these persecutions. Indeed, you yourselves know that this is what we are destined for.

4 In fact, when we were with you, we told you beforehand that we were to suffer persecution; so it turned out, as you know.

5 For this reason, when I could bear it no longer, I sent to find out about your faith; I was afraid that somehow the tempter had tempted you and that our labor had been in vain.

6 But Timothy has just now come to us from you, and has brought us the good news of your faith and love. He has told us also that you always remember us kindly and long to see us—just as we long to see you.

7 For this reason, brothers and sisters, during all our distress and persecution we have been encouraged about you through your faith.

8 For we now live, if you continue to stand firm in the Lord.

9 How can we thank God enough for you in return for all the joy that we feel before our God because of you?

10 Night and day we pray most earnestly that we may see you face to face and restore whatever is lacking in your faith.

11 Now may our God and Father himself and our Lord Jesus direct our way to you.

12 And may the Lord make you increase and abound in love for one another and for all, just as we abound in love for you.

13 To the end he may stablish your hearts unblameable in holiness before God, even our Father, at the coming of our Lord Jesus Christ with all his saints.

13 And may he so strengthen your hearts in holiness that you may be blameless before our God and Father at the coming of our Lord Jesus with all his saints.

TOPICAL OUTLINE OF THE LESSON

I. Introduction
A. Barnabas—an Exemplary Christian
B. Biblical Background

II. Exposition and Application of the Scripture
A. Paul's Concern for the Saints (1 Thessalonians 3:1-5)
B. Paul's Joy over Their Growth (1 Thessalonians 3:6-9)
C. Paul's Continuous Prayer (1 Thessalonians 3:10-13)

III. Concluding Reflection

LESSON OBJECTIVES

Upon completion of this lesson, the students will know that:

1. A true ambassador of Christ has concern for spiritual growth of the sheep;
2. A true ambassador prays consistently and passionately for the sheep; and,
3. A true ambassador yearns to see the spiritual and physical welfare of the sheep.

POINTS TO BE EMPHASIZED

ADULT/YOUTH

Adult Topic: Encourage One Another

Youth Topic: Hang in There!

Adult/Youth Key Verse: 1 Thessalonians 3:7

Print Passage: 1 Thessalonians 3:1-13

—"We" (verse 1) refers to Paul and Silas (Silvanus).

—Paul frequently sent Timothy to visit churches on his behalf.

—In Greek, the word for "persecutions" (verse 3) is *thlipisis,* indicating severe difficulties and a serious test of commitment and faith.

—Encouraging news delivered by Timothy led Paul to continue to pray for the church in Thessalonica.

—Paul's love for the Thessalonians and concern over the trouble they were facing caused him to send Timothy to them to strengthen their faith.

—Timothy returned with good news; the Thessalonians' faith and their love for one another were as strong as ever.

—Timothy's good news brought great comfort to Paul, who could not thank God enough.

—Paul let the Thessalonians know of his desire to visit them and his commitment to pray that God would make their love for one another continue to grow.

CHILDREN

Children Topic: Encourage One Another

Key Verse: 1 Thessalonians 3:7

Print Passage: Acts 18:1-4, 18-23; 1 Thessalonians 3:6-9

—In Corinth, Paul was encouraged by his relationship with Aquila and Priscilla.

—Many who heard Paul preach in Corinth became believers and were baptized.

—Paul continued to preach and to strengthen the disciples as he traveled with his friends to Ephesus and beyond.

—Paul told the Thessalonians that their faith and love were a real encouragement to him.

—Paul thanked God for the joy the Thessalonians brought to him because of their faith.

I. INTRODUCTION

A. Barnabas—an Exemplary Christian

The devotional reading for today's lesson comes from the Acts of the Apostles and gives us a glimpse of the social and religious life among the earliest Christians. The first-century Christian church was radically different from anything that we see today. Indeed, there are exceptions, but they tend to be few in number. The earliest Christians are described as people united behind the cause of Jesus Christ. They shared their possessions (see Acts 4:32). They were bold witnesses of the resurrection of the Lord Jesus Christ (see Acts 4:33). Everything possible was done to ease the stress of poverty and economic hardship among the saints (see Acts 4:34). Even if it meant selling their personal property and distributing it to others to meet the needs, they did it without any reservations (see Acts 4:35).

One of the real heroes of the early Christian movement was a man named Barnabas. Barnabas was one of those great giants whom society today would not deem to be a "Person of the Week." Clearly, he was a man greatly respected during his day. William Barclay calls Barnabas "the man with the biggest heart in the church." Barnabas was a native of the island of Cyprus, which is located in the Mediterranean Sea. Barnabas's name means "son of encouragement." This one aspect seems to get little attention. Barnabas was always willing to take a back seat to others. It is doubtful that we would be writing about or talking about Paul today were it not for Barnabas. One will recall further that it was Barnabas who introduced Paul to the church in Jerusalem (see Acts 9:26-27). Barnabas was a chief financial supporter of the work and ministry of the early church. He gave large sums of money to the work of the early church in Jerusalem (see Acts 4:37). He was a good man, full of the Holy Spirit and faith. When word of the expanding growth of the Gospel reached the apostles in Jerusalem, the council sent Barnabas to Antioch to investigate and offer some words of encouragement to the infant church (see Acts 11:19-24). It is possible that the love that we see flowing from the heart of Paul when he wrote his letter to the Thessalonians we saw first in Barnabas, who was his mentor in the early days.

B. Biblical Background

In the previous lesson, we studied 1 Thessalonians 2:1-12. In that study, Paul shared with his recent converts how he, Silas, and Timothy had been very loving and tender with the Thessalonians during their time there. Although their departure from Thessalonica was not according to his wishes, his absence did not minimize his continuing love and concern for them. The passage that we are studying today is a continuation of the discussion that began at 2:13, where Paul reminded them that they had received their message as the Word of God, and not as the word of men. It was this Word of God that had brought about their salvation through faith in the risen Christ (see 1 Corinthians 1:18-21). Just as their spiritual parents—Paul, Silas, and Timothy—had suffered in Thessalonica, so too had the saints in Thessalonica suffered persecution. Paul reminded them that they were not to be surprised by the persecution and trials that would come their way; they must expect them (see 1 Thessalonians 2:14). The Jews had been filled with such overt envy and resentment towards Paul and his companions that they forbade them to even speak to Gentiles (see 2:16). It is possible that Jews living in Thessalonica tried to play on the fears of the new converts by telling them that Paul would never return. This may be one of the reasons why Paul emphatically stated that they were overly eager to visit them again to see how they were doing. He described their departure in language that suggested that they did not leave the Thessalonians: "being taken from you" (see 2:17). This phrase conjures up the image of someone being kidnapped or taken against their wishes. Every attempt to get back to Thessalonica was thwarted by Satan (see 2:18). We are not told how Satan got in the way; it could have been a number of things. However, the love that Paul felt had not died, but had only intensified.

Today's lesson is a window through which we can see the exact circumstances surrounding the sending of the initial letter to the church of Thessalonica. According to Acts 17:10, when the missionaries left Thessalonica they went to Berea, the next major city on the Via Egnatia. The mission had success, but the Jews in Thessalonica soon found out about their presence and traveled to the city and caused an uproar (see Acts 17:11-13). Immediately the brethren in Berea sent Paul by sea to Athens, the quickest and safest route, while Silas and Timothy remained in Berea. Once in Athens, he sent word back via the brethren who had accompanied him requesting that Silas and Timothy join him in Athens. It was after joining him that Timothy received the assignment to go to Thessalonica and report back on the condition of the church. The general consensus is that Paul wrote the letter shortly after Timothy's return and his report on the conditions facing the church in Thessalonica. The most likely place where the letter was written was Corinth.

II. EXPOSITION AND APPLICATION OF THE SCRIPTURE

A. Paul's Concern for the Saints (1 Thessalonians 3:1-5)

WHEREFORE WHEN we could no longer forbear, we thought it good to be left at Athens alone; And sent Timotheus, our brother, and minister of God, and our fellowlabourer in the gospel of Christ, to establish you, and to

comfort you concerning your faith: That no man should be moved by these afflictions: for yourselves know that we are appointed thereunto. For verily, when we were with you, we told you before that we should suffer tribulation; even as it came to pass, and ye know. For this cause, when I could no longer forbear, I sent to know your faith, lest by some means the tempter have tempted you, and our labour be in vain.

The distance between Athens and Thessalonica is nearly 350 miles. The rugged terrain and poor methods of communication made it impossible to be sure of the situation in Thessalonica. Once Paul left the vicinity of Thessalonica, there was absolutely no way to know how the converts were faring. Were the new converts being persecuted? Had they been able to endure if they were being persecuted? Had they turned back to the worship of idols? Paul had no idea. The lack of information on what had happened to the new converts was eating away at his heart and consuming his thoughts. He had to know what was going on with them. Hence, when he could bear it no longer, he sent Timothy to ascertain their status and condition (see verse 1).

Paul considered Timothy to be like a son in ministry (see 1 Timothy 1:2). He met Timothy during his second missionary journey and made him a part of the team (see Acts 16:1-3). Timothy was given other significant assignments during his time with Paul (see Romans 16:21; 1 Corinthians 4:17; 16:10; 2 Corinthians 1:1, 19). Paul thought of Timothy as his son, a minister of God, and a fellow laborer in the Gospel. Timothy's assignment was threefold. First, he was to *establish* (Greek: *sterizo*—literally means "to make stable") the saints. Second, he was to *comfort* (Greek: *parakaleo*—literally means "to come alongside" or "to stand with someone"). Third, he was to help them to see

that they should not be moved by the suffering and the persecution that they were experiencing (see Romans 8:18; 2 Corinthians 4:7-16). Paul had learned from his personal experience that those who would trust in Jesus Christ must be prepared to suffer. He had prepared them for what was inevitable (verse 4).

We do not know what they endured, nor are we sure about the source of the persecution. It may have been a combination of Jews and local leaders in Thessalonica. Paul wanted to know if their faith was still strong. He reminded them a second time that when he could no longer stand the suspense—he wanted to know how they were doing. He did not want them to fall victim to the temptations of the devil (see Matthew 4:1-10). Satan does tempt and the easiest thing to do would be to return to one's former life when things became too hard. Paul did not mention how long Timothy was gone or how long he stayed. Those things were not as important as the status of the saints in Thessalonica.

Here is an area of ministry today that is often overlooked: the need to be concerned about the spiritual growth of new converts. The earliest Christians, particularly Paul in this letter, displayed a genuine concern about their converts.

B. Paul's Joy over Their Growth (1 Thessalonians 3:6-9)

But now when Timotheus came from you unto us, and brought us good tidings of your faith and charity, and that ye have good remembrance of us always, desiring greatly to see us, as we also to see you: Therefore, brethren, we were comforted over you in all our affliction and distress by your faith: For now we live, if ye stand fast in the Lord. For what thanks can we render to God again for you, for all the joy wherewith we joy for your sakes before our God.

Timothy's return was a welcomed sight and relief for Paul and Silas. We are not told how long it took Timothy to travel north and return with the news that Paul wanted to hear. First, he told them that the church was doing well. Timothy brought back news that their faith was strong and their love was increasing (verse 6). Gene L. Green remarked how the presence of love and faith were "'characteristics of those who are true members of the community of the redeemed'" (Galatians 5:6; Ephesians 1:15; Colossians 1:4-5; 1 Timothy 1:14; Philemon 5; Revelation 2:19). Second, Timothy reported that the church had good memories of the team and they longed to see Paul and Silas as much as they wanted to see the saints in Thessalonica. Paul framed his statement in such a way that he wanted the Thessalonians to know that he was not pleased that he was unable to see them. He desired greatly to come and would have given anything to have joined Timothy. Why he did not is not stated. Most likely it had to do with him being the chief spokesman and the most easily recognizable in the group. The church held no resentment or bitterness toward Paul and Silas because they had to leave suddenly and had not had a chance to return.

It had not been easy to work in Thessalonica and Philippi; while there, they were arrested, badly beaten, and jailed (see Acts 16:16-24; Philippians 1:30). The afflictions and distress had been well worth the results. The increasing faith of the Thessalonians was comforting (verse 7). The work had brought affliction and distress. Yet, had they continued to stand firm, it would have only increased Paul's desire to live a life that was committed to preaching the Gospel with boldness. The words *stand fast* were among Paul's favorite when it came to

encouraging steadfastness in the face of trial (see 1 Corinthians 15:58; Galatians 5:1; Ephesians 6:11, 13-14; Philippians 4:4).

There were no words that Paul could render to God for the great work of salvation wrought in the lives of the Thessalonians. This was the third time that Paul expressed thanksgiving to God in this letter (1:2; 2:13). Paul literally wanted to know what he could pay God for what had been done in the lives of the saints in Thessalonica (see verses 8-9). The answer was nothing. He simply had to rejoice over the outcome of the mission. The struggle, persecution, and trials were all worth the results.

C. Paul's Continuous Prayer (1 Thessalonians 3:10-13)

Night and day praying exceedingly that we might see your face, and might perfect that which is lacking in your faith? Now God himself and our Father, and our Lord Jesus Christ, direct our way unto you. And the Lord make you to increase and abound in love one toward another, and toward all men, even as we do toward you: To the end he may stablish your hearts unblameable in holiness before God, even our Father, at the coming of our Lord Jesus Christ with all his saints.

Verses 10-13 contain Paul's prayer that they might see the Thessalonians again and have the chance to personally perfect in them the work begun during the first visit (verse 10). That is the role of a pastor and leader—not to tear down faith, but to complete what is missing that the saints might be built up in Christ. God had begun a good work and it had yet to be completed. We know that Paul did not return during this journey, but he did return to Macedonia later and no doubt had a chance to visit the church in Thessalonica (see Acts 19:21-22; 20:1-6).

It was Paul's desire that they should know God as their Father (see 1 Thessalonians 1:1). Jesus is called *the Lord,* meaning that He is the One who desires complete loyalty and devotion. Additionally, He was the One to whom Paul directed his prayers and they were to do the same. His prayer was for the Father and the Son to make it possible for him to return to Thessalonica.

In verse 12, Paul poured out his heart to the Thessalonians: "May the Lord cause you to increase and abound in love for one another, and for all people, just as we also do for you" (NASB). The love herein lifted up by the apostle was a spiritual virtue. It was not a sentimental and sugary kind of emotion, but rather, it was one that grew out of a deep abiding faith in Jesus Christ (see John 13:34-35). Throughout the letter Paul mentioned the faith of the Thessalonians—how it was growing. To know Jesus Christ and the power of His resurrection is to conform in every way to His image and likeness (see Philippians 3:9-10). Spiritual love proceeds from a spiritual nature and is attracted by the sight of the divine image in the saints. Now we have not received the spirit of this world, but the very spirit of Jesus Christ that we might know the things that are freely given us by God (see 1 Corinthians 2:12).

This love is spiritual and comes through the believer's Spirit-filled life. It is a spiritual fruit that identifies who we are in Jesus Christ. We can no more fake this virtue than one can fake the ability to fly. There is but one way to fulfill this mandate to love others—and that is through life in the Spirit of Jesus Christ. Whatever we seek to become in Christ, it must be caused by Him and not ourselves. To be like Jesus is to love the brethren. Paul expressed

an awesome thought in this verse about ever-increasing love. He said, "May the Lord cause you to increase," or *pleonazo,* which means "to become more, multiply, cause to become rich." It carries the idea of: "May the Lord make you rich in love." Not only did Paul want the Lord to cause them to increase in love, but he wanted God to cause them to "abound," which further enriches the thought of increasing in love.

This thought of abounding in love is captured in Philippians 1:9 (NASB): "And this I pray, that your love may abound still more and more in real knowledge and all discernment." Love grows day by day as we grow in grace and in the knowledge of our Lord Jesus Christ. To be like Jesus is to love the brethren. The ultimate goal of their being established was so that they could live blamelessly and in holiness before God, to the end that they were prepared to meet Jesus when He comes with all of His saints. This was the second time that Paul had mentioned the coming of the Lord (see 2:19).

III. CONCLUDING REFLECTION

The New Testament lays bare the difficulty that the early Christians encountered to remain true to Christ. It was a persecuted, struggling minority that was on the brink of extinction. In order to survive the open hostility from every government where a local congregation existed, it needed a powerful, cohesive energy to bind the members to each other in an unbreakable bond. In that environment of hatred, animosity, and disrespect, if Christians ignored the necessity of a strong bond to unify themselves, they would have surely courted disaster. In point of fact, the church survived because Christians realized that they only had each other. It is no surprise that love was stressed among them as the norm for how they were to live among themselves.

From Paul's example, contemporary Christian leaders learn that there is no substitute for genuine concern and care on the part of the leader. Paul repeatedly reminded the saints how he longed to see them and to be with them and to teach them. In this short epistle there is a lifetime of seminary lessons on how to lead and love the people of God.

Every one of us needs encouragement. The world is in a state of flux, and no one knows exactly what individuals are going through in life. We assemble in church on Sundays and put up beautiful appearances. We mask ourselves with different clothes and makeup, we sing and shout together, but only God knows the battle that may be raging in the one sitting next to you. It is our responsibility to train ourselves to be sensitive to each other.

Sunday school teachers and participants are blessed to be in small groups. Sunday school is a good avenue through which to reach out to each other in love. Some congregations are so large that the senior pastor has no time to engage individuals on biting issues. However, our Sunday Bible teachers should be on alert, and as they teach, they should become encouragers to class members. Those who are discouraged should also take the initiative to speak to their teachers. One man said, "If we supply the will, God will supply the power."

PRAYER

Eternal and blessed God, may we learn to love as You have loved us. Grant to Your servants the kind of spirit that will empower us to speak life into the hearts of Your saints. Bless, with abundant power, leaders who seek to empower Your people. In Jesus' name we pray. Amen.

WORD POWER

Comforted (Greek: *parakaleo*)—this word in Greek contains two words: the preposition (*para*) and a verb (*kaleo*). In essence, Paul was saying that the brethren in Thessalonica were co-laborers, and they were called along with them. Their faithfulness to Jesus Christ brought comfort to Paul. Nothing comforts church leaders more than to see their converts walking the walk of faith.

HOME DAILY BIBLE READINGS
(June 14-20, 2010)

Sustained through Encouragement
MONDAY, June 14: "Son of Encouragement" (Acts 4:32-37)
TUESDAY, June 15: "Encouraging New Leaders" (Deuteronomy 3:23-29)
WEDNESDAY, June 16: "Encouraging the Fearful" (Isaiah 35:1-4)
THURSDAY, June 17: "Encouraged by the Scriptures" (Romans 15:1-6)
FRIDAY, June 18: "Supported by God's People" (Acts 18:1-11)
SATURDAY, June 19: "A Ministry of Encouragement" (Acts 18:18-23)
SUNDAY, June 20: "Encouraged in Distress" (1 Thessalonians 3)

LESSON 4   **June 27, 2010**

DEMONSTRATED IN ACTION

DEVOTIONAL READING: **Hebrews 11:1-6**
PRINT PASSAGE: **1 Thessalonians 4:1-12**

BACKGROUND SCRIPTURE: **1 Thessalonians 4:1-12**
KEY VERSE: **1 Thessalonians 4:1**

1 Thessalonians 4:1-12—KJV

FURTHERMORE THEN we beseech you, brethren, and exhort you by the Lord Jesus, that as ye have received of us how ye ought to walk and to please God, so ye would abound more and more.

2 For ye know what commandments we gave you by the Lord Jesus.

3 For this is the will of God, even your sanctification, that ye should abstain from fornication:

4 That every one of you should know how to possess his vessel in sanctification and honour;

5 Not in the lust of concupiscence, even as the Gentiles which know not God:

6 That no man go beyond and defraud his brother in any matter: because that the Lord is the avenger of all such, as we also have forewarned you and testified.

7 For God hath not called us unto uncleanness, but unto holiness.

8 He therefore that despiseth, despiseth not man, but God, who hath also given unto us his holy Spirit.

9 But as touching brotherly love ye need not that I write unto you: for ye yourselves are taught of God to love one another.

10 And indeed ye do it toward all the brethren which are in all Macedonia: but we beseech you, brethren, that ye increase more and more;

11 And that ye study to be quiet, and to do your own business, and to work with your own hands, as we commanded you;

12 That ye may walk honestly toward them that are without, and that ye may have lack of nothing.

1 Thessalonians 4:1-12—NRSV

FINALLY, BROTHERS and sisters, we ask and urge you in the Lord Jesus that, as you learned from us how you ought to live and to please God (as, in fact, you are doing), you should do so more and more.

2 For you know what instructions we gave you through the Lord Jesus.

3 For this is the will of God, your sanctification: that you abstain from fornication;

4 that each one of you know how to control your own body in holiness and honor,

5 not with lustful passion, like the Gentiles who do not know God;

6 that no one wrong or exploit a brother or sister in this matter, because the Lord is an avenger in all these things, just as we have already told you beforehand and solemnly warned you.

7 For God did not call us to impurity but in holiness.

8 Therefore whoever rejects this rejects not human authority but God, who also gives his Holy Spirit to you.

9 Now concerning love of the brothers and sisters, you do not need to have anyone write to you, for you yourselves have been taught by God to love one another;

10 and indeed you do love all the brothers and sisters throughout Macedonia. But we urge you, beloved, to do so more and more,

11 to aspire to live quietly, to mind your own affairs, and to work with your hands, as we directed you,

12 so that you may behave properly toward outsiders and be dependent on no one.

TOPICAL OUTLINE OF THE LESSON

I. **Introduction**
   A. Understanding Paul's Epistle
   B. Biblical Background

II. **Exposition and Application of the Scripture**
   A. Live to Please God (1 Thessalonians 4:1-2)
   B. Live Free of Sexual Immorality (1 Thessalonians 4:3-8)
   C. Live in Peace with Other Believers (1 Thessalonians 4:9-12)

III. **Concluding Reflection**

LESSON OBJECTIVES

Upon completion of this lesson, the students will know that:

1. To *walk worthily* is a heart attitude in forming a strong relationship with God;
2. Believers are required to live harmoniously with other believers; and,
3. Sexual sin is abhorrent in the church of God.

POINTS TO BE EMPHASIZED

ADULT/YOUTH

Adult Topic: Motivation for Action
Youth Topic: More Love
Adult Key Verse: 1 Thessalonians 4:1
Youth Key Verse: 1 Thessalonians 4:10
Print Passage: 1 Thessalonians 4:1-12

—The story of Apollos in the book of Acts is a glimpse into the history of the formation of the teaching and documents of the Gospels.

—Priscilla and Aquila were faith mentors for Apollos.

—The church in Thessalonica had a record of support of Christian communities in Macedonia.

—Paul urged his readers to continue living to please God in their daily lives.

—Paul wanted his readers to be holy and pure, avoiding fornication and lustful passion.

—Paul wanted his readers to seek to live quiet lives, minding their own business and doing their own work.

—Paul further defined for his readers that in living holy we can be positive examples to those who are not Christians.

CHILDREN

Children Topic: Help One Another
Key Verse: Acts 18:26
Print Passage: Acts 18:24-28; 1 Thessalonians 4:1-2, 9-12

—In Ephesus, Priscilla and Aquila helped Apollos, who had come from Alexandria, become a more accurate preacher and teacher for God.

—Apollos was then better able to help the believers in Achaia when he taught there about Jesus as the Messiah.

—Paul urged the Thessalonians to continue to live and please God more and more as he had taught them.

—Paul also urged the Thessalonians to love one another throughout Macedonia.

—In addition, Paul charged the Thessalonians to live quietly, mind their own affairs, work with their hands, and behave properly to others.

I. INTRODUCTION

A. Understanding Paul's Epistle

We learned in an earlier lesson that the epistles of the apostle Paul were really personally written conversations that he carried on with the churches he established. They were more than likely written to address some pressing issues or to offer advice on questions that had been raised (see 1 Corinthians 7:1). It was typical of Paul to use the first portion of his letters to address doctrinal matters and the second half of the letter for instructions on how to live out the teachings he had just shared. Very good examples are: the epistle to the Ephesians (chapters 1–3 are doctrinal and chapters 4–6 are practical instructions), and chapters 1–3 from the first half of the letter to the Thessalonians. Take note: in these chapters Paul took a great deal of time to reiterate to the church how they came to know Jesus Christ. He had shared with them intimately and passionately his love for them and his personal desire to see them. Finally, Paul shared his desire to come and personally establish the things that needed to be strengthened in the church.

In the second half of the letter, which begins with chapter 4, we are introduced to Paul's practical instruction or what is more technically called "paraenesis." *Paraenesis* was a traditional form of ethical and moral instruction that tended to be very general in nature. Often, the instruction may have come from some of the Greek or Roman philosophers. In ancient Jewish religion, paraenesis was found in the wisdom writings and in the oral traditions. Paul was a master at using the Greek literary and philosophical teaching techniques. In 4:1–5:28, the paraenesis is very specific, which leads some to believe that they were intended to speak to problems or concerns in the church of Thessalonica.

Generally, we would think of this type of instruction as application of the teachings of Scripture. The goal of reading, meditating, and studying the Word of God is application. We want to live the teachings of the Lord Jesus Christ (see Isaiah 29:13; Matthew 15:7; Luke 6:46).

B. Biblical Background

Today, we arrive at chapter 4 of 1 Thessalonians, which is rich with practical and moral instruction for Christians living in every age. The lesson can be subdivided into two main sections: 4:1-8 and 4:9-13. Paul began this section of the letter (verses 1-8) by encouraging and reminding the Thessalonians of the importance of living out what they had been taught. More specifically, he addressed the issues of sexual purity and the need for purity in this area, especially given that ancient Greeks were very open to sexual immorality. Ancient Greco-Roman society had very few restraints when it came to matters relating to sex. Paul instructed them that they were to live in honor and holiness—not causing a problem in the fellowship by interfering in someone else's marriage—and were not to practice fornication. They were not to live like Gentiles who were driven by lust.

In verses 9-12, he returned to the theme of love within the fellowship. Warm, nurturing relationships were the foundational cornerstone upon which the church had been built. Paul wanted to make sure that it remained that way. Love of the brethren had been mentioned previously in the letter, and in verses 9-12 he returned to it. He said to them that there was no need of further instruction on this matter. Once we have been born of the Spirit of God, the Lord Himself teaches us what is acceptable behavior toward other believers. To walk in obedience to God is to practice what His Word teaches us to do.

II. EXPOSITION AND APPLICATION OF THE SCRIPTURE

A. Live to Please God
(1 Thessalonians 4:1-2)

FURTHERMORE THEN we beseech you, brethren, and exhort you by the Lord Jesus, that as ye have received of us how ye ought to walk and to please God, so ye would abound more and more. For ye know what commandments we gave you by the Lord Jesus.

The word *furthermore* (Greek: *loipon*—pronounced "loe-pon") literally means "the rest that follows." This word marks the transition from the previous chapter. Sometimes the word is translated *finally*, which was a common word used by Paul to mark the conclusion of his letters (see 2 Corinthians 13:11; Ephesians 6:10; Philippians 3:1; 4:8; 2 Thessalonians 3:1). The word *then* (Greek: *oun*—pronounced "oon") literally means "therefore," in light of everything just mentioned. Paul gently, yet straightforwardly, reminded the Thessalonians to keep in mind all of the things that they had been taught. He appealed to and exhorted them as brothers and sisters in the faith that they were to live lives that were pleasing to God. He did not place himself above them, but saw them as his peers in the faith. The word *walk* in the original language means, "the action of walking started in the past and that must continue into the distant future." There was no end in sight; they were to continuously live lives that were pleasing to God. There was no spiritual vacation. The word *please* comes from a word that means "to accommodate oneself to the opinion and desires of another." On the one hand, their actions would be dictated by their desire to please God.

The instructions that Paul was referring to are what they received and appropriated from his very first visit. He urged them to "abound" more and more in the things that they had learned. They were exhorted to go beyond what they had been taught. The words that Paul was sharing were spoken to them in the name of the Lord Jesus Christ. Paul offered help for pastors, church leaders, and believers living in this age. First, we see a commitment to nurture and to discipleship. The new believers were not left to fend for themselves. Second, Paul called upon the believers to be accountable for what they did—there were no options given—"the lessons you have learned tell you how you ought to live." Third, the goal of every believer's life must be to live a life that is well-pleasing to God (see John 8:29; Colossians 1:9-10).

B. Live Free of Sexual Immorality (1 Thessalonians 4:3-8)

For this is the will of God, even your sanctification, that ye should abstain from fornication: That every one of you should know how to possess his vessel in sanctification and honour; Not in the lust of concupiscence, even as the Gentiles which know not God: That no man go beyond and defraud his brother in any matter: because that the Lord is the avenger of all such, as we also have forewarned you and testified. For God hath not called us unto uncleanness, but unto holiness. He therefore that despiseth, despiseth not man, but God, who hath also given unto us his holy Spirit.

The word *for* begins a new discussion or theme. In this case, it is an extended discussion about sexual purity and sanctification. These are two subjects that people, even some Christians, would love to avoid altogether. We live in a time when sexual freedom means one can do whatever one desires and wants. Before proceeding, we must answer the question of whether there was a situation in the church that prompted this discussion. If the letters of Paul were addressed to his congregations for specific purposes, does the inclusion of statements about sexual immorality indicate that this was a problem? We will answer yes and no. Yes, sexual immorality was a significant problem throughout the Roman Empire, given the lax and loose standards regarding sexual purity. People who were recently converted certainly may have felt the pull from time to time of the old ways and places. Perhaps in response to problems among the Thessalonians reported by Timothy,

Paul reinforced previous instructions (1 Thessalonians 4:1-2) concerning the maintenance of sexual purity in the Christian community. We will also answer no—that this was not a major problem. Remember, Paul had lavished extensive praise upon the Thessalonians because they had turned from idols to serve the true and living God (see 1:9). Their faith had been published throughout Macedonia and they had become examples for the other churches (see 1:7). It is highly unlikely that Paul would have been writing them to address this matter. More than likely, he was writing to address some general areas of personal and communal life that they must not take lightly. He often listed sexual immorality among the vices and works of the flesh that needed to be avoided (see Romans 1:28-31; Galatians 5:19-21).

In this section, Paul laid out three injunctions against the practice of an unholy lifestyle. Paul connected *sanctification* to the "will of God." What is the will of God? In this instance, it referred to a specific desire that God intended for the Thessalonians and all believers—that being to strive for holiness through the process of sanctification. What was God's will? This brings up the first injunction: that they abstain from or reject any temptations to become involved in fornication (Greek: *porneia*—this is where the word *pornography* is derived). This word literally referred to all types of inappropriate sexual behavior, whether it was adultery, lesbianism, homosexuality, bestiality, pornography, and acts such as these. The general definition has tended to limit fornication to sexual intercourse between two unmarried people. However, given the climate and culture of that day, Paul intended for the word to cover the whole range of sexual sins.

The second injunction has been a cause of much debate among scholars, both current and ancient. The heart of the debate centers on the proper interpretation of the word *vessel*. It would take more time and space than what is allotted to cover the history of this debate. Essentially, the two major interpretations are: (1) Paul was referring to one's physical body (see 2 Corinthians 4:7); and (2) Paul was referring to one's wife (see 1 Peter 3:7, where the wife is called the "weaker vessel"). The bottom line in the debate is that both interpretations are possible; however, the context best suits the first interpretation, where Paul was making reference to one's personal behavior. The focus was to know how to live in such a way that one not lose control or become tempted to revert back to the old ways of sexual looseness.

Verse 5 is further elaboration on the second injunction, where the people were not to be driven by the old lusts of the flesh. *Concupiscence* is an old word that simply means "craving" or "lust." They should not go back to their old ways, for to do such would identify them as being like the other Gentiles. Some interpreters have thought this was a racist statement, but this is highly unlikely given that racism is more modern than ancient. Paul likely used this to disconnect the Thessalonian saints from the old ways of the unconverted Gentiles who did not know God. Uncontrollable lust was a mark of the unsaved people.

The third injunction is found in verse 6: "That no man go beyond and defraud his brother in any matter." Here again, we are faced with a debate among interpreters as to whether or not Paul was still talking about sexual immorality or whether he shifted to discuss business matters, given his use of the word *matter* (Greek: *pragma*—literally "that which has been done"). In some instances, the word *pragma* has been used to refer to business or commercial transactions. Again, it is highly unlikely that Paul would shift dramatically to discuss business and then return to holiness in the very next verse. The generally accepted interpretation has been that Paul was referring to quite possibly defrauding a brother by interfering in his marriage.

Paul gave three reasons why sexual immorality was to be avoided. First, humans are not in a position to make others pay for their sins. All sin is against God (see Psalm 51). And because of this, we must all appear before the judgment seat of Christ to account for the deeds done in the body (see 2 Corinthians 5:10). Furthermore, regardless of how much we may be wronged and taken advantage of, God is the one who will avenge us (see Romans 12:17-21).

Second, God has called us to live beyond and above the world. He has called us to live in holiness, not in uncleanness (Greek: *akatharsia*—pronounced "ak-ath-as-see-a"). This word is a description of a condition that is just the opposite of what Jesus said in John 15:3 that one is "clean" through the Word. To be unclean renders one unfit to be used by God (see Leviticus 11:44-45; 1 Peter 1:14-15).

Third, the Thessalonians had received the gift of the Holy Spirit, who would keep them from committing these sins of the flesh. One cannot be filled with the Holy Spirit and live in sin. The two lifestyles are totally and completely incompatible with one another.

C. Live in Peace with Other Believers (1 Thessalonians 4:9-12)

But as touching brotherly love ye need not that I write

unto you: for ye yourselves are taught of God to love one another. And indeed ye do it toward all the brethren which are in all Macedonia: but we beseech you, brethren, that ye increase more and more; And that ye study to be quiet, and to do your own business, and to work with your own hands, as we commanded you; That ye may walk honestly toward them that are without, and that ye may have lack of nothing.

In the final section of this passage, Paul continued and concluded his lengthy discussion about love. Paul had been emphasizing practical Christianity. His theme had been a distinctive walk, whether as a walk of holiness or as a love for other believers and outsiders. Paul held the Thessalonians up as a model of congregational unity and strength. Their love and witness had been broadcast throughout Macedonia. He appealed to them to continue in brotherly love with one another. This was not something new or strange to them. In fact, they had been taught by God how to love. We are not told how this took place: quite possibly through the teachings of Paul and/or Timothy during his visit.

Their love should not stop growing. Moreover, they were to continue to love all of the brethren in Macedonia. Paul exhorted the saints to abound and love more and more. He was not chiding them nor declaring that they had not done enough; rather, his words were intended to spur them to higher heights of spiritual commitment and love.

In verse 11, the word *study* means "to keep doing what one is doing in leading a quiet life." Do not be swayed by the circumstances of life—rather, continue what is done. Throughout, Paul was laying out how they were to live in harmony with each other. Here the apostle elaborated on what it means to live in community—that is, within the community of faith and how the community of faith lives in the world. He said to be committed to living a peaceful life, to work at your own business, to be financially independent, and to not give the world an opportunity to criticize you.

III. CONCLUDING REFLECTION

These are very powerful, practical lessons that Christians today would do well to incorporate into their lives. Believers are called to live in harmony—first with each other. Jesus taught His disciples that the world would know them and of their relationship to Him by the love they had for each other (see John 13:34-35). Many times, rather than being a model of cooperation, compassion, and concern, the church can sometimes be cold, callous, and indifferent to the plight of the poor and the helpless. In this lesson, Paul encouraged the believers to be contributing members, not parasites; to be self-supporting, not dependent on others. Also, Christians should realize that they are sanctified by the blood of the Lamb and must continue in sanctification.

Many times the world looks in horror at persons who profess to be Christians and wonder what Bible these persons are reading. Our conduct must never be the cause of stumbling for unbelievers and the unchurched.

It is a common saying that "actions speak louder than words." Christianity is not a private religion. It is living by demonstrating and living practically the life of Christ. The Bible tells us that when the populace in Antioch observed the attitudes of the early Christians, they called them first "Christians"—that is, those who were emulating Christ in every aspect of life. In our time, Sunday worship services have become showtime in many churches. Many preachers have become motivational speakers instead of Gospel preachers. Many attendees have forgotten the admonition of Paul to his son in the Gospel—Timothy—that in the last days many would look for teachers who would soothe their ears with smooth talk. True to Paul's warning, we have seen many mega churches with smooth talkers in the pulpit, and hearers with itching ears in the pews.

The reason that so many shallow Christians today have lackadaisical attitudes is because of what they are being fed. Someone once said, "You become what you eat." Jesus Himself said, "A disciple is not above his teacher, but everyone who is perfectly trained will be like his teacher" (Luke 6:40). In light of this, we should not be surprised about the attitudes of many so-called Christians; they are suffering from a lack of in-depth Bible study and personal spiritual meditation on the Word of God.

As we reflect on this lesson today, Paul admonished all of us that we should strive to walk worthy of our calling. We must demonstrate Christlike attitudes. Our relationship with Christ must form the basis for our attitudes to outsiders. We are the only Bible that many people will read. There is more to Christian living than simply loving other Christians. We must be responsible in all areas of life. The Holy Spirit lives inside us and as long as we allow Him to direct our lives, others will testify that truly we are God's children (see Romans 8:28). How does your life measure up in view of this lesson? What would other people say about you when you are not around? Can you honestly say (like Paul), "Emulate me as I emulate Christ?"

PRAYER

Lord, eternal Creator, teach us how to live in such a way that You are always pleased with our lives. May the sunshine of Your love grant us the peace to live in harmony with those around us. May we love as You love, and walk as Your Son did. In Jesus' name we pray. Amen.

WORD POWER

Abound (Greek: *perisseuo* [perris-se-u-o])—here is another compound word. A compound word occurs when a preposition is added to a verb. The preposition strengthens the verb. In this context, the word *abound* can be compared to a flower growing from a bud to full beaming. Paul was asking the Thessalonians to go over and above in practicing their faith. They should bloom out for others to see.

HOME DAILY BIBLE READINGS
(June 21-27, 2010)

Demonstrated in Action
MONDAY, June 21: "Encouraging an Encourager" (Acts 18:24-28)

TUESDAY, June 22: "The Lord's Counsel" (Psalm 16:7-11)

WEDNESDAY, June 23: "The Lord's Instruction" (Psalm 32:6-11)

THURSDAY, June 24: "The Lack of Discipline" (Proverbs 5:21-23)

FRIDAY, June 25: "The Blessing of Obedience" (Deuteronomy 11:26-32)

SATURDAY, June 26: "The Final Payday" (Revelation 22:8-13)

SUNDAY, June 27: "Called to Holiness" (1 Thessalonians 4:1-12)

LESSON 5   July 4, 2010

GOD'S COSMIC PLAN

DEVOTIONAL READING: **Joel 3:11-16**
PRINT PASSAGE: **1 Thessalonians 5:1-11**

BACKGROUND SCRIPTURE: **1 Thessalonians 4:13–5:28**
KEY VERSE: **1 Thessalonians 5:9**

1 Thessalonians 5:1-11—KJV

BUT OF the times and the seasons, brethren, ye have no need that I write unto you.

2 For yourselves know perfectly that the day of the Lord so cometh as a thief in the night.

3 For when they shall say, Peace and safety; then sudden destruction cometh upon them, as travail upon a woman with child; and they shall not escape.

4 But ye, brethren, are not in darkness, that that day should overtake you as a thief.

5 Ye are all the children of light, and the children of the day: we are not of the night, nor of darkness.

6 Therefore let us not sleep, as do others; but let us watch and be sober.

7 For they that sleep sleep in the night; and they that be drunken are drunken in the night.

8 But let us, who are of the day, be sober, putting on the breastplate of faith and love; and for an helmet, the hope of salvation.

9 For God hath not appointed us to wrath, but to obtain salvation by our Lord Jesus Christ,

10 Who died for us, that, whether we wake or sleep, we should live together with him.

11 Wherefore comfort yourselves together, and edify one another, even as also ye do.

1 Thessalonians 5:1-11—NRSV

NOW CONCERNING the times and the seasons, brothers and sisters, you do not need to have anything written to you.

2 For you yourselves know very well that the day of the Lord will come like a thief in the night.

3 When they say, "There is peace and security," then sudden destruction will come upon them, as labor pains come upon a pregnant woman, and there will be no escape!

4 But you, beloved, are not in darkness, for that day to surprise you like a thief;

5 for you are all children of light and children of the day; we are not of the night or of darkness.

6 So then let us not fall asleep as others do, but let us keep awake and be sober;

7 for those who sleep sleep at night, and those who are drunk get drunk at night.

8 But since we belong to the day, let us be sober, and put on the breastplate of faith and love, and for a helmet the hope of salvation.

9 For God has destined us not for wrath but for obtaining salvation through our Lord Jesus Christ,

10 who died for us, so that whether we are awake or asleep we may live with him.

11 Therefore encourage one another and build up each other, as indeed you are doing.

BIBLE FACT

THE COMING OF THE LORD: The second coming of the Lord has always been a subject of discussion both among the saints of old and the present-day saints. In this epistle, some in the church of Thessalonica were worried about those who had died. Some of them had stopped working because they thought the Lord was coming soon. Paul, in his second epistle, told them to continue living and working until Jesus comes. Paul assured them of total victory at the final appearing of Jesus.

UNIFYING LESSON PRINCIPLE

Most people want to understand how they fit in and contribute to society as a whole. What is the context in which we obtain such an understanding? God's plan of salvation is embodied in the divine plan for all creation, which is directly related to Christ's return to earth.

TOPICAL OUTLINE OF THE LESSON

I. Introduction
   A. Living in Hope
   B. Biblical Background

II. Exposition and Application of the Scripture
   A. The Day of the Lord (1 Thessalonians 5:1-3)
   B. Children of the Light (1 Thessalonians 5:4-7)
   C. Appointed to Obtain (1 Thessalonians 5:8-11)

III. Concluding Reflection

LESSON OBJECTIVES

Upon completion of this lesson, the students will know that:

1. The coming of the Lord is sure and Christians must be watching for it;
2. Christians must not be idle as they look forward to Christ's coming; and,
3. Our election is based solely on God' grace and not our works.

POINTS TO BE EMPHASIZED

ADULT/YOUTH

Adult Topic: Finding Hope
Youth Topic: Committed Forever
Adult/Youth Key Verse: 1 Thessalonians 5:9
Print Passage: 1 Thessalonians 5:1-11

—The return of Christ will come as a surprise to some but not to others.
—Paul encouraged the church to live in the light of faith, love, and hope.
—Christ has done what is necessary for us to live with Him eternally.
—Paul told the church in Thessalonica that no one knows when the end of the world may come.
—Paul encouraged the Thessalonians by reminding them that they were children of light and did not need to fear the Day of the Lord.
—Paul told the Thessalonians to keep sober and remember that they were protected by faith, love, and the hope of salvation.
—Paul told the Thessalonians to encourage one another because God has given us the opportunity for salvation and eternity with God.

CHILDREN

Children Topic: Hey, I'm a Believer
Key Verse: 1 Thessalonians 5:8
Print Passage: Acts 19:1-10; 1 Thessalonians 5:8-11

—Disciples were baptized in the name of Jesus while Paul was in Ephesus.
—When the Holy Spirit came upon these disciples, they evidenced spiritual gifts.

—For two years, Paul and the Ephesian disciples taught at the public lecture hall.

—Christian believers are empowered by the Holy Spirit to lead clearheaded, disciplined lives, to have faith and love, and to look forward to salvation through Jesus Christ.

—Paul told the Ephesian believers to continue loving and supporting one another.

I. INTRODUCTION

A. Living in Hope

The finality of God's plan will take place when Jesus comes in glory and majesty with all of the holy angels (see Matthew 25:31; Mark 8:38). The second coming of Christ is at the very core of the Christian doctrine we call *eschatology*. Paul referred to the second coming of Jesus Christ as the "blessed hope" of the church (see Titus 2:13). Jesus never stated when He would return; it is an event and day left to the very prerogative of the Father (see Acts 1:7). What is of utmost importance is that one day He will descend from the heavens just as He ascended at the end of His earthly ministry (see Acts 1:11).

B. Biblical Background

Today's lesson is part of a larger portion of Scripture that begins at 1 Thessalonians 4:13, where the apostle Paul laid out several key points regarding the return of Jesus Christ. He had previously made three comments about the second coming of the Lord Jesus Christ which suggested that it was one of the main topics that needed to be addressed with the Thessalonians (see 1 Thessalonians 1:10; 2:19; 3:13). The technical term that is used in the Greek New Testament for the return of Christ (or the Second Coming) is *parousia*, meaning "arrival" (see 2 Corinthians 7:6ff; Philippians 1:26) or the presence of someone (see 2 Corinthians 10:10). The lengthy discussion about the *parousia* runs from 1 Thessalonians 4:13 through 5:11. One question has been whether or not there was a concern among the Thessalonians regarding the return. Another more probable question has to do with the status of those who had already died. Paul did address this. However, we cannot know with certainty whether there were numerous questions being raised among the saints about the dead. It is obvious from reading the letter that there must have been some concern given the fact that believers were dying and the saints may have wanted to know what would become of them. Paul reminded them in 4:13-18 that those who had already died were not people who died without hope. They too would see the Lord and all would go together to be with the Lord.

One of the key features of this section of the letter is its focus on the Day of the Lord. Did Paul mean the same thing as the ancient prophets of Israel did when he referenced the Day of the Lord? The mere mention of this subject suggests that during his stay he spent some time teaching them about the coming Day of the Lord. Paul's goal was to encourage the living that they would see the dead again and to prompt them into holy and righteous living. Those who await the Lord's return must be sober and watchful.

II. EXPOSITION AND APPLICATION OF THE SCRIPTURE

A. The Day of the Lord
(1 Thessalonians 5:1-3)

BUT OF the times and the seasons, brethren, ye have no need that I write unto you. For yourselves know perfectly that the day of the Lord so cometh as a thief in the night. For when they shall say, Peace and safety; then sudden destruction cometh upon them, as travail upon a woman with child; and they shall not escape.

Paul began with the phrase *de peri chronos kai kairos,* which is best translated, "But concerning the times and the seasons" (1 Thessalonians 5:1, NKJV). In this regard, the *King James Version* is a poor translation of what Paul actually wrote. In fact, a better translation would be "now concerning the times and the seasons." The use of this phrase indicates that there had obviously been a question raised by the Thessalonians regarding the return of the Lord Jesus Christ and the Day of the Lord. The question could have been raised with Timothy who might have informed Paul of a list of issues and questions when he returned from his brief mission trip to Thessalonica (see 3:6).

Chronos gives us the word *chronology* and refers to time as being either long or short. It is time as it is lived out in consecutive order. *Kairos,* on the other hand, refers to specific events or seasons. Kairos is the right moment in time when all of the factors are ripe for a specific event to occur. It is the word *kairos* that is used in Galatians 4:4 to refer to the specific point in time when Jesus was born. The Thessalonians did not need Paul to tell them what he was about to say. They had a very good understanding of these matters. They had already been instructed on a number of topics relating to Jesus Christ and God's salvation through Him. Paul wanted them to simply remember what they had already been taught.

In verse 2, he reminded them that they perfectly understood that the Day of the Lord would come as a thief in the night. Preoccupation with the timing of the Day of the Lord arose frequently in biblical and Jewish literature; thus, the question the Thessalonians raised is hardly surprising. In Old Testament prophetic writings, the Day of the Lord was seen as a future event when God would either judge Israel for her sin or Israel's enemies for their treatment of Israel (see Isaiah 13:6-13; Jeremiah 50:31; Joel 2:28-32; Amos 5:18-20; Zephaniah 1:14-18).

Paul used several analogies to describe the coming Day of the Lord. First, it would come "as a thief in the night," a phrase used also by Jesus (see Matthew 24:36, 43-44). Second, it would be at a time when people were crying "peace and safety" (see Jeremiah 6:14; 8:11; Ezekiel 13:10). Third, there would be sudden "destruction," a word used to describe complete separation from God. This destruction will come unannounced like the time when a woman is about to give birth. Fourth, there will be no escape. No place on the planet will be secure. Paul reminded us that all believers must be in a constant state of preparation for the return of the Lord Jesus Christ.

B. Children of the Light
(1 Thessalonians 5:4-7)

But ye, brethren, are not in darkness, that that day should overtake you as a thief. Ye are all the children of light, and the children of the day: we are not of the night, nor of darkness. Therefore let us not sleep, as do others; but let us watch and be sober. For they that sleep sleep in the night; and they that be drunken are drunken in the night.

Verse 4 begins a new section where Paul contrasted the situation of the believers of Thessalonica with the people who were not believers. "But ye, brethren," is a phrase that is inclusive of all of the believers, male and female alike. Unlike the unsaved in Thessalonica, the believers were not in the dark about what would take place at the coming of the Lord. Unlike the sinners in Thessalonica, who would not be prepared, the believers would always be ready. They knew what to expect; they did not know the day, but they knew it was coming. They would not be overtaken by this event, as the unsuspecting who were surprised when a thief came in the night.

Throughout verses 4-7, Paul drew a contrast between the unbelievers, who were in darkness, and the believers, who were in the light. Darkness or the dark is often used as a metaphor for the unconverted (see John 3:19; Romans 13:12; 2 Corinthians 6:14; Ephesians 5:11). In Romans 1:21, Paul referenced Gentiles as those whose understanding had been darkened by sin and rebellion against the Law of God. Christians are people who walk in the light and have passed from death to life in the Lord Jesus Christ. Just as there is a vast difference between the day and night, equally there should be as vast a visible difference between the believer and the unbeliever.

The Thessalonians were the children of light and the children of the day because they had been saved from the darkness of sin (see Acts 26:18; Ephesians 5:8; 1 Peter 2:9). Light is often used in the New Testament as a metaphor for the children of God in their new converted and redeemed state (see 1 Peter 2:9). Believers are the ones who have come out of darkness and now walk in the light of the Lord Jesus Christ. Since God is light and believers are in God there could be no darkness in them (see 1 John 1:5, 7; 2:10). Jesus Christ is the one who brought the light of immortality (see 1 Timothy 6:16). In 2 Timothy 1:10, Paul stated that the Gospel is the source of light because it has the power to bring men and women out of darkness.

The word *Therefore* in verse 6 sums up what must be the believer's stance; he or she must be wide awake at all times. *Sleep* is used in the Scriptures to refer to physical sleep (see Luke 22:46; Acts 20:9) or physical death (see John 11:11; 1 Corinthians 15:51). Sometimes, as in the present passage, it may refer to not being alert and prepared (see Matthew 25:1-13). The unprepared will not be able to meet the Lord when He comes. There is a broader application that speaks to believers who are asleep as those who are apathetic and uninvolved in what God is doing in the world. They may be members of a local congregation, yet they are fast asleep when it comes to the work of ministry and mission. They have not connected themselves to the deeper things of God.

In verse 6, the word *watch* means "to pay strict attention, and be completely alert." Those who are alert are especially alert during the hours of darkness—because the Lord will return at a time when they are least prepared and least expect Him. *To be sober* carries in it the idea of not being drunk or intoxicated with wine. This is another difference between the believers and the unbelievers. The unbelievers will not be watching and they will be drunk and asleep in the darkness of sin.

I spent six years in the U.S. Army as an airborne ranger infantry officer. In Ranger school, we were taught that one of the key elements for achieving success on the battlefield is the element of surprise. You want to always catch the enemy off-guard and unprepared. We were taught that night was the optimum time to attack because it creates covers for a surprising attack. Paul reminded the Thessalonians that Jesus will come during the time of greatest darkness, but unlike the unbelievers, they must be fully prepared, alert, and sober, ready to meet the Lord when He comes.

C. Appointed to Obtain
(1 Thessalonians 5:8-11)

But let us, who are of the day, be sober, putting on the breastplate of faith and love; and for an helmet, the hope of salvation. For God hath not appointed us to wrath, but to obtain salvation by our Lord Jesus Christ, Who died for us, that, whether we wake or sleep, we should live together with him. Wherefore comfort yourselves together, and edify one another, even as also ye do.

Verse 8 begins another and the final contrasting description between the believers and unbelievers. The unbelievers slept, got drunk, and were characterized by spiritual darkness (see Ephesians 2:1-4). The believers, on the other hand, were sober, did not get drunk, and were fully prepared to meet the Lord at His coming. The believers prepare for the coming Day of the Lord by putting on the breastplate of faith and love—and for a helmet, the hope of salvation. Beginning with verse 9, Paul shifted his

discussion to explain the destiny of the two groups—one would suffer God's wrath and the other would be saved from it. Believers were not destined or "appointed" to receive the wrath of God. Occasionally in these letters, the apostle reminded the Thessalonians of their election by God (see 1:4; 4:7; 2 Thessalonians 1:11; 2:13-14), a point to which he returned in the current verse. Believers would receive (possess) salvation by and through our Lord Jesus Christ. Paul made it clear that their future hope was anchored in the Lord Jesus Christ. The implication is that because Jesus died, we do not have to face the terror of death. Here death is seen as eternal separation from God. It did not matter to Paul whether the believer was alive or dead at the coming of the Lord (see Romans 14:8).

In the meantime, while they waited for the coming of the Lord they were to comfort each other and build each other up. The word for "comfort" is *parakaleo*, and it comes from the same root word that gives us the word *Paraclete*—which is another word for the Holy Spirit (see John 14:16, 26; 15:26; 16:7). *To comfort* is to come alongside and undergird and support. *Edify* comes from a combination of two Greek words that mean "to build a house or build up." While they waited for the coming of the Lord, they were to comfort each other with faith, love, and hope, continuously building each other up. The saints in Thessalonica were already doing what Paul requested. Continue to do this even as you already do.

III. CONCLUDING REFLECTION

The year 2008 will be a year to remember. America elected the first African-American president in its history. This symbol of change brought renewed hope and optimism to hundreds of millions of people around the world that under the leadership of President Barack Obama the world will be a better place to live. The year of 2008 will also be remembered as the year of the greatest and deepest global economic crisis since the Great Depression of the 1930s. World financial markets plummeted, businesses literally failed overnight, and national economies were plunged into a spiral of cataclysmic decline that will take years to reverse and recover from. Millions of Americans lost everything, including their hope in the future. When one has put all of his or her trust in this life, he or she will be most miserable (see 1 Corinthians 15:19-20). For the believer, his or her hope does not reside in the things of this world, nor the accumulation and possession of massive amounts of money, property, and the things of this world. We are reminded, just as Paul reminded the Thessalonians, that our hope is in the Lord Jesus Christ—who will one day take us to be with Him in glory.

PRAYER

Lord, teach us to trust You in the good times as well as during the days of great stress and difficulty. May we be prepared for the day when Your Son, Jesus Christ, will return in glory to receive us for Himself. In Jesus' name we pray. Amen.

WORD POWER

Appointed (Greek: *etheto* [e-the-to])—this word means "appointed, selected, or set aside for a purpose." It is a strong verb, which describes an act of God which is irrevocable. In the context of our lesson, Paul said, God has set us aside to receive eternal salvation and nothing can annul what God purposed for us.

HOME DAILY BIBLE READINGS
(June 28–July 4, 2010)

God's Cosmic Plan

MONDAY, June 28: "The Day of the Lord" (Joel 3:11-16)

TUESDAY, June 29: "Hearing the Word of the Lord" (Acts 19:1-10)

WEDNESDAY, June 30: "Watch for the Lord's Coming" (Matthew 24:36-44)

THURSDAY, July 1: "Prepared for the Lord's Coming" (Matthew 25:1-13)

FRIDAY, July 2: "The Coming of the Lord" (1 Thessalonians 4:13-18)

SATURDAY, July 3: "Blameless at Christ's Coming" (1 Thessalonians 5:12-24)

SUNDAY, July 4: "Obtaining Salvation in Christ" (1 Thessalonians 5:1-11)

LESSON 6   July 11, 2010

GLORY TO CHRIST

DEVOTIONAL READING: **1 Peter 5:6-11**
PRINT PASSAGE: **2 Thessalonians 1:3-12**

BACKGROUND SCRIPTURE: **2 Thessalonians 1**
KEY VERSE: **2 Thessalonians 1:11**

2 Thessalonians 1:3-12—KJV

3 We are bound to thank God always for you, brethren, as it is meet, because that your faith groweth exceedingly, and the charity of every one of you all toward each other aboundeth;

4 So that we ourselves glory in you in the churches of God for your patience and faith in all your persecutions and tribulations that ye endure:

5 Which is a manifest token of the righteous judgment of God, that ye may be counted worthy of the kingdom of God, for which ye also suffer:

6 Seeing it is a righteous thing with God to recompense tribulation to them that trouble you;

7 And to you who are troubled rest with us, when the Lord Jesus shall be revealed from heaven with his mighty angels,

8 In flaming fire taking vengeance on them that know not God, and that obey not the gospel of our Lord Jesus Christ:

9 Who shall be punished with everlasting destruction from the presence of the Lord, and from the glory of his power;

10 When he shall come to be glorified in his saints, and to be admired in all them that believe (because our testimony among you was believed) in that day.

11 Wherefore also we pray always for you, that our God would count you worthy of this calling, and fulfil all the good pleasure of his goodness, and the work of faith with power:

12 That the name of our Lord Jesus Christ may be glorified in you, and ye in him, according to the grace of our God and the Lord Jesus Christ.

2 Thessalonians 1:3-12—NRSV

3 We must always give thanks to God for you, brothers and sisters, as is right, because your faith is growing abundantly, and the love of everyone of you for one another is increasing.

4 Therefore we ourselves boast of you among the churches of God for your steadfastness and faith during all your persecutions and the afflictions that you are enduring.

5 This is evidence of the righteous judgment of God, and is intended to make you worthy of the kingdom of God, for which you are also suffering.

6 For it is indeed just of God to repay with affliction those who afflict you,

7 and to give relief to the afflicted as well as to us, when the Lord Jesus is revealed from heaven with his mighty angels

8 in flaming fire, inflicting vengeance on those who do not know God and on those who do not obey the gospel of our Lord Jesus.

9 These will suffer the punishment of eternal destruction, separated from the presence of the Lord and from the glory of his might,

10 when he comes to be glorified by his saints and to be marveled at on that day among all who have believed, because our testimony to you was believed.

11 To this end we always pray for you, asking that our God will make you worthy of his call and will fulfill by his power every good resolve and work of faith,

12 so that the name of our Lord Jesus may be glorified in you, and you in him, according to the grace of our God and the Lord Jesus Christ.

TOPICAL OUTLINE OF THE LESSON

I. Introduction
A. Christian Persecution
B. Biblical Background

II. Exposition and Application of the Scripture
A. Patient in Tribulation (2 Thessalonians 1:3-5)
B. The Destiny of the Persecutors (2 Thessalonians 1:6-10)
C. Prayer to Be Counted Worthy (2 Thessalonians 1:11-12)

III. Concluding Reflection

LESSON OBJECTIVES

Upon completion of this lesson, the students will know that:

1. We are called to persevere under extreme circumstances;
2. Persecutors will surely have their day with the almighty God; and,
3. Christians should always pray to be found worthy for God's use.

POINTS TO BE EMPHASIZED

ADULT/YOUTH

Adult Topic: Finding Purpose in Life
Youth Topic: Committed
Adult Key Verse: 2 Thessalonians 1:11
Youth Key Verses: 2 Thessalonians 1:11-12
Print Passage: 2 Thessalonians 1:3-12

—Paul taught that Jesus' return will be public and unmistakable.
—Paul taught perseverance in faith in times of affliction.
—God's justice will be final.
—Thankfulness to God is vital to Christians.
—Paul encouraged the Thessalonians to live in faith worthy of their calling.
—Paul sympathized with the hardships of the Christians in Thessalonica and told them that God was using them as good examples for others.
—Rest will come for those who persevere in the faith, and God will bring judgment on those who refuse to accept God's plan to save them.
—Paul assured the Thessalonians of his prayers for them and that God would make them the kind of children God wanted them to be.

CHILDREN

Children Topic: Keep the Faith
Key Verse: 2 Thessalonians 1:3
Print Passage: Acts 20:3-12; 2 Thessalonians 1:3-4

—Paul returned to Macedonia in the company of other believers.
—Paul traveled to Philippi and Troas, where he remained for seven days conversing with the believers.

—On his last day in Troas, Paul preached to the disciples until midnight.

—Eutychus was overcome with sleep while listening to Paul and he fell three floors to the ground below.

—Paul stopped lecturing the disciples long enough to restore Eutychus to life.

—Paul thanked God for the Thessalonian church's increasing faith and steadfast commitment during their trials and tribulations.

I. INTRODUCTION
A. Christian Persecution

The first disciples of Jesus were clear about one thing: their task of reaching the world with the Gospel of God's redemptive love would not be an easy one (see Matthew 10:22; 24:9; John 15:18). Not only would they have the challenge of traveling to places that many had never been, but also the difficulty would be compounded by the hostility that they would face because of the crucified Christ (see 1 Corinthians 1:18-23).

The lesson today serves as a reminder to us that persecution was a fact of life for the earliest Christians and it remains that for millions of Christians living around the world. If you were to do an Internet search of the words "Christian persecution" you would be surprised at the prevalence of the persecution of Christians, especially in countries that have a large and predominantly Muslim population. An organization known as Christian Solidarity International reported that nearly 150,000 Christians were martyred in 2008. The same organization offers a sobering report that even in the United States the persecution of Christians is on the increase. Clearly, we see that in many very subtle ways. There is a growing increase in films, television series, and even clothing styles that promote the occult and supernatural powers of evil. Our lesson today will give us the tools that we need to stand firm against the wiles of the devil, empowering us to defeat the unseen enemies of our faith.

B. Biblical Background

Today's lesson is the first of three lessons from the second epistle of the apostle Paul to the church of Thessalonica. The second letter is very similar in form and style to the first letter. Paul wrote this letter shortly after the first letter to the Thessalonians. More than likely the letter was written while he was in Corinth. As in the first letter, Silas and Timothy were with him and are mentioned as sending greetings along with him. Several questions about the second letter have been raised that we have no answers for. First, we do not know how Paul came to have knowledge of the circumstances of the church that would have prompted the writing of the second letter. In 3:11, he did mention that they had heard some things about the unruly members of the congregation. We are not quite sure what that meant. We neither know who he heard from nor how they communicated with him. Second, we have no record of who delivered the letter. It may have been someone who came from the church of Thessalonica to Corinth and while present with the group informed Paul about some of the issues facing the church.

Here is what we do know with some certainty. First, we know the author of the letter was Paul and that his companions at the time of writing were Silas and Timothy. Second, we know that the church was facing persecution. Third, we know that many of the saints in Thessalonica were concerned about the exact time that the return of the Lord Jesus Christ would take place.

II. EXPOSITION AND APPLICATION OF THE SCRIPTURE

A. Patient in Tribulation
(2 Thessalonians 1:3-5)

We are bound to thank God always for you, brethren, as it is meet, because that your faith groweth exceedingly, and the charity of every one of you all toward each other aboundeth; So that we ourselves glory in you in the churches of God for your patience and faith in all your persecutions and tribulations that ye endure: Which is a manifest token of the righteous judgment of God, that ye may be counted worthy of the kingdom of God, for which ye also suffer.

The letter began just as the first did—with words of thanksgiving and greeting from the three missionaries (see 1 Thessalonians 1:1-2). Paul wrote that they were obligated to give thanks to God for them. The work that had gone on and the commitment that they had to the spread of the Gospel throughout Macedonia were the reasons to be thankful to God. In verse 3, Paul mentioned two primary reasons for why they were thankful to God. First, their faith was growing by leaps and bounds. The word *exceedingly* means "to grow beyond measure and expectations." Given what they faced, it was inconceivable that the church would be reaching such heights. The second reason they were thankful was because their love for each other was growing. Unlike the saints in Corinth, where love was virtually absent, in Thessalonica it grew.

The strength of the congregation and their continuing growth in grace was a major reason for Paul's joy. They were his crown in the Lord Jesus Christ (see 1 Thessalonians 2:19). Paul found great joy in being able to brag and boast about the courage and faith of the saints in Thessalonica. He could not make the same claims about the Corinthians who seemed to always be in disarray and confusion when it came to the offering that was being collected for the saints in Jerusalem (see 2 Corinthians 7:14; 9:2, 4). The Thessalonians were a congregation that lived out its faith daily. There were three reasons why they rejoiced. First, they rejoiced over their *patience,* a word that refers to the steadfast capacity of a man or woman to face trials and not be moved (see Romans 2:7; 5:3-5; 8:25; 12:12; 1 Thessalonians 1:3). Second, Paul was thankful for their faith in the midst of their persecutions. Here, *faith* refers to the convictions that they had that Jesus was the Christ and the Savior of the world. They clung to these beliefs without wavering (see James 1:6). Third, they were enduring throughout the ordeal of their tribulations. We are not sure of the extent and intensity of their trials, but it clearly must have been the equivalent of what Paul faced when he initially went to that region (see 1 Thessalonians 2:14; 3:3-4; compare with James 5:11). The trial of their faith was daily, which is one of the reasons why Paul boasted to the other churches about the resolve of the Thessalonians.

In verse 5, Paul saw them as the manifest evidence that God would one day bring judgment upon those who persecuted the Thessalonians. There might have been some in the church who believed that their suffering was a sign that they had been rejected by God or that they were being punished for some reason unknown to them. In the ancient world, it was a common belief that suffering was the result of some moral collapse or some hidden and secret sin (see Luke 13:4; John 9:2). Paul wanted to assure the saints that their suffering had nothing to do with either sin or rejection.

B. The Destiny of the Persecutors (2 Thessalonians 1:6-10)

Seeing it is a righteous thing with God to recompense tribulation to them that trouble you; And to you who are troubled rest with us, when the Lord Jesus shall be revealed from heaven with his mighty angels, In flaming fire taking vengeance on them that know not God, and that obey not the gospel of our Lord Jesus Christ: Who shall be punished with everlasting destruction from the presence of the Lord, and from the glory of his power; When he shall come to be glorified in his saints, and to be admired in all them that believe (because our testimony among you was believed) in that day.

In verse 6, Paul made it clear that the suffering and the tribulations faced by the Thessalonians had not gone unnoticed by God. He was fully aware of their situation (see Psalm 34:15). The word *righteous* is a declaration that God is just: He would not allow the Thessalonians to suffer without *recompense,* a word that means "to repay." It would be against the very nature of God for Him not to repay those who had oppressed His people. The Scriptures abound with the truth of Paul's statement regarding the just nature of God (see Deuteronomy 32:41-43).

Paul was so confident in the justice of God that he told the Thessalonians to rest in God. He fully understood, as he was no doubt experiencing tribulation even as he wrote from Corinth. "Rest" has in it the idea of loosening the tension. Paul wanted the saints to release themselves from the burden of worry because God did have a day of rest for His people (see Hebrews 4:9). When would this time come? Paul stated that it would come at the appearing of Jesus Christ. When that day came, He would not come alone but with His mighty angels, an indication that those who had stood against the people of God would face a heavenly host that could not be defeated.

Paul used a series of prepositional phrases to describe the revelation of the Lord Jesus Christ. It would be: (1) from heaven; (2) with the mighty angels; and (3) in flaming fire. He followed up these phrases by identifying those who would be the recipients of the wrath of God. It would be those who did not know God who would receive the greater condemnation (see Exodus 5:2; Psalm 9:10; Jeremiah 9:6; John 8:19; Romans 1:28). There has been some discussion as to whether or not Paul was referring to a second group who would receive recompense who are described as those "that obey not the gospel of our Lord Jesus Christ" (verse 8). It may well be that these were people who had been exposed to the Gospel, heard it, and received it but refused to obey (see Luke 10:13-15).

The punishment of those who had troubled God's people and afflicted them would not be short-lived; rather, it would be everlasting destruction (see Isaiah 33:14; 66:24; Daniel 12:2; Matthew 25:41, 46; Philippians 3:1). There would be no deliberations, no appeals, no lessening of the sentence, and no possibilities for parole. Those whose names are not written in the Lamb's Book of Life will not receive second chances to repent and obey Jesus Christ (see Luke 16:19-31). There is a day and time to hear and respond; when it is passed the moment may never return (see Luke 19:41-44).

Verse 10 is a very complex verse and it is written in a very complicated fashion. Paul looked to the future when the Lord Jesus Christ would come. This seems to be a response to those who may have thought that the second coming or the revelation of Christ had already taken place. When He comes again, "He will be glorified in his saints" (verse 10). How do we understand this phrase "glorified in His saints"? The thought is that those who have followed Jesus will in that final day share in the manifestation of His glory. There will be a final vindication of the person and work of Jesus as the Christ (see Philippians 2:5-11). Some scholars see in these words an allusion to Psalms 68:35 and 89:7, where God is the one who is not only reverenced among His people, but He is also the one who gives them strength and power. Who are the saints? Paul often referred to the believers in the various churches as the saints (see Romans 1:7; 1 Corinthians 1:2; 2 Corinthians 1:1; Ephesians 1:1; Philippians 1:1; Colossians 1:2). Presently, the saints are all of the people of God who have washed their robes in the blood of the Lamb, endured the tribulations of this life, and remained faithful to Jesus Christ.

Finally, the saints will admire Jesus in that day, which is a reference to the Old Testament concept of the *Day of the Lord*. The Day of the Lord was often cited among the prophets as the day of God's vengeance and judgment (see Malachi 3:17). Jesus spoke of this day as well as the Day of Judgment when those who had done evil would be punished—even those who had pretended to speak in His name (see Matthew 7:22; 24:36).

C. Prayer to Be Counted Worthy (2 Thessalonians 1:11-12)

Wherefore also we pray always for you, that our God would count you worthy of this calling, and fulfil all the good pleasure of his goodness, and the work of faith with power: That the name of our Lord Jesus Christ may be glorified in you, and ye in him, according to the grace of our God and the Lord Jesus Christ.

Again in verse 11, Paul mentioned that they were praying for the saints in Thessalonica. They prayed always that God would count them as worthy of this calling. The Greek word for *worthy* at its core is the idea of weight or value. Therefore, "to be counted worthy" means that upon thorough examination, they had been proven worthy through their endurance. What did Paul mean by "calling"? It was a calling to live a life that reflected who they were in Jesus Christ, which came with great responsibility.

The second part of Paul's prayer was that God would fulfill what had already begun through the work of faith and the power of God. All that they were and did was not because of their own goodness, but was the product of the goodness of God. They had been called to good works and it was God who made it possible to perform the doing of them (see Ephesians 2:10).

Ultimately, the name *the Lord Jesus Christ* would be glorified as they let their lights shine (see Matthew 5:14-16). In verse 12, Paul used the title "Lord Jesus Christ" for the fourth time in this chapter. Clearly, he wanted his audience to know that Jesus was not only the one crucified and resurrected, but also He was the Lord, sovereign ruler over all that was, is, and will be.

III. CONCLUDING REFLECTION

The lesson is a highlight of both the challenges and blessings that believers have. When we are overly consumed and concerned about the plights we face and the predicaments that crop up from time to time, we run the risk of taking our eyes off the Savior. We must always be prepared for suffering. There is no truth to the notion that once we are saved, it is only a matter of time before we receive the abundance of God's grace and blessings. I have traveled extensively throughout Kenya, and have witnessed suffering and deprivation among the people of God in ways that many Americans can only imagine. Yet, I have seen people with virtually nothing praise God with excitement and look to Him with expectancy and hope. Paul pointed to that day when the Lord Jesus Christ comes and recompenses judgment upon all those who have troubled His people. This is our source of consolation in the midst of our challenges—that in the final day Jesus Christ will remember our suffering and pain. He will reward us for our faithfulness to the kingdom's agenda. This is what we call *perseverance of the saints.*

PRAYER

Lord God, we bless You for the grace that has been brought to light in the life of our Lord Jesus Christ. Thank You for the courage to endure and the faith that will not fade in the midst of our trials. We give Your name glory and honor. In Jesus' name we pray. Amen.

WORD POWER

Good Pleasure (Greek: *eudoke* [yu-do-ke-a])—the Greek word is a combination of two words: *eu* means "good," *dokea* means "pleasure." The word *eulogy* has two Greek words combined: *eu* means "good," *logos* means "word" (*eulogy*—"good word"). In the Key Verse, good pleasure is what Paul's prayer was all about. He prayed that God would find them worthy to fulfill His desire (good pleasure) to unbelievers.

HOME DAILY BIBLE READINGS
(July 5-11, 2010)

Glory to Christ
   MONDAY, July 5: "Remain Steadfast in the Faith" (1 Peter 5:6-11)
   TUESDAY, July 6: "A Nightlong Farewell" (Acts 20:7-12)
   WEDNESDAY, July 7: "Worthy Is the Lamb" (Revelation 5:9-14)
   THURSDAY, July 8: "The Saved Praise God" (Revelation 7:9-17)
   FRIDAY, July 9: "The Eternal Gospel Is for All" (Revelation 14:6-13)
   SATURDAY, July 10: "Give God the Glory" (Revelation 19:1-8)
   SUNDAY, July 11: "Worthy of Christ's Call" (2 Thessalonians 1:3-12)

LESSON 7   July 18, 2010

CHOSEN AND CALLED

DEVOTIONAL READING: **Psalm 33:4-12**
PRINT PASSAGE: **2 Thessalonians 2:13-17**

BACKGROUND SCRIPTURE: **2 Thessalonians 2**
KEY VERSE: **2 Thessalonians 2:15**

2 Thessalonians 2:13-17—KJV

13 But we are bound to give thanks always to God for you, brethren beloved of the Lord, because God hath from the beginning chosen you to salvation through sanctification of the Spirit and belief of the truth:

14 Whereunto he called you by our gospel, to the obtaining of the glory of our Lord Jesus Christ.

15 Therefore, brethren, stand fast, and hold the traditions which ye have been taught, whether by word, or our epistle.

16 Now our Lord Jesus Christ himself, and God, even our Father, which hath loved us, and hath given us everlasting consolation and good hope through grace,

17 Comfort your hearts, and stablish you in every good word and work.

2 Thessalonians 2:13-17—NRSV

13 But we must always give thanks to God for you, brothers and sisters beloved by the Lord, because God chose you as the first fruits for salvation through sanctification by the Spirit and through belief in the truth.

14 For this purpose he called you through our proclamation of the good news, so that you may obtain the glory of our Lord Jesus Christ.

15 So then, brothers and sisters, stand firm and hold fast to the traditions that you were taught by us, either by word of mouth or by our letter.

16 Now may our Lord Jesus Christ himself and God our Father, who loved us and through grace gave us eternal comfort and good hope,

17 comfort your hearts and strengthen them in every good work and word.

BIBLE FACT

CHOSEN (Greek: *Haireo*)—it means "to take for oneself, to prefer, choose" and "to choose by vote, elect to office." In the context here, *chosen* means "to take for oneself." One of the doctrines of the Bible that brings inexpressible joy to believers is "Chosen." It is a word which embraces the idea of grace in its widest scope. Christians are blessed because they are chosen for eternal salvation. They do not work for it, nor do they deserve it; it is purely based on the grace of God. We can do nothing to be saved on our own merit; we must accept the fact that we are chosen to be saved. This is the reason why some people give an acrostic to GRACE as "God's Redemption At Christ's Expense." The persecution which the Christians in Thessalonica were going through cannot be compared to the joy in heaven. We have been chosen too, and we must exhibit this doctrine by the way we live every day. Paul consistently affirmed that salvation begins and ends with God.

UNIFYING LESSON PRINCIPLE

Commitments grow from a number of factors. What is at the heart of a commitment that makes a needed and lasting difference? It is affirmed in the passage that our Christian commitment grows from a response to being chosen by God and empowered by the Spirit.

TOPICAL OUTLINE OF THE LESSON

I. Introduction
    A. A Shift in the Church
    B. Biblical Background

II. Exposition and Application of the Scripture
    A. Chosen to Salvation
       (2 Thessalonians 2:13)
    B. Called through the Gospel
       (2 Thessalonians 2:14)
    C. Stand Firm
       (2 Thessalonians 2:15)
    D. Jesus Christ, Our Everlasting Consolation
       (2 Thessalonians 2:16-17)

III. Concluding Reflection

LESSON OBJECTIVES

Upon completion of this lesson, the students will know that:

1. God chose us to inherit salvation—and not because of anything we have done;

2. Satan will challenge our position in Christ through many means; and,

3. We have the audacity to challenge Satan and remain firm in Christ.

POINTS TO BE EMPHASIZED

ADULT/YOUTH
Adult Topic: **Standing Firm**
Youth Topic: **Committed to Stand Firm**
Adult/Youth Key Verse: **2 Thessalonians 2:15**
Print Passage: **2 Thessalonians 2:13-17**

—Paul cautioned the church to not be deceived by false teaching.

—The Holy Spirit sanctifies and empowers Christians for service.

—Eternal comfort and good hope are available through God's grace.

—Paul encouraged thankfulness for having been chosen as the first fruits for salvation.

—Paul commended the Thessalonians for being chosen and called of God for salvation.

—Paul encouraged the Thessalonians to stand firm and keep a strong grip on the things he had taught them.

—Paul prayed for the Thessalonians, asking God to provide comfort and strength to them.

CHILDREN
Children Topic: **Finish the Job**
Key Verse: **2 Thessalonians 2:15**
Print Passage: **Acts 20:16-19, 22-25, 32, 36-38;**
2 Thessalonians 2:13-14

—Although Paul had decided to travel past Ephesus, he sent a message asking the Ephesian leaders to meet with him.

—Paul told the Ephesian leaders of his anticipated imprisonment while expressing his desire to finish the assignment given to him by Jesus.

—Paul commended the Ephesian leaders to God's grace and support.

—After praying with the Ephesian leaders, Paul embraced and kissed them because they were mourning the loss of companionship with their friend and teacher.

—Paul expressed his belief that God had chosen the Thessalonian church as the first fruits of salvation.

—Christian believers are called to proclaim the Good News and to glorify Jesus Christ.

I. INTRODUCTION

A. A Shift in the Church

The Christian church in America has undergone radical changes over the past twenty-five years. This period is marked by several significant changes. First, the church has seen a dramatic shift in congregational demographics wherein the greatest growth has occurred in non-denominational churches. What is a denomination? A *denomination* is made up of a number of congregations united under a common and distinct faith, name, and structure, like Baptists, United Methodists, or Anglican. Second, within many denominational churches there has been a shift by younger pastors to curtailing and moving away from these denominational structures. Why? The answer probably has to do with how one interprets a word that Paul used in today's lesson—*traditions*. *Church traditions* are those cultural mores that may be unique to a particular congregation. They can be the dates of an annual revival, the colors of the ushers' uniforms, or the day and time for the service of the Lord's Supper. All of these are congregationally determined and have no basis in Scripture; hence, they are man-made traditions.

We learn from our lesson about the Christian tradition which is an altogether different matter than traditionalism. By "Christian tradition," we mean the process by which the truths and beliefs of the faith have been passed on from one generation to the next. *Traditionalism* refers to those non-biblical customs and practices that we exalt to the status of the sacred. Today's lesson is important because it helps us to understand some of the foundational teachings of the early Christian church and why it is important to hold fast to our profession of faith.

B. Biblical Background

Chapter 2 is a continuation of the exhortation to hold fast and remain resilient in the face of persecution. In previous lessons, we have learned of Paul's desire to build up and encourage the saints to stand firm in the face of their opponents. Paul began the chapter by exhorting the believers in Thessalonica to continue in the faith, as they awaited the coming of the Lord. He encouraged the saints that although some people had made claims that the second coming of Christ had already occurred, they were not to be believed. These claims were completely false and they were not to be deceived by anyone who claimed that the Day of the Lord had passed (see 2 Thessalonians 2:1-3). We do not know the source of these false declarations and teachings. But whoever these people were, their words must have created quite a stir among the believers in Thessalonica.

In these verses, Paul reminded the saints that through God's grace believers receive eternal comfort and good hope. Just as God had called Paul, the Thessalonians had also been called by God's grace to eternal salvation. These were the traditions that were to be believed and passed on to the next generation of Christians.

II. EXPOSITION AND APPLICATION OF THE SCRIPTURE

A. Chosen to Salvation
(2 Thessalonians 2:13)

But we are bound to give thanks always to God for you, brethren beloved of the Lord, because God hath from the beginning chosen you to salvation through sanctification of the Spirit and belief of the truth.

In verse 13, Paul offered a second thanksgiving to God which is similar to the first one he offered in 1 Thessalonians 1:3. In the first thanksgiving, Paul expressed thanks to God because the faith of the saints was increasing in leaps and bounds. It is possible that embedded within these words were thanks for the consistent way in which they had become the means of the spread of the Gospel throughout Macedonia and Achaia (see 1 Thessalonians 1:9). As in the first thanksgiving, Paul talked about their obligation to thank God for them: "We are bound." The word *bound* conveys the sense of debt or an obligation which must be paid. This act of giving thanks was not a one-time prayer, but was constant. Every time he prayed, there was the mention of the saints in Thessalonica (see Romans 1:9; Ephesians 1:16; Philemon 1:4).

Paul understood the saints to be his brothers and sisters and therefore referred to them as "brethren," who were the ones loved by God (see Deuteronomy 33:12; Romans 1:7; Colossians 3:12; 1 John 4:10, 19). God chose them from the very beginning for salvation. The word *chose* comes from a Greek verb that means "to take for oneself." It has in it the idea of preferential choice. God chose them from the beginning—that is, the beginning of the time—that the Gospel was first preached in their hearing in Thessalonica. There is also the possibility that Paul could have been referring to God's choice of them from the very foundation of the world to be saved.

Whom God chooses for certain assignments and why is completely in His hands. God chose Israel to be His own special people, a peculiar treasure (see Exodus 19:5; Psalm 135:4). He redeemed them out of the bondage of Egypt and made them a kingdom of priests. In the same way, Paul said that God chose the Thessalonians to be His special people (see 1 Peter 2:9-10). They were chosen for salvation through sanctification. In these words, Paul reminded them of some instructions he gave in the first letter that they had not been appointed to receive the wrath of God, but for the purpose of salvation (see 1 Thessalonians 5:9). They had been saved not because of anything that they or Paul and his companions had done, but through faith in the death and resurrection of Jesus Christ (see Romans 10:9-13; Ephesians 2:8-10).

They were chosen to salvation through two means. The first was through the agency of the Holy Spirit who sanctified them and made them new creatures (see 2 Corinthians 5:17). *Sanctification* refers to being set aside or consecrated for divine purposes, an act that goes back to the time of Moses and the establishment and erection of the tabernacle. All of the holy vessels and utensils were consecrated to God for service, as well as Aaron and his sons (see Exodus 29:41; compare with Numbers 6:12; 1 Chronicles 29:5). The second means mentioned by Paul was through their belief in the truth of the Gospel that was proclaimed in their midst (see John 8:32, 45-46; 14:6; Acts 13:48; 15:9; Colossians 1:5; 2 Timothy 2:15; 3:15). Each of us has been chosen by God for his or her own purpose (see Romans 8:28).

B. Called through the Gospel
(2 Thessalonians 2:14)

Whereunto he called you by our gospel, to the obtaining of the glory of our Lord Jesus Christ.

In verse 14, Paul stated that the Thessalonians had been called by the Gospel. The Gospel is the Good News regarding the death, burial, resurrection, and return of the Lord Jesus Christ. It was through the message of the Gospel that they came to know God (see 1 Corinthians 1:18-23). Paul's use of the possessive pronoun "our" with *gospel* is not to be understood as something that he made up; rather, it was the message of the redemption of God in Christ that had been handed down to him (see Romans 1:16; 1 Corinthians 15:1-4). He understood himself to be a steward of the mysteries of the Gospel and an ambassador for Christ (see 1 Corinthians 4:2; 2 Corinthians 5:19-20). The purpose of their having been

saved and sanctified is also for the purpose of "obtaining of the glory of the Lord Jesus Christ." When Jesus Christ returns, all of His saints will share in the honor and glory that will be revealed. His coming will vindicate their faith in Him. Although they were facing severe persecution, the day was coming when Jesus would come with all of the holy angels and take them unto Himself (see Matthew 16:27; 24:30; 25:31; Mark 8:38; Titus 2:13).

C. Stand Firm
(2 Thessalonians 2:15)

Therefore, brethren, stand fast, and hold the traditions which ye have been taught, whether by word, or our epistle.

In verse 15, Paul began with the word *therefore*. In the New Testament and modern writings, the word *therefore* always serves as an indicator for the introduction to something new. It could be a warning or exhortation. It literally means, "in light of all that has been previously stated this is what you are called to do." Paul frequently used this technique in his writings to move from what can be called doctrinal statements to more practical steps for living out what he had just said. If we accept only doctrine without applying those doctrinal beliefs, then we end up with a lopsided faith. There must be balance to what we believe and practice. And here Paul provided balance. In light of everything that they had heard and experienced he exhorted them to do two things. First, he told them to "stand firm" (NIV), which is written in the present imperative tense (see 1 Corinthians 15:58; 16:13; Ephesians 6:10-12; Philippians 4:1). The words are written as a command to continue to resist the temptation to quit, give in, or turn around. The challenge that Paul faced and that every pastor faces came from believers who turned around and went back into the world because of the lures of the world or the pressure to quit (see Romans 14:4; 1 Corinthians 16:13; Galatians 3:1; 5:1; Philippians 1:27; 4:1). The most difficult spirit to deal with is an apostate spirit.

Next, Paul gave the means by which they were to stand, and that was to "hold the traditions which ye have been taught." The word *traditions* refers to the foundational truths of the Christian faith that are inclusive of salvation, sanctification, and service in the kingdom of God (see Luke 1:2; 2 Timothy 1:13-14). Paul was not referring to man-made traditions that we seek to pass on to another generation as sacred and untouchable. The Thessalonians had received these traditions by the word of preaching and teaching and through his letters. Believers must hold fast to that which was true and not those teachings and practices that conflicted with the Word of God.

D. Jesus Christ, Our Everlasting Consolation (2 Thessalonians 2:16-17)

Now our Lord Jesus Christ himself, and God, even our Father, which hath loved us, and hath given us everlasting consolation and good hope through grace, Comfort your hearts, and stablish you in every good word and work.

The lesson closes with the words of prayer. Paul used the complete title of the Lord Jesus Christ to show both His sovereignty and majesty. He was not just the crucified One; rather, He is the Lord. He and God our Father are One (see Ephesians 4:4-6). These final words were meant to reassure the saints that even in the midst of their trials and tribulations God loved them. His word through Paul and the visit of Timothy were a sure consolation that God was

concerned to give them good hope, which was grounded in their everlasting consolation. The reference here is most likely referring to their eternal hope that would be revealed when the Lord Jesus Christ came. Sometimes we can be filled with false hope that only brings further despair and disappointment. What they had received was good hope, which God had given through His grace.

Paul prayed that the Lord Jesus Christ would also *comfort,* a word meaning "to come alongside for the purpose of strengthening." Paul prayed that they might be comforted in their hearts, while being established or firmed up for the purpose of *doing good.* The *good* was defined as "good words and works." His grace and comfort would be the source and strength of their words and works. The phrase "in every good word and work" refers to the fact that everything that they did would be worthwhile and effective. *Good words* may also refer to speaking the truth in love and seasoning their words with salt so that they would not speak evil of other believers (see Ephesians 4:29; Colossians 3:8; James 3:3-12). Finally, Paul added to the good word the desire that their work would be equally good as well. We have been created to do good works, and it is our work that speaks volumes about our faith (see Ephesians 2:10; James 1:22-27).

III. CONCLUDING REFLECTION

It is stated in Romans 5:1-10 that we have been justified freely by our faith in the finished work of Jesus Christ, giving us access to God's peace and grace. In Ephesians 2:8, we are taught that we have been saved by grace. Since we have been saved by grace, given new positions and status in Christ Jesus, we are obligated to live lives that are consistent with our beliefs. In other words, salvation is not the end of the line. We must go on to spiritual maturity, moving beyond our conversion to full maturity (see Ephesians 4:14-16). It is stated in Hebrews 6:1-2, "Therefore leaving the principles of the doctrine of Christ, let us go on unto perfection; not laying again the foundation of repentance from dead works, and of faith toward God, Of the doctrine of baptisms, and of laying on of hands, and of resurrection of the dead, and of eternal judgment." It is true we have been justified by His grace, but we must move beyond that to sanctification in daily living.

Sanctification is the outworking and outliving of the doctrines of our faith in Christ. It is striving toward spiritual maturity in every sphere of our lives. In Philippians 3:12-14, Paul wrote about the process of sanctification: "Not as though I had already attained, either were already perfect: but I follow after, if that I may apprehend that for which also I am apprehended of Christ Jesus. Brethren, I count not myself to have apprehended: but this one thing I do, forgetting those things which are behind, and reaching forth unto those things which are before, I press toward the mark for the prize of the high calling of God in Christ Jesus." In other words, you must get beyond just being a church member, just coming to church, and just being satisfied with affiliation, and work out your soul's salvation daily.

PRAYER

Eternal God, fill us with Your Holy Spirit that we may live in victory. Grant that we may never be ashamed to declare You in this life. Sanctify us that our work for You will bear much fruit. In Jesus' name we pray. Amen.

WORD POWER

Tradition (Greek: *paradosis* [pa-ra-do-sis])—this word is a compound word—a combination of a preposition and a verb. *Para* means "alongside," and *didomi* means "hand over." In essence, Paul was saying that the Thessalonians must not accept any false doctrines. They should hold on to the apostle's teachings and doctrines and gathering of the saints. These are Christian *paradosis*.

HOME DAILY BIBLE READINGS
(July 12-18, 2010)

Chosen and Called

MONDAY, July 12: "Chosen as God's Heritage" (Psalm 33:4-12)
TUESDAY, July 13: "The Confidence of Hope" (Hebrews 3:1-6)
WEDNESDAY, July 14: "Called to Freedom" (Galatians 5:7-14)
THURSDAY, July 15: "Called to God's Purpose" (2 Timothy 2:8-13)
FRIDAY, July 16: "Finishing the Course" (Acts 20:17-24)
SATURDAY, July 17: "The Danger of Deception" (2 Thessalonians 2:1-12)
SUNDAY, July 18: "Stand Firm, Hold Fast" (2 Thessalonians 2:13-17)

LESSON 8   July 25, 2010

GOD'S OWN FAITHFULNESS

DEVOTIONAL READING: **Psalm 89:1-8**

PRINT PASSAGE: **2 Thessalonians 3:1-15**

BACKGROUND SCRIPTURE: **2 Thessalonians 3**

KEY VERSE: **2 Thessalonians 3:3**

2 Thessalonians 3:1-15—KJV

FINALLY, BRETHREN, pray for us, that the word of the Lord may have free course, and be glorified, even as it is with you:

2 And that we may be delivered from unreasonable and wicked men: for all men have not faith.

3 But the Lord is faithful, who shall stablish you, and keep you from evil.

4 And we have confidence in the Lord touching you, that ye both do and will do the things which we command you.

5 And the Lord direct your hearts into the love of God, and into the patient waiting for Christ.

6 Now we command you, brethren, in the name of our Lord Jesus Christ, that ye withdraw yourselves from every brother that walketh disorderly, and not after the tradition which he received of us.

7 For yourselves know how ye ought to follow us: for we behaved not ourselves disorderly among you;

8 Neither did we eat any man's bread for nought; but wrought with labour and travail night and day, that we might not be chargeable to any of you:

9 Not because we have not power, but to make ourselves an ensample unto you to follow us.

10 For even when we were with you, this we commanded you, that if any would not work, neither should he eat.

11 For we hear that there are some which walk among you disorderly, working not at all, but are busybodies.

12 Now them that are such we command and exhort by our Lord Jesus Christ, that with quietness they work, and eat their own bread.

13 But ye, brethren, be not weary in well doing.

14 And if any man obey not our word by this epistle, note that man, and have no company with him, that he may be ashamed.

2 Thessalonians 3:1-15—NRSV

FINALLY, BROTHERS and sisters, pray for us, so that the word of the Lord may spread rapidly and be glorified everywhere, just as it is among you,

2 and that we may be rescued from wicked and evil people; for not all have faith.

3 But the Lord is faithful; he will strengthen you and guard you from the evil one.

4 And we have confidence in the Lord concerning you, that you are doing and will go on doing the things that we command.

5 May the Lord direct your hearts to the love of God and to the steadfastness of Christ.

6 Now we command you, beloved, in the name of our Lord Jesus Christ, to keep away from believers who are living in idleness and not according to the tradition that they received from us.

7 For you yourselves know how you ought to imitate us; we were not idle when we were with you,

8 and we did not eat anyone's bread without paying for it; but with toil and labor we worked night and day, so that we might not burden any of you.

9 This was not because we do not have that right, but in order to give you an example to imitate.

10 For even when we were with you, we gave you this command: Anyone unwilling to work should not eat.

11 For we hear that some of you are living in idleness, mere busybodies, not doing any work.

12 Now such persons we command and exhort in the Lord Jesus Christ to do their work quietly and to earn their own living.

13 Brothers and sisters, do not be weary in doing what is right.

14 Take note of those who do not obey what we say in this letter; have nothing to do with them, so that they may be ashamed.

15 Yet count him not as an enemy, but admonish him as a brother.

15 Do not regard them as enemies, but warn them as believers.

TOPICAL OUTLINE OF THE LESSON

I. Introduction
   A. Maintaining Commitment
   B. Biblical Background

II. Exposition and Application of the Scripture
   A. Paul Appeals for Prayer (2 Thessalonians 3:1-2)
   B. Paul's Declaration that God Is Faithful (2 Thessalonians 3:3-5)
   C. Paul's Appeal for Discipline and Order (2 Thessalonians 3:6-12)
   D. Paul's Appeal for Steadfastness (2 Thessalonians 3:13-15)

III. Concluding Reflection

LESSON OBJECTIVES

Upon completion of this lesson, the students will know that:

1. The strength for serious commitment is found in a strong relationship with Jesus Christ;
2. Understanding the faithfulness of God is a ground for commitment on our part; and,
3. Leaders can set the example of commitment in local churches.

POINTS TO BE EMPHASIZED

ADULT/YOUTH

Adult Topic: Finding Strength
Youth Topic: Committed to Work
Adult Key Verse: 2 Thessalonians 3:3
Youth Key Verse: 2 Thessalonians 3:13
Print Passage: 2 Thessalonians 3:1-15

—The apostle Paul set an important example of working for his livelihood.
—Paul warned the church against idleness as they waited for the coming of Christ.
—Paul taught the Thessalonians to distance themselves from those who were not living according to the traditions of faith.
—Paul wrote that God was the source of strength and commitment for the work of the church.
—Paul asserted that God's faithfulness would strengthen believers for fruitful lives.
—Paul asked the Thessalonians to pray for him and the work God had called him to do.
—Paul told the Thessalonians not to regard those who were lazy as enemies, but to warn them as believers.

CHILDREN

Children Topic: Live like a Believer
Key Verse: 2 Thessalonians 3:3
Print Passage: Acts 21:1-14; 2 Thessalonians 3:1-3

—Through the Spirit, the disciples sensed the danger that awaited Paul in Jerusalem and urged him not to go.

—Paul, and the disciples traveling with him, prayed with believers in Tyre before continuing toward Jerusalem.

—While staying with Philip the evangelist and his four prophesying daughters, Paul was warned by Agabus of what would happen to him in Jerusalem.

—Paul declared that he was willing to be bound and even to die for the Lord Jesus.

—Paul urged the church in Thessalonica to pray for him and his companions so that the Gospel story would spread quickly and bring salvation to all persons.

—Paul reminded the Thessalonians that God was not only faithful but also would strengthen them and protect them from evil.

I. INTRODUCTION
A. Maintaining Commitment

One of the biggest challenges a pastor faces is building and maintaining commitment among the members of his or her local church. While some of the disciples are highly motivated and need very little encouragement, there are others who lose the will to continue and fight the good fight of faith every time there is a significant problem facing them. What is *commitment?* It is the act of binding ourselves to a person, cause, or course of action and staying on until it is completed. The word *commitment* is not found anywhere in the KJV in either the Old or New Testaments. However, the idea of commitment runs throughout the teachings of Jesus. The call to discipleship is a call to commitment to the things that matter most to God. During the first prediction of His passion, Jesus called upon His disciples to commit themselves to Him without reservation (see Mark 8:34-38; compare with Matthew 6:19-24).

What are the conditions which lead men and women to commit themselves without reservation to the cause of the Lord Jesus Christ? Individual believers who have authentic encounters with Jesus Christ stay committed without wavering. Committed disciples are men and women who fully invest in the spread of the Gospel and whose love of the Lord Jesus Christ is without limits. When we gave our lives to the Lord Jesus Christ, we took upon our shoulders everything that Jesus commanded the church to do. Thus, we can no more call ourselves Christians and not be committed to the cause of Christ any more than a bird can claim to be a fish. It is impossible to be a true Christian and not be committed to the cause of Jesus Christ. One of the most precious principles from today's lesson has to do with our commitment to Jesus Christ and to the lifestyle of believers. Paul prayed that the saints in Thessalonica would continue in the things that they had heard and seen. He urged them to face persecution with steadfast hope and resolve.

B. Biblical Background

Today's lesson brings us to the conclusion of our study of 1 and 2 Thessalonians. Chapter 3 is the conclusion of the second letter. We have no idea whether there was a third or even fourth letter. In his closing remarks, Paul wanted the Thessalonians to remember them—that is Silas, Timothy, and all of the other missionaries who may have been with them—in their prayers. It is clear from the content of the chapter that Paul wanted to address some very delicate matters relating to work and discipline among the believers in Thessalonica. Some had stopped working, maybe because they were expecting the Lord to return soon and thus they saw no need to continue working. Paul provided instructions (as to how they were to handle the situation) which certainly serve as a very positive model for this post-modern age in which we live.

II. EXPOSITION AND APPLICATION OF THE SCRIPTURE

A. Paul Appeals for Prayer
(2 Thessalonians 3:1-2)

FINALLY, BRETHREN, pray for us, that the word of the Lord may have free course, and be glorified, even as it is with you: And that we may be delivered from unreasonable and wicked men: for all men have not faith.

The concluding portion of the letter begins with "Finally," a clear indication that Paul had come to the closing exhortations. He requested that the saints in Thessalonica would pray for them (see Ephesians 6:19-20; Colossians 4:3; 1 Thessalonians 5:25). Paul's specific request was that they pray that the Word of God would have *free course;* this term literally means "to run without restrictions." The reason is obvious—there were many adversaries in and out of the church. Paul wanted to see the Word of God spread throughout the world without any hindrances. The Word must also be "glorified" or given the highest honor because of its effective power to save and sanctify (see Acts 13:48). The Thessalonians were living witnesses that the Gospel was the power of God unto salvation (see Romans 1:16; 1 Corinthians 1:18-23).

In verse 2, Paul made a second prayer request—that the Thessalonians would pray for the missionaries to be delivered from wicked men (see Acts 13:45, 50; 14:2; 17:5; Romans 10:16; 2 Corinthians 4:3-4). Why? Because wherever they went to preach they encountered men and women who did not have faith. The plan of the evil ones was to destabilize and uproot the faith of the Christians in Thessalonica. Faith in this instance was not saving faith, but faith as it relates to being a Christian warrior. Was there anything that would lead Paul to make this request? It is possible that Paul made his request based on his current experience in Corinth as they sought to establish a foothold for the Gospel. It may be that Paul was looking back over his experience as a preacher of the Gospel and recognizing that future preaching missions would not be any different.

Paul's request for prayer in the face of wickedness serves as a model and warning for all believers. We must recognize that there are evil and wicked people who would love nothing more than to destroy the church of Jesus Christ. Moreover, they would relish the thought of moral and spiritual failure on the part of God's servants. Believers must realize that they have giant bull's-eyes painted on their backs, and that Satan is taking aim (see 1 Peter 5:8).

B. Paul's Declaration that God Is Faithful
(2 Thessalonians 3:3-5)

But the Lord is faithful, who shall stablish you, and keep you from evil. And we have confidence in the Lord touching you, that ye both do and will do the things which we command you. And the Lord direct your hearts into the love of God, and into the patient waiting for Christ.

Contrary to the faithlessness and wickedness that was present in some people, God could be counted on to honor His commitments to His people. In verse 3, Paul gave to the Thessalonians one of the greatest affirmations of our faith—"The Lord is faithful." The faithfulness of God means that He can be counted on to always fulfill His Word and promises. He never leaves nor forsakes us (see Joshua 1:5). This is one of the most precious promises found in the Scriptures (see Exodus 34:6; Deuteronomy 32:4; Psalm 33:4; 36:5; 91:4; 117:2; 1 Corinthians 10:13; 1 John 1:9; Revelation 19:11). Because God was faithful, He would not allow the Thessalonians to fall or be snatched away by the enemy. He would establish or stabilize the saints and keep them, a term that is a military image and pictures a soldier standing guard (see Psalm 19:13; 121:7; John 17:15; 2 Timothy 1:12; 1 Peter 1:3-5; 2 Peter 2:9; Jude 1:24). The power of God would keep them from evil—that is: He would be a garrison that protected them from the evil schemes and devices of wicked men and women. We have already seen that the church in Thessalonica was living with the threat and stress of persecution; hence, they needed encouragement to continue (see 1 Thessalonians 2:14; 3:3-4; 2 Thessalonians 1:4-6). These words could also mean that God would keep them from committing evil acts as well.

Paul was very confident in the commitment of the Thessalonians to remain true and loyal to Jesus Christ. God's faithfulness to establish and keep them was a sure and certain sign that they would be able to continue in their missionary work in Macedonia. Here we have an example of people who respected and honored the leader enough to follow his teachings and commands. Paul's confidence in God and in the saints meant that they would be fruitful in every good work (see John 15:1-10; Colossians 1:9-10).

Verse 5 is the conclusion of Paul's prayer request for the saints. He wanted God to *direct,* a word that literally means "to give guidance." Paul wanted God to give guidance to the Thessalonians and keep them going in the right direction by removing every obstacle and hindrance to their growth and work. Paul realized that Satan would constantly plan to hinder the progress of God's work; therefore, he prayed passionately for them. He prayed that God would increase their love for Him, which would fortify each of them as they awaited the coming of the Lord Jesus Christ with patience.

C. Paul's Appeal for Discipline and Order
(2 Thessalonians 3:6-12)

Now we command you, brethren, in the name of our Lord Jesus Christ, that ye withdraw yourselves from every brother that walketh disorderly, and not after the tradition which he received of us. For yourselves know how ye ought to follow us: for we behaved not ourselves disorderly among you; Neither did we eat any man's bread for nought; but wrought with labour and travail night and day, that we might not be chargeable to any of you: Not because we have not power, but to make ourselves an ensample unto you to follow us. For even when we were with you, this we commanded you, that if any would not work, neither should he eat. For we hear that there are

some which walk among you disorderly, working not at all, but are busybodies. Now them that are such we command and exhort by our Lord Jesus Christ, that with quietness they work, and eat their own bread.

"Now" marks the transition to the final section in the letter. What follows was a major concern about the lack of discipline among some of the disciples. It was a major concern simply because of the amount of space Paul dedicated to this discussion. In these words, we get a very clear picture of some of the concerns that were pressing the local church leaders—laziness and behavior that brought disrepute upon the name of the Lord Jesus Christ. Paul gave an imperative command: "Now we command you brethren." The word *we* refers to Paul, Silas, and Timothy. These were not empty words; rather, they carried the authority of the Lord Jesus Christ. Christ is the Head of the church; hence, those who speak in His name speak also for Him. The command was to withdraw from every brother that led a disorderly life, who failed to honor the traditions or teachings that had been handed over to him. "Disorderly life" refers to deviating or turning away from the established rule of order. Gene L. Green noted that social separation was the principal means the early church employed to correct those members who did not conform to Christian moral teaching (see Matthew 18:17; Romans 16:17; 1 Corinthians 5:9-13).

Paul pointed to the personal conduct of the missionaries and reminded the Thessalonians that they should follow their example (verse 7). The missionaries had led exemplary lives before the believers in Thessalonica. They had done nothing that would have brought disrepute upon the believers in Thessalonica, or to the name of Jesus Christ. Paul issued a verbal command for them to straighten up, and then he followed up with a personal example. The example he provided was just as important as his words. This example went as far as his working among them to earn a living. Paul did not want to be dependent upon anyone for his livelihood. Paul was a tentmaker by trade and he would use those skills as the means for supporting himself and his companions. They never took food from people who might have already been struggling to make ends meet. They worked night and day, so that they would have no obligations to anyone in the church (verse 8). Paul and his companions led independent lives among the Thessalonians.

Was Paul entitled to financial support from the church? Yes. But rather than exercise what was a right to be supported by the believers because of his position and authority, he chose rather to work and not be a burden upon them (see 1 Corinthians 9:4-6; Galatians 6:6; 1 Timothy 5:17-18). Jesus believed and taught that the servants of the Word should be compensated for their service (see Matthew 10:10). Paul reminded the saints that even when they were in Thessalonica, they should all be responsible and work. If a man or woman would not work, he or she should not eat.

We have no record of how they came to hear that there were unruly and disorderly disciples in their midst. There were some who were not working at all; in fact, they were "busybodies," a word that implies uselessness. *Busybodies* are people who are preoccupied with the affairs of others. Rather than spending their quality time meddling in the affairs and lives of others, Paul commanded them to get to work, so that they could earn their own living. They were instructed to live quiet and peaceful lives (verse 12).

Paul reminded the saints to look at him and how he had tried to live a reputable life among them and the non-believers in Thessalonica. If there is one lesson believers need to incorporate into their lives, it is the necessity to honor the words of the covenant that we "walk circumspectly before the world." Many times non-believers and the unchurched cannot see the power of the Christian faith because they only see the weakness of our examples.

There is a further example of the necessity of work and the need to earn a living. There are so many people who believe that the world owes them something. African Americans have been discriminated against for many years, and, in some cases even now, have been denied equal access to opportunity. But that is no reason to believe that we are owed prosperity without work and accountability.

D. Paul's Appeal for Steadfastness
(2 Thessalonians 3:13-15)

But ye, brethren, be not weary in well doing. And if any man obey not our word by this epistle, note that man, and have no company with him, that he may be ashamed. Yet count him not as an enemy, but admonish him as a brother.

Paul recognized that not all of the brethren had fallen into the trap of laziness. "But ye, brethren, be not weary in well doing." These are words that Paul no doubt repeated again and again to believers who may have found themselves facing the long arm of hate, hostility, and persecution. What did he mean? He meant that they should not allow their circumstances or the treatment they may have faced to deter them from doing the right things. They should strive to live in such a way that people did see their good works, which would bring honor and glory to the name of God.

It is possible on this journey to be tired from the stress and strain of working, when the outcomes and results look small and not worth the efforts. Yet, we must always remember that we have never been called to be concerned about the results of our service—that is God's domain. One plants, one waters, but God gives the increase (see 1 Corinthians 3:5-10; 2 Corinthians 4:7-18; Galatians 6:9).

Paul charged the saints to take a stern position on discipline among the disciples. He told them that when the words of the current letter were read, if they were not heeded by the disorderly and undisciplined, those people were to be shunned. The goal was not to banish the disorderly from the fellowship; rather, it was to invoke shame and guilt to the extent that the person would correct his or her ways. The person should not be seen as an enemy, but as a wayward disciple who needed to be brought back into the fold. He or she was still to be considered as a brother or sister.

III. CONCLUDING REFLECTION

One of the most striking and often overlooked aspects of teachings in the New Testament has to do with discipline within the local church. Believers today are under the notion that they can do whatever they want in and out of the church, with impunity. No one has a right to question their personal lives or conduct. It is noteworthy that many churches experience turmoil because there are members who feel empowered to create dissension and disorder in the local church. It is clear that Paul did not want the church to ignore the people or the inappropriate behavior. We can pray about people whose conduct brings shame on the name of the Lord Jesus Christ, but at some point we have to take some action. This is precisely what discipline is about, and Paul taught us a great deal about confronting behavior that is inappropriate in the body of Christ. We must remember that the goal of any act of discipline is correction and restoration, not excommunication and permanent abandonment.

The apostle Paul warned that if anyone was walking disorderly, the church should have nothing to do with the person. In the main text of this study, Paul said, "We command you, brethren, in the name of our Lord Jesus Christ, that you withdraw from every brother (sister) who walks disorderly and not according to the tradition" (2 Thessalonians 3:6). The word *disorderly* is a military term which means "out of rank." Here, Paul neither admonished nor commended; rather, he issued a command to the effect that the church should isolate that individual. This may seem harsh to us, but we must remember that a little yeast works through the whole batch of dough (see Galatians 5:9). If any church will live up to the expectation of the founder, Jesus Christ, that church must not condone a lack of discipline. The reason why we are a weak church today is because we easily compromise. We do not want to offend anybody. We are bequeathing the legacy of a church without power to the next generation. We must at this point recall the words of Jesus Christ in Luke 18:8 (NIV), which reads, "When the Son of Man comes, will he find faith on the earth?"

PRAYER

Eternal God, Creator of the world and all that is within it, we give You praise and glory for this day. Grant that we may live in such a way that Your name will never be embarrassed. Give us the power to work and never grow weary. In Jesus' name we pray. Amen.

WORD POWER

Stablish (Greek: *sterizo* [ste-ri-zo])—this word means "to make stable, strengthen, or place firm." The reason for this strong word is because the evil one was working to destroy the foundation of what Paul did in Thessalonica through unstable people. Paul prayed that their faith would rest on the cornerstone (Jesus Christ), the founder of the church.

HOME DAILY BIBLE READINGS
(July 19-25, 2010)

God's Own Faithfulness
MONDAY, July 19: "God's Steadfast Love" (Psalm 89:1-8)

TUESDAY, July 20: "Ready to Die for the Lord" (Acts 21:1-14)

WEDNESDAY, July 21: "God Is Faithful" (1 Corinthians 1:4-9)

THURSDAY, July 22: "A Sure and Steadfast Anchor" (Hebrews 6:13-20)

FRIDAY, July 23: "Faithful Promises" (Hebrews 10:19-25)

SATURDAY, July 24: "Faithful to Forgive" (1 John 1:5-10)

SUNDAY, July 25: "God Will Strengthen and Guard" (2 Thessalonians 3:1-15)

LESSON 9   August 1, 2010

SHARING GOD'S GRACE

DEVOTIONAL READING: Acts 9:10-16
PRINT PASSAGE: Philippians 1:18b-29

BACKGROUND SCRIPTURE: Philippians 1
KEY VERSE: Philippians 1:27

Philippians 1:18b-29—KJV

18 Christ is preached; and I therein do rejoice, yea, and will rejoice.

19 For I know that this shall turn to my salvation through your prayer, and the supply of the Spirit of Jesus Christ,

20 According to my earnest expectation and my hope, that in nothing I shall be ashamed, but that with all boldness, as always, so now also Christ shall be magnified in my body, whether it be by life, or by death.

21 For to me to live is Christ, and to die is gain.

22 But if I live in the flesh, this is the fruit of my labour: yet what I shall choose I wot not.

23 For I am in a strait betwixt two, having a desire to depart, and to be with Christ; which is far better:

24 Nevertheless to abide in the flesh is more needful for you.

25 And having this confidence, I know that I shall abide and continue with you all for your furtherance and joy of faith;

26 That your rejoicing may be more abundant in Jesus Christ for me by my coming to you again.

27 Only let your conversation be as it becometh the gospel of Christ: that whether I come and see you, or else be absent, I may hear of your affairs, that ye stand fast in one spirit, with one mind striving together for the faith of the gospel;

28 And in nothing terrified by your adversaries: which is to them an evident token of perdition, but to you of salvation, and that of God.

29 For unto you it is given in the behalf of Christ, not only to believe on him, but also to suffer for his sake.

Philippians 1:18b-29—NRSV

18 Christ is proclaimed in every way, whether out of false motives or true; and in that I rejoice. Yes, and I will continue to rejoice,

19 for I know that through your prayers and the help of the Spirit of Jesus Christ this will turn out for my deliverance.

20 It is my eager expectation and hope that I will not be put to shame in any way, but that by my speaking with all boldness, Christ will be exalted now as always in my body, whether by life or by death.

21 For to me, living is Christ and dying is gain.

22 If I am to live in the flesh, that means fruitful labor for me; and I do not know which I prefer.

23 I am hard pressed between the two: my desire is to depart and be with Christ, for that is far better;

24 but to remain in the flesh is more necessary for you.

25 Since I am convinced of this, I know that I will remain and continue with all of you for your progress and joy in faith,

26 so that I may share abundantly in your boasting in Christ Jesus when I come to you again.

27 Only, live your life in a manner worthy of the gospel of Christ, so that, whether I come and see you or am absent and hear about you, I will know that you are standing firm in one spirit, striving side by side with one mind for the faith of the gospel,

28 and are in no way intimidated by your opponents. For them this is evidence of their destruction, but of your salvation. And this is God's doing.

29 For he has graciously granted you the privilege not only of believing in Christ, but of suffering for him as well.

Under adverse circumstances, our commitments may be challenged. When, if ever, should circumstances lead us to compromise our commitments? As we remain faithful, God sustains us in all circumstances.

TOPICAL OUTLINE OF THE LESSON

I. Introduction
A. Christians and Commitment
B. Biblical Background

II. Exposition and Application of the Scripture
A. An Uncompromising Relationship (Philippians 1:18b-21)
B. Purpose for Living (Philippians 1:22-26)
C. Striving and Suffering for Christ (Philippians 1:27-29)

III. Concluding Reflection

LESSON OBJECTIVES

Upon completion of this lesson, the students will know that:

1. Commitment to Christ is a sign of an authentic encounter with the risen Lord;
2. Adverse situations may threaten our commitment, but staying faithful is rewarding; and,
3. Paul stayed committed to Christ in spite of adverse circumstances.

POINTS TO BE EMPHASIZED

ADULT/YOUTH

Adult Topic: Overcoming Obstacles
Youth Topic: Good No Matter What
Adult Key Verse: Philippians 1:27
Youth Key Verse: Philippians 1:21
Print Passage: Philippians 1:18b-29

—It is revealed in the letter to the Philippians that Paul had a very close friendship with the church in Philippi.

—The Philippians questioned Paul's credibility because they supposed that a suffering apostle was a contradiction in terms.

—Paul reflected a high view of Christ and Christ's relationship with God.

—Paul and his coworkers stopped in Philippi and met some faithful Jewish women, proclaimed the Gospel to them, and established the first Christian congregation in Europe (see Acts 16:11-15).

—Paul thanked the Philippians for their prayers on his behalf and credited the Holy Spirit with helping him to endure.

—Paul admitted the appeal of leaving this world to be with Christ, but confessed his commitment to exalt Christ no matter what happened.

—Paul encouraged the Philippians to live in a manner "worthy of the gospel" (verse 27, NRSV) and to stand together firmly for the Gospel.

CHILDREN

Children Topic: Stand Firm in Trouble
Key Verse: Philippians 1:27
Print Passage: Acts 21:27-28, 31-33; 22:30; 23:1, 9-11; Philippians 1:27

—Paul told the Philippians that his imprisonment was for Christ.

—Paul was bold and spoke without fear.

—God told Paul to keep up his courage and continue to spread God's Word.

—God expects us to live our lives in a manner worthy of the Gospel of Christ.

I. INTRODUCTION

A. Christians and Commitment

In his epistle to the Philippians, Paul urged them to remain firm to their commitment to Christ. Christian commitment comes out of an authentic encounter with the Lord Jesus Christ.

In the Key Verse for this lesson, Paul spelled out two traits for Christian commitment. The first one was, "standing firm." To *stand firm* means "to remain unmovable." There are situations in life that will come and challenge one's firmness in Christ, but a Christian must remain firm. Second, Paul mentioned "striving." This is one of the actions that a Christian must practice all the time. Satan is walking around seeking whom he may devour (see 1 Peter 5:8). The phrase "striving side by side" carries the idea of praying for each other and remaining loyal in Christ's Spirit. To *strive together* involves operating in the same spirit. Striving together is a sure sign of commitment.

B. Biblical Background

Paul was a pastor and evangelist par excellence. While in prison suffering for the cause of Christ, he took time to write to the church in Philippi. It is also a letter to all believers in Christ. Paul's jail experience taught him to be content in all circumstances, and he encouraged Christians to have the same tenacity for the cause of Christ (see Philippians 4:11). Paul was on his second missionary journey when he received a vision from the Lord. Paul left Troas in the province of Asia (part of present-day Turkey) and traveled to Macedonia (present-day Greece). He went to the city of Philippi, spent a few days, and established the first church (see Acts 16:6-12).

Racial problems are as old as the Bible itself. Wherever people live, they form groups along racial lines, and then put up invisible but strong walls around themselves to keep others out. In our modern society, this is very discernible. We have upper-class neighborhoods, middle-class neighborhoods, and the projects—where houses are stacked upon each other. In our country, there are white neighborhoods, black neighborhoods, and recently we have seen Hispanic neighborhoods springing up across our land. When Paul arrived in Philippi, he went to the Jewish quarter and offered the Gospel to them.

We can emulate Paul by bringing down racial divides. Paul did not go to the Jewish neighborhood to praise them for their seclusion; rather, he went there to preach Christ to them.

This action would let the Jewish community be aware of the saving grace of Jesus Christ. We must understand that human nature is difficult to tame and that is why our churches are not enjoying the peace promised by Jesus Christ. In every church and in every generation, there are issues that divide us—like class, gender, experience, and education, and the list goes on. In our eagerness to serve Christ, we offend each other. Paul encouraged the Philippians to agree with one another, stop complaining, and work together. In the same spirit, Paul was encouraging us in this epistle to stop bickering and work together to advance the course of Christ.

II. EXPOSITION AND APPLICATION OF THE SCRIPTURE

A. An Uncompromising Relationship (Philippians 1:18b-21)

Christ is preached; and I therein do rejoice, yea, and will rejoice. For I know that this shall turn to my salvation through your prayer, and the supply of the Spirit of Jesus Christ, According to my earnest expectation and my hope, that in nothing I shall be ashamed, but that with all boldness, as always, so now also Christ shall be magnified in my body, whether it be by life, or by death. For to me to live is Christ, and to die is gain.

Paul had an amazingly selfless attitude. All he wanted to see was the advancement of God's kingdom. There were some who preached Christ out of envy and strife, and some out of goodwill. The Greek word for "striving" (*sunathleo* [sun-a-thle-o]) is drawn from athletic contests. Usually, athletes competed against one another. In this text, Paul was asking the church of Philippi to compete with him for the sake of the Gospel. What mattered most to Paul was that "Christ is preached." In view of his imprisonment, Paul expressed his positive attitude and confidence in the sovereignty of God. His belief in God did not waver; he knew that the Lord would deliver him from the hand of the wicked ones. The Greek word translated *deliverance* is usually translated *salvation*. In the New Testament, this word is used in various ways for "rescue from danger or death, physical healing, justification, sanctification, and glorification." In this context, Paul was using this word in assurance that God would rescue him from prison.

Paul was a strong believer in prayer. He encouraged the believers in Philippi to keep on praying for him. We should all learn from Paul by asking other believers to keep us in their prayers. Paul believed that the prayers of the brethren would lead to his deliverance from prison and produce positive results. We should know that God answers prayers and therefore we must continue to pray ceaselessly for brethren in our local churches and around the world. Originally, the word *supply (epikoregia* [e-pi-ko-re-gia]) in verse 19 was used to refer to a wealthy benefactor defraying the expenses of a chorus or dance team. Later and more generally, it meant to supply the abundant resources that would meet someone's need. Through the enablement of the Holy Spirit, Paul was released. Paul expressed his earnest desire in another way when he said, "For to me to live is Christ, and to die is gain." The encounter of Paul with Jesus Christ on the road to Damascus remained vivid in Paul's mind. He did not let that vision evaporate.

The phrase "earnest expectation" (in verse 20) gives us the image of the outstretched hand of someone straining to focus attention on an object. Paul believed in God's power to overcome any situation and for that reason he said, "In nothing I shall be ashamed." Paul determined not to be dishonored in anything or by anyone. Paul showed Christians that right actions are not determined by environment, but by right attitude of the mind. Christians should orient themselves in their new position in Christ. It is when we have right orientation that we can properly function as children of God. The only thing that Paul looked for is stated, "Christ shall be magnified." Paul was passionate for the cause of Christ. His aim was not selfish, but in every situation Christ would be made known. Whether through death or life, it made no difference to Paul; he was not depending on his own strength, but on the enablement of the Holy Spirit. We too can survive any situation and remain committed to Christ through the enablement of the Holy Spirit. Paul became bold because his imprisonment led to the advancement of the Gospel; He was doubly sure that even his death would lead to speedy acceleration of the Gospel.

B. Purpose for Living
(Philippians 1:22-26)

But if I live in the flesh, this is the fruit of my labour: yet what I shall choose I wot not. For I am in a strait betwixt two, having a desire to depart, and to be with Christ; which is far better: Nevertheless to abide in the flesh is more needful for you. And having this confidence, I know that I shall abide and continue with you all for your furtherance and joy of faith; That your rejoicing may be more abundant in Jesus Christ for me by my coming to you again.

Ambition is rooted in every human being, Christians and non-Christians alike. Each of us has one agenda or the other that we would like to execute. It is the pursuit of ambition that leads to achieving one's purpose in life. However, a look at the life of the apostle Paul reveals an agenda which is diametrically opposed to that of twenty-first-century Christians. Paul's ambition was to live for Christ, because it would mean opportunity to preach the Gospel. In his epistle to the Romans (1:16), Paul said, "I am not ashamed of the gospel of Christ: for it is the power of God unto salvation to every one that believeth; to the Jew first, and also to the Greek." When Paul realized the Gospel was the power of God, he was always ready to preach to the Jews and Gentiles alike.

"What I shall choose" (verse 22) is a phrase that depicts the joy of Paul. Paul was sure of eternity with Christ that he had preached; but at the same time, remaining in the world would mean more opportunities to preach. Paul was torn at the prospect of seeing Jesus face-to-face and staying with his beloved Philippians. We also need a purpose for living that goes beyond providing for our mundane needs. Every Christian must ask a fundamental question, which is: "What is my purpose for living?" The word *desire* here means "more than a wish"; it depicts an intense longing. To Paul, death was just a "door" to eternal rest. He had met Jesus; he had served Him with all his might and soul; he had established churches; he had taken the Gospel beyond the confines of Jerusalem and he had shown to the world that there was no wall between the Jews and Gentiles, males or females. What next? Paul wanted to exit. Paul was ready to depart and be with the Lord—whom he had preached with boldness.

The word *depart* in verse 23 means "to strike, or take down." Paul saw death not as the end of life, but as a time of moving from one home to the other. Paul found his purpose for living; therefore, departing to be with the Lord was a joyful thing to him. We also need a purpose for living, so that when we are about to depart, our consciences will be cleared, and we will freely tell the people around us, "I am ready to depart." Paul was confident that he would spend a little time with them. It is stated in verse 25, "And having this confidence, I know *(oida [oi-da])."* This word deals with knowing from the inner eyes. It depicted faith in action. Paul's staying with the Philippians would lead to their spiritual progress. It is one thing to be saved but quite another to progress to maturity. Every Christian should go beyond being saved to the level of maturity.

C. Striving and Suffering for Christ (Philippians 1:27-29)

Only let your conversation be as it becometh the gospel of Christ: that whether I come and see you, or else be absent, I may hear of your affairs, that ye stand fast in one spirit, with one mind striving together for the faith of the gospel; And in nothing terrified by your adversaries: which is to them an evident token of perdition, but to you of salvation, and that of God. For unto you it is given in the behalf of Christ, not only to believe on him, but also to suffer for his sake.

Paul encouraged the believers in Philippi to be in one spirit, and to stand firm. Their conduct must reflect their profession of Christ as their Lord and Savior. The church in Philippi was located in a Roman colony, and there were many unbelievers who were watching them. The Gospel of our Lord Jesus Christ is a way of life. Christianity is having relationship with Jesus Christ. Even though the church of Philippi was in a Roman region, their strategic placement would make them susceptible to sinful behavior. Therefore, they should live among other Roman citizens as citizens of another world, the heavenly kingdom. Their conduct should reveal their true identification with Jesus Christ. They should walk hand in hand by encouraging each other to stand firm. The use of the phrase *striving together* was an implication of the desire for the believers in Philippi to love each other. The Greek word used for "striving together" implies teamwork. It has an athletic connotation. In the SSPB's monthly newsletter "The Board Connection," February 2009 issue, Dr. Kelly Miller Smith Jr. encouraged the Sunday School Publishing Board employees by saying, "We should see ourselves as a track relay team which wants to make sure that we successfully pass the baton to the next runner." In essence, Christian workers should see each other as a chain linking from Christ to the present. Church workers should see and do their work in the spirit of oneness. When there is a cut in the chain, progress is retarded.

Paul encouraged us as citizens of heaven to run the race with team spirit. God never intended for believers to be alone. When Jesus was on earth, He moved around with His disciples. God's plan has not changed in reference to working together as a team. It is sad to note that much time and effort is lost in many of our churches by fighting against one another. We seem to lose focus on the real enemy, the devil. Peter warned, "Be sober, be vigilant; because your adversary the devil, as a roaring lion, walketh about, seeking whom he may devour" (1 Peter 5:8). We should stand together to face the devil and bring him down. Yes, we can! It takes a church which is purpose-driven to resist by fighting, and to maintain the common purpose of serving Christ. The devil has made us forget our mission in life, but we can recapture it.

Being in the Roman culture, the church of Philippi faced all kinds of intimidation. However, they must not be terror-stricken in the face of their enemies. Their standing firm would be a testimony to their strong relationship with Jesus Christ. Their strong determination to stand up for Christ would lead to the confinement of their enemies. The Philippians would be *living proof* (a legal terminology expressing proof obtained by an analysis of the facts) to their detractors that the message of Jesus Christ was authentic. In this passage, Paul brought out the issues of heaven and hell. Their enemies would end up in perdition while they would end up in the arms of their Savior, whom they had served with their hearts and souls.

III. CONCLUDING REFLECTION

The resounding theme in the epistle to the Philippians is joy in serving Jesus Christ. Paul wrote this epistle while in prison but one could not see his despondency. While in jail, Paul took the opportunity to preach Christ in spite of his incarceration. Paul wrote this epistle with fondness. The church in Philippi was a source of joy to him. The church was in the midst of enemies, yet they supported Paul more than all other churches he helped establish.

PRAYER

Father in heaven, we ask that You forgive us of our inability to stand together in one spirit. We ask that You help us to work together in one accord. Help us to operate as the Father, the Son, and the Holy Spirit stand together for a common purpose. In Jesus' name we pray. Amen.

WORD POWER

One Spirit (Greek: *eni pneumatic* [e-ni-pne-um-a-ti])—these two words give the heart of the letter of Paul to the Philippians. Their commitment to Christ could be sustained when they stood in one spirit. Once a church understands the importance of standing "in one spirit," their spiritual progress will soon be known to outsiders.

HOME DAILY BIBLE READINGS
(July 26–August 1, 2010)

Sharing God's Grace

MONDAY, July 26: "Paul's Call to Service" (Acts 9:10-16)

TUESDAY, July 27: "Paul's Arrest" (Acts 21:27-36)

WEDNESDAY, July 28: "Paul's Trial before the Council" (Acts 22:30–23:11)

THURSDAY, July 29: "Paul's Appeal to Caesar" (Acts 25:1-12)

FRIDAY, July 30: "Paul's Prayer for the Philippians" (Philippians 1:3-11)

SATURDAY, July 31: "Paul's Imprisonment Spreads the Gospel" (Philippians 1:12-18a)

SUNDAY, August 1: "Paul's Struggle with His Future" (Philippians 1:18b-29)

LESSON 10   August 8, 2010

GIVING OF ONESELF

DEVOTIONAL READING: Matthew 20:20-28
PRINT PASSAGE: Philippians 2:1-13

BACKGROUND SCRIPTURE: Philippians 2:1–3:1a
KEY VERSE: Philippians 2:5

Philippians 2:1-13—KJV

IF THERE be therefore any consolation in Christ, if any comfort of love, if any fellowship of the Spirit, if any bowels and mercies,

2 Fulfil ye my joy, that ye be likeminded, having the same love, being of one accord, of one mind.

3 Let nothing be done through strife or vainglory; but in lowliness of mind let each esteem other better than themselves.

4 Look not every man on his own things, but every man also on the things of others.

5 Let this mind be in you, which was also in Christ Jesus:

6 Who, being in the form of God, thought it not robbery to be equal with God:

7 But made himself of no reputation, and took upon him the form of a servant, and was made in the likeness of men:

8 And being found in fashion as a man, he humbled himself, and became obedient unto death, even the death of the cross.

9 Wherefore God also hath highly exalted him, and given him a name which is above every name:

10 That at the name of Jesus every knee should bow, of things in heaven, and things in earth, and things under the earth;

11 And that every tongue should confess that Jesus Christ is Lord, to the glory of God the Father.

12 Wherefore, my beloved, as ye have always obeyed, not as in my presence only, but now much more in my absence, work out your own salvation with fear and trembling.

13 For it is God which worketh in you both to will and to do of his good pleasure.

Philippians 2:1-13—NRSV

IF THEN there is any encouragement in Christ, any consolation from love, any sharing in the Spirit, any compassion and sympathy,

2 make my joy complete: be of the same mind, having the same love, being in full accord and of one mind.

3 Do nothing from selfish ambition or conceit, but in humility regard others as better than yourselves.

4 Let each of you look not to your own interests, but to the interests of others.

5 Let the same mind be in you that was in Christ Jesus,

6 who, though he was in the form of God, did not regard equality with God as something to be exploited,

7 but emptied himself, taking the form of a slave, being born in human likeness. And being found in human form,

8 he humbled himself and became obedient to the point of death—even death on a cross.

9 Therefore God also highly exalted him and gave him the name that is above every name,

10 so that at the name of Jesus every knee should bend, in heaven and on earth and under the earth,

11 and every tongue should confess that Jesus Christ is Lord, to the glory of God the Father.

12 Therefore, my beloved, just as you have always obeyed me, not only in my presence, but much more now in my absence, work out your own salvation with fear and trembling;

13 for it is God who is at work in you, enabling you both to will and to work for his good pleasure.

UNIFYING LESSON PRINCIPLE

We live in a culture in which we are encouraged to pursue our dreams at any cost and to fight for our rights. Where can we find more to life than a selfish pursuit of our own happiness at the expense of others? God calls us, through Jesus' example, to find life in serving others.

TOPICAL OUTLINE OF THE LESSON

I. **Introduction**
   A. Relationship
   B. Biblical Background

II. **Exposition and Application of the Scripture**
   A. The Basis of Congregational Unity (Philippians 2:1-4)
   B. Have the Mind of Jesus Christ (Philippians 2:5-11)
   C. Work Out Your Salvation (Philippians 2:12-13)

III. **Concluding Reflection**

LESSON OBJECTIVES

Upon completion of this lesson, the students will know that:

1. Serving others is the spirit of true Christianity;
2. Jesus Christ served and saved us through His death on the cross; and,
3. Serving others is an indication that one possesses the spirit of obedience.

POINTS TO BE EMPHASIZED

ADULT/YOUTH

Adult Topic: Serving Others
Youth Topic: Service with a Smile
Adult Key Verse: Philippians 2:5
Youth Key Verse: Philippians 2:3
Print Passage: Philippians 2:1-13

—A hymn to Christ is contained in verses 5-11.
—Note that Christ's humility resulted in His exaltation.
—These verses are the powerful synopsis of Christ's life and mission.
—Paul told the Philippians that it would make him truly happy if they would love one another and work together.
—Paul encouraged the Philippians to have the same mind as that of Jesus Christ—humble and ready to serve others.
—Jesus humbled Himself by going to the Cross to give His life for us, but God exalted Him and gave Him a name above every other name.
—Paul encouraged the Philippians to follow his instructions in God's power, and to continue to work out their salvation.

CHILDREN

Children Topic: Looking Out for Others
Key Verse: Philippians 2:4
Print Passage: Acts 23:12-21, 23; Philippians 2:4

—Paul's nephew became aware of the conspiracy of Paul's enemies to kill Paul and went to the barracks to warn Paul.
—Paul was taken to the governor in Caesarea, who protected him until his case was brought before him.
—Paul admonished the Philippians to be concerned about the interests of others.

I. INTRODUCTION

A. Relationship

There is nothing more painful to the Lord Jesus Christ than division among His people. Among all of the churches that we have records of, the Corinthian church was among the most divisive and quarrelsome in the New Testament. They were very much unlike the Philippians, who had differences but not the kind that generated congregational splits. Every year, hundreds of congregations split, sometimes over the most insignificant issues. Much of the disunity we see in congregations stems from the lack of healthy relations among the members and leaders, or between the leaders.

In many congregations today, the relationships are shallow and often very impersonal. In most congregations, the members only have a casual acquaintance with each other, being content to know each by face and not by name. This kind of shallowness produces cliques and special interest groups that usually work to foster their particular goals and not those of the larger congregation. Congregations that are always in turmoil and confusion are in no position to serve the greater ends and goals of the Lord Jesus Christ.

In today's lesson, Paul continued to stress the importance of relationship and the existence of harmony among the believers. He had been confined to house arrest for some time in Rome. Yet, his primary concern was not about himself, but those whom he helped birth into the Christian faith. Like a father looking after his family, so Paul continued to express concern over the spiritual growth and well-being of the saints in Philippi.

B. Biblical Background

All of Paul's letters were written to address some issues that might have risen within the community. Scholars are somewhat divided over exactly what the main issue was that Paul was seeking to address with the Philippians. Some think that there may have been a lack of unity among the saints, particularly between the women in the church, and hence he needed to address the matter of unity with them (see Philippians 4:2).

The verses that form the lesson today are a continuation of chapter 1. The break between chapters 1 and 2 is an artificial one and does not signal the start of a new thought; rather, it was the continuation of what was begun in Philippians 1:27. In the previous chapter, Paul addressed the matter of the Philippians who were able to withstand the onslaught of persecution that came from both Jews and Gentiles. He had applauded their fellowship and participation with him in the spread of the Gospel (see 1:5, 12, 29). They had stood with him throughout the years. Now his desire was to see them stand together with each other. Petty differences must not be allowed to get in the way of the greater cause of spreading the Gospel.

II. EXPOSITION AND APPLICATION OF THE SCRIPTURE

A. The Basis of Congregational Unity
(Philippians 2:1-4)

IF THERE be therefore any consolation in Christ, if any comfort of love, if any fellowship of the Spirit, if any bowels and mercies, Fulfil ye my joy, that ye be likeminded, having the same love, being of one accord, of one mind. Let nothing be done through strife or vainglory; but in lowliness of mind let each esteem other better than themselves. Look not every man on his own things, but every man also on the things of others.

The first four verses in Philippians 2 are a continuation of Paul's discussion about the need for the saints in Philippi to be united in their stand against persecution (see 1:27-30). This call to unity was not a superficial one; rather, it would be the fulfillment of Paul's joy (verse 2). The transition from verse 30 to 2:1 literally begins with the conjunction, "therefore." The words "there be" have been added by the translators to give greater clarity to Paul's original thought. If the Gospel is to go forth and have the impact that Jesus Christ intended, then the church must be united in its purpose. Paul's use of the word *if* was not intended to convey doubt in the minds of the Philippian congregation; rather, it denotes that what he was about to say was absolutely true. Some translators note that the word "since" would give greater clarity to what he said and meant. In verse 1, Paul affirmed a fourfold blessing that came from the unity created by their new lives in Jesus Christ. The thought goes something like this: "If therefore there be any consolation in Christ, if any comfort of love, if any fellowship of the Spirit, if any bowels and mercies.... fulfill my joy by standing together."

As a result of knowing the salvation of the Lord, they experienced and enjoyed the comforting presence of the Lord Jesus Christ. They knew the presence and solace brought by His unfailing love, the fellowship of God's presence through the Holy Spirit, and the tenderheartedness of His mercy. These four blessings in verse 1 must be the foundation of their unity (see Psalm 133:1; Acts 2:46; Ephesians 4:30-32; Colossians 2:2).

This unity must be characterized by four qualities. First, they must be likeminded, which denotes thinking the same way about purpose, vision, and direction (see; 1 Corinthians 1:10; 2 Corinthians 13:11; Philippians 2:20; 3:15-16; 1 Peter 3:3-9). Second, they should have the same love, referring to being mutually loving and supportive of each other (see John 13:34-35; 1 Corinthians 12:25-26). Third, they must be of one accord, which refers to being in complete harmony with each other. It denotes the absence of hostility and disagreement. This was the one indispensable trait that Jesus prayed that His followers would have and be identified with (see John 17:20-21; compare with Acts 1:4; 2:1, 46; 5:12). Fourth, the interests of others would be placed ahead of those of the individual. Rather than self-centeredness, Paul's desire was that they be selfless, governed by the principles of mutuality and possessing a spirit of reciprocity which is driven by love.

B. Have the Mind of Jesus Christ
(Philippians 2:5-11)

Let this mind be in you, which was also in Christ Jesus: Who, being in the form of God, thought it not robbery to be equal with God: But made himself of no reputation, and took upon him the form of a servant, and was made

in the likeness of men: And being found in fashion as a man, he humbled himself, and became obedient unto death, even the death of the cross. Wherefore God also hath highly exalted him, and given him a name which is above every name: That at the name of Jesus every knee should bow, of things in heaven, and things in earth, and things under the earth; And that every tongue should confess that Jesus Christ is Lord, to the glory of God the Father.

Paul turned from addressing the unity that should exist among the Philippians to pointing them to the supreme example of their unity. These verses are among the most important in the New Testament because they emphasize the preexistence of Jesus Christ, His incarnation, and His humanity (see John 1:1-14; 2 Corinthians 8:9). We think of these verses as Christological statements about the nature of Christ. Many scholars believe that these verses formed one of the earliest Christian hymns or confessional creeds.

Jesus Christ is not just the Lord of the church; He is the example for how to live in the world. The Philippians would be able to foster the kind of unity necessary to build up the body of Christ by having the same mind as Jesus Christ. "Let this mind be in you" (verse 5) is tantamount to saying that each of the members of the congregation must have the same kind of mind that Jesus Christ had about service and submission to the will of the Father.

Paul appealed to the church to have the same understanding as Jesus. In verses 6-8, he spelled out what that understanding meant. The "form of God" does not denote physical or material, but, rather, speaks to the essence or nature of God. Christ existed prior to His earthly ministry as God. Jesus did not think of His divinity as something that should be held onto or that His deity should be used selfishly (verse 6). Instead, He made Himself of no reputation; the Greek word is *kenoo* and literally means "to empty." Jesus Christ emptied Himself of the form of deity and humbled Himself as a *bondservant*—literally a slave. Jesus' own understanding of His ministry was one of servanthood (see Matthew 20:28; Mark 10:45).

Paul further defined what he meant by the self-emptying of Christ by saying He became a human being. Christ was made "in the likeness of men" (verse 7). This does not mean that at any point Jesus ceased to be God in the very fullest sense of God. He was always fully God and fully human. In His human existence, Jesus placed human limits upon Himself, which enabled Him to fully identify with the human condition (see Hebrews 4:15).

The use of the word *Wherefore* in verse 9 points to the results of Jesus' self-humiliation and crucifixion. The death of Jesus on the cross was not just submission and obedience without reward for His faithfulness. Rather, the point of the verse is to teach that God recognizes and rewards faithful service to His eternal purposes. "God…highly exalted him" are words that point to the elevation of Christ to the highest office (see Hebrews 1:1-2).

Jesus' name is greater than any other name in the universe. The name of Jesus is not mystical or magical; rather, it points to His work as Savior and His personhood as deity (see Matthew 1:21; John 1:14). The name of Jesus is the one name that believers are instructed to use in making petitions to the Father (see Matthew 18:20; John 14:13-14; 16:23). One day everyone—those who have acknowledged Him as Lord and those who have rejected His lordship—will stand before the throne and bow in humble submission to Him (see Isaiah 45:23-24; Matthew 25:31-46; 2 Corinthians 5:10; Revelation 20:11-15).

C. Work Out Your Salvation
(Philippians 2:12-13)

Wherefore, my beloved, as ye have always obeyed, not as in my presence only, but now much more in my absence, work out your own salvation with fear and trembling. For it is God which worketh in you both to will and to do of his good pleasure.

Paul really loved the Philippians. He referred to them as "my beloved," those whom he highly and graciously esteemed and cared about. He appealed to their faithfulness to Christ and their followership of him as their pastor/spiritual guide. In verse 12, we learn something very insightful about the personality and kind of people who made up the Philippian congregation. They were loyal, but they were also obedient and submissive to the leadership of Paul. This is not to be viewed as a negative trait, for indeed it was not. Paul was their spiritual mentor; he was their apostle who had led them to saving faith in the Lord Jesus Christ.

Paul called upon them to remain obedient and to continue working out their salvation with fear and trembling. The word *salvation* (*soteria* in Greek) is rich with meaning. It literally means "to deliver or rescue from danger." The Bible affirms that God is our Savior and Redeemer. He saves us not only from sins, but also out of our various trials and troubling situations (see Exodus 14:13; Psalm 34:4-6). The saints were exhorted to work out their salvation, which also has reference to doing the work of evangelism and mission. The Philippians were to show that they had been saved by engaging in the same type of work

among others that Paul had engaged in among them. The reference was not to work for the sake of work, but for work that produced fruit for the kingdom of God. Their working would be a reflection of their new lives in Jesus Christ. Paul would not be with them but they must keep to the teachings he had taught them.

III. CONCLUDING REFLECTION

The greatest weapon we have against the encroachment of disharmony and disunity in the body of Christ is the example of Jesus. Without a doubt, disunity is one of the greatest threats to the spread of the Gospel. Many congregations simply have a very difficult time working together and especially under the leadership of their pastor. They would much rather be at odds with the leader and keep the church off track than submit and be productive in the work of mission and ministry.

The Philippians could teach us much today. First, congregational wealth cannot be viewed as a sign of divine favor. The Philippians were a financially poor church, but they were rich in compassion. Second, they could teach us the lesson of mutual respect among people and leaders. Third, they knew how to persevere in trials. Paul wrote to encourage the saints, but he never said anywhere in the letter that they needed to return to their first love or come back to Christ. They withstood the onslaught of hostility flung their way. All three are very practical lessons by which believers in this generation would be greatly benefitted.

There are other lessons we learn from the church in Philippi. There are Christians who live for the express purpose of impressing others, or to please themselves, but we must realize that such attitude brings disharmony in the church. For this reason Paul stressed the importance of spiritual unity. He pleaded with this church to love each other and care for each other. We, the present-day Christians, cannot and should not do any less. We must endeavor to show love to each other and maintain unity of spirit at all costs. When we walk together in the spirit of unity, we demonstrate in a concrete way to the outside world that we truly are Christians. Do not be consumed with making names for yourselves at the cost of destroying Christian fellowship and unity.

What do we do when we do not feel like obeying God? The sure thing is that verse 13 helps us to know that God did not abandon us to struggle on our own. The Holy Spirit indwells us even when we do not want to do His will, and comes alongside to empower us. The question is: "Do we yield to the Holy Spirit or to our personal will?" The problem with us as human beings is that we have always caved in to the desires of the flesh, and therefore it is harder to yield to the Holy Spirit. This lesson today helps us to know how to give ourselves totally to God. When we surrender our will, God will supply the enablement.

PRAYER

Heavenly Father, help us to have the mind of Christ. Help us to promote Your kingdom. Help us to follow our leaders as they follow You. In Jesus' name we pray. Amen.

WORD POWER

Mind (Greek: *phroneo* [pro-ne-o])—this means "to have understanding and to think alike, to be harmonious, to care alike." Paul (through this Greek word) was saying to the Philippians to think like Christ, who had no separate interest: Christ promoted the glory of God, and He elevated the welfare of the human race in the Spirit of God. Therefore, they must strive to have the exact mind as Christ.

HOME DAILY BIBLE READINGS
(August 2-8, 2010)

Giving of Oneself

MONDAY, August 2: "The Greatness of a Servant" (Matthew 20:20-28)

TUESDAY, August 3: "Revealing a Conspiracy" (Acts 23:12-24)

WEDNESDAY, August 4: "Sacrifices Pleasing to God" (Hebrews 13:12-18)

THURSDAY, August 5: "A Living Sacrifice" (Romans 12:1-2)

FRIDAY, August 6: "Poured Out in Sacrifice" (Philippians 2:14-18)

SATURDAY, August 7: "Concerned for Others' Welfare" (Philippians 2:19-30)

SUNDAY, August 8: "Looking to Others' Interests" (Philippians 2:1-13)

LESSON 11   August 15, 2010

LIVING INTO THE FUTURE

DEVOTIONAL READING: 1 John 4:7-12
PRINT PASSAGE: Philippians 3:7-16

BACKGROUND SCRIPTURE: Philippians 3:1b–4:1
KEY VERSES: Philippians 3:13-14

Philippians 3:7-16—KJV

7 But what things were gain to me, those I counted loss for Christ.

8 Yea doubtless, and I count all things but loss for the excellency of the knowledge of Christ Jesus my Lord: for whom I have suffered the loss of all things, and do count them but dung, that I may win Christ,

9 And be found in him, not having mine own righteousness, which is of the law, but that which is through the faith of Christ, the righteousness which is of God by faith:

10 That I may know him, and the power of his resurrection, and the fellowship of his sufferings, being made conformable unto his death;

11 If by any means I might attain unto the resurrection of the dead.

12 Not as though I had already attained, either were already perfect: but I follow after, if that I may apprehend that for which also I am apprehended of Christ Jesus.

13 Brethren, I count not myself to have apprehended: but this one thing I do, forgetting those things which are behind, and reaching forth unto those things which are before,

14 I press toward the mark for the prize of the high calling of God in Christ Jesus.

15 Let us therefore, as many as be perfect, be thus minded: and if in any thing ye be otherwise minded, God shall reveal even this unto you.

16 Nevertheless, whereto we have already attained, let us walk by the same rule, let us mind the same thing.

Philippians 3:7-16—NRSV

7 Yet whatever gains I had, these I have come to regard as loss because of Christ.

8 More than that, I regard everything as loss because of the surpassing value of knowing Christ Jesus my Lord. For his sake I have suffered the loss of all things, and I regard them as rubbish, in order that I may gain Christ

9 and be found in him, not having a righteousness of my own that comes from the law, but one that comes through faith in Christ, the righteousness from God based on faith.

10 I want to know Christ and the power of his resurrection and the sharing of his sufferings by becoming like him in his death,

11 if somehow I may attain the resurrection from the dead.

12 Not that I have already obtained this or have already reached the goal; but I press on to make it my own, because Christ Jesus has made me his own.

13 Beloved, I do not consider that I have made it my own; but this one thing I do: forgetting what lies behind and straining forward to what lies ahead,

14 I press on toward the goal for the prize of the heavenly call of God in Christ Jesus.

15 Let those of us then who are mature be of the same mind; and if you think differently about anything, this too God will reveal to you.

16 Only let us hold fast to what we have attained.

UNIFYING LESSON PRINCIPLE

Many people are preoccupied with past failures or achievements. How can our lives achieve fresh focus? The Christian faith draws us into the future, preoccupied with God's mission in Christ.

TOPICAL OUTLINE OF THE LESSON

I. Introduction
A. Symbolic Places
B. Biblical Background

II. Exposition and Application of the Scripture
A. Suffering Loss for the Sake of Christ (Philippians 3:7-8)
B. Righteousness that Is Built upon Faith (Philippians 3:9-12)
C. Forgetting the Past and Looking Forward (Philippians 3:13-16)

III. Concluding Reflection

LESSON OBJECTIVES

Upon completion of this lesson, the students will understand that:

1. Paul did not hold on to his former life; rather, he pursued his mission with zeal;
2. Christians should learn how to let go of their past and focus on God's missions; and,
3. Preoccupation with God's mission is a panacea for spiritual success.

POINTS TO BE EMPHASIZED

ADULT/YOUTH
Adult Topic: A Focus for Life
Youth Topic: Back to the Future
Adult/Youth Key Verses: Philippians 3:13-14
Print Passage: Philippians 3:7-16

—Paul had reason to boast and yet he saw the relative unimportance of His accomplishments in contrast to the joy of serving Christ.
—The thrust of this passage is that Christ is the basis of our future in this life and the next.
—The reference to becoming like Christ in His death in verse 10 may be a baptismal reference.
—Paul told the Philippians that everything else in his life paled in comparison to knowing Jesus Christ.
—Paul told the Philippians that he trusted in Christ alone to save him, not in his own righteousness.
—Paul admitted that he was not perfect because he had not yet learned all that God had to teach him.
—Paul's purpose was to focus on the goal of "the prize of the heavenly call of God in Christ Jesus" (verse 14, NRSV).
—Paul believed that God reveals the truth to believers, and that we should hold fast to whatever truth we have.

CHILDREN
Children Topic: Look Ahead
Key Verse: Philippians 3:14
Print Passage: Acts 27:1-2, 13-14, 18-26; Philippians 3:13

—Paul was on a ship traveling to Rome when he experienced a violent storm.
—An angel of God told Paul that all the people on the ship would survive the storm.
—The people on the ship were calmed by the words and actions of Paul and his trust in God.
—God's goodness allowed all of them to reach land safely.

I. INTRODUCTION

A. Symbolic Places

My wife Rosetta and I have had many wonderful opportunities to travel all over the world. Some of our most memorable journeys have been with Christian tour groups going to places visited by the apostle Paul and many of the earliest Christian missionaries. One of the things that strike one about going to the places that have been venerated by the Christian faith is the churches where many of these sites have been preserved. One of the holiest places for Christians is the church of the Holy Sepulchre in Jerusalem. It is believed to be built over the site of the crucifixion of Jesus and is believed to be the location of the actual rock upon which the cross of Jesus stood. The original church built in AD 355 was destroyed by the Persians in 614. In 1099, the Crusaders began a fifty-year construction project that gave us the current church. The church is owned by three denominations: Greek Orthodox, Roman Catholic, and the Armenian Church. Within the confines of the church is a small Ethiopian Coptic church.

Every day thousands of Christian pilgrims and tourists file through its doors in search of the ultimate experience that will boost their faith and give them even more reasons to believe in the teachings of the New Testament. Each of the major denominations has its own space and has its own times for worship. The irony of this most sacred place is that the three major denominations have feuded with each other for years on who has primacy in the church. Each of the denominations has its own ceremonies, rituals, and processionals that have become more important than the God they represent. The symbols, traditions, rituals, candles, and all of the trappings of this magnificent structure often get in the way of people seeing the power of the cross of Jesus Christ. In today's lesson, we hear anew the words of the apostle Paul as he reminded the Philippians that there was nothing in life greater than knowing the power of the resurrection of Jesus.

B. Biblical Background

Chapter 3 marks a turning point in Paul's epistle to the Philippians. Throughout the first two chapters he had appealed to them to stand unified against the crush of persecution and oppression. We have seen his warm and tender compassion on display as he shared with them how much he loved them because of their care and concern for him. The third chapter begins with the word *finally,* a word which meant that he had come to the remainder of what he wanted to say to them—the calling for the saints in Philippi to live in victory by having a joyous spirit. He warned them to be on the lookout for *dogs,* a metaphor for men who possessed impure minds. They must be vigilant and watchful for the presence of false teachers and preachers, especially those who taught that circumcision was necessary in order to be saved. Paul had already known and experienced the kinds of trouble that these Judaizers could produce in a young congregation (see Galatians 1-3; compare with Acts 15:1-29). He shared with them that a man's personal credentials did not matter when it came to salvation in Jesus Christ. Paul had every possible educational, social, and religious advantage. Yet, when he met Jesus Christ on the road to Damascus, Jesus changed Paul's life.

Paul's conversion experience came to symbolize the radical change that took place in his life. The experience left an indelible mark upon Paul's mind and heart, so much so that it shaped his beliefs, teaching, and preaching for the rest of his life. Paul was so committed to the point that everything that he once held in the highest regard was thrust aside for the prize of knowing Jesus Christ.

The resurrection of Jesus Christ from the dead is the foundation and cornerstone of the Christian faith. It is the one great truth upon which hangs the very essence and existence of the Christian church. The resurrection of Jesus Christ from the dead is the source of our power to pull down strongholds and take captive every thought to the obedience of Christ. The Resurrection is God's victory over the powers of sin and evil. The resurrection of Jesus Christ is the source of our power over the demonic powers of darkness—the flesh, the world, and the pride of life. The resurrection of Jesus Christ gives us power over sin and death. The apostle Paul wrote in 1 Corinthians 15:13-14, "But if there be no resurrection of the dead, then is Christ not risen: And if Christ be not risen, then is our preaching vain, and your faith is also vain."

II. EXPOSITION AND APPLICATION OF THE SCRIPTURE

A. Suffering Loss for the Sake of Christ (Philippians 3:7-8)

But what things were gain to me, those I counted loss for Christ. Yea doubtless, and I count all things but loss for the excellency of the knowledge of Christ Jesus my Lord: for whom I have suffered the loss of all things, and do count them but dung, that I may win Christ.

Paul was among the religious elites of his day. He had met and exceeded all of the standards that would declare him righteous according to the Law. However, the very things that Paul considered to be advantages turned out to mean absolutely nothing when it came to salvation by grace.

In verses 4-6, he listed all of his credentials and the things that he felt had given him a status of ritual righteousness that placed him above the average Jew, to say nothing of Gentiles. These things formed the basis of Paul's relationship with God. The Philippians were his badge of honor that he wore with pride, and quite possibly with exuberant joy. But, when he met Jesus Christ on the road to Damascus, he saw those things that he trusted in for what they were (see Acts 9:1-9). He counted them as loss. There was nothing that he had not done to be righteous in the eyes of God, but it was all for naught. Christ Jesus was a far greater and more precious gift.

Paul was prepared to give up everything for the sake of Jesus Christ, who was His new Lord. And give up everything he did. Paul said that he suffered the loss of all things (see verse 8). What did that include? Clearly, it included everything that went with his being a highly regarded Jewish scholar and rabbi. How does a man give up so much for what appears to be a life of struggle and hardship? Prior to his experience on the road to Damascus, the Law had been his lord and ruler, but now in Jesus Christ Paul had come to the perfect knowledge of God's eternal will and purpose which was manifested through Jesus Christ. His accomplishments prior to his conversion were no more than dung. Paul did not make light of his education or training; rather, he insisted that the things that he had put all of his confidence in proved to be worthless when it came to the value of knowing Jesus Christ.

Paul had found the true source of righteousness, which was in Christ Jesus (see verse 9). He had written earlier to the church of Rome that they had a zeal for God, but it was not according to the true righteousness of God. Rather than establishing his own standards, he had come to know the true righteousness which was by faith in Jesus Christ (see Romans 10:2). Paul came to a point wherein he denounced all of the former ways, beliefs, and practices that had held him in bondage—although he could never escape the struggle he had with indwelling sin and its power to control a man or woman (see Romans 7:13-25).

Paul then experienced a new power and righteousness. This was righteousness that came through the finished work of Jesus Christ on the cross (see Romans 1:16-17; 3:20-28; 4:1-9; 5:1-10). Paul referred to the true righteousness as having right standing before God. In Jesus Christ, we stand before God completely forgiven of all of our sins.

B. Righteousness that Is Built upon Faith (Philippians 3:9-12)

And be found in him, not having mine own righteousness, which is of the law, but that which is through the faith of Christ, the righteousness which is of God by faith: That I may know him, and the power of his resurrection, and the fellowship of his sufferings, being made conformable unto his death; If by any means I might attain unto the resurrection of the dead. Not as though I had already attained, either were already perfect: but I follow after, if that I may apprehend that for which also I am apprehended of Christ Jesus.

Paul declared that he wanted to know the power of the Resurrection, that same power that raised Jesus Christ from the dead. In this epistle we read, "That I may know him, and the power of his resurrection, and the fellowship of his sufferings, being made conformable unto his death." Paul wanted to be like Jesus in his sufferings. His desire was to be a partner with Jesus Christ in the pains that come with the preaching of the Gospel. He had known suffering, but he also knew suffering to be nothing more than a momentary "light affliction" for the unsurpassing worth of knowing Jesus Christ (see 2 Corinthians 4:10, 17).

The most important point regarding the experience of the power of His resurrection is to know Jesus Christ. Paul used a Greek word for *know* (*ginosko,* which means "more than intellectual knowledge"); it means "more than mere acquaintance, more than having heard something about someone, and more than the knowledge of some facts and figures." Rather, the word *ginosko* means "the kind of knowledge that comes with an intimate and loving relationship with the Savior." It is the kind of "knowing" that is used to describe how a man knows his wife (see Genesis 4:1, 25).

"That I may know him" (verse 10); here, Paul was referring to knowing none other than the risen and triumphant Lord of creation. He was not talking about knowing something about Jesus. He was not talking about having a conversation about Him and reading some books about Him, but about knowing Jesus in a real, personal way. He was talking about knowing Him from an experiential standpoint.

Verse 11 is not a statement or expression of doubt. "If by any means" points to God's sovereign authority and right to raise him and others however He chose. Paul's intent was to keep the Philippians completely focused on the fact that one day the resurrection of the dead would occur.

The resurrection of Jesus Christ is foundational to the Christian faith. It is our very basic core belief. That Jesus Christ was raised from the dead has been attested to and witnessed by many of the New Testament writers and early witnesses of the Christian faith (see Matthew 28:1-8; 1 Corinthians 15:3-8). The people who saw Jesus crucified on Good Friday saw Him condemned and executed as a common criminal, among criminals. His disciples ran off and left Him. But the story of God's redemptive plan did not end at Calvary; three days later Jesus was alive and full of God's power. When believers gather on Sunday it is for the purpose of reaffirming their belief in the Resurrection and to celebrate its historicity.

C. Forgetting the Past and Looking Forward (Philippians 3:13-16)

Brethren, I count not myself to have apprehended: but this one thing I do, forgetting those things which are behind, and reaching forth unto those things which are before, I press toward the mark for the prize of the high calling of God in Christ Jesus. Let us therefore, as many as be perfect, be thus minded: and if in any thing ye be otherwise minded, God shall reveal even this unto you. Nevertheless, whereto we have already attained, let us walk by the same rule, let us mind the same thing.

Paul was never satisfied with the achievements he had made, let alone with his relationship with the Lord Jesus Christ. The word *perfect* comes from the Greek word *telioo*, and it means "to carry through to completion, add to make full"—and in some instances it may refer to maturity. Forgetting is often very difficult for many people to do because it means we will not allow the past to influence our present attitudes or conduct. Forgetting means that everything that has gone wrong in previous years is over and with each new day we begin with "new mercies" and fresh energy. We must forget all that we have done and remember only what we still have to do.

The use of the word *forgetting* suggests a continuous action. What this means is that every time something from Paul's past came up, he would remove it so that he could concentrate on the future. Every time a failure came up, he would forget it so that he could concentrate on the future. Every time heartache wanted to intrude, he would forget it.

In verse 13, Paul told the Philippians that he had not yet grasped the full significance of Jesus Christ for his life. The NRSV translates verse 13 this way: "Beloved, I do not consider that I have made it my own; but this one thing I do: forgetting what lies behind and straining forward to what lies ahead." Here again the apostle was referring to having not reached his full spiritual potential. He had not made it yet. But there was one thing that he was going to do and that was to continue to press forward. He began running the race on the road to Damascus, and many years later he was still running just as hard and fast. Paul pointed to his power to concentrate on the one thing that was most important to him, which was his ministry. There is power in concentrating on what one does well.

Verse 14 is one of the most well-known verses in the entire letter. Paul used the language of the Greek athletic games to drive home the point that they must all persevere in the good fight of faith (see 1 Corinthians 9:24-27; 1 Timothy 4:7-10; 2 Timothy 4:7-8). "Pressing toward the prize" is the picture of a runner who is straining with every ounce of her or his strength to reach the finish line and attain the status of champion. The "high calling of God" is the call to embrace God's wonderful gift of salvation in Jesus Christ. The goal of the Christian life is to move continuously forward to sanctification and ultimately to glorification.

The lesson ends with Paul's appeal to continue to embrace the mind of Jesus (see 2:5-11). The word *perfect* is best understood as "those who are mature in the faith." He called upon all who thought in a mature fashion to be on the same page. Those who were not like-minded would be revealed by the Holy Spirit. "Same rule" comes from the Greek word *kanon* and refers to "the standard or rule that has been set." Thus, the sense is that unity, fellowship, and peace are maintained when the believers follow the supreme example of Jesus Christ. It is further enhanced when all seek to live by the same standards and rules.

III. CONCLUDING REFLECTION

Constant preoccupation with the past will cripple and paralyze any individual, organization, nation, and even a church. If we continue to dwell on our past failures we will inevitably close the door to our future. One of the great dangers that any church faces is its inability to be forward-thinking and progressive. There is this tendency to want to stay mired in the past because the future looks too uncertain and too unfamiliar. Many congregations stifle progress because they cling to some idealistic notion that the past is always better and brighter than the future. We may fail to remember that God is always calling us to tomorrow and not yesterday. We long for the "good old days" when life was simpler and the pace was not as hectic or demanding. I want to caution you against wanting to remain in the past. I want to caution you against wanting to return to yesterday as though that would be a remedy for your tomorrow. There are some things in life that we have to just forget so that we might move forward.

It is clear from this lesson that Paul understood life to be progressive, wherein the prize was at the end of the race, not the beginning. Each of us must seek a greater and more dynamic relationship with the Savior, who constantly encourages us to reach for the next rung on the ladder of our growth. We must all embrace the future, for that is where our greatest work will be done.

Why do we look back and bemoan our present, as if God is out of our equation? Paul looked back but with a different purpose in mind. He said, "What things were gain to me, those I counted loss for Christ." The word *loss* calls for sober reflection. In this context it means, "that which is damaged or of no use." In other words, those things that Paul thought to be important became unimportant after encountering the resurrected Christ. Our past, whatever it was, should not hold us back in progressing in the Christian faith. Many look at "good old days" when they used to be highly valued, but now nobody pays attention to them. There are those who look at the sins they have committed and are paralyzed and ashamed of their lives. Some have been financially supportive of the church, but eventually quit giving because there was no public recognition of them. Paul encouraged every Christian to look forward and endeavor to forget both achievements and failures. Be careful of considering past achievements so important that they obstruct the view and your relationship with Christ.

PRAYER

Eternal God, creator and sustainer of all life, we thank You this day, for Your tender mercies and lovingkindness. Grant that we may walk together in love, fellowship, and peace. Give us the mind that was in Christ Jesus, so that we may run the race before us with patience. In Jesus' name we pray. Amen.

WORD POWER

Apprehend (Greek: *katalambano* [ka-ta-lam-ba-no])—to lay hold of so as to make one's own, to obtain, to appropriate or take possession of. In the key text, Paul had yet to take hold of eternity. He was looking forward to it. No sincere Christian should take leave from holy aspirations to enter eternity. Paul was encouraging believers in every generation not to rest until they see Jesus face-to-face.

HOME DAILY BIBLE READINGS
(August 9-15, 2010)

Living into the Future

MONDAY, August 9: "God's Love Perfected in Us" (1 John 4:7-12)

TUESDAY, August 10: "Trust in the Lord" (Jeremiah 17:7-13)

WEDNESDAY, August 11: "A Place Prepared for You" (John 14:1-4)

THURSDAY, August 12: "Trust with All Your Heart" (Proverbs 3:3-8)

FRIDAY, August 13: "Breaking with the Past" (Philippians 3:1b-6)

SATURDAY, August 14: "Our Citizenship in Heaven" (Philippians 3:17-21)

SUNDAY, August 15: "The Heavenly Call of God" (Philippians 3:7-16)

LESSON 12   August 22, 2010

GROWING IN JOY AND PEACE

DEVOTIONAL READING: Psalm 85:4-13
PRINT PASSAGE: Philippians 4:2-14

BACKGROUND SCRIPTURE: Philippians 4:2-14
KEY VERSE: Philippians 4:9

Philippians 4:2-14—KJV

2 I beseech Euodias, and beseech Syntyche, that they be of the same mind in the Lord.

3 And I intreat thee also, true yokefellow, help those women which laboured with me in the gospel, with Clement also, and with other my fellowlabourers, whose names are in the book of life.

4 Rejoice in the Lord always: and again I say, Rejoice.

5 Let your moderation be known unto all men. The Lord is at hand.

6 Be careful for nothing; but in every thing by prayer and supplication with thanksgiving let your requests be made known unto God.

7 And the peace of God, which passeth all understanding, shall keep your hearts and minds through Christ Jesus.

8 Finally, brethren, whatsoever things are true, whatsoever things are honest, whatsoever things are just, whatsoever things are pure, whatsoever things are lovely, whatsoever things are of good report; if there be any virtue, and if there be any praise, think on these things.

9 Those things, which ye have both learned, and received, and heard, and seen in me, do: and the God of peace shall be with you.

10 But I rejoiced in the Lord greatly, that now at the last your care of me hath flourished again; wherein ye were also careful, but ye lacked opportunity.

11 Not that I speak in respect of want: for I have learned, in whatsoever state I am, therewith to be content.

12 I know both how to be abased, and I know how to abound: every where and in all things I am instructed both to be full and to be hungry, both to abound and to suffer need.

13 I can do all things through Christ which strengtheneth me.

Philippians 4:2-14—NRSV

2 I urge Euodia and I urge Syntyche to be of the same mind in the Lord.

3 Yes, and I ask you also, my loyal companion, help these women, for they have struggled beside me in the work of the gospel, together with Clement and the rest of my co-workers, whose names are in the book of life.

4 Rejoice in the Lord always; again I will say, Rejoice.

5 Let your gentleness be known to everyone. The Lord is near.

6 Do not worry about anything, but in everything by prayer and supplication with thanksgiving let your requests be made known to God.

7 And the peace of God, which surpasses all understanding, will guard your hearts and your minds in Christ Jesus.

8 Finally, beloved, whatever is true, whatever is honorable, whatever is just, whatever is pure, whatever is pleasing, whatever is commendable, if there is any excellence and if there is anything worthy of praise, think about these things.

9 Keep on doing the things that you have learned and received and heard and seen in me, and the God of peace will be with you.

10 I rejoice in the Lord greatly that now at last you have revived your concern for me; indeed, you were concerned for me, but had no opportunity to show it.

11 Not that I am referring to being in need; for I have learned to be content with whatever I have.

12 I know what it is to have little, and I know what it is to have plenty. In any and all circumstances I have learned the secret of being well-fed and of going hungry, of having plenty and of being in need.

13 I can do all things through him who strengthens me.

14 Notwithstanding ye have well done, that ye did communicate with my affliction.

14 In any case, it was kind of you to share my distress.

TOPICAL OUTLINE OF THE LESSON

I. Introduction
   A. An Uncertain Season
   B. Biblical Background

II. Exposition and Application of the Scripture
   A. Paul's Plea to Two Co-Workers (Philippians 4:2-3)
   B. The Perfect Cure for Anxiety (Philippians 4:4-9)
   C. The Key to Finding Contentment in Life (Philippians 4:10-14)

III. Concluding Reflection

LESSON OBJECTIVES

Upon completion of this lesson, the students will know that:

1. Disagreement between brethren could prevent the church from fulfilling their goal;
2. Christians are to rejoice always because the source of their joy is the undefeated Christ; and,
3. We should be thankful to people for the support we receive from them.

POINTS TO BE EMPHASIZED

ADULT/YOUTH

Adult Topic: Finding Peace
Youth Topic: Why Worry?
Adult Key Verse: Philippians 4:9
Youth Key Verse: Philippians 4:6
Print Passage: Philippians 4:2-14

—Paul was saying that the peace that comes from God was superior to anything else to which it might be compared.

—The word translated as "peace" can also be translated as "security."

—In the list, in verses 8-9 are described the qualities that Paul believed should indicate the attitudes and actions of Christians.

—Euodia and Syntyche were two women in the Philippian church who had been disagreeing.

—Paul urged the Philippians to get along with one another.

—Paul urged the Philippians to focus on things that were positive and to keep on doing them.

—Paul had learned how to be content with whatever circumstance he was in and knew he could do anything in the strength of God.

CHILDREN

Children Topic: Praying at All Times
Key Verse: Philippians 4:6
Print Passage: Acts 27:27, 29, 33-36, 39, 41-44; Philippians 4:6

—As the ship neared land, Paul told the people not to panic, as their lives would be spared.

—The centurion saved Paul's life by not agreeing with the people who were planning to take Paul's life.

- Every day on the ship, Paul provided encouragement to everyone on the ship.
- Paul prayed a prayer of thanks in the midst of the storm.
- As Paul stated, no one was harmed on the ship and everyone reached land safely.
- Paul suggested in Philippians 4:6 that we should not worry, but give thanks in all things.

I. INTRODUCTION

A. An Uncertain Season

The end of 2008 and the beginning of 2009 were some of the most emotionally agonizing days in American history. Anxiety swept across the globe like an out-of-control brush fire. Around the world people were hurt by the massive array of perplexing economic problems and sticky political situations. Among the many questions people asked were: "Will the economy stabilize in America, which has produced a near-global economic depression?" The election of the first African-American president only brought temporary relief from the anxiety. What are we going to do about crime and gang violence in our schools? Who has the answer to the unsolvable drug problem? How will the military meet its requirements for national security when it is strung out on multiple continents? Who is going to be available to teach our children when so many capable teachers have all but given up? How can we keep our families intact when we have so many internal and external pressures pushing and pulling at us? How are we going to pay our bills, when there was never enough income to meet current expenses? When will global warming finally reach the irreversible point of no return? On and on goes this never-ending litany of questions that produce more anxiety, tension, and stress.

Many people today are highly frustrated. They are frustrated at home because their home lives are in shambles. They are agitated on the job because they are expected to do more with less. How are we to feel good with all of this pressure? How are we to be inspired with all of these financial problems? How are we to get pumped up with all of these problems in our lives? How can we be at peace when we can hardly sleep at night?

There is a simple explanation that answers every one of those questions: we have not started to enjoy the peace that God has given us through the Holy Spirit. This sounds so simple that it is almost hard to believe, accept, or comprehend. The way one gets this peace is not some mystery that is beyond human comprehension. There is no six-step process for getting and enjoying the peace of God. You do not have to go to a conference on peace in order to know His peace.

In today's lesson, Paul shared with the Philippians his frame of mind. We see a man who had learned to be at peace with his circumstances. His experiences would open the door for increased joy and abounding peace in Christians' lives.

B. Biblical Background

Today's lesson brings us to the end of our study of Philippians. In this concluding passage, Paul continued to express his concern that the church in Philippi would remain steadfast and immovable in the face of entrenched demonic powers. He exhorted the saints to stand firm and not to be moved by trials that they had experienced because of the Gospel. Paul continued to lavish his love on them, reminding them that they were his joy and crown. His most fervent desire was to visit them one more time. We learned earlier that Paul wrote this letter from his prison cell in Rome and this church continued to maintain contact with him.

There are several memorable verses in this section that have encouraged believers for thousands of years. One of the unique features of this section of the letter is the number of short, pithy sayings that highlight Paul's continuing role as their pastor and teacher. Paul piled one statement upon the next, knowing that the time was drawing near—therefore, he wanted to say as much as he could in spite of the limitations of time and space. Paul needed to give as much practical advice and support to the Philippians as possible so that in the days to come they could stand firm and resolute in the face of persecution.

II. EXPOSITION AND APPLICATION OF THE SCRIPTURE

A. Paul's Plea to Two Co-Workers
(Philippians 4:2-3)

I beseech Euodias, and beseech Syntyche, that they be of the same mind in the Lord. And I intreat thee also, true yokefellow, help those women which laboured with me in the gospel, with Clement also, and with other my fellowlabourers, whose names are in the book of life.

As he neared the conclusion of his letter, Paul mentioned two women by name: Euodias and Syntyche. It is possible that these two women were at the center of the disagreement that may have existed within the church. We do not know what it was, but it was prominent enough that Paul knew about it and felt the need to call out their names in a publicly read letter. His approach was not one of scorn or taking sides. This was the first time in any letter that Paul had done this. It has been suggested that use of the word "beseech" before each name reflected Paul's intention to be evenhanded and not condescending to either of the women. His appeal was that they be of the same mind in the Lord. This was a reminder that they should not only be in agreement, but also their agreement should reflect the mind of Christ in Philippians 2:5.

Paul called upon someone he referred to as a "true yokefellow," a reference to someone that Paul considered a reliable comrade in the ministry. We do not know who this person was or his relationship to the church. Some interpreters have assumed it was Epaphroditus, but this seems highly unlikely because Paul would have mentioned him by name. He mentioned the two women and it stands to reason that he would do the same in this case. Whoever he was, his stature and reputation were highly regarded in the church. Paul wanted him to help the women to reach an agreement and settle their differences. These were two very important workers. He offered to the church words of commendation for their service. They had spent time in the trenches with Paul, along with Clement and other fellow workers in the ministry. No mention was made of where they worked together, which was quite possibly in Philippi or maybe throughout Macedonia.

B. The Perfect Cure for Anxiety
(Philippians 4:4-9)

Rejoice in the Lord always: and again I say, Rejoice. Let your moderation be known unto all men. The Lord is at hand. Be careful for nothing; but in every thing by prayer and supplication with thanksgiving let your requests be made known unto God. And the peace of God, which passeth all understanding, shall keep your hearts and minds through Christ Jesus. Finally, brethren, whatsoever things are true, whatsoever things are honest, whatsoever things are just, whatsoever things are pure, whatsoever things are lovely, whatsoever things are of good report; if there be any virtue, and if there be any praise, think on these things. Those things, which ye have both learned, and received, and heard, and seen in me, do: and the God of peace shall be with you.

Verses 4 and 5 contain a short series of exhortations to be filled with joy or the exhortation to "rejoice in the Lord always." Paul spoke in such a way that his words were an imperative command. Rejoicing was not an option; rather, it was something that they had to do. He added "always" indicating that there were to be no circumstances that kept the saints from rejoicing and celebrating the goodness and mercy of God. Even in the most vexing situation, the believer was encouraged to rejoice in the Lord (see Habakkuk 3:17-18). The call is not to be "happy," because happiness is situational. We are happy when everything is well and there are no problems that have cropped up in our lives. *Joy* on the other hand is a direct result of the indwelling presence of the Holy Spirit (see

Galatians 5:22). Joy is the inward assurance that in the midst of the worst that life can throw at us, God will work things out for our good (see Psalm 30:1-6; Romans 8:28).

Moderation is better translated as the term "forbearing spirit" (NASB) or "gentleness" (NRSV). Paul was conveying the necessity that the Philippians be fair, just, and patient in their dealings with all people. By demonstrating the spirit toward outsiders, it would naturally filter into the relationships that existed among them. The fourth exhortation was a reminder—"The "Lord is at hand" was a glance toward the future, when the Lord Jesus Christ would return. By living with eternity in view they would always be driven to do what was pleasing in the eyes of God.

In verses 6-7, Paul told the Philippians that God's peace removes feelings of anxiety. They were exhorted to "Be anxious for nothing, but in everything by prayer and supplication, with thanksgiving, let your requests be made known to God; and the peace of God" (NKJV). Humans are by nature prone to worry. We are encouraged not to spend a lot of time giving matters beyond our control grave and serious thought. There are some people who worry about, debate, and struggle with everything. They give everything such deep, probing thought that they become stuck in the pits.

The words *do not be anxious* mean "do not spend a lot of time thinking about these matters, do not brood over them, and do not spend a great deal of time pondering the possible outcomes." One way to think of it is this way: there are people who will not fly because they have spent time thinking that if they get on an airplane it is going to crash. There are people who when they have a pain in the chest or elsewhere that is out of the ordinary, they think it is terminal. We spend an enormous amount of time processing information about our situations. We can give too much credibility to our everyday circumstances that claim an enormous amount of time and energy.

Paul exhorted the saints with the contrasting conjunction *but*: "But in every thing by prayer and supplication with thanksgiving let your requests be made known to God." We are to ask in the full assurance of faith that God not only hears us, but that He will also answer (see Psalm 34:1-8; John 14:13-14; 15:16; 16:23-24; 1 John 4:6; 5:14). The Greek word Paul used for *prayer* is a word that can mean "worship." The Greek word *proseuche* means "to bow down before, to prostrate oneself before God." Worship then must be seen as one of the means for dealing with fear and anxiety. The idea that is expressed in these words is that of prayer as an act of worship. Inward peace comes as we acknowledge our deep-seated need for worship. God says to bring Him everything, great and small. There is nothing that we cannot put on this agenda of prayerful worship. Supplications are the specific needs that we have. It is revealed in the text that thanksgiving is at the heart of experiencing the abiding peace of God. We are to release our cares to God. Pray about everything; make specific requests to God, then close with thanksgiving. Thanksgiving is the cure for ingratitude. When we are grateful, it leads to developing a heart and spirit full of joy and peace.

"Finally" is not another conclusion. Rather, it more than likely means that "as a result of all of the preceding discussions" there are some things that each of us must do to cultivate the peace of God in our lives. Often believers tend to think that God does everything and there is nothing for them to do. However, we must be active participants in growing in grace (see Ephesians 4:22-32; 2 Peter 1:3-10). In verse 8, Paul stated that the mind that lives in the realm of peace must also be a mind that concentrates on the right thoughts. He provided a list of positive virtues that must be cultivated. "Things that are true" refers to being honest in our thought processes. Honesty has reference to one's character, and while "things that are" just can refer to righteousness, more than likely it means for one to live in such a way that he or she obeys the laws of the land. "Things lovely" is a reference to being free of carnality and sin, and that which is pleasing and acceptable. "A good report" can refer to speaking those things that reflect favorably upon others or oneself, or not to allow corrupt communication to come from the believer.

Paul made a fourfold appeal to the Philippians, not just to hear his words, but to remember everything that had transpired in their lives over the past few years. He called on them to remember what they had learned, received through his teachings, and heard him say and write—and more importantly, what they had seen in his life. He was the epistle that they could read.

C. The Key to Finding Contentment in Life (Philippians 4:10-14)

But I rejoiced in the Lord greatly, that now at the last your care of me hath flourished again; wherein ye were also careful, but ye lacked opportunity. Not that I speak in respect of want: for I have learned, in whatsoever state I am, therewith to be content. I know both how to be abased, and I know how to abound: every where

and in all things I am instructed both to be full and to be hungry, both to abound and to suffer need. I can do all things through Christ which strengtheneth me. Notwithstanding ye have well done, that ye did communicate with my affliction.

In the final section of the lesson, we see one of the primary reasons why Paul wrote the letter to the church of Philippi. They had ministered to his physical needs. He had called upon them to rejoice. Now he turned and said that he too was filled with joy. His joy was occasioned by the renewal of a relationship that he cherished. How long they had been out of touch is not stated. Evidently, there was something that had prevented them from being able to connect or it may have been the impoverished condition of the saints that prevented them from assisting Paul with his needs. Whatever it was he was very happy.

Verse 11 must not be understood as a statement of disrespect for the gift given by the Philippians; on the contrary, just as Paul had shared with them about rejoicing always, he told them that he had learned to do the same thing as well. He had had to learn how to live in any condition and find contentment. This level of contentment meant that he knew how to live with plenty and he knew how to live with very little or nothing. He knew how to live with ample food stores and how to live with hunger. Verse 12 is written in the present tense, which is an indication that Paul was not talking about a past experience, but a present reality.

In the midst of some of the worst times of his life, Paul was still standing on the mountaintop of courage and strength. Verse 13 is one of the most quoted verses in the letter. Many times these words are used by the preachers of prosperity who proclaim that you can do all

things when you put your mind to it. Clearly, that is not what Paul believed. The use of the prepositional phrase "through Christ" shows a relationship between his ability to overcome the challenges he faced and the source of his power. He could face the many problems confronting him, but only through Jesus Christ. Christ is the vine and we are the branches. It is only as believers remain connected to Him that we can face the enormous obstacles that seek to impede the spread of the Gospel.

Paul thanked the church that they ministered to him in spiritual and physical matters. They did not just know that he had a need and not respond. They did whatever was necessary to make sure that he understood they cared and cared just as deeply for him as he did for them.

III. CONCLUDING REFLECTION

I have led many short-term mission trips to Nigeria and Kenya, and one of the most remarkable experiences that first-time missionaries recall is the celebrative spirit and joy that characterizes African worship. The amazement stems from the fact that here are people who by virtue of what they have should have every reason to question the righteousness of God. They should have every right to say that God is not fair to them, yet the opposite is always the case. They rejoice in the Lord because contrary to western thinking, which believes that God's favor is evidenced by our fat piggy banks and numerous toys, God is worshiped and celebrated for who He is and not for what He gives. We are intoxicated with the desire for more, but more never satisfies.

Believers today would do well to heed

the lessons of contentment that come from knowing the Lord Jesus Christ as Savior and Redeemer. Being content means knowing that in Jesus Christ God has called you to embrace the greatest purpose in the world—telling others who He is and why He desires for them to be saved. Try living on less and giving more to further the cause of Jesus Christ.

One of the most effective means through which the evil one destroys Christian fellowship is lack of peace and joy among brethren. Many Christian families have been destroyed through lack of peace and joy in the home. A Caucasian preacher once told me that if he had to be a pastor again, he would not allow his wife to be on the committee that planned church socials. He said many problems come from disagreeing on what types of foods to cook and the ingredients to add. We do not know the exact problem between Euodias and Syntyche, but Paul knew that their disagreement was a detriment to the body of Christ. We must always remember that Jesus is our Lord and Savior and He is the Prince of Peace. In the body of Christ, there must not be irreconcilable differences. As Christians, there should be no excuses for remaining at odds with each other.

PRAYER

Lord, God of the universe, owner of the cattle on a thousand hills, teach us to love what is dear to You. May we embrace the discipline of simplicity with the desire to live in harmony with Your will. In Jesus' name we pray. Amen.

WORD POWER

(KJV) Do; (NKJV) Practice (Greek: *parasso* [pa-ras-so])—this word has athletic connotations. Paul encouraged the Philippians to get busy in doing what they saw in him. They ought to carry on, leading Christlike lives. They must continue exercising Christian behavior. A footballer who refuses to practice will lose his physical conditioning. So Christians are called to do spiritual exercises.

HOME DAILY BIBLE READINGS
(August 16-22, 2010)

Growing in Joy and Peace

MONDAY, August 16: "God Speaks Peace" (Psalm 85:4-13)

TUESDAY, August 17: "Facing Danger with Peace" (Acts 27:33-44)

WEDNESDAY, August 18: "Reap in Shouts of Joy" (Psalm 126)

THURSDAY, August 19: "Finding Joy and Peace" (Isaiah 55:6-13)

FRIDAY, August 20: "Peace Be with You" (John 20:19-23)

SATURDAY, August 21: "Focusing on the Spirit" (Romans 8:1-8)

SUNDAY, August 22: "Experiencing God's Peace" (Philippians 4:2-14)

LESSON 13   August 29, 2010

UPHELD BY GOD

DEVOTIONAL READING: Acts 9:23-30
PRINT PASSAGE: Acts 28:16-25a, 28-31
KEY VERSES: Acts 28:30-31

BACKGROUND SCRIPTURE: Acts 28;
Philippians 4:15-23

Acts 28:16-25a, 28-31—KJV

16 And when we came to Rome, the centurion delivered the prisoners to the captain of the guard: but Paul was suffered to dwell by himself with a soldier that kept him.

17 And it came to pass, that after three days Paul called the chief of the Jews together: and when they were come together, he said unto them, Men and brethren, though I have committed nothing against the people, or customs of our fathers, yet was I delivered prisoner from Jerusalem into the hands of the Romans.

18 Who, when they had examined me, would have let me go, because there was no cause of death in me.

19 But when the Jews spake against it, I was constrained to appeal unto Caesar; not that I had ought to accuse my nation of.

20 For this cause therefore have I called for you, to see you, and to speak with you: because that for the hope of Israel I am bound with this chain.

21 And they said unto him, We neither received letters out of Judaea concerning thee, neither any of the brethren that came shewed or spake any harm of thee.

22 But we desire to hear of thee what thou thinkest: for as concerning this sect, we know that every where it is spoken against.

23 And when they had appointed him a day, there came many to him into his lodging; to whom he expounded and testified the kingdom of God, persuading them concerning Jesus, both out of the law of Moses, and out of the prophets, from morning till evening.

24 And some believed the things which were spoken, and some believed not.

25 And when they agreed not among themselves, they departed, after that Paul had spoken one word.

Acts 28:16-25a, 28-31—NRSV

16 When we came into Rome, Paul was allowed to live by himself, with the soldier who was guarding him.

17 Three days later he called together the local leaders of the Jews. When they had assembled, he said to them, "Brothers, though I had done nothing against our people or the customs of our ancestors, yet I was arrested in Jerusalem and handed over to the Romans.

18 When they had examined me, the Romans wanted to release me, because there was no reason for the death penalty in my case.

19 But when the Jews objected, I was compelled to appeal to the emperor—even though I had no charge to bring against my nation.

20 For this reason therefore I have asked to see you and speak with you, since it is for the sake of the hope of Israel that I am bound with this chain."

21 They replied, "We have received no letters from Judea about you, and none of the brothers coming here has reported or spoken anything evil about you.

22 But we would like to hear from you what you think, for with regard to this sect we know that everywhere it is spoken against."

23 After they had set a day to meet with him, they came to him at his lodgings in great numbers. From morning until evening he explained the matter to them, testifying to the kingdom of God and trying to convince them about Jesus both from the law of Moses and from the prophets.

24 Some were convinced by what he had said, while others refused to believe.

25 So they disagreed with each other; and as they were leaving, Paul made one further statement.

UNIFYING LESSON PRINCIPLE

People struggle to keep commitments. How can we hold to our commitments? In recognizing God's commitment and faithfulness to us, we are challenged to commit our lives to God's care.

.....

28 Be it known therefore unto you, that the salvation of God is sent unto the Gentiles, and that they will hear it.

29 And when he had said these words, the Jews departed, and had great reasoning among themselves.

30 And Paul dwelt two whole years in his own hired house, and received all that came in unto him,

31 Preaching the kingdom of God, and teaching those things which concern the Lord Jesus Christ, with all confidence, no man forbidding him.

.....

28 "Let it be known to you then that this salvation of God has been sent to the Gentiles; they will listen."

29 (*Other ancient authorities add this verse): And when he had said these words, the Jews departed, arguing vigorously among themselves.

30 He lived there two whole years at his own expense and welcomed all who came to him,

31 proclaiming the kingdom of God and teaching about the Lord Jesus Christ with all boldness and without hindrance.

TOPICAL OUTLINE OF THE LESSON

I. Introduction
   A. Commitment to Christ
   B. Biblical Background

II. Exposition and Application of the Scripture
   A. Arrival in Rome
      (Acts 28:16)
   B. Meeting with the Jewish Leaders
      (Acts 28:17-22)
   C. Preaching and Teaching among the Jews
      (Acts 28:23-25a)
   D. Paul Preaches with Boldness
      (Acts 28:28-31)

III. Concluding Reflection

LESSON OBJECTIVES

Upon completion of this lesson, the students will know that:

1. Commitment to the course of Christ is the soul of Christianity;
2. Paul becomes an example to follow in total commitment and confidence; and,
3. Commitment leads to complete surrender to God.

POINTS TO BE EMPHASIZED
ADULT/YOUTH

Adult Topic: Keeping Commitments
Youth Topic: Committed to the End
Adult/Youth Key Verses: Acts 28:30-31
Print Passage: Acts 28:16-25a, 28-31

—Paul viewed his imprisonment as serving the cause of Christ.

—Paul believed that Christ was sovereign over all the circumstances of his life.

—Acts 28 contains what appears to be the last of the "we" passages in the book of Acts.

—Paul was a prisoner sent to Rome at his own request.

—Paul called the Jewish leaders in Rome to a conference to explain why he was there.

—The Jewish leaders were impressed with Paul's testimony and wanted to hear more.

—Some Jews were convinced by Paul's testimony, while others refused to believe.

—Paul told the Jews that God's salvation had been sent to the Gentiles.

—Paul proclaimed the kingdom of God and taught about Jesus Christ up to the very end of his life.

CHILDREN
Children Topic: Trusting Always
Key Verses: Acts 28:30-31

Print Passage: Acts 28:1-2, 10-16, 30-31

—The people on the island of Malta showed unusual kindness to the people from the wrecked ship.

—After three months, Paul and the other travelers again set sail for Rome.

—After arriving in Rome, Paul was allowed to live by himself under guard and to continue his witness to the kingdom of God.

—Paul welcomed all who came to him and he boldly taught about Jesus Christ.

I. INTRODUCTION

A. Commitment to Christ

One of the challenges many contemporary churches face is developing a core group of believers who are unreservedly committed to the cause of the Lord Jesus Christ. There are some schools of thought that believe and espouse that people will not make commitments today to the church and its ministry. They believe that the days of that kind of radical commitment to Jesus Christ have ended. I have an opposing view. However, there may be several reasons why people do not make serious commitments to their local churches today. First, the pace of American life is so fast that people hardly have time to keep up with themselves, let alone catch up. The pace of our society means that what free time people have is going to be divided up between a host of activities, trips, and family time. Second, Americans have come to expect and even look for a variety of options and alternatives, even when it comes to their faith. This buffet mentality of the Christian faith means that people are more likely to believe that they can pick and choose the things that they like and leave out those that they find too demanding and that impose upon their personal lifestyles. Third, many church leaders today have lowered their expectations of themselves and the people they lead.

B. Biblical Background

We have come to the closing chapter of the book of Acts and Luke's final words about the life and ministry of the apostle Paul. At long last his personal desire to go to Rome was fulfilled, although not as he had hoped (see Romans 1:15; 15:24, 28). Paul had been a champion of the cause of Jesus Christ for nearly twenty-five years. He had faced much and endured much for the Gospel of the Lord Jesus Christ. His arrest in Jerusalem and subsequent appeal to Caesar brought him to the point where we meet him in today's lesson. He never grew weary of preaching the Gospel and explaining to others the unsurpassing greatness of God's power.

Paul's journey to Rome was filled with intrigue and excitement (see Acts 27:1–28:15). There are several reasons why the journey was out of the ordinary. First, the journey itself was not without its dangers. Consider that the ships of that day were nothing compared to the ocean-going vessels we see in our time.

Second, the distance of two thousand miles made every mile perilous and these long sea journeys were often filled with tension. Third, they left during the most inopportune time and the weather did not bode well for the journey from the start. The journey to Rome lasted several months.

II. EXPOSITION AND APPLICATION OF THE SCRIPTURE

A. Arrival in Rome
(Acts 28:16)

And when we came to Rome, the centurion delivered the prisoners to the captain of the guard: but Paul was suffered to dwell by himself with a soldier that kept him.

Verse 16 marks the end of Paul's long and arduous journey to Rome. The presence of the pronoun "we" indicates that Luke was part of the entourage that reached Rome. We have no further record of whether or not he was present throughout Paul's time there, or of where he ultimately went. What is clear is that Paul's vision of preaching the Gospel in Rome, the imperial city, had been fulfilled. We are told that the Roman soldiers who brought Paul and the others to Rome turned them over to the captain of the guard. We know nothing of the relationship that Paul may have developed with Julius, the centurion assigned to make sure he and the other prisoners arrived safely in Rome (see Acts 27:1).

Paul was allowed to live in Rome, on his own. He was placed under some form of limited house arrest and guarded by a single soldier. This indicates that whatever the charges were against him, they were not serious enough to warrant confinement in a prison cell in Rome. The freedom in Rome helped Paul to preach the Gospel to the men around him.

B. Meeting with the Jewish Leaders
(Acts 28:17-22)

And it came to pass, that after three days Paul called the chief of the Jews together: and when they were come together, he said unto them, Men and brethren, though I have committed nothing against the people, or customs of our fathers, yet was I delivered prisoner from Jerusalem into the hands of the Romans. Who, when they had examined me, would have let me go, because there was no cause of death in me. But when the Jews spake against it, I was constrained to appeal unto Caesar; not that I had ought to accuse my nation of. For this cause therefore have I called for you, to see you, and to speak with you: because that for the hope of Israel I am bound with this chain. And they said unto him, We neither received letters out of Judaea concerning thee, neither any of the brethren that came shewed or spake any harm of thee. But we desire to hear of thee what thou thinkest: for as concerning this sect, we know that every where it is spoken against.

According to verse 17, Paul was in the city just three days when he requested a meeting with the chief Jewish leaders. This is reminiscent of Paul's earlier strategies when he first launched his missionary work. He would go to a city and meet with the local Jewish leaders first (see Acts 13:42-48; 18:5-7; 19:8-10). Paul wanted to meet with the leaders so that he could offer some explanation for why he was there and why he was under house arrest. Paul began his meeting with a defense of his ministry by stating that there was nothing that he had done that would warrant his current status. He had done nothing to shame, destroy, or distort the traditions of the Jewish faith. The Jews in Jerusalem had a different opinion of Paul's preaching and his purposes. They fully believed that he was out to destroy the Jewish faith through his preaching of Jesus Christ as the Messiah and hope of Israel (see Acts 21:28-31). Paul pointed out that the Romans arrested him because a riot had broken out in Jerusalem. The Romans were very quick to quell any disturbances that cropped up around the annual feast days in Jerusalem (see Acts 21:31-34).

Paul stated that when he was initially arraigned, the Romans could find nothing with which to charge him, let alone charge him with something worthy of the penalty of death (see Acts 22:24-30; 23:29; 25:25; 26:31). The Jewish case against Paul was extremely weak. But the Jews were a very powerful presence in Jerusalem and most of the Roman leaders would try to appease them when possible (see Acts 25:9). In verse 19, Paul pointed out how the Jews were adamantly against his being released. Therefore, in order to preserve his life and go to Rome, which was something he greatly desired, he appealed to Caesar (see Acts 25:10-12, 21; 26:32). Paul's appeal to Caesar was not for the purpose of charging the Jews with some crime or injustice. He was proud of his Jewish heritage, and all he wanted was for them to embrace the redemptive plan of God through Jesus Christ.

In verse 20, he pointed out that the reason he wanted to meet with them was for the purpose of seeing them and knowing who they were. That very moment must have been a great delight in the heart of Paul. The other reason he called them together, which has already been stated in the previous verses, was to offer some explanation as to why a prominent Jewish rabbi would come to Rome bound in chains. As he stated, it was for the hope of Israel.

Verse 21 comes as a surprise. One would think that the Jews who were so adamant that Paul be killed would have sent someone along to make sure that he was tried before Caesar and sentenced to death. Yet, the Jewish leaders acknowledged that there had been no correspondence between them or the Jewish leaders in Jerusalem. There were some Jews on the ship who arrived in Rome at the same time as Paul. Yet, there was not a single person who spoke ill of Paul who had been on the journey with them. As far as they knew, he had done nothing to cause them to question his mission. They did want to know more about his thoughts and ministry. However, there was one thing that was clear in their minds: Christianity was not highly regarded. More than ten years earlier, Claudius, the Roman emperor, had expelled the Christians because they had been accused of starting a major fire that destroyed nearly half the city (see Acts 18:2). They wanted to meet with him at a later date to discuss these things.

C. Preaching and Teaching among the Jews (Acts 28:23-25a)

And when they had appointed him a day, there came many to him into his lodging; to whom he expounded and testified the kingdom of God, persuading them concerning Jesus, both out of the law of Moses, and out of the prophets, from morning till evening. And some believed the things which were spoken, and some believed not. And when they agreed not among themselves, they departed, after that Paul had spoken one word.

In this section of the passage, Paul's meeting with a large number of Jews who lived in Rome is highlighted. The Jewish leaders left their initial meeting with Paul, agreeing to meet at an appointed day and time. Many Jews came to his lodging, and he expounded the Word of God about Jesus Christ. Paul was a skilled theologian, and was very knowledgeable of the Law and the prophets. What was the content of Paul's message? It centered on the kingdom of God. This is a phrase that is a reference to the rule and reign of God in the world and in the lives of His people. Further still, Paul preached Jesus Christ to them. Paul taught and preached from morning until the evening. He was able to hold people's attention for hours. He sought to persuade the Jews, not just recite some Scriptures and give some thoughts. Rather, his intent was to convert them to Christianity through a reasoned approach and exposition of the Scriptures.

Paul's preaching and teaching was the embodiment of what he believed about faith and salvation. We do not know whether Paul baptized them. More than likely he would have sought to connect the new believers to the local church, which was in Rome. Likewise, there were some who would not believe (see verse 24). They simply rejected everything that Paul said. Paul's preaching aroused sharp disagreements among the Jews who came to meet with him. They departed and we are not told whether or not they had any further contact with Paul (verse 25).

D. Paul Preaches with Boldness
(Acts 28:28-31)

Be it known therefore unto you, that the salvation of God is sent unto the Gentiles, and that they will hear it. And when he had said these words, the Jews departed, and had great reasoning among themselves. And Paul dwelt two whole years in his own hired house, and received all that came in unto him, Preaching the kingdom of God, and teaching those things which concern the Lord Jesus Christ, with all confidence, no man forbidding him.

Luke ended his portrayal of the life and ministry of Paul by telling us that Paul lived for two whole years in his own rented house. He was free to receive as many people as he wanted. There are a few things that must be dealt with concerning this statement. Did Luke mean that Paul only lived for two more years and then went to trial and was executed? Or did Luke mean that after two years Paul was released? What is certain is that Luke wrote to point to the triumph of the Gospel of the kingdom of God. Paul had been one of its most ardent and determined proclaimers; but the book of Acts was really not about Paul, but about how the Gospel of Jesus Christ came to dominate and conquer the mighty Roman Empire. Jesus had said that His disciples would be His witnesses, beginning first in Jerusalem, Judea, Samaria, and the uttermost part of the earth. Rome was the final frontier and last great bastion of imperial might that had to be conquered for Jesus Christ.

Paul preached to both Jews and Gentiles. He preached the kingdom of God and the message about Jesus Christ (see 2 Corinthians 5:19-20). Paul, like all of the other apostles and missionaries, was a witness of what God had done through Jesus Christ. He preached with confidence and without hindrances. This is further evidence that Paul had done nothing according to Roman law that would warrant death.

Some people believe that Paul was released and that he eventually made his way to Spain and preached the Gospel there—and then came back to Rome and was re-arrested and eventually beheaded (see Romans 15:24, 28). This is of course more speculative tradition than fact. Luke did not tell and it may be best that he left it that way—for in the life of Paul we see that the Gospel went forth unbound, unfettered, and undeterred by the schemes of Satan.

III. CONCLUDING REFLECTION

In 2004, I went to Turkey for the first time. When I shared with my friends and colleagues that I was going to Turkey, many of them asked why I would want to do that. My answer was simple: Turkey is the land of biblical Asia Minor and home of many of the places visited by Paul and the early Christian missionaries.

I have since traveled to Turkey on three other occasions. During each of those trips, I have come away with a greater appreciation of and deeper respect for the work of Paul and other missionaries who traveled throughout that country preaching Jesus Christ. The one overarching lesson that this quarter has taught us is that whenever the people of God are gripped by an insatiable desire to serve the purpose of God, there will never be any question regarding their commitment or determination. In Paul, we see a man who made God's purpose his only purpose for living.

PRAYER

Eternal God, may the sunshine of Your grace saturate our hearts so that we will be moved to serve You and only You in all we do and say. In Jesus' name we pray. Amen.

WORD POWER

Confidence (Greek: *parresia* [par-re-si-a])—the word means "bold, freedom in speaking, or unreservedness in speech." It also means "to speak without ambiguity." The encounter and knowledge of Paul about Jesus Christ gave him such confidence to speak with boldness. Our lack of serious encounters with Jesus Christ explains our lack of the kind of boldness Paul had.

HOME DAILY BIBLE READINGS
(August 23-29, 2010)

Upheld by God
    MONDAY, August 23: "An Encouraging Advocate" (Acts 9:23-30)
    TUESDAY, August 24: "Our Refuge and Strength" (Psalm 46)
    WEDNESDAY, August 25: "The Lord Is Your Keeper" (Psalm 121)
    THURSDAY, August 26: "God's Promise and Protection" (Psalm 119:114-117)
    FRIDAY, August 27: "Protected on the Journey" (Acts 28:1-15)
    SATURDAY, August 28: "God Will Satisfy Every Need" (Philippians 4:15-20)
    SUNDAY, August 29: "The Unhindered Gospel" (Acts 28:16-31)